THE
IRISH REVOLUTION
AND ITS
AFTERMATH

For my wife Anne
and our sons Eoghan, Emmett, Conor and Ronan

THE
IRISH REVOLUTION
AND ITS
AFTERMATH
1916–1923

Years of Revolt

FRANCIS COSTELLO

IRISH ACADEMIC PRESS
DUBLIN • PORTLAND, OR

First published in 2003 by
IRISH ACADEMIC PRESS
44 Northumberland Road, Dublin 4, Ireland

and in the United States of America by
IRISH ACADEMIC PRESS
c/o ISBS, 5824 N.E. Hassalo Street, Portland
Oregon 97213-3644

Website: www.iap.ie

British Library Cataloguing in Publication Data

Costello, Francis J.
  The Irish revolution and its aftermath, 1916–1923: years
  of revolt
  1. Ireland – History – 1910–1921   2. Ireland – History – Civil
  War, 1922–1923   3. Ireland – Politics and government –
  1910–1921   4. Ireland – Politics and government – 1922–1949
  5. Great Britain – Politics and government – 1916–1936
  I. Title
  941.7'0821
  ISBN 0-7165-2633-6

Library of Congress Cataloguing-in-Publication Data

Costello, Francis J.
  The Irish revolution and its aftermath, 1916–1923: years of revolt / Francis Costello.
    p. cm.
  Includes bibliographical references and index.
  ISBN 0-7165-2633-6
    1. Ireland–History–Civil War, 1922–1923. 2. Ireland–History–Easter Rising, 1916. 3.
  Ireland–History–1910–1921. I. Title

  DA962.C67 2002
  941.5082'1–dc21   2002032735

Typeset by Variorum Publishing Ltd., Rugby, UK

Printed by ColourBooks, Dublin

Contents

List of Illustrations

Preface

Although it is now more than seven decades since the Irish Revolution, it remains an era that can still be touched by those living in the present. This is so if for no other reason than the inescapable fact that the decisions made at that time to wage war and then to end it continue to colour not only Anglo-Irish relations, but the daily existence of ordinary people on the island of Ireland and particularly those in Northern Ireland. The momentous 'Good Friday Agreement' endorsed overwhelmingly on both sides of the Irish border in 1998 was in large part an effort to prevent the past from continuing to shape the future. For that reason the events spanning the years 1916–22, which gave rise to an armed revolt against British rule and subsequently to the creation of two separate jurisdictions on the island of Ireland, remain very close to the surface.

At the time of writing this volume, the seventy-fifth anniversary of Dáil Éireann has taken place with little notice in Ireland itself. Likewise, the seventy-fifth anniversary of the establishment of the Irish Free State passed with little public commemoration. Both non-occurrences in the way of significant public events or public forums at the very least aimed at assessing the state of Irish democracy may indeed suggest a certain ambivalence in modern Ireland about the origins of the State itself.

Indeed, efforts may be undertaken to rewrite Irish history, to try to sanitise the events of those years, or even to attempt to characterise the Irish Revolution as irrelevant to modern Ireland. But its achievements are nonetheless felt in Ireland today. Ireland today operates as an independent state within the European Union and as a member of the United Nations. Since the start of 2001 it has held a seat on the UN Security Council and its army is an effective contributor to UN peacekeeping activities. This may in part be due to the fact that many of the key actors who participated in the Irish independence effort, or who were involved in charting the course of an independent Ireland immediately afterwards, were still among the living until quite recently. For example, Eamon de Valera, the last living link to the leaders of the Easter Rising; Richard Mulcahy, who had been the IRA's Chief of Staff, and later leader of the Fine Gael Party; Ernest Blythe, ardent nationalist and defender of the Free State; Sean MacEntee, member of the First Dáil, opponent of the Anglo-Irish Treaty and later high-ranking minister in several Fianna Fáil governments; and General Tom Barry – these, among others, all lived well into the 1970s or 1980s. On more personal levels, memories linger of grandfathers, grandmothers, uncles, aunts, fathers or mothers who by one means or another challenged British rule. And there are also, for others, the memories, equally valid, of family members who served in the Royal Irish Constabulary or in the trenches for the British Army in the Great War and other conflicts.

In addition, unlike other epochs in Irish history, we can still see incidents and actors from this period come to life. In the newsreel footage many of those from the Irish Revolution, both British and Irish, Catholic and Protestant, continue to cast a presence. Michael Collins is seen collecting funds for the Dáil Loan, using the chopping block upon which Robert Emmet was beheaded, as the widow of the more recently executed Irish patriot Tom Clarke offers her subscription money for the cause. He cranks his head back offering his nonchalant, boyish smile. Then he hands her a receipt more like the bank clerk that he was before he became a revolutionary, doling out death to his opponents. We see the body of IRA guerrilla fighter Sean Treacy lying in the back of a British lorry after a deadly encounter with detectives and Auxiliaries on the streets of Dublin. Young men wearing caps and trench coats are questioned with hands raised by 'Black and Tans' on a windswept Irish country road. The Irish Delegates in another segment move briskly from their cars to enter No. 10 Downing Street to begin negotiations with their British counterparts. Later, Collins' funeral cortege moves slowly down Dublin's O'Connell Street.

The film archives of the recent 'troubles' also reflect the living connection with the earlier period of upheaval in Ireland. In a recent television documentary on the 1974 Dublin/Monaghan bombings in the Irish Republic – one of the worst atrocities emanating from the Northern Ireland conflict to date – the viewer sees a stately old man kneel in prayer at a funeral for some of the victims in Dublin's Pro-Cathedral. The image is that of Eamon de Valera, then the last surviving leader of the Easter Rising.

Unlike previous insurrections, the Irish Revolution was a revolt that would not be suppressed after a skirmish or two in a few Irish towns between poorly armed rebels and the local constabulary. Instead, it caught the British Empire's attention in a way which no insurrection in Ireland had previously. British rule was driven into retreat as the tools of terror and counter-terror were employed by IRA flying columns and Crown forces to deadly effect. From this grim, savage and often grindingly slow course of events emerged the current political configuration on the island of Ireland: a twenty-six County Republic and a Northern Ireland state now emerging from twenty-eight years of direct rule from London.

As one of the first conflicts for national independence in this century that featured the large-scale use of guerrilla warfare by an organised rebel force with popular indigenous support against the might of an Empire, the Anglo-Irish War of 1919–21 has been the subject of numerous interpretations. Memoirs and autobiographies by those involved – particularly on the Irish side – histories of Ireland and Britain covering this period, and more detailed analyses of the Anglo-Irish War published in recent years, have shed further light on that violent revolt and the British effort to suppress it. Within these pages the effort is made to chronicle many of the events of that war.

But an analysis of the British government's effort to pacify Ireland through the combination of political and military force during 1919–21, and of the IRA's guerrilla campaign during what is known as the 'Black and Tan War' and the 'Irish War of Independence', must be placed within the context of other developments. As important as the campaign of guerrilla warfare waged by the IRA during 1919–21 was in forcing the British Government at least into a position of stalemate in Ireland, it was but one key factor that resulted in the decision of the British Government to reverse its policy by mid-1921 and seek a negotiated settlement with the representatives of Sinn Féin. It is my intention herein to shed new light on British policy in Ireland, both civil and military, during the Anglo-Irish War, along with providing additional insight into the Irish revolutionary effort at all levels.

For Britain itself, it should be seen that its sights were not focused on Ireland alone at this time. Other problem areas requiring British attention in the aftermath of the Great War included the question of world disarmament, German war reparations, intervention in Russia, threatening situations in Silesia, Greece, and Palestine, as well as efforts to set in place a Commonwealth system by which the Empire itself might be preserved. In addition, the Indian subcontinent was a source of colonial unrest. Downing Street understood that Britain's success in dealing with Ireland could have a profound long-term effect on the Empire. Closer to home, British domestic unrest, particularly the protracted and costly railway workers' strike of 1919, added further to the burdens of the Coalition. In effect, the attempt to prosecute a policy of official coercion in Ireland amounted to more than a draining away of British energy and resources from other spheres of interest.

A wider examination of the efforts of Sinn Féin, through Dáil Éireann, and in defiance of the Crown, to set in motion institutions for Irish self-government is also in order. The popular support it garnered played a critical role in the British Government's ultimate policy reversal in Ireland. Similarly, the social and economic forces with which Sinn Féin had to contend during 1919–21 while confronting the British Empire also require attention, along with a closer look at the use of propaganda by both sides at home and abroad. In an analysis written less than a decade after the signing of the Anglo-Irish

Treaty of 1921, Winston Churchill asked the following series of rhetorical questions concerning Ireland's relationship with Britain:

> How is it that the great English political parties are shaken to their foundations and even shattered in almost every generation by contact with Irish affairs? ... Whence does this mysterious power of Ireland come? It is a small, poor, sparsely populated island, lapped about by British sea power, accessible on every side, without iron or coal. How is it that she sways our parties, and inflicts us with bitterness, and deranges our actions? How is it she has forced generation after generation to stop the whole traffic of the British Empire to debate her domestic affairs?[1]

Whatever Churchill's reasons for asking these questions, they offer an insight into how generations of British politicians had come to view Ireland. Ireland in essence was the problem, rather than British misgovernment in Ireland or the refusal to accept that a majority of its people saw themselves as members of a separate nation. The degree to which such concerns as American government attitudes and American public opinion towards Britain's Irish policy in the aftermath of a World War in which American financial largesse was sought will also be considered in these pages. Likewise, an examination of the competing obligations placed on Britain's financial, military and other resources during 1919–21 in the effort to preserve the Empire is also attempted herein, along with an assessment of the extent to which the Irish independence efforts evoked official British concerns that events in Ireland could spark colonial discontent elsewhere under the British flag.

In the end, the use of force on the part of the British government to pacify Ireland during these years failed. By mid-1921, the British government sought to accomplish at the negotiating table that which it had been unable to achieve during the almost two-and-a-half-year joint military and police campaign in Ireland, employing a combined force of 100,000 men at its high point. Both sides found themselves locked in stalemate, and both in the end sought a negotiated settlement made possible by the Anglo-Irish Truce that took effect on 11 July 1921. An analysis of the events leading up to the Truce, and of the tenuous circumstances that characterised the period of the Truce itself, will, I hope, provide a clearer perspective on why, by June 1921, the British government and the Sinn Féin regime both came to the conclusion that a negotiated settlement was in their mutual interest.

By interpreting sources not previously examined, and by attempting to cast a fresh gaze on some that have been covered elsewhere, I hope to provide the widest possible picture of the 1919–21 conflict and its aftermath. Within the context of Ireland itself, the papers, archives, and correspondence of British and Irish figures – both Nationalist and Unionist – have been consulted, as well as the official records of all undertakings relevant to the prosecution and resolution of the conflict.

In regard to the Republican effort, the records available from the IRA's General Headquarters and at the Brigade and Division level have been invaluable. The materials consulted on the British side, in addition to Cabinet, Colonial Office and British military reports, include the records of the British legation in the United States. Also most useful in offering a unique perspective were the US State Department files containing the reports of the US Consular staff in Ireland during the period in question. From the Irish standpoint, I have also sought to make use of such collections as those of Richard Mulcahy, Michael Collins, Ernie O'Malley, Erskine Childers, Terence MacSwiney, the Dáil Éireann Files and the Minutes of the Free State Cabinet both at the State Papers Office and also the Archives of the Irish Department of Defence.

A debt of gratitude is owed by me to the staff of the National Library of Ireland, the State Papers Office, Dublin, the Archives Departments at University College, Dublin and Trinity College, Dublin, the Military History Bureau of the Irish Department of Defence, the O'Neill Library at Boston College, the Lamont Library of Harvard University, the New York Public Library, the Boston Public Library, the British Public Record Office at Kew, the National Library of Wales, the House of Lords Record Office, the Archival Department at Oxford University and the Linen Hall Library Belfast. At each facility, kind and courteous help was afforded me by all whose assistance I sought.

I would also like to recognise the individual courtesies and encouragement extended to me by a range of people over a period of many years, including the late Paul O'Dwyer, Ray Flynn, Phil Flynn, Liam O'Murchu, John Owen, the late Liam de Paor, Eamon Phoenix, John Connorton, Sean Cronin, John Cullinane, Jim Lyons, Gerard Kearney, Paul Kelley, Paul Bew, the late Jim Cook, Tony Canniffe, and the late Peter Young. Most of all I wish to thank my devoted wife Anne, and our sons Eoghan, Emmett, Conor and Ronan. A special thank you is given to my devoted assistant Audrey Megquier for her patient and thorough help in preparing the manuscript.

FRANCIS COSTELLO
Belfast
September 2002

A Storm Builds within the Calm: the Prelude to Revolt

We do not seek any alternative of the constitution or supremacy of the Imperial Parliament. We ask merely to be permitted to take our place in the ranks of those other portions of the British Empire – some twenty-eight in number – which, in their own purely local affairs, are governed by free representative institutions of their own.

John Redmond, 'What Ireland Wants', *McClure's Magazine*, October 1910

It remains one of the paradoxes of Irish history that, despite a range of social and institutional reforms introduced by Britain in the late nineteenth century designed to pacify the country, Ireland nonetheless produced a revolt in 1916 that gave rise to a wider war of independence three years later.

By the turn of the century much that had antagonised nationalist Ireland had been ameliorated. The Anglican Church had been disestablished since 1867, and its once vilified Catholic counterpart held control of virtually all levels of education, including the provision of financial aid by the Crown for seminary training, by the turn of the century. Watershed land reform measures like the Wyndham Act created a nation of small landowners at the expense of the absentee landlords. In addition, the social reforms initiated by Gladstone in Britain were extended to Ireland with funds targeted for relief of the so-called 'congested districts'. Throughout the period 1880–91 the prospects of Home Rule for Ireland owed more to Charles Stewart Parnell's parliamentary tactics than to British altruism. Even after the demise of Parnell – 'the uncrowned King of Ireland' – the likelihood of Home Rule, sooner rather than later, continued to hold a certain inevitability.

Indeed, the success of the Irish Party at Westminster, and the combination of British reforms at virtually all levels of Irish society, resulted in the situation in which, by 1900, Irish constitutional nationalism held effective control of local government and the social institutions of much of Ireland. Why then a revolt in the streets of Dublin in 1916 and the subsequent Irish War of Independence? What were the issues and the circumstances that fuelled it?

The last decades of the nineteenth century represented the end of the monopoly of economic power which the Act of Union had placed in the hands of the Protestant gentry. It was James Fintan Lalor, a member of Young Ireland and an early agitator for land reform, who in the famine-racked Ireland of 1848 helped articulate the importance of the land issue to the cause of Irish nationalism:

> The land question contains, and the legislative question does not contain, the materials from which victory is manufactured, and that therefore, if we be truly in earnest and determined in success, it is on the former question, and not on the latter that we must take our stand, fling out our banner, and hurl down to England our badge of battle.[1]

The combination of the liberal Land Acts of 1870 and 1881, together with the Ashbourne Act of 1885 and the Syndham Act of 1903, contributed greatly to satisfying the demands of Irish agrarian agitators for 'a fixity of tenure, fair rent, and free sale'. Significantly, the transformation of Irish land ownership was accomplished within the context of constitutional politics. However, in addition to the agitation of the Irish Party and the Land League, the scenario for the attainment of these measures was made possible, ironically, by the awful effects of the Great Famine of 1847–50. Without that famine and the loss of over two million people to starvation and emigration, the establishment of large-scale proprietorship would have been rendered untenable. Furthermore, the agricultural disaster which beset Irish land-owners in the 1870s and 1880s contributed to a weakening of the resolve of the entrenched landowners; moreover, the achievement of land reform measures notwithstanding, the Irish census of 1891 showed a decline of 600,000 people during the previous decade. But while the provisions of land to significant numbers of the Irish peasantry reduced agrarian tensions by the end of the nineteenth century, the Irish Party's desire for Home Rule persisted.

Well before Gladstone's introduction of the First Home Rule Bill in April 1886, Parnell and the Irish Party had featured significantly on the British parliamentary landscape. The County Wicklow aristocrat's use of obstructionism within the legislature was ironically enhanced by the fact that, with 105 seats, Ireland held a disproportionately large share of seats in the House of Commons relative to its population. That disproportionate number was derived from the grim legacy of famine and emigration. Indeed, if divine wrath was measured out to successive British governments for its previous maladministration of Ireland, it would have appeared at times that the Irish Party's ability to stalemate Parliament was the divinity's chief instrument.

Parnell's downfall and the bitterness it provoked within the Irish Party left a serious wound in the Irish Nationalist movement. Without concerted and aggressive pressure on Westminster from a unified Irish Nationalist front, results were simply not forthcoming. The Party was unable to resurrect Home Rule as a likely occurrence with the Liberals' return to power in 1906. The

Liberals now had a huge electoral majority and so the Irish Party counted for much less. Likewise, the Liberals were internally divided over what form Home Rule should take. Similarly, after the Liberal landslide of 1906 Redmond was in no position to throw out a Liberal government that was recalcitrant on the Home Rule question. Indeed, even if he had been able to, the alternative would have been an openly hostile Tory regime.

Added to this were the changes within Britain's own political order. Out of power for almost two decades, the Liberals found a country ready for social reform. The split within the ranks of the Irish Parliamentary Party provoked by the Parnell tragedy would last for almost a decade, until John Dillon and John Redmond achieved unity in 1900. Until then, there were three factions – Redmondite, Dillonite, and Healyite. Yet from this disillusionment came a revival in Irish nationalism that expressed itself in cultural, athletic, economic and political terms.

In 1911, owing to the British domestic political crises that occurred between 1908 and 1911, the Irish Party was able to return to its position as the tie-breaker at Westminster. The two general elections held in 1910 greatly reduced huge Liberal majorities. In addition, the Parliament Act of 1911 limited the power of the House of Lords over the Home Rule Bill. But the measure did not fully calculate the capacity of Unionist resistance both within Ulster and at Westminster itself. While a Home Rule Bill was introduced in 1912, it was not until July 1914 that it reached its full gestation, and by that time developments on the European continent had drawn the British government's attention elsewhere. Ulster's resistance was by this time quickening, and becoming more volatile.

It was a truism that constitutional nationalism was at its strongest when the Irish Party could coerce a Liberal government. But the final and futile battle fought by the Irish Party for Home Rule laid bare its ineffectiveness. Protestant resistance to Home Rule in Ireland would also provide the out-of-power Tories in Britain – split over tariff reform – with a much needed political vehicle, which in turn conspired to make legitimate Unionist threats to defy the British Parliament.

The development of the Ulster unionist resistance proved the major stumbling block to the enactment of a Home Rule measure and the government's later decision not to implement the measure that won passage. On 23 September 1913, 500 delegates of the Ulster Unionist Council approved the establishment of a Provisional Government within the northeast if Home Rule became law. The Provisional Government was to consist of seventy-seven members, with Sir Edward Carson as Chairman of the central governing body. A military council was also established, with specific responsibilities in such areas as business, education, law, customs and the post office assigned to special committees. The effort to form a 'Provisional Government' had its roots in the militarism of these same conspirators the year before.

In Belfast on 28 September 1912, 218,000 Ulster Protestant men signed the 'Solemn League and Covenant', pledging to defend 'for ourselves and our children our cherished position of equal citizenship in the United Kingdom'. The Protestant women of Ulster were not invited to sign, but 228,000 of them signed a separate declaration pledging support to their men. The Covenant's signatories promised to use 'all means which may be found necessary to defeat the present conspiracy to set up a Home Rule Parliament in Ireland'. Rudyard Kipling's poem, 'Ulster 1912', served to characterise the outlook of the majority of Ulster Protestants toward the prospect of Home Rule:

> Believe we dare not boast
> Believe we dare not fear –
> We stand to pay the cost
> In all that men hold dear.
>
> What answer from the North?
> One Law, one Land, one Throne.
> If England drive us forth
> We shall not fall alone.[2]

The formation in 1912 of the Ulster Volunteer Force, under the instigation of Carson, represented a violent act against the British rule of law. It was aimed at preserving the Unionist minority within the Empire and outside the control of an Irish nation dominated by a Nationalist majority. In April 1913, one year before the arming of the Irish Volunteers, the collier ship *Clydevalley* made its way from Germany to Belfast for the Ulster volunteers. It is one of the ultimate ironies of Irish history that it was not the Irish separatists who would be the first to arm themselves at this early stage of the twentieth century against the actions of the British Government. It was instead the Protestants of Ulster.

In March 1914, Asquith offered an amendment authored by Lloyd George giving an option to the nine Ulster Counties to remain outside of Home Rule for six years, barring an Act of Parliament to the contrary. Carson rejected this on the basis that 'we do not want a sentence of death with a stay of execution for six years'. But as events will show, he would prove a willing architect of a partitioned Ireland with a six-county Northeast Ulster State.* Five days later, Winston Churchill, then a member of the special Cabinet Committee on the Ulster situation, caused a stir when he stated in a speech

---

* Carson, as early as 1913, had already lent his support to partition in some form, starting first with the Agar-Roberts proposal calling for the exclusion of the four Ulster Counties of Down, Antrim, Londonderry and Armagh from the provisions of a Home Rule Bill.

that there were 'worse things than bloodshed even on an extended scale'. In his view, the Ulster Provisional Government was 'engaged in a treasonable conspiracy'.[3] But Churchill's words were not backed up by British action. When confronted by Ulster loyalism's determination to disobey British law, the British Government looked the other way. Indeed, in a sop to the Unionists, the Government eventually appointed Carson as British Attorney General. Redmond was likewise offered a Cabinet position. He refused. Carson's determination and the lack of fear he exhibited in his opposition to Home Rule had worked to his advantage. His remarks uttered in Newry on 7 September 1913 serve to encapsulate both the level of his defiance of British law and his clever reading of the situation: 'There will be the danger and difficulties of trying to run a government of our own . . . I am told that it will be illegal . . . Don't be afraid of illegalities.'[4]

But while Carson's remarks were not lost on the Unionist faithful, they did contribute ironically to militant Irish nationalism's efforts to raise the stakes concerning Ireland's future. Conversely, the emergence of an armed Protestant militia was an incentive to militant Irish separatism, slowly emerging from its dormancy to act. Indeed, as one writer has noted, 'deep was calling deep'.[5] The formation of the Irish Volunteers in 1913 can be said to have been in large measure the answer of the South to the intransigence of the North. Redmond's decision to assume the leadership of the Volunteers was in fact a sign of weakness to the extent that it meant the resort to militarism over constitutionalism was the way forward. He was now attempting to stay ahead of the pace the militants were setting.

While Irish separatists of Eoin MacNeill's and Patrick Pearse's stripe were willing to be part of an umbrella group of armed Irishmen, which might result in Home Rule as a step towards independence, they would not swallow death on the fields of France in service to the Crown as some other Irishmen had. A minority – but significantly an armed one, the breakaway Irish Volunteers – would eventually provide the backbone of the Easter Rebellion of 1916. The unpopularity of the Great War in Ireland and the failure to gain Home Rule enabled Sinn Féin, the Irish Republican Brotherhood (IRB), and their kindred spirits, to gain ground at the expense of the constitutionalists.* In the aftermath of the Rising, the constitutionalists made a desperate effort for a settlement, one that included the exclusion of north-east Ulster. That attempt also failed. What would be the Irish Party's, and also Redmond's,

---

* The Irish Republican Brotherhood was formed in the United States after the American Civil War. Comprised largely of Irish-American veterans who fought in the Union Army, its aim was to foster physical force driven Irish separatism from British rule in Ireland. An excellent account of the history of the IRB is found in Leon O'Broin, *Revolutionary Underground: the Story of the Irish Republican Brotherhood*, 1858–1924 (Dublin, 1976).

last attempt at a constitutional resolution, came a year later at the Irish Convention.

In all, the years 1911–16 can be seen as a period of disintegration for constitutional nationalism. Redmond, a man of great personal integrity, was as much a victim of the difficulties of his times as of his own errors in judgement. He was a parliamentarian caught at a time when Irish parliamentarians of his type at Westminster were no longer needed. The Curragh mutiny in the spring of 1914 and the suspension of Home Rule were especially severe blows to his belief in Parliament.* In effect, the pace of events served to defy the grasp of Redmond and his party. Likewise, Redmond's decision to offer the Irish Volunteers as a unified force to the battlefields of Europe was rebuffed by many of his own countrymen.

During Redmond's tenure as leader of the Irish Party, one source of disagreement within his own ranks concerning strategy on the national question came from John Dillon. F. S. L. Lyons, who saw Dillon as the 'archetype' of young men of the 'Parnellite generation', provides a useful description of the parliamentarian's emergence as a constitutional nationalist. In effect, for young men like Dillon, it was a decision tempered more by pragmatism than a revulsion at physical force.

> Brought up in the traditions of Young Ireland, in youth an extremist by temperament, his later career is the record of a gradual evolution towards constitutional nationalism ... He did not regard physical force as immoral, rather as unfeasible; and even at that, as his record in 1916 reveals, he could not withhold either his sympathy or his respect from those who were prepared to die for their beliefs.[6]

---

* The Curragh mutiny within the British ranks took place in March 1914 and affected the 5th Division of the British Army, which covered the whole of the province of Ulster. Led by the Anglo-Irish commander of the 5th Division's cavalry brigade, Brigadier-General Hubert Gough, almost all the cavalry officers resigned their commission as a protest against any effort to 'coerce' Ulster into Home Rule and against involving them in reinforcing weapons depots in Ulster for possible use against the Ulster Volunteer Force (UVF). Gough secured a guarantee from the British Secretary of State that the army would not be used against the UVF. However, owing to a major uproar, the Cabinet repudiated the guarantee and the Secretary of State for War, the Chief of the Imperial Staff and the Commander-in-Chief in Ireland all resigned. Over time the order was rescinded and the resignations cancelled. While no British soldier refused an order, the events were clearly viewed by the German high command as evidence of division in the British Army. It should be noted that not all officers in the Curragh supported Gough's actions. Indeed, Major-General Sir Charles Ferguson, adhering to strict devotion to the rule of law persuaded the remaining divisional officers not to follow the cavalry's actions. For further reading on the Curragh mutiny see: Ian F. W. Beckett (ed.), *The Army and the Curragh Incident, 1914* (Army Records Society/Bodley Head, 1986); Sir James Fergusson, *The Curragh Incident* (Faber, 1964); and A. P. Ryan, *Mutiny at the Curragh* (Macmillan, 1956).

Opposition to nationalist violence was also tempered by some constitutional politicians who believed that the British Government was operating under a double standard: Nationalist violence or the threat of it would be harshly dealt with, but lawlessness by the Ulster Unionists was not only left unpunished, it was at times rewarded. The same Prime Minister Asquith who would condemn the actions of Sir Edward Carson and the other Ulster Covenanters on the grounds that 'a more deadly blow has never been dealt in our time by any body of responsible politicians at the very foundation on which democratic government rests' would appoint Carson, along with F. E. Smith and Bonar Law, in May 1915, to his War Cabinet.[7] Pearse had been handed a superb pretext for embarking on his revolutionary course. The 'lawful constitutional government' had condoned both revolutionary and military action to deny the democratic wishes of the people. It had also secretly committed itself to the partition of a previously united country.[8] With the British refusal to implement Home Rule for Ireland, Redmond no longer had anything to offer. The Party's *raison d'etre* now lay smashed upon the rocks of political expediency.

Redmond and his fellow moderate Irish Nationalists also suffered from the same inability of more radical Irish Nationalists to come to terms with the reality of Ulster unionism. In Redmond's view, Carson's efforts were all a bluff. Likewise, in the eyes of the IRB and Sinn Féin the activities of the Ulster resistance to Home Rule were at their core a plot of British manufacture aimed at dividing Ireland and denying the island complete autonomy. Erhard Rumpf has written that unionism in Ulster 'was not merely a political creed of a small social and economic elite, but a mass movement with an extremely broad social base'.[9] This analysis explains Ulster unionism in a way that was lacking in the attitudes of Irish Nationalists of all schools. It is also an assessment that is relevant in the present.

> The Protestants in Ulster could not be termed an elite except in a very special sense that they constituted and still do a disproportionately large element of professional, managerial, and skilled manual workers, and a corresponding smaller proportion of the unskilled and semi-skilled groups. The relationship between Protestants and Catholics in the North was thus not, as it was in the rest of the country, simply a more than virulent form of class antagonism, but an extremely complex structure of sectarian suspicion, animosity, and segregation.[10]

The inability of virtually all elements within Irish nationalism to understand the determination on the part of Ulster Unionists to remain outside the confines of an Ireland ruled by a Catholic majority would prove to be a source of enduring myopia. The wishful thinking which the Redmondites and Sinn Féin alike held on the subject of Unionist inclusion within a united Ireland framework is also well captured in J. J. Lee's important work on Ireland in the twentieth century.

The essential assumption was that Ulster Protestant attitudes were basically the consequence of British duplicity. The Unionist mentality was attributed to the divide and conquer policies pursued by Britain. Once the British notified the Unionists that their interests would be satisfactorily guarded in a home rule state, the scales would drop from their eyes and they too would enter the promised land. Ulster Unionists, on this assumption, were the creatures of Westminster, utterly incapable of objectively assessing their own situation, puppets dangling from British strings.[11]

Conversely, the collective self-image of Ulster Unionists was equally fanciful. Despite the initial objections of figures such as Carson, many Protestant leaders proved ready to accept a partition arrangement which would guarantee the maximum degree of Protestant hegemony possible. This was so even if it meant excluding large numbers of other Ulster Protestants in Counties Monaghan, Cavan and Donegal. To the significant Unionist minorities of these three Ulster counties – all signatories to the Ulster Covenant – it was, to say the least, a jolt to the cherished values of honour and the belief that the collective word of unionism was tied to an unbreachable bond. Realpolitik had prevailed and their future as British citizens was scuttled in the equation, except for those who would later vote with their feet and move into the territory of the six north-eastern Ulster counties.

But while the contentious issue of Home Rule loomed large across the Irish political scene, the impact of certain cultural movements also began to take root in the new century. The last decades of the nineteenth century had witnessed the emergence of a number of literary societies and cultural organisations extending down to the grass-roots level. Donal McCartney has observed that 'out of these tiny seed-beds, which were half literary and half political, sprang such influential movements as the Anglo-Irish literary revival, the Gaelic League and Sinn Féin'.[12]

These developments on the cultural and intellectual front during the 1890s and the first decade of the twentieth century, through the intervention of the Irish Republican Brotherhood in both the Gaelic League and Sinn Féin, eventually provided the basis for the creation of revolutionary Irish government. This new entity proclaimed and asserted its independence from Britain. One organisation which demonstrated a commitment to developing a sense of Irish identity, as well as staying power, was the Gaelic Athletic Association (GAA). Founded in 1884, the organisation's overriding objective was the institutionalisation of the Gaelic games of football and hurling from the parish level up. From the outset the RIC, at least, viewed the Gaelic Athletic Association as a Fenian plot.[13] One IRB sympathiser at Dublin Castle, who would eventually work as an intelligence source for Michael Collins, wrote that the election of Michael Cusack to a position of prominence in the GAA was engineered by the Irish Republican Brotherhood. Cusack was favoured at a meeting of a leading IRB cell in Blackrock, County Dublin in 1883, because it was felt that 'prominent anti-constitutionalists should not, in the initial stages at all events, openly appear to dominate'.[14] His own separatist credentials were apparently held in very high regard by the IRB.

The situation confronting the Gaelic League was somewhat different. The decline of the Irish language in the nineteenth century is best illustrated by census figures showing that between 1861 and 1891 Ireland as a whole contained fewer Irish speakers than the province of Connaught (the smallest Irish province in terms of population) had during the previous thirty years. A lion-hearted effort at turning this tide was launched on 31 July 1893 at a sparsely attended meeting at No. 9 Lower O'Connell Street when the Gaelic League was founded. Its founder and first President, Dr Douglas Hyde, was both a Protestant and a nominal Unionist. The Gaelic League would grow to have a great impact on the course of Irish separatism.

The organisation was to prove itself as more than an agency for Irish instruction. It's role grew to include stimulating native Irish economic development and the study of Irish history, together with organised social and cultural activities, Irish in character. Both the Gaelic League and Sinn Féin became important tools for the adherents of physical force, because they formed, as Richard Davis notes, 'both the cover and the starting point for later violent efforts'.[15] The eventual domination of these movements by the separatists who joined and had slowly taken over would leave their respective founders, Hyde and Griffith, bitter, although both would play a role in the creation of an independent Irish state.

In July 1915, Douglas Hyde resigned his Presidency of the Gaelic League because of its politicisation as a vehicle for extreme nationalism. The IRB gained control of the Executive, adding a political definition of freedom rather than a cultural one. Such notables in the 1916 Rising as Patrick Pearse and Tom Clarke, with good reason, saw the value of the Gaelic League as a binding agent for Irish separatism. In February 1914, Pearse called the organisation the 'most revolutionary influence that has ever come into Ireland. The Irish revolution really began when the seven Gaelic Leaguers met in O'Connell Street ... The germ of all future Irish history was in the back room ...'.[16] While its founder, Dr Hyde, wanted the organisation to have a major impact, he was less than enamoured by the League's takeover by the IRB and its adherents. At the time of his resignation in 1915, he wrote to a friend: 'My work for 22 years was to restore Ireland to her intellectual independence. I would have completed it had I been let. These people queered the pitch on me, mixed the physical and the intellectual together, interpreted my teaching in terms of bullets and swords, before the time, and have reduced me to impotence.'[17] Hyde was undoubtedly even less comforted by the knowledge that the man elected Secretary of the Gaelic League, Tom Clarke, did not even speak the language.

Hyde's views on the IRB and other Irish separatists were subject to change over the years. Later, perhaps based on the level of success attained by the Irish separatist movement in the aftermath of 1916, Hyde moved away from the accommodations he felt he had to make with Irish moderates. While he may not have been a nationalist in the political sense, Hyde struck a tender chord in many ordinary Catholics seeking a sense of cultural identity. In a later view, expressed in an unpublished account, Hyde wrote revealingly about his own contribution and the role played by the physical force separatists who essentially ousted him from his leadership position in the language movement:

> I am not sure that the turn things have taken may not be the best thing for the language movement ... It has put an end to my dreams of using the language as a unifying bond to join all Irishmen together, but it at least rendered the movement homogenous ... I am not at all sure that the League did not do the right thing for the language in practically throwing me over. I did not see it at the time, however, for I did not foresee the utter and swift debacle of the Irish Parliamentary Party and the apotheosis of Sinn Féin ... [18]

Patrick Pearse's own involvement in the Gaelic League did not have a hidden agenda, his later actions within the Irish Volunteers and his treatment of Eoin MacNeill and others notwithstanding. In the 8 November 1913 issue, for example, of *An Claidheamh Soluis*, the League's official publication, he outlined clearly his view of what the organisation's utility had been to the cause of Irish separatism. His remarks were also significant in revealing his belief that the League was, by that time, becoming a 'spent force' from a nationalist standpoint. This latter point may be useful in explaining Pearse's actions within the context of the Irish Volunteer movement and the course of Irish separatism from 1914 onward.

> I have come to the conclusion that the Gaelic League, as the Gaelic League, is a spent force; and I am glad of it ... I mean that the vital work to be done in the new Ireland will be done not so much by the Gaelic League as by men and movements that have sprung from the Gaelic League ... [19]

Pearse was particularly candid, and perhaps even prescient in describing what he saw as likely to take shape in the following years:

> There will be in the Ireland of the next few years a multitudinous activity of Freedom Clubs, Young Republican Clubs, Labour Organizations, Socialist groups, and what not; bewildering enterprises undertaken by sane persons and insane persons, many of them seemingly contradictory, some mutually destructive, yet all tending towards a common objective, and that objective: the Irish Revolution.[20]

Sinn Féin likewise grew to include radical and moderate Irish separatists, while still containing many who were not separatists at all. P. S. O'Hegarty has noted that Arthur Griffith did his utmost to drive out the physical force men who might frighten away the priests, and moderate businessmen whom he was hoping to conciliate.[21] Each year, between 1908 and 1914, under Griffith's tutelage, the organisation sponsored an annual industrial exhibition empha-sising Irish domestic development. At the turn of the century Sinn Féin grew from a single Irish separatist club into an organisation that subsumed groups like the Dungannon clubs and Cumann na Gaedheal. In 1903, Griffith had emerged as the most experienced man in the movement upon the death of his mentor, William Rooney. Earlier, Griffith had played a principal role with Rooney in the setting up of the *United Irishman*, a small but influential Irish nationalist weekly among the IRB and other advanced nationalists.

Unlike the IRB, Sinn Féin's early heroes were not the physical force advo-cates but intellectuals like Thomas Davis, and Charles Stewart Parnell. Donal McCartney has written that 'essentially Griffith was more like Davis than Parnell: he was not so much the leader of a political organisation as a pro-pagandist, a national philosopher'.[22] But while Griffith's thinking followed a path towards Ireland's national development that was at variance with phy-sical force, he was anything but a member of the camp of constitutional nationalism in the tradition of the Irish Party at Westminster. While he advocated an Irish constitution in the tradition of Grattan, along with the creation of a dual monarchy between Ireland and Britain on the model of Austria and Hungary, Griffith argued at the same time that those Irish MPs who took their seats at Westminster were, in essence, parties to an act of criminality against the Irish nation. On the grounds that the Act of Union of 1800 which bound Ireland to Britain was achieved only by British Imperial aggression rather than mutual consent, Griffith argued that 'no lapse of time, no ignorant acquiescence, can render legal an illegal act'.[23]

It was these latter arguments that eventually made Sinn Féin politically attractive to the IRB as a vehicle for physical force separatism, much as the Gaelic League had attracted them at the cultural level. Soon, Griffith came to realise that, like Douglas Hyde, his own organisation had been seized from him by younger and more militant men. Without them, however, the decline occurring within Sinn Féin prior to 1916 might not have been reversed. Indeed, the revolution they would instigate gave Sinn Féin new life.

The framework which Arthur Griffith's Sinn Féin movement provided through the advocacy of obstructionist tactics, the boycott of British goods, abstentionism from Westminster, and the development of native Irish legal and local governmental administrative institutions in defiance of the Crown, enabled advanced Irish nationalism to offer an actual alternative to the Irish Party and a basis for building wide public support. This was particularly true after the collapse of constitutional nationalism's Home Rule effort. By providing

Irish Republicanism with the ideological basis from which to lay the groundwork for a native Irish Government, Irish separatism was taken for the first time beyond the confines of a dedicated group of conspirators committed simply to violent revolt.

Griffith's philosophy of non-cooperation with British rule in Ireland found its roots in the policy outlined by James Fintan Lalor in 1847. It was further influenced by the Dungannon clubs later in the nineteenth century. But it would not be until 1919–21 that an effort aimed at boycotting the British civil administration and its courts and replacing it with a native Irish system was attempted. Nonetheless, the attractiveness of the Gaelic League and Sinn Féin to Irish separatists of the physical force side was motivated by far more than the opportunities offered by their takeover. There was, at bottom, a fundamental commonality of interests which Pearse, among others, shared with Hyde and Griffith. As in the case of Thomas Davis and the Young Irelanders before them, British rule was a source of cultural as well as political domination. Britain, through its laws, its materialism and its educational system as implemented in Ireland – along with its 'depraved' literature – had effectively polluted Ireland, and at the same time served to eradicate any sense of Irish identity. The recreation of Irish society, for Griffith and many cultural nationalists, was also rooted in the values of Irish Catholicism. They also favoured a restructuring of the Irish educational system, which they held was laden with a stifling pro-British bias.

It was indeed an analysis that also reached beyond those with only passive remedies in mind. Ernie O'Malley, the son of a unionist County Mayo middle class Catholic family, who left medical school to take up arms against the Crown and who would play a leading role as an organiser of the subsequent guerrilla war campaign, offered this view of the Ireland he saw under British rule. His was one of the most literate voices of the generation of Irish revolutionaries that came of age after the Easter 'Rising'.

> Ours was the country of broken tradition, a story of economic, social and mental oppression, propped up by a mythological introduction innocent of archeological or historical interpretation. To compensate for the submerged centuries our early historical significance had been emphasised. We were a nation of saints and scholars, we had often been told, but our experience had disproved the cliche. If sainthood was intolerance, we had a great share of it. If scholarship was living on the unearned appreciation of people who wrote or taught eleven hundred years ago, and whose works were hardly known to us, then we were scholars. We did not see through either the unbroken arrogance of chiefs, or a purely literary tradition unsifted by literary criticism .... The laws of aristocratic tradition were in our teeth. We favoured the royalists in the English civil war, the beaten South in America, and the Irish battalion that had fought against Italian freedom ... [24]

The cost to Ireland, O'Malley argued, was a dear one. 'Cut off from scientific and intellectual eddies,' he wrote, 'we had built a world of our own, an emotional life but no philosophy or economic framework. Physically we have never had control of the land in peace (with the exception of Grattan's Parliament). As an agricultural people, we lacked scientific training. We were a ranch sending bullocks to England, boys and girls to America.' But O'Malley also added a note of anti-clericalism with his argument that the 'Catholic Church, unlike the Empire, made use of both ends of the social system ...'.[25]

By the early 1900's Irish nationalism had moved closer to Catholicism, rendering it almost synonymous with Catholic Ireland. The synthesis that had occurred between Irish cultural nationalism and Catholic Ireland is reflected in the creative work of Canon P. A. Sheehan, the Catholic cleric. His 1914 novel, *The Graves of Kilmorna*, served as a vehicle for attacks on what he saw as the moral corruption of the Irish Parliamentary Party as well as British imperialism and socialism in general.[26] Earlier he had written in terms similar to those of Pearse, promoting blood sacrifice: 'I have never thought of anything higher or greater than to strike one smashing blow for Ireland, and then lie down to die on some Irish hillside ...'[27] Yet, while much attention has been drawn over the years to Pearse's own use of the language of 'blood sacrifice' in his exhortation of Irish manhood to take up arms against British rule, it should be noted that such rhetoric resembled the equally effusive comments on the cleansing effects of blood uttered by political leaders and leading literary figures elsewhere at that time. Such sentiments were particularly prevalent in Britain during both the Boer War and the Great War and one need look no further than the Kipling poems 'Ulster 1912' and 'British-Roman Song' or, on a broader scale, to the rhetoric used by the British Government in urging the 'liberation' of Belgium in the midst of the Great War.

Viewing Pearse narrowly as an Irish Catholic social conservative also provides a limited picture of the man. His role as an Irish educationalist is a subject for analysis in its own right. At the end of his young life, Pearse, the Irish Catholic separatist, would accommodate himself with socialism, as conversely James Connolly, Ireland's premier socialist thinker and activist, would come to embrace the religious tenets of Catholicism not long before they both faced a British firing squad. In *The Sovereign People*, shocked by the conditions of the Dublin working class, Pearse wrote: 'The end of freedom is human happiness. The end of national freedom is industrial freedom ... National freedom implies national sovereignty. National sovereignty implies control of all the moral and material resources of the nation ... In other words, no private right to property is good against the public right of the nation ...'[28]*

---

* It will be seen elsewhere that Pearse's philosophy, as outlined, also served at least in part as the basis for the Democratic Programme, ratified by the First Dáil in January 1919. His views perhaps had a wider impact on that body on social questions than the views of James Connolly.

The combination of land reform, a generally stable economy, and the like-lihood of a Home Rule measure becoming a reality contributed greatly to the calm that seemed, on the surface at least, to characterise Ireland during the first decade of the twentieth century. For advocates of physical force, how-ever, who were clearly in the minority, it was anything but a happy time. P. S. O'Hegarty, an early Sinn Féin propagandist writing in 1912, stated: 'It was indeed a period to try the hearts of the stoutest. It seemed as if the famine clearances and constant emigration drain had broken Ireland's back.'[29] He also showed himself to be particularly adept at characterising the contempt held by the surviving Fenian veterans for both constitutional nationalism and a younger generation they found quite wanting:

> You will find them ... in the cities, but you will find them also in the country places, in villages that look as if a breath of passion had never stirred there, in lonely farm-houses ... And they will tell you fiercely and passionately, that there is but one way. The old way. 'What is the good of your Sinn Féin movements,' said one of them to me not long ago, 'unless you arm the people. Talk will never free the country, and all your plans are useless unless you can back them up with guns.'[30]

Such a man from that older generation was Tom Clarke, imprisoned for much of his life up to that point for his Fenian activities. Clarke, who had been inspired by the example of even older men like O'Donovan Rossa and John O'Leary, in turn inspired the young Michael Collins, staff captain to Joseph Plunkett in the General Post Office (GPO) during the Rising. Collins would go on to become the mastermind of a more successful brand of physical force separatism. Indeed, it would be the memory of seeing an old and vanquished Tom Clarke stripped and degraded after his surrender that lead him to mark the offending British officer for assassination three years later. A younger generation of IRB men, perhaps more ruthless, would avenge the suffering and the humiliation of the old.

The writings of O'Hegarty and Pearse had the effect of making Tom Clarke a happy man during the final years of a life ended by a British firing squad at the age of fifty-eight. In a letter to Joseph McGarrity, the Clan na Gael leader in the United States, he described the change he witnessed among young Irishmen as the result of the combined influence of the Irish Volunteer movement and the multiplicity of political and cultural groups which had spurred a greater sense of Irish identity. He especially rejoiced at a mass meeting of the Volunteers held in Dublin in November 1914:

> Joe, it is worth living in Ireland these times – there is an awakening – the slow, silent prodding and the open preaching is at last showing results. Things are in full swing on the upgrade ... I can't, I won't try to give you a history of the causes that have brought about what I refer to – Just take it for granted that the prospect today, from the national point of view, is brighter than it

has been in many a long year ... tis good to be in Ireland these times ... hundreds of young fellows who could not be interested in the national move-ment ... are in these volunteers and are saying things which prove that the right spot has been touched in them by the volunteers. Wait till they get their first clutching the steel barrel of a business rifle and then Irish instincts and Irish manhood can be relied upon.[31]

Even in the original Irish Volunteers, the influence of the more militant Irish separatists was felt. As MacDonagh writes, 'using leading members of the Gaelic League, especially Eoin MacNeill, as 'front men', the Irish Republican Brotherhood intended to control the new body through Sean MacDermott and a very recent and most important convert, Patrick Pearse'.[32] The two came to occupy leadership roles in the Volunteer Executive. The advo-cates of physical force were now positioned to take centre stage on Irish nationalism.

Pearse did not start out as an advocate of physical force, however. At one stage he warned Eoin MacNeill of the danger of allowing extreme nationalists such as Hobson into prominent posts in the Volunteers out of a fear that they might seize control of Irish volunteers. As late as January 1914, Pearse stated in Limerick that '[i]n the Volunteer movement we are going to give Red-mond a weapon which will enable him to enforce the demand for Home Rule.'[33]

Yet, by August of that year, he was in fact making it clear in his corre-spondence with John Devoy, the IRB leader in the United States, that guns were needed and that physical force was necessary to advance the separatists' ideal. Redmond's open intention to place the Volunteer movement at the disposal of the British Empire for the war in Europe was unacceptable to him. 'To everyone in Ireland that has any brains it seems madness or treachery on Redmond's part', he wrote in a letter to Devoy on 12 August. For Pearse, Eoin MacNeill's acquiescence in Redmond's efforts to steer the Volunteers toward taking up arms for England was a great part of the difficulty. 'I blame MacNeill more than anyone', he told Devoy. 'He has the reputation of being 'tactful', but his 'tact' consists of bowing to the will of the Redmondites every time.'[34]

In MacNeill's oration at the launching of the Volunteers, he emphasised the influence which the Ulster Volunteers had in spurring on the formation of the nationalist military organisation. 'The Ulster unionists were always Home Rulers at heart. They have gone straight for Home Rule and have got it. We of the Irish Volunteers must admit candidly that it is the Ulster Volunteers who have opened the way for the Irish Volunteers.'[35] But while Pearse was also impressed with the action taken by the Volunteers, he was at the same time dismayed by the ineffectiveness shown by the physical force adherents in securing arms in any significant quantity for themselves. The 900 guns that landed in Howth on Erskine Childers' *Asgard* seemed to him 'antiquated' and 'inferior to the British service rifle and even to those which Carson's men have'.[36] Pearse made it clear to Devoy that guns were needed from America.

> It is obvious that before we can intervene, or even pretend to intervene, in the crisis to any purpose we must have guns. Hence the one great urgent duty of the hour, the duty which overshadows every other duty, is to get guns and ammunition into the country. It is up to the American Committee to act at once and on a large scale. You are as much alive to the need as I am. Every penny you can command must be expended now and the goods sent to us with as little delay as possible. A supreme moment for Ireland may be at hand. We shall go down to our graves beaten and disgraced men if we are not ready for it.[37]

In the meantime, the increasing prospect of the extension of conscription to Ireland served to spur on the preparations of the separatists for revolt. In those early stages of 1915 and 1916, the foundation for a guerrilla war was laid. Bulmer Hobson credited J. J. O'Connell, later a General of the Irish Free State Army, for laying the basis for guerrilla warfare by his advocacy of 'hedge fighting'.[38] These efforts, he wrote, were 'calculated to turn the men's minds to the possibilities of putting up a resistance which could be prolonged and would be very difficult for a foreign force to suppress'.[39] Hobson elaborated further on the internal planning of the IRB in the year before the Rising:

> Out of the many discussions a general plan began to emerge. In the event of conscription being imposed on the country, it was intended that men drafted for the army should join small flying columns in various parts of the country, defend themselves from being captured, with whatever arms we could obtain, and conduct a guerrilla war against the forces sent to draft them into the British armies . . . [40]

But while Hobson and others were committed to a plan of action for a rising, they did not agree with Pearse and the rest of the minority in the IRB executive that it should actually take place as early as Easter Week 1916. Indeed, assurances given by Pearse and MacDonagh that they would not commit the volunteers to any plan of action not approved by the Executive Committee were later recalled with bitterness by Hobson. He wrote candidly of this occurrence together with the lack of support the rising received from the general population: 'I thought of this later as I watched the Dublin mob, not join Connolly in the Post office, but looting the shops in O'Connell Street. I thought of it again when I read in the press box how the British soldiers after surrender had to protect their prisoners from the violence of the Dublin populace.'[41]

However, it would be a mistake to overstate the difference in philosophy between the Hobson–MacNeill camp and the Pearse–Connolly camp, among other conspiratorial combinations, as to the correct timing for a rebellion.

Connolly had, to the consternation of Pearse and others, made plans for the Citizens Army – no more than 300 strong – to commence a rebellion in the Spring of 1916, separate and apart from the IRB's own hidden agenda. Hence it can be seen that during the period January–April 1916 sub-plot after sub-plot was added to counter-plot. What is most significant is that to the majority of separatists who had joined the Gaelic League and Sinn Féin, including Hobson, there was a commitment to physical force through the involvement of the Irish Volunteers. A military council set up by a minority within the IRB in 1915 planned a rising for Easter 1916. That body consisted of Pearse, Plunkett, Ceannt, and later MacDermott, who formed half of the block of signatories to the Easter 1916 Proclamation.[42]*

But it was the killing of the fires of Irish Home Rule by the British Government that made the appeal of Irish separatism to physical force more compelling. The process was an incremental one, but it was no doubt fuelled by the state of ineffectiveness that Irish constitutional nationalism had reached at Westminster. No matter how brave a face John Redmond and company attempted, the government had spoken: Home Rule for Ireland, for all intents and purposes, was a dead issue. For the advocation of physical force, the stage was now set for a journey headed away from the skullduggery of politics and towards the world of idealism. It also would mean a road to carnage and death in Ireland.

One man who made it his business to ensure that a revolt took place was James Connolly. He had emerged as an independent force. Connolly, as Sean Cronin has noted, 'had spent a lifetime studying revolution. Irish history was filled with men who had waited for the right moment and then lost.' In Connolly's own words, an insurrection was 'a leap in the dark'.[43]

There is much to this argument. In the case of the 1916 leaders, the difficulties they had encountered in realising the dreams of the Gaelic League may have had an impact in their decision to pursue violent methods sooner rather than later. Tom Garvin, in his study of the physical force tradition, has expounded upon this viewpoint:

> Many of the leaders had invested much psychic capital and personal energy in the Gaelic League's forlorn attempt to bring about a spiritual and cultural revolution through the campaign to revive the Irish language ... Many of them knew, at least subconsciously, by 1914 that this campaign was running into impassable social obstacles and may have fast impelled the resort to insurrectionary political activity in part as a compensatory device.[44]

But idealists often do not make for good military tacticians. The failure of the rebels to take over the Dublin Telephone Exchange and to seize the wireless station in the area made it possible for British reinforcements to be

---

* All were subsequently executed.

sent from the Curragh and England.[45] It is more than ironic that Sean MacDermott, who was inside the GPO as Pearse surrendered, recognised that the goal of the Rising had been met, and that continued struggle would be futile. Aware of his own likely execution, he offered the members of the ranks inside the GPO a remarkably dispassionate assessment of what the future might bring to the survivors of the Rising:

> You've already fought a gallant fight ... You gain nothing, you lose every-thing if you try to continue ... They'll send you to prison for a few years, that's the worst. But what does it matter if you survive? The thing you must do, all of you, is survive, come back, carry on the work so nobly began this week. Those of us who are shot can die happy if we know you'll be living on to finish what we started.[46]

While MacDermott's remarks would be taken to heart by many of the young men who in fact survived to fight another day, so was the advice given by Major John MacBride after he and his men surrendered at the Jacob's Bis-cuits Factory: 'Take my advice, never allow yourselves to be cooped up inside the walls of a building again.'[47] Similar sentiments, perhaps more pointed at the leaders of the rebellion, were expressed later by Michael Collins: 'The Rising Week was not an appropriate time for the issue of a memorandum couched in poetic phrases, nor of actions worked out in similar fashion. Looking at it from inside it had the air of a Greek comedy about it.'[48]

If the British government had underestimated the potential for an armed revolt in the streets of Dublin, it was not because it had occurred without warning. One newspaper, in fact, editorialised a month before the Rising that the conditions for an insurrection were ripe:

> There is the devil's own row in Dublin over the action of the Sinn Féiners. If the government of the country is not placed in stronger hands, I would not be surprised if we have an explosion ... The Sinn Féiner's may muster courage to commit some outrage ... the military authorities in Ireland are handi-capped by the civil authorities at the Castle.[49]

In the aftermath of the Rising came an even stronger warning from within the counsels of the British Government, one that would have a prophetic air to it. To James Campbell, a Unionist and a Protestant Irishman who was then Attorney General for Ireland, the imposition of partition as outlined in the amendment to what was to be the last Home Rule Bill would only worsen the situation in the country. In a confidential memorandum addressed to the Cabinet in June 1916, Campbell wrote:

> Englishmen may well think that the experiment is worth the risk, but no Irishman who is conscious of the dreadful results that must inevitably follow from its failure can regard it as anything short of a desperate and dangerous

gamble while its success must permanently divide the Irish nation into two hostile sections, each bearing the statutory brand of a distinctive religious sentiment. One side or the other is going to be deceived in this matter, with the inevitable consequences of bitter recrimination and renewed agitation.[50]

Ironically, Campbell's analysis was not all that far removed from that of James Connolly. Two years earlier in *The Irish Worker* Connolly wrote that partition would lead to a 'carnival of reaction in both North and South, would set back the wheels of progress, would destroy the oncoming unity of the Irish labor movement and paralyse all advanced movements while it lasted'. Connolly also emphasised that 'Labour should give its bitterest opposition against it. Labour in Ulster should fight even to the death if necessary, as our fathers fought before us.'[51]

While it may have been a rare instance where an Irish Unionist like Campbell and an Irish Republican Socialist such as Connolly saw eye to eye, an open expression of respect for the rebel leader came after his death from another leading Irish Unionist, Sir Horace Plunkett. That the vehicle for this expression was in fact a letter to King George V is itself noteworthy. The correspondence, written during Plunkett's tenure as President of the Irish Convention (1917–18), also provides a useful insight into the impact of Connolly's loss to Ireland as well as to Irish separatism:

> When the governing body met on Saturday before the tragic Easter Monday, the to be or not to be of the attempt to set up an Irish Republic by a majority of one, the fatal resolution was carried. The decision was due to the powerful influence of James Connolly – a far abler labour leader than Larkin ... Conolly was a unique combination of international socialist and Irish nationalist. He carried with him the working classes of Dublin, whose condition, ever deplorable, was aggravated by the war which brought them little of the highly paid employment elsewhere ... [52]

The leaders of the Rising were sentenced by tribunals set up under the Defence of the Realm Act (DORA). In all, 1,800 members of the Volunteers were deported to Britain following the 'Rising'. The majority of them would remain there in various internment camps for the next eight months.

Beyond the executions and the deportations, the British also sought out their own scapegoats. They, however, would be dealt with without violence. A Royal Commission appointed by Prime Minister Asquith after hearing evidence in closed hearings from 9–11 May 1916, held Augustine Birrell, the British Chief Secretary for Ireland, directly responsible for not taking steps in advance to disarm the Volunteers. The Commission's findings led to Birrell's ouster. In his defence, when asked to explain why the Volunteers were allowed in the months up to the Rising to train openly with their weapons unimpeded by the Government in Ireland, Birrell answered: 'I quite agree, it seems almost ridiculous, but on the other hand the alternative would have been to have employed soldiers. The police could not have done it. You would have had to attack these people, disarm them, and whether that was done north, south, east or west, it would have resulted in bloodshed.'[53]

Birrell presented himself at once as both too logical and too civilised. He knew well that such an action would have achieved little in the way of a positive response from the great number of Irish people to British rule. Consequently he became the convenient scapegoat for a British administrative apparatus in Ireland that had begun falling apart well before he arrived on the scene to preside over it.

Evaluating the success or failure of the 1916 Rising in military terms alone is clearly inadequate. Indeed, by any military definition, the Rising was a fiasco. It lacked organisation and manpower, as well as public support, and outside of Dublin there was little in the way of a revolt. Nonetheless, the 'Rising' of that Easter Week represented an important watershed for Irish nationalism. When tied to the resulting British over-reaction in executing its leaders, it may well have marked the death knell for the Irish Party well before the 1918 General Election. Significantly, the Rising and its aftermath served to galvanise all shades of Irish separatism. Even prior to Pearse's surrender, Arthur Griffith had directly offered his services as a combatant to the GPO Command. The pendulum had shifted in the world of Irish nationalism, away from Home Rule to complete independence.

The Easter Rising also came wrapped in the ideals expressed in the Easter Proclamation, the document read aloud by Pearse in front of the General Post Office to a combination of confused and bemused passersby as the rebels seized the building. In time that document would be on the walls of hundreds of thousands of Irish households and public places throughout the world. It explained in clear-cut terms the objectives of the six men who signed it with Pearse, including three members of the Irish Republican Brotherhood.

In straightforward terms the Easter Proclamation heralded the announcement of a new State, using language that was evocative of the American Declaration of Independence and the French Declaration of the Rights of Man. Liam de Paor, in his invaluable analysis of the Easter Proclamation, argues that the purpose of the Rising 'was to issue the Proclamation, with sufficient force and courage to give it meaning'.[54] By issuing the document in the midst of a violent revolt it was the rebels' intent to magnify their effort to achieve an independent Ireland and to reach an audience beyond Ireland itself while also arousing the nation at home.

The final text drafted largely by Pearse proclaimed the creation of a 'Provisional Government'. But it was not the first 'Provisional Government' declared on the island of Ireland, given that the Ulster Unionist Council had proclaimed one of its own in November 1913 in defiance of Home Rule. The 'Irish Republic' which the Easter Proclamation proclaimed under arms, however, gripped the consciousness of Irish nationalism. This was owed to the confluence of two events: the Easter Rising itself and the failure, soon to be realised, that despite the sacrifice of tens of thousands of young Catholic Irishmen on the fields of Europe under the Redmondite banner in defence of the British Empire, Home Rule for Ireland was no more likely than before.

Indeed, the events of Easter Week would in short order help obscure that sacrifice in Europe. Shortly before he would himself die in an English uniform in battle on the Continent, the poet Tom Kettle penned these wistful lines for his daughter, grasping to the end to a heroic justification for the sacrifice of his Irish countrymen. It was written not long after the events of Easter Week, where other Irishmen died under an Irish sky to sever the connection to the Crown.

> So here, while the mad guns curse overhead, and tired men sigh with mud for couch and floor, Know that we fools, now with the foolish dead, died not for flag, nor King, nor Emperor, But for a dream, born in a herdsman's shed, and for the secret Scriptures of the poor.[55]

In addressing 'Irishmen and Irishwomen' the Easter Proclamation evidenced a commitment to inclusiveness, and reflected the influence of James Connolly. Perhaps an even more progressive note was sounded later in the Proclamation's pledge of 'religious and civil liberty, equal rights and equal opportunities to all its citizens ... to pursue the happiness and prosperity of the whole nation and of all its parts, cherishing all the children of the nation equally, and oblivious of the differences carefully fostered by an alien government, which have divided a minority from the majority in the past'. While the claim by its authors that the new Ireland they offered would be 'oblivious of the differences' that in fact divided the people of Ireland tested credulity as much as any similar statement uttered in the present day, the authors were nonetheless sincere in the vision they offered of a non-sectarian Ireland.

What mandate gave these men the right to act in the name of Ireland? Certainly, they had no referendum from the Irish people supporting a violent revolt and the hardship it would almost certainly bring them. But neither, it must be said, did the 'Minutemen' at Lexington and Concord have a mandate to initiate a violent revolt themselves against the same British Empire, or the workers at Petrograd in seeking to overthrow the Czar and the Russian social order. Revolutions, popular or otherwise, are rarely preceded in an orderly fashion by referenda and open public discourse. Indeed, when they involved the attempt to topple a colonial order, especially in a situation when the adversary was the same British Empire who had succeeded in infiltrating other Irish revolts, secrecy was essential.

It is also noteworthy that, as extreme as the British reaction was to the rebellion, from a political standpoint it was actually tame in comparison to some of the remedies advocated by a number of government advisors. Efforts were made by British military intelligence even to destroy the Irish Party by implicating John Dillon and Joe Devlin in the original plot. In a touch of supreme irony, Sir Henry Wilson, Director of Military Operations of the British General Staff, one of the principals in encouraging British officers to take action against the British government in the Curragh Mutiny, actually went as far as to advocate that Augustine Birrell be executed.[56] The genie was now getting out of the bottle for Britain, and it revealed that the use of force in Ireland remained as much as ever a ready option. As a catharsis for Irish nationalism, the effect of the rebellion had been even more significant. We have seen that Catholic Ireland, conservative by nature, was apparently placated with land and relative economic prosperity from the turn of the century up to the Rising. How did a violent, revolutionary movement develop and succeed to the extent it did in such a climate?

It did so because it combined the ideals expressed in the Easter Proclamation with an actual revolt on the streets of Ireland's capital. Connolly's 'leap in the dark' in fact set the table for a wider revolt, bolstered by the fact that Britain showed itself no more favourably inclined to implement Home Rule for Ireland than it did at any time in the previous quarter century.

Furthermore, the executions of the 1916 leaders served to inspire most sections of Irish nationalist opinion while either radicalising the moderates or driving others among them to irrelevancy. This was so to the extent that such developments as the Irish Convention of 1917–18 held little bearing, while a few years earlier it might well have succeeded. William Butler Yeats' view that 'all has changed, changed utterly' in the aftermath of the Rising proved a most accurate description.

It bears emphasis at this juncture that the 'Rising' represented a reversal for the IRB, given that it had been forced upon the organisation by the secret group led by Pearse from within. Pearse's successful manipulation led the IRB to go against its own strong anti-insurrectionary policies.[57] In this respect, despite Lenin's later description of the Irish Revolution as a bourgeois enterprise, the actions of Pearse and Connolly and company were not all that dissimilar to the Bolsheviks who 'kidnapped' the Russian Revolution.

While the components of the next round, the decisive round of physical force separatism, would prove different to those of the 'Rising', the cults of personality its martyred heroes left behind became the standard by which subsequent leaders judged themselves and each other. For some, like Collins and Mulcahy, that legacy proved to be more than burdensome. In perhaps one of the most candid moments in the Dáil, a weary Collins uttered these comments to those colleagues opposing the 1921 Anglo-Irish Treaty on the basis that it was a betrayal of the men of 1916:

> Deputies have spoken about whether dead men would have approved [the Treaty] and they have spoken whether children yet unborn will approve it,

but few of them have spoken as to whether the living will approve it. In my own small way, I tried to have before my mind what the whole lot of them would think of it ... There is no man here who has more regard for the dead men than I have ... [58]

In essence, Collins' remarks demonstrated the difficulty which confronted the military and political pragmatist who was at one and the same time tied to a movement in which the veneration of the past often took precedence over present realities. Against the still close backdrop of 1916 and the imagery associated with it, the ability of young realists like Collins to function had been greatly impaired. But they would, ironically, be given room to grow in the confines of British internment camps like Frongoch in Wales, where new ideas and methods would be studied and debated.

By the end of 1916, most of the 2,000 Irish prisoners were released under a general amnesty by Lloyd George, who became Prime Minister in December. The bulk of them would soon show themselves ready to force the issue of Irish independence to a different plane, with Collins figuring as a central player in that development. Lloyd George would come to regret his decision to set the young rebels free. He came to realise bitterly that the move had the effect of allowing the Irish Volunteers to revitalise themselves. The IRB's Supreme Council became reconstituted with young blood, largely under Michael Collins' tutelage. In short order Collins also became Director of Organization of the Irish Volunteers after brief service as Adjutant General.

Collins was in large measure responsible for much of the early organisational work that bound the newly arrived Irish prisoners to the Volunteer movement through the Prisoners Dependents Association. The Irish National Aid Association provided the basis through its fund-raising efforts by which the returning Republican prisoners could be kept before the public. It also provided Collins and others with a means for getting the Irish Volunteers back on track. At Frongoch Prison in Wales, which the Irish Parliamentarian Timothy Healy referred to as 'University of Revolution', Collins had begun to manoeuver himself up the leadership ladder of the IRB. He played a vital role in filling the vacuum created by the execution of the 1916 leaders. As we will see, Collins also provided a different type of leadership, a type that while no less committed to Irish nationhood, was less interested in symbolism and more concerned with successful military tactics. Soon he would divide his time between political, financial and military matters, while in the latter he especially evidenced a capacity for knowing his enemy.

The experience of large-scale imprisonment at Frongoch and other prison camps in the aftermath of the Rising may also have had the effect of breaking down regional barriers between the Volunteers. At the same time, as one writer has noted, the high concentration of Volunteers interned together from

West Mayo, for example, would later serve to make that part of the county a hotbed of revolutionary activity, while much of Mayo would remain inactive.[59]

A fundamental difference between the new Sinn Féin leadership in the post-Frongoch phase of Irish Republicanism and those who organised the Easter Rising lay in the fact that the former came from a different, much broader, less violent, more centrist world. They were not necessarily averse to the Irish parliamentary tradition. The conspiratorial mindset, which deliberately kept the tight circle that started the 'Rising', was not out to create a broad-based democratic movement. The leaders of the Rising were not, by background or temperament, consensus builders. And yet, as Brian Farrell has noted, their 'symbolic coup ... accelerated the process of political change ... It did not seriously alter the mainstream of the Irish political tradition'. 'They remained,' he writes, 'as events were to show, firmly committed to a liberal democratic, representative and essentially conservative course.'[60]

While Eamon de Valera, one of the few surviving leaders of the Easter Rising, entered the political arena in May 1917, one month earlier on the first anniversary of the revolt he had made clear why he feared that political defeat might squander what he saw as having been achieved by the execution of his 1916 comrades. In a letter that was in fact written on toilet tissue and smuggled out through the scapula of an inmate released on medical grounds, he explained his concerns.

> Defeat may well mean ruin, and to us defeat does not appear at all impossible ... we are not willing to risk that what has been purchased by our comrades' blood should be lost on a throw with dice loaded against us. We have been of the opinion from the beginning that electoral contests in which we are represented officially as taking part are most dangerous and likely to damage the good done by last Easter's events. The revival of old party contests is but a rallying cry to bring the former combatants each round his former flag – a thing not quite to be wished for in our opinion. As soldiers [Irish Volunteers etc.] we should abstain officially from taking sides in these contests and no candidates should in future be officially recognised as standing in our interests or as representing our ideals. This is our opinion.[61]

It was an ironic statement given the later role de Valera would play as the leader of an independent Ireland and also on the world stage within the League of Nations. De Valera, in his use of the word 'our', may have ordained himself to speak for his fellow inmates. But in addition to winning local government seats, Sinn Féin also tasted its first success at the parliamentary level by winning a series of elections in 1917. Their victories came in County Roscommon in January of that year by the success of Count Plunkett, father of Joseph Plunkett – one of the executed leaders of the Easter Rising: Plunkett topped the poll there. In a County Longford by-election later that year, Collins persisted against de Valera's opposition, and apparently without the approval of the proposed candidate himself, Republican prisoner Joe McGuinness. With no opposition from Arthur Griffith's more moderate faction, McGuinness, with only his name on the ballot, defeated the candidate of the increasingly moribund Irish Party under the slogan, 'Put him in to get him out.'[62] It was a gamble that worked on several fronts, with de Valera also gaining his first taste of electoral success. He won an East Clare by-election by a two-to-one margin over the Irish Party candidate Patrick Lynch.

Not only was the Irish Party's eclipse exacerbated, but the physical force school of Irish separatism, which by this time Collins and Thomas Ashe, among others, had come to dominate, gained actual electoral prominence over Griffith's force of moderation. Ironically, in this case it was with the latter's unwitting cooperation. Griffith supported Michael Collins' demand for the release of all Irish political prisoners and wanted to avoid weakening the electoral impact of that issue by actively opposing McGuinness' candidacy.

As the credibility of the Irish Party continued to erode in the year following the Easter 'Rising', a tentative alliance between nationalist organisations favouring non-participation at Westminster took shape after the gathering of the various strands of Irish separatism assembled there in October 1917. They opposed physical force and operated under the title of the 'Mansion House Convention'. Yet the Sinn Féin organisation, headed by Arthur Griffith, was itself forced to give way to the young men who had participated in 'The Rising' and were now released from jail. The first step in the effort at control over Sinn Féin by the Volunteers lay in the ceding by Griffith of half of the Sinn Féin Executive to the Volunteers. The physical force adherents elected included Eamon de Valera, Michael Collins, Rory O'Connor and Countess Markieviez. De Valera's victory in an East Clare parliamentary by-election in 1917 spurred the calling of the Convention. A central purpose was the rewriting of the organisation's Constitution.[63] A key objective ratified by the Convention was drafted by de Valera himself and held that 'Sinn Féin aims at securing the international recognition of Ireland as an independent Irish Republic.'[64]

The October Convention marked a narrow victory for the advocates of physical force, as well as a narrow defeat for Griffith's programme. Griffith had sought the adoption of a dual monarchy with Britain, establishing a 'King, Lords and Commons' for Ireland – a proposition which IRB man Diarmuid Lynch saw as 'an unbelievably retrograde step a year and a half after Easter Week'.[65] In essence, what Griffith sought to achieve was a return to the governing structure in place in Ireland before the Act of Union. Instead, the Convention resulted in Griffith, under pressure, standing down as President of Sinn Féin in favour of Eamon de Valera, who was by now also head of the Irish Volunteers organisation. In addition to gaining election, P. S. O'Hegarty has written that at this time another armed revolt seemed highly unlikely: 'Mention of another insurrection was greeted with laughter, a proposal by a clerical delegate to make it clear that a phrase about 'using any and every means' against foreign government did not cover anything from pitch and toss to manslaughter was opposed by Cathal Brugha'.[66] Yet de Valera sought an assurance that they would not propose to fight English rule by assassination.[67]

With the election of de Valera over Griffith as President of Sinn Féin, the official policy of the organisation moved from the dual monarchist pro-Grattan Parliament restoration that had been its trademark to the 'securing of the international recognition of Ireland as an independent Republic'. Added to this came the proviso that 'the Irish people may by referendum freely choose their own form of government'. In light of the bitter Civil War that was to follow the Dáil's ratification of the Anglo-Irish Treaty, and despite the substantial public acceptance of the Treaty at referendum, this provision must now be seen as particularly ironic. Supporting de Valera over Arthur Griffith was the Irish Republican Brotherhood, the organisation that had proclaimed the Irish Republic more than half a century earlier. The Supreme Council included such younger men as Liam Mellowes and Harry Boland, in addition to Collins.

In 1918, Sinn Féin grew to function as a pro-separatist umbrella organisation that encompassed a multiplicity of interests favouring Irish independence. In its ranks were a combination that included Arthur Griffith, militant members of the Irish Volunteers, the newly organised IRB, the constitutionalist Irish Nation League, Count Plunkett's Liberty League, Cumann na nBan, as well as former supporters of the Irish Parliamentary Party. In rural areas such as Bodyke, Co. Clare, the Sinn Féin organisation had come under the control of former Irish Parliamentary Party activists. The only major Irish interest otherwise absent was organised labour.[68]

The autumn of 1917 marked a change not only in the direction of Sinn Féin. It was also a time for a reshuffling in the power centre of the Volunteers, brought on by the vacuum in leadership left by the execution of the leaders of the 'Rising' two days after Sinn Féin Volunteers held their own convention in Dublin. Now even younger and perhaps more ruthless men moved to the forefront. Michael Collins was named Director of Organization. Some months later, Richard Mulcahy was named Chief of Staff. But most important, the gathering of militarists elected de Valera President of the Volunteer Executive. Within a period of seventy-two hours he was chosen as leader of both the political and armed dimensions of the Irish independence movement. From now on the latter would be seen to drive the conduct of the former. At the Volunteer Convention, Cathal Brugha was elected Chief of Staff, with Diarmuid Lynch chosen as Director of Communications. But while de Valera was elected as leader, the power centre of the Volunteer organisation would continue to be the IRB. A new constitution for the Volunteers was drafted by Collins. He also drew up a governing document for the IRB. As we will see, de Valera and Brugha harboured a deep-seated animosity towards this secret society.

While the reconstituted voice of Irish Republicanism was planning its future course, Britain remained determined to keep Ireland within the Empire. Ireland was still important from a strategic standpoint and the fact that Germany sought to exploit the country's internal divisions during the Great War rendered it more so. But in the context of Britain's domestic and international difficulties, it can be said that Ireland, both during and in the aftermath of the Great War, did not represent an asset. The country by now constituted a net loss from the manpower point of view, requiring more troops to pacify it than it was sending to the front.[69] Such a situation must have weighed on the later calculations of Lloyd George, who grew to realise that a contented Ireland would be more to Britain's advantage.

Yet as we shall see, it would take a considerable amount of bloodshed on all sides, as well as a persistent British policy of trial and error, before the Prime Minister and a majority of his colleagues in the Coalition were to reach this conclusion together. As we have seen, Lloyd George succeeded Asquith as Prime Minister in December 1916. One of his first major initiatives towards Ireland as head of the Coalition came in May 1917 with his call for an Irish Convention involving the Nationalist Party and the Unionists, but excluding Sinn Féin. The objective was to produce a scheme for Irish self-government but with the country remaining within the Empire. Sir Horace Plunkett, an Irish unionist of unquestionable decency and good will to all segments of the population, was elected as the Convention's Chairman. But the effort was doomed from the start by the Government's announcement early on that it would not act on any Convention report unless it was unanimously approved by the parties participating. This left little impetus for the Ulster Unionists to compromise on the question of Home Rule. But as we will see, there were other, even more compelling impediments put in the Convention's way by the government that summoned it.

The Irish Administration

If Anglo-Irish relations had reached their lowest ebb in the aftermath of the Easter Rising, the Irish administration, charged with representing the Crown in Ireland and responsible for implementing its policies, did little to reduce those tensions. In fact it can be argued that, acting from its seat of power at Dublin Castle, the Irish Administration actually served to exacerbate this situation with the full backing from London of Sir Walter Hume Long, the hard-line unionist and former Irish Chief Secretary. Long was later to head up a Cabinet-level committee on the Irish situation and was in fact responsible for drafting the language contained in the Government of Ireland Act (1920) and its provision for Ireland's partition.

What was the structure behind British rule in Ireland leading up to the opening shots of the Irish Revolution? For the first two decades of the twentieth century, the power of the Crown in Ireland continued to be vested nominally, as it had been for much of the previous century, in the office of the Lord Lieutenant. The Lord Lieutenant was also known as the Governor General and as the 'Viceroy'. But in reality, the real power on a day-to-day basis was held by the Chief Secretary. The elevation of the Chief Secretary was initiated by Arthur Balfour as Prime Minister in 1905 because in his view the nature of events in Ireland required that the 'real headship' of the government should be transferred to a minister who happened to be both in the Cabinet and in the House of Commons. But each entity held a different relationship with ministers and with parliament and consequently their autonomy also varied. Some were adjuncts of the Irish administration answerable to Dublin Castle, while others were branches of departments in London.

For the remainder of 1918 and throughout most of 1919 British policy in Ireland remained uncertain. Party bickering came to the fore, and Ireland receded as a priority.[70] Part of the problem lay in the lack of accurate information reaching the cabinet from Dublin Castle. The Irish Administration together with a majority in the Cabinet were blind to the differences between moderate Sinn Féin and the more hard-line physical force adherents. The effect was counterproductive toward any hope of peaceful settlement, as moderate Sinn Féiners and other nationalists became increasingly alienated. Thus the stage was set for a new round of conflict, one that contained some different ingredients for those Irish nationalists favouring physical force.

2

War by Any Other Name

Dáil Éireann, in its message to the free nations of the world declares a state of war to exist between Ireland and England ... Every volunteer is entitled, morally and legally, when in the execution of his military duties, to use all legitimate methods of warfare against the soldiers and policemen of the English usurper and to slay them if necessary.

From a lead article in *An t-Oglach*, 31 January 1919, the *Journal of the Irish Volunteers*

Clearly, the war in Europe had a significant impact on Irish politics, especially in relation to Irish nationalism. John Redmond's decision to support the British war effort split the ranks of the Irish Volunteers. The Great War itself also spurred on the desire of the Irish separatists to exploit England's preoccupation with its own survival as an opportunity for revolt in Ireland.

From an economic standpoint the war held mixed results for Ireland. Overall, it drove prices up in the agricultural sector significantly and provided a boom in those industries tied to it. At the same time, the war-time emphasis by the Government in favour of tillage over grazing was also a source of protest. Furthermore, those living in urban districts derived little benefit in the way of a positive economic impact. For its part Britain still harboured larger plans for Ireland in the prosecution of its war effort in spring 1918. By March of that year, mercifully, in light of the fate that would soon befall the Irish Party, Redmond would be dead.

While it is difficult to imagine a greater blunder than that committed by the Government in its execution of the leaders of the 1916 Rising, its decision to impose conscription demonstrated there were few limits to its imagination. As in the failure to implement Home Rule and the Government's apparent willingness to buckle before unionist resistance, the Cabinet continued to hand Irish separatism issues which it would use to its advantage. None was more useful from both a propaganda and an organisational standpoint than conscription. Up until that point, the British Government sought to avoid extending conscription to Ireland for a variety of reasons. Keith Middlemas, in his analysis of the political structures of modern Britain, underscored the dilemma faced by the British Cabinet in deciding whether to meet its man-power shortage at the front by imposing conscription in Ireland or ending the release from service given to the British trade unions early in the war.

> Torn between offending the T.U.C. and handing Ireland irrevocably to Sinn Féin, the Government delayed until the German offensive in March 1918 forced it to choose. Lloyd George feared a seething mass of ferocity – for over seven hundred years Irishmen had been unwilling partners in what was essentially a British show. And Ministers busily looked for alternatives ... So heavily did Ireland weigh on an imperially-minded War Cabinet that the Military Service Bill of January 1918 actually omitted Irishmen living in Britain ... [1]

Lloyd George's decision to attempt to implement conscription came despite reservations expressed in January by Sir Henry Duke, who had been appointed by Asquith as the Chief Secretary for Ireland in the aftermath of the Easter Rising. Duke agreed that without dealing with the issue of Home Rule first, the extension of conscription to Ireland would amount to 'an error in policy'.[2] In April, Duke renewed his opposition to the idea because by then a 'complete organisation of resistance to Conscription was in place'.[3]

The timing could not have been worse from the standpoint of a peace initiative for Ireland launched by the Government. On 5 April the Irish Convention issued its report, as the Government prepared to introduce legislation to impose conscription on Ireland. While the report proposed an Irish Parliament for the whole of Ireland, it was one which would have to defer to the British Government on such substantive matters as customs, excise, defence, policing, and even postal matters. Whatever hope Horace Plunkett's much undermined effort at finding a 'constitutional' solution to the Irish situation had at this stage was dealt a death blow in the eyes of the Nationalist majority in Ireland by the Government's decision to impose conscription. Indeed, if the Irish Convention was Lloyd George's way of derailing Sinn Féin's momentum, conscription was the issue which assured an increase in the movement's popular support. In fact, the Convention's report appeared in the press on the same day that the Government announced its plans for con-scription. But even without the blow which the timing of the Government's decision to impose conscription in Ireland held for the Convention, the effort itself had been doomed from the outset.

By the exclusion of Sinn Féin, the result of Plunkett's effort was an Irish Convention report that was satisfactory to few. The Ulster Unionists had made it clear they wanted no part of a Nationalist-dominated Ireland in any form. Desperate to gain some form of Home Rule, John Redmond joined the southern Unionists in proposing a moderate scheme. In so far as the proposal sparked division within his own ranks, especially on the issue of fiscal auton-omy, it also offered sobering notice to northern Nationalists there that their future was negotiable in the eyes of some leading southern Nationalists for the sake of expediency. In that respect, we will see that their own faith bore an inverse relationship to that of the southern Unionists who found their own position in Ireland would be determined by the self-interests of the Unionist majority in Northeast Ulster. The Ulster Unionists were also crystal clear in their submission to the convention. It was their minimum requirement that there be protection for 'the safety of Irish industrial enterprises, the vast proportion of which are situated in the North-Eastern Counties of Ulster, and from which the bulk of Irish Revenue is derived'.[4]

It was with a degree of wishful thinking that Sir Horace Plunkett wrote to Lloyd George in his transmission letter for the Convention's report, 'notwithstanding the difficulty with which we were surrounded, a larger measure of agreement has been reached upon the principles and details of Irish self-governance than has ever yet been attained'.[5] Indeed, the worst was yet to come for Anglo-Irish relations, while the wishes of the Nationalist majority in Ireland were to vent themselves in a vehicle far different from the Irish Convention.

An important vehicle for the coalescing of nationalist opposition of all shades of green on the conscription issue was provided by the Lord Mayor of Dublin, Laurence O'Neill, on 18 April 1918. By convening what became known on that day as the Mansion House Conference, a watershed was reached on a number of fronts, not least of which was the fact that under one banner it brought together Eamon de Valera and Arthur Griffith of Sinn Féin with the leadership of the Irish labour movement and the Irish Parliamentary Party.

In the anti-conscription effort, Irish Labour occupied a pivotal position with Sinn Féin, the Irish Parliamentary Party, and the Catholic hierarchy in common cause. The level of unity among Irish Nationalists and the Catholic hierarchy in their opposition to conscription culminated on 21 April 1918, when a combined pledge was signed. Two days later, a shut-down in the normal life of Nationalist Ireland occurred. Key to this effort was the general strike action by the trade union movement which closed down factories, and suspended public transport in most of the country.

But during their meeting came another perhaps even more important development from the standpoint of the legitimacy of Sinn Féin. A call was placed to Archbishop Walsh of Dublin by Lord Mayor O'Neill, where the prelate was meeting with Catholic bishops who were at that point preparing their own statement in opposition to conscription. The call led to a panel of representatives from the Mansion House meeting, including de Valera, being sent to Maynooth that day to meet the bishops to win their endorsement for the Mansion House statement.

Two statements were released concurrently, one by the Mansion House group, the latter by the Catholic Bishops. The documents clearly echoed each other. In the Mansion House statement, signed by Eamon de Valera, John Dillon, Timothy Healy and William O'Brien, Lord Mayor O'Neill, and Arthur Griffith among others, held that the Conscription Act

> must be regarded as a declaration of war on the Irish nation. The alternative to accepting it is to surrender our liberties and to acknowledge ourselves slaves. It is in direct violation of the rights of small nationalities to self-determination, which now even the Prime Minister of England – now preparing to employ naked militarism and force his Act upon Ireland – himself officially announced as an essential condition for peace at the Peace Conference.

The document called upon all Irishmen to resist the measure 'by the most effective means at their disposal'. The message issued by the Catholic bishops ordered that the pledge against conscription be read outside every mass throughout Ireland on the following Sunday. The bishops also authorised, with Cardinal Logue's approval, that a collection be permitted to raise funds for the campaign against conscription. In addition, the hierarchy also made it clear that it viewed conscription as 'an oppressive and inhuman law which the Irish people have a right to resist'.[6]

Significantly, the conscription issue allowed Sinn Féin to rise to an undisputed position of national leadership, a role it would soon parlay into overwhelming electoral success. The immediate effect was to strengthen its position since all nationalist feeling against conscription became more readily shaped to fit the Republican vision. The revolutionists of Ireland were emerging into the light of respectability and found support for their call of 10 April 1918, that 'everyone throughout the country ... refuses to purchase any commodities, with the exception of necessary foods on which the British Government levies any tax'. In addition, they called on the Irish people to refuse to honour the payment of instalments 'due in respect of land purchase' along with 'any and every direct and indirect tax'.[7]

It is in the conscription crisis that de Valera emerged as a leader in his own right. No longer simply a living icon of the 1916 Rising, de Valera was now thrust to centre stage in Irish politics. He was by then already the President of Sinn Féin and the head of the Irish Volunteers. His dealings with the Catholic hierarchy and southern Ireland's political establishment, took him to a point where he could no longer be marginalised in Irish society by the British Government.

But while Sinn Féin grew in prominence, so grew the desire of the Irish Volunteers to exploit the conscription crisis for its own sake. The Volunteers' choice of words cannot be written off as merely the expressions of men on the extreme end of Irish nationalism. Ernest Blythe, a key activist in the Gaelic League, an IRB member as well as an Ulster Protestant, would later demonstrate a desire for blood as his own in response to the British Government's support for conscription. He argued that anyone who 'connived in this crime against us ... merits no more consideration than a wild beast, and should be killed without mercy or hesitation as opportunity offers'.*

On 17 May the British Government, in response to the weight of the opposition to conscription, decided not to enforce it. In the words of Lionel Curtis, editor of the pro-Liberal *The Round Table*, and a legal advisor to Lloyd George, 'this was due, no doubt, partly to the conviction that they could not spare the necessary troops, and also to evidence that Irish conscripts would not be trustworthy'.[8] Yet on the same day the Government decided to forgo conscription for Ireland, it decided to order the mass arrest of Sinn Féin members and their supporters under the pretext of a so-called 'German plot'. The claims of the conspiracy, later documented in only the most specious terms by an official White Paper, combined the appearance of obvious hysteria on the part of the Government with a deliberate effort to manufacture the evidence. One rumour cited by Dublin Castle officials and British Intelligence involved the hypothesis that 'communications between the Sinn Féiners and Germany are kept largely through Maynooth and the Vatican'.[9]

The mass arrests undertaken against the leaders of the alleged plot were overseen directly by Lord French. The effort backfired. Not only were moderate Sinn Féin figures of a non-violent bent like Arthur Griffith caught in the British net, but two of the leading physical force advocates in the persons of Michael Collins† and Cathal Brugha escaped. Ironically, with key moderate Sinn Féiners imprisoned, the two were now given freer reign to exploit the situation.[10]

The 'German Plot' arrests can be viewed as a hastily conceived British remedy for checking the progress of Sinn Féin. The Government acted by using the Defence of the Realm Act to arrest and transport the greatest number of suspected Irish Republicans since the Easter Rising. Along with Arthur Griffith, other Sinn Féin leaders including Eamon de Valera, William T. Cosgrave, and Count Plunkett, were arrested and deported to English jails during the period 17–19 May. Only the most specious of evidence was offered by the British authorities to support Lord Lieutenant Sir John French's contention that Sinn Féin leaders were engaged in treasonable contact with Germany. That evidence itself consisted largely of previously published

---

* Ernest Blythe, 1889 to 1975, who would distinguish himself later as the Director of the Abbey Theatre from 1939 to 1967, displayed himself during the Irish Civil War, 1922–23, while a member of the Free State Cabinet as one of the most outspoken advocates for extreme measures against his former colleagues, including his support for the summary executions of seventy-seven Republican prisoners. See Roy Foster, *Modern Ireland* (Dublin, 1988). Protestant by religion, Blythe was a life-long devotee of the Irish language and author of several books in that medium.

† Michael Collins, in the absence of more senior leaders on the outside, was able to grow in importance in the Republican effort as well as becoming an important figure in the Sinn Féin propaganda effort himself.

contacts between the Germans and Sinn Féin leaders, including the late Roger Casement. Furthermore, for the better part of a year following the Easter Rising, the vast majority of the Sinn Féiners arrested in the 'German Plot' conspiracy had been in English prisons and had been unable to make contact even had they wanted to with the Germans. In all, by October 1918, some 500 had been arrested.

While the British allegations of a conspiracy may have lacked concrete evidence, sufficient on its merits to convince a court of law, a review of British official sources indicates that even weeks prior to Lord French's proclamation, Cabinet members such as Austen Chamberlain had raised the prospect of a 'German Plot' in a different vein. According to Lloyd George's papers, on 3 May 1918 Chamberlain suggested outright to the Prime Minister that while the evidence to support his argument as to the existence of such a conspiracy might have been inadequate for purposes of legal prosecution, they would still be found 'sufficient for America'.[11] Here, then, is one of the earlier efforts to link Sinn Féin to an enemy power for propaganda purposes, with an eye towards affecting American opinion. The dead Casement's solitary connections with Germany were now, two years later, still the stuff of conspiratorial manufacture.

The US Consul in Queenstown was not impressed by the British Government's conduct in regard to either conscription or the 'German Plot' affair. In a report to US Secretary of State Colby on 12 September 1918, US Consul Charles Hathaway tied the collapse of the Government's Irish Convention initiative to the decision to extend conscription to Ireland. 'The result was instantaneous', he wrote, and added that 'the report of the Convention was dead before it left the printer's hands'.[12] Hathaway was equally incisive elsewhere in his account:

> In a few weeks it became apparent that the Government could only enforce Conscription in Ireland at the price of chaos. From that movement they sought for an avenue of escape and found it in a 'German Plot'. It is quite true that there has been a 'German Plot' in Ireland since the beginning of the war as there has been in America and other countries and as there are no doubt Allied plots in Poland and Bohemia, but it was no worse in May 1918 than at any previous time.[13]

The Government's handling of conscription and the 'German Plot' arrests combined to give Sinn Féin an electoral advantage it was not to waste. The conscription issue aside, in the years before the 1918 general election Sinn Féin had succeeded in making an impact at the local government level. Individual urban district councillors were elected in Loughrea, Dundalk, Donegal and Castlebar. But Dublin was the major source of Sinn Féin's success between 1906 and 1918. Among the Aldermen it succeeded in electing was William T. Cosgrave, later to become leader of the Irish Free State.

Winning such seats, in addition to giving Sinn Féin electoral credibility, also provided important governmental experience to the successful candidates. Soon it became clear that, in advance of the next British general election, Sinn Féin could already count on taking at least one quarter of the parliamentary seats. In many constituencies it was clear that Redmondites would be unable to field a candidate.

The Nationalist Party had itself failed to see the writing on the wall, or to gauge properly the sentiment that Sinn Féin had generated among the Irish Nationalist population. At the same time, the Party's leaders may have been the victims of a sudden electoral swing from the village level up. For decades the Irish Party enjoyed an unchallenged role at the ballot box as the voice of Nationalist Ireland. On the surface at least, in many parts of rural Ireland, it appeared that the party of Redmond maintained its grip over a Sinn Féin movement that was still more of an enigma than a political organisation, with the Irish Party winning a series of by-election seats during the spring and summer of 1918. The intensity of the competition between the two sides that continued into 1918 is described by Patrick Kavanagh in an account of a rally held by the Ancient Order of Hibernians, near the Co. Monaghan town of Carrickmacross. The Hibernians as stalwarts of lay Catholicism were synonymous with the Irish Party.

> There were thirty hands in the procession, and as many banners. The music didn't impress me. But the banners were beautiful. Green silk and shiny gold. All the constitutional saints of Ireland had their images painted on those banners ... The Hibernian orators were florid men ... One speaker rose and made a dramatic gesture with his arms ... I listened intently. He condemned Sinn Féin. He said it would end badly. 'Remember what your Cardinal said,' he shouted, 'Sinn Féin will end in red ruin, defeat and utter collapse.' The crowd cheered.[14]

But buoyed by the combination of credibility and momentum which the Government had inadvertently handed them by the Conscription Act, Sinn Féin set about building popular electoral support itself. The 1918 general election provided the movement with the platform it needed. Unknown to both the public and the contestants, it was to be the last election in which Ireland voted as a single jurisdiction.

The election Manifesto issued by Sinn Féin, now growing into the role of a political party, placed special emphasis on the upcoming Paris Peace Conference, while also seeking to bleed every last ounce of propaganda value out of the conscription fiasco. From the outset, the document offered the Irish electorate a clear choice between Sinn Féin and the Irish Party, between abstention from the British Parliament and maintaining an Irish Nationalist delegation at Westminster. 'Sinn Féin aims at securing the establishment of the Irish Republic', the Manifesto proclaimed. That goal would be established by the withdrawal of the 'Irish representation from the British parliament and by denying the right and opposing the will of the British Government ... to legislate for Ireland'. Instead, Sinn Féin would establish a separate 'constituent assembly' which would 'act in the name of the Irish people and to develop Ireland's social, political, and industrial life for the welfare of the whole people of Ireland'. While the document was vague on the use of physical force per se against British rule, it nonetheless supported outright the 'use of any and every means available to render impotent the power of England to hold Ireland in subjection by military force or otherwise'.

The pledge to appeal Ireland's case to the Paris Peace Conference for 'the establishment of Ireland as an independent nation' was tied directly to the commitment to withdraw from the British Parliament. By demonstrating openly that a clear majority of the Irish people supported an independent Ireland with its own separate legislative body and governmental apparatus, Sinn Féin hoped to strengthen the case for support of the Irish cause at the Conference. The Manifesto also sought, with some skill, to weave the age-old credo of Irish separatism together with a pledge for social justice and democratic rights in the present: '[Sinn Féin] stands by the Proclamation of the Provisional Government of Easter 1916, reasserting the inalienable right of the Irish people to achieve it, and guaranteeing within the independent nation equal rights and equal opportunities to all its citizens'.

Any lingering impression on the part of moderate Irish unionists or the Government itself that the implementation of the Second Home Rule Act would prove sufficient to mollify Sinn Féin was also dismissed in the Manifesto. The measure's provision for Ireland's partition was singled out for attack.

> The enforced exodus of millions of our people, the decay of our industrial life, the ever-increasing financial plunder of our country, the whittling down of the demand for the 'Repeal of the Union' ... to that of Home Rule on the Statute Book, and finally the contemplated mutilation of our country by partition, are some of the ghastly results of a policy that leads to national ruin'.[15]

And on that basis the stage was set for the formal end to Irish involvement on any significant scale with British parliamentary democracy.

John Dillon, now the Irish Party leader, manifested his party's myopia in pre-election remarks regarding Eamon de Valera, then in Lincoln Jail. 'I wish to God he was out now', Dillon stated, 'because the more speeches he makes the more will be my majority'.[16] Dillon went on to remark that he desired that his home constituency of Mayo might set an example 'for the country on this occasion'. In fact, Mayo did. Dillon lost his own seat, a result that was to be the reality for virtually every other Nationalist Party candidate with the exception of only six seats. On 30 December 1918 the staunchly unionist *Irish Times* delivered this post mortem in an editorial:

> If Mr. Asquith's Liberals would go back to Parliament on a big aeroplane, the Nationalists would go back on an Irish jaunting car . . . Mr. Dillon has lost his seat to Mr. de Valera. He fails with the party of which he himself was chief executive.[17]

In Patrick Kavanagh's Co. Monaghan hamlet, the political upheaval in Nationalist Ireland was also evident. On election day 1918, Irish Party supporters, equipped with blackthorn sticks and ash plants, were met head on by the younger enthusiasts of Sinn Féin, the latter armed physically as well as metaphorically with hurley sticks. Kavanagh, an eyewitness to the ensuing confrontation, related:

> The Sinn Féin hurley men moved towards the center of the road. Zero hour. A Sinn Féin hot-head made a rush for the Hibernian banner . . . around their standard bearer the stickmen rallied, the last defenders of Dan O'Connell's Ireland. 'Get goin, get goin,' I heard. The Hibernians fought well. The blackthorn and ash plants whistled through the dusk. The Sinn Féiners were in on the Banner now and one of them had seized St. Patrick by the leg, dragging his whole body out of shape. The pole of the banner dented its bearer's solar plexus and he dropped to the ground with a groan. That was the beginning of the end. The Hibernians fled in the direction of the pub.[18]

As a result of the Representative of the People Act of 1918, the Irish electoral pool increased from 701,474 in the previous election to 1,936,673. This marked an unprecedented opportunity for change in Irish life and government.

In the 1918 general election, out of the a total of 105 parliamentary seats, Sinn Féin carried a total of 73. The fact that Sinn Féin contested less than 100 seats rendered their result all the more dramatic. The Irish Party total went from eighty to only six seats, five of which were uncontested seats in Ulster, the result of an electoral pact there with Sinn Féin to avoid their loss to Ulster Unionists. Of Sinn Féin's impressive tally, twenty-five seats were uncontested. Only in four counties in northeast Ulster did the Unionists receive a majority. The 1918 election can be seen as fundamental in providing the Republicans with the ability to claim in Britain, the Dominions, the United States and elsewhere, that they had the moral authority to govern Ireland and that the British Government did not.* But at the same time it

---

* In addition to the strength Sinn Féin showed among the Irish electorate in the 1918 general election, continued momentum was shown in the next local government elections held in January 1920. Sinn Féin took control of 72 out of 127 urban councils. Significantly, in May 1920 the largest unit of urban government in Ireland, the Dublin Corporation, voted to accept the authority of Dáil Éireann as the duly elected Government of the Irish people and asked that Britain disengage from Ireland. Also in that month, the Sinn Féin record of electoral success continued unabated as they won control of 18 of the 32 County Councils of Ireland, including two of the six counties Britain partitioned in Northeast Ireland under the Government of Ireland Act, along with the controlling influence of 182 out of 206 rural councils.

cannot be concluded that this vote was a mandate for violence, nor was it necessarily a vote for a republican form of government. Sinn Féin candidates received at total of 485,105 votes while the Irish Party obtained 237,343 votes. When the 320,092 votes cast for Unionist candidates is added to the Irish Party's tally, Sinn Féin can be seen to have won a minority of the total votes cast. Nonetheless, it should be noted that 25 Nationalist seats were won by Sinn Féin in non-contested races; this represents some 80,000 additional voters. An element that remains striking from the Sinn Féin campaign was the lack of a unified position on the Ulster Question. This would persist for the next several years.

The role of the IRB must also not be overlooked in discussing this election. Michael Collins and Harry Boland, serving as members of the Supreme Council, were also officials within the Sinn Féin hierarchy. They were in fact directly responsible for the selection of the panel of Sinn Féin candidates for each of the parliamentary constituencies contested nationwide. They ensured acceptance of the Sinn Féin programme and loyalty to the primacy of national independence as the overriding issues. There was little regard for social standing.

Prowess at organising an electoral campaign, however, was not the only, or even major cause of concern that the Sinn Féin organisation posed to the British Government. Their internal discipline had greatly diminished the Castle's ability to acquire political intelligence. Whereas in the aftermath of the Easter Rising an intelligence officer for the British garrison in the midlands was able to boast of the authorities' ability to put a swift end to any separatist outburst, one year later he was to note that Sinn Féin had become 'peculiarly well-disciplined'. The official also stated that he had found drunkenness to be 'almost unknown' among the new Sinn Féin organisation while it had also become 'very hard to obtain any insights into the organisation's meetings'.[20]

In the aftermath and euphoria of the 1918 general election victory, Sinn Féin as a movement, as one of the leading propagandists P. S. O'Hegarty wrote,

> did not contemplate an insurrection, a guerrilla war, or anything in the nature of violence. It contemplated making the continuance of English government impossible in practice by passive resistance to its operation, by assuming such powers of government as would be assumed within the fabric of the police and military forces which maintained the English Government as a de facto government.

Furthermore, Sinn Féin sought 'the exploitation in Ireland, England and abroad ... of the difficult situation England would be in in the international world if, now that Ireland had made the clearest possible self-determination for a Republic ... Her answer to it was to be the maintenance of English Government on the old scale'.[21] In each of these objectives, it will be seen that

Sinn Féin fared remarkably well. But while Sinn Féin may not have set out to support a violent revolution, once again violence would play a major part in the Irish independence effort. The 1918 general election results provided some physical force adherents with both a sense of impetus and legitimacy for conducting a full-scale revolt against British rule.

On 21 January 1919, the opening session of the First Dáil Éireann was held despite the fact that many of its members were either in prison or on the run. Ironically, as the Dáil met at the Mansion House, and proclaimed a 'Democratic Programme' while reasserting the Irish Republic, the opening shot of the Anglo-Irish War was fired against the RIC. It was carried out by a body of Volunteers at Soloheadbeg on a quiet country road in County Tipperary, under the command of Dan Breen. This was done without the approval of any Sinn Féin central authority. While drawing inspiration from 1916, it was to spark a different kind of Irish insurrection. Many who would eventually take up weapons against Britain in what would also be known as 'The Black and Tan War' had not participated in the Easter Rising. Dan Breen, speaking of himself and Sean Treacy in 1916, wrote that 'we were both bitterly disappointed that the fighting had not extended to the County. We swore that should the fighting ever be resumed, we would be in the thick of it, no matter where it took place'. Indeed, by the killing of two members of the Royal Irish Constabulary, together with the seizure of a load of gelignite, Breen and Treacy not only were in 'the thick of it', they would, in fact, serve as catalysts for the most protracted and effective revolt yet against British rule in Ireland.[22]

Yet it bears noting that two years and eight months had passed since the Easter Rising and the Soloheadbeg slayings. No policemen, soldiers or Irish Volunteers had been killed during that time. But while there were few violent incidents, there was still, as we have seen, considerable revolutionary activity, provoked in many ways by developments like the conscription crisis. The Soloheadbeg ambush was a good example – as one writer has noted, paraphrasing Che Guevara – that 'it is not necessary to wait till all conditions required by revolution are present; they can be created'.[23] Nonetheless, the killings resulted in South Tipperary being proclaimed a 'military area' by the British Government. In reality, the Volunteer Headquarters – Oglaigh na h-Éireann – was forced to follow the actions of the rank and file in the aftermath of Soloheadbeg. But Breen also describes the initial reaction from Headquarters over the killing of the two RIC men. His description is useful in demonstrating that the chain of events leading to what was to become a largely guerrilla-based war of independence during the years 1919–21, was not the product of a deliberate plan of action.

> The people had voted for a Republic, now they [Sinn Féin] seemed to have abandoned those who tried to bring that Republic nearer, for we had taken

39

> them at their word. Our former friends shunned us. They preferred the
> drawing room as a battleground; the political revolution rather than the gun
> as an offensive weapon. We had heard the gospel of freedom preached; we
> believed in it, we wanted to be free ... But those who preached the gospel
> were not prepared to practice it.[24]

It was this attitude toward the General Headquarters' staff that led Breen to conclude that an incident like that which occurred at Soloheadbeg was necessary. Ironically, Breen argued, one of the biggest causes of the malaise he saw at the upper levels of the Republican movement was the outcome of the 1918 General Election and Sinn Féin's overwhelming victory:

> Many had ceased to be soldiers and had become politicians. There was a
> danger of disintegration, a danger which had been growing since the threat of
> Conscription disappeared a few months earlier. I was convinced that some
> sort of action was absolutely necessary.[25]

In an observation which goes to the heart of a problem that existed between men like himself, active with the gun and the command at General Headquarters, charged with the responsibility of overseeing the entire campaign and tied, at least to some extent, to the oversight of Dáil Éireann and its ministries, Breen was particularly candid: 'The Volunteers were in great danger of becoming merely a political adjunct to the Sinn Féin organisation'.[26] His own example itself served to underscore the early lack of co-ordination between the General Headquarters staff and the Irish Volunteers, and the consequent weakness of a delineation of authority between the civil and military sectors of the Republican effort. Within the IRA, deep-rooted tensions between the rural communities and Dublin also rose to the surface. As we will see later these tensions between the soldiers of the 'Republic' and the politicians was given particular vent by Ernie O'Malley, along with Dan Breen and others.

Nonetheless, while the incident at Soloheadbeg may have met initially with the general disapproval of the Sinn Féin organisation and of Volunteer Headquarters, that view was not a unanimous one. Although Breen and Treacy acted without his prior knowledge, they earned the support of Michael Collins. In fact, although he was in England at the time of the attack, overseeing the successful escape effort of Eamon de Valera and other prisoners from Lincoln Jail, Collins was actually accused of helping orchestrate what happened in Tipperary. Furthermore, the incident at Soloheadbeg did not unleash widespread violence, given that there were no immediate incidents perpetrated by the IRA, nor was there a sudden British response. At the same time, Soloheadbeg marked a watershed in Irish history, given that it would be cited as a catalyst by other Republican physical force adherents for further violence. It would in time also have an impact on unionist opinion throughout the island. Paul Bew argues persuasively that the failure to understand the role of violence in the Irish Revolution exacerbated the Ulster problem in particular.

In light of the great degree of mythology that has developed around Collins, it bears noting that he did not start the violent campaign against British rule that has come to be known as the Anglo-Irish War. But unlike de Valera, large segments of the Catholic clergy and perhaps even a majority in the First Dáil, Collins was not revolted by what Breen and Treacy had done in shooting to death the RIC men on a quiet country road. Instead, he took them under his wing and encouraged them. If men like Dan Breen and Sean Treacy provided the brawn for the IRA, Michael Collins provided the brains in a significant way. It proved a lethal combination.

Collins believed that what Breen and Treacy needed was a better choice of target. With that in mind, he involved them directly in Dublin's effort to ambush General Sir John French, the British Lord Lieutenant for Ireland. Lord French had been appointed to his post in May 1918 as part of a demonstration by the British Cabinet that it intended to restore 'law and order' there. During one attempt, Collins joined the two Tipperarymen and the rest of an ambush party in Dun Laoghaire in an effort to assassinate the Viceroy as he returned from London. Their quarry did not appear, however, having apparently been re-routed. With them that evening in an action in which Collins sought to draw in the best men available, was Tomas Mac-Curtain, Lord Mayor of Cork, and Commandant of the IRA's Cork No. 1 Brigade, who would be killed in his home the following year by a party of disguised RIC men. Some months later, Breen and Treacy once again met up with Lord French, as they tried to ambush him near a railway station in their own County. But French again escaped unharmed.

After Soloheadbeg the Dáil issued a declaration of independence and stated that a state of war existed between Ireland and England. According to Piaras Béaslaí, at a meeting soon after of the Volunteer Headquarters' staff, Cathal Brugha stated that 'the Volunteers ... had now become the army of a lawfully constituted government elected by the people, and were entitled morally and legally when in the execution of their duty to slay the officials and agents of the foreign invader who was waging war upon our native government'.[27] It was to be two years, however, before the Dáil would accept the Volunteers openly as the Army of the Republic.

Nonetheless, tacit responsibility was assumed some time earlier. In August 1919, the IRA was placed directly under the Dáil's nominal authority. The loyalty oath each member was required to take to the Dáil as the Government of the Irish Republic was orchestrated by Brugha as Minister for Defence. It might be viewed as having been a direct means of minimising the hold the IRB had over the men in arms. It is from this point that the Irish Volunteers became known officially as the Irish Republican Army. Frank O'Connor contends that 'Collins knew perfectly well that Brugha wanted to tie up not only the Volunteers, but the secret society which Collins controlled. He had never liked it. Now he hoped to smash it by making its members, who were mostly Volunteers, swear allegiance to the Dáil'.[28]

Whether recognised formally by the Dáil or not, the role of the IRA at the local level, as an active agent of the Government of the Irish Republic, was evident. In effect, the IRA served as the instrument with which the decisions of the civil government were enforced through a police function. The mandate of the Republican courts and the County Councils was often intertwined with the IRA. Furthermore, the raising of the national loan by the Department of Finance under the direction of Michael Collins was often facilitated by the efforts of the IRA at the brigade level in villages and townlands throughout Ireland. In effect, the department that Collins headed in the civilian sector saw one of its objectives serviced by the military organisation of which he was a ranking official as Director of Intelligence, and also head of the Irish Republican Brotherhood. The military activities of the IRA also facilitated the Dáil's efforts to control the countryside. As Richard Mulcahy later explained, the strategy at work 'involved, insofar as possible, the removal of the powers of control that the police barracks represented'.[29]

Frank Pakenham has observed that 'as a matter of fact, it is impossible to mark off logical stages in the developments that culminated in the guerrilla war'.[30] However, the build-up towards open hostilities was unmistakable from Soloheadbeg onwards. On 30 July 1919, a detective of the Dublin Metropolitan Police was shot dead on the orders of the Volunteer Headquarters. While there were differences in class and outlook between the rank and file of the Volunteers and their leadership, it can be stated that together they constituted an army that was quite different to that which took part in the 'Rising'. As Lionel Curtis, a leading architect of the British Commonwealth system, wrote wistfully in his retrospective on Ireland in the June 1921 issue of the *Round Table*, 'control passed from the intellectuals to leaders of a different type'.[31]

> With such forces at their disposal, the leaders (of Sinn Féin) would probably have ventured on open rebellion if matters had come to an issue before the war. But in 1919, realizing the terrific power of modern artillery against troops in the open field, they resorted to the weapons with which centuries of agrarian oppression had familiarised Ireland. As formerly the landlords and their agents, so now officers of Government became marks for the bullets of assassins.[32]

While Breen and Treacy acted alone at Soloheadbeg the organ of the Irish Volunteer movement – *An tÓglach* – made it clear not long after the incident that violent action in the name of Irish independence was to come very much into vogue:

The principle means at the command of the Irish people is the Army of Ireland, and that Army will be true to its trust ... If they are called upon to shed
their blood in defense of the new-born Republic, they will not shrink from the
sacrifice. For the authority of the nation is behind them, embodied in a lawfully constituted authority whose moral sanction every theologian must
recognise, an authority claiming the same right to inflict death on the enemies
of the Irish State, as every free national claims in such a case ... We have thus
a clear issue laid down, not by anybody that could be termed 'militarists' or
extremists, but with the utmost care and responsibility, and unanimously
adopted. The 'state of war' which is thus declared to exist, renders the
National Army the most important national service of the moment. It justifies
Irish Volunteers in treating the armed forces of the enemy – whether soldier
or policeman – exactly as a National Army would treat the member of an
invading army ... Every Volunteer is entitled, morally and legally, when in
the execution of his military duties to use all legitimate methods of warfare
against the soldiers and policemen of the English usurper, and to slay them if
necessary.[33]

In short, even though Dáil Éireann may not have yet endorsed the Irish
Volunteers as the Army of the Republic, the body sought to legitimise its
actions by aligning itself with the authority of Dáil Éireann. Significantly, it
was a claim that the Dáil did not seek to repudiate. By this statement, the
Irish Volunteers, with the apparent acquiescence of moderate elements in
Sinn Féin, had made it clear that the mandate given the movement in the
1918 General Election was interpreted to mean an endorsement of an independent Irish Republic with a right to bear arms to defend it. The views
outlined in the above passage would continue to have an impact on the future
of Ireland for some time. Not least, it would haunt the actions of others trying
to build an Irish nation-state that adhered to the wishes of a majority in Ireland. In short order, the course of events would show that the Volunteers
were indeed in earnest.

Throughout much of 1919, the IRA confined most of its efforts to securing adequate quantities of weapons with which to conduct an effective
guerrilla campaign. The acquisition and distribution of arms and munitions
was a task that was often overseen directly by Collins himself. An exchange
of correspondence from August 1919, between Collins and Frank Barrett,
the head of the Mid-Clare Brigade, on the acquisition of hand grenades,
provides a useful example of this. On 1 August of that year, Barrett
informed Collins:

Your dispatch dated July 29 came safely to hand on the 31st instant ... I am
quite delighted that the hand grenades are available. What do they cost each?
Would it be safe to pack them in a box and have them sent by rail? If there is
no danger of an explosion as a result of rough handling, I may be able to have
them taken here under cover ... [34]

Eight days later, Collins replied:

> Cost of the samples I have mentioned will be 6/6 or 7/ each. It is possible that
> your idea may be all right as allowances can be made to avoid breakage.[35]

The movement towards an aggressive physical force campaign against the Crown's forces in Ireland in 1919 was also shaped in part by the reality that the Paris Peace Conference had concluded without including Ireland among the list of small nations with a right to self-determination. The formation of the First Dáil in 1919 as an independent Irish constituent assembly formed on the basis of a democratic mandate also held ramifications, or so the leadership of Sinn Féin believed, on the international scene. The existence of Dáil Éireann provided part of the basis for presenting Ireland's claim to self-determination before the Paris Conference. In addition, the body's existence was used to legitimise the naming of Irish consuls abroad and participation in various international labour conferences.*

In seeking admission to the League of Nations in February 1919 during the Paris Conference, delegates sent by Sinn Féin laid emphasis on the existence of Dáil Éireann as the constituent assembly of a democratically elected Irish Government that had repudiated Britain by the wishes of the vast majority of the Irish people. Nonetheless, the plea made for the recognition of an independent Ireland by Count Plunkett, Eamon de Valera, Arthur Griffith and others fell on deaf ears as President Wilson weighed in on the British side, giving evidence to the view that the rights of some small nations would be no more respected in the new international order then they had in the old one. The rejection left the voices of moderation in Sinn Féin severely wrong-footed as to what strategy to pursue. For Michael Collins and others in the Volunteer movement, more disposed to violence to begin with, the defeat at Versailles left them in a position where they could move the Irish separatist movement in a different direction. In Ireland, the Volunteers responded to the verdict by the heightening of their violent campaign. It was another episode where Sinn Féin and Dáil Éireann were forced by the course of events to follow the lead taken by the advocates of violent revolution.

Absent from that opening session of Dáil Éireann, along with thirty-four other elected members who were either in jail or on the run, were Eamon de Valera and Michael Collins. The former was in prison in England, while the latter had gone there to get him out.

Rescue efforts, whether successful or not, formed a dramatic aspect of the IRA's campaign. The rescue of Sean Hogan on 13 May 1919 from the grip of an RIC escort on a train at Knocklong Railway Station in County Limerick

---

* For a detailed analysis of the establishment of the First Dáil and its subsequent role see Arthur Mitchell's *Revolutionary Government* (Dublin, 1995).

was one of the most successful attempts undertaken by the IRA. Hogan had been one of the principals that took part in the Soloheadbeg ambush five months earlier, and in addition to serving as a key Flying Column leader in Tipperary also operated in Dublin.

On the day of the IRA's attempt to rescue him, Hogan had been in British custody for only twenty-four hours. His escape was masterminded by the three men he had joined at Soloheadbeg – Sean Treacy, Dan Breen, and Seamus Robinson. Convinced that Hogan would be transferred to Cork for prosecution under the Defence of the Realm Act, the three Tipperarymen moved swiftly to intercept the train transporting Hogan at Knocklong, after previously considering the station at Emly on the borders of Cork, Limerick and Tipperary. But, with Treacy as the architect of the rescue attempt, they settled on the isolated station at Knocklong, where the nearest barracks was some miles away.

Using the code name 'Greyhound' for Hogan, Treacy set in place an elaborate communications system to keep him apprised of his comrades' movements. Joined by five other IRA men, Treacy, Breen and Robinson met at Knocklong at 7.45 p.m. on 13 May, waiting for the train that bore Hogan some forty minutes later. They had come in a desperate attempt to rescue the young man from certain execution. As the train pulled into Knocklong, Hogan was apparently made aware by a signal from a passenger planted on it by Treacy that a rescue was about to be attempted. The prisoner sat with his back to the engine in handcuffs between an RIC Sergeant and Constable. Two other constables with loaded carbines sat opposite him. As the train stopped, one of the rescue party who had entered the train at Thurles jumped to the platform and signalled to his colleagues the compartment where Hogan was. Treacy entered the train, his revolver drawn, accompanied by another IRA man, as Dan Breen and Seamus Robinson waited on the platform to facilitate the rescue attempt. As Treacy opened the sliding door to Hogan's carriage he shouted, 'Hands up! Come on, Sean, out!'

A melee broke out as the RIC's Constable Enright grabbed Hogan and attempted to use him as a human shield. Treacy opened fire immediately and shot the Constable dead. For the next five minutes he engaged in a deadly hand-to-hand struggle with Sergeant Wallace, with both men grappling for a pistol. In the end Treacy sustained a serious wound to the throat, while Wallace was shot dead by the Tipperarymen. Hogan broke free, crashing his handcuffed hands into the faces of his captors. As Hogan emerged from the train with the wounded Treacy the surviving RIC men opened fire on the crowded platform with Breen and Robinson returning fire. Breen stood on the platform, wounded in his right arm and lung, returning fire with his left hand as the IRA party made a successful escape from the station.

The rescue would not be without costs, however, as one IRA man connected with the Knocklong raid – Ned Foley, and another, Patrick Maher, who had facilitated the escapees later, were executed in June of the following year at Mountjoy Jail.*

The IRA's rank and file

Who exactly were the IRA at the local level, and who were the men that led them? The description of one writer in attempting to characterise the IRA man and British soldier at this time is helpful in forming at least part of the answer to this question:

> On both sides there was a 'Jack the Lad' air, caps at jaunty angles, cigarettes hanging from lips, riding boots, Sam Browne belts: a fusion of casual fashion and military attire. Sir John French's dress is matched by Martin Savage's who was killed attempting to assassinate him. A photograph of the Castle Murder Gang shows gangsterish attire and pictures. Breen's machine pistol was included in his wedding photograph. Behind him stood his best man, Sean Hogan, wearing the military tunic and cross-belt.[36]

The IRA's adoption of many aspects of British military procedure may be seen as the result of an inevitable resort to the most available type of military literature. Tom Barry was also not alone as an IRA leader who had served in a British uniform. So had Emmet Dalton and J. J. 'Ginger' O'Connell, among others.

It is noteworthy that there was a lack of a paternal influence on a significant number of volunteers in Cork. One study of 524 Cork Volunteers reveals that, according to the 1911 census, twenty-three per cent had mothers at the head of their households.[37] It might be more than a coincidence that the fathers of both Dan Breen and Sean Treacy died when they were in early childhood, thus making them more susceptible perhaps to the attraction of revolutionary activity. Such was also the experience of Michael Collins and Liam Lynch. But there were other male authority figures. Breen's own description of the impact of his national school teacher on his development of a hatred towards British rule is insightful:

> He did not confine his history lessons to the text book. He gave us the naked facts about the English conquest of Ireland, the manner in which our country was held in bondage. We learned about the Penal laws, the systematic ruining of Irish trade, the elimination of our native language ... By the time we had passed from his class, we were no longer content to grow up happy English children as envisaged by the Board of Education.[38]

---

* Ned Foley and Patrick Maher, who died together on 7 June 1921, were the last Republicans executed before the Anglo-Irish Truce by the British Government. In October 2001 their bodies, along with eight other executed IRA members, were reinterred at Glasnevin Cemetery after a State Funeral arranged by the Irish Government (see Illustrations).

The influential position held by the local schoolmaster is also described by Tom Garvin, who offers an assessment of the frustrations which drove these mostly rural educators to the radical positions they espoused on the national question. Comparing them to some equally disgruntled Irish-born civil servants, he writes:

> Schoolteachers themselves had a similar uncomfortable position in society, in that they possessed education and quite considerable cultural influence in village society while often having little real security or political independence. National teachers were conspicuous among Gaelic League and Sinn Féin ideologues of the post-1898 period, and were involved in the project to revive the Irish language through the schools. NTR's were often IRA leaders during 1919–1923, and many other leaders had parents or other close relatives in the profession.[39]

In the Irish context, the National teacher was in the employ of both the clergy and the Crown. In one late nineteenth-century account a visiting American writer described the impact of the more Anglophobic elements of the Irish–American press on many Irish National school teachers. Twenty years later in the midst of the Irish Revolution, Ulster Protestant Home Ruler and writer George Birmingham noted that 'it is impossible to estimate, though it is interesting to guess, how far the present condition of Ireland is due to the influence of the National School Teachers'.[40]

De Valera

Perhaps one of the best examples of a fatherless boy, who was influenced by both his National school teachers and a strongly Nationalist local Catholic priest, was Eamon de Valera. In his later years, de Valera, whose mother sent him to Ireland in early childhood to be raised by maternal relatives in humble conditions in rural County Limerick, referred to his local parish priest, Father Eugene Sheehy, as the man who 'taught me patriotism'.[41]

Eamon de Valera was not only one of the few surviving leaders of the Easter 'Rising', he was the one who best served to link that event to the Irish war of independence. In swift order, by January 1919, he stood as head of the Volunteers, President of Sinn Féin, and President of Dáil Éireann – a post he was elected to in absentia. Early in 1919, this taciturn leader found himself behind bars in England with other Republican prisoners. On 3 February, de Valera was able to escape from prison with the personal assistance of Michael Collins and Harry Boland. He was bundled off to America from Liverpool aboard a vessel, on which he masqueraded as a seaman. One month later, on a street corner in Manhattan, the leader of the Irish Republic was turned over to the care of Harry Boland and Joe McGarrity. Boland, like de Valera, a committed revolutionary, had journeyed ahead of his leader. McGarrity was the wealthy head of Clan na Gael, the IRB's principle support group in America.[42]

De Valera would remain in America for the next eighteen months conducting a campaign aimed at rallying support for the Irish independence cause while the IRA waged a campaign of guerrilla warfare in Ireland. De Valera agreed with the assessment of Collins and others: he could do more to advance Ireland's case by rallying public opinion in America then he could on the run in Ireland. Nonetheless, de Valera's stay in the United States was fraught with controversy, sometimes of his own making. Indeed, it can be written that his activities placed him at odds in a number of instances with Irish–American organisations and their leaders. From the earliest stages of his visit, he made the mistake of taking sides between Irish–American organisations when his service as a unifying force would have proved far more productive to the interests of the cause he came to represent.

But while it is quite often presented by recent writers* that Eamon de Valera helped cause division in the ranks of Irish–Americans, the record indicates that serious fissures between Irish–American support organisations were in place well before he arrived in the United States. The 'Irish Race' Convention held in Philadelphia in February 1919 to support the formation of Dáil Éireann the previous month, received little or no support from either Judge Daniel Cohalan or John Devoy, despite a major outreach effort conducted by Joseph McGarrity, the leader of Clan na Gael, the IRB's outlet in the US. In fact, there persisted throughout the War of Independence a key philosophical difference between McGarrity and Cohalan: the former, an Irish native, was committed outright to the ideal of an independent Irish Republic, while the latter, an anti-Wilsonian Democrat, opposed American entry into the League of Nations, placed his emphasis on self-determination for Ireland but not so much on what form of government the country should have.

One organisation able to straddle the differences between McGarrity and Cohalan and later between de Valera and Cohalan was the American Committee for Relief in Ireland, founded by Dr William Maloney. The group, through pressure placed on the British Government by President Warren Harding in 1921, was able to provide $5 million in humanitarian assistance to Ireland.[43] We shall see in a later chapter that Maloney, by remaining outside the orbit of Irish–American organisations, tied to no one particular faction, was able to exert pressure on the British Government of a political and propagandistic nature.

---

* Tim Pat Coogan and Owen Dudley Edwards, in their respective biographies of de Valera, provide two cases in point.

In his various tours across the American continent during 1919 and 1920, de Valera reached millions of people and set in motion the means by which he was responsible for generating some $5 million for the Dáil Loan. In city after city, he was feted at city halls and state legislative chambers, by mayors and governors alike. These proved to be invaluable public platforms. Baseball stadiums and armouries afforded him his best opportunity for connecting with larger audiences, as was the case in Boston on 27 June 1919, and in Chicago two weeks later, when 70,000 and 50,000 respectively turned out for outdoor events in those two cities.

But de Valera's visit was motivated by more than fund-raising. Indeed, his primary task was to secure recognition of the Irish Republic by the US Government. Conversely, the priority of President Woodrow Wilson was approval of the League of Nations by the US Senate. Furthermore, to make the new world order he envisaged in what was now the aftermath of the First World War a reality, Wilson needed Britain as a staunch ally. These reasons, beyond Wilson's own Ulster Presbyterian background, rendered either the US special recognition of the Irish Republic, or support for its case for nationhood before the League of Nations, extremely unlikely. In the end, despite the best efforts of de Valera and the thousands of Irish–Americans in various pro-recognition organisations, the bid for US recognition ended in failure. As we have seen, that result assured that physical force, not political agitation, would become the engine driving the Irish independence effort.

Not surprisingly, the attention which de Valera's extended stay in the US garnered from a propaganda and, over time, a financial standpoint was a source of consternation to the British Government and its officials in the United States. At the outset, however, the tone of the reports back to the Foreign Office from the British Legation in Washington was dismissive in nature. On 28 June 1919, one official told Lord Curzon, the Foreign Minister, that it was 'unlikely that [de Valera] will be able to exert any serious influence on events. Already the papers on the Atlantic coast have relegated their accounts of his doings to the fourth page; the tone adopted by them in their reports is usually rather humorous and they do not take him very seriously.'[44]

Less than one year later, however, the same official conveyed to Lord Curzon a far more urgent message concerning the extent of the influence of Irish America in general on the American political process. Coming in the midst of de Valera's visit and the many months of rallies and 'barnstorming' tours he participated in along with countless press interviews, the man British officials in the United States termed the 'so-called President of the Irish Republic' clearly made an impact shaping the attitude to the Irish situation in the United States. In a separate communication, the Foreign Secretary was informed of the British Embassy's concern with the influence of Irish America in general on the American political process:

49

It is impossible to exaggerate the extent to which the Irish question and Irish vote dominate the situation. Other agitators, such as the Germans and Indians, attach themselves to the Irish organisation [sic], and obtain from it support and a veneer of respectability. Considered in a broad manner and disregarding comparatively minor issues ... or disputes among Irish politicians in America, the outstanding fact is that the Irish vote in America is enormous, and that at a moment of crisis, American politicians even against their convictions will bid for it.[45]

By November 1920, de Valera's comments in America had caused so much consternation that Sir Auckland Geddes, the British Ambassador to Washington, sent a cable to the Foreign Office asking that Britain seek the Irish leader's expulsion from the United States along with Sinn Féin's suppression there:

I think time [sic] has now come when an effort should be made to supply me with evidence of support in the form of money or munitions reaching Sinn Féiners [sic] from this country. If any such evidence is available it is I think both practical and desirable to bring greater pressure to bear on the United States Government than we have hitherto been able to do with a view to securing expulsion of de Valera and suppression of principal Sinn Féin organisations in this country.[46]

Geddes' superiors had other ideas as to how de Valera should be handled, however. In fact, their objective was the opposite, to keep him out of Ireland at all costs. 'If he applies for a visa or a passport, it is to be refused. If he returns clandestinely he will be deported to his country of origin'. The instructions sent to Geddes also included this requirement: 'In any communication to the United States Government you should emphasise the fact he is not a British subject'.[47]

It was unknown to British officials that Eamon de Valera was to end the discussion himself over whether he should or should not be deported from America. In December 1920 he returned to Ireland as he had left it eighteen months earlier, smuggled on board a merchant ship. De Valera's eighteen-month visit to the United States also contributed to Collins' rise in status in Ireland. Arthur Griffith, the acting President during de Valera's absence, was a quiet, middle-aged man but his own arrest in November 1920 catapulted Collins into the position of Acting President, and quite possibly hastened de Valera's return.

The propaganda war

If there was an added value to de Valera's time spent in the US it lay in the amount of propaganda he garnered for the Irish independence effort there.

Propaganda was also a commodity which the Irish independence movement sought to trade in at home. During the first six months of 1920 a heightened IRA offensive against the Royal Irish Constabulary barracks yielded valuable propaganda material and also served to undermine British effectiveness in much of rural Ireland.

The IRA's attack on the RIC Barracks at Ballylanders, County Limerick, on 27 April 1920, marked the first such attack in the Anglo-Irish war. The facility and the police complement within it were taken after a half-hour attack by the IRA's Saltee Battalion.[48] The attack was spearheaded by a significant IRB cell within the East Limerick IRA organisation. It was an assault which also employed for the first time a technique the IRA would use in future actions against an RIC barracks: break through the roof of the barrack, ignite the structure from the top floor and drive the occupants out while a frontal assault was waged simultaneously from the front. The attack was also launched close to midnight – what became the usual hour for such actions by the IRA. Ballylanders was soon followed by another Barracks attack in County Limerick, which neatly fitted Tom Barry's characterisation of the desirability of Flying Columns that could strike anywhere at anytime.

The destruction of the RIC Barracks in Kilmallock, County Limerick, during the early hours of 28 May 1920 is also illustrative both of the efficiency and the ferocity with which the IRA could strike. It also marked a clear departure from earlier Irish armed revolts. For in Kilmallock, as in other encounters with agents of the Crown, the IRA made it clear that it was playing to win.

After occupying buildings opposite and adjacent to the barracks at Kilmallock, the IRA launched an initial assault on the structure's rooftop. A hole was made in the roof and a combination of Molotov cocktails and buckets full of paraffin oil – conveyed from an oil truck hidden around a corner which had been commandeered earlier in the evening by the IRA – were thrown in. As the barracks' rafters ignited the IRA began a frontal assault from the buildings across the road. Sandbags were placed in windows for maximum cover.

From the position of the higher roof of an adjacent house the IRA laid on a relentless attempt to destroy the building and to force the surrender of its occupants. But from behind the steel shuttered windows, filled with turret holes, the RIC men fought valiantly back, oblivious to the flames that threatened them from the top. From midnight to dawn the fight raged.

The IRA assault had begun when a heavy iron weight was dropped through the barracks' roof. By 1.00 a.m. part of the structure had started to collapse, but the RIC men refused demands that they surrender. Casualties were suffered on both sides. The RIC were able to effect a retreat from the barracks, however, through a separate office.

In all, some sixteen barracks still in use were destroyed along with forty-seven courthouses and scores of other facilities previously abandoned. As

Charles Townshend has written in his analysis of the Anglo-Irish War, 'Here the psychological element was well to the fore. These evacuated buildings were no longer of use to the Government, but as scorched shells they became a chilling advertisement of its retreat'.[49] Sinn Féin's own propaganda effort was quick to pick up where the IRA left off since the ruins resulting from these attacks provided stark testimony of what little effective administrative control Britain had left in much of Ireland.

Townshend has also noted that 'by 1920, the IRA's more determined units were sufficiently well endowed to embark on operations with objectives which were more psychological than logistical'.[50] Within that context the use of propaganda by the IRA's leaders, and most particularly by their colleagues in Sinn Féin, is itself worthy of discussion. The successful generation of propaganda by the Irish Republican movement's civilian officials was as important to its success as the level of IRA activity. Indeed, making the public in Ireland, Britain and elsewhere aware of the IRA's activities was a key function of Republican civilian propagandists. But in addition to fighting a war of independence with limited resources, it was important to communicate the impression that Sinn Féin could govern Ireland effectively and that it enjoyed popular support.

Perhaps one of the most significant propaganda coups and morale boosters for the IRA occurred in June 1920, when the IRA's No. 2 brigade in Cork under Liam Lynch captured a British general. General Lucas found himself the highest ranking British official captured to date by the IRA after he was seized during a fishing trip outside Fermoy, County Cork. Lucas was taken along with two other British officers. But the General was not taken without a struggle. While Lynch and his comrades sought to move Lucas to a detention house hidden in the countryside, Lucas and an officer with him attempted an escape from the vehicle they were riding in. A scuffle ensued between Lynch and Lucas within the vehicle. Lynch prevailed, shooting and wounding Lucas' companion in the process. After a month, and a number of transfers within Cork, Clare and Limerick, Lucas made a successful escape.

It became the responsibility of the Sinn Féin Publicity Bureau under the instructions of Michael Collins to make every skirmish between the IRA and the British forces appear as a pitched battle.[51] In fact, with Collins' additional support as Minister of Finance, the Sinn Féin Publicity Bureau was to function as a fully fledged department within the Republican Government. On 11 November 1919 the official organ of the illegal Irish Republican Government came into existence. It was known as the *Irish Bulletin*. It would grow soon after to be published on a twice-weekly basis. The publication became a useful source of information for both the Irish and British daily press. The volume disputed Britain's own propaganda and provided the public in Ireland and abroad with Irish data on the scale of actions by the Dáil and the IRA. The *Bulletin*'s impact was felt to such an extent by the British

Government that its intelligence network operating out of Dublin Castle at one stage decided to issue fake numbers of the organ. Although this action caused some initial confusion among Sinn Féiners and their supporters, over-all the forgeries were a source of embarrassment to the British. In exposing the bogus issues of the *Bulletin* before the House of Lords in April 1921, Lord Henry Cavendish-Bentnick requested the Chief Secretary for Ireland to 'ask the benevolent politicians not to waste their money in sending me any more of their forgeries'.[52]

That Sinn Féin sought to develop as accurate a network as it could for monitoring the coverage it was receiving, especially within Ireland, was made evident by a directive sent from General Headquarters by P. S. O'Hegarty to all Brigade Commanders with the objective of creating a framework for assessing the political sympathies of the local newspapers. In explaining his directive, O'Hegarty noted that 'under the heading class it should be stated whether the newspaper is friendly or friendly by intimidation, neutral, or hostile'.[53] The language of the directive itself, issued at the height of the Republicans' physical force effort, underscored the importance attached by Sinn Féin to the way the fight was presented, right down to the most local level. It also demonstrated the organisational prowess behind the Republican attempt to ensure the attainment of the most favourable publicity possible. The 'schedule' accompanying the directive came with this instruction from O'Hegarty: 'Brigade Commanders will fill up and return the attached sche-dules with regard to the local newspapers and coverage in their areas.' The attached standardised form included such questions as: 'Is circulation of paper large or influential? Is paper doing good or harm?'[54] The information sheet also sought the name of the correspondents in each brigade area.

This effort was undertaken with the approval of General Headquarters. It was sparked by O'Hegarty's desire to see as much control as possible imposed on the flow of information to the press. On 18 March 1921 he wrote to Headquarters outlining a proposed strategy for dealing with the press in a more thorough manner than had existed to date. In candour, O'Hegarty suggested that 'where local correspondents are useless for our purposes, they shall be as far as possible superseded by men under our control'. He also noted: 'I have gone into the whole question of press correspondence with a number of pressmen at several meetings and they have convinced me that little can be done with local correspondents, save in a few outstanding cases. A good number of them are unsympathetic or hostile, the majority are too intimidated to be of any use.' His analysis of the pressure which many corre-spondents found levelled at them by the British authorities during the course of their reporting on developments in Ireland is particularly helpful: 'Accounts of fights and shootings are usually telegraphed to Dublin. The local man has to hand in his message in the local P.O. [sic] and present a pass signed with his name. This makes him an easy target for the Black and Tans if he reports anything they object to. By the way, many of the correspondents are also reporters for the Press Association, a hostile agency.'[55] From this analysis by O'Hegarty, we see the basis for the 4 May 1921 directive to all Brigade Commanders.

The official status of Sinn Féin's own publicity bureau was made evident in the financial statements submitted to Dáil Éireann by Michael Collins as the Dáil Government's Minister for Finance. These statements are also important for illustrating the increasing weight attached to propaganda by Collins and his fellows during the peak of Anglo-Irish hostilities in 1920–21. In Collins' report of 19 January 1921, he summarised the position of the Republican Government's finances and stated that the allocation given to the publicity Bureau came to £407. This was indeed a minuscule amount compared to the allocations granted the Departments of Foreign Affairs and Home Affairs during the same period, which came to £12,081 and £9,313 respectively. Yet in the same report, Collins projected that the allowance for propaganda should be increased substantially by a thousand fold for the first six months of 1921, to an estimated £4,000. This contrasted more favourably in this instance with the Department of Foreign Affairs, which saw a projected budget of £10,000.

That a connection existed as well between the generation of favourable propaganda and revenue raising for the Republican efforts was demonstrated by the record of Collins' own correspondence in his overlapping responsibility as Adjutant General. In that role he encouraged the purchase at the grass-roots level of the Republican organ *An tÓglach*. A letter of 26 April 1920 from a County Monaghan Brigade Commander, enclosing payment for several issues of the publication, was later given this note in Collins' hand: 'The amount would appear to be correct'.

In an effort to counter the gains made by Sinn Féin, the British Government sought to wage a propaganda war of its own. Its resources for so doing were considerable, particularly from a publishing and communications standpoint. In the aftermath of World War I, the ability of the British Government to focus these resources on the Irish situation was greatly enhanced. And as the Coalition became more mired in a position of stalemate in Ireland, the need to accentuate the war of words with Sinn Féin took on added meaning.

Whatever the problems facing Britain in Ireland at that time, a concern for sufficient funding for its own propaganda campaign was not among them. The Government had at its disposal, in addition to its own access to the resources at Dublin Castle, where a full time press relations officer was placed: the frequent use of the public platform in the House of Commons and the House of Lords; the regular publication of materials favourable to Government policy and critical of Sinn Féin and its supporters at home and abroad by His Majesty's Printing Office; the utilisation of friendly newspapers and journalists; and the allocation of Government funds, sometimes covertly, for the publication of books and other printed matter by private publishers in Britain and overseas.

By the end of 1920 the Government was acting to heighten its propaganda effort at home and abroad further. In the House of Commons on 18 November 1920, Sir Hamar Greenwood, Chief Secretary for Ireland, announced the appointment of a 'Press Officer of long experience whose duty it is to communicate to the press officially authenticated information with regard to events of public interest in Ireland'.[56] The individual assigned was Basil Clarke, whom Greenwood described as 'for several years a well known London journalist . . .'.[57]

The amount of Government funds used to finance the propaganda effort against Sinn Féin is not easily quantifiable due to a dearth of documentation. However, we can with some degree of certainty assume that it was substantial, based on other propaganda efforts sanctioned by the British Government at that time. According to Keith Middlemas, Lloyd George, in seeking to undermine the more radical elements within the British labour movement – specifically with regard to the 1919 railway workers' strike – turned to secret propaganda. To that end, he set up an organisation 'concerned with anti-Bolshevism . . .' intended to incite public hostility against the trade unions and political left wing and to encourage 'constitutional as well as direct action'. Sidney Walton, a former undercover agent and government fugleman, was appointed to run it, with a fund of £100,000.[58]

In a memorandum to Hamar Greenwood on 21 April 1921, Lloyd George emphasised the need for a heightened propaganda effort.[59] Propaganda was indeed only one way of sharpening the focus by the British Government on the Irish situation in the aftermath of the Great War and the Versailles Conference. An extract from the notes of Walter Hume Long, the Irish Situation Committee's Chairman, is useful in illustrating the manner in which the British Government now viewed its problems in Ireland:

> The Committee felt strongly that the moment has arrived for the Government actively to assume the offensive in its Irish policy, and to come to grips with Sinn Féin. They considered that Government should show the world at large it is in deliberate earnest in its assertion that the republican movement in Ireland should be destroyed and that the authority of the Imperial Government cannot be flouted with impunity.[60]

While the essential ingredients in that heightened British effort to show the world how 'earnest' it was in dealing with the increasing menace of Irish Republicanism included resort to a policy of coercion, official reprisals, and martial law, propaganda was also to play a prominent role. The generation of British official publications during this period, purporting to show that the Republican movement was aided and abetted by foreign governments and ideologies, initially the Germans and later the Russian Bolsheviks, illustrates the degree to which official British propagandists sought to counteract the success of Sinn Féin in Ireland, Britain and the United States. That these British-inspired conspiracy theories represented ideological leaps of faith was apparently inconsequential when weighed against the need to manufacture an aura of guilt by association. On a regular basis throughout the Anglo-Irish conflict, the British Government through its own printing office directed the publication of various allegations seeking to show Sinn Féin ties to both German Imperialism and Russian Bolshevism. Two examples of this, forgeries included, were printed by His Majesty's Stationery Office under the Command Series and were entitled 'Documents Relative to the Sinn Féin Movement' No. 1108 (1921), which attempted to demonstrate the 'active connection between the leaders of the Sinn Féin movement and the German Government' from 1914–19, and 'Intercourse Between Bolshevism and Sinn Féin' No. 1326. More than contributing to the war of words alone, these publications served as part of the basis for the official effort to paint Sinn Féin and Irish Republicanism as hostile to British and democratic interests.*

Later, in an effort to link Sinn Féin to the hysteria of the Communist 'Red Menace' that engulfed Britain and other western democracies at the time, Lloyd George went on to intimate the possible impact of an outcome favourable to Sinn Féin on Britain itself:

> There is a small but vigorous Communist Party in these islands, which bitterly and with the most intense conviction believes that it ought to overthrow democratic institutions and seize power by force and violence because of the manner in which they consider that the ruling classes of the past, the aristocracy and the owners of capital, oppressed and exploited the poor. Are

---

* Lloyd George's own involvement in trying to add greater effect to the Government's propaganda campaign through his considerable public relations skills was evidenced by the manner of his response to a letter critical of the Coalition's Irish policy from Britain's Protestant bishops in April 1921. The Prime Minister's official answer, after no less than eight attempted drafts within the Cabinet, was released extensively as part of an offensive against criticism of British conduct in Ireland. The Prime Minister stressed that his response was necessary 'on account of the responsibility and public influence of the signatories'. He proceeded to tacitly condone the record of the 'Black and Tans' on the basis that 'individuals working under conditions of extraordinary personal danger and strain, where they are in uniform and their adversaries mingle unrecognisable among the ordinary civilian population, have undoubtedly been guilty of deplorable acts'. Summoning all the skill of a propagandist in his own right, Lloyd George proceeded to allege that the Protestant bishops were aligning themselves with Sinn Féin in their criticism of the government. 'I do not contest Sinn Féin's right to its opinions and I have never done so', the Prime Minister stated. 'But what amazes me', he continued, 'is that a body of responsible men, earnest leaders of the Church, should state publicly that Sinn Féin had some kind of justification for murdering innocent men in cold blood, because its novel and extravagant political ideals have been denied.'

the Communists, because of sufferings and the grieving of the working classes and sincerity of their own industrial ideals, to be justified in employing murder and assassination to achieve these ends?[61]

While Lloyd George might not have privately agreed with his own Government's view that Sinn Féin was part of a foreign conspiracy, he did believe that 'the policemen on strike, the many agitators actively engaged in various parts of the country were generally of Irish extraction and they were creating a vicious atmosphere'. But while he held little regard for Irish national rights, he believed that a satisfactory 'settlement of the Irish Question is important from the standpoint of world opinion and also for our relations with the Dominions and the United States'.[62]

In the documents released in the British 1921 White Paper, 'Intercourse Between Bolshevism and Sinn Féin', Dr Patrick McCartan, the head of the Washington Bureau of Sinn Féin, was held to be the architect of the Republican effort to establish reciprocal recognition between the Irish Republic and the new Soviet State. That the Republican Government sought Soviet recognition is made clear by the minutes of the secret session of Dáil Éireann for 25 January 1920, when a motion of Arthur Griffith's was carried, authorising the President to appoint consuls and diplomatic agents to several countries. Within that motion, provision was made for the appointment of a diplomatic mission to the Soviet Union with a view to establishing diplomatic relations. However, it should be emphasised that Sinn Féin's efforts to make contact with the Soviet Union appear to have been motivated more out of a desire to gain the widest possible degree of recognition for the Irish Republic rather than out of any ideological commitment. Indeed, on the same day the Dáil Éireann authorised the delegation to go to Moscow, it also approved a sum not to exceed one million dollars in the effort to obtain recognition of the Republic by the US Government.[63] Furthermore, as the British Government already knew, and as Dr McCartan came to know, so anxious was the Soviet Union throughout 1920–21 for a trade agreement with Great Britain that it did not view the Irish situation sympathetically or favourably. In addition, the Soviets were also more intent at this time upon consolidating their internal position than seeking involvement in conflicts elsewhere. It is also noteworthy, as Dr McCartan observed in *With de Valera in America*, that recognition by the US was deemed of such importance by the President of the Irish Republic that he was willing to slow down any process of discussion with the Soviets.[64] Nonetheless, for the British Government, the mere occurrence of contact by Sinn Féin with the Soviets provided a basis for concerted action in the propaganda sphere.

Aside from the issuance of the 1921 White Paper, seeking to tie Sinn Féin to Russian Bolshevism, the British Government's effort to undermine Sinn Féin, particularly in the US, was exemplified by the 1921 publication at its expense of two separate volumes in the form of books authorised by Dublin Castle propagandist C. J. C. Street, under the pseudonym 'I.O.'. Published in New York by the Dutton Company, the two books sought to defend British policy in Ireland, while linking Sinn Féin to subversive forces. The books, entitled *The Administration of Ireland, 1920* and *Ireland in 1921*, drew largely for their details on the Command Series documents relating to Sinn Féin. According to Street in *The Administration of Ireland, 1920*, the publication of the 'Documents Relative to the Sinn Féin Movement' was sufficient in itself to reveal 'the whole story of the negotiations between Sinn Féin and Germany, and it is therefore unnecessary to pursue the matter further'. C. J. C. Street cited a 28 November 1914 letter of Sir Roger Casement to Eoin MacNeill relating to the publication of an official German declaration of that country's goodwill towards Irish national aspirations. Almost equally dated was another document cited by Street: a Republican notice from 1915 to the people of Wexford, urging them to disobey orders published under the Defense of the Realm Act concerning any invasion of Ireland by Germany.[65]

To this British propagandist, however, these dated examples 'were typical of the evidence contained in the White Paper which should be perceived by all who wish to understand that Irish point of view'. 'For all history,' Street wrote, 'both recent and remote, shows that the Irish appeal to America is based upon self-seeking and not at all upon racial affinity.' He went on to make what was perhaps one of the most ironic characterisations regarding the Irish Republican movement ever to come from a British propagandist seeking to defend Britain's performance in Ireland: 'The Irish Republican movement is and always has been the child of an almost incomprehensible selfishness, as the very title of its later advocates, Sinn Féin – "ourselves alone" – indicates.'

At Street's time of writing, Germany had been vanquished in Europe. It therefore became necessary to develop a new technique for denigrating the Irish cause in the United States. In this instance, Street sought to question the loyalty of those Irish activists then operating in the US. He wrote:

> Finding Germany a broken reed, the Irish malcontents have turned once more to America, as being the country whose population might be expected to be most in sympathy with Irish ideals. The so-called President of the Republic himself made the United States his headquarters for over a year ... and for the last few years there has been a fog of misunderstanding between two great cousin nations, America and England, it should be the earnest endeavour of every true citizen of either to dissipate.

Street also belittled the involvement of American elected officials on behalf of Irish independence: 'It cannot be too widely realised that a very great part of the Irish Question in America is nothing but the conventional cry of politicians, that the great bulk of the reasoning multitude are no more interested in Ireland than they are in the South Pole.'

Street's analysis of the reasons for the apparent interest of American politicians in the Irish Question was even more pointed: 'Owing to the fact that there are some twenty million of Irish descent, the Irish vote is something to be angled for. Politicians of every shade of opinion always have and always will dangle the bait of speeches in the Irish Republican interest before the noses of the electorate, whenever such tactics seem likely to procure them votes'.[66] Street was even less kind to Irish–Americans concerned with Irish independence:

> We have one guarantee which will never fail us: that the only type of man who can influence American policy is the man who is first a citizen of the United States and an Irishman incidentally ... The converse, the man who places his abandoned nationality first and his American citizenship second, is a man who gains nothing but mistrust in the State in which he dwells.[67]

It can be seen from this glimpse how the British Government, through its own propaganda machine, attempted to characterise those active in support of the Irish cause in America as being less than loyal to the US, while painting those interested elected officials as self-centered vote-seekers interested in exploiting the Irish issue for their own ends. The limited success of this effort, however, was demonstrated by the response garnered by such organisations in the US as the Friends of Irish Freedom, which Street noted with evident frustration.

Using what he termed 'a single extract' from what was in fact another outdated correspondence, Street quoted the 'Friends' as calling for an 'Irish Race Convention' while seeking 'close relations between the German Government and various Irish–American Sinn Féin organisations'. To Street, the sinister force behind these developments was the secret American-based Fenian-rooted Society, the Clan na Gael.

In the effort to win the hearts and minds of the American public, both the British and Irish Republican efforts sought to draw respective parallels with American history. British propagandists argued stridently against the attempt of Irish sympathisers in the US to compare the Irish independence struggle with the American Revolution and a common British enemy. Consistent with comments made by Lloyd George, Street argued that 'the position of that section of the Irish people who wish to secede is far more approximate to that of the Confederate States in 1861. They wish to rebel against a longstanding partnership, to the detriment of both partners. And no one will doubt the wisdom of the policy which held the South by force to the Union.'[68]

Nonetheless, the importance of propaganda to both sides sets the table for a wider discussion of the conflict itself. But before continuing with a further analysis of the Anglo-Irish war, some of the social aspects of the conflict should be visited at this juncture.

While the relationship of the Irish labour movement to the Irish Revolution is dealt with at length later, a brief discussion of developments vis-à-vis labour and Ireland is warranted. Despite demonstrations of worker solidarity with the Irish struggle, radical industrial and agrarian action was not a common-place feature of the Irish Revolution. When it did occur, it was usually in response to coercive actions taken by the British authorities against the local population. This was the case in April 1919 when a general strike was called in Limerick after the city was divided in two, a military zone imposed and all manner of civilians subjected to harassment. The strike was combined with the proclamation of a 'Limerick Soviet!' The strike was abandoned in less than two weeks. However, between 1920 and 1921, the model of worker 'Soviets', which saw the takeover by workers of such enterprises as creameries, foundries and mills, was replicated elsewhere in the County at Knocklong, and at the Arigna coal mine in County Leitrim. But these actions were for the most part a response to British policy as a whole in Ireland and not industrial grievances alone. Despite the use of the term Soviet, the takeovers of private businesses were largely motivated by a desire for increased wages. When the gains were made, the control reverted back to the owners.[69]

3

Britain's Dual Policy: Politics with Coercion

If we steadfastly adhere ... to the double-barrelled policy of firm and effective
dealing with the Sinn Féiners, murderers and other scoundrels, and at the
same time pursue our policy of reform by passing our measure through
Parliament with as little delay as possible ... I am satisfied that we shall win
through.

Walter Hume Long, Chairman of the British Cabinet's Irish Situation
Committee, 18 June 1920

Enough had occurred in the way of violent insurrection throughout the first
ten months of 1919 to make it clear to Lloyd George that the use of force was
not the answer if Ireland was to be pacified.

If we take stock of what had happened in the country up to the end of
1919, we see that not only were the lives of those in a police or British military
uniform at risk, so were all agents of the Crown in Ireland susceptible to
assassination. From the ambush at Soloheadbeg onward, it became clear that
the type of IRA Volunteer the British Government was now facing in Ireland
was not interested in heroic last stands aimed at martyrdom. The IRA was
ruthlessly determined to utilise every means at its disposal to end British rule.
From January to October 1919, a steadily increasing pattern of Volunteer
violence had developed. Consequently, the British Army grew to a total of 27
battalions in Ireland. But it proved insufficient as police barracks throughout
the country underwent sandbagging and other fortifications. Lord French, as
we have seen, narrowly avoided assassination. In September of that year
came the first evidence of a British policy of counter-terror, as shops and
houses in the County Cork town of Fermoy were put to the torch in reprisal
for the earlier ambush of a Light Infantry Brigade. As one observer has
commented, the IRA campaign which the Crown found itself responding to
represented 'a steadily increasing pattern of violence and mounting passion
that does not easily fall into discernible discrete stages'.[1]

The insurrection in Ireland was, of course, also manifested by another reality besides violent revolt: the existence of Dáil Éireann and the early manifestation of an alternative government in defiance of the Crown. Worse still

for the British Government, this alternative system had the legitimacy of democratic support of the majority of the Irish people, who backed Sinn Féin's decision to boycott Westminster completely. Sinn Féin was outlawed, but neither the combination of official proscription or deadly force by the Crown and its agents succeeded in weakening popular support for Dáil Éireann. Nationalist Ireland had given its allegiance to it.

As Arthur Mitchell has written in his outstanding account of Dáil Éireann and its importance to the Irish Revolution, the middle of 1920 represented the high-water mark for the outlawed body.

> The alternative government of Dáil Éireann blossomed in the summer of 1920; its growth was rapid and its season short. Its success with the courts, the police, army and local government created a public demand for its services far beyond these areas of administration. It is now seen by many, if not most people as the de facto government of the country ... it was now viewed by many people as being at least one of the governing forces in Ireland. To meet this demand for its services, the underground state had to expand quickly, and there were severe growing pains.[2]

Yet those growing pains notwithstanding, backed by the voice of the vast majority of the Irish people, the Dáil Government persisted as an open and democratic challenge to British rule. In Britain Lloyd George grappled with the fact that a different approach might be needed. Yet at no time did his Government seek totally to substitute accommodation for coercion or the threat of greater force.

Britain's Irish administration had by now come to exist in much of Southern Ireland in name only. Driven out of much of the South by the combination of Sinn Féin's electoral success with a campaign of terror and intimidation conducted by the IRA, the King's writ was in essence confined to a new pale consisting of Dublin City, Northeast Ulster, and certain towns in the south-east.

A report submitted to the Government by a panel sent to evaluate the state of the Irish administration at this time, issued this dour finding:

> The Castle Administration does not administer. On the mechanical side it can never have been any good and is now quite obsolete: in the infinitely more important sphere of a) informing and advising the Irish government in relation to policy and b) of practical capacity in the application of policy, it simply has no existence.[3]

More than Home Rule was now needed if a remedy was to be attempted. But it was to Home Rule that Lloyd George in fact returned, if only as a starting point. On 9 October 1919, in a stroke befitting his usual resourcefulness, the Prime Minister appointed Sir Walter Long to head a special Cabinet-level committee known as the committee on the Government of Ireland

Amendment Bill. The elderly Long, a country squire and a former Chief Secretary for Ireland, had long been seen as an ally of the unionists and an enemy of Home Rule. But now, against the backdrop of open revolt in Ireland, he was charged with the task of legislating and implementing a Home Rule measure that would take into account the whole island.

Long's pedigree as a hardliner in support of British rule was no doubt strengthened in the eyes of Conservative backbenchers by his support early in 1919 for supplementing the RIC through the hiring of British ex-servicemen. The outfit would become known as the 'Black and Tans'.[4] The reasoning behind his decision to embrace Home Rule at this stage is instructive: it helps explain the reversal of other unionists like him who before the First World War would never have done so.

> I have come to the conclusion that after the passing of the act of 1914 it has been impossible to avoid one of two courses: a) to allow that act to come into force; b) to amend it or substitute another for it – simple repeal being, in my judgment, impossible ... Therefore, I set myself to work to try and frame a practical, working scheme.[5]

In brief, realpolitik had colored his decision. As Long told the Archbishop of Westminster some time earlier, 'I feel that it cannot, must not, be beyond the power of statesmanship to avert the awful disasters with which we appear to be threatened'.[6] Like Lloyd George, he had come to believe that force alone was not enough to extinguish the flames of rebellion in Ireland. Long's appointment effectively represented the beginning of what has been termed the Government's dual policy.

The efficacy behind a dual policy was best described by Long himself when he emphasised to Lloyd George that if the Government adhered to a 'double-barrelled policy of firm and effective dealing with the Sinn Féiners, murderers and other scoundrels, and at the same time pursue our policy of reform by passing our measure through Parliament with as little delay as possible ... I am satisfied that we shall win through'.[7]

On 4 November 1919 Long submitted a report for an amended Home Rule Bill to the Cabinet. What would become known as the Government of Ireland Bill contained provisions for a divided Ireland to be served by two parliaments along with a Council of Ireland, which would function as a means for promoting Irish reunification. What some might term adroit, others could term this language disingenuous. In the end the Bill became the vehicle for the partition of Ireland. But the creation of the two parliaments was used as a device for mitigating nationalist objections to remaining under British rule. 'No nationalist', the report claimed, 'would be retained under British rule. All Irishmen would be self-governing.'[8] The comment, of course, ignored the significant Nationalist minority that would be created in a six-county North-east Ulster jurisdiction. While the report could be viewed as an example of

Walter Hume Long's talent for legislative draftsmanship, its implementation nonetheless would have far-reaching effects for both Irish nationalists and unionists alike.

It is here that a brief digression into the origins of how partition came to be legislated for Ireland is necessary. In June 1916, the attempt was made by then Prime Minister Asquith to amend the language of the 1914 Home Rule Act that had been placed on the statute books to include provision for Ireland's partition into two separate jurisdictions. This was not undertaken as a separate bill but as an amendment to the 1914 measure which was not implemented, as we have seen, under the pretext of the Great War. This legislative approach was accompanied by a fairly duplicitous attempt by Lloyd George, then Britain's Munitions Minister and appointed by Asquith, to seek an Irish settlement in May 1916 after the execution of the leaders of the Easter Rising. It was not, of course, the last attempt at coercion and conciliation by Britain in Ireland.

Ostensibly, Lloyd George was to try to gain agreement between Sir Edward Carson and John Redmond. On the one hand he promised to Carson the exclusion of the six north-eastern counties, and a united Ireland under Home Rule to Redmond. He almost achieved this inherently contradictory objective. Under a plan he had worked out with the two leaders separately, Ulster was to be excluded from a unitary jurisdiction with one parliament for all of Ireland until one year after the war. John Dillon sought a formal guarantee that the country would be united, but was instead only met with the promise from Lloyd George that it was a temporary measure and that the 1914 Home Rule Act would take effect for all of Ireland. The plan, when made public met with expressions of outrage from the Nationalists in the six north-eastern counties affected – Antrim, Down, Fermanagh, Armagh, Tyrone and Derry. On 23 May 1916, Nationalist delegates convened a meeting in St Mary's Hall, Belfast, and voted down the proposal.

In the end it was the Government of Ireland Act, four years later, that formally provided for the exclusion of those six north-eastern counties under partition, and for a Northern Ireland Parliament.

The Government's immediate objectives in initiating the Amended Home Rule Bill in 1919 while continuing the use of repression offered clear evidence of a policy mixing politics with coercion. Long's Bill was not a sop to terrorism, but was instead the anchor of an objective aimed at undermining Sinn Féin.

By December 1919, with Long's initial prompting, the Cabinet had decided at least on a provisional basis in favour of including all of Ulster's nine counties in the area to be covered by the Northern Ireland Parliament. Such an arrangement was the most logical one, Long contended, if the island's eventual unity was to be achieved. But neither this goal nor a nine-county Ulster state was desirable to a majority of Ulster Unionists, a fact made clear to the Government on 15 December. A secure Northeast Ulster State was what Craig and his allies saw as essential to their remaining outside of a united Ireland.

The Ulster diehards got their way and a six-county Ulster, excluding Counties Monaghan, Cavan and Donegal, was substituted in the Bill following a meeting of the House of Commons on 19 February 1920. By this point, after a visit to Ulster, Law himself came to embrace the six-county alternative. This was done despite the fact that the majority of the Irish Situation Committee had favoured a nine-county Ulster. Therein lay a crucial and inherent contradiction of what was to emerge as Britain's policy towards the partition scheme which parliament had itself accomplished: The unification of Ireland was the Government's stated goal and Ireland's partition was only temporary. At the same time it acquiesced to Ulster Unionism's demand for a six-county Ulster enclave in the full knowledge that such an outcome made acceptance of a united Ireland by a majority in that territory virtually impossible. In effect, the Unionist veto over a self-governing Ireland covering the entire island had been set in stone by the British government, under the guise of a Government of Ireland Bill designed ostensibly to achieve a peaceful resolution of the Anglo-Irish conflict. The price for the support of Sir James Craig and other Ulster Unionists was a measure that would condemn future generations in Britain and Ireland to more bloodshed and upheaval.

The partition imposed by the map, as has been noted elsewhere, in many cases did not adhere precisely to actual demographic patterns of Protestants and Catholics, nor to the wishes of the inhabitants of many border areas. The significant Protestant minorities of east Donegal and Counties Cavan and Monaghan, who found themselves left out of the six-county area under the Government of Ireland Act, tried to no avail to argue the case for their inclusion. In effect, the Unionist leaders of Northeast Ulster were successful from the earliest stages in hijacking the Government of Ireland Act.

A submission to Parliament by a Unionist delegation from the three Ulster counties cut off by the proposed partition held that a nine-county Ulster would have a Protestant majority of 200,000 and would assuredly elect a unionist majority in the parliamentary elections. But that ratio of Protestants to Catholics proved too close for comfort for Sir James Craig and his loyalist vanguard. Thus the Government of Ireland Bill was amended in favour of a six-county Northern Ireland state, despite the earlier recommendation by the British Cabinet for the inclusion of all of Ulster.[9]

And so the unionists of three Ulster Counties, despite their inclusion in the Ulster Covenant of 1912, were sacrificed in the interests of assuring the greatest possible degree of Protestant hegemony in a northern state. One writer has remarked that the Ulster unionists acted with 'the same sacred egoism with which Sinn Féin sacrificed the Catholics of the Six Counties'.[10] Despite passing the House of Commons by a vote of 348 votes to 94 on 31

March 1920, a debate over amendments to the Government of Ireland Act meant that the Bill did not reach the House of Lords for its approval until 16 December 1920. Shortly before Christmas of that year, after receiving the royal assent, the Government of Ireland Act (1920) became law.

How were the unionists of the six Protestant counties able to achieve this result? As Professor Nicholas Mansergh has pointed out, by the late nineteenth century, 'over most of Ireland, the ascendancy was expendable and politically it had been, or was being, expended'.[11] Mansergh's analysis of how the Protestants of northeast Ulster transformed their position is instructive:

> In the period 1886–1920 it advanced its position from that of an unidentifiable minority group within a recognised political entity to one of control of a semi-autonomous state equated by Act of Parliament with the remainder of the island of which it formed a part. Minority determination to resist incorporation in a unitary Irish state, the reality of which was recognised most clearly by republican opponents, could not have achieved as great a transformation without the backing of formidable English allies. At a favourable moment politically the minority were in consequence enabled to obtain not only a separate state but also the area for which they asked, on the grounds that it was the largest in which stable unionist government could be maintained.[12]

Some twenty-seven years later, Lord Mountbatten,* as the last British Viceroy in India, rejected Mohammed Ali Jinnah's effort to secure the whole six provinces of north-west and north-east India, which together held a Muslim majority, in favour of a separate Muslim state of Pakistan. In Ireland partition would apply but without any local divisions to determine its scope.[13] In effect, the arbitrariness with which partition was implemented added insult to injury for many Irish nationalists. Ironically, it took more than a year to see the government's civil remedy in its 'Dual Policy' pass through Parliament. But it took less than a few weeks for the Government to accomplish 'martial law' and other elements of coercion for Ireland during the same year.

A wider role was assumed by Walter Long during the debate on 24 June. Long was named by Lloyd George to head the Cabinet's Irish Situation Committee for the purpose of making recommendations for ending the state of disorder in Ireland. Among the other Committee members were Winston Churchill, Lord Birkenhead, Hamar Greenwood, Sir James Craig, and H. A. L. Fisher.† The Irish nationalist viewpoint – that of the vast majority in Ireland – was obviously absent, given the fact that this body of opinion had

---

* Lord Mountbatten was murdered along with his grandson while on holiday in the Irish Republic in 1979 by the Provisional IRA.
† Fisher would serve as the principle draftsman for the new legislation.

gone over to Sinn Féin, in no small part thanks to British policy in Ireland itself. One could argue that Sinn Féin's policy of abstention from the British Parliament ensured the enactment of major legislation without the voice of Nationalist Ireland's elected representatives.

If the British Government was serious in its contention that it saw partition as only a temporary measure under the terms of the Government of Ireland Bill, *The Times* of London cautioned that the inclusion of the whole Province of Ulster within the boundaries of Northern Ireland was the most desirable option. 'In our view', the paper editorialised on 18 May 1920, 'the nine county area is a necessary corollary to the principle of evolution from partition into a unit upon which rests the fairest hope of settlement'. *The Times* stated while it heard the arguments advanced by 'the disciplined chorus of the Ulster Unionist Party', it could not support the creation of a six-county area. But Craig and his followers prevailed on the Government, however, and a six-county entity was established. It was a result which meant to *The Times* that 'at all events, darkness must obscure the brightest hope for the future success of this measure'.[14] Charles Mowat's description of the enactment of the Government of Ireland Act in the context of other events in Ireland in 1920 is valuable here:

> The bill had about it from the start, an air of unreality as far as it concerned Ireland outside the six counties of the North. Opposition speakers in the debate reminded the government of the fighting in Ireland; and it took little prescience to foretell that Home Rule would no longer satisfy the greater part of Ireland. The Bill seems to have been enacted as a temporary sheltering of an awkward legislative problem, and as a means of convincing the United States that the Government had some Irish policy besides violence; its very slow progress through Parliament, occupying much of 1920, seems to suggest this.[15]

Although the Government of Ireland Act was viewed as a dead letter by Sinn Féin and most of Nationalist Ireland, owing to the weakness of its provisions – Home Rule being viewed by this time as too little too late – the measure would still have a profound effect on Ireland's future. But a measure of Home Rule in a divided Ireland was as far as Lloyd George and the Government were prepared to go by the end of 1920. Any grant of dominion status would render it only a matter of time before full independence for Ireland became a reality. Lloyd George said as much himself in the House of Commons on 11 November 1920:

> If you give the right to Ireland to determine what form of government she likes, the majority of those who speak for Ireland make it clear that that is what they would claim [a Republic] neither for the sake of Britain nor for the sake of Ireland can we contemplate anything which would set up in Ireland an independent Sovereign state . . .[16]

Nonetheless, we will see that, as the violence increased in Ireland, Lloyd George would need to contemplate further remedies.

A new regime for Dublin Castle

Equally important, in British eyes, from the standpoint of peace in Ireland was the appointment of a new team of civil servants at Dublin Castle. Most notable was Sir John Anderson, who was named Undersecretary in May 1920. Anderson's primary task was to add professionalism and efficiency to the moribund Castle administration. Joining Assistant Undersecretary Anderson were Andy Cope* and Mark Sturgis, whose diary record of the period provides many invaluable insights from a Dublin Castle perspective.[17] Cope has been termed by one writer as having been in reality 'Lloyd George's special agent, charged with informally exploring avenues of settlement with Sinn Féin'.[18]

Anderson's appointment was due to preliminary work which Alfred 'Andy' Cope had done in surveying the Dublin Castle organisation for Warren Fisher. Cope and Sturgis came to personify the very nature of the bureaucracy Anderson was responsible for heading. In essence Cope, a former Customs Detective, was sent to Dublin by Lloyd George to act as a personal envoy to Sinn Féin, in order to assess who it was the Government could negotiate with. Sturgis, a former Assistant Private Secretary to Asquith, was, like Anderson, a career civil servant, who served as a liaison for Anderson with Sinn Féin sources.

Anderson once explained in answer to a question as to how the Dublin Castle team was formulated: 'I came in by the front door; Andy came in by the back door; and Mark came in through the drawing room window'.[19] Nonetheless, it was Sir John Anderson who played the leadership role in the Castle's Secretariat. His biographer has written that 'occasionally he could break out in forceful condemnation of his masters' futile attempts to combine coercion with conciliation and at their inevitable vacillation between the two'.[20] Nonetheless, ever the British career civil servant, he set about helping to implement what were Britain's conflicting policies in Ireland.

Like the garrisons that attempted to enforce the King's writ in the Irish hinterlands, Anderson and his colleagues found themselves living behind the walls of Dublin Castle in siege-like conditions. Their activities, with the exception of Cope's meeting with Republican contacts, confined them within those walls out of personal safety. An immediate task for Anderson, as Greenwood's chief deputy, was the reorganisation of a badly demoralised RIC. General Tudor, another friend of Churchill, was named police adviser,

---

* Cope's appointment was not formalised until some time later.

and he in turn set about coordinating police and military intelligence in the hands of Brigadier-General Ormonde Winter. While the move may not have enhanced the conditions for peace, over time it made life far more difficult for the IRA.

But while Anderson and his colleagues may have helped direct British policy from the top, they did not preside over a system that was by any means paying total obeisance to the Crown. The extent to which Catholics of a nationalist bent had advanced by the sheer force of numbers into the British Civil Administration in Ireland by this time is significant. Michael Collins' ability to gather intelligence of a high calibre owed much to the fact that he had access to individuals in the Royal Irish Constabulary and the civil service, who indeed – in the case of two young detectives, David Nelligan and Joe Kavanagh amongst others – placed themselves at great risk.

Coercion and counter terror: the British counterattack

At the beginning of 1920, the British Government found itself spending £20 million per annum in Ireland to support its military campaign.[21] In March of that year its controversial specially recruited auxiliary police force arrived in Ireland. Soon to earn infamy as the 'Black and Tans', owing to their dark tunics and tan trousers, these largely unemployed veterans of the Great War responded to the lure of a wage of ten shillings per day. To Winston Churchill, the 'Tans' had been chosen on the basis of intelligence, character, and their war-records. Yet to many in Ireland they were 'the sweepings of English jails'.[22] Somewhere in between lay the truth. In the end the 'Blacks and Tans', it will be seen, did much to unite opposition in Ireland and Britain alike to the conduct of British policy by the appalling conduct of some in their ranks.

Despite the superior strength in numbers of the British Army, the RIC and auxiliary police personnel, the IRA persisted throughout 1920 as a frustrating opponent. C. J. C. Street, the British propagandist and a former army major, offered a glimpse of the official British exacerbation of IRA activity. In his British government-financed volume aimed at counteracting Sinn Féin's propaganda success, he described the conduct and tactics of the IRA over the course of a number of assaults on the RIC:

> Such is the bold language of the police reports in the record of an average week of murder and attempted murder by the Republicans. In no single case is there any indication of open warfare, the methods of the assailants are those of the common assassins, careful never to act until they are in overwhelming numbers and have covered their line of retreat. Fuller accounts of the murders of policemen merely emphasise the cowardly and brutal methods of the ruffians, who style themselves soldiers of the Irish Republic.[23]

But the IRA's tacticians had a different perspective on what was needed for confronting the forces of an empire. They had determined out of necessity, as would the leaders of guerrilla armies in other places later in the century, to fight according to their own rules. Tom Barry, the leader of the IRA's West Cork Brigade and architect of the 'Flying Columns' that engaged the enemy and disappeared to fight again, and who ironically received his own military training as a British enlisted man during the First World War, offered this assessment of the IRA's tactics:

> It was accepted in West Cork that the paramount objective of any Flying Columns, in the circumstances then prevailing, should not be to fight, but to continue to exist. The very existence of such a column of armed men, even it if never struck a blow, was a continuous challenge to the enemy and forced him to maintain large garrisons to meet the threatened onslaught on his military forces and for the security of his civil administration. Such a column moving around must seriously affect the morale of garrisons, for one day it would surely strike.[24]

Under Barry's personal direction, the 'Flying Column' would 'choose its own battleground and, when possible, would refuse battle if the circumstances were unfavourable'.[25] Similarly, Michael Collins had perhaps one of the most candid of all explanations for its use as a remedy for changing British policy in Ireland. Through the unending resort to violence against the British forces, Collins held that he and the rest of the Republican leadership had 'discovered that we had grown strong enough to make England too uncomfortable'. Collins added: 'More than this, we discovered that while England expatiated on the futility of force by others, it is the only argument they listen to. Above all, the valiant efforts of Irishmen under the terror – their deaths – these finally awoke the sleeping spirit of Ireland'.[26]

That those in the King's remit had no hesitation about murdering leading public men in Ireland in cold blood was made evident by events which occurred on 20 March 1920. During the early hours of that day a contingent of RIC men in disguise broke through the doors of the home of Cork City's Lord Mayor Tomas MacCurtain. MacCurtain fell dead from two shots fired at him as he stood at the top of his landing. MacCurtain's murder set in motion a chain of events in Cork City and elsewhere which exacerbated the violence that now held Ireland firmly in its grip. It also made possible the ascension to office of Terence MacSwiney as MacCurtain's successor. Mac-Swiney, as we shall see, would occupy centre-stage in the Anglo-Irish conflict in short order by pursuing a hunger strike to the death.

Five months after MacCurtain's murder RIC Detective Inspector Swanzy, who had been named by a coroner's jury as a responsible party for the death, was himself assassinated by members from the Cork No. 1 IRA Brigade. With the apparent sanction of Michael Collins, Swanzy was tracked down to

Lisburn, County Antrim, where he had been re-assigned to what was assumed
to be the safety of a loyalist enclave. Later, Collins explained the rationale
behind the killing of Swanzy.

> As I was in command, I decided to collect my evidence and play them at their
> own game. This was the start of the vicious circle – the murder race. I inter-
> cepted all the correspondence. Inspector Swanzy put Lord Mayor MacCur-
> tain away so I got Swanzy and all his associates wiped out, one by one, in all
> parts of Ireland to which the murderers had been secretly dispersed. What
> else could I do?[27]

Irish Republican actions on both the military and propaganda fronts led to
the heightened annoyance of the British Cabinet. This was evident in the
minutes of the 20 July 1920 meeting of the Cabinet's Irish Situation Committee. Under Walter Long's chairmanship, the group had been formed
shortly before by Lloyd George to monitor the situation in Ireland and to
report back directly to the full Cabinet. In his notes on the 20 July session,
Long stated:

> The Committee felt strongly that the moment had arrived for the Govern-
> ment actively to assume the offensive in its Irish policy, and to come to grips
> with Sinn Féin. They considered that the Government should show the world
> at large that it is in deliberate earnest in its assertion that the Republican
> movement in Ireland should be destroyed and that the authority of the
> Imperial Government cannot be flouted with impunity.[28]

Long's account made specific reference to the remedies of the Irish Situation Committee considered for carrying out the Government's policy against
Sinn Féin: they included the imposition of martial law, the closing of the
postal system, the withholding of pension payments in all counties where
Sinn Féin had obtained an effective hold, as well as the 'round-up of Sinn
Féin courts in that all persons taking part in these proceedings should be
arrested'.[29]

One month earlier, Sir Hamar Greenwood, the Chief Secretary for Ireland,
told the Cabinet that the worst areas for the rebellion were Limerick, Kerry,
Cork and Dublin. Greenwood and General Sir Nevil Macready agreed that
the honoring of all requests for a heightened British military presence in Ireland offered the best chance of undermining the IRA. Two months later
British military strength in Ireland consisted of forty infantry battalions and
eight cavalry regiments.[30] But the difficulties which the Crown forces met,
including a railway workers' strike which we will discuss in detail later, serve
to underscore that superior force alone did not offer a panacea for the British
Government in its effort to pacify Ireland. General Macready openly admitted the difficulties he faced, even if more troops had been provided, in this
exchange with the Cabinet:

Sir Nevil Macready: My requisitions were put in two weeks ago. The troops are now stationary except the cavalry. The War Office is fulfilling my demands as fast as they can but they are held up by the [Railway] strike, but even if we get what I have asked for the result of our policy will be gradual and depend very much on luck.

Mr Bonar Law: Good management is the mother of good luck.

Mr Nevil Macready: The two police forces are rotten. General Tudor is taking that in hand. There is no detective department in Ireland. We have a good deal of wirelesses in the country, but the operators are very difficult to obtain ...

Mr Long: The complaints from soldiers and sailors are that owing to the non-existence of martial law they are liable to be tried for murder and found guilty. They have no protection if they shoot first.

The Prime Minister: The Cork jury has found the Lord Lieutenant and myself guilty of murder.[31]

But with the Restoration of Order in Ireland Act in several southwestern counties Lloyd George no longer needed to worry about such charges being directed at him. Under the new measure, Coroner's Juries, such as those which had charged Lloyd George and his government with collusion in the killing of Lord Mayor Tomas MacCurtain, were abolished. The frustrations within the British Government over the loosening of its grip in Ireland also unleashed some of the most bloodthirsty attitudes found within the Cabinet towards that country and its inhabitants. In discussing the options available for expanding martial law in Ireland in the Irish Situation Committee on 31 May, the following exchange occurred in which Winston Churchill went so far as to embrace the summary execution policy of the same Soviet regime that his Government had only recently sought to overthrow.

Mr Churchill: What strikes me is the feebleness of the local machinery. After a person is caught he should pay the penalty within a week. Look at the tribunals which the Russian Government have devised. You should get three or four judges whose scope should be universal and they should move quickly over the country and do summary justice.

Mr Denis Henry: Shows all the more the need for extraordinary action. Get three generals if you cannot get three judges.

Mr Churchill to the Prime Minister: You agreed six or seven months ago that there should be hanging.

The Prime Minister: I feel certain you must hang [sic]. Can you get conviction from Catholics?

Mr Denis Henry: Substantially no.

Lord Curzon: What are the objections against martial law? We are all brought to the edge of it and then fear to adopt it. The Chief Secretary wants to try the alternative method. We have got a state of open civil war in Ireland and not merely civil, it is as bad as against the Germans.[32]

It was here that the question of implementing martial law in Ireland, together with the decision to hang IRA members, found its origins. Macready,
however, sought to make the Committee aware of the ramifications which
imposing martial law in Ireland entailed.

> The question is, can martial law be brought into operation in any part of the
> United Kingdom without legislation? Martial law meant the will of a general.
> It would be a military court. Under martial law you would surround Limer-
> ick and get the whole place searched effectively. All civil courts of the area
> would cease. The difficulty behind martial law is that you would put certain
> people in prison and they would hunger strike. What would the people in
> England say? Could you go through with it to the death? Imprisoned men
> cannot be held indefinitely. Will they return as martyrs?[33]

Macready and the Government received their answer by the example provided by the hunger strike of Terence MacSwiney, the Lord Mayor of Cork,
and other Republican prisoners, commencing in August 1920. More than
any other instance of self-martyrdom by an Irish patriot, MacSwiney's case
came to personify the conflict of the weak against the strong. His public
utterances issued regularly from Brixton Prison, which adopted the use of
religious symbolism, were undoubtedly aimed at engineering greater public
support for the Irish independence movement.

An increase in the number of RIC recruits entering the force by the middle
of 1920 was not enough to stem the tide of resignations. Sir Hamar Greenwood told the Cabinet on 31 May, that 'we are getting a number of recruits
but also resignations from the RIC at the rate of [hundreds] a week as against
25 before the War'. 'The men are resigning because of the terror felt by their
families', he said. Greenwood also noted that 'we are recruiting well for the
RIC, but our forces are still glued to the ground and we cannot succeed until
our mobility is greater than theirs'.[34] These mobility problems were exacerbated, in General Macready's view, by the Railway Strike underway at that
time, an effort that we shall discuss in a later chapter. But while fear of IRA
revenge was undoubtedly a serious contributing factor behind the large
number of resignations by RIC men at this time, so also were shame and
outrage over British conduct against civilians in Ireland. In Listowel, Co.
Kerry, on 17 June 1920, several RIC men resigned on the spot following
instructions given them in person by General Tudor and Colonel Smyth, the
RIC divisional head for Munster, that no quarter should be given to civilians
believed to be connected with Sinn Féin. Likewise, the men were told that
under the terms of martial law they would not be subjected to disciplinary
action for any excesses they might commit.

An account appearing in the 13 July 1920 issue of the pro-Sinn Féin *Irish
Bulletin* by one of the RIC constables who mutinied, describes this exchange
with Colonel Smyth after the latter had finished his remarks. 'By your accent,

I take it you are an Englishman and in your ignorance forget that we are Irishmen', one constable said. After laying his holster and bayonet on the table, the constable added, 'These too are English. Take them as a present from me and to hell with you – you are a murderer'.[35] One month later Colonel Smyth was assassinated by the IRA in Cork. His demise, however, did not come as a surprise to some in Dublin Castle. Andy Cope, the Assistant Under Secretary and a man destined to be involved in the effort to establish a dialogue with Sinn Féin, commented after Smyth's killing: 'It's a bad job, but he asked for it.'[36]

On 21 May, ironically on the day that Greenwood and Macready were in London discussing the RIC, a similar situation had unfolded in County Tipperary, where a body of RIC men refused to assist the Black and Tans in the cold-blooded shooting of two local Sinn Féin officials. One Constable who had resigned over this and other such incidents told a visiting American Commission later that year of the extent to which the RIC were expected to perform in conjunction with the activities of the Black and Tans:

> They were to go in an armoured car with a machine gun … and every man who took a prominent part in the Sinn Féin movement were to stand up in front of his house and turn the machine guns on it. In this armoured car there were put one hundred and twenty cans of petrol and also one hundred and twenty mills bombs, and the reasons for this was that they were for burning houses.[37]

In May, the Irish Executive at Dublin Castle submitted to the Cabinet a statement outlining the need for additional British troops in Ireland to make up for what it termed a 'deficiency of personnel'. The document sought three battalions of troops for the British Fifth Division, three for the Sixth, and two for the Dublin Districts, along with additional transportation equipment. The Executive went on to state that 'the two forces of the Irish Police, viz, the RIC and the DMP have reached a state where it is absolutely necessary that a thoroughly competent official should be appointed to supervise the entire organisation and to recommend to the Irish Government such changes as are essential'. Such an appointment was made in the person of General Henry Tudor, who assumed responsibility for all police forces in Ireland. Tudor had already been a catalyst in the formation of the Black and Tans. As the new Executive Officer for the police and the auxiliaries, he issued rifles and machine guns to the RIC, installed steel shutters on most of the surviving barracks, and provided transport vehicles.[38]

The following month Sir Hamar Greenwood, as Chief Secretary for Ireland, made the virtual collapse of the British Administration in Ireland and its replacement by Sinn Féin appear all too clear. At the same time he also asked the government to withdraw some of the amendments to the 'Crimes

Act' on the basis that given the apparent magnitude of Sinn Féin's popular support, it would be impossible to enforce the regulations.

> This is a great embarrassment for us in administration for we cannot as a practical matter suppress all expressions of Sinn Féin sentiment, and under the present conditions, the law is openly flouted every day, moreover, it is not consistent with the policy of His Majesty's Government as we understand it to strike the mere expression of political views and aspirations, however obnoxious. Nor can we ignore the fact that the local councils, which, in a wide sphere are the recognised instruments of Government, and are in receipt of large Exchequer grants, containing now a preponderating (sic) Sinn Féin element everywhere except in the northeast.[39]

One of the most significant undertakings on the part of Sinn Féin to assist in ending British rule in Ireland by the force of arms and aid in running a de facto government was the initiation of the Dáil Loan Scheme. This scheme represented the most important effort on the part of the fledgling Republican Government to obtain public support among the Irish at home and abroad. It was launched at a session of Dáil Éireann in the autumn of 1919, and was placed largely under the domain of Michael Collins as Minister for Finance. In all, from the date of the initiation of Dáil Loan funding drive until its completion in July 1920, over £1,000,000 were raised in support of the Republican Government, with three quarters of that amount coming from the United States through the efforts of the Irish Self-Determination League and the work done there by Eamon de Valera and James O'Mara.

In a prospectus for subscriptions co-signed by Collins and Arthur Griffith as Acting President, the purposes for which the loan funds were to be applied were explained:

> The Loan, both internal and external, will be utilised solely in the interests of Ireland – an indivisible entity. It will be used to unshackle the Irish Trade Union Congress, and give them free access to the markets of the world; it will be used to provide Ireland with an efficient Consular Service; it will be used to end the plague of emigration, by providing land for the landless and work for the workless; it will be used to determine the industrial and commercial resources of our country and to arrange for their development; it will be used to encourage and develop the long-neglected Irish Sea Fisheries, and to promote the re-afforestation of our barren wastes; it will be available for, and will be applied to, all purposes which tend to make Ireland morally and materially strong and self-supporting.[40]

But to Hamar Greenwood, the Dáil Loan served as the means for which IRA 'thugs' were able to carry out their operations. 'We are certain', he told the British Cabinet on 31 May 1920, 'that these (IRA) are handsomely paid, that the money comes from the USA, and that it is passed through Bishop

Fogarty and Arthur Griffith by means of cheques issued to Michael Collins, the Adjutant General of the Irish Republican Army'. 'The money', he claimed, 'is paid out to the murderers in public houses'. Greenwood's view of how the IRA was able to carry out its activities is also useful:

> ... there is shooting after dark by local people drawn from a district 10 to 20 miles around and who have energetic leaders from outside. The community is hostile, indifferent or terrorised. The majority, I believe, are terrorised. The hierarchy and farmers are now rapidly organising independently of the labourers and are adding about 1500 a week to their organisations.[41]

British comments on terror at this time might be seen as odd given an attempt on the life of Bishop Fogarty of Killaloe already carried out by the Black and Tans in the name of the Crown. But Fogarty himself was not the only Catholic bishop targeted for elimination, nor were such acts contemplated solely by those who were agents of the Crown. Bishop Cohalan of Cork may have figured in the elimination plans of Terence MacSwiney, who was Commandant of the IRA's Cork No. 1 Brigade as well as Lord Mayor of Cork. P. S. O'Hegarty described a meeting with MacSwiney in May 1920, at which the latter outlined to him a proposal which the former stated 'seemed to me then to be fiendish, and indefensible and inadvisable from every point of view'.[42] While O'Hegarty was not explicit as to whom the plan was directed at, one author has surmised, however, that its target was to have been Bishop Cohalan himself. Cohalan had proved particularly uncooperative in Mac-Swiney's efforts to gain his public support for the Dáil Loan and in refusing to endorse the Irish Republic,[43] and had also played a central role in persuading MacSwiney and Tomas MacCurtain as leaders of the Volunteers in Cork not to participate in the Easter Rising but to turn in their weapons instead.*

The implementation of martial law in Ireland served as the focal point of a Cabinet-level discussion at Downing Street on 26 July 1920, in which the willingness of virtually all in attendance to remain in violation of the normal processes of British law was apparent. Indeed, the success of the Republican Courts in undermining British rule in Ireland, coupled with the fact that the majority on the island of Ireland had come to accept the legitimacy of the Sinn Féin regime, left the British Government with a sense that it had few measures at its disposal other than martial law. 'All the experts agreed', Sir Hamar Greenwood noted, 'that the only tribunal which could carry on was a court martial with powers to deal with ordinary and extraordinary crime'. 'They would not supersede the other tribunals where they existed and

---

* This latter issue appears to have served as a driving force in leading MacSwiney to give his life in a 74-day hunger strike. MacSwiney carried a great deal of guilt for his failure to join the Easter Rising in 1916.

functioned and they would have the power to impose the death penalty', he wrote.[44]

At the 26 July Cabinet meeting, the discussion focused in part on how the application of the death penalty and the special tribunal would be administered.

> Prime Minister asked how a man would be killed. Would he be shot or hanged?
>
> Hamar Greenwood: He would be tried as under ordinary law. Balfour asked if it was proposed that a tribunal should be composed entirely of soldiers.
>
> Balfour: That staggers me. I must agree we get a substitute for the jury system. They do not administer anything. It is wise to use D.O.R.A. [Defence of the Realm Act] if you can do it. Where I hesitate is to come forward and use war machinery after peace is declared, and, in order to do that, you hand over the administration in Ireland to soldiers . . .
>
> Prime Minister: I am entirely of Balfour's view. People will get shocked at the whole criminal administration being put into the hands of soldiers. We must have some civilians.
>
> Sir J. Anderson: Any civilian associated with the court would have to be surrounded by soldiers.

A British intelligence report submitted to the Irish Situation Committee in the summer of 1920 also provided a useful overview of the scale of the IRA's activities in Ireland, along with the organisation's mode of operation. The account could have only been viewed as disturbing to its readers.

> The Irish practise a fairly minute system of espionage and nine tenths of their ordinary intelligence reports deal with the movements of lorries of military or police and the comings and goings of the forces of the Crown. Sometimes the personal touch is invoked thus, as for instance: 'Peeler O'Sullivan was gone across to Patrick Murphy's last night at eight o'clock . . . He carried no rifle but had his pistol.' I am thinking it's a bullet that man needs. Signed, Intelligence Lieut. A. Coy.
>
> Then there are the Post Office spies and some of the Irish Post Offices are very obliging with information to the murder gang. There is a report of one such traitor: At 4:00 p.m., District Inspector Williamson received a code telegram from the Castle. It read SLMPX. QSTVA. PMSTQ. At 8:30 p.m. Tullamore Barracks rang up on the telephone to warn they might be attacked any minute. The postal services, be it noted, are officials in the pay and service of the British Government.
>
> Then there are the records of the various Brigade Staffs of the IRA, scribbling note books full of parade states, records of arms, and prolific schemes of instruction . . .[45]

The report also dealt at length with the accounts system by which weapons were purchased and IRA intelligence members compensated. 'The source of these monies', it stated, 'is from Dáil Éireann . . . and therefore, anyone, anywhere in the world who has subscribed to any Sinn Féin funds has given his mite to murder'.[46]

The difficulty which Sinn Féin's methods posed for Britain in Ireland was driven home by an editorial of 1 May 1920, in the *Irish Times*, the respected voice of Irish Unionism. Referring to Dublin Castle's predicament, the paper declared:

> The Irish Executive must begin with a full recognition of the dismal truth that hitherto it has been fighting a losing battle. If the confession calls for new methods, then new methods must be formed without delay ... A map of seditious successes – since the usually alert intelligence of the Republican movement has not prepared such a map, perhaps the Executive will forestall it – would show that the King's Government virtually ceased to exist south of the Boyne and west of the Shannon.[47]

Further evidence that the British rule of law in Ireland had broken down came to the Irish Situation Committee's Coordinator, Walter Long. In a 30 June 1920 session of the Committee, Long revealed that an acquaintance of his in Ireland reported to him: 'Everybody is going over to Sinn Féin, not because they believe in it, but because it is the only authority in Ireland'.[48]

The need for an assessment of the British Military Campaign was evident in a communication from General Macready to Hamar Greenwood two weeks later. Macready's initial report to the Chief Secretary for Ireland is noteworthy both for its candor and its willingness to concede how far the British grip on Ireland had deteriorated. 'I have not yet got Strickland's definite report', Macready wrote, 'but I know that while he has not found anything startling as a result of the search, he has arrested a fair number of men who will all be run in for possessing arms'.

In Macready's view the general situation in July 1920 would have been a great deal worse if 'we had not been so reinforced [with thousands of additional soldiers]'. In the General's estimate Sinn Féin 'has gained ground ... either from fear or conviction'. 'Nearly every day', he stated, 'one sees in the papers that the Sinn Féin police are able to round up malefactors where the RIC are powerless and that, of course, is merely because Sinn Féin have now at their disposal the very men who were formerly used by the RIC to get their information.' Macready argued that 'the state of affairs in this country has been allowed to drift into such an impasse that no amount of coercion can possibly remedy it'. In a perhaps even more candid assessment he offered the view that coercion was implementable in Ireland as in a Theatre of War: 'I am not prepared to say that the troops would stand it long, because there are indications in one or two units who have Irish recruits from Liverpool and in that part a certain amount of sympathy with the Irish exists.'[49]

Macready went on to emphasise that Britain's coercion policy 'is merely one of attrition, and it remains to be seen whether the necessary time can be made available, and whether the rearrangement of police and military for the winter months will not lessen the grip upon certain parts of the country'. He apologised to Greenwood for his pessimism, emphasising the conviction 'that nothing but what might be called a bold, dramatic, political stroke will solve this matter, and I do not for one instant think that the British public would stand martial law, as I understand it, for a week over here, and anything less than that in the direction of coercion would be a little better than what we are doing at present'.[50]

On 20 July similar sentiments were expressed to Hamar Greenwood from the civil sector by no less than his chief civil servant at Dublin Castle, Sir John Anderson. While Anderson claimed that the 'reconstituted' Irish Executive should bear credit for an improvement in the political climate that saw the Catholic hierarchy become more critical of the IRA and Sinn Féin, he feared that an over-reliance by the Government on coercion would be counter-productive. 'If such measures of coercion were relied upon and proved successful in achieving their immediate purpose, the course of events would, I believe, be such as to relegate to the distant future all hope of a political settlement'.[51] But Anderson was especially disheartened by what he saw as the likely failure of any all-out effort at coercion.

> To make the attempt and fail would be disastrous and, if I am right ... it is essential that the firm measures which recent events demand should be accompanied by a declaration of policy and an appeal to moderate opinion in Southern Ireland which will create an atmosphere favourable to suppression of crime and prepare the way for an ultimate settlement by consent. Possibly the forthcoming deputation to the Prime Minister from the Trades Union Congress might afford an opportunity for at least a first step in the direction suggested.[52]

Nonetheless, the policy of coercion continued while, simultaneously, Anderson and his fellow civil servants in Dublin Castle worked to find someone in the Sinn Féin leadership with whom their Government might negotiate. As we have noted, John Anderson, Andy Cope and Mark Sturgis were placed in Dublin Castle for this very purpose. They often acted against the sanction of Greenwood, their ministerial superior. One week after Anderson's memorandum to Greenwood, he also made a point of informing the Cabinet of the state of affairs in Ireland. Many employed by the British in Ireland's local government, he noted, 'cannot be relied upon to cooperate in the carrying out of even the most reasonable and moderate measures'.[53] 'The mischief goes much deeper', he stated. 'The machinery of the Courts has been brought virtually to a standstill and rival courts are functioning openly, and where forcibly suppressed will continue to function in secret', Anderson continued. The Crown's chief civil servant in Ireland also made the Cabinet aware that the 'Local Civil Service composed entirely of Irishmen, while in a sense not disloyal, is politically directed and exposed as it is to every kind of pressure and in many cases of intimidation, cannot be relied upon in the execution of a vigorous policy'.[54]

General Macready had a special explanation for the effectiveness shown by the IRA by the summer of 1920. In a memorandum to the Irish Situation Committee on 6 August 1920, the General contended that the 'increased efficiency of our opponents is without doubt very largely due to the release of leaders who were interned without trial during the early part of this year'. 'Individuals', he stated, 'who come back from internment are reported as being more active than they were before arrest'. 'Under present circumstances', Macready wrote, 'the army continues to act "in aid of civilian power" and the initiative lies mainly with our opponents'. It was Macready's assessment that 'while both men and officers are keen upon their work, and are daily improving in powers of initiative and self-reliance, the police forces of the country are in a much worse state than they were three months ago, with the result that the task of the army is increasingly difficult'. It may also have been due to the fact that some key IRA men, both in the field and helping oversee the training sector, had recently returned from their service in the Great War in the British Army.[55]

The steady flow of such views from senior officials in Ireland in both the civil and military sectors led the Cabinet to conclude in a meeting of the following month that the Coercion Act, without popular support, was unlikely to succeed.

> Strong measures would be required to put down the policy of the extremists, and there might come a point when public opinion would desert the Government. Even if the Act was successful, there would be no party left in Ireland with which the Government could negotiate a settlement. The position at present was that the Six Counties wanted Home Rule for themselves, and would not be content simply to remain part of the United Kingdom. In the South and West there was no Unionist Party in the old sense left. Many of them were embracing, however reluctantly, the new ideas, and were not unwilling to make use of the Sinn Féin Courts. In the circumstances it was necessary that the Government should review its policy and the length it could go to in the way of concessions.[56]

On the day the Cabinet met to discuss the efficacy of coercion, Terence MacSwiney commenced the first day of his hunger strike. He refused to recognise the right of the Government to try and convict him by way of court martial for alleged offences against the Crown. The Government, however, showed itself quite willing to accommodate the Lord Mayor's commitment to dying as an Irish rebel martyr. It was a decision made out of a fear of showing weakness. It was also a decision which Lloyd George and his colleagues would come to regret, as MacSwiney's protest from behind the doors of his hospital ward at London's Brixton Prison would command international attention.

The breakdown in morale throughout much of Southern Ireland, and the degree of fear which the advances made by the combination of the Sinn Féin and IRA campaigns had engendered in the RIC, was described in graphic terms by a petition submitted by rank-and-file RIC members from the Athlone Station to their superiors. Few sources provide as direct a glimpse of the obstacles confronting those who had been given the day-to-day task of enforcing British rule in Ireland.

> We consider it is almost an impossibility to carry out our functions as a civil police force under the present circumstances. The strain on the force is so great, by the daily assassinations of our comrades who are ruthlessly murdered and butchered by the roadside without getting a chance to defend themselves, and the boycotting and threats arraigned against us, against our families, our relatives and our homes, that the agony of a suffering force cannot be much further prolonged ...[57]

'We are now useless as a civil police force', the petition continued. The situation for the RIC was such that 'every day we are being more alienated in platform and press, and even the moderate section of the community are so terrorised or apathetic that not even a voice of sympathy nor ray of hope comes from any side'. Even in death there was little peace for the RIC. 'The dead bodies of our murdered comrades are insulted, kicked and jeered', noted the RIC representative's statement. At the same time, they contended, the same ill feeling was not directed against the foreign-born British military.[58]

As coercion continued in 1920, the Government of Ireland Act was in the process of implementation. The measure marked the first effort towards Irish self-government since the Home Rule Act of 1914, which was subsequently shelved due to the Great War. But the Government of Ireland Act differed from the earlier Home Rule measure since northeast Ulster was removed from the jurisdiction of the Southern Irish Parliament and given a parliament of its own, consisting of two houses. To Irish Nationalists, the measure had become known as the 'Partition Act'. These institutions later served for what Northern Ireland's first Premier, Sir James Craig, hoped would be 'a Protestant Parliament for a Protestant people'.[59] So while Home Rule under the Government of Ireland Act was to become a reality for Ireland at long last, it provided for an Ireland divided into two parts by an Act of the British Parliament and sustained by the force Britain provided. As noted earlier, two of the six counties subsumed from the nine-county Province of Ulster, Fermanagh and Tyrone, had clear Nationalist majorities. The measure took effect in December 1920.

Sinn Féin, still representing the majority of Irish Nationalists, refused to recognise the Southern Parliament created by the Act. Instead, it used the parliamentary elections associated with it as a vehicle for electing the Second Dáil in the June 1921 election. But a policy which combined coercion with the limited prospect of Irish self-government offered under the Government of Ireland Act 1920 was not sufficient to secure peace in Ireland. In September 1920, W. E. Wylie, Law Advisor to the Dublin Castle Executive, stated to Hamar Greenwood that the continuances of coercion in Ireland would only serve to repulse British subjects at home. 'British law', he argued, 'is framed for a constitutional people by a constitutional people'. 'Its ultimate sanction', he stated, 'is the people in any democratic country and undoubtedly the root reason why the present administration of Ireland is so difficult is that there is no body of people (or call it public opinion) behind the administration'. Wylie stated that the Irish public would not support the Irish Administration unless the following measures were taken:

> 1. Govern constitutionally. Drop all anti-democratic and semi-martial measures.
>
> 2. When and where they can, deal out *prompt* punishment to all offenders who can be tried and convicted. In other words, suppress crime, not confusing crime with politics.
>
> I am also convinced (although it is not within the scope of this minute) that side by side with the foregoing there should be a legislative measure which will be acceptable to a large body of Irishmen, viz. Colonial Home Rule in the widest sense.[60]

While the internal debate continued within the Government, the IRA persisted with its campaign of violence. The monthly survey submitted to the Cabinet by the Dublin Castle Executive for the week ending 30 August 1920, presented a dour view of the situation from a military standpoint. The scope of the IRA's activities, along with the impact of the hunger strikes undertaken by Terence MacSwiney* and other Republican prisoners were all documented.

> Outrages committed during the week showed a considerable increase on those of the previous week, the numbers being 192 as compared with 140. The most noticeable increase was in the number of raids for arms. These were made for the most part during the night by masked and armed persons. In a few cases the raiders showed a certain measure of consideration for the victims of their illegal acts but in the majority of cases their purpose was achieved by terrorism accompanied, if need be, by violence. One victim, a retired Army Officer, nearly 70 years of age was shot dead; another was wounded by a revolver shot.
>
> Attacks on police were again heavy. Seven officers were killed and 14 wounded, most of them in circumstances which gave them no chance of self-defense. The total casualties for the year are 85 killed and 248 wounded. Military casualties for the week numbered 1 killed and 4 wounded bringing

---

* For a fuller account of the impact of MacSwiney's hunger strike see Francis Costello, *Enduring the Most: The Life and Death of Terence MacSwiney* (Dublin, 1995).

the totals for the year to 12 killed and 50 wounded. Four unoccupied Royal Irish Constabulary Barracks were destroyed and 4 occupied Barracks were attacked, the raiders being beaten off in three cases. Two Coast Guard Stations were destroyed. Courts martial during the week number 13 and the convictions 212.

Hunger strikers in Mountjoy Prison and in Limerick Prison were discontinued after some days. 14 prisoners in Cork Gaol, however, are still on hunger strike and 11 of these men are in a state of physical exhaustion ... The case of the Lord Mayor of Cork who is also on hunger strike, has attracted an even wider attention. Threats are being freely circulated that his death will be followed by murder.[61]

Prior to the implementation of the Restoration of Order Act, which produced an increase in the number of convictions for membership in the IRA, the majority of IRA men were active on a part-time basis. But by September 1920, driven from their homes, these wanted men had formed into Active Service units functioning as 'Flying Columns'. In effect, the actions of the British Government had ironically spawned the most effective armed response yet against its forces in Ireland.

The method of reply chosen by the British Government to these developments was to allow the continuance of official reprisals. Throughout the autumn of 1920, that policy continued apace in Ireland. But rather than serve to pacify the country, the reprisals, directed with apparent disregard for whether the person or property of those victimised had in fact committed any breach of the law, had an opposite result. The King's writ had ceased to run in much of Ireland. And those who wore the British uniform in its various shades, be they Auxiliaries or Black and Tans had done their part in making that a reality. Each village burned and each citizen killed in cold blood by those charged with the responsibility for enforcing British law in Ireland resulted in more young men joining the IRA and in more people providing the guerrilla army with safe havens. The burning and looting of Cork City by British forces in the autumn of 1920, and the torching of the towns of Miltownmalbay and Balbriggan, and of Cork City later in the year, provided the Irish citizenry with the basis for a healthy contempt for the British rule of law. In counties Kerry, Clare, Galway and Tipperary, the torture and killing in cold blood of young men, including members of the clergy, by the British forces left a lasting legacy of bitterness. Quite often, it was the actions taken by military and police that also helped to exacerbate the erosion in the ranks of the RIC. While many policemen resigned from the police simply out of fear for their lives, it has been shown that some departed in disgust.

On 23 September 1920, the residents of the three small West Co. Clare towns of Miltownmalbay, Lahinch and Ennistymon had the opportunity to see first-hand how the Government's reprisals policy worked. Miltownmalbay was the hardest hit, as the local drapers shop, several licensed premises and a score of homes were put to the torch at random by a group of Black and Tans. Upon entering various homes, the military personnel seized various items of personal property before setting the dwellings alight. 'No fewer than eight houses have been burned', a correspondent for the *Cork Examiner* wrote, 'and there are not ten houses in the little town that have not suffered in greater or less degree'. In the aftermath of the visit of the soldiers, the reporter observed that the town 'now presents a spectacle akin to that of a town in Belgium after the Germans had visited it'.[62] As Miltownmalbay burned, a similar scenario was being played out in the towns of Lahinch and Ennistymon. At the day's end, three innocent men were shot dead by Crown forces, one of them while in the process of trying to quench the flames that engulfed his home. A few days later, in the County Galway village of Kiltartan, a young mother was shot to death as she stood in her doorway by a passing convoy of Black and Tans, who apparently fired at random. The infant in her arms was not wounded, but her unborn child died along with her. The shooting of Mrs Quinn was explained by Dublin Castle as 'one shot fired as a precautionary measure'. It was characterised by a military court as 'a manslaughter and accidental shooting by some occupant unknown of said police car'.[63]

But the IRA were by no means silent that September. The attack by Cork's No. 2 Brigade IRA under the command of Liam Lynch on the British Seventeenth Lancers stationed at Mallow RIC barracks on 28 September 1920 provided a severe jolt to British rule in the south-east of Ireland. Joined by Ernie O'Malley, the IRA guerrilla fighter supreme, Lynch and a small group of handpicked IRA men broke through the guard room that morning after O'Malley immobilised the sentry.

In short order the soldiers in the guard room were taken prisoner and marched out on to the square by Lynch's men. An army sergeant was shot dead while trying to elude capture. The barrack's gates were opened and three carloads of IRA men entered the yard. The large store of weapons and ammunition which the IRA had seized was put into the cars, including 27 rifles, 2 Hotchkiss light machine guns, and 4,000 rounds of ammunition. It was a good day's work for the Volunteers of the Cork No. 2 Brigade, yielding weapons that would be used in further attacks on British forces and the police. Amazingly, the attack on the barracks at Mallow took place at such a pace that the RIC in Mallow were left totally unaware until afterwards. Nevertheless, there was a British official response to the IRA attack in Mallow: the town hall and local creamery were burned by British forces, accompanied by the burning and looting of private property.[64]

By the end of September 1920, the outrages committed by the Black and Tans had provoked criticism from as diehard an anti-Republican as Sir Henry Wilson.* In an entry in his diary for 29 September, Wilson described

---

* He would himself die at the hands of a London unit of the IRA less than two years later.

his conversation with Lloyd George and Bonar Law regarding the reprisals policy:

> I told them what I thought of reprisals by the Black and Tans, and how this must lead to chaos and ruin. Lloyd George danced about and was angry, but I never budged. I pointed out that these reprisals were being carried out without anyone being responsible; men were being murdered, houses burnt, villages wrecked (such as Balbriggan, Ennistymon, Trim, etc) ... It was the business of the Government to govern. If these men ought to be murdered, then the Government ought to murder them ... I got some sense into their heads and Lloyd George wired for Hamar Greenwood, Macready, Tudor and others to come over tomorrow night.[65]

What Wilson objected to, then, was not the reprisals policy in itself. He wanted it taken out of the hands of the Black and Tans and overseen directly by the Government. An editorial in the London *Times* on 28 September 1920, presented that paper's latest attack on the reprisals policy. 'Methods', a lead article of that date stated, 'inexcusable even under the loose code of revolutionaries, are certainly not fit methods which the Government of Great Britain can tolerate on the part of its servants'.[66] One month later, former Prime Minister Herbert Asquith launched an attack on the Government's reprisals policy that was in itself one of the richest of ironies. Four years earlier, as the King's Chief Minister, he had sanctioned the execution of the leaders of the Easter Rising, including the badly wounded James Connolly who needed to be strapped to a chair in order for his execution to be carried out. Nonetheless, speaking in Leicester in October 1920, Asquith stated that 'outrages have been committed by the officers of the law in the uniforms of soldiers and policemen – outrages not committed in hot blood, but calculated, planned and organised, and of which the victims have not been those who committed the murders or maltreated policemen or soldiers, but absolutely innocent, unoffending civilians who had no part or lot of any kind in the matter'.[67]

More often then not, however, denial became the Government's chief response for the reprisals policy carried out by its forces in Ireland. Nonetheless, the record indicates that both the Cabinet, and to a greater extent Dublin Castle, recognised the effect that official acts of violence were having in further alienating large segments of the Irish population. In the autumn of 1920, Deputy Inspector General C. A. Walsh of the RIC cautioned the District Commander and the other ranking police officials at all police stations in the country against reprisals. At least on the record, one top RIC official sought to condemn such actions.[68]

Far more tolerant remarks on the actions of the RIC and of the Auxiliaries came from Chief Secretary Hamar Greenwood. In a public address to the rank and file of the RIC's Dublin Depot the Irish Chief Secretary claimed that 'Accounts of reprisals in certain newspapers are often misleading and acts of justifiable self-defence are frequently misrepresented as reprisals'. Greenwood stated that those cases where misconduct had occurred were 'being carefully investigated'. At the same time, Greenwood reminded the men of the danger of over-reaction: 'The great provocation under which men suffer who see their comrades and friends foully murdered is fully recognised, but the police are urged to maintain, in spite of this provocation, that self-control that has characterised the Force in the past. By so doing, they will earn the respect and admiration of the majority of their fellow countrymen'.[69]

On 1 October 1920 a Cabinet Conference, called by the Prime Minister himself, came away with the conclusion that 'reprisals by burning must be put a stop to at the earliest possible moment'. The minutes of the meeting also stated that 'confidence was expressed that reprisals by burning would generally be put a stop to, although in the exceptional conditions prevailing in Ireland, it could not be guaranteed that occasional and spasmodic incidents of the kind could not occur'.[70] But such equivocation served only to send a mixed message from the Government to those who wore the uniform in its name in Ireland. It did not end reprisals by the Black and Tans or other components of the security apparatus in Ireland. A ballad composed by one unit of these auxiliaries, titled The Black and Tans and directed at the Irish population as much as for the entertainment of the outfits' ranks, is useful in underscoring their cavalier attitude to the use of deadly force:

> In the hush of the night when the curfew tolls and the churchyards yawning upheave men's souls
> Hark! a rattle of wheels on the cobblestones and heedless of churches and dead men's bones
> With an armoured car leading and massed in vans come the 'devil-may-cares' called the Black and Tans.
>
> What are they after, why are they here and at dead of night do they now appear?
> They are here of set purpose for hunting down Assassins defying the empire's Crown to
> Trace them out to the hidden lair and shoot at sight when they find them there.
> They are after the cult that is called Sinn Féin which bears on its forehead the brand of Cain
> And deludes young men into ghastly deeds whose expanding bullet the victim bleeds whilst
> The widow's wail and the orphan's cry ascent to the throne of God on high.
>
> They see these sights but the arm-chair men, the newspaper critics who wield a pen and
> Speak of reprisals with bated breath, what do they care for the victim's death?
> But by God, to avenge him the job's a man's and we'll see it through, say the Black and Tans.[71]

86

The IRA likewise practiced its own form of harsh justice on those found to have run afoul of it. In one account, based on British official allegations, an elderly woman who had been in the employ of the local RIC barracks at Ballyshannon, County Donegal, found herself the recipient of physical punishment by the local IRA.

> Further official details have been received of the outrage on Ellen Gillen, a woman of 60 who was police barrack servant at Ballyshannon. It seems that at 10:30 at night a knock was heard at the door of the house in which she lodged and a boy whom she did not know, delivered a message that the woman was wanted at Mrs Cleary's. She did not leave the house immediately and in a few minutes four armed and masked men entered, two of whom held up the householder with revolvers and dragged her to an adjacent field. They asked if she would cook the breakfast for the police anymore and when her replies were not satisfactory they cut off her hair, abused her and even kicked her as is evident from the bruises on her body. She had been servant at the police barracks only for about a month, her predecessor having been driven out through terrorism. Special precautions have been taken by the police to provide the old lady with protection for the future.[72]

Another elderly woman, a member of the loyalist gentry in County Cork, was murdered by the IRA for her cooperation with the Crown. When asked during the Anglo-Irish Truce why he had sanctioned the killing of the old woman as a spy, Michael Collins's responded:

> 'I was sorry about that,' he replied, as he cast his eyes on the ground as if ashamed, 'but she wasn't murdered in cold blood. She was executed. She lived in County Cork in the martial law area ... she acted as an informer ... she warned the police of an ambush and was the cause of military reprisals ... so she was taken off by my men. Strickland tried five men and was going to shoot them and did so. My fellows sent word to him if he did they'd shoot Mrs Lindsay whom they'd tried and found guilty as a spy and informer. The men were shot, so was Mrs Lindsay. But there is this about it, they should have referred it to me for a decision, but did not do so ... that's why I said I was sorry about it, as I don't think I'd have shot her on account of her age.'[73]

The IRA's need for arms and for cash with which to buy arms also led in some locales to raids on the homes of the more prosperous residents, particularly those of unionist background. A complaint to Arthur Griffith from one such individual in County Donegal inquired as to under what authority the IRA were acting.

> We have recently received notices to pay to officers and volunteers sums of money up to £2.10 to buy arms, etc. We should like to know are these orders from Headquarters or have they power to act on their own initiative? Having nothing against a Republic, as such, but representing raids made on our

premises by armed and masked men, articles taken (not arms), dragged from our homes, revolvers fired from our hands, we naturally would like to know are we supposed to support acts of this description by subscriptions.[74]

Griffith, in turn, forwarded the letter for action to the IRA's General Headquarters. On 9 November, Geroid O'Sullivan, in his capacity as Adjutant General, wrote to the Brigade Commandant in Leitrim, asking for a report on the matter. 'I am not prejudicing the case in question', he wrote, 'but it is a fact that a number of complaints of this kind are being made from a number of places in the North Midlands, and it is absolutely necessary that whatever cause of such complaints should be removed at once'.[75] Evidently, the IRA had greater scruples in such matters than their British counterparts in the ranks of the Black and Tans and the Auxiliaries.

The command structure and brigade strength of the IRA

Assessing the scale of manpower under arms for a guerrilla army is at best difficult, at any time. Attempting to reach an accurate portrait of where the IRA stood in terms of total strength during the years 1919–21 is especially so. It was a movement that functioned on the run. Despite a General Headquarters staff in Dublin, the IRA functioned as a diffuse operation with a system of written records that varied from one Brigade area to another. Within what became the 1st Southern Division were 30,620 officers and men, a number equalled only in Dublin in terms of divisional strength.[76] The Cork No. 1 Brigade was the largest, with 7,500 men, followed by Cork No. 3 under the command of Liam Lynch, with 5,270, followed in turn by Cork No. 2, with 4,700. Thus, with a total of about 13,000 men, Cork was by far the most active Southern County in terms of total manpower. Kerry's No. 1 Brigade included 4,000 men in its ranks; two Waterford Brigades containing 2,270 men combined, West Limerick with 2,100 and Kerry No. 3 with 1,350 rounded off the Southern Division. The combined British strength in the area consisted of 18,750 troops, 1,600 RIC, 340 Auxiliaries and 570 marines, for a total of 21,260 combined.

While the brigade structures cited imply a level of organisation not evidenced in prior revolts, even for areas as highly motivated as Cork and Tipperary, there remained throughout the Anglo-Irish conflict something less than full accountability to either Dáil Éireann or to General Headquarters. The IRA that evolved from the Volunteers in 1919 remained by necessity first and foremost a guerrilla army. And just as the IRA's strength in numbers and organisation was not uniform throughout the country, there was as a consequence a lack of a regularised command structure. Poor communications, combined with the limited access to weapons, munitions, and modern transportation, often meant that decision-making began and ended at the local brigade level.

Nonetheless, the IRA proved itself a highly motivated force and, most significantly, enjoyed popular support in much of the country, without which it would have been crushed by the British military machine in short order. Furthermore, the role of Michael Collins, aided by Richard Mulcahy in the General Headquarters staff, must be reiterated here from the organisational standpoint. Collins brought, and in some cases forced, a coherent vision for undermining British rule on a national basis, and in the process earnestly sought to steward resources such as weapons, munitions, and manpower, training talent where they could be best utilised. And as we shall see, he and Mulcahy tried to make local commanders accountable for how supplies were used and to introduce efficiency and discipline into the operations of the guerrilla army. He worked hard to motivate those areas that in his view should have been more active, the west of Ireland in particular.

But perhaps it was in the City of Dublin, the nerve-centre of British governance in Ireland, that he had his greatest effect. It marked the first instance where an assault on British rule largely succeeded in the Irish capital. Without that success within the Pale the achievements in other areas would have been effectively minimised. In Dublin, Collins ruthlessly deployed his 'Squad', also nicknamed 'the Twelve Apostles'. It consisted of twelve men handpicked by Collins for their combination of loyalty, courage, ruthlessness and efficiency. While they were dedicated to the cause of Irish freedom, they were also dedicated to Collins over anyone else.* The group operated under the cover of a building tradesman's outfit. When on assignment for Collins they often wore carpenters aprons under their coats, carried rules and pencils in their pockets and notebooks replete with phony building specifications. Against the resources of an Empire now finished with the World War, and which possessed thousands of troops, fleets of armoured cars, an air force and tanks, the work of the 'Squad' proved necessary for the IRA's survival. Central also to the IRA's effort in Dublin was the leadership of Dick McKee. McKee combined with Collins and Mulcahy to provide the brains and, in his case, also the firepower for the most effective campaign ever against British rule in the Irish capital.

But in the subterranean war that Collins so effectively waged against the British Government, the strength of his intelligence apparatus lay within the G Division of the Dublin police. Within that elite body Collins had two brave informants who reported to him regularly: Eamon 'Ned' Broy and Joe Kavanagh. They were later joined by James McNamara and David Nelligan.

---

* Indeed, in the years after Collins' death, many of the 'Squad' had a hard time adjusting to life without their leader. Tobin and Cullen played a prominent role in the 'Army Mutiny' within the Free State in 1924, and were forced out.

Nelligan in fact had quit the RIC in disgust prior to meeting Collins. But Collins instructed him to re-enter the force and to act as a spy. Both McNamara and Nelligan ended up on invaluable assignments from the standpoint of access to information within Dublin Castle itself. Through the services of these men Collins was able to keep Brigade Commanders around the country supplied with police codes and, on a more lethal basis, to know who within the British ranks posed the greatest threats, and where they could be found when it was decided to summon the 'Squad' to carry out an assassination.[77]

The close connection between the respective roles of Collins' network of spies within the Dublin detectives apparatus and his squad of assassins was made clear by the assassination of Detective Hoey of the Dublin Metropolitan Police on 13 September 1919. Hoey was gunned down gangland style as he walked along Brunswick Street that night. He had shown himself to be a belligerent adversary of the IRA, and on that day joined Detectives Smith and Barton of G-Division, who had met a similar end at the hands of the 'Squad' some months before.

But Collins' list of eligible targets for assassination was not confined to G-men threatening counter-attacks on the IRA. Indeed, his roles as Director of Intelligence for the IRA and Minister for Finance overlapped on occasion in a most brutal fashion. When the underpinnings of the Dáil Loan Scheme that Collins oversaw were threatened, he ordered the assassination of a resident magistrate named Alan Bell. A former RIC investigator, Bell came close to uncovering Collins' elaborate system of bank accounts designed to hide the fund. While en route to work in a Dublin tram one morning, Bell was shot dead by Collins' hit squad in broad daylight. No other British agent came close to exposing the workings of the Dáil Loan Fund.

The roles of hunter and the hunted underwent a reversal on the streets of Dublin in October 1920, when Sean Treacy, who had led the opening attack of the Anglo-Irish War almost two years earlier with Dan Breen, was killed while trying to escape a British manhunt for him. Eerily, much of the attempt to capture Treacy is recorded on the newsreel footage of a French camera crew that had apparently travelled with the Auxiliary force leading the effort. Treacy, a member of the IRB, and a leader of the 3rd Tipperary Brigade, was standing near the doorway of The Republican Outfitters Shop when two lorries full of auxiliaries arrived. One plainclothes officer leapt at Treacy as he sought to make his getaway on a bicycle that was too big for him. A gun fight at close quarters ensued as Treacy wounded the first attacker. Nicknamed 'the parabellum man' for his dexterity with that weapon, Treacy also killed a plainclothes officer named Price virtually as he himself collapsed mortally wounded from stray gunfire sprayed from a military vehicle. In the shooting frenzy which the auxiliaries orchestrated in the attempt to capture Treacy dead or alive, one child and one adult fell dead on the sidewalk. They also injured some of their own comrades. The mayhem is captured on the newsreel footage, and ends with images of Treacy's body being lifted onto the back of the lorry with that of Lieutenant Price. The scene is poignant, capturing the end of two young lives pitted by circumstances against each other.[78] But by November 1920 Collins' squad, aided by additional support from IRA units, displayed a greater propensity for blood. It also took the initiative in the bloodiest month of the fighting to date. On 1 November, as Terence Mac-Swiney was buried, following his seventy-three-day hunger strike, 18-year-old Kevin Barry, a member of the IRA's Dublin Brigade, was executed in Mountjoy Jail for his participation in an attack on a military bread van that resulted in the killing of a soldier. The death of the two men served as a catalyst for an IRA offensive that centred in Southwest Munster and Dublin City.

As young Barry awaited his execution, he responded with both wit and sarcasm to a former Professor at UCD who had taken the time to convey her view to him that he in fact deserved to die.

> Thanks much for your most interesting letter. It reached me yesterday whilst I was deeply engrossed in making my bed and recalled my mind at once from the lofty to the mundane. Yet in spite of the act that it was in parts grossly insulting, it was welcome. Yes, by all means come and see me, but come early in the morning, before 12 or you may not manage it ... Bring someone with you and get value for your money. I have to finish this in pencil. A kind friend has removed the pen and ink. Also I make no apology for the writing as I never could write ... As to answer your query as re my hairsuit adornments, I beg to report the appearance on my upper lip of 12 silky hairs. Not very encouraging but hope springs eternal. I have reformed my life – given up wine, women ... Physics, Chemistry, Biology, also work of every description. you will remember what the latter sacrifice means to me.[79]

The IRA was not long in responding to Barry's execution as County Longford registered significantly in the roster of large-scale IRA attacks on British forces in early November. Following a raid it had conducted in Granard on the evening of 5 November, in which a number of private homes were put to flame, a party of some 100 Black and Tans were ambushed outside the village of Ballinalee by a force of not more than twenty IRA men under the command of Sean MacEoin. It is likely that as many as twenty Black and Tans were killed in the incident, with those surviving forced to make a hasty retreat. The incident was not fully acknowledged in any official reports, possibly because of the inebriated state of a number of the Black and Tans at the time of the ambush and because the group had been caught right after carrying out the reprisal attack in Granard.[80]*

---

* MacEoin was later arrested and charged with the murder of a British Lieutenant during another IRA ambush. Sentenced to death, he figured prominently in the Anglo-Irish truce negotiations when his release was demanded by Collins and de Valera. He was eventually set free.

Bloody Sunday

Motivated in part by a desire to avenge the deaths of Barry and MacSwiney, and especially to destroy the British military intelligence apparatus in Dublin, the IRA attacked in a most ferocious manner on Sunday 21 November, beginning at 9.00 a.m. On that day 180 IRA men from the Dublin Brigade and other specially selected units imported from the country set about assassinating British officers. Many of the men were shot in their beds and in the presence of their wives or other female companions. The British officers were believed, according to an intelligence analysis by Michael Collins, to have been members of the 'Cairo Gang', an elite British Secret Service squad dispatched to the Irish capital during the preceding weeks, assigned the task of eliminating the IRA's command staff and leading Sinn Féin figures. Within one half-hour fourteen British officers lay dead and a dozen wounded.

A review of the dispatches contained in the files of the Criminal Investigations Department of the Dublin Metropolitan Police on that day's shootings, along with other British official accounts, makes clear the havoc that Collins' own personally cultivated hit squad wreaked on both the civilian Executive at Dublin Castle and the police and military command. One report from an attack at the rooming house at 28 Upper Pembroke Street describes the deadly efficiency of the IRA on that damp and overcast winter morning.

> At 9:00 a.m. today two Military Officers were shot dead and 4 wounded at 28 Upper Pembroke Street, the residence of Mrs Gray. A porter named Greene was cleaning the hall at the time. The front door was open and a number of men, about 20, entered the hall. They were armed with revolvers and were not masked. They held up the maid who was coming down the stairs and seven or eight of them rushed up the stairway and through the house. Mrs Gray was also held up when leaving her room. Ten or twelve shots were then heard in various parts of the house after which the party left immediately.
>
> After the men had left, Mrs Gray and her maid discovered two men shot in their rooms on the third floor. One was known as Major Dowling, Grenadier Guards. He was found shot dead at his bedroom door, and was fully dressed.
>
> Captain Price was found dead in the room next to Major Dowling. Both were dressed in uniforms and were about coming down to breakfast.
>
> Captain Kinnelly was found wounded on the second floor. He was shot in the arm.
>
> Colonel Woodcock, who occupied a room on the same landing, was shot in the back and is badly wounded.
>
> On the first floor, Colonel Montgomery was wounded in the body. He was at the door of his room.
>
> A Mr Murray, believed to belong to the Royal Scots was found wounded in the hall, having come down the stairs while the shooting was on.[81]

The wife of Captain B. C. P. Keanlyside witnessed the attempt to kill her own husband that morning. She recalled being awakened 'by a loud knocking and 20 to 22 men dressed in overcoats and rain coats and wearing cloth caps and felt hats filed methodically into the bedroom'. Her husband was ordered out of bed and forced downstairs with his hands up. 'I protested and begged them not to hurt him', she recalled, 'while tugging at the arm of one of the IRA men'.[82] But the young rebels had come determined to do their grizzly deed:

> I followed them immediately out and saw another officer being taken down-stairs with his hands up. They then placed him and my husband side by side in the hall, demanded their names, and fired at them, wounding the officer in the back, and my husband in the jaw, both arms and the upper part of his forearm. I ran down and helped him quickly upstairs to our bedroom ... and he was conveyed to an adjacent nursing home. My husband noticed especially that only one man fired and he was quite young and seemed cool, grim and determined.[83]

Among the raiding parties at the officers' home that morning was a young man named Sean Lemass. Four decades later he would become Prime Minister of the Irish Republic. The complement of IRA men used at each detail averaged between twelve and twenty. Todd Andrews, then a 19-year-old serving in the Dublin IRA Brigade's 'E Company', recalled years later his own involvement in the events of Bloody Sunday as a young, would-be executioner. The quarry which he, his brother, and another companion were to share that evening was a Captain Nobel. Both Andrews brothers were then also students at University College, Dublin.*

> We were very excited by the assignment but the prospect of killing a man in cold blood was alien to our ideas of how war should be conducted. We were apprehensive, too, because it could be a very dangerous operation. We were already being affected psychologically by the terror of the Tans. On the other hand, it was an article of my national faith that separatism had always been wrecked on a reef erected by informers and spies. I believed that it was justifiable to kill informers, spies, touts, traitors, and collaborators with the occupational forces.[84]

But Andrews, who was later to serve for years as the head of leading Irish government-backed agencies, was to be disappointed. Captain Nobel was not found in the house where he was a lodger. Andrews remembered with displeasure, however, the conduct of two members from Michael Collins' own handpicked hit squad, which he had witnessed at the house.

---

* In 1991, Andrews' son David became Foreign Minister of the Irish Republic, and in 1992 Minister of Defence, and would again return as Minister of Foreign Affairs in 1997.

They were from Collins's squad and their object was to get hold of Nobel's papers, but in fact none were found. There were only women and children in the rest of the house but that did not prevent the pair from the squad behaving like Black and Tans. In their search for papers they overturned furniture, pushing the occupants of the house around, and either through carelessness or malice, set fire to a room in which there were children ... Nearly half an hour was wasted putting out the fire before we were able to get out of the house, turning our 'dogs' [guns] in the waiting taxi and disperse singly on foot.[85]

To Michael Collins the 'twelve assassinations' were legitimate acts of self-defence forced by English oppression. He was blunt about why the British officers were selected for death and the means used to kill them.

Let it be remembered that we did not initiate the war, nor were we allowed to choose the lines along which the war developed ... Our only way to carry on the fight was by organised and bold guerrilla warfare ... However successful our ambushers, however many 'murders' we committed – England could always reinforce her army. She could always replace every soldier she lost ... To paralyse the British machine it was necessary to strike at individuals outside the ranks of the military. Without her Secret Service working at the top of its efficiency England was helpless ... robbed of the network of this organisation throughout the country, it would be impossible to find 'wanted' men. Without their criminal agents in the capitol it would be hopeless to affect the removal of those leaders marked down for murder. It was these men we had to put out of the way.[86]

It was Collins' candid assessment that 'spies are not ready to step into the shoes of their departed confederates as are soldiers to fill up the front line in honourable battle'.[87] General Macready's report to the Irish Situation Committee surmised that the IRA attacked in 'parties of from about six to twenty' and judged them to have been 'well acquainted with the interior of the houses'.[88]

The slayings had their desired effect. The scale of the effectiveness of the IRA's action in Dublin induced panic among the British ranks and, not surprisingly, within the Dublin Castle Administration. Mark Sturgis remarked in his diary from within the walls of the Castle that 'It has been a day of black murder. What they hope to gain by it, God alone knows'.[89]

Immediately after the attack on the British officers, British armoured cars and squadrons of troops took to the streets. All motor cars were stopped, searched and sent back to their garages. Until 11 a.m. the following morning, all trains were prevented from leaving Dublin until noon that Monday. The measures no doubt provoked new hardships for the local citizenry. But the shootings by the IRA had the most chilling effect of all, and doubtless a desirable one from the Republicans' point of view, on those British forces in the capital. All British officers from then on were ordered, for reasons of their own safety, to live in barracks or in buildings commandeered for such use.[90]

But by late afternoon on that Sunday 21 November, with their dead removed to a military morgue, the British military set about unleashing what could only be viewed as retaliatory terror of their own. The venue was the GAA Headquarters at Croke Park, scene of a Gaelic Football challenge between Dublin and Tipperary. Under the pretence of going to Croke Park to seek out suspects for the shooting of the British officers that morning, a large contingent of the RIC, followed by British army regulars, entered the field and stands at the outset of the game, and in short order commenced firing into the crowd, apparently without warning. Thirteen people in all, including eleven spectators and one player, died from British gunshots, with some seventy injured.

The *Freeman's Journal* of the following day offered a graphic report of the massacre. Comparing the British performance to the Amritsar massacre of the previous year, when British soldiers shot dead hundreds of Indian nationalists, the paper's lead paragraph proclaimed: 'Scenes of bloodshed on a football field, unparalleled in the history of the country, were enacted at Croke Park yesterday by armed forces of the Crown.' Another account in the paper stated that 'The armed forces, according to many of the onlookers, gave no warning to the spectators to disperse, beyond a preliminary volley of shots in the air.' 'Then the bullets came in as thick as hail, dealing out death in their swift passage; a wild scene of panic ensued, and women and children were knocked down and walked on', the account continued.[91]

To the Crown forces on that Sunday afternoon, Croke Park seemed like a logical place both to search for IRA suspects and from which to conduct reprisals. As W. F. Mandle has written in his history of the Gaelic Athletic Association and its involvement with Nationalist politics, the GAA 'had set itself up as a nationalist organisation; many of its members, both of the leadership and in the rank and file, had fought and suffered for Ireland; police raids upon Gaelic matches had, over the previous few months ... become commonplace'.[92] Mandle also pondered the question of whether Croke Park might have been a useful hiding place for at least some who had participated in the assassinations that morning.

> Whether the British officers killed were all specially recruited intelligence officers whose deaths were necessary for Collins and IRA intelligence to survive, or whether they were ordinary serving officers, or a mixture of both, the Sunday morning operation required the services of perhaps 120 men, not all of whom could be obtained in Dublin. The possibility that the cover of a Gaelic football match could be used to get men into Dublin cannot be discounted. There is evidence Collins knew of the game; and the use of such fixtures as a cloak for the gathering of members of revolutionary organisations was a hallowed G.A.A. precedent. It seems unlikely that the game was set up as a cover since planning for the assassination seems to only have begun four days prior to the event. Although one authority suggests that the concentrated

killings and attacks on police in Donegal, Longford, Tyrone, Kerry, and Tipperary on 31 October, were a rehearsal for Bloody Sunday.[93]

The gruesome events at Croke Park, however, did not mark an end to the day's bloodshed. That evening, within the gates of Dublin Castle, three Republican suspects were shot dead in cold blood by their military captors, among them Dick McKee, the much valued leader of the Dublin Brigade. The Government falsely claimed that the three men died while trying to escape. It even went so far as to issue photographs taken of the dead men after their corpses had been arranged to give the impression that they died while an escape attempt was in progress.

The British Government's attempt to deny the assassin's role played by most of the British officers killed by the IRA earlier that day was later criticised by one its former principles in Ireland, Brigadier-General Frank Crozier. 'It must be remembered', Crozier argued, 'that while all revolution carries with it, liked or disliked, wanted or unwanted, revolver rule, largely carried on sub rosa, there is no justification for similar methods on the part of "Crown" authority'. The willingness of the British Cabinet to sanction such activities on the part of those who wore the British uniform in Ireland was a source of particular criticism by the General.

> Captains A and B and many others at the War Office (backed up secretly by the C.I.G.S., Sir Henry Wilson) set out in the name of 'law and order' on a similar mission before Michael Collins with this difference – Collins never denied what he did ... The reader may not remember the solemn pomp and circumstance which accompanied the cavalcade of death through the streets of London when coffins or gun carriages draped with the Union Jack, containing the remains of murdered officers and ex-officers, were solemnly paraded before the populace followed by Ministers of the Crown and attended by the King's representative and guards of honour. I do. Either those Ministers knew they were following the mortal remains of men who had died in the service of the Crown while engaged in a 'murder stunt' or they did not. Sir Henry Wilson knew and went to his own death within two years under very similar circumstances. If they did not, they should have. It was their duty to know.[94]

As we have noted, the British military offered a clinical explanation for their own role in the day's murder and mayhem: The Tipperary–Dublin football match at Croke Park was believed to have provided what General Macready described as 'a suitable occasion for the introduction of a gang of murderers into Dublin'.[95] Nonetheless, of particular significance is the fact that Macready sought to distance the British army from the RIC's actions, claiming that the police had helped provoke the chaos in the stadium by their precipitate action.

Arrangements had been made that the police should not enter the ground until after it had been surrounded and that an officer should warn the crowd by megaphone that they must keep their seats and afterwards leave by the proper exits and that if they did so elsewhere they would be shot ... The police arrived ten minutes before the time arranged and the troops were not in position and no caution was given. The RIC state that they were fired at on arriving near the gates and about the same time a signal for dispersal appears to have been given by a spectator in the grandstand firing three revolver shots in the air. The RIC returned fire and the crowd stampeded breaking down a railing on one side of the ground. As a result about 10 civilians were killed or injured and 65 wounded or injured chiefly as a result of the stampede.[96]

Macready's report claimed that '30 or 40 revolvers' that were thrown away were picked up off the ground. The 'premature' action by the RIC, Macready claimed, allowed many individuals to escape from Croke Park without being searched.[97] Macready's report, however, was clearly at odds with the submission forwarded to the Cabinet the previous week by Hamar Greenwood on the shootings at Croke Park. In that account, the Chief Secretary claimed that the violence was initiated by 'Sinn Féin pickets at the entrance to the field' before the police cordon had been completed. 'The police returned the fire,' Greenwood stated, 'and I regret to state with the result that ten persons were killed and eleven seriously wounded.'[98]

Michael Collins' hand in the Bloody Sunday executions of British personnel was made evident some time later by a note to Richard Mulcahy, after the latter in his role as Minister of Defence in a native Irish Government sought advice from Collins as to how the mother of one of the British officers killed should be answered. The communications between the two men regarding the killing of ex-Captain Patrick McCormack also make clear that some of the British officers killed on 21 November were in fact not members of the Secret Service. Collins gave Mulcahy these instructions, while deflecting the blame for the incorrect selections onto the Dublin Brigade, rather than his own men:

> With reference to the case, you will remember that I stated on a former occasion that we had no evidence that he was a secret service agent. You will also remember that several of the names of the November 21st cases were just regular officers. Some of the names were put by the Dublin Brigade. So far as I remember, McCormack's name was one of these ... In my opinion, it would be as well to tell Mrs McCormack that there was no particular case against her son, but just that he was an enemy soldier.[99]

Ironically, Officer McCormack's mother was a cousin of Michael Davitt, the architect of the Irish Land League and a committed Fenian. McCormack himself was Irish by birth.

The frustrations caused to the British Government in the aftermath of the almost total destruction of its intelligence network in Dublin in November were also felt by the British Ambassador to the United States, Sir Auckland Geddes. On 24 November he complained to the Foreign Office that the newspaper accounts in the US on the incidents of Bloody Sunday featured information transmitted by the Press Association that was 'especially bad from its strong pro-Sinn Féin bias'. In Geddes' view, any evidence tying US contributions and munitions to the insurgents in Ireland should be used by the British Government 'to bring greater pressure to bear on United States Government [sic] than we have hitherto been able to do with a view to securing expulsion of de Valera and suppression of principal Sinn Féin Organisations in this country'.[100] However, in the estimate of one ranking British Foreign Office official who successfully overruled Geddes' effort, it was 'very doubtful if we could really secure that anything serious would be done by the US authorities to deal with the Sinn Féiners'.[101] The official presented what was a balanced assessment of the situation in quite heated circumstances:

> It is very natural that Sir Aukland Geddes should feel so strongly about the position in which he finds himself, both on public and personal grounds. But I am sceptical as to the advisability of general representations as to the United States Government with regard to the Sinn Féin proceedings. We must bear in mind that we have to deal not only with a Government that exercises but a feeble control over the local bodies, but also with an administration that is discredited.[102]

But 'Bloody Sunday' did not by any means mark the end of the shock and raw terror which the month of November brought to the British Government and to those acting to enforce its by now tenuous grip on Ireland. One week later eighteen British Auxiliaries met their deaths in an ambush at Kilmichael in the lush countryside of West Cork. Ironically, the ambush occurred as General Macready was informing the Cabinet that he had decided to withdraw some of his forces back to the Curragh. 'Owing to the situation having developed more favorably than was anticipated', Macready announced the withdrawals, including the transfer of the Lancers from County Cork to Galway, along with the 6th Dragoon Guards from Galway and the 10th Hussars from Limerick, both to the Curragh.[103] It was the first significant attack on that force.

The attack at Kilmichael was led and masterminded by 22-year-old Tom Barry. The one-sided engagement occurred at a sharp bend in a road at 5.30 p.m. on a Sunday evening. One account forwarded to Dublin Castle by a British officer who arrived at the scene afterwards stated that the dead soldiers had been 'terribly mutilated, as though hacked with hatchets'.[104] But according to an account by Barry himself, an attempt to take prisoners ended when the British officer in charge urged his men to commence firing'. The false surrender compelled the No. 2 West Cork Brigade to shoot all remaining British soldiers, Barry contended. Immediately after the incident, he sought to restore discipline to the young IRA men who, in the majority of cases, had just shot another man dead for the first time. To the haunting sounds of a single bagpiper Barry led the men to drill along the roads, walking over the bodies of the British soldiers, before he ordered them from the grizzly scene.[105]

Barry's memoir of the IRA's campaign in West Cork gives a gripping description of the ambush.

> So close were the combatants, that in one instance the pumping blood from an Auxiliary's severed artery struck one attacker full in the mouth before the Auxiliary hit the ground. The Auxiliaries were cursing and yelling as they fought but the IRA were tightlipped, as ruthlessly and coldly they out-fought them.[106]

Consistent with the policy followed by the British Government up to this point, sterner measures were sought. At a Cabinet session on 5 December Lloyd George stated that he had received 'a further private letter from the Chief Secretary from Dublin in which he reported that the military authorities in Ireland wished to extend to the whole of Ireland the policy of some form of martial law, which the Cabinet had sanctioned for a district in the Southwest of Ireland'.[107] Martial law, however, by decision of the Cabinet in December 1920, still remained limited to South Munster. Dublin was the one exception.

There were reasons why martial law was not expanded beyond these areas. In reality the great preponderance of the armed conflict in the Anglo-Irish War then or later took place in Dublin City and in the six counties comprising the province of Munster: Kerry, Cork, Tipperary, Limerick, Clare and Waterford. Pockets of armed resistance, sometimes dramatic, were offered in Galway, Mayo, Roscommon, Kilkenny, Wexford, and Longford, among other areas. But it would not match the intensity or the continuity of the activity witnessed in Dublin and Munster. At the same time, as Michael Hopkinson has noted, 'Even within Munster, IRA size and effectiveness varied from area to area. West Clare was much less active than the rest of the County. Kerry, for all its fighting reputation, saw only patchy activity and much disorganisation and internal conflict within the IRA.' Such factors as geography also entered into the picture, and may have affected the IRA's development. One senior IRA officer in Kerry noted the differences between the 'glen' and the 'flat' people in that County, contending that while the former were more prone to taking up arms, the latter were more interested in attaining prosperity and stability.[108] The areas in County Kerry with better agricultural land and larger farms were not by any means unique in the country during the conflict for their relative inactivity. A review of the British reports of 'outrages', submitted by its Military Command to the Cabinet on a weekly basis during 1920–21, offers little evidence of serious resistance from the IRA in more prosperous counties such as Wicklow, Carlow, and Kildare, with the exception of those who were from the poorest ranks of the agricultural sector.

Nonetheless, as 1920 drew to a close the worst violence to date had been experienced. By that time few places in Ireland were shown to be immune from violent attack by either side in the Anglo-Irish conflict. Raids on great houses throughout the countryside were by no means the preserve of the IRA. An attack by the RIC on a crowd attending a St Stephen's night dance at Caherguillamore House in Bruff, County Limerick, represented a particularly bloody end to the year.

Acting on information that the holiday dance, which involved 300 young men and women from throughout that East Limerick community, included prominent IRA members, a large party of Black and Tans, joined by RIC members and British army regulars, set out from Limerick to attack the Great House and its occupants. Overcoming a number of IRA scouts along the way, and striking silently with their lorries left far behind, the combined force of some 300 men opened fire with .303 ammunition. Bursting through doors and windows, the joint force entered with guns blazing and bayonets fixed. Bloodhounds stood at the ready outside to track any Volunteers attempting to escape to the nearby forest. The dogs led a party of British Auxiliaries to one wounded IRA man who was executed on the spot. Inside the large house broken banisters were used by the Black and Tans to bludgeon a group of 120 young men who had been rounded up, while rifle butts and bayonets were also given liberal use. In all five Volunteers were killed that night, along with one Black and Tan. Over one hundred bloodied male prisoners were taken under martial law.

The burning of Cork City: 11 December 1920

Within the confines of the Cork No. 1 Brigade, which included the city of Cork and the town of Macroom, a total of forty-one members of the British military forces and RIC were killed in action in 1920 alone, as against five fatalities for the IRA. That statistic is useful when placed against the backdrop of reprisals committed by the police, the Auxiliaries and front line British military personnel against persons and property in that area during November and December 1920. The ambushes by the Cork No. 1 Brigade and by the other Brigades in Cork already described, added to the virtual elimination of the British intelligence apparatus in Dublin on Bloody Sunday, also had an inevitable effect in prompting British efforts, through secret intermediaries, to begin negotiations with Sinn Féin. These efforts, and the response of the Dáil Government to them, will be discussed in greater detail later. But it is useful to remember the context of these developments and the fact that the Government of Ireland Act was already on the statute books at Westminster, with provision for the island of Ireland's partition already in place. The combination of these developments, in so far as the British Government could still exert control over Irish affairs at least on an external basis, underscores clearly that a dual policy of coercion and conciliation was very much in effect.

With Eamon de Valera still in the United States, and Arthur Griffith by this time in jail, the leader to whom the task fell of responding to British secret peace feelers was Michael Collins, the Acting President of Dáil Éireann. It was a new role for Collins, and the continuation of British atrocities throughout the country left him at this stage no less determined to plough on with the IRA's guerrilla campaign. While some actions committed by those in British uniform may not have been sanctioned by the Government, the recklessness and the bitterness they engendered did much to prolong the conflict. The sacking of Cork City, with the burning of its City Hall and the business district along Patrick Street on the night of 11 December 1920 by large numbers of British Auxiliaries and other military personnel, made other acts of wanton destruction by the agents of the Crown pale in comparison. And it did even less to pacify Ireland, owing to its sheer magnitude, and was comparable only with the murder unleashed by the Crown's forces on Bloody Sunday at Croke Park.

Cork was the third largest city in Ireland. Just two decades earlier the city had played host to a warm welcome for the King. But now it was a cauldron of rebellion. Early on 11 December a party of Auxiliaries were ambushed by the Cork No. 1 Brigade outside Cork City. Following the 10.00 p.m. curfew that night a combined force of Auxiliaries, Black and Tans and regular Army members set about the wholesale burning and looting of the City in retaliation. Two civilians were murdered by the force that night without provocation. Cork's City Hall, among other public buildings along with much of Patrick Street in the main business district, was completely destroyed. A strong wind conspired to ensure that the city burned for much of the night. Fire hoses were cut by British personnel to deter the fire brigade's effectiveness. The litany of actions in what was effectively a joint police and military riot included the removal of four hundred gallons of petrol via military lorries from Victoria Barracks, to be used to start the fire. Among the public buildings also destroyed was the Carnegie Library. General Frank Crozier, who a few months later would resign from the British army in revulsion for the Government's conduct in Ireland, wrote of the grisly affair.

> Once the orgy had begun there was nothing to choose between looters of the army, the police or the civil population. All were mad, many were drunk,

most were dishonoured, but none so much as the Government which subsequently tolerated the regime of lying, and the wretched weaklings who allowed it.[109]

There were also individual acts of valour by some members of the police and military that night who in a number of instances stood guard over banks and stores, shooting looters, both civilian and in uniform.

In Westminster the Government sought to minimise the damage to its prestige and to its Irish policy caused by the incident. But while the Government had not approved the burning of Cork in advance, its tolerance for the reprisal campaign carried out by those who wore the British uniform in Ireland set the chain of events in motion. The fact that the Government in the end saw fit to pay out some £2,000,000 in damages offered at least partial evidence of its culpability.

A report ordered by Lloyd George, which would not be published despite his promise to do so, condemned the RIC but exonerated the army. It also censured General Tudor, the patron and commander of the Black and Tans, for dispatching a hastily arranged company to Cork. In his memoir, General Crozier took issue with this action, since it was he, not Tudor, who sent the company to Cork, knowing them all to be experienced men.[110]

Seventy-two hours after the burning of Cork City the Auxiliaries added further to the image of British forces as bent on violent crime. Members of the Catholic clergy were also not exempt from murder by those representing the King in Ireland. Only weeks apart two priests, Father Michael Griffin in Galway City and Canon Magner in Dunmanway in West Cork, were murdered in cold blood in November and December of 1920. The slaying of the elderly Canon Magner, along with another innocent civilian, on 15 December 1920, however, provoked a public outcry that led to official action. Within a week the young British soldier accused of the murders was found guilty before a British military court set up by General Strickland. Soon after, he became the only soldier tried and executed for the murder of a civilian during the Anglo-Irish war.[111]

But overall, the County of Cork had proved a particular thorn in the side of the British. Some 13,000 men found themselves on duty in Cork, one third of all British regular forces in Ireland.

The IRA, where it operated in sufficient numbers, had inflicted severe damage on British facilities and morale. Jolted by the experience, the British Government responded by employing still more counter-terror. Stalemate had set in, and with it came strong public opposition in Britain itself. On the surface at least, it was evident that the early stages of the 'dual policy' of combining constitutional reform with coercion was having little effect in pacifying Ireland.

The events of Bloody Sunday and Kilmichael combined pointed the way in the British Government's eyes to more coercive remedies rather than conciliation. By the end of November over 500 men had been arrested within a period of days. On 10 December 1920, with the approval of the Cabinet, Lord French placed the southwest Munster counties of Cork, Tipperary, Limerick and Kerry under martial law. Counties Clare, Waterford, Wexford and Kilkenny were added to the list one month later.

However, despite the harshness which martial law represented for the residents of these counties, whether they were sympathetic to the IRA or not, martial law added to the confusion that was British policy in Ireland at the close of 1920. Frank Sturgis noted that Lloyd George sought to limit martial law to 'the distant provinces, a storm on the horizon'.[112] In his view, the Prime Minister sought to leave Dublin outside martial law as a means of encouraging a negotiated settlement. It was still a mixture of coercion and politics.

The introduction of martial law, though, had a motive beyond serving as the most forceful attempt to date to thwart rebellion in the most troublesome parts of Ireland. It was also seen as 'an attempt to silence that section of British public opinion which had found the reprisals policy odious and to prevent further outbreaks of British military undisciplines, and to keep the Army, RIC and Auxiliaries under the control of a specific authority in the selected counties'.[113] But this objective suffered a severe jolt when, on the day after martial law was proclaimed, the British forces and RIC burned Cork City.

But as bloody as the months of November and December 1920 had proved, General Macready's year-end report to the Government conveyed the ironic message that the state of affairs had become predictable. 'The general military situation is developing as was anticipated', the General stated. 'That is to say', he noted, 'certain rebel flying columns still carry out enterprises in outlying districts against small forces of troops or police, while the districts where troops are in strength are for the most part quiet'. Macready conceded that the capture of such IRA flying columns was a 'matter of considerable difficulty owing to the fact that in the areas where they operate, the inhabitants are either openly on the side of the rebels or are terrorised into acquiescence in their methods'.[114]

Coming as it did from the top British military official in Ireland, the statement represented a glaring admission of the precarious state of British rule in Ireland by the end of 1920.

4

The Stalemate

There is a risk that a position of virtual stalemate may continue throughout the summer and that winter will be a time of decisive advantage to the rebels.

General Nevil Macready in a memorandum to the British Cabinet (24 May 1921)

With the Coalition's decision to continue the military campaign in Ireland, the criticism of British policy from both inside and outside Britain grew. Such pro-Liberal Party newspapers as the *Manchester Guardian*, the *Daily News*, and the *Westminster Gazette* had opposed a military approach to the Irish situation from the outset. In addition to C. P. Scott's *Manchester Guardian*, Lord Northcliffe's newspapers, the *Times* and the *Daily Mail*, among other publications, also opposed the continuation of the campaign. It was within this context that the part played by Wickham Steed, editor of the *Times*, in shaping British public opinion against the continuation of the Anglo-Irish War cannot be overestimated. Steed's role included far more than sermonising against the British military campaign in Ireland through the editorial posture of the *Times*. He lobbied members of the Cabinet, as well as the King. He also expressed concerns about the damage Britain's conduct in Ireland was causing to Anglo-American relations.[1]

The 20 November 1920 edition of the *Times* contained an article by a correspondent in Ireland that reflected the presence of the paper's editorial policy on its news pages:

> If only the people in Britain knew ... everywhere in Ireland today you hear that cry, 'why do these things happen? ... Why are servants of the Crown charged with pillage and arson and what amounts to lynch law even with drunkenness and murder! How can the reign of terror be stopped?'[2]

In Ireland, however, the story was known too well. On 20 October 1920, despite the risk of official censorship, the *Irish Independent*, one of the country's largest dailies, declared: 'Nobody in Ireland accepts as truthful any statement made by the British Government'.[3]

Other efforts aimed at bringing external and internal pressure on the Government's Irish policy ran virtually in tandem at the end of 1920 and the beginning of 1921. Though clearly partisan, the findings of both the *American Commission on Conditions in Ireland, 1920-1921,* and the Report of the Commission sent to Ireland by the emerging British Labour Party were effective in focusing attention on the conduct of Britain's military campaign. Both served also to counter British propaganda efforts aimed at describing the campaign as a police action in the name of law and order against IRA murder gangs.[4]

The well-attended and extensively reported hearings of the American Commission served to keep the Irish Nationalist point of view before the American public during a period of extensive division between the competing Irish-American Nationalist groups in the United States. Modelled after the investigation conducted by Lord Bryce into alleged German atrocities in Belgium, and known initially as the 'Committee of One Hundred on Conditions in Ireland', the Commission's membership numbered nine US senators, including some from such non-Irish areas as Louisiana and Oregon. Membership eventually grew to include 150, including five governors, members of the US House of Representatives, labour leaders and church leaders from an array of different creeds.

It is clear that Dr William Maloney, architect of the Commission, strove to use it as a vehicle to make the conduct of Britain's present policies in Ireland difficult, though this may not have been the outward intent. Describing in a memorandum to potential supporters the concept behind the panel, Maloney wrote: 'The main object to be kept in mind is that the Commission is merely a mask to place the Irish case before the tribunal of the civilised world.'[5] As F. M. Carroll has observed, for Maloney, 'an impartial account of British activities in Ireland might work to inhibit further British operations until there was a change in the British Government or until world opinion was moved to action'.[6]

To Sir Auckland Geddes, the British Ambassador in Washington, the intent of the Commission was also clear. Geddes told the Foreign Office that the Commission was 'obviously designed to embarrass us as, naturally, no evidence can be forthcoming from this side'.[7] Geddes, however, actually favoured the admission of a group of Commission members to Ireland, but was firmly overruled by the Chief Secretary for Ireland, Sir Hamar Greenwood. The British rejection of the American request provoked a joint letter of protest to the US Secretary of State by the ten senators who were members of the Commission, including George Norris, Robert La Follette, and David I. Walsh. They argued that the British denial of the panel's entry was a 'violation of the right of free communication between the liberty-loving people of two democracies'.[8]

When the hearings commenced in Washington, DC, on 18 November 1920, they did so without any official British participation. Ironically, the

Commission also conducted its affairs without testimony from the Sinn Féin mission in the US, who feared British reprisals against any private citizens they might recommend. Nonetheless, the Commission, in the course of fourteen days of public hearings (from 19 November 1920 to 21 January 1921) took testimony from thirty-seven witnesses, eighteen of whom came from Ireland. Included among them were Muriel and Mary MacSwiney, the wife and sister of Terence MacSwiney, the late Lord Mayor of Cork. MacSwiney's death had received world-wide attention and nowhere, save Ireland, did it receive more attention than in the United States, where effort was made by local, pro-Irish Republican organisations to present MacSwiney as a martyr to British oppression. The appearance of the two MacSwiney women, dressed in black, coupled with the lengthy, emotional yet poignant testament of Mary MacSwiney which lasted several hours (covering a session and a half) were not helpful to Britain's image in the United States.[9]

From December 1920 to March 1921, *The Nation* published the transcripts of the testimony in weekly instalments. In fact, during the Commission's formative stages, *The Nation* provided office space for the effort at its Washington office, and also assisted in collecting funds.[10] Although the Commission concluded its hearings by January 1921, the group's final report was not released until July 1921. However, the Interim Report of March 1921 was sufficient to provide discomfort for the British Government. As anticipated, by virtue of the official British decision not to participate in the proceedings of the Commission, the British case was not covered in the Interim Report. As a result, the findings represented an indictment of British rule in Ireland, as evidenced by this damning conclusion:

> We would extend our sympathy to the British people. The army, which is the instrument of their government in Ireland, would also seem to be the instrument of that moral heritage which was their glory and which cast its luster on earth and all of them. The sun of that glory seems finally to have set over Ireland. British 'justice' has become a discredited thing. The official Black and Tans in Ireland compete for dishonor of Anglo-Saxon civilisation with our unofficial lynch mobs ... We welcome the British Labour Report on Conditions in Ireland and the reports of the Englishwomen's International League and the British Society of Friends ... We would congratulate the *Manchester Guardian* ... the *London Daily Herald*, the *New Statesman*, and the *Westminster Gazette* for the courageous stand they have taken in exposing and denouncing to the British people the murder done in their name. In spite of this campaign of murder, arson, terror and destruction, the Imperial British Forces would appear to have failed to preserve British rule in Ireland.[11]

The report of the British Labour Party's 'Commission to Ireland' published in January 1921 also carried considerable influence due to its increasing strength as a major party. The Labour Commission Report was the outgrowth of the Party's decision to send a fact-finding group of its own to Ireland from November to December 1920, simultaneous with the hearings of the American Commission on Conditions in Ireland. The Labour Commission consisted of seven members, including Labour MP Arthur Henderson as Chairman. On 25 October 1920 Henderson had proposed that 'an independent investigation should at once be instituted into the causes, nature and extent of reprisals on the part of those whose duty is the maintenance of law and order'.[12] When Parliament rejected this proposal, the Labour Party decided shortly thereafter to send its own panel, with a military advisor included. The report concluded that 'the final solution of the Irish problem will not be found through a policy of violence or of vengeance. Ultimately, it will have to be found along the lines of conciliation and consent by the more enlightened method of negotiation'.[13] But perhaps the Labour Commission's severest rhetoric, echoing that of its American counterpart, was deployed in this statement:

> Things are being done in the name of Britain which must make her name stink in the nostrils of the whole world. The honour of our people has been gravely compromised. Not only is there a reign of terror in Ireland ... but a nation is being held in subjection by an Empire that is the friend of small nations.[14]

It should be noted that the Labour Party's Commission of Inquiry was motivated at least in part by a desire to diffuse those elements in the British labour movement that sought a more militant opposition to the Coalition's policies in Ireland. In fact, despite the publication of the Commission's Report in January 1921, the majority of local trade union councils voted that same month in favour of a general strike against sending more troops to Ireland, as well as over other domestic British issues. At the same time, the British labour movement's leadership as a whole remained hesitant to express support for Irish independence.[15]

For the Cabinet, the document was a source of concern, despite the observations of British Commander-in-Chief in Ireland, General Nevil Macready, that 'the report of the Labour Commission and the tone of the speeches at the Labour Conference were so obviously biased that, though well-advertised, they have not had the influence which a more impartial attitude might have achieved'.[16] However, Macready's regular army was spared the brunt of the Labour Commission's strong attack on the policy of coercion in Ireland. While most of the army officers, in the view of the Commission's military advisor, Brigadier General C. B. Thomas, were 'ignorant of their professional duties', the Auxiliaries or Black and Tans were deemed to be out of control. 'Under whom do they serve?' the report asked, noting that the outfit did not even recognise the authority of Dublin Castle.[17] The unabashed hostility the report demonstrated for the policies of the Coalition Government fed Lloyd

George's belief that the Irish, among the rank and file of the Labour Party movement in Britain, were a source of domestic unrest, underscoring the need to rid himself and the country of the Irish problem for good.

The assassination of public figures by the RIC and British forces in Ireland continued as part of the official campaign of counter-terror. The year 1920, as we have noted, saw the murder of Cork City's Lord Mayor Tomas Mac-Curtain. A coroner's jury in Cork returned a verdict of 'wilful murder' against the RIC in that city. The British official response was to eliminate the coroner's juries. That new incidents occurred well into 1921 indicates a conscious decision to ignore public outrage in Ireland and Britain itself, and to persist with a policy of cold blooded reprisals. In March 1921 the City of Limerick was the next to be visited, with the slaying of its public men.

Seoirse Clancy had been recently sworn in as Mayor of Limerick. As he lay in bed in his home on the north side of the city on the evening of 6 March, death had already visited his family. His wife's father had been buried the previous day. A committed Gaelic Leaguer, and a leader in the campaigns against conscription and to raise the Dáil Loan, Clancy was a respected first citizen in the Shannon-side city. He was also a thorn in the side of the local British authorities for these reasons and more.

Clancy's house was no stranger to British raids and searches. RIC members and British auxiliaries during the course of the previous months had threatened to burn the house, removed property and abused the staff. But most ominously of all, they had told Mrs Clancy that during a subsequent visit they planned to give 'a Lord Mayor's show'.[18] It was a threat that held a clear meaning to those who knew the fate of other Irish municipal leaders as a result of such visits.

As Mayor Clancy and his wife slept on that Sunday night, the representatives of the Crown returned in earnest. At 1.30 a.m. the Clancys were awakened by a pounding on the door. Refusing his wife's plea that she respond, instead the Mayor insisted that they were the subjects of another 'routine' raid. Nonetheless, the worried woman trailed her husband to the door. When Clancy asked who was outside, the word 'military' was returned in response. A flickering candle-light revealed through a crack in the door that a party of men were in disguise, wearing goggles over darkened faces and pulled-down caps. When Clancy answered that it was him, he was ordered outside. When he refused, the raiders forced themselves into the house and there began a scene of death and mayhem. One man fired a single shot into the Mayor. Suddenly, Mrs Clancy thrust herself in front of him as he fell to the ground. In the darkness she grappled with the official gunmen, but they were still able to fire several shots into him. He crawled outside to the gate as the intruders fled, and died inside his house soon after. In the confusion one of the assassins left without his glasses, owing to Mrs Clancy's desperate attempt to save her husband.

But the Clancys' was not the only household to be visited by cold-blooded murder that night. On the other side of Limerick, at that late hour, Clancy's immediate predecessor, Michael O'Callaghan, lay asleep. He too had been the victim of many raids by the army and police. He was also a prominent player in Sinn Féin's efforts in his city. Twelve months earlier he represented Limerick as the City's Mayor at the funeral of Tomas MacCurtain in Cork. O'Callaghan was also an out-spoken critic of British reprisals against the people of his city and a leader of the Irish Industrial Development Association.

At 1.00 a.m. on 7 March, an ominous knock came to the O'Callaghans' door, as it had to the Clancys'. From the bedroom window Mrs O'Callaghan asked who it was. She was told by a group of men that they wanted her husband – 'We want him', came the reply from a familiar voice. She recognised it as the cultivated voice of a young British 'cadet' in the Auxiliaries who had led a raid on their home a few weeks earlier. O'Callaghan went downstairs, a candle in one hand, accompanied by his wife. She opened the door. Again there was the vision of men with blackened faces and goggles demanding that an unarmed man come out to them. Again, a frightened woman sought frantically to save her husband's life by acting as a human shield. The raiders tried to knock her out of the way. One shot rang out and O'Callaghan slumped to the floor. Instantly, one of the men emptied the contents of his revolver into O'Callaghan. His wife still clawed at his soon-to-be assassins; at one point all of them rolled on the hallway floor. Finally they fled into the night from which they had come. Elsewhere in Limerick, this time on a public street, the bullet-riddled body of another man – Joseph O'Donoghue, an IRA member – was found, as the old Irish city fell victim to a reign of terror and confusion. Official inquiries would be launched by the British Government, along with attempts even by Lloyd George to blame the IRA for the killings. But there was little credibility behind the effort as it became commonly known that the enforcers of the tattered King's writ were themselves the perpetrators.[19]

During this same period, Bishop Michael Fogarty of Killaloe, an outspoken critic of British rule, escaped a similar fate by his fortuitous absence the night four British auxiliaries arrived at his home. The attempt on Fogarty's life occurred on the night of 3 December 1920. Later Frank Crozier confirmed the attempt on Fr Fogarty's life after he had resigned from the military in protest against the Government's policy in Ireland.[20]

While the attempt to pacify Ireland by force continued, by the end of 1920 the British Government had initiated a second and simultaneous policy. It was, in fact, aimed at finding someone in Sinn Féin with whom they could negotiate. The preferred framework for such a negotiated settlement in British official eyes was within the context of the Government of Ireland Act (1920). But as a practical matter, the Government of Ireland Act was regarded by the overwhelming majority of Irish nationalists as too little, too late. A year and a half of a state of insurrection in which the IRA had forced the might of the British Empire into a position of stalemate had changed the equation drastically. This situation, combined with the erosion of British Governmental institutions and their replacement by the rudiments of court and local government systems implemented by Sinn Féin with popular support, made more fundamental change necessary. While more blood would be shed on both sides before a majority in the British Cabinet would accept this reality, it became clear within its inner counsels, through the reports of its own military command in Ireland, that force alone was not the answer. Its application had only succeeded in alienating the majority in Ireland from British rule even further.

One of the first initiatives towards a negotiated peace appears to have been initiated by Arthur Griffith as Acting President of the Irish Republic during Eamon de Valera's absence in the United States. Dublin Castle Law Advisor W. E. Wylie became aware through his own sources, late in September 1920, that Griffith was by this time willing to meet a high-ranking British official with whom he could hold preliminary discussions for a truce as a forerunner to formal peace negotiations. Wylie and Anderson both entered into discussions with Griffith at a solicitor's office on St Andrews Street on 26 September 1920. Anderson's biographer cites conflicting accounts as to whether Griffith and Anderson ever met face to face.[21] In any event, the meeting did not result in a breakthrough. But soon after Anderson and his subordinates at the Irish Office, Mark Sturgis and Andy Cope, developed contact with two men capable of acting as intermediaries between the parties: Dublin physician Dr W. M. Crofton and Former General Wanless-O'Gowan. The two men informed Dublin Castle that, based on conversations with leading Sinn Féin figures, a Dominion Home Rule proposal accompanied by provisions for financial autonomy and a general amnesty would provide the basis for a settlement. This view, together with an estimate by the Irish Executive of the political realities confronting the moderates in Dáil Éireann who wanted to support a peace initiative, was conveyed by Sir John Anderson in a 5 November letter to Bonar Law. 'A very influential section of Dáil Éireann is definitely prepared', he wrote, 'to accept the essential conditions outlined by the Prime Minister before the recess.'[22] Anderson, based on information received from those he labelled his 'informants', contended that those Dáil members 'could for the sake of peace be prepared to accept the present bill, enlarged in certain directions, particularly in regard to Finance'. The overriding difficulty, he noted, was that 'the present members of Dáil Éireann were elected on the Republican ticket and before they could "deliver the goods", they would have to consult their constituents and for this they would require special facilities'. Anderson suggested that consideration might be given in that case to lifting the legal ban on the Dáil. The Government's top civil servant in

Ireland went on to request a meeting for General Wanless-O'Gowan and Dr Crofton with the Prime Minister. He placed the request in the form of a personal favour from Bonar Law:

> I have advised them to get in touch with you first, and if you will be so good as to give them an interview I shall feel personally grateful ... I understand Ireland is a country of disappointments and I am not building extravagant hopes on this recent development but it will always be a great satisfaction and comfort to those of us who are working here under conditions of great strain to feel that no possible avenue to peace has been left unexplored and this, at any rate, is the first definite indication of a 'Sinn Féiner on the bridge'.[23]

Four days later Wanless-O'Gowan and Crofton met with Lloyd George. They were joined by Bonar Law and Hamar Greenwood. 'I think it is better to write nothing about the interview', Law told Anderson afterwards, 'but it looked more like a reality than anything I had heard of before'.[24]

The British Foreign Office's Intelligence Department was also involved in the discussion concerning peace feelers at the end of 1920. One intelligence official, C. J. Phillips, informed the Cabinet of six meetings he had had between September and November with 'Mr P. Moylett, claiming to represent Mr Arthur Griffith'.[25] The official stated that Moylett had been introduced by Mr John Steele, London correspondent of the *Chicago Tribune*, who had paid several visits recently to Ireland and been in touch with various Sinn Féin leaders, including Mr Arthur Griffith himself. 'I have no doubt at all', Phillips stated, 'that Mr Moylett has all the credentials necessary to justify the Government in considering the proposals which he brings as authentically emanating from the headquarters of Sinn Féin.' In a scenario outlined by Moylett on behalf of Sinn Féin, Dáil Éireann would convene an open meeting, sanctioned by the British Government, whose sole purpose 'would be to receive and answer an invitation from the British Government to nominate representatives to a conference called by the British Government for a settlement of the whole Irish question'. Under the proposal submitted by Moylett, the conference would consist of 'one or two men, both representing Ulster, one or two representing Sinn Féin and (say) five others representing England, Scotland, Wales and possibly the two Dominions, specially interested in the Irish question, viz. Canada and Australia'. In Phillips' view, Sinn Féin's proposal was proof positive that 'the Sinn Féin leaders realise quite well the hopelessness of their attempts to carry on the struggle on present lines and are seeking a plan by which they may, at the same time, end the present crisis, save their own faces as far as possible and checkmate the extremist section among their followers'. But force, rather than conciliation, continued to be the British response.

The *Times* of London criticised the Government for allowing the prospect of an end to hostilities to dissipate at the end of 1920. The paper's editor, Henry

Wickham Steed, noted in his memoir that he had kept so abreast of the exchanges between Sinn Féin and the British Government that 'a summary of the conversations was brought to me almost daily and placed in custody in my safe'.[26] Lloyd George's declaration on 9 November 1920, in an address at the London Guild Hall, that the Government had 'murder by the throat' was particularly obnoxious to Steed and the *Times*.[27] An editorial of the following day argued:

> It is not true that there was no response to the Prime Minister's invitation. There was a response, but he ignored it . . . The gravest of the grave charges to which the Government has laid itself open is that of not having sought, fairly and honestly, to enlist on the side of peace in Ireland the great bulk of Irish opinion that abhors murder.[28]

At the 6 December meeting in which the Cabinet approved the wider application of martial law in Ireland, the prospect for establishing peace feelers with Sinn Féin resurfaced. Attention was drawn to 'communications which had been published in the newspapers from more or less responsible Irish quarters, in favour of approaches to a peaceful settlement of affairs in Ireland'.[29] One such communication cited was a telegram from Fr Michael O'Flanagan, the Acting Secretary of Sinn Féin during Arthur Griffith's imprisonment, to the British Government, which in part stated: 'You state that you are willing to make peace at once without waiting for Christmas. Ireland is also willing. What first steps do you propose?'[30]

O'Flanagan's statement provided the senior civil servants at Dublin Castle with a further basis for cultivating contacts with Sinn Féin; his comments were seen as having had Sinn Féin's approval. The British Government in December also placed particular emphasis on the resolution passed by the Galway County Council calling on Dáil Éireann to seek a truce.[31] The body's action was in fact a source of indignation for Michael Collins and for others within both the Dáil Cabinet and the IRA's General Headquarters staff, who held that the guerrilla war should continue. At the same time, Fr O'Flanagan's efforts resulted in a decision by British officials to engage Arthur Griffith in a dialogue aimed at reaching moderate Sinn Féin opinion. Griffith, then in Mountjoy Prison, was in fact provided with special facilities wherein he could meet with visitors acting as peace emissaries.[32]

In December, the Most Reverend Patrick Clune, Catholic Archbishop of Australia,* travelled to Dublin, with the apparent encouragement of Lloyd George, on a peace mission, where he met with Arthur Griffith and Michael

---

* Archbishop Clune, an Irish native, had an additional personal interest in the Irish situation. He was the uncle of Peadar Clune, a politically uninvolved young man who was killed in cold blood by British authorities inside the walls of Dublin Castle on the evening of Bloody Sunday in November 1920.

Collins. In January 1921 Eamon de Valera returned to Ireland from his eighteen months of activity in the United States. Although high on the British Government's wanted list as President of the Irish Republic, the Cabinet ordered its officials in Ireland not to arrest him.[33] But while Lloyd George seemed interested at this time in pursuing the discussion route, he made it clear to Sir Hamar Greenwood that a truce would be required if discussions were to take place – one that would have to include an 'undertaking (by IRA leaders) that no new murders would be committed'.[34]

At the same time, an interest in discussion was still evident on the Irish Republican side, as witnessed by the January meeting of the Dáil Éireann, where de Valera called for an 'easing off' by the IRA on the enemy. De Valera's proposal was rejected, however, underscoring the persistent difficulty during the Anglo-Irish War that Sinn Féin civilian authorities had in exerting control over the military side. Among his strongest opponents was Michael Collins – a situation of the utmost irony, given the way events were to play out. Yet Collins himself was critical afterwards of the failure of the Republican leaders to seize the opportunity for a truce in December 1920. In what remains one of the few published accounts of his comments on that subject, he told an American journalist what his view had been at that time:

> A truce would have been obtained after the burning of Cork by the forces of the Crown in December, 1920, had our own leaders acted with discretion. There is every reason to believe that the British Government was minded to respond favourably to the endeavours of Archbishop Clune ... but the English attitude hardened through the too precipitate action of certain of our public men and public bodies.[35]

While Collins did not cite the public men and the public bodies by name, it is evident that he was referring directly to de Valera's own actions in the Dáil and the votes taken by a number of county councils in favour of negotiations with Britain. According to Collins:

> Several of our most important men gave evidence of an over-keen desire to peace, while proposals were being made and considered. So it was that, although terms of the truce had been virtually agreed upon, the British statesmen abruptly terminated the negotiations when they discovered what they took to be signs of weakness in our councils. They conditioned the truce, then, on surrender of our arms; and the struggle went on.[36]

While Dublin Castle sought to build an avenue to negotiations, the British military and Dublin police endeavoured to capture Michael Collins. On 16 December a block of houses in the vicinity of the Four Courts was completely cordoned off during the night. A memorandum from the Irish Executive's propagandist, Basil Clarke, to his opposite number in London, C. J. C. Street, describes the attempt: 'At dawn, other troops arrived and a stolid house to house search by an advancing party began. Object: Michael Collins and other extremists. Operation may last two days or more. Meanwhile, no one goes in or out of isolated area. Two brigades and police on street which may yield nothing or may develop into shooting match at any moment'.[37] But Collins continued to avoid the British dragnet.

The desire to apprehend Collins on the British Government's part was well placed. In addition to serving as the IRA's Director of Intelligence, overseeing the virtual destruction of the British intelligence system in Ireland, he was also, as previously noted, the architect of the Dáil loan effort as the Republican Government's Minister of Finance. A measure of Collins' financial acumen in other areas was manifested in a 31 December report he submitted to Dáil Éireann, entitled 'A Statement of Receipts and Expenditures for the Half Year 1st May 1920 to 31st December 1920'.[38] In his report, which recorded amounts down to the penny, Collins said: 'It will be noted that the total receipts for all sources allowing for accrued interest, refunds and transfers from the USA amounted to £335,115:15:0, while the gross expenditures amounted to £51,905:17:7, and excess of receipts over expenditures of £282,149:18:5, which adds to the amount of £176,637:10:10 brought into accounts making a total gross amount expended at that date of £459,787'. Collins' report noted that during the month of November 1920 some £29,805 had arrived from the United States. In effect, he had shown himself to be as important to the Dáil Government's ability to operate as he was to the IRA's viability.

Nonetheless, circumstances were combining at this time which evidenced greater effectiveness on the part of the Crown's Forces, particularly in Dublin. It made life for Collins and his colleagues all the more precarious. A note by him on 21 January to a contact connected with the Dáil Loan in Mid-Cork on the proper placement of loan receipts serves to underscore the burdens which the Republican Government and those who served it were under at this time: 'I have a large number of Loan receipts and I am at a loss to know where I should send them. Most of the people with whom I was in touch during the time of the Loan activity are now either dead or in jail'.[39]

In the meantime, while the British Government saw Fr Michael O'Flanagan as someone with whom possible dialogue could be initiated, it also made a point of monitoring his activities. An intelligence report by the Superintendent of the London Metropolitan Police covering a visit by the cleric to London on 5 January 1921 provides a case in point:

He arrived by the Irish Mail train at Euston Station at 6:05 p.m. It was not seen who left the train with him, but he was accompanied to the Russell Hotel, Russell Square, by Mr Justice Connell and another man who I think was Mr MacDonnell, the Irish solicitor. Another Reverend gentleman accompanied them in the cab but did not live at the Russell Hotel. The driver was instructed to take him to the Imperial Hotel, Russell Square. I understand that Mr Justice Connell arrived at the hotel on the 4th instant and was occupying Room 608. The Reverend O'Flanagan has been allotted Room 332. All three went upstairs for about thirty minutes and then the one who I think is MacDonnell left and entered a taxi-cab. He directed the driver to go to Whitehall and said 'I will give you the address when we get there'. A few minutes later the Rev. O'Flanagan and his other companion left. The observation will be resumed at 8 a.m. tomorrow and any information regarding persons visiting the Rev. O'Flanagan will be immediately submitted.[40]

While monitoring Fr O'Flanagan, Dublin Castle at the same time exchanged communications with him, using Lord Justice O'Connor as an intermediary. On 26 January Sir Hamar Greenwood forwarded to Lloyd George proposed terms for an initial meeting involving President de Valera and Fr O'Flanagan himself. Greenwood noted that 'either or both will come with written authority to negotiate on behalf of the Dáil Éireann'.[41] The memorandum which O'Flanagan submitted to the British Government, stated:

(1) Representatives of Dáil Éireann with authority to negotiate to meet representatives and the British Government with similar authority.
(2) No conditions of settlement accepted or excluded as a preliminary condition to the meeting.
(3) The negotiations to take place under such circumstances as not to give an opportunity to the extreme press to destroy their chances of success.
Note: I suggest as a means of securing this last object that the meeting take place in Paris during the visit of the P.M.[42]

Despite this initiative, Greenwood cautioned the Prime Minister against altering the Government's course in Ireland. He contended that the Government of Ireland Act should be afforded the chance of full implementation.

O'Connor is going to London tonight to see Carson or Craig to find out if they will agree to fiscal autonomy after the Act is in operation. O'Connor says he thinks the Sinn Féiners will work the Act if fiscal autonomy is promised after the Act is in operation. O'Connor says he is also trying to get his Hierarchy to come out to condemn murder. He also said that Michael Collins was getting anxious for peace.[43]

Greenwood argued that Lloyd George ought not see de Valera yet at any rate. 'You will be suspect by your best supporters and in my opinion, de Valera cannot stop the murder gang', he wrote. 'Everything is moving our way,' he argued, 'which is the way desired by the vast majority of the Irish people.' At the same time, he held that 'The question of seeing O'Flanagan is different. On balance I should put it off a bit.' Greenwood also outlined a set of specific reasons for holding off negotiations with Sinn Féin at this point.

I urge you not to be rushed into negotiations that are certain at this stage to be abortive. Leave things to me. I'm here on the spot and can see O'Connor every day. He is most anxious for peace. So am I, but the gunmen are still at large, though fewer in number every day. Macready admits all police are much better. This is praise indeed! Discipline is enforced with vigour. The different Courts are functioning again. Jurors are again coming up in numbers. The Sinn Féin court doesn't exist. Rent is being paid that has been in arrears since 1914.[44]

While the Chief Secretary succeeded in thwarting the desire of some in the Cabinet for negotiations with Sinn Féin, a recognition that, as an instrument for an Irish settlement, the Government of Ireland Act (1920) amounted to too little, too late, was clear as early as February 1921 to one of the principle advisors to the Prime Minister and the Cabinet on the Irish situation, J. T. Davies. The seemingly unalterable electoral strength of Sinn Féin as the voice of nationalist Ireland rendered this particularly the case. The Southern Parliament provided for by the Act was simply unacceptable to Sinn Féin. Nonetheless, apparently aware of an increasing belief by a majority within Sinn Féin that the Republic would not be recognised by Britain, certain of the imperatives behind the Government of Ireland Act, namely, the imposition of partition and the maintenance of Southern Ireland within the Empire, Davies provided the Irish Situation Committee with some telling observations behind what he saw in February 1921 as the reasons why a majority in Sinn Féin would accept partition.

1. The Nationalist case against Partition which in 1914 was supported by the predominant political party in Great Britain is now deprived of all effective support in that country.
2. The political and religious animosities in Ulster are much stronger today than in 1914 when an appreciable minority of the professed Unionists of Ulster were known to be very doubtful adherents of the Covenant policy, and to be as averse to Partition as were their fellow countrymen of the South.
3. The Act has placed Protestants of Ulster in Statutory possession of the right to exclusion, and the whole strength of the Imperial Government is behind them in their determination to exercise that right.
4. Southern Ireland as represented of its own choice by the Sinn Féin organisation has fallen upon evil days and can therefore accept terms dictated to it by the Imperial Government without sacrifice of principle.

For Davies, the last reason was the decisive one. He believed that the acceptance of partition by Sinn Féin's representatives was now likely, while six months previously it would have wrecked the party 'as completely as its acceptance would have wrecked the [Irish] Parliamentary Party in 1914'. On that basis, he offered the view that Sinn Féin was now in a position to negotiate a settlement with the Government that was in fact predicated on the two essentials of the Government of Ireland Act (1920): 'the unimpaired integrity of the Empire and the exclusion of Northeast Ulster'.[45]

To a great extent we can see that, ten full months before an Anglo-Irish Treaty was negotiated, Davies held a fairly accurate sense of what a majority in Sinn Féin could actually accept. We may also see that partition was a reality well before the December 1921 Anglo-Irish Treaty document was signed in London. The guarantee of British Government support for the partition provision was seen at an early stage as an incentive for Northeast Ulster Unionists to remain outside any entity resembling a united Ireland. In a subsequent chapter the process leading up to the Treaty and its actual negotiation will be discussed at greater length.

Apparently out of a desire to quell any public impression that Sinn Féin had been overcome by a sense of desperation, on 15 February 1921, Eamon de Valera issued a report of a private session of the Dáil from January in which the question of a possible truce was discussed. The report included reference to discussions which both sides had had in December with Archbishop Clune. The document is useful in outlining Dáil Éireann's view as to why a truce was not reached in January 1921:

> On December 1st, perturbed at the effect on world opinion of his unrestricted Black and Tan warfare upon the Irish people, the British Premier commissioned the Archbishop of Perth to come to Ireland as an official intermediary 'to arrange a truce'. His Grace accepted the commission, came and had interviews with the Acting President, with the Minister of Finance and others … The attitude of Mr Lloyd George seemed to have changed somewhat during the week. He had before him the document that emanated from six of the thirty-two members of the Galway County Council – that document was passed on the world as a resolution of the Council, 'quite unanimously' as Mr George handsomely appended, and also Fr O'Flanagan's telegram – both of which he believed, or pretended to believe, were indications of a general break-up of the morale of the Irish people and a cry for 'peace at any price.' In his speech on December 10th in the British House of Commons, he flourished as you remember, these signs, as he chose to regard them, of our demoralisation, and outlined his plan for the victorious final assault.[46]

The Dáil report then went on to describe Archbishop Clune's return visit in mid December to meet with Arthur Griffith, among others. On 16 December Sinn Féin submitted terms for a truce through the Archbishop to Dublin Castle. In it, they proposed that during such a truce the British side would conduct 'no raids, arrests, pursuits, burnings, shootings, lootings, demolition, courts martial or other acts of violence'. For their part, Sinn Féin agreed likewise to refrain from acts of violence or provocation. The objective stated was to create 'an atmosphere favourable to the [British Government] meeting together with the representative of the Irish people with a view to bringing about a permanent peace'.[47]

On 17 December Dublin Castle conveyed its acceptance of this approach, but in Dáil Éireann's view 'added the impossible condition that we should surrender our arms and leave ourselves without any means of resistance or of defense'.[48] Archbishop Clune sought earnestly to get the British Government to delete this requirement. On 31 December he was informed that the Government would make no such concession. And so the undertaking of Archbishop Clune ended on the rocks.[49] But according to notes kept by Tom Jones, as the Cabinet's Secretary, the Government's decision to go no further had, in fact, been reached one week earlier. Lloyd George's attitude had been shaped, according to Jones, by a British Labour Commission which had visited Ireland at that time headed by Arthur Henderson and William Adamson. Jones stated that it had been Archbishop Clune's view that 'of all the "Irish leaders" he had met, he found Michael Collins the only one with whom business could be done'. In Jones' estimate, it was the Archbishop's view that Collins 'desired peace, but the main obstacle was the handing over of arms'. It is noteworthy that Clune's assessment ran contrary to Collins' public position of opposition to a truce at this time.

But Jones' record of 24 December 1920 also reveals concerns with the Cabinet over its Irish policy, including the fear of possible American intervention should the situation deteriorate further, along with fears over the 'danger of trouble' between the RIC and the British Army. The decision to expedite the implementation of the Government of Ireland Act also appears to have taken root at this session, which in turn led to the conclusion that approaches to Sinn Féin should be suspended until the Act was operational. The Government's plans for holding elections early in the following year were tied to how the military situation was being handled. This was also underscored by Tom Jones' comment that 'the character of such an election would be largely determined by the conduct in the meantime of the military and police forces in Ireland'.[50]

At the conclusion of the meeting, the Cabinet agreed to another session on Ireland the following week, with General Macready, Sir John Anderson, General Tudor and General Boyd in attendance. Macready and Tudor, of course, represented the military and police in Ireland. It is unfortunate for the historical record that Jones did not attend that meeting. His next entry concerning Ireland covered a meeting of 30 January. The intervening period had seen an expansion of the policy of coercion in Ireland. Martial law was extended to Counties Clare, Kilkenny, Waterford and Wexford. In all, nine counties along with Dublin City were included in the martial law area. In addition, the commencement of an officially sanctioned policy of reprisals, combined with the introduction of the death penalty for the harbouring of IRA men, also served to show that the Crown still saw force as its main device for leveraging a state of peace in the land that was its first colony. It is probable that the policy of authorised reprisals would have been implemented earlier but for the US Presidential election held the previous November.[51] January 1921 was also the month in which General Macready sanctioned the destruction of houses owned by individuals found guilty of rebelling or aiding those acting against the Crown.[52]

The Cabinet's 30 January meeting focused on whether the Prime Minister should meet with Eamon de Valera. The view expressed by Sir Hamar Greenwood in opposition to such a meeting is seen from the record as not entirely in keeping with how Lloyd George saw things, although the Irish Secretary's position on maximising the use of force still carried the day. The meeting is one of the most significant in providing insight into the Cabinet's policy towards Ireland and in understanding the attitude of some of its principals towards the Irish. What follows is an extract of Tom Jones' account of the proceedings:

> Prime Minister: I have a letter somewhere from de Valera ... He wants to come and see me secretly. Hamar Greenwood is against his coming. I am not sure that we ought not to see him. After all, we have said repeatedly that we would see anyone who could deliver the goods. O'Flanagan could not do that. Miss Stevenson* produced a letter from Lady Hamar Greenwood to herself in which it was quite plain that while protesting her neutrality, she was keen that the P.M. should see de Valera. She said that de Valera wanted a 'face-saver,' that he was willing to drop the Republic and even fiscal autonomy if that could be done.
>
> Bonar Law: Tried to put the subject off, but the P.M. persisted.
>
> Prime Minister: Auckland Geddes gives a most gloomy account of the situation in America and in the interests of peace with America I think we ought to see de Valera and try to get a settlement.
>
> Bonar Law: Eric Geddes once told me that Auckland is apt to be panicky and that what he says ought to be taken with a grain of salt.
>
> Prime Minister: If we take it with a salt cellarful it is still sufficiently serious. Jeudine† says it will take 12 months to put our present policy through.
>
> Bonar Law: This is also Macready's view.
>
> Prime Minister: That is a long time. If we could settle quickly it might clear up our American debt. I have all sorts of other reactions.
>
> Bonar Law: Macready tells me that Michael Collins is quite definitely responsible for the murders but that he does not at all regard himself as a murderer.
>
> I then said something about these men being idealists who were laying down their lives for what they considered a great cause and that they had put up a wonderful fight and that there had never been anything quite like it before.

* Then Lloyd George's mistress/secretary and later his second wife.
† General Jeudine at this time was the British Military Commander in the Midlands of Ireland and Connacht.

Bonar Law: I do not agree. I looked up Macauley's account of the O'Connell period and it was very much the same thing as now.

Prime Minister: Said he had been very much impressed with O'Flanagan's personality.

At 10:15 Bonar Law and the rest of us got up to leave, postponing the Irish business till the next morning when de Valera's letter would be available. (On the following morning Prime Minister, Bonar Law and Carson were closeted together.) Coming along the passage with Bonar Law, I told him I felt intensely about the Irish business and that the ghastly things that were being done were enough to drive one to join the Republican Army. [*sic*] In effect, his answer was that coercion was the only policy: that in the past it had been followed by periods of quiet for about ten years; that that was the most we could hope for from the present repressions, and that he had come to the conclusion 'that the Irish were an inferior race'.[53]

The continued acts of reprisal carried out in Britain's name by the Black and Tans and the RIC, with apparent official sanction, did little to engender the support of Irish opinion. Evidence that his Government's policy of fighting terror with counter-terror had backfired was made clear in a letter of 25 February 1921 from the Prime Minister to Sir Hamar Greenwood. In it, Lloyd George made clear his concern with 'the state of discipline of the Royal Irish Constabulary and its auxiliary force'. The scope and credibility of the reports left him in little doubt that 'the charges of drunkenness, looting and other acts of undiscipline are in too many cases substantially true'. While Lloyd George expressed his sympathy with the difficulties under which the men operated, he emphasised to Greenwood that it was 'vital that the violence and indiscipline, which undoubtedly characterize certain units of the RIC should be terminated in the most prompt and drastic manner'. Foremost in his mind was the concern that the indiscipline cited was largely serving to alienate public opinion in Britain and Ireland alike.[54]

One on the Sinn Féin side who believed that Lloyd George recognised the need for a change in policy by this time was Michael Collins. 'I have always believed', Collins stated, 'that Mr Lloyd George foresaw the inevitable at least a year before his colleagues even considered the possibility of granting Irish freedom'.[55] Collins based his assessment on Lloyd George's impetus for the passage by Parliament of the Government of Ireland Act (1920).

In my opinion, Mr Lloyd George intended the Act to allay world criticism. As propaganda, it might do to draw attention away from British violence for a month or two longer. At the end of that period, most of the English Ministers mistakenly believed Ireland would have been terrorised into submission.[56]

Collins' assessment is also borne out by an account by W. E. Wylie, who was Law Advisor to the Dublin Castle regime. Through the intervention of General Macready, Wylie went to England in the summer of 1920 for a private meeting with Lloyd George. The purpose? To impress upon the Prime Minister the view that a reconquest of Ireland was impossible.

> I spent two hours with him after lunch and expounded my views, which were that a settlement must be made. Macready's plan and mine was that the British Parliament should put on the statute book a measure of complete Dominion Home Rule for Ireland patterned on Canada, but not a Republic.[57]

While Lloyd George expressed agreement with Wylie's analysis, he emphasised that as the head of a coalition his problem was with his Conservative partners, most notably Bonar Law. Following a meeting with Bonar Law arranged for him by Lloyd George, a private but nonetheless dramatic exchange occurred between the two. Upon being told by the Prime Minister that he refused to 'break the coalition for Ireland', Wylie responded: 'Ireland will break the Coalition and more than the coalition'.[58] Within months, a despondent Wylie resigned his post in protest.

While the Coalition Government continued to hold out hopes for a military victory, the IRA also persisted with its own violent campaign. The extent to which the IRA intelligence apparatus overseen by Michael Collins featured in the tactics employed at the local level is made evident by a training report issued by Emmet Dalton as Director of Training in January 1921. Dalton began his lengthy communication to the IRA Brigade and Divisional heads by quoting from a captured report of General Strickland to Dublin Castle: 'The rebels during the past months have been very active. They are concentrating in larger numbers than they have been doing up until now, our training must therefore be adapted to searching out their parties by scouting and attacking them vigorously wherever they are found'.[59] Strickland's comments were used by General Headquarters to lay heavy emphasis on the need to avoid complacency within the ranks and also to alert IRA Brigade Commanders to an impending change in British military tactics. To Emmet Dalton, the General's statement held a special meaning. His remarks to the Brigade Commanders also demonstrate the direct bearing of an effective intelligence gathering network in the IRA's structure and tactics in the fighting district:

> This extract has a very important bearing on the management of our active service units. These units are not exactly a standing force of shock troops, they are also training units and it is this that is their most important function. Even on active service only a very small proportion of a soldier's time is spent in actual fighting; as much as possible of it must be devoted to actual training. This is the case with our active service units more than with troops pursuing a regular system; to a great extent they are Officers Training Corps on active service. In every area where an active service unit exists, every officer in that

area should spend a period of service with it. When all the officers have been passed through the unit all the N.C.O.'s must be similarly passed through it, and after them, the best men of the rank-and-file. In this case we can count on with entire safety a uniform standard of command, and a high and workmanlike standard at that.[60]

As a specific remedy to General Strickland's plan for 'searching out' the IRA's active service units 'and attacking them vigorously wherever they are found', Dalton said, 'there is an answer to this, for which it is not too difficult to find and practice effectively'.[61] He emphasised 'ever increasing attention to training in protection and patrol fighting'. 'Up to the present', he continued, 'our troops have uniformly proved superior to the enemy forces in this type of fighting, so that preserving suitable vigilance and care should be able to drive off the enemy patrols and blind his forces, leaving them unable to act with effect.' Dalton was also explicit as to what the real role of the active service unit was. Based on his own military training, he was in a position to reiterate the importance of a rigid adherence to the chain of command.

They [the active service units] are as large as can conveniently be trained and supervised by an officer under A. S. conditions. They are also large enough to take care of themselves in all ordinary circumstances. But they are not and were never meant to be suitable for operations on a mass scale. Hardiness and mobility should be their characteristic marks and in dealing with their transport and supply the need for mobility must be steadily kept in mind. 'Everywhere, all the time, but nowhere at a given moment.' That must always be the motto. Within each active service unit it is most important to preserve proper subordination of command, and thus proper internal discipline ... The only sound method is to observe existing seniority ... For example: a Lieutenant should not be in a position to give orders to a captain or a captain to give orders to his commandant.[62]

Dalton argued that the officer 'must have every chance of practicing command and assuming responsibility; he can never get this unless he takes charge'. Subsequent training memoranda dealt respectively with the most effective use of the semi-automatic weapon much favoured by the IRA, the parabellum, and the need for improved scouting techniques. 'Scouts', Directive No. 13 stated, 'should be on the watch for movements, changes and contrasts ... or unnatural objects ... signs of the enemy in dust or smoke'. The glint on a clear outline of such objects 'as the barrel of a rifle or a helmet was another item the scout was encouraged to look for'. The parabellum, another training memorandum reminded the Brigade Commanders, was 'sighted to 800 metres (practically 800 yards) [sic] and has a flat trajectory up to 100 metres'. Then followed what were termed 'full instructions for use, including holding, stripping, receiver, reassembly, etc'.[63]

It is noteworthy that of the men that Collins elevated to the top of the IRA during his time as Director of Organisation, Michael Brennan, John Prout, J. J. 'Ginger' O'Connell, and Emmett Dalton, three of the four had had prior experience in either the British or American Armies. In effect he added a level of experience and a penchant for organisation that would have otherwise been sorely lacking with the Irish independence struggle. The level of military organisation shown by the IRA at this time was also noticed by the American Consul in Dublin, Charles Dumont. In a report of 22 March 1921 to the State Department, the diplomat noted that the 'Irish Republican Army have become much improved. He enclosed IRA orders, presumably intercepted by British Intelligence, 'which would indicate a fair measure of military organisation on the part of the insurgents'.[64] The digest of Dumont's analysis of the overall political and economic situation in Ireland at the time is also useful in giving a somewhat impartial account of the overall situation in Ireland:

> Economic: Irish Trade is suffering from the general depression and also from sabotage. The country is just beginning to feel this.
> Financial: It is not believed that Sinn Féin finances will hold out more than another 12 months. British forces in Ireland are reduced to less than 45,000 including the police. General Macready states 100,000 are needed to quiet the country but are unavailable. He pins his hope on the exhaustion of the revolutionary funds.
> Conclusion: Except for the extremists the differences of opinion between Lloyd George and Sinn Féin are not great. The power of de Valera is only nominal and Sinn Féin leaders cannot agree among themselves. Irish fighting has been done mainly by the extremists [sic] faction which is in the hands of three or four men in Ireland . . .[65]

One month later, the diplomat forwarded to his superiors a report which focused totally on the IRA's guerrilla warfare campaign during March and early April 1921. He painted a vivid picture of the scale of events, which included ambushes of police and military personnel in Counties Kerry and Cork, and also Dublin City.

> The most notable ambushes which have taken place during the period under review were those of Headford Junction, Roscarberry, and Harcourt Street Station, Dublin. A train containing an officer and 29 men of the British Army, pulling into the Headford Junction Station, County Kerry, was heavily fired upon from both sides of a steep cutting, losing in a fight which lasted an hour the officer and 8 men killed and 10 wounded. Only the arrival of reinforcements prevented the wiping out of the entire force, when the attackers, numbering nearly 150 men, withdrew. One civilian passenger was killed and two wounded. The balance escaped injury by throwing themselves flat on the floor of the cars, remaining there until the attack was over. The lives of many more civilians would have been lost had not the troops detrained and fought from the open. The attack at Roscarberry was made on the Police Barracks. After a desperate defence in which 3 were killed and 11 wounded,

lasting from 2 a.m. to 7 a.m., the few survivors effected their escape through an open window at a time when the building was almost consumed by fire. On April 6th at dusk, a military lorry containing troops was bombed and fired at while passing the Harcourt Street Railway Station in Dublin by Sinn Féin forces in plain clothes. Great numbers of pedestrians were passing on the street at the time of the attack. The attackers used the great stone columns of the station for cover. The soldiers opened fire at once, killing two of the attackers and wounding one, who has since died. Only the officer in command of the British troops was injured.[66]

Dumont stated that 'the bombing of military and police lorries is of daily occurrence in Dublin'. But given the level of protection the lorries enjoyed, it produced a situation in which 'the bombs, glancing off the sides or roofs of the lorries, explode in the crowded streets, injuring or killing passersby or their throwers'.[67] Relying on both British and Sinn Féin information, the US Consul then presented a view of the military scene in Ireland that was openly at odds with the official British version of events. It is an account that showed a clear astuteness on the diplomat's part.

> While ambushes during the period under review have been more and more frequent all over Ireland, the Flying Columns of the Irish Republican Army have been singularly unsuccessful during the time mentioned, if results are considered. The casualties to the British Forces are less and less in proportion to the number of men engaged and the number of ambushes. The British, in their confidential reports to London, attribute this to a deterioration in morale of Republican Flying Columns, stating that the novelty of continuous active service is wearing off in the latter and that the effect of hardships and casualties is being severely felt. I do not agree with the British in this opinion. The fact that the number of ambushes is increasing, while at the same time the number of men engaged also increases, argues that the falling off in British casualties is due to better care and organisation on the part of the British in order to meet such attacks, and to the improvement in their Intelligence Service. Sinn Féin Flying Columns have been unusually active, especially in the Province of Munster. In that Province, particularly North and West of Cork and in the immediate vicinity of the city, the Republican forces, in their efforts to impede the transit of lorries containing British troops and Police, have almost destroyed the public roads; tearing down walls, blowing up bridges, cutting down trees, etc., and, to stop the movement of troops, police and supplies by train, have torn up rails, rolled great rocks on the tracks, destroyed telegraph and telephone wires, signals, etc.[68]

Dumont also provided his government with figures showing the impact of the IRA campaign as of 11 April 1921, based on statistics compiled by the British authorities:

Courthouses destroyed, 74
Police Barracks destroyed, 537

Police Barracks damaged, 246
Raids for arms, 9,196
Policemen killed, 276
Policemen wounded, 456
Soldiers killed, 99
Soldiers wounded, 216

Somewhat sardonically, Dumont stated, 'it would be interesting if Dublin Castle gave out the number of houses and buildings destroyed in official and unauthorised reprisals executed by the British forces but this is most unlikely to be done'.[69] He noted a claim made by Sinn Féin that some 2,000 private homes had been put to the torch by British reprisals.

But there were also instances that evidenced less atavistic impulses. Todd Andrews, who had served in the IRA's Dublin Brigade, relates an episode he witnessed involving a fellow prisoner after the two of them had been released abruptly from Mountjoy Jail in the Spring of 1920 in the midst of a mass hunger strike. His colleague, an Ulsterman, arrived with him to a hero's welcome at the Mater Hospital, where they were taken for recovery from their protest. Andrews described the other man as possessing a 'magnificent head of titian red hair'. 'His beard, of the same colour, was beautifully trimmed', Andrews added, 'and his large brown languid eyes expressed fortitude, compassion and sadness'. 'He could well have been a model for a statue of the Sacred Heart', he noted. Later that evening, Andrews bore witness to a less than saintly performance by his colleague.

> I must have been asleep for a couple of hours when I was awakened by some noises coming from the bed next to me ... My Christ-like companion ... a leader of the hunger strike, had succeeded against, it must be said, mere token resistance in pulling one of the nurses on to his bed.[70]

A raid on the house of IRA Chief of Staff Richard Mulcahy in March 1921 resulted in one of the most significant seizures up to that point by the British of IRA documents. Included in the files was a listing of individuals targeted for assassination by the IRA, along with plans for the large-scale poisoning of British troops, and the blowing up of the canal at Manchester.[71] The raid on Mulcahy's residence was made possible by the work of Brigadier General Sir Ormonde de L'Epee Winter, who in 1920 was given the task of overseeing the Crown's intelligence apparatus in Ireland as its single director. Winter operated under the code name 'O'. Despite possessing no previous experience at intelligence gathering on a full-time basis, he nonetheless set about reorganising the shambles that British intelligence in Ireland had become.[72] The raid on Mulcahy's office was indeed an important breakthrough. In a 5 March 1921 entry in his diary, Mark Sturgis noted that 'O says that the last capture of the Mulcahy documents shows a really big determined and fairly well organised conspiracy.' 'The only thing he liked in them', Sturgis noted, 'was the issue of orders to the IRA to attack in large numbers as small ambushes had been a failure.'[73]

While orders were issued from General Headquarters to local IRA divisional Brigade Commanders in the field, and reports in turn submitted back to Dublin, communications between the two were often sporadic at best. This situation, compounded by the part-time nature of the role of Minister of Defence as performed by Cathal Brugha, is vividly described by Ernie O'Malley.

> Brugha ... did not know the senior officers well. He worked as a traveller while his deputy was paid his salary. That desire to work without pay was understandable, but his position as Minister of Defence needed all his energies. Many members of the G.H.Q. staff did not know the country. They could add to their knowledge by talking with T.D.'s, but few of them knew the tides of our military effort. H.Q. staff had ceased to inspect the country; only by inspection and by actual touch with men on their own ground could a complete idea of the senior officers, their difficulties and drawbacks be properly appreciated.[74]

Despite official British claims that new patrol tactics by the government forces had made a serious dent in the activities of the IRA, the casualties that Britain incurred in Ireland for the first four months of 1921 suggest that the year was likely to be even more costly than the previous one. The year 1920 saw a total of 182 Royal Constabulary members and 57 soldiers killed in Ireland, with 251 police and 118 soldiers wounded, while the period between January and April 1921 alone saw 94 police officers and 45 soldiers lose their lives as the result of IRA activity. Yet the figures were also comparatively high for the IRA and Irish civilians alike during this latter period, with 317 dead and 285 wounded.[75]

The decision of the British Government to keep the emphasis on a military solution persisted into the Spring of 1921. It continued as a source of frustration to its senior Civil Servants at Dublin Castle. Anderson, Cope and Sturgis all believed that their Government did not fully grasp the risks inherent in pursuing their course.[76] Their situation was made more awkward by the fact that the Chief Secretary for Ireland, Sir Hamar Greenwood, was among the Cabinet's most aggressive advocates of the use of force as the way to pacification. In a diary passage that is one of the most prescient comments by a British official during the Anglo-Irish conflict, Mark Sturgis remarked: 'I can't help being uneasy that we are not taking a big enough view of the position ... Not only the future of the Irish is at stake but the future relations of the two countries which must ever live side by side and there is much talk as if we had nothing to do but beat the enemy.'[77]

Sturgis's diary is also peppered with descriptions of people and events that are in some cases provocative, while puzzling in others, particularly as they relate to the efforts by him and his colleagues to establish contact with credible figures in Sinn Féin. Writing of the Sinn Féin leadership on 16 February 1921 Sturgis remarked that 'above all, they distrust themselves'. On that date he described his fellow civil servant at Dublin Castle and would-be peacemaker Andy Cope as 'a queer sensitive old thing'. 'He was up to the neck in all this from the start,' Sturgis wrote, 'and he is, I think, jealous of the Lady's hand in the game and perhaps of mine too.' The Lady referred to by Sturgis in his 16 February entry was in fact Lady Margery Greenwood, wife of then British Chief Secretary Sir Hamar Greenwood. Her judgement was in fact held in high regard by Lloyd George and her contact with the Prime Minister even included her forwarding private recommendations from Sturgis to Lloyd George directly.[78]

Curiously, at this time Sturgis also referred to Michael Collins as 'Michael' with an implied familiarity that remains unclear, particularly since it marks only instances in his diary in which a prominent Irish rebel leader's Christian name is so used. The reference was made within the context of a description of a conversation he had with Fr O'Flanagan: 'If a big wig got killed, any such accident which might happen any day would blow peace to blazes. "Yes" said O'Flanagan, "on either side." I suppose he was thinking of Michael.'[79]

Sturgis' references to Collins in his diary also spanned the prurient as it also did, it would appear, for the senior intelligence officials tracking the IRA leader's movement. In another city, still referring to Collins as 'Michael', he related these findings by Sir Ormonde Winter, the head of British Intelligence in Ireland:

> 'O' [Ormond Winter] is on the track of Michael – he was musing about a report he wanted to send to the Under Secretary but couldn't as it would have said that Michael slept with a girl, address known, once a week, and that he shrank from dictating to his chaste female shorthand writer. So he had to give his news by word of mouth.

Such references to Collins by a senior Dublin Castle official using only the name 'Michael' no doubt add to the aspersions as to Collins' loyalties levelled by some Republican irredentists after his death. Whether in fact Collins at this time had any direct contact with Lady Greenwood is unclear. Nonetheless he did have access to a number of titled ladies who would have been in her circle, most notably Lady Hazel Lavery, wife of painter Sir John Lavery, with whom he was romantically linked, an impression she also apparently sought earnestly to promote. And also Moya Llewelyn-Davies, the young Irish-born wife of Crompton Llewelyn-Davies, Crown Solicitor for the British Postal System, and a personal friend of Lloyd George. She was also the daughter of James O'Connor, the former Irish Party MP who was then working with Dublin Castle on the prospects of a truce with Sinn Féin. Moya Llewelyn-Davies appears to have had a friendship with Collins dating back to

Christmas 1918. One account describes her as having hosted a reception for Collins and others in the Sinn Féin delegation, who visited London in 1919 in the hope of a meeting with President Woodrow Wilson, then en route to the Paris Peace Conference. By the time the reception had ended, Wilson had already left the city.[80] In Collins' defence, however, one need only surmise how the Irish Revolution would have been affected had it been without the varied talents of this undoubtedly complex individual in both the civil and armed sectors of that struggle.

Sturgis continued to reveal the level of despair he felt with Dublin Castle, noting on 5 March 1921 that he had taken to writing an anonymous letter to the *Irish Times*, titled 'An Irish Peace', in which, giving the impression he was an ordinary citizen, he urged a negotiated settlement. 'All our nerves are wearing thin', he wrote. He noted the fact that General Macready was by then also confined for security reasons to Dublin Castle.[81] It was a development that drew sarcastic comment from Collins during an interview with an American newspaperman while on the run, in which the Corkman sarcastically sent the British Commander his best wishes.[82] But 5 March was also the day on which six IRA men were executed at Victoria Barracks, Cork. Two weeks earlier, thirteen IRA men were killed in related incidents in Cork City. Reference to the level of disagreement which existed within the British Government in Ireland was shown by an occurrence described by Sturgis the following day:

> Yesterday a string of cars were ambushed near Killarney and one of Strickland's Brigadiers was killed . . . I haven't heard that we punished the enemy at all . . . How scathing Macready would be if they had been police, yet what does it matter which it was, it was us.[83]

Sturgis underlined the word 'us'. He also noted that 'Cardinal Logue in March 1921, issued condemnation of the IRA bombing and ambush campaign'.[84]

February and March 1921 indeed marked a difficult time for the Cork No. 1 Brigade. During the first of that month a total of eleven officers and men were killed by the RIC and British forces. It was evidence of how effective the Crown's forces had become by early 1921. The level of success which the British forces began to realise in the field against its enemy underscored to those possessing a level of detachment that the IRA's ability to strike at British convoys or facilities had been seriously thwarted. The combination of rigid curfews and a change in tactics that saw the British deploy their own version of the 'Flying Column' represented a clear demarcation from the state of affairs that had existed in 1920, when the IRA had been able to function with far greater fluidity.

The setback suffered by the Cork No. 2 Brigade under Liam Lynch on the Cork–Fermoy Road on 15 February 1921 offers a case in point. Instead of acting as the attackers, the IRA column became the attacked as a convoy of British auxiliaries came at the ambush party from the opposite direction. The would-be Irish ambush turned into a rout as British machine guns killed three IRA men, while eight were captured. Two of the men were later executed. The work of an informer had been suspected.[85]

Overall, the British forces had become more effective in rural areas by this time. British mobile units struck in the countryside in an effort to counter the IRA's Flying Columns. After a sweep they were picked up at a certain point by larger military bodies backed up by transport. The IRA's flow of communication in the countryside was disrupted as scouts were captured along with other IRA men.

Another measure of how lethally effective British efforts at out-manoeuvring IRA Flying Columns had become came on 21 February 1921, when a group of British auxiliaries and regular Army surrounded and attacked a Flying Column of the Cork No. 1 Brigade, killing five of them. Seven IRA men taken prisoner that day were executed afterwards.[86] That this incident happened only a week after the attack described on Cork's No. 2 Brigade underscores how severe the pressure on the IRA had become, especially in an area that was at the heart of the IRA's campaign.

The organisational and other problems which affected many of the IRA's County units and which appear to have been beyond the knowledge of the British Military and the RIC, formed the basis for a memorandum from Richard Mulcahy as Chief of Staff, issued to IRA Brigade and Divisional Commanders on 7 March 1921. Among the problems cited at the organisational level was the failure to recognise responsibility for coordination at the brigade level, together with a lack of 'good non-commissioned officers'.[87] Elsewhere in the memorandum, Mulcahy continued his criticisms of what he saw as being wrong at the organisational level:

> Intelligence: very faulty grasp generally. Neither officers, non commissioned, nor men realise its imp. [sic] Men who clamour for arms neglect this branch which they can perfect unarmed. Brigade Organisation: Vice Commandant and Quartermaster do not ... fulfil proper functions: no definite agenda to work on; set orders not issued or issued imperfectly. Too much laissez faire attitude.[88]

An analysis of the correspondence of Michael Collins as both IRA Director of Intelligence and Organisation, and Richard Mulcahy as IRA Chief of Staff, in the Spring of 1921, provides a glimpse of the situation in the field from their perspective. It also shows the level of flexibility the two men sought to maintain within the scope of the available human and material resources. On 21 March Mulcahy wrote to Collins proposing a new structure for mapping the strength of local IRA divisions:

> The numbering is simply on grounds of convenience for making an outline map. More definition as to demarcation seems desirable in the case of areas 6, 8, 12.
> 2. Tyrone, Derry
> 4. Armagh Down
> 3. Antrim, East Down, Monaghan
> 11. Offaly, Tipperary
> 12. Carlow, Kilkenny
> 13. Cork, Kerry, Waterford.[89]

Five days later Collins replied that 'It might be possible to combine numbers 2 and 3, but the Adjutant would have tremendous responsibility in the way of organising and regrouping.' 'The same applies', Collins stated, to numbers 4 and 5, 'if we can get suitable direction of the Director of Training, it would be more important, I think, to establish the engineering arm first'. Collins emphasised that 'all these instructions will have to come up a good deal at tomorrow morning's meeting'.[90] On the same day Collins replied to Mulcahy, General Headquarters also heard from Tom Barry, Commandant of the Cork No. 2 Brigade, on matters more personal in nature: 'The Brigade Commander asked me to drop you a line with regard to some acknowledgement of some kind to the relatives of volunteers killed in action or shot by the enemy. He thinks it very desirable that this be done. We have now a fairly large number of cases.' Barry alone raised the question of the possibility of 'providing for the relatives as much as necessary in an adequate way'.[91]

On 24 March Mulcahy issued a memorandum to the General Headquarters staff entitled 'The War as a Whole', in which he sought to analyse in some detail the Republican military and strategic position at that time. The document was in fact issued a few days before the capture of Sean MacEoin, a key IRA leader in the North Midlands. The manner in which Mulcahy addressed the question of resource allocation in the context of what he saw as the primary war zone is particularly significant:

> When we come to discuss ways and means, allocations of supplies, direction of effort, it is necessary to review the whole of Ireland in a sort of bird's eye view. *The War Zone*: Properly speaking, this embraces the counties of Kilkenny, Limerick, Cork and Tipperary – Cork far more than any of the others. Here the enemy has accumulated strong, numerical material resources, techniques of command and in general is executing serious military effort.[92]

Nonetheless, Mulcahy observed with a note of optimism that 'For all that, our forces are so far holding their own without danger and there is reasonable grounds to assume they can continue to do so forever.' The ability to assume a 'passive role' if necessary was also stated. Nonetheless, Mulcahy emphasised that the war zone to be outlined 'is on all grounds entitled to support of all kinds and must be kept munitioned as fully as possible'. Mulcahy added the proviso that the continuance of such a strategy was a wise one so long as it did not result in a 'serious draining of our resources or weakening our striking power elsewhere'.[93]

The strategic and political importance attached to the success that the IRA had achieved to date in Dublin was also given special emphasis by Mulcahy:

> In one vital respect, the present struggle differs from any other military attempt to obtain the independence of the country. For the first time, the national military command is securely established in Dublin ... The precise measure to be adopted for strengthening Dublin requires determined concentration but it cannot be too clearly stated that no number nor any margin of victory in any district at provincial areas have any value if Dublin is lost in a military sense.[94]

The IRA's Chief of Staff also appreciated the importance, as well as the difficulty, of exerting the maximum effort possible in Ulster at all levels. 'Ulster', he wrote, 'is the English lever for governing Ireland.' 'Here then', he argued, 'it is necessary to attack them with all the force that can be developed ... militarily, economic, propagandist and the attack should be steady and persistent.'[95] It was an attack, however, that was never fully to materialise.

A British document obtained by Collins reflecting 'increases in Civil Service for Ireland for the year ending March 31, 1921', proved a source of interest to the IRA General Headquarters. It revealed dramatic increases in British administrative expenditure in Ireland, excluding the cost of keeping its garrison there.

	June 1919–20	Est. 1920–21
RIC	£367,901	£3,402,253
DMP	29,206	335,250
Prisons	21,431	203,448
Criminal Prosecutions	5,201	69,954
Sup. Ct.	32,810	182,759
Co. Court Officers	46,811	172,722
Chief Sec. Office	109,406	189,020
Totals	£612,406	£4,555,496[96]

Collins presented this analysis of the increases:

> The last item is of particular notice. It used always to stand at about £25,000. The year previously it was suddenly increased to £79,604 [actual]. Following the rural elections in June [1920] in the interval of 14 weeks between June–Sept, 74 towns and villages were sacked and 13 murders committed.

He also offered in the report his assessment of the changes in the British security apparatus in Ireland:

> Inquests were replaced by military tribunals. But in Macready's case, the British Government had appointed a policeman who had no experience of police work ... was not in a position to administer direction of ROIR Act, which had to be administered by Macready ... and his Court of Inquiry ... at the mercy of the police administration which had taken the place of the regular RIC.[97]

Conversely, from a British vantage point, Mark Sturgis' accounts are again useful in gaining an understanding of the Irish situation as seen through the eyes of Dublin Castle at this point. Although his entries for April 1921 are without specific dates, they help in measuring the extent of the pressure exerted on the IRA through the British policy of arrest and internment. Citing figures supplied by Ormonde Winter, Sturgis wrote: 'Apart from IRA officers killed and imprisoned there are interned today: 18 Brigade Commanders; 44 Staff officers, 71 Battalion Commanders; 166 Battalion Staff Commanders; 1166 Company officers; 1479 other ranks and unknown.'[98]

On that date, Sturgis also cited US Consul Charles Dumont as having told him of Sinn Féin's willingness to seek a settlement, stating that it was 'only a question of tactics'. He also gives further indications of division in the British ranks. Describing an exchange between Greenwood and Macready, Sturgis wrote: 'I can still hear the winged words in which he stimulated the gentle Hamar to action – 'the expedition of General Headquarters – the stubborn inefficiency of the Castle'.[99]

Later, Sturgis cited a report by his colleague James MacMahon of a meeting by Dáil Éireann: 'He says that Sinn Féin leaders have had a meeting at which a large majority of moderates were for taking a settlement against an extremist minority who were for a Republic or nothing, and that the minority have accepted the majority vote. It is said that at this meeting Michael Collins spoke on neither side but said only that he would abide by the majority vote whichever way it went ...'. MacMahon's report indicated that by this time the British Government had a good sense of the direction Sinn Féin were pursuing at this time, and also on the weight they attached to Collins as a force to be reckoned with. Sturgis also made appropriate reference to the key role played by Andy Cope in the search for peace, stating that it was to him 'beyond question to whom the honours of peace would go if it really comes now'. 'Who will get the most credit is a matter of pleasing speculation,' Sturgis added, 'who ought to get it is not in doubt – Andy first, last and all the time.'[100]

In that same April entry, however, Sturgis made another reference to Michael Collins in which he referred to him as 'Michael'. Writing of how James MacMahon had made contact with a Sinn Féin source who had arranged a meeting with de Valera, Sturgis wrote: 'He was asked would he see Michael Collins and he said indeed he would not – that if Michael was arrested when he was with him both sides would call him a traitor. I asked what about the Ackerman story and MacMahon said it was exactly what Michael Collins would say to any newspaperman.'[101] What was meant by this comment remains unclear, yet it appears indicative of an awareness of the regular contact Collins was having at this time with Andy Cope. Nonetheless, the inference can be made that Sturgis and MacMahon, at least, entertained a belief that Collins deliberately chose to appear publicly as an irreconcilable hardliner, while at the same time engaging in discussions with Dublin Castle officials.

The large number of IRA officers imprisoned led the IRA command to consider various options. On 4 April 1921 Rory O'Connor, in his capacity as Director of Engineering for the Republican effort, wrote to Richard Mulcahy requesting various materials for 'Jail Deliverance'. O'Connor requested the acquisition of such accessories for potential prison breakouts as rope ladders, expansion ladders, sash cords, hacksaws, bolt-cutters and handcuffs.[102]

The attention to detail shown by General Headquarters in seeking to ensure that the maximum use of resources was achieved was also exemplified by a series of circulars issued by O'Connor. Engineering Circular No. 7, a directive issued in April 1921 covering the 'Protection of Munitions from Damp', stated:

> It has been found in some [sic] consistent basis that munitions which have to be laid several hours before being exploded have failed to explode owing to dampness. In order to ensure against this, the explosive, more particular, those of the nitre glycerine variety, e.g. gelignite, should be placed in a wooden or preferably tin box, the inside of which has been painted, modifications of this may of course be adopted, e.g. a box containing the explosive might be placed in a larger one and the space between them run with pitch, lino foil, or sheet lead might also be employed as a lining for the box.[103]

Likewise, a corresponding directive from April, 'Engineering Circular No. 8', offered detailed instructions on how to tap a telephone.[104]

That the weight of increased arrests of principal IRA men, tied to better 'policing' methods, was forcing Sinn Féin to look more seriously to the negotiating table became clear to Dublin Castle. On 17 May 1921 Sturgis noted that 'We are so near settlement, it's a jumpy time'. His diary for this date also discusses Andy Cope's report on a meeting with the representatives of Michael Collins:

> He saw the head lad from Michael Collins who agreed the killing of women was deplorable. Andy said: 'So your gunmen are out of hand.' He replied 'Individuals in our army sometimes go too far just as they do in yours.' He gave it as the view of Michael Collins that the IRA soldiers must carry on just as ours while negotiations are afoot. Then if negotiations are successful down comes the curtain.[105]

In informing General Macready of Copes' progress, Sturgis was met with this reply: 'Bless you, my children. Go and make peace if you can – I doubt you're doing it. I am but a simple soldier and you cannot expect much active help from me – but you certainly will get no hindrance.' Macready's estimate of the military situation was referred to by Sturgis in a diary entry of 19 May, in which he was characterised as saying that 'if it is to be war and not peace, he won't be properly slipped [*sic*] till the end of June – 14 days after the real setting up (or not setting up) of the Parliament – which will only give him til October for active operations'. More sobering perhaps was Sturgis' reference to the fact that Macready had already cautioned Sir Henry Wilson that the army 'cannot go through another winter campaign, but must go into winter quarters'. 'This may', he reflected, 'help London to press on for a settlement.'[106]

Later that month, Arthur Griffith and Eoin MacNeill were released from prison. In the view of the Dublin Castle Administration, the release of these two key moderates was a useful peace gesture. Sturgis wrote that 'we suggested the release of Griffith and MacNeill as a good stunt – our contribution to a free election ...'.[107]

However, a 25 May IRA attack on the Custom House in Dublin made it clear that the advocates of continued force within the Irish independence movement were more than content to keep the fight going. The attack, waged largely by the Dublin Brigade's 2nd Battalion, marked the largest armed deployment by the rebel forces since the Easter Rising. With some 200 men involved in all, the attack in retrospect might be judged to have been as foolhardy for the IRA as it was dramatic in scale. While the objective of damaging the Custom House and destroying thousands of tax records was achieved, in all the attack resulted in the loss of some seventy-five members of the Dublin Brigade due to arrests at the scene and the deaths of six others. An entry in the diary of Mark Sturgis the day after the attack noted that the structure was 'still burning this morning'. '"O" is in high glee having had a most successful raid this afternoon and cleared out Michael Collin's [*sic*] new headquarters office. Among the captured documents a letter written to M. C. [Michael Collins] saying what a bloody business it was "that we lost all those gallant fellows yesterday at the Custom House."'[108] Collins' attitude to the attack beforehand remains unclear. But given his gut reaction afterwards, the assessment offered by Dublin Brigade Commander Oscar Traynor that 'the objective we set out to accomplish has been achieved' was less than a cause for celebration.[109]

The objective for attacking the Custom House in fact dated back to the end of 1918, when the Irish Volunteers devised a plan for the building's destruction if and when the British Government imposed conscription on Ireland. Vincent Byrne, a member of the execution gang attached to Michael Collins' Intelligence Department, recalled his role in the attack and subsequent escape.

> I got a tin of petrol and proceeded to the second floor. I opened the door and sitting inside were a lady and gentleman, civil servants having tea. I requested them to leave, stating that I was going to set fire to the office. The gentleman stood up and said, 'Oh, you can't do that.' I showed him my gun and told him I was serious ... The lady then asked me if she could get her coat, and I replied: 'Miss, you'll be lucky if you get out with your life.'[110]

Byrne, like other Brigade members, was able to escape in the confusion caused by the smoke that engulfed the building and the mayhem that prevailed outside, as harried British Auxiliaries sought to round up suspects, who were indistinguishable from the rest of the population. Byrne, in fact, relied on his wits to escape from a situation in which he had been detained by joining a crowd that was being questioned by an officer.

> Now it came my turn to come before the officer. I humbly asked him: 'Could I go home now?' He looked at me and said, 'What are you doing here?' I replied: 'Sir, I was on my way to Brown Thomas to buy some timber.' He ran his hand all over me and out of my back pocket he pulled a carpenter's rule and a few pieces of paper. The paper showed different sizes of pieces of timber, which I usually carried as a decoy. Handing me back my rule and papers he said, 'Get to Hell out of this.' I said, 'Thank you, sir.' I was once more clear.[111]

Byrne was much luckier than several IRA men in Cork one month earlier, who were executed by the British authorities in Cork City. One of them, Patrick O'Sullivan, writing to his mother shortly before the hour of his death, displayed a nobility well worth noting. 'I am in great spirits', he wrote, 'and pray for the hour to come when I will be released from this world of sorrow and suffering. We must all die some day and I am simply going by an early train. If I could choose my own death I wouldn't ask to die otherwise.'[112]

The isolation of the British officials assigned to enforce the King's writ in Ireland was becoming ever more acute as 1921 wore on. It was apparent that no matter what symbols of imperial power continued in name or on public edifices, they were largely in a foreign country. The inability of Lloyd George to fully understand the dimensions of the Irish situation was due, according to W. E. Wylie, to the fact that 'the intelligence system from which he derived his information was faulty'.[113] Indeed, the entire Irish Executive, along with General Macready, were forced out of fear for their safety to live in Dublin Castle. The information reaching them often came from individuals who themselves had only limited access to the Irish public, and even less to those in the Irish independence movement. Thus the problems besetting the IRA's General Headquarters staff and the British representatives were similar – structural problems were confounded by the actions of the other side, with a resulting stalemate.

In terms of total British strength in Ireland in May 1921, there were 14,000 members of the RIC backed by 2,600 Dublin Metropolitan Police, in addition to Auxiliaries and Black and Tans. In addition, according to General Mac-ready, by this time there were some 40,000 regular British military personnel in Ireland. In the British Army's Sixth Division in Southwest Munster alone, there were 14,483 British soldiers, in addition to the Auxiliaries and the RIC.[114] Despite this significant armed presence, British policy had at best reached a stalemate in Ireland.

Macready was candid in his reflections on the inability of Britain's armed might, even aided by martial law and a wide scope of coercive measures, to regain control of Ireland. He noted that 'the opposing array on paper of 51 battalions and six cavalry regiments did not take into account the fact that, owing to the weakness of nearly every battalion, and the number of guards locked up in protecting barracks and public buildings, not more than 250 to 300 men per battalion were available for offensive action against the rebels'. Furthermore, Macready admitted that his men 'were suddenly faced with situations foreign to all preconceived ideas of military operations, but demanding as great a display of cunning, vigilance, patience, and resource as the most delicate operation of war'. But perhaps the most ominous of warnings confirming this reality came to the Cabinet's attention in a memorandum of 24 May 1921, prepared by Worthington Evans, who had succeeded Winston Churchill as Secretary of State for War: 'There is a risk that a position of virtual stalemate may continue throughout the summer and that winter will be a time of decisive advantage to the rebels.'[115]

By this time the Cabinet had been made aware of another challenge. On 27 April Greenwood told his colleagues that 'There is going to be civil war in Ulster, if there is no truce. It will be a bloody business.* Unknown to them, the desire for a settlement was becoming stronger on the part of Sinn Féin as well. A report from the No. 1 Brigade of the IRA's First Northern Division on 22 May 1921 shows that the pressure applied by successive deployments of British Forces in Northern Donegal and County Derry had apparently had an effect in weakening the IRA's position there.

> On the morning of 16th inst. [sic] a big drive was made by the sea and land on this area taking all by surprise and resulting in the capture of the Division Commander and his staff, and also the commandant of my 1st Bat., his father and brother. I escaped only by hiding myself in the house from Mon. until Thurs., then I got out through the lines in disguise ... and came in small motor launches to Burtonfort Quay ... I have been informed that a special flying column of police and military headed by Head Constable Duffy of Killybegs has been established to deal with our area. This head constable is the most dangerous man in the country and is subordinate only to Gen. Tudor. These big drives are beginning to tell on our men ... The forces

---

* Tom Jones, *Whitehall Diary*, Vol. III, p. 61.

[British] which operated here are also K.O.Y.L.I. who lately arrived in Derry, Rifle brigade from Bunbeg, Letterkenny, Stranorlar and Donegal ... RIC were present ... The whole force would approximate about 500 men ... The military not being able to use the telegraph wires had with them a field wireless set. There were 27 lorries with the force as well as several motor cycles.[116]

But if the Donegal and Derry IRA units suffered from an increase in the British military presence, the situation in some parts of the West of Ireland took on a different complexion. In response to the East Connemara Brigade Commandant's report of 17 May that at 4.00 a.m. of that day his Brigade had opened fire on the local barracks without inflicting any casualties on them, Mulcahy stated: 'There is no use having a gun in the hands of a man who cannot hit a policeman at 80 yards no matter how willing he is'. In response to the British crackdown, Mulcahy stated:

> You must arrange that it will be impossible for the enemy to transverse any road in your area without the date and time being reported to you at once. And you must use this information for the purpose of getting a systematic knowledge of his movements in order that you may hit at him on every possible occasion, with as little hanging around and waiting as possible ... I also want to draw your attention to General Order No. 14. Will you see that this Diary of activities comes ... regularly every other month in future and in order that I may be able to see what each individual battalion in your area is doing. I want you to show the diary for each battalion separately.[117]

Western Galway was a source of special concern to Collins and Mulcahy from April to June 1921. On 15 April, Michael Collins told Mulcahy that matters in 'Connemara, West Galway have been very bad but I am having these fixed up in Tuesday next, and I think there will be no further complaint'. 'Those who are no good have fled', Collins stated, 'and the few left should be supported.'[118] As late as 1 June, Mulcahy found it necessary to instruct the commanding officer in East Connemara that he 'must arrange beacons in your area or other signals for the purpose of approach of any enemy forces'.[119]

That spring, in a letter addressed to the Commander of the Kilkenny Brigade, Mulcahy also emphasised the need to implement an aggressive campaign of 'road cutting':

> [Road cutting] ... should now be taken to ring round every enemy post in your area whether great or small, with extensive road cutting, so that it will not be possible for them to leave their bases suddenly. Interaction between the enemy posts which you have ringed round systematically and extensive breaking of the roads must be carried out practically along all roads.[120]

Mulcahy's road cutting directive, however, did not meet without opposition, and the difference between sound theory and actual practice was underscored to him by the head of the Mid-Clare Brigade: 'I know local circumstances do not attach the same importance to enemy activity as you are inclined to. The major portion of the enemy activity was clearing roads and on these occasions he was mixed up with an army of civilians. There is no fear that our men in the area will become demoralised ... as they feel and know exactly the position in which they have placed the enemy.'[121]

An increase in the activity of spies and informers also became a source of heightened concern to General Headquarters. Early in June, Richard Mulcahy saw the need, as Chief of Staff, to issue a General Order covering 'The Communication of Information to the Enemy'. The document was explicit in the type of punishment to be meted out for varying offenses:

> 1. Death Penalty: The communication to the enemy of information concerning the work of the army of the Civil Admn of the Republic is an offense against the life of the nation and in the ultimate is punishable by death.
> 2. Fines: Cases will occur in which owing to the important character of the information given and the circumstances ...
> 3. When a fine in excess of £50 is proposed, the case shall be submitted to the Adj. Gen. for covering authority.
> 4. Amount of fines so collected shall be accounted for in the Brigade accounts.
> 5. All sentences in cases of communication with the enemy shall be subject to notification by the Brigadier Commander.[122]

A report from a Brigade leader in Galway to Headquarters on 29 May 1921 concerning the execution of an alleged enemy agent found in the area demonstrated the level of cooperation between the Republican effort and some members of the local Catholic clergy on such unsavoury issues:

> This man told me he would not give me no information of any kind. Going about [the] district for five days ... spying about and going into houses for a glass of milk. He was seen in the County with the military and police on two occasions by local volunteers. The volunteers arrested him and held a court martial on him. The man was given a court martial and told 'to clear out of the district.' ... I then asked him where he was going to ... and he said he couldn't think of it. After a while, he said Clonalee ... I asked him was he in the county with military and police at the Blue Bull and that a military officer left him up the road leading to Mountbellew, and he denied it. I then told him I was going to shoot him as he was looking for information for men on the run. Seeing that I had found him out in his maneuver he asked for forgiveness. I told him it was too many chances he had ... I then told him to prepare for confession and I went for a priest and brought him forward. After he had his confession told, the priest called me aside and asked me did I hold court martial on him and I told him I did. He said that I was right, that I was

doing my duty then gave him the Blessed Sacrament and he told me to take him immediately out of his sight. Concluding, I thought myself perfectly right in shooting him as myself and my men were in danger, considering I had the priest's advice as well on the matter.[123]

The treatment of spies, however, was a matter of concern within the ranks of the IRA throughout the conflict. In the winter of 1920, the following request for instruction came to Collins and Mulcahy from an IRA Brigade in the West of Ireland: 'Have you decided whether capital punishment should be inflicted on women spies? A number of us through the work of women spies had a miraculous escape in a hail of bullets. Had we fallen, the whole brigade organisation was gone.'[124] But there were some cases in which direction from General Headquarters was not sought when it came to executing those believed guilty of spying. Such arbitrary decisions were of concern to Mulcahy, as shown by a correspondence of 1 June with the Brigade Commandant for Kilkenny. 'It is a very serious matter that a junior officer should take upon himself the responsibility for executing two spies and I want to have a special report on this case. It must generally be understood that executions where our forces are in actual peril and action cannot be delayed that the Brigade Commandant's authorisation is necessary.'[125]

The period from April to June 1921 marked a particularly heavy one for the 'execution' by the IRA of those it judged to be guilty of espionage or acts of reprisal. Mulcahy's files detail a litany of such cases: 'Constable George Duckham, June 28, 1921; Gallivan and Daly, May 4, 1921; 10th June 1921 captured and executed Cadet Leonard French ... April 27, District Inspector Potter at Clogheen Co. Tipperary executed as reprisal for hanging of a prisoner, T. Traynor; 9th May, C. Murdoch ... executed'. On 16 June, for example, came a report from H Company of the 'Execution of spy McMahon, Bolton Street, carried out this afternoon. 8 rounds of 45 ammunition used. He was taken to George V. Hospital'.[126]

Under Mulcahy's direction as Chief of Staff for the IRA, explicit instructions were also issued from General Headquarters for 'Attacking English Non-Commissioned Officers': 'The English Army is very dependent for discipline and training on its Warrant Officers and Sergeants. The ranks are far more valuable to them than Senior officers who for the most part are quite unequal to carrying on the more routine part of their administration. Large numbers of Warrant Officers and Sergeants can be seen in uniform in the streets of Dublin any evening.'[127] It was Mulcahy's contention that striking at these key components of the non-commissioned ranks would inflict a severe 'loss on the enemy by depriving them of valuable personnel. It is very possible', he concluded, 'that this driving of its important non-commissioned ranks underground would very seriously affect the discipline of the English Army. The young soldiers ... would have their confidence seriously shaken in superiors if accurate.' Mulcahy's assessment revealed a perhaps surprising understanding of the British Army.

The first two weeks of June represented a particularly active period of localised IRA activity in the south and southwest of the country which along with Dublin City had become the focal point of the campaign of guerrilla warfare. Between 5 and 7 June 1921, twenty-one ambushes were reported by North Wexford Brigades at Gorey and Bunclody, resulting in the death of two RIC men and the wounding of three others. A report submitted by the Cork No. 3 Brigade on 7 June 1921 detailed in West Cork 'some 20 incidents including Dunmanway, Clonakilty, Bandon (MC own area). Effort seen to repeat success of Dunmanway and Kilmichael ambushes, involving a "column of Cork No. 3 Brigade of 85 riflemen"'.[128]

A digest of reports from the Dublin Brigade covering June 1921 includes the following: '6/18 Ormond Quay; 6/15 Adelaid Road; 6/16 Report of H Company 'Execution of spy McMahon, Bolton St., carried out this afternoon. 8 rounds .45 used. He was taken to George V Hospital. O/C'[129] In all, some nineteen separate incidents occurred in Dublin City alone between 15 and 18 June 1921, including attacks on various police barracks in suburban areas.

IRA Headquarters continued to press on with the acquisition of arms, despite an intensified and more successful British effort at preventing their arrival into the country. This success was due in large measure to improved intelligence gathering methods. Michael Collins continued as the central player in overseeing the purchase and distribution of those arms the Republican side was able to obtain in his overlapping responsibilities as Director of Organisation for the IRA, Minister for Finance in the Dáil Government, and Republican Director of Intelligence. In effect, his existence as a one-man interlocking directorate enabled him to expedite the location, purchase and distribution of the weapons. His handwritten accounts reflecting the period 5–17 June 1921 indicate that the preponderance of weapons successfully acquired were largely revolvers of American origin, along with the necessary ammunition.[130]

The events of June 1921 are also usefully chronicled from the British side by Mark Sturgis, who noted an RIC Constable was executed at Mountjoy Jail by British authorities for the murder of a civilian. He also noted in reference to the Southern Irish Parliament created under the Government of Ireland Act, that 'Ireland has a Parliament for the first time since the Act of Union'.[131] He neglected to mention, however, that in Dáil Éireann, the majority of the Irish people already had a Parliament of their own choosing. Sturgis cited Dublin Castle legal counsel W. E. Wylie as having spoken of 'the vast improvement in the manner and discipline of the Black and Tans, now a first class force which everybody can respect'. On 13 June Sturgis pointed to what he saw as inadequacies within the leadership of Sinn Féin for its failure to move on the issue of peace. 'I cannot believe', he wrote, 'that the Sinn Féin reluctance to come out and play the statesman is due to the simple fact that they are to a certain extent all to pieces ... If we want to deal with England, there's Lloyd George – if we want to talk to Ulster there's Craig or Carson, but when we want to talk to Sinn Féin, it's a heterogeneous collection of individuals.'[132]

Perhaps one of the most telling accounts to sway Lloyd George, and consequently the British Cabinet, to the view that now was the time for a change of policy in Ireland came in June 1921. The Liberal publication *The Round Table*, ran a lead article written by the pro-imperialist Lionel Curtis.[133] Curtis, upon returning from colonial appointments in South Africa in 1909, had joined with Sir Edward Grigg, later private secretary to Lloyd George, in founding the 'Round Table', also known as 'Kitchener's Kindergarten', a Liberal Imperialist intellectual group which pressed the case for closer unity within the Empire. During the Anglo-Irish Conference of 1921, Curtis would serve as Secretary to the British delegation. Soon after, he was the chief British constitutional expert during the setting up of the Irish Free State, and served as Colonial Office advisor on Irish affairs from 1921 to 1924. Curtis is credited with inventing the phrase 'British Commonwealth of Nations' to cover the amalgamation of territories under the British crown. A vehicle for the 'Round Table' was its quarterly publication of the same name. The March visit of Lionel Curtis to Ireland resulted in his June article advocating dominion status for Ireland, along with fiscal autonomy for Northern and Southern Ireland. In remarks to Lord Riddell on 23 October 1921, Lloyd George stated his view that the Round Table combination was 'probably the most powerful in the country'.[134]

Although the *Round Table* had previously included accounts of the deteriorating state of affairs in Ireland throughout 1920, the June 1921 issue included a lengthy opening article by Curtis providing both an historical analysis of the Irish problem and a prescription for Dominion Rule for Ireland. Curtis' suggestion at the end of his analysis that it was time for Britain to respond 'to the call of a great opportunity' would appear almost prophetic as events unfolded during the next three weeks. As we shall see, King George V delivered a conciliatory message at the opening of the Northern Ireland Parliament in Belfast on 22 June, and soon after Lloyd George issued his invitation for discussions to Eamon de Valera and Sir James Craig. Craig was the newly installed Premier for the Northern Ireland state established under the Government of Ireland Act (1920). The final draft of the King's speech was prepared by Curtis' associate and fellow *Round Table* founder, Sir Edward Grigg. Grigg by this time had become Lloyd George's private secretary.

Lionel Curtis' analysis at the outset in the June issue of the *Round Table* provided a retrospective on the historical and political realities of the Anglo-Irish conflict that was fairly objective, given his pro-imperialist views. Most importantly, it represented a candid admission by someone close to the colonial scene that the policy of coercion in Ireland, and the essence of the union between Britain and Ireland itself, had failed. Curtis wrote:

> The history of Great Britain and Ireland shows how completely a political union may succeed in one case and fail in another. In various respects, the Scots or Welsh have remained as different from the English as the Irish have done. But the devotion of all three to the British Commonwealth exceeds that which they feel to England, Scotland and Wales. In the great mass of the Irish people, political union has developed no such affection for the larger community in which they are merged. Their final devotion is still to Ireland.[135]

Perhaps among the most useful contributions of Curtis' essays in bringing home the failure of British policy in Ireland was the directness with which he addressed the limitations of the policy of coercion, while pointing the way to a different course. 'The movement may be crushed for the moment', Curtis warned, 'but no remedy will go to the root of the evil which does not give Irishmen a freedom to manage their own affairs which may be used to the injury not only of ourselves, but of Great Britain as well.'[136] However, Curtis also made it plain that in following a negotiated approach, the Government would have to be mindful of a predominant resentment on the part of the Irish of the word of British politicians, owing in some measure to Lloyd George's own involvement with the failed Irish Convention of 1918. 'It is this', Curtis wrote, 'which Irishmen largely have in their minds when referring ... to the great betrayal. This more than anything is due to the present distrust of any attempt to end the struggle by negotiations.' In Lloyd George's defence, Curtis noted that while he admitted making the pledge, his resignation was refused by Asquith 'on the grounds that he was the one indispensable man in the government'.[137]

Indeed, with an increasing desire to rid himself of the Irish problem came the open recognition by Lloyd George that a new strategy was needed. By June 1921 it was evident that the decision to continue with coercion in its present form had not produced the desired results. The British military campaign, the driving force behind the coercion effort, had also failed. An assessment offered to the Cabinet at the end of the previous month and endorsed by both General Macready and General Sir Henry Wilson of the Imperial Staff, was particularly pessimistic:

> While I am of the opinion that the troops at present in Ireland may be depended upon to continue to do their best under present circumstances through this summer, I am convinced that by October, unless a peaceful solution has been reached, it will not be safe to ask the troops to continue there another winter under the conditions which occurred there during the last. Not only the men, for the sake of their morale and training, should be removed out of the 'Irish atmosphere', but by that time there will be many officers who, although they may not confess it, will in my opinion be quite

unfit to continue to serve in Ireland without a release for a very considerable period ... Unless I am entirely mistaken, the present state of affairs in Ireland, so far as regards the troops serving there, must be brought to a conclusion by October, or steps must be taken to relieve practically the whole of the troops together with the great majority of the Commanders and their staff.[138]

The final sentence of Macready's remarks are key to understanding how dire he thought circumstances had become. Years later, however, Winston Churchill sought to diminish the note of alarm sounded by Macready. In Churchill's estimate, 'There could, of course, be no question of giving effect to it'. In his view,

These despairing counsels were not justified by the facts; nor in any case was there any possibility of relief. No relief, but reinforcement on a large scale, all the old forces – with new forces added – was the obvious step; and this, though costly and troublesome, was quite practicable. Still, while the Cabinet did not accept, they were bound to weigh these sweeping and alarmist assertions of the Commander-in-Chief, endorsed as they were, by the Chief of the Imperial General Staff.[139]

Churchill, however, offered no evidence as to what he thought the 'facts' were. In the absence of such evidence from someone who was so close to the situation, his remarks may be taken as having been less than candid.

To the upper echelons of the IRA, the limits of their own resources were also apparent. In May 1921 Michael Collins made it clear that there was little or no financial support available for the legal expenses incurred by Republicans in jail.

What I would say in regard to defence of such IRA men charged in 'capital offences' is that they be allowed to defend themselves and that volunteer officers should be permitted to help them by getting them in touch with lawyers and in ... writs and so on. But such prisoners should not be allowed to regard the IRA without very special reasons. (Of late this is being done indiscriminately by almost every man tried in Cork). With regard to legal expenses, the prisoners should write to their relatives and friends in the first instant. The people of their districts would readily subscribe the costs if an effort were made to collect the money.[140]

Dublin City and its vicinity between 24 and 27 May saw IRA attacks on a section of RAF men in a lorry heading to the aerodrome at Baldonnell and the RIC Barracks in Enniskerry, and Bray, Co. Wicklow. An IRA 'patrol report' of 30 May 1921, forwarded by the Dublin Brigade to General Headquarters, demonstrated the adoption of standardised forms by the Brigade O/C:

On the 30th instant, two men of the Active Service Unit armed with one 'Peter the Painter' and one parabellum, took up a position in the ruins of a house known as Pages Bootshop, corner of Skipper's Alley, Merchants Quay. At about 10:10 a.m., three lorry loads of Black and Tans came along from the depot going towards the Castle. Both men fired two shots at the first car; one Black and Tan who was sitting by the driver, crouched himself up. The other two cars immediately opened fire and three minutes of machine gun fire was brought into action. This state of affairs lasted for fifteen minutes. Our men got away safely. Casualties: One Black and Tan wounded or killed.[141]

A synopsis of the reports prepared by Michael Collins for Mulcahy that focused on the situation in the west of Ireland shows a continued concern with the performance of the IRA units there. Concerning accounts of activities by the IRA he had received from West Mayo, Collins stated that 'It is very unfortunate this has been delayed so long ... There are some extracts which would valuably be sent ... and other possibilities to inform. It is almost too late to deal with them now'. Collins noted that the information regarding an action was 'highly satisfactory'. He did, however, have some criticisms to offer concerning the engagement, and the report submitted: 'A great pity though that the arms were not captured. The report is very poor as they guess too much at the casualties. However, the great thing is that there is fighting in Mountbellew. Ogs Hanratty, Egg Merchant, Galway, Peace Resoluteer'. The latter comment referred pejoratively to a recent resolution by the Galway County Council, asking Sinn Féin to seek a negotiated settlement. As for Sligo, Collins remarked unhappily: 'Same type of report as always comes from there.'[142]

On 2 June 1921, Collins forwarded a report from the head of the East Waterford Brigade to Richard Mulcahy and added these remarks: 'I suggest you write to O/C 1st Southern Division and send him a copy of the report of the irregular meeting referring also to the Position of the Brigade officers note marked 'X'. This is because you have already written about it.'[143] The Waterford report, dating from 22 May, dealt largely with an unauthorised decision on the part of the 2nd Waterford Brigade to remove the then current Brigade Commander. It stated in part: 'The proceeding was entirely irregular. Personally I could not get any good of any officer in Waterford, or get any scrap of organisation in the Brigade as a whole until the present Brigade Commander took command some months ago.'

Between 5 and 7 June 1921, a total of twenty-one ambushes were undertaken by the North Wexford Brigade, which resulted in the death of two members of the RIC and the wounding of three others. On 6 June, a report from the South Wexford Brigade also showed an extensive array of actions during this time, with particular emphasis by the Wexford No. 4 Brigade on road cutting which saw the main Enniscorthy–Wexford Road severely damaged. Their actions, completed between 11 and 27 May, included the cutting of telegraph wires and poles between Wexford and Enniscorthy.

A report from Rory O'Connor on 3 June, however, was less sanguine about the IRA's actions in Britain itself. In his view, the IRA's operations there left him 'satisfied ... that the total loss of property there is not less than £5 million'.[144] The report from the man who would emerge as one of the most militant opponents of the Anglo-Irish Treaty within the IRA's leadership is important in shedding light on the limited extent of Republican activities of a military nature in Britain during the War of Independence.

> In addition to the operations carried out by the volunteers, the example shown has been taken up by some other organisations or individuals particularly in the case of farm fires or window smashing, the miners have done comparably little. It was often stated in the British House of Commons that up to 11 April forty pits had been allowed to flood. A fire was carried out in Shields where the damage amounted to £4 million and some minor operations were carried out by them. I would not hope for anything from these men.[145]

O'Connor's attacks against economic targets in Britain during 1921 ranged from the destruction of the Labour Exchange office in Camberwell, near London, to attacking a cotton warehouse in Liverpool. Large farms outside Kingsbury were also attacked along with an aerodrome in Newcastle. Yet overall, these attacks had little impact on British policy. Acting under orders from General Headquarters, O'Connor carried out no operations in Scotland or Wales, while such obviously 'economic' and strategic targets as power stations and petroleum companies apparently went unharmed. His report is also useful in painting a picture of the limited attention given to the IRA's campaign in Britain by the British press, as well as to the need to expand the effort at sabotage there.

> The enemy press is suppressing reports of activities ... the operations in Newcastle were not reported by the leading London dailies, the only reports being in the local papers ... The organisation should be extended in Britain. That there is material there, there is no doubt. Newcastle which six months ago had only six Volunteers now has 680. I am taking up this matter at once.[146]

In Ireland itself, the IRA's ability to provide its members with basic essentials was a matter of increasing focus. A draft order on the commandeering of supplies was submitted by Richard Mulcahy to Michael Collins on 10 June 1921. 'I have given the order a bit of a twist', he noted. 'When in its final form,' Mulcahy advised Collins, 'we must submit it to the Minister for Defence before issue.'[147] The desire to avoid conflict with Brugha appears to have been of greater concern to Mulcahy than it was to Collins. The draft order stated:

> 1. When stores are required for any purpose which it is not possible to pay in cash at the moment, such stores may be commandeered.

2. Officers commandeering stores will, if called upon to do so, explain that the Irish Government accepts responsibility for such goods on the part of the army and that claims for goods so commandeered will be one of the first charges on the Republic, when peace is declared...[148]

One day later, the IRA's first Southern Division in County Kerry forwarded a report to GHC that yielded favourable news for the Republican effort. An ambush set on the road from Kilorglin to Tralee resulted in the killing of four RIC men and the capture of a cache of weapons. Elsewhere in Munster, British forces were strengthened. Mulcahy divided the British armed presence in County Cork into four groups: Military, RIC and Black and Tans, Auxiliaries and civilian agents.

> The military strength of the British military in Cork has been variously estimated at twelve to fifteen thousand troops. It is difficult to give an estimate of the strength of the RIC and Black and Tans due to the fact that they were located in smaller detachments of 15 to 20 in various buildings throughout the City and in more important centres of the County. I consider 500 to be a fair estimate for the City and 1500 for the County. They possess the arms and equipment which is usually associated with that personnel. There were three companies of Auxiliaries located at Dunmanway, Macroom, and Newmarket, each company had approximately 100 ...[149]

In matters related to IRA morale and discipline, Collins continued to play a direct role. In May, he received from Mulcahy a copy of a correspondence relating to poor organisation and attention to detail in one Sligo Brigade. The matter in question concerned Mulcahy's intimation to a Sligo officer that he would be relieved of command if the officer told him he felt he was unable 'to be responsible for the situation in Sligo'. Mulcahy further stated:

> Not once since the issue of General Order No. 14 have I got a monthly report on your area that dealt in any way satisfactorily in the matters required of this report. Operations reported on are reported in manner with no details that may be useful for estimating what the state of training in your area is ... Coupled with this, I find a tendency to poor mouth and complain on your part, and I realise the difficulties you are up against and that I know that such an attitude of mind cannot conquer or overcome these difficulties.

Mulcahy then spoke for Michael Collins on the point that more guns and ammunition alone were insufficient by themselves for success: 'The keynote of today must be that with organisation and system, we shall win this war, if we are left with nothing but pick and shovels to wage it. This does not mean that we underestimate the value of .303 ammunition or that we are waiting for it to grow on trees. For goodness sake, don't undermine your morale by developing grievances that may not be remediable.'[150]

While ammunition may have been in short supply, Collins and Mulcahy were determined to find other means with which to inflict damage on the Crown's forces. From General Headquarters, on 21 June, the two sent a blunt communication to Brigade Commanders suggesting the intimidation of the wives and families of members of the RIC and British Army stationed in their areas in civilian quarters.

> In what places have private homes been commandeered and the occupants expelled? In order to provide accommodations for the wives and families of RIC and Black and Tans ... ? Do families visit the homes? That such people must not be allowed to live unmolested in houses commandeered from the people. That it will be more necessary to drive out all such occupants.[151]

Yet such aggressiveness may also have indicated that the IRA had become as frustrated as the British. In reality a lack of central control governed much of the IRA's guerrilla campaign during 1919–21. Fundamentally, the IRA campaign in its most effective guise relied on local guerrilla efforts. The weariness which the conflict had brought to the Irish population as a whole was an important factor in Sinn Féin's decision to pursue the possibility of a truce. According to Sean O'Muirithile, the Secretary for the IRB, 'The economic conditions were causing alarm owing to the difficulties of tilling the land or selling its produce.' 'The holding of fairs and markets', he noted, 'had become dangerous if not an entirely useless event.' The entry of more young men into the ranks of the IRA also meant an increase in the amount of land that went untilled. An increase in unemployment during this time, as O'Muirithile writes, produced a situation 'in which the decision to emigrate was stronger than ever before'.[152] An order passed by Dáil Éireann the previous summer restricting emigration was by June 1921 being more rigorously enforced by the IRA, in their police capacity for the Republic. The guidelines issued by the Republican Department of Home Affairs required proof of health grounds, foreign studies, or hardship as the basis for an individual gaining an exemption allowing him to emigrate. In the view of Austin Stack as Minister for Home Affairs, 'the intention of the Dáil in controlling emigration is really to stop it entirely'. The bitterness which Sinn Féin's decision had evoked among the more youthful segments of the population desiring to leave Ireland permanently was not lost on the British Government. A report from Dublin Castle to the British Cabinet noted that 'a party of young men on their way to America were held up by armed men at Knocklong Railway Station yesterday morning and compelled to return home'.[153]

The effect of the intensified British effort was clear to the IRA's leadership according to O'Muirithile, making a truce all the more necessary:

> There were no delusions on the part of those on the Irish side who were leading the warfare as to the actual position of the IRA, but their duty was to

show no weakening and to keep as much as possible from the rank and file the dangerous position of supplies of armament running out owing to the discovery of many sources ... Like some members of the Dáil Cabinet, the English authorities overestimated the real strength and capability of the Volunteer forces and saw no weakening on their part. Cathal Brugha would not hear of the suggestion that the chances of military victory were not bright. The Volunteers said nothing but carried on as directed to the best of their ability, as Collins used to quote, 'Tis but in vain for soldiers to complain.[154]

The success of the change in tactics employed by the British military, and their impact on the Republican effort in both the country and the city, was also evident in reports sent to Headquarters from the field. Óghlaigh na h-Éireann, in turn, laid heavy emphasis to all Brigade Commanders on the steps needed in order to thwart the enemy crackdown. A belief that a majority of Sinn Féin and Dáil Éireann saw a cessation of hostilities as necessary was confirmed for the British Government in an intelligence survey. The memorandum contended that the information 'is direct from Headquarters'. The document is also useful for its description of Michael Collins' distrust of the civil authority of the Dáil at the time.

> De Valera told the members of the Standing Committee that it was absolutely necessary that an effort would be made to bring peace and that he was being strongly pressed by the Church to stop all the crime that was going on. He laid great stress on the number of young men who had either lost their lives or were in prison. He also dwelt on the condition of the country and the state of the crops which, from reports that had reached him, gave great cause for alarm as to the danger of famine. He was of the opinion that to refuse to confer would turn nations that were friendly away from Ireland.[155]

The report went on to note that while de Valera's opinion was shared by a number present, 'Collins and the leaders of the Irish Republican Army are dead against a compromise and Collins said that to treat with the Prime Minister while the majority of their men were in prison, would be a scandal'. Collins would not agree, the account stated, 'on any of the points put forward when it was suggested that they should seek to interview the Northern Parliament. He replied that had already been tried with no good result.' In light of the discussions held between Collins and Andy Cope on the matter of peace talks and the earlier reports of Collins' conduct in Mark Sturgis' diary, this informant's comments are interesting, if not also contradictory:

> In the press it is said that de Valera is asking certain people to meet him at the Mansion House on Monday. I can tell you for a fact that Collins is not a party to that and further that he met several officers of the Irish Republican Army at 4 p.m. on the 28th of June over a saddler's shop, 40 Usher Quay, Dublin, and consulted with them. He left at 5:40 and went to Clondalkin, but a message from him was read to volunteers assembled in stables at the back of

Westmoreland Row Chapel in Cumberland Street which was as follows –
'Until our arms have brought us victory we shall never surrender. Fight on,
show no quarter to enemies of Ireland and keep a special look-out for the
starred ones. Work hard for the liberty of your country and don't heed talk.
Be true and faithful to your leaders and obey your orders and victory shall be
yours'.[156]

Such observations served only to confirm the view of Lloyd George and other
Cabinet members that Collins was a man with whom they had to deal if
peace was to be achieved. Unless Collins could be so engaged, the situation
was likely to become less predictable. According to Sturgis, the informant also
offered this appraisal:

> My private opinion is that things are in a very bad way and de Valera knows
> it. The volunteers are out of hand and robberies are being carried out without
> orders. De Valera is of the opinion that he will be able to arrange a scheme
> with the Northern Parliament and then present it to the British Government
> for their acceptance. I am sure he has no power over Collins, if he had, and is
> sincere, would he not have ordered the murders to stop at once. His telegram
> was hardly written when a poor constable was riddled with bullets on the
> Canal coming from his sister's house by three lads on bicycles. That is the
> reason I say all these moves will require to be carefully watched as I am cer-
> tain that there is no honest deal in the matter and all is a game to try and gain
> time.[157]

Sturgis also noted his informant's contention that de Valera had no control
over the IRA. It is noteworthy that Sturgis' source for this information was
apparently also in the habit of talking to Maud Gonne McBride, the widow of
the executed Easter Rising leader, John McBride. 'Maud Gonne', he wrote,
'said Collins did not take the meetings [in Dáil Eirean] seriously and his
opinion is [Collins'] that it is the mood of the government to bull [sic] their
activities and get at news of the foundation of the Irish Republican Army and
its headquarters.' It was also believed that Collins had taken a belligerent
stand against communicating the policies adopted at General Headquarters
to Dáil Éireann. 'In Collins' estimate,' the source commented, 'Dublin Castle
gets more news through the gossip of Dáil members and their friends then
from the host of spies they employ.'[158]

At the end of June, Dublin Castle had also become aware that Collins had
taken aggressive and indeed coercive action to thwart emigration. Collins sent
IRA men to the various travel offices across Dublin with an order to book no
more emigrant departures. It also appeared that he was running his own
conscription programme. He knew firsthand how British restrictions on emigration from Ireland during the Great War fuelled the decision of young men
to take up arms against the Crown, rather than court death on the killing
fields of the continent. At a minimum, by keeping young Irishmen at home,
Collins hoped to give an infusion of new members to the IRA.[159]

Yet while Collins sought to stem the flow of emigration, a different Ireland was still being born. It was an Ireland that could no longer be kept in tow by promises of Home Rule. Ernie O'Malley describes in graphic terms from his Republican vantage point how much of Ireland stood by the middle of 1921:

> Gone was the country of the soft brogue or blarney, the foxhunting days and the pleasant parties or tennis tournaments. Instead was a hard, steady Ireland, cool, assertive. It had pitted its strength against the Empire and the latter was beginning to waver. The mentality of the island seemed to have changed; the political type with his flow of eloquence and his mouthings, his bland assurances, his ability to 'pull wires,' and his gymnastic feats of conscience seemed to have disappeared. There was no room for oratory. The nation was at war ... Simple country boys, simple in that they were not sophisticated, had found they possessed organising and administrative ability. They had made themselves respected by their own people and, more difficult still, by those of their own class.[160]

To O'Malley the revolution that he had witnessed and participated in had already produced a very real victory over colonialism. In its effective prosecution, the IRA men in the field had also won the hearts and minds of many of their fellow citizens.

5

The Irish Revolution, Labour, and the Social Order

The cause of labour is the cause of Ireland. The cause of Ireland is the cause of labour.

James Connolly

We have seen the extent to which force, rather than the machinery of constitutional democracy, became an agent for political change in Ireland during the years 1919–21. At this juncture, however, the impact of the Irish Revolution on the social order during these years, and the relationship of the Irish independence movement to the Irish labour movement require attention in their own right.

The Irish labour movement's assistance proved essential to the gains made by Sinn Féin in governing Ireland. The type of support given to the Republican effort was reflected in the wide spectrum covered by both the Irish trade union leadership and the rank and file. Nonetheless, the level of support for Irish independence defined by Tom Johnson, leader of the Irish Labour Party, in October 1919, was fairly reflective of Irish labour's attitudes towards Irish self-determination.

> Mr Thomas Johnson said when they spoke of a free Ireland they meant an Ireland free for the workers – an Ireland that would have real self-determination. He believed the success of the labour movement would be the means of bridging the Belfast workingman and the rest of Ireland.[1]

The story of the relationship between Irish trade unionism and Irish Republicanism during 1919–21 was one of an unrequited display of affection. In reality, Labour's rank and file demonstrated themselves to be more willing to embrace the Republican national ideal than the Dáil Éireann was to embrace the agenda of the Irish worker, either by direct efforts to support the Irish worker or through the collective organs of the Irish Labour Party and the Irish Trades Union Congress (ITUC).

In the aftermath of the Easter Rising and the arrest and internment of most of Irish Labour's leadership, Tom Johnson and D. R. Campbell emerged as the heads of the movement. Both men were Protestants who hailed from England and Ulster respectively. Each supported Home Rule and opposed partition.[2] In essence, their outlook was one of studied moderation. In the cases of Tom Johnson, the Secretary of the Irish Labour Party, and William O'Brien, who would serve as General Secretary of the ITGWU, neither could be described 'as revolutionary socialists'. 'They were', as Adrian Pimley has noted, 'parliamentary social democrats with a social policy of labourism who found themselves cast in the role of revolutionaries', he noted.[3] O'Brien actually helped Connolly in planning the Rising by providing him with plans of the Dublin workhouse where he worked as a tailor.[4]

There were, of course, ideological differences within the ranks of the Irish labour movement itself. At a minimum, the Irish Labour Party, under Tom Johnson's orientation, had in fact and in substance, steered away from James Connolly's position that Irish independence was a driving force that bound the interests of Irish workers to Irish separatism. Yet there were, of course, similarities between Johnson's and Connolly's rhetoric. When the English-born and raised Johnson spoke of 'an Ireland free for the workers of Ireland – an Ireland that would have real self-determination', he echoed a view that Connolly had sought to advance from the early part of the century.[5] Similarly, Johnson's contention that the labour movement's steady advancement would serve to ameliorate the differences between the Belfast workingman and the rest of Ireland was also true to Connolly's sentiments against sectarianism within the ranks of the working class. However, less than three months after Connolly's execution an effort was made by the Irish Trades Union Congress, with Johnson at the helm as leader of its political arm, the Irish Labour Party, to disassociate the movement from Connolly's Republicanism. Desmond Greaves has noted that at the TUC Conference in August 1916, 'eloquent tribute was paid to Connolly, but not for his part in the Rising'.[6]

Recent writers have advanced the view that Connolly subordinated his own plans for a socialist revolution in Ireland to the separatist ideals of the IRB. Oliver MacDonagh writes that in the final years of his life Connolly came to see 'the Irish conflict as an inextricable portion of a general war, a war between capital and labour ... which already existed in Ireland. But this was but a local manifestation of the death struggle between the bourgeoisie and the proletariat the world over'. For MacDonagh, 'In August 1914, Connolly, like many other socialists, "Utopian" as well as "Scientific", expected the workers to prefer class to country. It was only when these hopes disintegrated that his socialism wore thin'.[7] Indeed, Connolly himself was well aware of the concerns his active involvement in the Irish separatist cause provoked among many in the Irish left. From within the GPO during the rising, he remarked that 'the Socialists will not understand why I am here. They forget I am an Irishman'.[8]

Ironically, while Connolly opposed British imperialism up to the moment of his death, he nonetheless showed himself ready to enter an alliance with the

Kaiser's Germany in the effort to advance Irish independence. His readiness to commit the Irish Citizens Army to a course doomed to failure, as well as to involve himself in a conspiracy with imperial Germany, has led Austen Morgan to conclude harshly that 'Connolly deserves the harshest criticism since he had the deepest political understanding'.[9] On Connolly's transformation from an internationalist socialist to a nationalist revolutionary, Morgan is particularly severe:

> It is disingenuous to maintain that Connolly was working for a socialist revolution ... He became a Germanophile, and collaborated with a wartime imperialist state. Connolly had little faith in popular revolutionary activity, and he based his expectations on the MacNeill Volunteers. The IRA secured his admission to the IRB's military council, and Connolly went to his death an unapologetic Fenian.[10]

Similarly in Oliver MacDonagh's view, James Connolly transformed the Citizens Army, from a strike defence force 'to a worker's revolutionary brigade and ended practically, though not formally, as an auxiliary of the IRB'. For MacDonagh, that transformation represented a 'bridge' between political and economic radicalism in Ireland, even if – or particularly if – the traffic flowed in only one direction.[11]

But these criticisms of Connolly do not fully take into account the context in which he found himself operating from January 1916 onward. Nor do they seek to assess his own analysis of the situation. First and foremost James Connolly sought to stop the Great War, recognising the extreme threat it represented to working-class solidarity. He was indeed a Germanophile, not out of regard for the Kaiser, but because the centre of international socialism was to be found in Germany. He fully embraced the denunciation of the war by the German syndicalists Rosa Luxemburg and Karl Liebknecht as driven by imperialism. But the clear intent of the British Government by January 1916 to impose conscription on Ireland left Connolly with little option but to fight against the British Empire. Connolly was committed to thwarting conscription by any means he could, with his front line of attack being the Irish Citizens Army. For Connolly the outfit's banner 'We Serve Neither King Nor Kaiser' represented a greater depth of commitment than a mere slogan. From this point commences his involvement with Irish revolutionary nationalism. It bears emphasis that Connolly was co-opted effectively by the IRB and the Irish Volunteers. He did not seek them out, although in the end he joined them willingly. Indeed, by the end of 1915 the IRB's Supreme Council – Bulmer Hobson and P. S. O'Hegarty in particular – saw Connolly and his Citizens Army as unguided missiles. Given his previous experience as a British soldier, he should have known from the outset that the plans for the Easter Rising were tactically foolhardy. But in that case it is Connolly's judgment, and not his commitment as a socialist, that should be called into question.

It is a matter for conjecture what the relationship would have been between the Irish labour movement and the Republican Government established by the First Dáil Éireann had Connolly lived. The First Dáil had, of course, attached itself formally to the Republic proclaimed by Connolly and Pearse in Easter Week. Clearly, no one emerged from the labour movement to take Connolly's place as an advocate for the economic advancement of the worker in the context of the struggle for national independence from Britain. One individual who emerged from the post-1916 generation with the greatest base of power, in both the political and military dimensions of the Republican effort, had in fact seen Connolly as the most impressive and practical leader of the Easter Rebellion. To Michael Collins, idealist and pragmatist, Director of Intelligence for the IRA, and the Republic's Minister of Finance, Connolly was one of the few from the 1916 vanguard whose leadership was to be respected. Collins had served inside the GPO as a staff captain under the command of Joseph Plunkett.

There can be little doubt that the emphasis of Collins, among others, on the attainment of political independence alone would have been deemed inadequate by the socialist leader. Few among James Connolly's surviving disciples within the Republican movement were as able to articulate the view he had advanced until his death that 'the Irish Question is a social question'.[12] This viewpoint was not the result of a sudden realisation attained in 1916. At the turn of the century, he had arrived at a specific analysis for combining Irish nationalism with socialism. In light of the eventual Anglo-Irish settlement of 1921 in which Collins and Griffith figured so largely, these views take on an added significance:

> If you removed the English Army tomorrow and hoist the green flag over Dublin Castle, unless you set about the organisation of the Socialist Republic, your efforts would be in vain. England would still rule you. She would rule you through her capitalists, through her landlords, through her financiers, through the whole array of commercial and individualists institutions she has planted in this country and watered with the tears of our mothers and the blood of our martyrs ... Nationalism without Socialism – without a reorganisation of society on the basis of a broader and more developed form of that common property which underlay the social structure of Ancient Erin – is only national recreancy.[13]

Connolly's analysis is also relevant to the partition question. As early as 1912 he held that the division of Ireland into two different jurisdictions 'would destroy the Labour movement by disrupting it. It would make division more intense and confusion of ideas and parties more confounded'.[14] D. G. Boyce has argued that, 'Before 1916, Connolly had made no secret of his contempt for the social conservatism of Sinn Féin'.[15] Nonetheless, despite the criticism levelled at Connolly for leaving international socialism and throwing his energy behind a nationalist, separatist revolt, it appears from Connolly's own perspective that the effort spawned by the IRB held out the best bet for a Socialist Republic over time. He accepted that British withdrawal would have to be accomplished first, while never actually departing from his view that economic independence was also essential to Irish nationhood.[16] The Easter Rising, of course, resulted in his death, thus removing the leading advocate of fundamental social change in a separatist movement that placed a higher premium on national independence than on an agenda for economic reform. As Patrick Lynch has observed, 'The way was now open for the original supporters of Sinn Féin to take the leadership. With Griffith dominating the national movement, the social aims of the Revolution, as Connolly conceived them, were put aside; opposition to England and National Solidarity became the only issue.'[17] Indeed, to Griffith, writing in 1918 'The man who injures Ireland whether he does it in the name of Imperialism or of Socialism is Ireland's enemy.'[18] This attitude was translated into action by the very manner in which the Dáil sought to end land agitation.

It can be stated that James Connolly's personal and labour organising experience was totally urban in nature. Among Connolly's shortcomings, Joe Lee has noted his lack of 'an adequate theory of political power'. Combined with this Lee saw a 'fatal tactical error' in Connolly's 'reluctance to acknowledge the existence of rural Ireland'. In his estimate, Connolly's 'solitary journey to Southwestern Ireland brought clear insight into the economic problems of small farms, but no understanding of peasant psychology'. Connolly's experience outside Ireland was limited to British and American labour circles, among the few socialist movements not faced by major agrarian issues.[19]

But there would be no successor to Connolly who would be able to carry forward his vision of a Socialist Republic. While there were others, such as Liam Mellowes, who had a Socialist outlook, none held either Connolly's grasp of revolutionary socialism or his force of personality. As one writer has noted, Mellowes's significance 'was limited and lies more in his uniqueness than his influence or achievements'.[20] Connolly's death proved an irreplaceable loss to the Irish left in its effort to build social democracy in Ireland.

Paul Bew has argued that 'when, after 1916, Sinn Féin emerged as a new force in nationalist politics – sanctified by the "blood sacrifice" of the Easter Rising – it was able to outflank the Irish Party both on the left and on the right in agrarian matters according to convenience'.[21] But in completing such manoeuvres, Sinn Féin remained subject to the whims of the Irish middle class.

> Like the Home Rule movement, which it so closely resembled, Sinn Féin was heavily dependent upon the shopkeepers, employers and large farmers for income, and the Republican County Councils for their rates. Systematic intimidation might have alienated a substantial and articulate group of

Irishmen from the Irish Republican cause, thus breaking the underlying principle of consensus nationalism.[22]

The desire, for example, on the part of the recently landed Irish farmers to forgo the repayment of loans for land purchase to the British Government is one factor behind the substantial rural support garnered by Sinn Féin. One cynical observer who had been rooted in the by then vanquished Irish Party noted that 'Sinn Féin is in the main a farmers' movement and has for its most enthusiastic advocates the young peasants who have secured their farms on British credit. They need have no further dealing with the Saxon Government than pay the half yearly interest of the money it has advanced them.'[23]

Other issues were emerging to Sinn Féin's advantage. Sinn Féin displayed significant political skills vital to its success in the 1918 general election, in which it took 73 of 105 parliamentary seats. Its ascent owed much, it has been noted, to the antipathy toward British rule sparked by the conscription proposal. Labour demonstrated its commitment as well as its strength on the conscription issue on 20 April 1918. As the result of a vote taken against conscription by the delegates to a special convention of the ITUC held in the Mansion House, a twenty-four hour strike was launched as a protest across Ireland, the only exception being Northeast Ulster.

The decline of the Irish Party as the central political voice for Irish Nationalism was in evidence even before the 1918 general election. However, of particular importance to Sinn Féin's success was the decision of the Irish Labour Party not to contest the election itself. On 1 November 1918, by a vote of ninety-six to twenty-three, the Party's National Executive withdrew candidates from the ballot on the grounds that in the aftermath of the war 'circumstances have decided that the Election now upon us be the "peace election" not the "war election"'.[24] 'In light of these new circumstances', the Labour Party Executive stated, 'the National Executive has decided to recommend the withdrawal from the election of all Labour candidates. They do so in the hope that the democratic demand for self-determination to which the Irish Labour Party and its candidates give its unqualified adherence will thereby obtain the greatest chance of expression at the polls.'[25]

This decision paved the way for Sinn Féin's emergence as the sole nationalist alternative to the Irish Parliamentary Party in the general election campaign. It was also left as the political manifestation of Irish Republicanism, unchallenged from the Irish left in an election that featured the largest registration of voters ever available in Ireland.

As for the Irish Labour Party itself, the decision not to contest the 1918 general election was counterproductive to its own long term interests, undermining its ability to establish a long-term base.[26] But in the short term the Party, in fact, sought to avoid having to take a stand on the issue of abstention from the British Parliament, an issue which was national rather than social in character. At the same time, the official Labour statement was not without a reaffirmation of the kind of independent Ireland which the Irish trade union movement desired:

> We had hoped to use the period between the two elections for an active educational propaganda directed towards ensuring that the building of the new Ireland shall be in the hands of the men and women who view the problems of political and social development from the standpoint of the working class, to determine, as far as our means and abilities allowed, that the Irish Republic – if such were to be the form of Government determined upon by a people guaranteed the right to choose its own sovereignty – should be a Workers Republic, not an imitation of those Republics in Europe and America, where political development is but a cloak for the capitalist oligarchy.[27]

It is ironic that Connolly's dream of a 'Workers Republic' was better kept alive in the statement of a Labour Party that was not itself contesting the election. It would soon be seen that such a vision was in reality not part of the Sinn Féin agenda.

Among the more radical provisions of Labour's 1918 platform for the election were these: 'To win for the workers of Ireland collectively, the ownership and control of the whole produce of their labour ... to secure the democratic management and control of all industries and services by the whole body of workers, manual and mental, engaged therein ...'.[28]

Labour's decision to withdraw had a monumental effect on the course of events. Brian Farrell has offered this very penetrating analysis of what the result was for Labour in the years to come:

> The majority of Labour leaders, despite Connolly and Larkin, failed to recognise the need to synthesise socialism and nationalism. They over-emphasised the electoral confidence of Sinn Féin and underestimated the powerful persistence of the separatist impulse it represented ... They did not recognise in it a political weapon that might be captured by a vigorous Labour leadership and shaped into a socialist sword ... They played no central role as Sinn Féin went on to construct a policy within a policy. Labour was excluded from the First Dáil, from direct representation in the Treaty negotiations and from participation in the first, seminal Irish governments ... It permitted the shaping of a basic cleavage in Irish political life that ran along a constitutional axis and cut across other potential sources of political disagreement.[29]

Accepting Labour's decision to absent themselves from the 1918 general election at face value would be unwise since it ignores certain significant contradictions in its attitude towards Sinn Féin. As recently as 1917, for example, the President of the Irish Trades Union Congress told the organisation's annual Congress that in his estimate Sinn Féin were part of the same capitalist establishment that sought to keep labour from advancing its position.

> In times of industrial strife the capitalist class drops all political and religious divisions. Sinn Féiners, Redmondites, Carsonites, Catholics and Protestants all join together with one common objective and that is to grind down the organised workers – all of which points to the necessity of a strong, virile Labour organisation keeping itself independent and always ready to grapple with any tyranny no matter what flag it sails under.[30]

What were the circumstances that transpired by the autumn of 1918 that led Labour to retreat from this objective of 'keeping itself independent' and to allow Sinn Féin a free run at cancelling out the last vestiges of the Irish Parliamentary Party? As early as August of that year, Labour had entered into formal negotiations with Sinn Féin towards an agreement over seats for the Dublin constituencies. No formal agreement was reached, however. Ironically, only months before, Sinn Féin appeared to be in danger of decline. But actions taken by the British Government even before the decision to impose conscription served to erode the Irish Parliamentary Party and, as its leader John Dillon noted, served only in 'manufacturing Sinn Féiners'.[31]

It can be argued that the notion that Labour withdrew in favour of Sinn Féin is without basis. The Irish labour movement fully understood the dimensions of its decision, even if it could not foresee all the ramifications of its action. Emmet O'Connor has argued that the overriding motive behind Labour's withdrawal in the end was to keep it 'out of unconstitutional agitation'. The opposition to Johnson's proposal came from Thomas Farren and Cathal O'Shannon, the two most ardent separatists on the executive.[32] In his estimate, the negative consequences attributed to Labour's decision to sit out the 1918 election 'have been exaggerated'.[33] 'By 1921,' he writes, 'the Congress Executives had given freely to nationalism what it refused to sell in 1918.'[34] Nonetheless, by allowing the political mantle of the Irish national struggle to be carried solely by Sinn Féin, Labour, perhaps inadvertently, allowed the goals and priorities of the Irish independence effort to be shaped and enunciated by Sinn Féin through the vehicle of the Dáil Éireann.

William O'Brien, among others in Irish Labour, appears to have held the view that in light of the burgeoning of trade union membership still well underway in 1918, Labour could have exercised its leverage on Sinn Féin by the position it held in the nation's economic life.[35] The Irish Labour Party abstained from the 1918 general election, providing Sinn Féin with the ability to run head to head against the Irish Parliamentary Party. It abstained again in the general election of 1921, when Sinn Féin was once more allowed to run unopposed. But Labour's decision not to contest the 1918 election did not leave the Party totally in the political wilderness. Instead, as Michael Laffan has noted, in the 1920 Municipal elections, Sinn Féin took 422 seats to Labour's 324. Nonetheless, in the elections held in the rural constituencies in 1920, Labour obtained only 11 per cent, showing the dichotomy that persisted in its appeal nationwide.[36] And while abstaining from national electoral politics, the years 1916–20 saw the Irish trade union movement enjoying a period of unparalleled growth. During that time the numbers represented in the Irish Labour Party and the Trades Union Congress rose from 100,000 to 225,000 – one quarter of Irish wage earners. In 1918 the Irish Labour Party and the Irish Trades Union Congress merged to form a single structure.

How did Irish Labour come to enjoy such an unprecedented boom period? Adrian Pimley's account of the myriad circumstances that made this growth possible is particularly helpful in arriving at an answer:

> Firstly, socio-economic conditions for such growth were good. Economic activity was high in Ireland until 1920 and farm prices remained correspondingly high due to the war, and this was the period when the Transport Union achieved its fastest growth in membership. In the years up until 1920, the union was concerned with raising wage levels, whereas after 1920, when farm prices slumped, it was almost solely concerned with maintaining wage levels. The Transport Union could also lay claim to the legacy of James Connolly's involvement in the Rising, while the administrative skills of O'Brien gave the union a new financial and organisational soundness that had been gravely lacking under Larkin's leadership.[37]

It was in the context of such rapid growth in trade union membership that William O'Brien spoke of realising the syndicalist ideal of 'One Big Union'.[38] It is against such a backdrop that credence should be given to the view that while Sinn Féin would indeed tell Irish Labour to wait, Labour's leadership during 1916–20 did so willingly.[39]

The Sinn Féin that stood in the general election of December 1918 was in reality a different entity from the movement spawned by Griffith and Rooney at the turn of the century. During the short spans of time from the aftermath of Easter Week to the autumn of 1918, with the efforts of many physical force adherents, it developed into a political organisation with a nationwide appeal across urban, rural and class lines. It did not, however, transcend the religious divide. In Brian Farrell's view, 'this "second Sinn Féin" owed little beyond its name to the little group of advanced nationalists brought together by Arthur Griffith with his ideals of a 'King, Lords and Commons of Ireland".[40] 'With masterly ambiguity', Farrell writes, the new Sinn Féin 'avoided any narrowly "Republican" definition.'[41] Years later, Fr Michael O'Flanagan, the Catholic priest who held the most prominent role of any cleric associated with Sinn Féin, bitterly decried that very ambiguity: 'It was built upon compromise from the start. The so-called treaty was only the wedge that burst the two sections asunder'.[42]

With the election in October 1917 of Eamon de Valera over Arthur Griffith as President of Sinn Féin, the official policy of the organisation moved from the dual monarchist pro-Grattan Parliament restoration that had been its trademark to the 'securing of the international recognition of Ireland as an independent Republic'.[43] Added to this came the proviso that 'the Irish people may by referendum freely choose their own form of government'. In light of the bitter Civil War that was to follow the Dáil's ratification of the Anglo-Irish Treaty, and despite the substantial public acceptance of the Treaty, this provision would become particularly ironic. Supporting de Valera over Arthur Griffith was the Irish Republican Brotherhood, the organisation that had proclaimed the Irish Republic more than half a century earlier. The Supreme Council included such younger men as Liam Mellowes and Harry Boland, in addition to Collins – men whom D. R. O'Connor Lysacht has termed less than 'democrats'. In his estimate, Mellowes and Boland were 'at best prepared to use social programmes to reinforce the political aims and at least (like Collins and the majority) eager to avoid such programmes for fear of jeopardising those aims'.[44]

Collins and Boland, serving as members of the Supreme Council, were also officials within the Sinn Féin hierarchy. They were in fact directly responsible for the selection of the panel of Sinn Féin candidates for the 1918 general election. Central to the selection of candidates for each of the parliamentary constituencies contested nationwide was acceptance of the Sinn Féin programme and loyalty to the primacy of national independence as the overriding issue. But there was no ideological litmus test on economic or social issues.[45]

The composition of the First Dáil, proclaimed in January 1919 as the direct result of Sinn Féin's impressive showing in the 1918 general election, has been the subject of varying interpretations. To Desmond Greaves, the First Dáil was not, as constituted, a cross-section of Irish society:

> This was a white-collar representation to be sure. But the bourgeoisie were not in it. They had become a class without a Party. If they could not revive Redmondism they must capture Sinn Féin ... But the working class also was missing. Labour had failed to claim its rightful place. And thus was created the gap through which the bourgeoisie was finally to emerge to power.[46]

John A. Murphy has written that the membership of the First Dáil was 'highly educated, with the professions and the lower levels of the commercial world far better represented than workers and peasants'.[47] In his view,

> the Dáil's outlook on social matters was due less to its social composition than to the conservative social climate in Ireland generally. It was Sinn Féin's conviction that sectional issues must not endanger the broad national objective of liberation, and also perhaps to the determination that the Dáil's

actions must be seen by the watching world to be 'responsible' and far removed from anarchy and bolshevism.[48]

One account lists the First Dáil as having included thirty-one professional men, nine journalists, seven teachers, eighteen men involved in commerce, two from local government bodies, five individuals connected with nationalist organisations and two legal clerks.[49]

The bourgeois character of Dáil Éireann also created tension with the rank and file of the IRA. There was indeed an apparent disparity between the IRA members and Dáil Deputies.[50]

Perhaps a fundamental reason for the division between the Sinn Féin leadership and IRA's General Headquarters Command in Dublin, on the one hand, and the IRA's local membership on the other, lay in who they were. Lysacht contends that the IRA at the local level 'were most generally farmer's younger sons, farm labourers, unemployed men and others of the propertyless'. 'Above all', he writes, 'they could not be separated from local problems or social aspirations'.[51] He is not alone in making this argument. David Fitzpatrick and Henry Patterson, among others, have also seen a division in the ranks. Nonetheless, a closer look at the social origins of the guerrilla leaders and figures at the grass-roots level of the IRA suggests a situation that was somewhat mixed. While figures such as Sean Treacy, Liam Lynch, and Dan Breen indeed came from humble origins, and appeared to face economic futures that held little chance of upward mobility, others who took up arms against the Crown can certainly be said to have held more of a stake in Ireland. For example, Eamon de Valera, Ernie O'Malley, Richard Mulcahy and Liam Cosgrave were all in an economic position that would have enabled them to remain part of the status quo had they not chosen the path of rebellion. Each one either hailed from a family background that gave him a stake in society or held professional credentials that stood him in relatively good stead.

Michael Laffan has drawn an ironic parallel between the respective attitudes of Sinn Féin and its predecessor, the Irish Parliamentary Party, on the question of social change:

> Sinn Féin's interventions in labour, agrarian and other social problems were not designed primarily to help the underpaid or the landless, but to calm them, and its leaders showed little concern with improving the living standards of the poor before the British departed. Here Sinn Féin followed an established tradition. It's predecessor, the Irish Parliamentary Party, had feared the British remedies for Irish grievances might blunt the demand for Home Rule.[52]

According to an analysis by J. C. McCracken, Ireland's professional and commercial classes, based on the 1926 census, amounted to only six per cent of the total population, while in the First and Second Dáil they amounted to sixty-five and fifty-eight per cent of the members respectively.[53] For Laffan, 'such a background made it easy, even natural, for Sinn Féin spokesmen to urge patience and restraint on others less fortunately placed than themselves'. Furthermore, 'it reinforced their strategic or tactical aversion to involving themselves in questions which would turn one class against another'.[54]

The fact that the first Dáil was comprised of a membership which in Lysacht's analysis 'had nearly two-thirds of it made up by men from the urban professional and white collar classes, another quarter by capitalists, and the remaining 10 per cent by farmers' in reality meant that 'the bourgeoisie was disillusioned with orthodox parliamentary tactics'. In effect, the Irish Parliamentary Party no longer proved viable to them, with the collapse of the Home Rule Bill as a particular reason for driving them away. What one writer has termed the 'natural division of interests between propertyless volunteers and T.D.s' was generally smoothed over in the interest of national unity'. The overriding attitude of de Valera and Sinn Féin from the Dáil's opening session, Lysacht contends, was that 'as with the pre-1916 volunteers and indeed with most "pure" national movements, the morale was everything: policy nothing'.[55]

But if Dáil Éireann was unwilling to actually embrace large-scale economic change, it did show itself ready, at least rhetorically, to support it. From a tactical standpoint, Sinn Féin's support for the Democratic Programme may have been made as a gesture to Irish socialism in order to strengthen Irish Labour's claim to full representation at the International Socialist Conference in Switzerland. This in turn would build support for the claim to international recognition for the cause of Irish independence.[56] By the Dáil's adoption of the Democratic Programme at its opening session in January 1919 it appeared to be tilting its economic and social outlook towards the objectives of the Irish labour movement. As enacted by the Dáil and read aloud by Richard Mulcahy, the document echoed both the Easter 1916 Proclamation and Pearse's philosophy as outlined in the *Sovereign People*:

> We declare that the nation's sovereignty extends not only to all men and women of the nation, but to all material possession, the nation's soil, and all its resources, all the wealth producing processes within the nation, and we reaffirm that all right to private property must be subordinated to the public right and welfare ... In return for willing service, we in the name of the Republic declare the right of every citizen to an adequate share of the produce of the government of the Republic to make provision for the physical, mental, and spiritual well-being of the children, to secure that no child shall suffer hunger or cold from lack of food, clothing, or shelter, but that all shall be provided with the means and facilities requisite for their proper education and training as citizens of a free and Gaelic Ireland.[57]

The document then went on to criticise the British Poor Law system then in place in Ireland as 'degrading'. However, the Democratic Programme sought only to replace that system with the vague terminology of a 'sympathetic nation for the care of the nation's aged and infirm'. Ambitiously, the Programme called for 'the development of the nation's resources, to increase the productivity of its soil, to exploit its mineral deposits, peat bogs and fisheries, its waterways and harbours, in the interest of and for the benefit of the Irish people'.[58]

A review of the original material submitted to Dáil Éireann by Tom Johnson and William O'Brien on behalf of the Irish labour movement for inclusion in the Democratic Programme suggests the advocacy of a more advanced programme than that actually adopted. But as John A. Murphy has noted, 'Even in its diluted form ... the program stood for a policy of extensive social and economic change.'[59] Cathal O'Shannon, who was also involved as a draftsman in the effort, stated that approximately one third of the final document was written by Sean T. O'Kelly, while Irish Labour contributed two thirds.[60] Among the Labour recommendations rejected was Tom Johnson's contention that the 'Nation must ever ascertain the right to resume possession of its soil or wealth whenever the trust is abused or the trustee fails to give faithful service'. Perhaps even more significantly, as Desmond Greaves has noted, the Dáil eliminated an argument advanced by Johnson which amounted to a restatement of part of the *Communist Manifesto*: 'The Republic will aim at the elimination of class in society which lives upon the workers of the nation but gives no useful social service in return, and in the process of accomplishment will bring freedom to all who have been hitherto caught in the toils of economic servitude.' As a result of an objection made by Michael Collins, a passage was also deleted which sought to give a syndicalist interpretation of 'the process of working class power'.[61]

The *Irish Times* also took the Dáil's action seriously, terming the Democratic Programme a 'rhetorical pretext for which the Dáil would pave the way for a programme of action consistent with the ideology of Lenin and Trotsky'.[62] In less than five months, however, the Dáil, under Arthur Griffith's instigation, was to take an approach to the land question that was anything but 'Communistic'. Griffith told the Dáil on 29 June 1920 that the creation of the Land Bank and National Arbitration Courts had 'prevented the land questions from being used to divert the energies of the people from the national issue'.[63]

In the view of Erhard Rumpf, the Dáil's agrarian policy served as the principal example of 'the essential conservatism of the revolutionary regime'. Consequently, to Rumpf, the application of that policy underscored the fact that the Democratic Programme was merely an expedient. 'At all events,' he wrote, 'it remained merely a form of words which may have served a useful short-term political purpose so far as relations between national and labour leaders were concerned, but which never at any stage bore much resemblance to the social policy actually pursued by Sinn Féin'.[64] But such criticism seems unduly harsh, given that the implementation of any social policy by a regime born in an ongoing insurrection was practically impossible: this was the case with the Republican Government during the years 1919–21. This is particularly the case when it is realised that the Republican Government sought to function at a time when the military might of the British Empire held a substantial portion of the country under martial law. Indeed, the problems encountered by the burgeoning Soviet State, in working to consolidate power while fighting a civil war, offers an even more compelling example of the dilemma of revolutionary states of the same period. Social change in Ireland was also sublimated by the fact that the Irish labour movement agreed, at least tacitly, to the short-term good of national liberation first, to be supplemented by socialism later, as was made apparent by its acceptance of the Democratic Programme.

Citing Michael Collins as his authority, D. G. Boyce contends that 'the class struggle in Ireland was a nationalist struggle; therefore, the only class which stood in the way of freedom was the class which stood for the Union'.[65] However, Collins and his adherents in Dáil Éireann, who appeared to have constituted a significant majority, may have shaped their views on social policy more out of political reality than out of any antipathy to the views of Irish labour organisations or to the socialist ideal itself. The irony was certainly not lost on them that they sought to wage a revolution at a time when the age-old land issues which had dominated previous revolts were no longer significant in much of the country. As Patrick Lynch has noted, 'By 1916 most agricultural holdings had been purchased by their occupiers, subject to land annuities, which were not then a matter of contention'. 'The tenant', he observed, 'had become a proprietor, the owner of his land'. Rural Ireland had so much benefited by the time of this latest and most protracted round in the Anglo-Irish conflict, by such measures as old age pensions and an unmatched wartime level of agricultural prosperity, that in 'rural Ireland thoughts of social revolution were held only by a minority – the articulate few and by those who had no stake in war prosperity'.[66]

By 1911 there were 324,743 Irish farms, of which over 100,000 comprised less than a total of 100 acres. There were some 450,000 workers in agriculture, including farm labourers and their family members. Seven years earlier, the Wyndham Act had to a considerable extent removed the landlord class as the principle source of enmity for the rural Irish population. As Henry Patterson has observed, 'It was precisely because the Irish Party Programme on the land question had been largely met by the British Parliament that an Irish constitutional party at Westminster became irrelevant.' But Patterson has also noted that this development preceded two other 'possible lines of fissure in the Irish countryside; between rich farmers and labourers, and particularly in the West between the land hungry small-holders and the ranchers in their midst'.[67]

Ironically, a considerable portion of the advantage gained by the British government in removing what appeared to be the most likely reason for renewed conflict was undermined by 1917, when legal emigration from Ireland was effectively ended by the British Government, closing what one writer has aptly described as 'a traditional safety valve on Irish rural society'.[68] Rural unemployment increased markedly, and with it a new wave of land agitation that outstripped the ameliorative capacity of the Wyndham Act, particularly as it concerned the number of 'landless' young men. Counties Clare, Roscommon, Mayo, and Galway witnessed the return of land seizures. Soon, however, the increase in land agitation would also have a negative effect. Wherever the King's writ and the presence of the RIC collapsed under the weight of popular opposition, the Dáil Éireann sought to diffuse the agrarian agitation through a combination of Republican arbitration courts and the assignment of a 'police' role to the local IRA.

Henry Patterson writes that 'Sinn Féin's first association with agrarian protest in 1917 and early 1918 was short-lived and typically instrumental'.[69] Michael Brennan, the principal IRA officer in Co. Clare, stated candidly after the Anglo-Irish War that he 'hadn't the slightest interest in the land agitation, but I had every interest in using it as a means to an end ... to get those fellows into the Volunteers ... and up to that they were just an unorganised mob'.[70] Two years later, rather than exploiting a burgeoning level of post-war unemployment, and committed to demonstrating its capacity for governing, the Dáil Éireann recommended a programme which combined increased tillage with the expansion of public works and the development of profit-sharing industries.[71]

The establishment by the Dáil of land and arbitration courts in 1919 was one remedy offered to stem the tide of land agitation actions that were clearly seen as counter productive to the national struggle. Sinn Féin's response to these intensified outbreaks of agrarian unrest, in Michael Laffan's estimate, 'was to dampen rather than arouse or even channel this social radicalism, and they stumbled, reluctantly and hesitantly, into efforts to contain it'.[72]

At the same time the Dáil was not at all hesitant about stating its opposition to the outburst of agrarian discontent in direct terms. In a proclamation issued on 29 June 1920, it stated that the nation's 'energies must be directed towards the clearing out – not the occupiers of this or that piece of land – but the foreign invader of our country'.[73] The success of the land courts in quelling the drift towards increased agrarian discontent was twofold: it provided an important source of propaganda, allowing Sinn Féin to demonstrate its capacity to develop a key part of the machinery for governing in a stable manner, and effectively replaced the British legal system in Ireland. The courts also succeeded in reducing agrarian protest to a minimum. None-theless, to Peadar O'Donnell such developments made it clear that the 'Free State was in existence long before the name was adopted'. The Dáil's oppo-sition to social unrest meant in his estimate that the Republican ideal 'lost out in 1921 because there was no day to day struggle making for differentation so that in those days we were forced to defend ranches, enforce rents and be neutral in strikes'.[74]

Sinn Féin's lack of a demonstrable commitment to an expanded land reform effort including small farm labourers in the western Province of Con-naught led, in Patterson's view, 'to a distinct lack of enthusiasm for the national struggle in the province where small-holders had seen their agrarian struggles denounced by Sinn Féin and sometimes suppressed by the IRA'. 'Connaught,' he notes, 'the most aggressively nationalist province in previous periods of agrarian agitation, was relatively restrained in the War of Inde-pendence, the central role passing to the province of Munster with its more substantial, medium sized farmers' class'.[75] Erhard Rumpf, in attempting to tie the land question to the independence struggle, also offers some useful insights into this development.

> The districts where the most violent unrest occurred during the period were not the centres of the national struggle. The social aspirations of the landless men were not primarily expressed in terms of hostility to the British adminis-tration. To a certain extent such aspirations were directly excluded from the national struggle, for the spirit which dominated the IRA leadership at all levels inculcated a deep suspicion of any attempt to mix social aims with the pure cause of the national struggle. The social conditions of many areas of the West were not favourable to an active national fight. The main national resistance was concentrated in more prosperous districts, such as de Tocque-ville noted was the case in the French Revolution, and was also true of the German peasants' war.[76]

Patterson writes that 'the largely integrative approach of Sinn Féin and the Dáil to labour issues, their refusal to take sides with labour against capital, was viewed as a poor response to the positive role of the ILPTUC [Irish Labour Party and Trade Union Congress] and individual unions in the War of Independence'.[77] But while Dáil Éireann may have been determined to avoid class issues, the actions of some IRA units in the West of Ireland still had an economic goal. David Fitzpatrick has argued that in County Clare, for example, IRA operations were 'in many cases thinly disguised land seizures which Dublin had neither the ability nor, perhaps, the intention to prevent'.

Connaught's relative inactivity in the Anglo-Irish War, given the fact that as recently as three decades before it had been at the centre of both the land reform and separatism issues, poses a challenging question. Unlike Leinster, with its proximity to Britain and the dependence of its economic interests on the British connection, Connaught represented the one Irish province with the weakest ties to the Empire, as well as the principal remnant of the old Irish culture. David Fitzpatrick offers two explanations for Connaught's limited contributions to the separatist struggle during 1919–21. First, during the War of Independence, 'there was the absence of a middle class capable of footing the Revolutionary bill'.[78] Second he cites 'the growing hostility of the nationalist revolutionary leadership towards the demands of land-hungry labourers and 'uneconomic holders demands more stridently voiced in Connaught than elsewhere since nowhere was poverty so prevalent or land more prized'. It is noteworthy that, just as Connaught was at the centre of the land reform issues in the 1880s, it was also at the height of electoral opposition to the Anglo-Irish Treaty of 1921. In Fitzpatrick's eyes, 'Connaught was, therefore, always incapable of footing Revolutionary bills; whether or not it could do so presumably depended upon the cost involved'. Fitzpatrick also offers this observation:

> It may be that the independence movement of 1918–21 was unusually expensive, being conducted as effectively in the form of costly foreign propaganda as in the form of cheap but violent domestic protest. Without doubt, the revolutionary organisers in Dublin considered the support of well-off shopkeepers and farmers essential to their success, and attempts of the poor and the hungry to weld national and social struggles together threatened to alienate the rich, unless repeatedly and unambiguously denounced by national headquarters.

This sense of realpolitik in effect served to separate Dáil Éireann in its actions from the rhetoric of the Democratic Programme, and particularly from Patrick Pearse's view as outlined in *The Sovereign People* that 'the Nation's soil and its resources, all the wealth producing processes of the nation ... and ... right to private property must be subordinated to the public right and welfare'.[79]

A frank assessment by a principal theorist for Sinn Féin came from Darrell Figgis, later a drafter of the Free State Constitution, in explaining the conscious effort on the part of the Dáil to steer clear of class issues:

> Action became imperative for a number of reasons ... The Republican Government, in the first place, had either to be a Government or not to be a Government, and in the second place, it had to keep the national demand for freedom from class issues or be caught in the snare of class war ... Such was the origin of the Republican Land Commission that during the year [1920] it saved what seemed an almost impossible situation and made landowners realise that the National Government, to which they were so bitterly hostile, not only meant impartial justice to all parties but was, in fact, the only body to which they could look in confidence for the administration of such justice.[80]

Nonetheless, while the Dáil adhered to its conservative approach on economic issues there was a considerable expansion which the ITGWU had enjoyed during the years 1918–20, tied to the attraction of some 40,000 agricultural workers'.[81] These newly organised farm labourers would become one of the most militant elements of the Irish Labour Party. In Waterford, better organisation among the agricultural workers proved crucial in turning back efforts to reduce their wages by the Irish Farmers Union (IFU) after the War of Independence. Emmet O'Connor has noted that when the IFU joined with the newly formed Free State Government at the end of the Irish Civil War to undermine the labourers, they 'sparked off outright class warfare, creating a situation where the 1913 lock-out in Dublin seems tame by comparison'.[82]

In October 1917, farm labourers saw a 70-per cent gain in their wages on average, price inflation notwithstanding. However, the collapse of farm prices in 1920, combined with the impact of a full-fledged recession the following year, served to weaken the conditions for continued trade union expansion in both the industrial and agricultural sectors. David Fitzpatrick has commented on the impact these developments had on Irish labour:

> By the end of 1921, about one-third of Irish workers in the major insured industries were out of work, roughly the same proportion as in Britain ... Labour's position was progressively weakened until its best hope was toppled for mitigation of wage reductions rather than demand wage increases. Even had the labour market been less unfavourable to union organisation, it is unlikely that the Irish Trade Unions would have kept their wickets intact under the hail of bullets and revolutionary rhetoric.[83]

What was the response of Sinn Féin to the collapse of the economic position of Irish workers? Sinn Féin certainly welcomed those measures of sympathy taken by the Irish trade union movement on its behalf. But strikes, carried out purely for reasons outside the objective of national independence, were simply unwarranted in Sinn Féin's view.[84] In order to keep such actions in check the Dáil set up a Department of Labour in 1919. Rather than championing the cause of the Irish worker outright, the Ministry's mandate was to help moderate disputes between labour and capital. Two years later, for example, the Department reported to the Dáil Cabinet that almost all its efforts during the previous two months had been aimed at enforcing the Belfast boycott.[85] The presence of Constance Markievicz during most of the 1919–21 period as Minister for Labour was largely symbolic. As Emmet O'Connor has observed, the combination of the Dáil's implementation of the arbitration courts and a Central Conciliation Board under the Labour Department, Markievicz's credentials as the only proclaimed socialist in the Cabinet notwithstanding, 'had the practical effect of asserting Dáil Éireann's legitimacy to employers and employees, reducing strife, and settling grievances, usually on the basis of precedents set out by (British) Government machinery'.[86] Among the members of the conciliations boards set up under the Labour Department's aegis were such conservatives as Darrell Figgis and Ernest Blythe. In Cork, Sean Moylan, Commandant of the Cork No. 2 Brigade, complaining of the bureaucratisation which the panel involved said, 'We started the war with hurleys, and by God, we'll finish it with fountain pens.'[87]

Emmet O'Connor has noted that during the Anglo-Irish War, the Labour Department 'never occupied the key positions in the resolution of popular discontent held by the Dáil Ministries of Home Affairs and Lands'. A key reason for this was the fact that, throughout much of the conflict, Constance Markievicz was herself 'on the run'. Nonetheless, O'Connor concedes that 'during the six months leading up to 20 January 1921, the Department intervened successfully in sixty disputes and made unsuccessful attempts at intervention in a further eight'.[88] The decision to implement the conciliation board system, as opposed to a wage bargaining approach, was part of a collective decision by the Republican Government to avoid placing it in an untenable position with either labour or the employers.[89]

Through the implementation of the Conciliation Boards, the Labour Department sought in earnest to operate impartially across class and religious lines. In one instance during the Anglo-Irish truce, Constance Markievicz threatened to use the IRA in a police action against a Catholic quarry manager in County Tyrone whom she believed to be discriminating against a Protestant workman. 'We wish to state', she wrote to him in a public warning, 'that the Government of Dáil Éireann cannot stand for intimidation and for the penalising [sic] of men because of their religion, and unless this intimidation is stopped, we shall have to put the matter into the hands of the Republican police.'[90] Ironically, despite its Nationalist majority, the provisions of the 1920 Government of Ireland Act and the subsequent terms of the Anglo-Irish Treaty placed County Tyrone under the jurisdiction of the Northern Ireland state. On 26 September 1921, the Republican Labour Ministry intervened satisfactorily in the dispute between the Tyrone Co. Council and local quarry workers, although the Council continued to enjoy official relations with the British local government authorities. To Markievicz, the action marked an example of 'the popular respect that the National Government enjoys' for its impartiality.[91]

While the Labour Department was not a front line aspect of the Republican Government, it nevertheless provided a direct awareness to Sinn Féin of the plight of the Irish workers in 1921. In a memorandum submitted to the Cabinet during the truce, Constance Markievicz emphasised measures that should be taken:

> [to relieve] the distress of the Agricultural worker, and to put the farming industry on a sound footing, it would be necessary to examine carefully into the question as to where the unjust profit is taken off our Agricultural products, and to discover if it would be possible to reorganise the whole producing industry so as to establish a proper relationship between the price

paid to the worker for their labour and the price they must pay for the products of their labour when it has been subsequently converted into food.[92]

While Markievicz's analysis was that of the only socialist in a position of authority in the Republican Government, her assessment of the increasing scale of militancy shown by workers throughout Ireland who suffered from a recession economy doubtless served as sobering evidence of the instability that was unfolding. 'In the last few weeks', she wrote, 'conditions have been growing worse and worse, and in many places – Bruree, Cork, Limerick, Wexford, Drogheda, etc. – the workers have taken forcible possession of industries, put machinery out of order, and burnt farms and ricks'. It was her contention that this state of affairs had, in fact, been 'intensified by the truce'. 'We do not know whether it is to be war or peace during the next few months that are coming ... In the meantime, we have an enemy in partial occupation of our country, our Government cannot function freely and our supply of money is limited'.

Markievicz went on to outline a series of short-term measures which the Government might support in order to stabilise the situation. She suggested the development of cooperatives for the sale and distribution of meat, along with the seizure by Dáil Éireann of 'the Irish Packing Factory, which would give a good deal of employment if it were started, and show the workers that we had their interests at heart'. Markievicz also suggested that 'the roads through the country districts might be repaired – this would give work to roadworkers who are in many places in great distress'.[93]

In the anti-conscription effort, Irish Labour occupied a pivotal position with Sinn Féin, the Irish Parliamentary Party, and the Catholic hierarchy in this common cause. The level of unity among Irish Nationalists and the Catholic hierarchy in their opposition to conscription culminated on 21 April 1918, when a combined pledge against conscription was signed. Two days later, a shut-down in the normal life of Nationalist Ireland occurred. Key to this effort was the general strike action by the trade union movement which shut down factories, and suspended public transportation in most of the country. The next call for a general strike by the Irish labour movement occurred on 12 April 1920, when the Irish Labour Party and the Irish Trades Union acted in support of the hunger strike initiated by Irish Republican prisoners in British prisons in Ireland. Within three days of the commencement of a general strike, the full complement of sixty-six prisoners were released outright. The British Government had evidently decided on this course of action rather than the granting of political status. But the move allowed Irish Labour along with Sinn Féin to claim a victory, much to the regret of Lloyd George and the Coalition.

A unique development which provided a localised example of worker solidarity with the Irish independence effort were the self-styled 'Soviets' initiated by the workers themselves in and around Limerick City in May 1920. While the nine-day work stoppage, as part of the 'Soviet' campaign, was tied to a lingering demand for higher wages, particularly in the creamery sector, it also contained a strong component of protest against repressive measures taken by the Crown's forces within the county.

Aside from the involvement of Irish Labour's rank and file with the independence effort through strikes and by outright participation in the Republican movement, the movement's work in supporting the recognition of the Irish Republic at various international forums between 1917–20 must also be emphasised. In Stockholm in 1917 the Irish delegation actively lobbied on behalf of Ireland's right to nationhood. Two years later, to somewhat greater effect, the Irish Labour delegation worked on behalf of the Republic at the International Labour and Socialist Conference held in Berne, on 3 February 1919, with Cathal O'Shannon and Tom Johnson representing Irish Labour. The press coverage they garnered there was particularly useful to the Irish independence effort.[94]

While generally termed a strike, the action taken was in fact an embargo created by the decision of the Irish rail and dock workers to refuse to carry military goods and to object to the transportation of troops carrying arms. It was with no little irony that the origins of the action arose out of the support Irish Labour had lent their British counterparts during the 'Hands Off Russia' campaign, when they refused to load munitions onto British vessels destined for Poland for use against the fledgling Soviet regime earlier that year. The Irish Trades Union Congress singled this out as the basis for supporting the Irish workers' decision not to unload munition-bearing ships upon their arrival in Dublin in May 1920. Reciprocal support by the British National Union of Railroads was not forthcoming, however. Instead, the British Labour organisation offered to call a special session of the British Trade Union Congress at which the Irish question would be considered, in exchange for the Irish railwaymen ending their actions against the Crown's military apparatus in Ireland. The National Executive of the joint Irish Labour Party and the ITUC was not long in stating why they supported their own railwaymen's action. The joint manifesto issued by the Irish Labour Party and the ITUC as published in the 10 June 1920 *Freeman's Journal* clearly laid out what the Labour movement's position was and why the action by the railwaymen was being sustained by a £1,000-per-week subscription fund to assist the workers:

> The men who work in the transport industries have laid it down emphatically that they will not be parties to the attempted reconquest of Irary Forces. Railwaymen, dock workers, and carters are quite fixed in their resolve and they will be supported by the organised workers in every other industry … It has happened that the railwaymen at the North Wall have been the first to be victimised in this phase of the National struggle. Over 400 men have

been locked out of their work for nearly three weeks because they will not bind themselves to handle war material ... The issue that is raised is ... identical with the issue that was fought to victory two years ago in the struggle of the Irish Nation against conscription. Then it was sought to take our bodies and compel us to bear arms in a fight not of our own choosing; now they seek to compel us to become co-workers with them in the destruction of our Nation.[95]

The Irish Railwaymen avoided an actual strike on a policy of management-instigated dismissals. In the process, the railway companies had to deal on a case-by-case basis with each worker who refused to carry British munitions. During the seven-month action, over 1,000 men were dismissed, while 17,000 railwaymen remained on the payrolls, a process which successfully halted the movement of troops and munitions. The harassment of Irish railway workers by the British forces was one method of retaliation. The Irish Trades Union Congress *Report* released in 1921, perhaps the most authoritative primary source on this period from the vantage point of the Irish Labour movement, stated:

It was a common practice for the military authorities to get upon the footplate of an engine and say to the driver, 'you have got to drive this train', put a revolver to his head and say, 'you will get the contents of this if you don't drive', and to the everlasting credit of the railwaymen, they said no.[96]

The essential terms of what would and would not be transported by the railway workers was made clear on 26 May 1920, following a lengthy tour of inspection of the cargo of trains near the North Wall by labour representatives, company managers, and military officials. During this episode, the authorities demonstrated to the labour representatives that the train cargo contained only pressed beef. It was therefore allowed to leave Dublin operated by the usual workforce. The description supplied by the *Irish Times* of 27 May on the 'inspection' is useful in underscoring the public embarrassment which the situation inflicted upon the British Government and its military forces in Ireland:

The first of the wagons was already open and a glance at the rough wooden casings and loose packing in the van showed that there could be nothing like ammunition there. The officer said that they might handle anything and also that they could if they liked get into the trucks. This was done and a very thorough search was made ... 'Are you quite satisfied before we leave it?' said the officer. Mr McDonald checked his notes and the men said that they were.[97]

The paper expanded on its earlier predications of dire economic consequences for the Irish economy on the grounds that 'if the strike becomes general, the closing of the railways will affect Irish industry and commerce with an instant paralysis. Within a fortnight, the country will be starving for lack of coal and other important necessaries; the Irish cattle trade will be killed, and farmers' produce will be left rotting on their hands.' Irish farmers, particularly in the west of the country, were indeed affected by the Irish railway workers' action.

In contrast to the editorial content and general coverage in the *Irish Times*, the *Freeman's Journal* proved far more sympathetic to the action by Irish labour. In its 6 June edition, the *Freeman's Journal*, in reporting on the rebuff by British labour of its Irish counterparts, noted that

> neither Mr Johnson or Mr Foran was very much attracted by the spirit in which the gathering responded to their appeal. Both declare that the impression left in their minds was one of indifference where it was not actually bad or positively unsympathetic. In net terms, the summing up of the discussion was that the Irish labour leaders look for no action of a decisive kind by the English transport workers as a body.[98]

In essence, British Labour had repudiated the Irish workers' claim and refused to provide financial assistance for their activities against the British Government and the railway companies. Similarly, as the *Irish Times* noted, there were to be 'no sympathetic strikes in Great Britain, whose railways and mercantile marine will continue to carry troops and stores and munitions for them to our Irish harbours'. The paper's editorial comment also paid a backhanded compliment to British labour leader J. H. Thomas' decision not to support the Irish rail and dock workers:

> It was a wise and chastened Mr Thomas who addressed his fellow railwaymen at Battersea. He was repudiated and would like to be able to forget his Police adventure. He sees now that the challenge which the Irish strikers asked him to endorse would be a challenge against the British Constitution ... Once more, the common sense of British labour has checked it on the slope that leads to anarchy.[99]

Finding public support at home to back up the Irish workers financially as well as morally also proved a source of difficulty, at least during the first two months of the action. A declaration by the ITUC appearing in the *Freeman's Journal* of 12 June starkly stated that 'funds must be raised immediately to provide for their (the workers) sustenance ... At least one thousand pounds a week will be required. Up to the present, the general public have subscribed less than one hundred pounds ... Trades Councils throughout the country are hereby requested to take a hand immediately in the formation of local committees for the purpose of organising collections ...'[100]

In serving to actually deprive the British Government of the use of Irish railways for moving both its armed forces and military supplies, the action served throughout its duration as a source of practical difficulty, as well as embarrassment, to the British Government. It occurred at a time when significant inroads were also being made by Sinn Féin on the question of who was actually governing Ireland. The establishment of Republican national arbitration courts, coupled with the 'police' activity of the IRA, created the impression that Britain had ceased to govern much of Ireland. A review of the British military and Cabinet records from the period May–December 1920 underscores the tension between the Government's air of outward indifference and its private concern towards the rail boycott.

At the outset of the railway embargo, a report to the Cabinet from the Dublin Castle Executive stated that 'the general situation throughout Ireland remains in a very disturbed condition'. The political assessment given by the Irish Administration to the Cabinet took the view that the Irish workers' 'failure to obtain such support from British labour and the preparations of the Government to cope with the emergency of a railway strike have resulted in their adopting a waiting policy. Employees have been instructed that they are not to drive trains with armed troops or police to handle "munitions" but otherwise to remain at work until they are dismissed'.[101]

During its first two months, the embargo saw the Government go from tacitly accepting the use of force to compelling the railway engineers to move the trains to actually stopping other rail traffic as a means of causing public opposition to the workers' actions. Finally, they criticised the railway owners for their ineffectiveness in dealing with their employees. This last strategy served more than anything else as a cover for the Government's own inability to bring the action to a swift halt. The approach led to the full consideration of a proposal submitted by Chief Secretary for Ireland Hamar Greenwood, that the British subsidy be revoked from the Irish rail companies. A Cabinet-level conference held in September 1920 concluded that

> the Chief Secretary's view was right in principle that it was absurd that the government should continue to subsidise, at the expense of the general body of taxpayers, the shareholders of a railroad company that refused to carry government traffic or to provide funds where with to pay increased wages to the very men who refuse to handle the traffic. The Chief Secretary was asked to see the Minister of Transportation in order to ascertain the precise position in regard to the powers of the government on this question.[102]

Greenwood's proposal, however, was rejected after it was determined by the Crown's legal officers that special legislation would be needed for the removal of any subsidies. Nonetheless, while the Chief Secretary's recommendation was not adopted, his analysis of the impact of the munitions embargo on British rule in Ireland remained valid. The 'strike', he told the Cabinet on 25 September 1920, had put the Government 'in a humiliating and discreditable position'. It was a viewpoint which Greenwood's top deputy, Sir John Anderson, also shared. 'At the present rate,' he stated, 'we would be broken sooner than the railway companies.' It was likewise his opinion that 'the railway managers and directors have not put their backs into this and ought now to do so'.[103]

Winston Churchill also favoured a hardline approach to the Irish railway crisis that would supplement the effort at coercion against Sinn Féin. Of this account, Tom Jones wrote in his diary:

> He (Churchill) would raise a crisis on the railways and on the Post Office. It was clear from what Sir John Anderson had said that the prevailing discomfort was already beginning to tell ... He would stop the subsidy to the railways, shut them up and turn the men off. After three or four days without wages they would want to begin to come to terms.[104]

Harassment from Sinn Féin was one reason advanced by the Irish Administration to the Cabinet for the almost total stalemate in the Irish rail system between July and October 1920. 'Generally speaking,' Greenwood stated, 'the staff know that it is safer to refuse to work Government traffic than to do their duty.' But lacking evidence of any serious instances of IRA harassment of railway workers, the Government also resorted to the use of forgeries of Republican documents and publications in connection with the railway 'strike'. Workers in the Derry and Donegal areas were treated to the circulation of the following apparently British-manufactured ultimatum, allegedly from Republican Headquarters: 'Acting under instructions, you are hereby notified that after this date, you are forbidden to drive any train or assist in any way the transport of armed forces of the British Government.'[105] While intimidation may actually have been a feature of the Republicans' effort to heighten workers' cooperation with the embargo in some areas, by and large the position of the workers themselves was one of sympathy with the Irish revolutionary struggle.

Nonetheless, the British Government was also well aware of the popular support for the transport workers in Co. Mayo, for example. Evidence came to the Irish Situation Committee of developments in that western county from a source, who wrote complaining of actions taken by local government authorities there: 'Government officials have given large sums to the munitions strike fund. R. M. [Royal Magistrate] considers that the amount of support given to the munitions strike could not have been so great except for the belief current that Government will eventually give in and send munitions and soldiers by road.'[106]

A review of the work stoppage figures indicates that for the months of October and November 1920, the south-western counties represented far greater numbers than any other segment of the country, with thirty-five and ninety rail stoppages, as compared with twelve and twenty-five for the Dublin and South-Eastern Railway, and twenty and fifty-four respectively for the Midland Great Western Railway, among others. These figures are themselves consistent with the fact that the Southwest comprised the epicenter of the Republicans' armed effort in the Anglo-Irish War. In general, the inability to move British military supplies caused by the railway embargo was a major part of the breakdown of British governance in Ireland.

By November 1920, with over 1,000 workers dismissed from their jobs, it became evident to the railwaymen, as well as the British Government, that the action could not continue much longer. The *Freeman's Journal*, the workers' strongest supporter in print outside the trade union press, made it clear on 17 November that the continuance of the strike was counter productive:

> For six months Irish railwaymen have borne a heavy responsibility and borne it manfully ... without the strongest guarantees that her sufferings shall produce some tangible benefit for her people, we realise that a withdrawal would be an apparent defeat for the men, but to persist would be an actual victory for the Government. The strike means starvation.[107]

In a milder statement than would be ordinarily expected, the *Irish Times* in its issue of the same day cited Tom Johnson's view that 'an economic war with England would throw back the social life of Ireland for perhaps a hundred years'. 'The Irish railwaymen', the paper stated, 'must choose within the next few days whether that fate is to be invited or averted.'[108] By December, evidence that the action was nearing the breaking point for the railway workers, the rail companies, and the Irish economic sectors that depended on them became even more compelling. 'The paralysis of the railways has been creeping slowly', the *Freeman's Journal* proclaimed on 3 December 1920. 'But inexorably,' it continued, 'over the whole of Southern Ireland ... already the Great Southern and Western Companies have served notices of dismissal on their staffs. We announce today that the Dublin and Southwest Co., will follow their example before the end of next week. Thus Dublin's three principle links with the South and West of Ireland are in imminent danger of being broken.'[109]

These actions drove home to the Irish labour movement the odds against its being able to carry on the effort against the British Government's munitions and troops much longer. A National Labour Conference held on 16 November, followed by the railwaymen's own conference one month later, made it clear that the embargo had been stretched to the limits of the railway workers' endurance. The meeting of the Irish TUC held in the Mansion House, Dublin, on 16 November presented a cross section of opinion that was cognizant that the end was near. At the same time, there was pride in what had been accomplished. One principal delegate stated that the likely dismissal of an additional 1,600 men would be a burden that the labour movement could not sustain. And while they 'were not afraid of the issue ... they were not going to be content with false talks about fighting on ...' Tom Johnson, Secretary to the National Executive and English by both birth and upbringing, stated a view that sought to move the action of the Irish railway workers to a plane well above that of nationalism alone. By withholding their labour from 'certain work of an abominable kind', the workers he held 'were making an assertion that as workingmen they had a right not to be conscious coop-erators in the end that was being sought, that in their work they were not merely cogs in the industrial machine, but were human beings'.[110]

But the economic realities of a continued embargo were also evident to other members of the Executive. Delegate Hart, representing the Dockers' Union, appealed to the Congress 'to look at the situation from the point of view of the people who were suffering, and those who were likely to suffer'. 'The idea of the Government', he contended, 'was to bring about starvation and break the spirit of the Irish people through their children.' For Hart, the negative impact of a continued job action was clear:

> If men were thrown out of employment, and if they saw their little children going hungry, they would clamour for a settlement. The railwaymen would not alone be affected by the struggle. The industries of the country would be involved. The present question was one of vital importance to Ireland, and was vital to Labour.[111]

Secretary Birmingham, of the Irish National Union of Railwaymen, noted that while the strike had not in reality prevented the distribution of munitions throughout the country, 'at least ... they were not conveyed by railwaymen'. However, he was quick to caution that 'if the struggle was continued it would mean that at least fifteen thousand railwaymen – all except those in the North-East corner – would be within a week or two thrown on the industrial scrap heap'. Like Hart, Birmingham dreaded the economic impact of a continued railway embargo on labour and the nation alike:

> Not alone the railways but the county's industries would have to close down. There would be thousands swelling the ranks of the unemployed. Even the farming community would be vitally affected ... Very little privation has taken place amongst the railwaymen so far, but under altered circumstances that condition of affairs could not exist.[112]

Some members of the Executive resolved to fight on to the end: 'It would be better', Cathal O'Shannon declared, 'that we all go down in this fight than that we should stain our souls, our movement, and our whole generation with dishonour.' His views were echoed by a delegate identified as 'Miss Maloney', who argued that the material question was whether they were prepared to keep the body of Ireland alive 'at the expense of the soul'. 'They were not waging the fight', she stated, 'because they had a chance of success, but because they were right, and that was the only basis upon which they should wage any fight.'[113] Such arguments were apparently in the minority, yet they were the rhetorical prefigurations of the larger debate that would take place one year later in Dáil Éireann over ratification of the Anglo-Irish Treaty articles.

The British Government largely became aware of the defeat of the railway workers on 9 December, in a report from Dublin Castle official Mark Sturgis. The report documented the transportation of armed troops on the Great Southern and Western for the first time in several months. At their Conference on 21 December, the Irish railway workers voted unanimously and unconditionally to end their action.

The 1921 *Report* of the Irish Trades Union Congress offers the official Irish labour interpretation of the 1920 Munitions Strike. With an eye to posterity, the *Report* itself noted that it had in mind the future historian of these times, whom it held 'will without doubt, give some attention to the struggle of the railway workers on this issue'. According to the ITUC's view, the workers' policy 'that had been carried through from the beginning, of accepting individual dismissals, was continued with the result that notwithstanding the efforts of the military to force the issue, the railways of the country were never compelled to close down'.[114] The *Report* characterised as 'malicious and characteristic lies' statements by Chief Secretary Greenwood that a facsimile released to the press in Britain and the United States, and which threatened in the name of 'Minister of War of the Government of the Irish Republic' railway workers who moved troops and munitions against their orders. The ITUC labelled the charges 'a simple forgery' on the basis that the railwaymen acted from the beginning on their own initiative, and were supported by the National Executive and by the country generally'. A second falsehood the *Report* refuted was the allegation advanced by both Greenwood and Lloyd George that the railway workers categorically refused to transport any soldier. 'During the whole of the munitions struggle police and soldiers were constantly seen on the railways', the ITUC stated. 'So long as they were not carrying arms,' they held, 'nobody sought to interfere with them.'[115]

In the eyes of ITUC Executive, efforts at organising alternative methods for the distribution of foodstuffs around the country were, in fact, thwarted by the British Government. They argued that Irish Labour sought to establish 'a National Food Committee whose duties it would be to organise the food supplies nationally and locally, and to make provision for the necessary transportation'. 'Local authorities', the ITUC *Report* noted, 'showed every willingness to take action in this Report, and to cooperate with the Trade Unions in so doing.' However, the document further stated that 'large numbers of men who were capable of giving active assistance in the organisation of distribution, active Trade Union officials and others, were either arrested or driven "underground"'. As a result of this official coercion, the ITUC argued that the Food Committee, which was to have been formally called 'The Lord Mayors' National Committee' was prevented from getting off the ground. The burning of Cork City on 10 and 11 December was also cited by the Irish Labour movement as a reason for ending the munitions embargo, particularly in the context of the railway workers' own formal gathering on

21 December. It was not fear of increased British repression but recognition that it was not in the interest of the Irish labour movement to be seen as the reason for a violent Governmental response that victimised greater numbers of Irish men and women.

> At an early stage of the struggle, it became evident that the British Government's design was to force a quick close down of the Railway Services while, at the same time, seeking to make it appear that the Railway workers were responsible. We advised you to frustrate this plan by refusing to strike ... The British Authority which assumes Governmental power in Ireland has with deliberate intent sought to interfere with and destroy the preparations being made to cope with the problem of providing food, milk, and fuel to the people: they have seized the papers and records of our Food Committees, have arrested and imprisoned without charge the members of the Committees and have placed a barrier against the Organisation of the Motor Transport Service ... These acts have been followed by the Proclamations of Martial Law ... by a threat to intensify the campaign of frightfulness. His [Lloyd George's] cue is immediately taken up in the City of Cork, the published threats to utterly destroy the City being carried a long way towards fulfilment.[116]

These developments led the National Executive to conclude that 'changed conditions require a change of tactics'. On that basis, the leadership decided 'to advise the Railway and Dock workers to alter the position and to offer to carry everything that the British Authorities are willing to risk on the trains'. 'Whatever the risk that might be involved,' the National Executive's 16 November statement stated, 'we feel confident that the Railwaymen are not less willing to face them than the travelling public.'[117] In effect, rather than risk provoking public wrath against the Irish labour movement, the Executive adopted a policy that both suited the reality of the situation and brought continued disruption to the British military effort in Ireland. While its use of the word 'risk' in reference to the practice of the Military actually carrying weapons on the trains was not expanded upon, the implication of support for Irish separatism is also clear.

While the Irish railway workers did in fact end the embargo as a means of protest, the impact of what they had actually accomplished in upsetting the British military effort in Ireland, as well as the Empire's prestige, must not be overlooked. People throughout the country had not only seen Irish workers flout British authority, they also witnessed a seven-month-long labour action that was part of the general collapse of British rule in most of Ireland in 1920. It occurred at a time when, in the eyes of much of the population, the Dáil Éireann's National Arbitration Courts were effectively replacing the British legal system in Ireland. Seen in the context of these and other developments affecting the British administration in Ireland, the munitions embargo takes on a wider significance. Charles Townshend has written that had 'the embargo been made total in scope and indefinite in duration, it is hard to see how a functional Military presence in the hinterland could have been maintained'.[119] The occurrence of the munitions embargo itself, and the determination displayed on the part of the railway workers over a protracted period and against the backdrop of over 1,000 dismissals, also revealed dimensions of an Irish workforce that was clearly supportive of Irish national aspirations.

The importance of the direct cooperation of the Irish railway workers with those engaged in armed activities against the Crown was underscored by Piaras Beaslai, an associate and early biographer of Michael Collins. Beaslai's account is particularly useful in showing the importance of 'railway communications' in the effective operation of Collins' intelligence network. Beaslai writes:

> Mention should be made here of Collins' work with regard to Railway communications. On all the lines there were guards and other officials who regularly carried the volunteer messages, even during the time when trains and passengers were systematically searched by the Black and Tans. Among the men he was closely in touch with in connection with this work may be mentioned: Sean O'Connell, who was employed at Kingbridge; Claffey, Daly, and Finnegan on the Midland Great Western; Paddy Dunne, Quigley, Ambrose and Semple on the Great Southern.[120]

The IRA, in turn, reciprocated the assistance given by those employed on the railways, especially when matters involved their own operations. In *No Other Law*, Florence O'Donoghue, a senior IRA officer in the Southern Command, described one incident when this mutual cooperation between the railwaymen and the Volunteers occurred: 'When they arrived at O'Connell's it was found that the house held another prisoner, a Railway official from Mallow who had been arrested by the IRA for cooperating with the British Forces by dismissing railmen [sic] who also refused to work trains carrying troops and equipment.'[121]

The cooperation between the Republican movement and Irish Labour also reached to the highest levels, as shown by correspondence of 6 July 1921 sent by Michael Collins, in his capacity as Director of Intelligence, to William O'Brien, on one of the most sensitive of topics: the infiltration of British spies into the Irish trade union movement. The letter, written five days before the commencement of the Anglo-Irish Truce, stated:

> I got the following from a very reliable source: 'Enemy Spies in Trade Unions': Dublin Castle is selecting men from the military there to go around the country anywhere there is a Trade Union of any description to pose as coming from the Executive of the particular Union. [sic] Men so selected are to be supplied with faked union badges and forged instructions written on identical or Union Note [sic] paper signed by forged signatures of the Secretariat of the different Unions which they are to visit in order to find out the class of men attending meetings and anything else that would matter in their eyes.

In his letter, Collins also told O'Brien that he did not know how far 'this thing has gone, but you may take it that if it hasn't gone beyond the initial stages it is because the Enemy Authorities are not certain of their ground'. The Republican Intelligence Chief suggested that 'as a first step on your part a couple of reliable Branch Secretaries should be informed'. 'From what I know', he offered, 'of the way the Enemy regarded the Unions, I am sure the Transport would be the first body to be dealt with.' In a postscript, Collins added that Branch Secretaries should be 'put on their guard with a view to immediate discovery when the attempt is made'.[122]

It can be inferred, given the evidence of British Government subterfuge against the labour movement in Britain itself, that the consternation and embarrassment provoked by the 1920 munitions embargo could indeed have led the Crown to attempt to undermine trade unions in Ireland. Likewise, Michael Collins' own understanding of the role of the Irish labour movement as an important source of support for the Irish independence effort, led to his own concern that any attempted British effort at espionage within that movement should be dealt with as swiftly and as effectively as possible.

Nonetheless, Collins had something less than a full admiration for the leadership of the Irish railworkers. 'Unfortunately,' he wrote in a letter of 26 February 1921 to Art O'Brien, Sinn Féin's principal official in Britain, 'the leaders of the Irish Railwaymen are what might be described as "old-timers" and are without vigour and national spirit.' 'Their guiding principle', he added, 'would be weak action, if I may be permitted to use such a term.'[123] The remark was typical of the hostility he often held for Irish labour organisations, which he felt were largely subservient to the demands of their parent organisations in Britain. It also may have shown an awareness on Collins' part that the Irish Labour movement's leadership was far removed from the legacy of James Connolly on the national question. In retrospect Collins' assessment may not have been overly harsh. British Cabinet records indicate that Irish Labour's decision not to contest the June 1921 General Election was apparently never a *fait accompli*. Tom Johnson, William O'Brien and Thomas Foran, the leader of the Irish Transport and General Workers' Union, met with senior British government officials in the spring of that year to seek an accommodation that would have enabled the Irish Labour Party to go forward in the upcoming Westminster election, Sinn Féin's position notwithstanding. A discussion within the British Cabinet on 27 April 1921 makes clear that these three senior Irish Labour leaders expressed a willingness to accept a Southern Parliament under the terms of the Government of Ireland Act (1920) if an amendment providing for wider Irish fiscal autonomy was added. The account of Tom Jones, Lloyd George's Private Secretary, of the private exchanges between the Irish Labour leaders and British Home Secretary Edward Shortt, at the home of a railway company official, provides a useful insight into their political strategy at this point.

Mr Fisher:* Some weeks ago, before Easter, the Home Secretary received intimation that some Irish Transport workers were anxious to meet some Ministers. The Transport workers arrived on Saturday and we met them on Monday, but it never came off because on that day there was a number of executions in Dublin. We understood that they were prepared to say 'if we can get an assurance from the government that there will be fiscal autonomy we will come out in the open and publish a manifesto'. Burgess (a railway company official)[*sic*] said that the Transport workers had made an arrangement with Sinn Féin that if the Transport workers came out with the manifesto the Sinn Féiners would denounce it but would allow the elections to be worked. One of the difficulties is that you have Sinn Féin who want to save their faces and get an excuse to get out of the Republic pledge and do not know how to begin ...
Mr Shortt:† I saw the Transport workers at Burgess' flat. Foran, Tom Johnson and O'Brien. Fisher's account is accurate. They were content with fiscal autonomy. They were agreed that they could not differentiate against this country or against Ulster. They were willing to issue a manifesto over their names. They are powerful men. Foran the strongest and Johnson the ablest. Had they issued the manifesto it would have led to a bitter quarrel in their ranks. I do not know what their view is now.[124]

There were also specific instances where trade union members involved actively in the independence effort sought the direct support of the Republican Government on behalf of workers who had found themselves imprisoned or unemployed as a result of their activities in defence of the Republic. In one case, for example, Terence MacSwiney, in his capacity as Lord Mayor of Cork and as Commandant of the Cork No. 1 Brigade of the IRA, received a solicitation on 25 May 1920 from Cork Labour leader James Fitzgerald, in search of funds to supplement the Prisoners' Dependents Fund for workers incarcerated for Republican activities. Fitzgerald also sought to impress upon MacSwiney the need to make 'suitable arrangements' with the Labour Bureau in Cork in an effort to provide work for 'our out of work soldiers'. 'The drain on our Prisoner's Dependents Fund is 20 pounds weekly', he stated. He added that 'as you can imagine, such cannot continue and has no permanent, only immediate, good effects'.

Fitzgerald outlined for MacSwiney the case of one worker who was imprisoned for involvement with an IRA arms raid. It was an example that no doubt served to expose the Lord Mayor to the hardships that such involvement could bring to workers and their families.

---

* H. A. L. Fisher, 1865–1940; Historian, Liberal MP, authored 1918 British Education Act, and Member of Irish Situation Committee.
† Edward Shortt, 1862–1935; Liberal MP, 1910–22, Home Secretary 1919–22.

For example, the bearer of this note is one Sean O'Connell, just released from Wormwood. He organised and carried out successfully the capture of six rifles at Rushbrooke last February and his arrest was accomplished soon after. This resulted in his dismissal from Haulbowline Dockyard. Although we allow himself and his people 3 pounds per week, we cannot do so for long more; and to keep his family (a large one) in comparative decency, his aged father (65 years old) is intending going to sea before the mast in a week's time. His brother was out in Easter Week with himself and our small section and surely his case deserves attention.[125]

Fitzgerald concluded his letter by asking MacSwiney to assist in finding gainful employment for the man in Cork City, and made specific reference to the Ford Motor Co. He added that O'Connell's situation 'is but one of many similar cases, and where we suffer in common for the cause, we might also unite in helping each other'. An internal memorandum sent by Dublin Castle to the Cabinet following the document's seizure emphasised that Fitzgerald's letter revealed the severe financial situation with which the Republican effort was faced. 'As a result of the vigorous efforts of the police and military, a great number of Irish Republican leaders [six] are on the run with the result that they and their families are dependent on Republican funds for maintenance.'[126]

Sinn Féin's lack of sympathy overall for the cause of the Irish left was not lost on the Soviet Government. During a visit in 1919 to Moscow in search of official recognition for the Irish Republic, Dr Patrick McCartan encountered this awareness from one Soviet official:

He said they had been informed we were hostile to the Irish Communists. If that were so, I replied, we were hostile to something that did not exist in Ireland. We concentrated on the fight with England and gave no attention to anything else. The mass of the people were friendly to Communist Russia, not because they understood Communism, but because they saw England endeavouring to overthrow the present regime in Russia. They concluded therefore, that the government of Russia must be a good government.[127]

Emmet O'Connor challenges what he sees as the weaknesses inherent both in the traditionalist and revisionist interpretations of Irish Labour during 1917–23, largely on the basis that both views 'stem from their concern with leaders rather than workers, with structures rather than movements, with politics rather than industrial conflict, and from their common exaggeration of the importance of Nationalism on Labour'. His analysis is predicated on 'the assumption that a mass transformation of values cannot be explained by theories of leadership, charisma, or leadership betrayal'. 'In all trade unions', he writes, 'tensions exist between the attractions of militancy and the requirements of organisation.' O'Connor argues in his study of Irish syndicalism during the years 1917–23 that 'the expansion of industrial conflict from

1917 to 1923 stemmed from social and economic forces created by wartime conditions, the post war boom, and the slump that followed'. 'In its values, its tactics, its goals,' he contends, 'labour operated independently of the Republican campaign.'[128]

The argument against placing an over-reliance on developments concerning Irish Nationalism and Irish Labour during the War of Independence is also underscored by Adrian Pimley, who argues that 'more important than this lack of leadership on the part of the labour movement was the lack of any revolutionary party and the lack of any significant social base for a revolution'. The fact that the great majority of Ireland's population were rural dwellers would likewise work strongly against a successful socialist revolution. As Pimley notes, 'For a social revolution the Irish working class needed an alliance with the rural population.'[129] Even at the height of the gains made by Irish agricultural workers during the period 1918–20, no effort to unite the rural and the urban worker was undertaken. As we have seen, Connolly himself left no such legacy of cooperation. It was with supreme irony that upon entering the Dáil of the Irish Free State in 1927, an out-of-power Eamon de Valera expressed his frustration over the fact that the course of events had placed his new Fianna Fáil Party and Labour in a relationship of opposition, which he saw as divisive and regrettable. 'I have never regarded freedom as an end in itself', he told the Dáil, 'but if I were asked what statement of Irish policy was most in accord with my view as to what human beings should struggle for, I would stand side by side with James Connolly.'[130] There were to be few other instances in his long career where de Valera publicly sought to link himself in such a way to the man he had joined in arms during Easter Week. In effect, the outlook of de Valera, and others of a more conservative nationalist bent, lay at the heart of the limited social goals of the Irish Revolution.

One of the most candid analyses of the limited vision of Sinn Féin on the economic front is that of Ernie O'Malley, who held a unique perspective due to the role he played throughout Ireland as a key IRA training officer.

> Perhaps the situation would have been different if Sinn Féin had been able to develop slowly, if their main energies had not been put to the electioneering side. Driving force was there, but no vision or attempt at economic solution. There was an economic root to the fight. Though many on our side would not better their position by a result in our favour. Freedom comes religious, political, and economic. We were at the political stage. We had not the faculty for thinking things through sufficiently.[131]

In such an assessment may have lain some of the seeds for later internecine strife when the political objectives of Sinn Féin were subsumed by the question of support for or opposition to the Anglo-Irish Treaty.

THE PROCLAMATION OF

POBLACHT NA H EIREANN.

THE PROVISIONAL GOVERNMENT
OF THE

IRISH REPUBLIC
TO THE PEOPLE OF IRELAND.

IRISHMEN AND IRISHWOMEN: In the name of God and the dead generations from which she receives her old tradition of nationhood, Ireland, through us, summons her children to her flag and strikes for her freedom.

Having organised and trained her manhood through her secret revolutionary organisation, the Irish Republican Brotherhood, and through her open military organisations, the Irish Volunteers and the Irish Citizen Army, having patiently perfected her discipline, having resolutely waited for the right moment to reveal itself, she now seizes that moment, and, supported by her exiled children in America and by gallant allies in Europe, but relying in the first on her own strength, she strikes in full confidence of victory.

We declare the right of the people of Ireland to the ownership of Ireland, and to the unfettered control of the Irish destinies, to be sovereign and indefeasible. The long usurpation of that right by a foreign people and government has not extinguished the right, nor can it ever be extinguished except by the destruction of the Irish people. In every generation the Irish people have asserted their right to national freedom and sovereignty : six times during the past three hundred years they have asserted it in arms. Standing on that fundamental right and again asserting it in arms in the face of the world, we hereby proclaim the Irish Republic as a Sovereign Independent State, and we pledge our lives and the lives of our comrades-in-arms to the cause of its freedom, of its welfare, and of its exhaltation among the nations.

The Irish Republic is entitled to, and hereby claims, the allegiance of every Irishman and Irishwoman. The Republic guarantees religious and civil liberty, equal rights and equal opportunities to all its citizens, and declares its resolve to pursue the happiness and prosperity of the whole nation and of all its parts, cherishing all the children of the nation equally, and oblivious of the differences carefully fostered by an alien government, which has divided a minority from the majority in the past.

Until our arms have brought the opportune moment for the establishment of a permanent National Government, representative of the whole people of Ireland and elected by the suffrages of all her men and women, the provisional Government, hereby constituted, will administer the civil and military affairs of the Republic in trust for the people.

We place the cause of the Irish Republic under the protection of the Most High God, Whose blessing we invoke upon our arms, and we pray that no one who serves that cause will dishonour it by cowardice, inhumanity, or rapine. In this supreme hour, the Irish nation must, by its valour and discipline and by the readiness of its children to sacrifice themselves for the common good, prove itself worthy of the august destiny to which it is called.

Signed on Behalf of the Provisional Government.

THOMAS J. CLARKE

SEAN Mac DIARMADA.	THOMAS MacDONAGH.
P. H. PEARSE.	EAMONN CEANNT.
JAMES CONNOLLY.	JOSEPH PLUNKETT

1. The Proclamation of the Irish Republic, issued 24 April 1916.
(Courtesy of Paul Kelley, USA)

In committing an independent Ireland to a non-sectarian and socially inclusive society, the Proclamation stands as a progressive document and a manifestation of the attitude of its signatories. Each of them would die before a British firing squad.

6

The Republican Courts and the Breakdown of British Rule

Not less important to the nation than a national civil service are national courts of law.

Arthur Griffith in The *Resurrection of Hungary* (Dublin, 1907)

In addition to establishing an independent Irish legislature in Dáil Éireann, Sinn Féin also took significant steps to break down and replace the British legal system in Ireland. The Dáil established under its control the National Arbitration Courts, which began functioning in June 1920. Within a month, twenty-one such courts were adjudicating what were in essence land disputes, a vital concern in a still largely agrarian society. Since the original structure of the Land Courts had been under the force of British law, in June the Dáil took legislative action to ensure, at least on a de facto basis, that their judgments were enforced in the name of the Irish Republic.

Arthur Griffith, the intellectual father of the passive dimension of the Sinn Féin movement, formulated the rationale for such a system in the *Resurrection of Hungary*, (1907). For Griffith, the establishment of independent courts was part of the process of peaceful refusal to participate in the institutions of the British Government. In effect, these courts were tied to his outlook, expressed in the *Resurrection of Hungary*, on the need for Nationalists to refuse to sit in the House of Commons. In Griffith's view, a native Irish government, elected by 'the Irish people, abstaining from Westminster, would serve as the vehicle by which the powers of the British Government would be gradually, but successfully, eroded'. The establishment of a native legal system would be concurrent with that goal. Griffith was explicit on the advantages of such a development:

> The prestige, the dignity, the strength such a national legal system would confer upon a movement for national independence is obvious ... but, in addition, it would deprive the corrupt Bar of Ireland of much of its incentives to corruption, save the pockets of our people, and materially in bringing about the spirit of brotherhood of national oneness in Ireland ... The decisions of an arbitration court are binding not only in morals, but in law, on

those who appeal to it. I say to my countrymen as the 'Nation' said to them in 1843, 'You have it in your power to resume popular courts and to fix laws and it is your duty to do so ... It is the duty of every Irishman to himself, to his family, to his neighbour, his boundless duty to his country to carry every legal dispute to the arbitrators and obey the decisions.'[1]

It was Griffith's contention that 'eighty per cent' of the cases 'which are now heard in the Common Courts of Ireland involve the expenditure by the people of an enormous sum of money which is utilised to keep up a corrupt judicial system'. The majority of those cases, he argued 'could be equitably and legally decided in voluntary arbitration courts at practically no expense at all. The course', Griffith wrote, 'is legal and feasible – its advantages are great and obvious.'[2] This non-violent resistance, by providing for the take-over of functions performed by the British Government, made British rule in much of Ireland impossible. This achievement cannot be omitted from any discussion of the Anglo-Irish conflict during the years 1919–21, particularly in light of the legitimacy the courts helped bestow on the Dáil Government. At the same time, it should be noted that the implementation of this aspect of Griffith's non-violent policy was made possible by a chain of events linked closely to a more militant Sinn Féin movement that drew its inspiration from Easter Week 1916.

Dáil Éireann initially established the system referred to as the 'National Arbitration Courts' in June 1919. But a full year would pass before the Dáil would offer specific guidelines for the operation of such courts. Nonetheless, even before the Dáil's action some local Sinn Féin organisations had already commenced an arbitration process. Dorothy Macardle places the formulation of the Republican courts within the context 'of the land agitation spreading rapidly in the West'.[3] Indeed, Sinn Féin was motivated in the establishment of a legal system of its own by more than a desire for establishing Republican legality in Ireland. It was also driven by a keen awareness of the importance of the agrarian issue. It was probably not an accident that the first Repub-lican 'land court' under the arbitration system set up by the Dáil was held in the West of Ireland in the Spring of 1919. Conor Maguire, who served as a Republican judge, was the first to organise a system of tribunals to deal with civil disputes. 'To our surprise,' Maguire wrote, 'we found it comparatively easy to persuade litigants and solicitors to bring their cases before the new tribunals.' Maguire also provides a useful insight into the rationale used by Sinn Féin in setting up the National Arbitration system.

> The idea was to set up arbitration tribunals to which litigants would submit their disputes. Dáil Éireann gave sanction to this course of action, preferring not to challenge the courts directly for fear of repression ... behind it also was the belief that as arbitration was a recognised procedure under British Law, the authorities would hesitate to use force to prevent arbitration tribunals from functioning.[4]

Indeed the land courts at first, and later the wider body of civil courts established by Dáil Éireann, were driven in large part by the need for order in the country. As Mary Kotsonouris has written in her account of the Dáil Courts, 'Small groups of Volunteers formed themselves into village constabularies who pursued and punished thieves, vandals and wife beaters and made themselves responsible for crown control at race meetings and fair days.' 'Increasing frustration', she notes, 'about the division of land combined with general lawlessness led to serious outbreaks of Whiteboyism; cruel attacks were perpetrated on landowners – mostly small farmers themselves – and their stock'.[5]

As arbitration tribunals, the 'courts' were without a coercive jurisdiction and could thereby function simultaneously with the Crown's Courts. The swift popularity of the 'tribunals', as the arbitration courts became known, required the setting up of 'regular sittings of Parish courts ... each with their justices and clerks'.[6] The courts won such a degree of public acceptance, and served so forcefully in weakening the British Administration, that on 29 July 1920 the Dáil formally established the Courts of Civil and Equity jurisdiction. Some weeks earlier, the Dáil had authorised Austin Stack as Minister for Home Affairs 'to employ such organisers as he required for the Arbitration Courts Scheme'. Instructions were also given for women to be made eligible for appointment as Arbitrators and for the appointment of Irish speakers in Irish-speaking districts.[7]

Stack estimated that the annual cost for implementing the scheme including the Supreme Court, Court of Appeal, District Courts and Petty Courts to be £112,000. In addition, he calculated that a pilot scheme of so-called 'Rotary Courts' would cost a further £11,300. This figure included funding for seven justices at a rate of £750 each.[8]

Initially, the courts were allowed to sit in public without any risk of dismissal by Crown forces. But over time, as British opposition to the courts grew, it became necessary to hold their sessions clandestinely. While the courts were derived from the Sinn Féin doctrine of passive resistance, and performed functions previously under the purview of the British Government, they were, at the same time, status quo oriented. Rather than serving as agents for fundamental change at the agrarian level in Irish society, the Land Courts, in essence, performed as guardians of the existing private property system. For that reason, their acceptance over time by Protestant landowners during the height of the Anglo-Irish conflict might be better understood. The picture painted by Darrell Figgis, who was later involved as a drafter of the Free State's Constitution, of the role of the Republican Courts as proof positive of the essentially conservative Nationalism motivating Sinn Féin at that time, is indeed a useful one. Figgis wrote that a grasp of the general success of the arbitration courts in gaining acceptance of their decisions 'can only be realised by those who know how intensely agrarian disputes can bind a community in Ireland, particularly in the congested districts'.[9]

The Republican Courts were themselves also a source of propaganda in Ireland, Britain, and the United States, in presenting an image of Sinn Féin that was committed to order and the rule of law, and suggesting that for that reason the claims made by Conor Maguire and other participants should be viewed with some suspicion. Nonetheless, the identity of the courts was clearly at odds with the British attempt to portray Irish Republicanism as a force driven by anti-democratic extremism in league with Russian Bolshevism. In the pre-Anglo-Irish Truce period, the role played by the Courts in helping to keep the Irish separatist movement united and apart from class divisions tied to land agitation was useful in making the national question the focal point of concern. In addition, it will be seen that the standard set by the Republican Courts for the equitable administration of justice also proved useful in gaining the support of many Southern Unionists for what would become the Irish Free State a few years later.[10]

From the Irish left, however, the Republican Courts' performance appears counterproductive. In Desmond Greaves' estimate, 'while claims to ranches and demesne lands were not affected, it was clear that the land policy of Dáil Éireann was in no fundamental way different from that of the British Government'. Indeed, Austin Stack, who succeeded Arthur Griffith as Minister of Home Affairs, played a leading role in discouraging the Republican Courts from hearing claims involving the transfer of occupied lands on the basis of prior tenancy. Directing his remarks to the situation in Southwest Munster, Stack told the Dáil in 1920, according to Desmond Greaves, that he believed there were some who were 'out to create a state of anarchy which ought to be put a stop to'. As Greaves has also noted to Peadar O'Donnell, Republican and Socialist, the Republican Courts combined with the Dáil's land policy to have a negative effect on the Irish struggle for independence. In Greaves estimate, 'For the first time the power of Dáil Éireann had been directed against the masses.' Griffith, he wrote, 'had started the process which was later to produce partition and the Free State'.[11]

In August 1920, the Dáil passed a decree against emigration. The decree was initiated by Austin Stack, Minister for Home Affairs and one of Collins' and Griffith's most bitter enemies, even before their role as catalysts of the Anglo-Irish Treaty. Under Stack's name, the Department of Home Affairs enunciated a policy on emigration with the explicit admission 'that the intention of the Dáil in controlling emigration is really to stop it entirely'.[12] The guidelines issued by his Ministry in seeking proof of such reasons as health, foreign studies, and hardship, made clear the seriousness of the effort to restrict emigration.

The interaction that occurred between the Dáil Ministries and those active as judges in the Republican Courts was made evident by a communication of 7 September 1920 between Austin Stack and Conor Maguire: 'I am directed by the Minister for Home Affairs to enclose herewith copy Decree [sic] restricting Increase of Rent.' In their application of the Law, the Republican Courts were instructed by Dáil Éireann to enforce 'the Law as recognised on 21st January, 1919'.[13] Exception was made for those provisions in the British Law that were animated by a spirit of religious or political intolerance. To Greaves and O'Donnell, the acceptance of the British Law guaranteed that the forces of reaction would prevail, even in a state Irish in name. Greaves writes: 'This was as high as the petite bourgeoisie could rise. The acceptance of the continuity of the English Law ... involved the acceptance of the most reactionary Department, the English Law of Property.'[14]

Nonetheless, Greaves and O'Donnell, among other writers, do not accept arguments that cattle driving threatened to undermine the focus of the separatist struggle in 1919 and 1920. But a loss of life was also a real part of the upheaval generated by land disputes, particularly in the West. The *Irish Times* of 24 May 1920 details two separate incidents in which young men, in both cases farmers' sons, were shot dead in land disputes. Both were Catholics. The frequency of violent incidents on the land front at the time was fundamentally counterproductive to what Collins termed the objective of gathering 'strength by the justice of our cause'.[15] Likewise, such incidents threatened to undermine the effort to build support for the ability of Sinn Féin to implement the machinery of a native government more responsive and effective than that administered by Dublin Castle. At the same time, the fact remains that these measures against land agitation enacted by Dáil Éireann and enforced by local IRA 'police' alienated many western activists from Sinn Féin. The immediate residue of the resentment engendered among those seeking land would be seen during the Irish Civil War.

In Limerick, early in 1920, renewed land agitation clearly played a major role in the decision of the West Limerick Sinn Féin Executive, a body headed by a local Catholic priest, to establish an arbitration court. The move was initiated with formal approval from the Central Executive. Sean Brouder, who had observed the founding of the Sinn Féin Court in Limerick and made note of the close relationship of the Catholic clergy to the administration of the system there: 'I can vividly recall the first sitting of the Sinn Féin court. It was held in the upper room of the Carnegie Library, Newcastlewest. Father Punch, who, like all the young priests of the time, enthusiastically supported Sinn Féin, presided and was supported by his fellow judges ... Among the litigants, I remember the committee of the West Limerick creamery.'[16]

But from the standpoint of the Dáil's social policies, exemplified by the mandate given to the Land Courts, Desmond Greaves has noted a dichotomy between Sinn Féin's overall treatment of those without land and the waged worker. In his estimate, 'If the small farmers and landless men were to be shown their place in the Republic, it was not possible yet to deal so unceremoniously with the workers.' According to Greaves, 'Collins' proposal that the Dáil should attempt to collect income tax', met with Brugha's insistence 'that the scheme proposed depended on the good will of Labour'. In this session at any rate,' Greaves writes, 'Collins emerged as the spokesman of the left. Not only was he prepared to trust to Labour support, he was prepared to implement a socialist programme.'[17] The extent, however, to which Collins supported a socialist programme is not readily discernible. In a collection of essays, in defense of the Anglo-Irish Treaty published posthumously in his name, Collins offered an insight into what he saw as the main issues of the Anglo-Irish struggle:

> The National instinct was sound – that the essence of our struggle was to secure freedom to order our own life, without attaching undue importance to the formulas under which that freedom would be expressed. The people knew that our government could and would be molded by the nation itself to its needs. The nation would make the government, not the government the nation.[18]

In this instance, we see a Collins who viewed the role of a native government in terms of a pragmatic nationalism, free of doctrinaire restriction. It is within that context that the Republican Courts operated. As the elected voice for most of Irish Nationalism, Dáil Éireann's decision to implement a legal system based on Griffith's early Sinn Féin policy was itself a manifestation of pragmatic nationalism. Within short order, the Republican Courts were to play an important part in the lives of Irish citizens of all classes and traditions. In the process, this development increased the credibility of Dáil Éireann. Piaras Beaslai describes the courts' importance at the local level in 1920, as well as the growing alarm of the British Government towards them:

> It was the general feeling that more fair play and more reasonable decisions would be obtained at these popular tribunals than at the Courts held under British Law, while the cost of litigations was immensely reduced. The English Government was embarrassed by the fact that under English Law an arbitration court was perfectly legal, and its decisions as binding on the parties concerned as those of the law court. At a later date, war was declared on these courts, but for the present they were not interfered with, and the newspapers began to publish regularly reports of cases tried at Sinn Féin courts.[19]

One partisan observer who had covered the proceedings as a young journalist at the Limerick Courthouse during the time when the British legal system had proceeded unencumbered, and who would later participate in the Republican Courts himself, offered this comparison:

> I had seen the Assize judges, Chief Baron Pallas, Lord Chief Justice O'Brien of Kilfenora ('Peter the Painter'), or Lord justices Ronan, Dodd, Boyd, or Cherry, arrive, escorted by mounted British soldiers – symbols of our subjection. As I sat at the table of the Sinn Féin court I knew that all that was finished. I knew the King's writ would no longer run in West Limerick or elsewhere in the South.[20]

The evident success of the land tribunals led Dáil Éireann, prompted by Austin Stack in Home Affairs, to place the Republican legal system on a more regular footing by creating a structure that operated from the parish level to 'District Courts' at the top. The Dáil decree of 29 June 1920, significantly expanded the legal apparatus of the Republic to include Courts of Justice and Equity, along with enabling the Home Affairs Minister to establish Criminal Courts, with police powers given to the local IRA units.

Proof that the courts were more than mere symbolism and would in fact adjudicate such sensitive matters as slander actions against Republican activists is provided by an action by Austin Stack. On 6 April 1920, a trial was held in Dublin, with Kevin O'Shiel serving on the judicial panel, for a slander suit brought against Mary McSwiney and Countess Markievicz by members of the Cork Branch of Cumann na mBan, the women's arm of the Republican movement. The plaintiffs sought restitution for 'slander and victimisation' from the two prominent women. Markievicz in fact was Minister for Labour in the Dáil Government at this time.[21]

In seeking the expansion of the Republican legal system, Padraig Colum paraphrases Austin Stack as having stated that the courts 'hitherto established were purely arbitration courts which depended on the consent of both parties. The country was in such a state ... that the people looked to the Republican Government for their law and equity, and in a very short time, they would have ousted the English Courts altogether.' Stack also held, according to Colum, 'that it was, therefore, necessary to take immediate steps to set up courts throughout the country which would be competent to hear every class of case similar to the cases dealt with in the English Courts of petty sessions and assize as far as Civil Jurisdiction was concerned'.[22]

The 'Rules and Forms' for Parish and District Courts, published by the Department of Home Affairs, made clear the delineation of authority that was to exist between the various courts. Consistent with the authority granted it by the Dáil's June 1920 decree, the Department promulgated the following guidelines for a 'Supreme Court' and four Circuit Districts:

1. A Supreme Court sitting in Dublin and having jurisdiction over the Republic.
2. District Courts having jurisdiction in their respective Districts; and having special sittings called 'Circuit Sittings' presided over by a Circuit Judge.
3. Parish Courts having jurisdiction in their respective Parishes.
4(a) The Supreme Court shall consist of not less than three members who (after the first appointment) shall be persons legally qualified of at least twelve years standing.
(b) A decision of the majority of the Court shall be the decision of the Court.
(c) Where a case of exceptional public importance comes before the Supreme Court, that Court may direct that it be heard and decided by a full Court which shall consist of not less than two members of the Supreme Court, and

two Circuit Judges. In such case the decision of the majority shall be the decision of the Court, but in the case of an equality of votes the President shall have a casting vote in addition to his ordinary vote.[23]

In all, the circuit courts would hold 'three circuits in each year' running from January to August. The Justices of the Supreme Court and the Circuit Judges were to hold office for life, and would be removable only by a special decree from Dáil Éireann. The District courts were to be established 'for each constituency returning, or capable of returning a member to Dáil Éireann'. At the parish level, the courts were given jurisdiction over a range of petty criminal offenses, civil claims 'not exceeding £10 in value or damage' and for the taking of evidence and for returning it for trial to 'ordinary and circuit sittings of the District Court' concerning criminal offences of a higher nature.[24]

Cathal Brugha, as Minister of Defence, sought police powers for the IRA 'to do work which it should not have to do, normally to perform police duties, capture criminals, and put down crime and offenses ...'. In fact, the securing of available locations for court sittings was usually handled by the local IRA units, as part of their 'police' function, along with the execution of court orders. And while the Sinn Féin 'police' grew to be as commonplace and as accepted in rural Ireland as the decisions of the National Arbitration Courts, the Republicans were to find that the public was no more enthusiastic about the rate collection efforts of a native government than they were for those of the British. A report sent to London by an informant noted that 'considerable annoyance is expressed at the rate levied by Sinn Féin – 6d to the pound [sic] from householders for payment of their police'.

That an understanding of the value behind the successful implementation of the Republican courts to the Sinn Féin propaganda effort existed from the very outset was made clear in a letter of 17 February 1920 from Sinn Féin publicity chief, P. S. O'Hegarty, to Austin Stack. The letter is also useful in illustrating the obstacles the Republican Government encountered in implementing its policies as a de facto regime: 'I shall be glad to know whether any further steps have been taken with a view to completing the scheme therein outlined, i.e., in the arbitration courts committee report of October 30, 1919. I fear that owing to the disarrangement [sic] consequent on raid of 11th November, the matter may have been overlooked.'[25]

The final phase of the Dáil's legal scheme lay in the creation of parish courts, as part of the effort to enable each constituency to expedite the formation of a Republican legal presence at the local level. Dorothy MacArdle described the evolution of this process in *The Irish Republic*:

> In West Clare, action was taken without delay. Three parish courts were set up, and a district court, having jurisdiction over the constituency. The latter consisted of a member of the Dáil for the constituency, the President of the

Comhairle Ceanntair of Sinn Féin and three other justices. A constitution was drawn up; rules of the court, scales of fines, costs and fees were settled. The litigation of the district was gradually transferred from the British courts to those which served as a model for the courts later set up by the Dáil Minister of Home Affairs.[26]

By June 1920 arbitration courts dealing with land questions were functioning in twenty-eight of Ireland's thirty-two counties; the exception being the hard-core loyalist Northeast. Their existence thwarted what Darrell Figgis termed Dublin Castle's hope that 'the Republican Government would crumble into the general disorder of the agrarian war'.[27] Ironically, to a pro-Unionist organ like the *Irish Times*, the formation of the land courts was seen as an intensifier, rather than a modifier, of the land question. A report in its 20 May 1920 edition informed its readers:

> While the agrarian agitation in the West and South of Ireland is being pursued with the utmost vigor by the labourers and small tenants, Sinn Féin has taken a step that sets at defiance all constitutional authority. It has set up district courts for taking evidence and delivering judgments in land disputes, and in the counties of Clare, Kerry and Rosscommon, it has issued proclamations inviting those who believe that they are entitled to property in the lands of other persons to file their claims with the registrar of the Sinn Féin courts ... Today a report is furnished of the first public meeting of a Sinn Féin land tribunal. The court was held in the town of Ballinrobe in County Mayo, and the arbitrators are said to have been Mr Arthur O'Connor, Sinn Féin, M.P., and Mr Kevin O'Shiel, a barrister-at-law. The court was crowded and Irish volunteers regulated admission and kept order.[28]

Cahir Davitt, son of Michael Davitt, who served as a Circuit Judge of the Dáil Éireann Courts from 1920–22, has noted that between June 1919 and June 1920 the Republican courts 'functioned smoothly and with great success in many areas, particularly in Clare, Galway and Mayo'. However, as Cahir Davitt and Conor Maguire have also stated, during the last six months of 1920 a dramatic shift was evident in the British response to the continuance of the Republican Courts. In Davitt's account from August 1920 until January 1921, 'sittings in the Parish and Dáil Courts had been held in several areas; but as the Crown forces became more active and hostile, it became increasingly dangerous to hold them openly and the courts had to go underground'.[29]

An analysis of the reports presented to the British Cabinet by Dublin Castle underscores the extent to which the Irish Administration was caught off guard by the swift success of the land tribunals and their acceptance, together with the subsequent expanded Republican legal effort, by the population at large. And with the acceptance and recognition of these courts by much of the Irish public, many in the Irish legal profession also attended their sittings. As one British official informed the Cabinet: 'They cannot afford to lose their clients' connection, and whether the courts are legal or not, it is not their business to enforce the law.'[30]

An observer for the Crown in one district reported that 'unionists have laid their complaints on the Sinn Féin Courts on the express ground that they are the only authority that can protect their fishing rights in the district'.[31] Reports in June and July 1920, forwarded to the Cabinet's Irish Situation Committee, made it plain that the success of the Republican Courts was a phenomenon that had taken root in all areas except Republican Northeast Ulster. On 7 July 1920 an account from County Sligo to the First Lord of the Admiralty stated that 'The Sinn Féin courts are allowing legal business in certain districts to a seriously apprehensible extent.' Remarkably, the source, a solicitor, informed the Government that at the Assizes in Sligo 'out of forty civil bill appeals listed, five were heard by the Judge of the Assize, but the remainder were withdrawn and transferred to the Sinn Féin tribunals'.[32]

From Ballina, Co. Mayo, came equally glum news for the British Government:

> The condition of the district is deplorable. There is a wide-spread spirit of lawlessness and contempt for constitutional authority; the ordinary process of the law is in abeyance; the courts are boycotted ... In many of the courts the local magistrates have ceased to attend, rather [than risk] the unpopularity or worse, that attendance would entail. Arbitration courts have been set up all over the district and their decrees enforced by threat of action from the Republican volunteers.[33]

The Report went on to summarise the situation across the country, painting a grim picture for the British Government as to the slender thread by which its writ held in most of Ireland in the summer of 1920.

> Kanturk, Co. Cork: (Col. Owens) The R.M. sees no prospect of the present conditions improving until those who desire to be loyal to the government are certain that if they side with the loyal element they will receive support and full protection. Ballinasloe, Co. Galway: (Mr Armstrong) Sinn Féin courts are being held regularly and are presided over by the priests. The various parties appearing before these courts seem to be satisfied with the decisions; but I am informed that the courts are finding it more difficult to arrive at a decision and are postponing a good many cases which are too involved for them. Portarlington, Co. Laois: (Mr Butler) ... has become entirely dominated by Sinn Féin Petty Sessions. Courts are deserted and people either put up with their grievances or refer them to arbitration. Wexford: (Major Crosbie) District is in a terrible state. The R.M. has been warned of death three times ... Solicitors have been warned not to appear before English courts. Doctors are censured for attending to give evidence in cases where their testimony was essential ... An ex-Indian Army Officer (Major Little) is acting as President of the Sinn Féin Appeal Court at New Ross. Ballybunnion, Co. Kerry: (Mr O'Hara) The business of the Public Court has to a great extent been taken

over by the Sinn Féin Arbitration courts. Castlerea, Co. Roscommon: (Major Johnston) Country is becoming a little more settled owing to the operation of the arbitration courts; but it would appear that these courts have impressed the people to such an extent with the power of Dáil Éireann that it would be difficult to shake their belief in the reality of a Republic.[34]

This reference to conditions in Castlerea is an important one since it underscores the acceptance on the part of the observers of the Crown, at least in some quarters, that the Republican courts were having a stabilising effect rather than a disruptive one on the day-to-day life of the country. It further indicates the desire on the part of the Republican Government to show that it had the capacity to govern, as well as the ability to undermine British authority. In effect, Sinn Féin wanted to replace that authority with effective institutions that would enjoy popular support, even among Unionists. The Republican courts were for that reason a vital part of that effort. The reports from the Irish hinterlands continued to be perplexing for the British Government:

Kilkee, Co. Clare: Increased motor transport is greatly needed for patrol work. It is obvious that a great deal of harm is done by large areas being left with no police or military. Limerick: (Colonel Williamson) The members of the newly appointed County Councils are all Sinn Féiners. They have notified the town clerk, the secretary, and other justices of the peace to resign their commissions forthwith – also their solicitors to keep away from British courts of justice. All justices of the peace are terrorised in their districts except two ... Ballincollig, Co. Cork: (Mr O'Hare) Reports of several court houses. The opinion now experienced by nearly all, irrespective of creed or class, is that as the present conditions of things is intolerable, they would be better off under an Irish government, even a Sinn Féin one. Ballinasloe, Co. Galway: Sinn Féin policy seems to be advancing steadily. There is a steady movement going on to gradually ignore and oust every British institution, and British authority was never at a lower ebb. Local authorities are being asked to bring any cases in dispute before Sinn Féin Courts. An attempt is even being made to prevent dangerous lunatics from being committed to asylums in the usual way. Tralee, Co. Kerry: District is in a most disturbed and lawless state ... Very little business comes before petty session courts as all cases are taken to the Sinn Féin Courts. Magistrates will not attend courts as the R.M. cannot deal with certain cases by himself, it makes it a very difficult situation ... The R.M. considers that the military forces in the districts should be increased. Carrick-on-Shannon, Co. Leitrim: [Major Dickie] Saw a connection between the lack of troops to assist the RIC who from their isolated situation and scanty numbers can do nothing ... As a result, even loyal citizens are now asking for Republican permits and are attending Republican court ... The bitterness and despair of people of this sort is painful to witness. They state they have been driven into becoming Sinn Féin as they have been abandoned by their own people ... Galway: [Mr Kilbride] Sinn Féin activities have brought about almost a revolution in local affairs. They are able and prepared to adopt any measures which may be directed from headquarters.[35]

Such accounts underscore that the Republican courts figured largely in the assessments which the British Government received about the collapse of its administrative system in Ireland. In addition, they demonstrate that in counties that were not part of the main 'fighting districts' as in the cases of Leitrim, much of Galway, and Laois, British rule was still threatened by one of the more potent aspects of non-violent Republicanism.

But the British Cabinet did not need to rely on the pessimistic reports of informants throughout Ireland to learn of the loss of credibility to the King's writ there. Reports appearing regularly in the pages of the British and Irish press made plain the level of acceptance gained by the Republican courts, together with the corresponding decline in the authority of the British legal system in Ireland. The *Irish Times* of 24 May 1920 reported: 'A Sinn Féin arbitration court was recently held in Drumshambo, Co. Leitrim, the court being composed of a member of Dáil Éireann and a well-known professional man. After investigating matters of local disputes and hearing the evidence, the court adjourned the parties and the decision would be duly promulgated.'[36] One month earlier, an *Irish Times* correspondent wrote from County Clare that 'all local cases are brought before the self-constituted courts of Sinn Féin, and when the County Court Judge [*sic*] sat recently at Kilrush, he was informed that many of the cases which were to have come before him had either been "settled or withdrawn" ... The taking of land for grazing is now absolutely forbidden and the large farmers have withdrawn their cattle from the chief grazing districts.'[37]

Taken in the aggregate, the reports of the situation in Ireland to the Cabinet, along with the press reports, produced one clear verdict for the British Government that a situation of political and military stalemate had taken hold of much of the country. As the Republicans continued to gain the initiative throughout the first six months of 1920, the Coalition began to focus greater attention on Ireland. The increase in British manpower that was to commence following the appointment of both a new Chief Secretary and Commander-in-Chief in the persons of Hamar Greenwood and Nevil Macready was as much a response to the breakdown of British authority in Ireland, caused by the success of the Republican courts, as to the increasing success of the IRA Flying Columns. On 23 July 1920 at a meeting of the Cabinet's Irish Situation Committee, which had been created the previous April to monitor developments in Ireland, W. E. Wylie stated that in regard to the civil courts, 'the entire administration of the Imperial Government had ceased'. In one town, he stated, out of forty-five appeals down for hearing, only two cases came in. 'As for the revenue, everyone was determined to pay no taxes, and it was not fair to ask the revenue officers to collect them. For if they attempted to do so, they did it at the peril of their lives.'[38]

Walter Long, who served later that year as the principal parliamentarian in the enactment of the 'Government of Ireland Act', provided the Committee, at its meeting of 30 June 1920, with the text of a letter from a Unionist friend in Co. Limerick. Its author had come into direct contact with the Republican courts and with the Sinn Féin administration at the local level. The letter provided a picture that was considerably at variance with the image of Republicanism which the Coalition had itself sought to present at home and abroad. The letter stated:

> Sinn Féin rules the County and rules it admirably. At our local races the Sinn Féin police controlled the traffic, the crowds, etc., 'parked' the motor cars, and, in fact, did all the work which has usually been done by the police, and did it excellently. Petty thefts, or indeed crimes of any kind, are dealt with by the Sinn Féin courts, who try the accused with perfect fairness and administer justice in the most thorough fashion ... Missing property, if the facts are reported to the Sinn Féin authorities, is invariably found and restored to the owners ... They approached the High Sheriff of the County and asked him if he would preside over one of their chief courts: he told them it was quite impossible for him to do so as he was High Sheriff ... The fact is that everybody is going over to Sinn Féin, not because they believe in it, but because it is the only authority in the County; and they realise that if their lives and property are to be secured, they must act with Sinn Féin. Their general statement is: 'How can we avoid joining Sinn Féin when everything is extremely well done?'[39]

The manner in which the Sinn Féin Courts functioned also caused a shift in the focus of even the staunchly Unionist *Irish Times*. Evidence of the change which the Courts' operations occasioned can be measured by two reports appearing less than six weeks apart. One account, published on 7 April 1920, lamented that 'The general failure of law and order is beginning to have serious effects in the West of Ireland, where it is being expressed, as is usual, in terms of greed for land.' The *Times*' correspondent predicted that the combination of a rise in cattle driving 'with a formidable land agitation by the laboring classes and by that large army of younger sons who are known as "landless men" would cause the now prosperous farmers to discover the drawbacks of the revolutionary movement'.[40] However, on 31 May of that year, the *Irish Times* reported that a successful effort was under way in the prime lands of County Kildare against cattle driving. Ironically, the catalysts for that action were the Republican courts, with local IRA units acting as police. The report stated:

> A few nights since the cattle were reported missing from the Kilcullen district, as well as a number of sheep from the Curragh borders, with the result that the matter after fullest inquiry was placed in the hands of the Sinn Féin Executives. The latter, it would seem, immediately investigated the matter with the result that ... two volunteers motored to certain houses in the district ... arresting five men where it was stated a 'court martial' would be held and an inquiry made into the matter by the Sinn Féin Court ... Already, it is said,

some of the cattle have been returned to the owners from whom they were stolen.[41]

It is against this backdrop that, by the early summer of 1920, a clear dichotomy had emerged between the public posture of the British Government, which sought to communicate a message of unconcern with the Republican Courts, and the recognition within the Cabinet that greater action was needed if the Government was to appear in control. In the House of Commons on 17 June 1920, one Conservative backbencher asked the Coalition whether it was true that in three quarters of Ireland 'law and order are being maintained by the Sinn Féin Courts?'. Although the Government denied that such a situation existed, Hamar Greenwood actually offered the argument that a lack of evidence had prevented them from thwarting the activities of the Sinn Féin courts! He stated: 'In the absence of evidence from the persons aggrieved, identifying the parties serving the summonses, or at whose insistence they are served, no prosecution can at present be sustained.'[42]

In other instances, in answer to direct questions pertaining to the Sinn Féin courts, the Government took the route of obfuscation. When asked, for example, whether the Donegal County Council had provided the use of the Court House at Ballyshannon for the Republican Courts, Greenwood replied: 'My attention has been drawn to prior notice to the effect mentioned ... but there is no evidence available to prove that the House has been used for illegal purposes. If and when such evidence is obtained, then action will be taken.'[43] On the question of whether the Republican Courts even existed, the following exchange from the House of Commons Debate of 1 July 1920 shows Greenwood to have been even more evasive:

> Mr Palmer: May I ask if the Right Honorable gentleman is yet convinced of the fact that there are such things as illegal courts in Ireland?
>
> Greenwood: I am convinced that there are a great many irregular gatherings called courts in Ireland.
>
> Mr Palmer: At which barristers appear!
>
> Mr Palmer: Do appear!
>
> Greenwood: It is impossible for the Secretary for Ireland to take legal steps until we have evidence which is legal.[44]

The loss of cases in the established British courts to the Republican judicial network was itself a source of embarrassment to the Government. In a debate of 24 June 1920, when asked if he could provide the House of Commons with the number of cases withdrawn from the British High Courts in Ireland, along with the number of cases tried in those courts as compared with previous years, Greenwood answered: 'The information asked for is not available, and could not be procured without an expenditure of time and labour out of all proportion to its public utility.' But his admission of 1 July of that year that there were 'a great many irregular gatherings called courts in Ireland', indicates that the Chief Secretary could no longer go on without admitting the problem publicly.[45]

Within the counsels of the Cabinet, the news concerning the courts continued to be a source of consternation. From Dublin Castle, Assistant Secretary Andy Cope stated, according to Cabinet records, that 'the Sinn Féin Courts were doing more harm to the prestige of the British Government than the assassinations'.[46] As the weeks passed, the effectiveness of the Republican Courts continued to improve as their level of public acceptance grew correspondingly wider. With the virtual collapse of the British legal system in Ireland came also the breakdown of Crown control over the entities of local government in much of southern Ireland. At the meeting of the Irish Situation Committee on 23 July 1920, W. E. Wylie told Lloyd George directly that 'the local authorities ... were prepared to function so far as their local affairs were concerned, but they would give no assistance in carrying out the instructions of the Irish Government'.[47] By the term 'Irish Government', Wylie was referring to the Dublin Castle administration, which had by now become increasingly irrelevant in the day-to-day life of the Irish citizenry, except as an armed fortress from which instructions for increased coercion were dispatched to an expanded military garrison. Padraig Colum captures these developments succinctly in his biography of Arthur Griffith:

> It was evident that Dáil Éireann and the administration that had come into being in its name had created a situation that could not be reversed. When the Land Court could divide a farm between quarreling brothers, when a unit of the IRA could halt a cattle drive, it was clear that British authority in the main part of Ireland was pushed back, never to be restored.[48]

Colum also provides a useful example of the degree to which the Republican Government had become confident enough to come out in the open, witnessed by an incident on 1 June 1920 at Callan, where the Republican Courts held a public hearing: 'The prisoners were marched through the town by volunteers who, on their way, passed the District Inspector and Head Constable of the RIC.'[49] However, a description of the makeshift manner of the facilities used in West Limerick for the holding of the sessions of the Sinn Féin courts there sheds light on the extremely tentative circumstances in which the proceedings were held.

> The courthouses were chosen more for their inconspicuousness than for the accommodation they had available, which was at times a bit on the short side; screened parking accommodations for horse drawn vehicles. There was always an I.R.A. man on duty to direct each car as it arrived. Sometimes there would be as many as a dozen cars, mainly because elderly people coming a distance to the courts had to travel by car. Others came by bike or walked.

The cars had to be stowed away somewhere near the court but out of sight of the road. The Tans who were careering [*sic*] about the country in their Crossley tenders might happen along at any hour; to them everybody was suspect, but a group of three or four cars would most certainly attract their unwelcome attention.[50]

One approach taken by the British Government, with little apparent success, lay in an effort to characterise the operation of the Republican Courts as a tool for the 'terrorisation of the Irish populace'. On 8 October 1920 the Dublin Castle Authorities, in conjunction with British Army headquarters in Cork, issued an account describing the coercion employed by Sinn Féin in County Clare to enforce a verdict by the Republican Courts there against one individual:

A defendant who had refused to pay a certain sum of money awarded on a claim against him was kidnapped by Sinn Féin Volunteers and taken to a remote churchyard in Clare. Here he was led to a large family vault which had been opened, and was ordered to get inside the vault. A lighted candle was then given him and he was told 'by the time that candle burns out you will perhaps have decided to change your mind and abide by the decision of the Court.' The vault, which contained five coffins, was then closed, and his captors departed, leaving the unfortunate victim entombed. His tormentors did not return for twenty-four hours by which time the candle had long since burnt out leaving him in the dark with the coffins. Under threats of a repetition of the treatment he had suffered, he paid the sum demanded.[51]

Had the effort by the British Government to reassert its authority in Ireland not become synonymous by this time with police coercion and official reprisals carried out against the Irish population, the point which Dublin Castle sought to make in this instance would have had more credibility. This general breakdown in the British administrative apparatus led directly to the decision made by the Coalition in the summer of 1920 to apply coercion in Ireland. Ironically, however, while the Government was able to limit severely the functioning of the Republican Courts from June of that year until the truce of the following July, its efforts did not result in a return of public acceptance of the instrumentalities of British rule. The many incidents of lawlessness perpetrated by Crown forces against Irish civilians also contributed, undoubtedly, to the lack of credibility of British institutions, including those claiming to provide justice. An editorial appearing in *The London Star* during the height of the Coalition's policy of coercion provided its readers with a sense of how far their government had fallen in the effort to counter Sinn Féin, the presence of 40,000 British troops notwithstanding:

Sinn Féin appear to be following the Lloyd George line – through terror to triumph. From all accounts Sinn Féin has succeeded brilliantly in

> demonstrating its ability to administer justice. The increasing support of the Sinn Féin courts to which not only Sinn Féiners but unionists resort and before which solicitors and barristers are rapidly transferring their practice, leaving official courts deserted, has the dash of drollery about it, but its significance is extremely serious ... [52]

Nonetheless, increased coercion by the British Government had a chilling effect on the day-to-day effectiveness of the Republican Courts, particularly from August 1920. Military raids throughout the country made public sittings no longer possible. The intensity of the crackdown was even greater in Dublin where, for example, a raid was directed against a sitting at a private home on North George's Street, where lawyers and litigants sat awaiting one Republican judge's decision.[53] However, Conor Maguire has noted that 'the blow had been too long delayed to be effective'. 'The courts', he wrote, 'were established so firmly that although their activities were necessarily restricted, they continued to function.' An account by Maguire of a British military raid on a private session of a Republican court at Mullingar, presided over by Kevin O'Shiel,* is useful in demonstrating the awkward position in which the Government found itself.

> Suddenly the door at the end of the hall was flung open. A young officer appeared brandishing a revolver. 'What's going on here?' he demanded. 'This,' said Kevin O'Shiel, 'is a court of the Irish Republic. Who are you?' 'You had better get out of this quickly, or you will be removed by force,' came the reply. Turning to us, Kevin O'Shiel said quite calmly, 'Gentlemen, we must yield to superior force. It can now be judged, who wish to maintain law and order, and who are the disturbers of the peace!'[54]

Despite such harassment, the work of the Republican Courts continued on throughout 1920 as the Home Affairs Department continued to seek new means for enhancing the effort. In September of that year, Stack sought Conor Maguire's participation in an effort to set 'scales of Solicitors' costs for Parish and District Councils. I am making this request', he noted, 'at the suggestion of members of the High Court. They are anxious that you should come to town at your convenience to discuss matters with them.'[55] But as the end of 1920 neared, Maguire notes that it 'became more difficult for the courts as well as for the IRA. During the winter months, enemy suppression was slowing down many of our activities.'[56] On 6 December 1920, members of a Black and Tan raiding party shot one participant dead and wounded several others at a Republican court session in Co. Clare. It is surprising, however, that only one Republican judge was captured by the British forces during the conflict. The judge in question had, in fact, been one of the 'Circuit' judges created by Dáil Éireann through Stack's efforts. He was charged

---

* Later to be the Irish Free State's Attorney General.

before a court martial with unlawful possession of documents relative to Dáil Éireann, a crime punishable under the Restoration of Order in Ireland Act, and sentenced to two years in prison.[57]

Pressure in driving the Republican Courts underground did, in fact, succeed to such an extent that Lloyd George was able to claim on 28 April 1921, and with some accuracy, that the Sinn Féin Courts had vanished.[58] During the Dáil debates on the Anglo-Irish Treaty, Michael Collins, in defending his position that a settlement was necessary, stated that the courts in South Cork had not met for eight or nine months.[59] In the last session of Dáil Éireann held prior to the Anglo-Irish Truce, in May 1921, the harried body met with only twenty-one deputies present and heard Eamon de Valera implore them, according to Padraig Colum that 'It was only a question of keeping up the constructive effort. The enemy government was afraid of the Republican courts working again. The day they got the courts working again all over the country, they had the British beaten.'[60]

But the Republican courts would not, as such, function as openly again until the truce of 11 July 1921. As León Ó Broin has written, 'from the closing weeks of 1920 until the truce in July 1921, the functioning of the courts was adversely affected. In a few other areas,' he notes, 'where circuit sittings became necessary and possible, the courts were held in all sorts of places: in the town in county council offices, workhouses, hospital buildings, schools and Sinn Féin club premises, in county districts in creameries, farmhouses, outhouses, barns or at any place with four walls and a roof which could be made serviceable'.[61] Some ninety parish courts and seventy district courts were in operation under the sanction of Dáil Éireann by the time of the truce in July 1921.[62] Ironically, it was the man who was their original advocate who would prove in the end to be their chief antagonist following the Anglo-Irish Treaty. On 14 July 1922, Arthur Griffith, President of the Dáil Éireann established after the Anglo-Irish Treaty, suspended the sittings of the Supreme Court, which had been set up by the Department of Home Affairs under Dáil Éireann's June 1920 decree. His action was taken in the name of Dáil Éireann, with, as Dorothy Macardle has written, this reason in mind: 'The courts have been invoked by the Republicans in a manner which, had their claims succeeded, would have affected the government's policy of arrests.'[63] In an article written soon after his resignation as Minister of Foreign Affairs in the Free State Provisional Government, Gavan Duffy, a signatory to the Anglo-Irish Treaty, made it clear why he felt 'compelled to break upon issues involving a very grave matter of principle'. Duffy held that 'On July 25, 1922 it was determined to abolish the Supreme Court and its judges rather than meet in open court an application for release on writ of habeas corpus made on behalf of one of the military prisoners in Mountjoy.' He argued that this action was an affront to the 'first principles of freedom and democracy', and that Dáil Éireann had democratically established the Republican Courts.

Hence, they could not be removed by executive fiat by the Provisional Government. 'Habeas corpus', Duffy stated, 'was deemed so vital and fundamental a right that it had to be scrupulously secured to the Irish people, and even in time of war, by being incorporated in the constitution itself.'[64]

Soon after, in the course of the Dáil proceedings, Kevin O'Higgins announced as Free State Minister for Home Affairs that he did not support suggestions that some aspects of the Dáil court structure be incorporated into the judicial system of the Free State on the basis that 'The Dáil courts have left little impression upon the modern Irish legal system.'[65] O'Higgins' memory was in this instance a short one, however. The successful establishment of the Republican Courts and the public acceptance they gained during 1919–20, resulted in the fact that the British Administration in Ireland had suffered a setback from which it never recovered. Indeed, it can be argued that their contribution in undermining British authority in Ireland helped to provide the basis for the negotiations that saw the British Government agree to the creation of the Irish Free State itself. In effect, we see the importance of non-violent action to the Irish Revolution.

On that account, there can be no better authority on the impact of the Republican Courts in shaping British policy in Ireland during 1920–21 than the British Government itself. The 'Conclusions' of a Cabinet meeting, chaired by Lloyd George, on the evening of Friday, 13 August 1920, express the assessment that the Dáil Courts were key among the inroads made by Sinn Féin in gaining acceptance among much of the population, and were likely to render the Government of Ireland Act (1920) and Restoration of Order in Ireland Act ineffective. Further concessions would be necessary, given that increased coercion was likely to alienate the population from British rule even further.

> Strong measures would be required to put down the policy of the extremists, and there might come a point when public opinion would desert the Government. Even if the Act was successful, there would be no party left in Ireland with which the Government could negotiate a settlement. The position at present was that the six counties wanted Home Rule for themselves, and would not be content simply to remain part of the United Kingdom. In the South and West, there was no unionist party left in the old sense. Many of them were embracing, however reluctantly, the new ideas, and were not unwilling to make use of the Sinn Féin Courts. In the circumstances, it was necessary that the Government should review its policy, and the length it could go in the way of concessions.[66]

The need for further change, then, was becoming an increasing reality. The success of the system of courts instituted by Dáil Éireann had proved to be a catalyst behind that imminent policy shift. It was known only at this stage within the counsels of the British Government, however. For now, the military approach continued, as the Cabinet floundered and searched for a way out.

7

The Search for a Negotiated Settlement

> Gone was the country of the soft brogue or blarney ... Instead was a hard, steady Ireland ... It had pitted its strength against the Empire and the latter was beginning to waiver.
>
> Ernie O'Malley in *The Singing Flame* (Dublin, 1979), p. 10

With the end of the Great War, we have seen that Lloyd George focused greater attention on the state of affairs in Ireland. But the war in Europe itself had not been the sole impediment preventing more concerted action in an effort to end what was one of the oldest and most bitter of conflicts.

The Coalition, comprised of Liberals and Conservatives, held conflicting views as to what should be done. But by the spring of 1921 it had become clear to even the most hardline members of the Cabinet that its policy in Ireland was not working.

The evolution of Lloyd George's attitude towards Ireland requires a special focus. Throughout his years as a Cabinet member and as Prime Minister, his enigmatic reputation as a politician is nowhere more evident than in regard to Ireland. His attitude raises a number of fundamental questions concerning British conduct there during the years 1919–21. Did he, for example, realise by the end of 1920 that a military victory by Britain in Ireland was not attainable without an even greater loss to Britain and consequently to his own prestige? Or did he decide after discussing the situation with his military advisors and the Cabinet that progress in pacifying Ireland through coercion was actually being made, and that his Government was better suited to remain with its 'dual policy' against the Irish rebels? Or finally, did pressure from the more conservative elements of the Coalition force Lloyd George, against his own sentiments, to prolong the military approach until the right opportunity for a negotiated settlement presented itself?

Describing the British Government's blueprint for tranquillity within the Empire and in Britain's external affairs in the aftermath of the First World War, Kenneth Morgan writes that for the Coalition 'a policy of studious concession to the forces of nationalism in the Middle East, in India, was the agreed concomitant of conciliation in Europe and peace at home'.[1] It is ironic, given the situation in Ireland, that despite Lloyd George's dislike of nationalism in India, his Cabinet used a conciliatory approach in its relations with that country as early as 1918.

The one obvious arena of British rule which stood in direct contrast to the Coalition's pursuit of a peace based on consensus was Ireland. Indeed, it was Lloyd George himself who had gone to Paris as the defender of the oppressed minorities and an advocate of the right of small nations to self-government. But in Ireland, his Government maintained its presence there during much of 1919–21 by coercion and by martial law.

As late as October 1920, Lloyd George referred to himself as 'still a Gladstonian Home Ruler' on the Irish Question.[2] There was indeed some validity to his claim, although it was not until the spring of 1920 that Ireland became a primary focus of the Prime Minister's attention. It is noteworthy that unlike many of those in positions of power in Britain, Lloyd George did not share the view that alleged collusion between Sinn Féin and Britain's external enemies was the source of the conflict that erupted in armed revolt in 1916 and Sinn Féin's subsequent electoral success. On 24 July 1920 he told a group of Unionist elected officials that 'we should make a mistake if we come to the conclusion that Sinn Féin is purely a Bolshevist conspiracy against Britain'.[3]

In the aftermath of the Easter Rising, Prime Minister Asquith engaged Lloyd George, then the Minister of Munitions, in an attempt to undermine that 'old friend' by promoting a settlement still within the Imperial framework. Lloyd George dealt directly in this effort with the constitutional nationalists led by John Redmond and the Unionists headed by Sir Edward Carson. However, his efforts at a settlement during May–July 1916 and again through the vehicle of the Irish Convention of 1917–18 were virtually doomed from the start owing to the intervention of the Southern Unionists within the British Cabinet led by Lord Lansdowne and Walter Long, who insisted on permanent partition. John Redmond was forced to disown the settlement which he had agreed to on a provisional basis. That tentative agreement involving Redmond collapsed on 24 July 1916. The collapse of the subsequent Irish Convention, despite the best efforts of its Chairman, Horace Plunkett, was even more counterproductive to the effort for a peaceful settlement, since the Ulster Unionists had little incentive to accept constructive agreement. Lloyd George encouraged the Unionists' intransigence by his position that Parliament would not give effect to any decision of the Convention unless there was substantial agreement. Such a requirement was indeed an impossible one for any honest effort by an assembly of intelligent people charged with the task of finding a settlement to a complex problem. As such, it served to underscore the disingenuousness with which Lloyd George and his Government had approached a solution to their problems in Ireland at that time.

Lionel Curtis' June 1921 article in the *Round Table* spoke candidly of Lloyd George's less than productive role in Anglo-Irish areas while a member of the Asquith Cabinet and as Prime Minister himself. Curtis referred specifically to the failure of the Irish Convention of 1917–18, which had been set in motion by Lloyd George. He also cited Lloyd George's duplicity as Minister for Munitions in the 1916 negotiations with Carson and Redmond, in which he pledged support for the Unionist right to remain outside a Home Rule Parliament for the rest of Ireland. At the same time Lloyd George told the moderate Nationalists he would not allow the Unionists to undermine a settlement in an all-Ireland context.[4]

Yet from the standpoint of political self-interest, by not forcing the issue with the Unionist members of the Asquith Cabinet, Lloyd George may well have prolonged his own career.[5] Fresh from that experience with Ireland, Lloyd George decided out of sheer necessity to focus his energies on the conclusion of the war in Europe and on a peace settlement. He was also provided with the more or less convenient rationale for postponing a decision on Ireland until after the war.

The changes within the British Cabinet and wider political structure occurring from 1919 onward must also be examined for the effect they had on the Coalition's Irish policy. By 1919, Lloyd George had moved away from his 'Garden Suburb' Secretariat approach in coordinating war-time governmental activity back to the more recognisable outlines of Cabinet government, although Sir Maurice Hankey, Lloyd George's chief aide, remained as the principal secretary for the Cabinet.* His return to Cabinet government at this time was an important factor in the Government's decision to persist with a military policy in Ireland in the early months of 1921. During the war, as an irreplaceable Prime Minister, Lloyd George was in a position, as A. J. Taylor observed, where 'his situation condemned him to success'.[6] Most importantly, Lloyd George's Liberals were a vital part of the coalition with the Conservatives. However, by 1919 the Conservatives were in a position to form a government on their own without Lloyd George, despite his efforts to position himself as the best hope for the moderates against a burgeoning Labour party.[7] These political realities thus appear to have motivated his decision to stay the course in Ireland which the Conservative hard-liners – Bonar Law in particular – still wanted to pursue.

Lloyd George, then, did not turn his full attention to Ireland until the spring of 1920. Alarmed by the state of affairs there, which seemed increasingly beyond the control of Britain's civilian and military authorities, the

---

* Sir Morris Hankey served as senior Secretary to the Cabinet from 1918, but he was essentially private secretary to Lloyd George. Prior to that he was the Secretary to the War Cabinet and the Imperial War Cabinet.

Prime Minister sought the support of Winston Churchill. In a letter of 10 May 1920, Lloyd George wrote to his then Minister of War:

> I am very anxious about Ireland, and I want you to help. We cannot leave things as they are. De Valera has particularly challenged the British Empire and, unless he is put down, the Empire will look silly. I know how difficult it is to spare men and materials, but this seems to me to be the urgent problem for us. I understand from Bonar [Law] that there will be an important conference tomorrow to discuss the situation. Macready has certain proposals which he is bringing over from Ireland. I am very anxious you should see him before the conference. Do your best to put them through without any loss of time.[8]

Like both Churchill and Greenwood, Lloyd George grew accustomed to the concept of police warfare, including the use of reprisals. Counter-terrorism by the police and British Auxiliaries in Ireland, sanctioned by the Prime Minister, produced what has been termed by some British historians some of the darkest hours for Britain in the twentieth century. To Kenneth Morgan, in his work on the Lloyd George Coalition Government, the coercion policy in Ireland 'was the blackest chapter of the Government's policy in any theatre, a monument' to ignorance, racial and religious prejudice, and ineptitude'.[9]

Lloyd George's loss for one year of the friendship of the *Manchester Guardian* publisher, C. P. Scott, over the policy of reprisals carried out by the Black and Tans in Ireland, showed that there were personal as well as political costs for him. Writing in his diary of a June 1920 breakfast meeting with Lloyd George and the Anglican Archbishop of York, Scott stated that although there were rumours of 'a new Irish policy' he found Lloyd George 'entirely occupied with plans for repression'. According to Scott, Lloyd George offered the following:

> There must be, he regretted to say, stronger measures. Crime was unpunished – 29 police murdered and no one brought to justice. He proposed to set up a special tribunal – a judge to try murder cases without a jury. 'What about the evidence?' I asked. 'We have got the evidence,' he said.[10]

An uncertain policy, characterised by a willingness to move from active coercion in Ireland to the issuance of feelers for a negotiated settlement and then back to an intensified military campaign, is evident from an examination of the British Government's conduct in Ireland from October 1920 to late June 1921, when the Prime Minister felt he was secure enough to pursue formal talks with Sinn Féin. As we have seen, despite an interest in a negotiated settlement shown by Lloyd George late in 1920, he backed away from these initial attempts in favour of a continuation of the policy of open coercion. Perhaps the estimates of his Irish Secretary, the Canadian-born MP Sir Hamar Greenwood, were still credible to him. On 26 January 1921,

Greenwood claimed that the tide had 'turned against Sinn Féin'. He saw the implementation of the Government of Ireland Act of 1920 as a primary means for ensuring the ultimate destruction of the Republican effort.[11] However, by June 1921, after the total number of officially classified IRA 'outrages' had risen to 500 for the month of May, and with British fatalities for June climbing, the Irish Secretary took a different view, conceding that there was in fact 'a very marked increase in rebel activity throughout the whole country'.[12]

According to Maurice Hankey, the previous autumn Lloyd George had actually considered abandoning the rural areas of Ireland – in effect most of the country – and holding only the ports of the largest cities.[13] It was an idea that would emerge again for consideration. But just weeks later he made two speeches that were openly supportive of the hard-line approach to Ireland: the first in his constituency at Carnarvon on 19 October, the second at the London Guildhall on 9 November. Neither could be viewed by third parties during the closing days of 1920 as helpful to a peace initiative. At Carnarvon, the Prime Minister openly excused the conduct of the British forces, including the Black and Tans, and in London he claimed that as a result of its present policies in Ireland the Government now had 'murder by the throat'. Lloyd George's support of the methods of counter-terrorism adopted by the police had already been made clear to General Tudor. Sir Henry Wilson, one of the staunchest of Irish Unionists, was taken aback when Lloyd George told him of his 'amazing theory that Tudor, or someone, was murdering two S. F.'s (Sinn Féiners) to every Loyalist the S. F.'s murdered'.[14] The Prime Minister also told General Wilson that such official violence was 'the best means for dealing with the IRA'.[15]

In his diary, General Wilson also related a conversation he had had with Winston Churchill two days after Lloyd George's Carnarvon speech, in which, according to Wilson, Churchill said of Lloyd George:

> Lloyd George had told him last night [11 October] that during the war he had hated being up near the front and was frightened of shells and he supposed this was because it was not his duty and business to get killed. Whereas he had no fear of denouncing the S. F.'s as assassins, etc., although he knew it sensibly increased his own chance of being murdered. In this case, he conceived it to be his duty.[16]

In June 1920, Lloyd George expressed to the Cabinet his resentment of the criticisms Macready continued to level against the RIC.[17] By this point, the Prime Minister had tired of the General's admonitions that, as a result of the self-propelled reprisals campaign of the Black and Tans and the RIC, the police force in Ireland was operating outside civilian control. In Macready's memoirs of his service in Ireland, he related that by 1920 his disaffection with the conduct of the Black and Tans and the RIC had reached its peak.

Macready went so far as to petition the British authorities in Ireland to replace the khaki uniforms of the special force in order to avoid any confusion between them and his troops. For Macready, the integrity of the army was at least as important as the success of the Government's policy.[18]

That considerations other than Ireland weighed heavily on Lloyd George at this time – Britain's effort at economic recovery in the aftermath of the Great War in particular – is demonstrated by a review of the events of the period. Throughout 1919 and 1920, as the Government sent more troops to Ireland, industrial disturbances continued in Britain. A somewhat revealing account in Tom Jones' diary shows Lloyd George as willing to use the British military to put down industrial unrest at home as he was the rebellion in Ireland. However, he was somewhat restricted in this desire by the lack of military manpower available due to the demands in Ireland. According to Tom Jones, at a special Cabinet meeting with the Government's military advisors on the industrial situation on 17 January 1920, the Prime Minister asked Air Marshall Sir Hugh Trenchard 'how many airmen are there available for [containing] the revolutionaries?' Upon hearing from Trenchard that only 100 were operational, Lloyd George 'presumed they could use machine guns and drop bombs'.[19]

Britain's domestic unrest at this time was not totally separate from the Prime Minister's view of Ireland. He contended at one stage in 1919 that 'the policemen on strike, the many agitators actively engaged in various parts of the country', were generally of Irish extraction, and were 'creating a vicious atmosphere'. Accordingly, Lloyd George's endorsement of repressive measures for Ireland, which he probably would have found abhorrent elsewhere, might be seen as consistent with his view that the claim of Irish Nationalists to nationhood was a 'sham and a fraud'.[20] Nonetheless, it was the pragmatic side of Lloyd George that also held the view that a 'satisfactory settlement' of the Irish question was important 'from the standpoint of world opinion and also for our relations with the dominions and the United States'.[21]

Lloyd George, as demonstrated in other instances at home and abroad, did not believe in bargaining for peace unless he was able to bargain from a position of strength. But the virtual military stalemate Britain encountered in Ireland, despite the addition of thousands of troops and the recruitment of the Black and Tans, did not amount to such a position. In February 1921 General Tudor, whom Lloyd George had praised the previous year as the catalyst of the Black and Tans, was removed. The British military campaign in Ireland continued still for another four months, amidst recommendations by General Macready for more regular troops and the extension of martial law throughout the country.

As late as May of that year, Lloyd George was still opposed to a truce with Sinn Féin. According to H. A. L. Fisher, the Prime Minister argued at that time that if Britain sought a truce, then 'we lose the day'. At a meeting of

12 May 1921, the Cabinet voted nine to five against pursuing a truce with the rebels. It was the last full discussion by Cabinet members of the situation in Ireland until the mid-June meetings held in preparation for George V's 22 June speech before the opening session of the Northern Ireland Parliament. As we will see, a lot would transpire, much of it behind the scenes, to effect a change in British policy in Ireland during that intervening six-week period.

Tom Jones' account of that 12 May Cabinet meeting provides a revealing look at how seriously Lloyd George and his Cabinet viewed the need to bring some form of conclusion to the situation in Ireland, as well as at the difficulty they had in determining what it was they should do differently. This extract from Jones' *Whitehall Diary*, in which Lloyd George and Robert Munro, an MP and Secretary for Scotland, weighed the merits of seeking a truce with Sinn Féin, is instructive:

> Munro: Whatever differences we may have as to the present proposal [a truce] the Cabinet is about to make a decision of far-reaching importance. You yourself, Prime Minister, said that the present policy has failed.
>
> Lloyd George: I did not say that.
>
> Munro: Something like it. It is an appeal to the honour of the Irish people, not force. In the documents from Ireland there is a unanimous view against cessation of hostilities. Difference is as to time. Chief Secretary does not say it shall not take place after election [the May elections for a North and South Parliament under the Government of Ireland Act]. You now have a rare combination of circumstances: New Viceroy [Lord Fitzalan, an English Catholic], de Valera and Craig interview [the two had a secret meeting early in May], election pending. I can't leave out of sight this: at the present moment the public is alienated and disgusted by our present policy and would welcome new effort ...
>
> Lloyd George: It is a very difficult decision. Let us see where we stand in the evidence. You've got Commander-in-Chief [Macready] against it on merits ... a police report is to the same effect. Political consideration: the Chief Secretary (Hamar Greenwood) is against it ...
>
> Lloyd George added (later in the meeting): There ought to be very strong reasons (for a truce.) At best, it is a gamble. Fisher (H. A. L. Fisher) says 'Something may come of it.' A beautiful gesture may make us look ridiculous.
>
> Fisher: The present evil is so degrading. You ought to seize the first opportunity.
>
> Prime Minister: I've taken part in two or three acts of this kind. We sent back deportees and they laughed at us. Did the same after the Easter rebellion. Every one a failure; there was no response from the Irish and they took full advantage of us.

It is important to note that while Lloyd George voted at that session against pursuing a truce, Winston Churchill made the case as to 'the great public importance of getting a respite' in Ireland. This was a viewpoint which would become the predominant view of the Coalition over the next six weeks and, most importantly, would come to be accepted in large measure by Lloyd George himself. Churchill's arguments were prophetic and merit careful reading:

> I don't agree that it would be a sign of weakness. It would be six or eight months ago. Then we were not in a position to make any concessions and we had to stand firm and did so. Now our forces are stronger and better trained; auxiliaries are stronger; the police are extending their control over the country; our position is vastly better in a material sense; our position is not better from the point of view of reaching finality ... very unpleasant as it regards the interest of this country all over the world; we are getting an odious reputation; poisoning our relations with the United States; it is in our power to go on and enlist Constable and Black and Tans; but we should do everything to get away to a settlement.[22]

Indeed, as we shall see, George V's speech opening the Northern Ireland Parliament, and the favourable reaction it garnered in both Britain and Ireland, were singularly important to Lloyd George and his Government. Rather than grab 'murder by the throat' as Lloyd George had hoped, the British policy of coercion had virtually dried up whatever credibility the British Government had left in Ireland as a peace keeper and peace maker.

Lloyd George, forever the pragmatist and intent in his desire to extricate himself from the Irish quagmire his government found itself in, was now clear in his desire to avoid a return to open military conflict. 'It is a very important decision to make', he warned the Cabinet, 'and may lead to war in Ireland. I do not agree with the Colonial Secretary that it is a small operation. It is a considerable operation.' If a break was to occur between the Government and Sinn Féin, the Prime Minister hoped that it would be 'more thorough than anything we have had yet and a complete smash-up of the revolutionaries'.[23] Nonetheless, these sentiments expressed by Lloyd George provide further evidence of his ambiguous response to the Irish question: if conditions for a military victory did not exist, Lloyd George was then willing to pursue the path of negotiation.

The manner in which that process was 'fast tracked' by the Coalition, prompted by some external pressure, is our next topic.

Enter the King

The opening session of the Northern Ireland Parliament in Belfast on 22 June 1921, as provided for under the Government of Ireland Act (1920), served as a catalyst for a decision by the British Cabinet to seek a negotiated settlement with Sinn Féin. King George V's remarks, tendered at the opening, served as the vehicle for that policy shift. Indeed, the King's Belfast speech continues to

2. Liam Lynch, commander of the 3rd Cork Brigade of the IRA during the Anglo-Irish War. Lynch was later killed during the Civil War by Free State forces on 10 April 1923.

3. Dinny Lacey, leading figure of the IRA in Tipperary who fought in both the War of Independence and the Civil War.

4. The IRA Flying Column in Tipperary.

5. Irish Volunteer Dan Breen. Breen, along with Sean Treacy, was among the Irish Volunteers who killed two members of the Royal Irish Constabulary at Soloheadbeg on 21 January 1919.

6. Sean Treacy, another leading member of the Tipperary IRA.

7. A newsreel camera captured this footage of Lieutenant Price, a plainclothes officer, firing at Sean Treacy on Dublin's Talbot Street on 14 October 1920. Within seconds both Treacy and Price lay dead.

TERENCE MacSWINEY. M.I.P.
Lord Mayor Of Cork.

8. Terence MacSwiney (Lord Mayor of Cork) died in Brixton prison on 25 October 1920 after 74 days on hunger strike. This was a postcard which was printed by supporters in his memory.

9. Terence MacSwiney's body being brought back to Cork by British Auxiliaries in November 1920. On the left in the foreground a soldier rests on the coffin.

10. Eighteen-year-old Kevin Barry in the uniform of 'H' Company, 1st Battalion of the Dublin Brigade of the IRA. Barry's execution on 1 November 1920, shortly after Terence MacSwiney's death by hunger strike, fanned the flames of revolution in Ireland in 1920.

11. A section of the crowd outside Mountjoy Prison in Dublin awaiting word of Kevin Barry's fate, 1 November 1920.

12. Michael Collins throwing in a ball at a Croke Park Hurling match during the Anglo-Irish truce. The truce was signed between the IRA and the British Army on 11 July 1921.

13. Michael Collins pictured in London during Anglo-Irish negotiations in the Autumn of 1921.

14. Arthur Griffith, Chairman of the Irish delegation to the Anglo-Irish negotiations in 1921. Griffith founded Sinn Féin in 1902.

15. Provisional Government (later Free State) Troops prepare to fire on Anti-treatyite positions at Four Courts, Dublin, during the Civil War in June 1922. The look of confusion on their faces is a reaction to the recoil from the artillery gun fired by other government troops.

16. State funeral, organised by Taoiseach Bertie Ahern's Fianna Fáil led government, which was held in 14 October 2001 for Kevin Barry and nine other IRA men who had been executed in 1920 and 1921. Irish President Mary Mcaleese appears at the right.

17. How many Royal Ulster Constabulary members did it take to arrest Eamon de Valera? Nine, judging by this photo taken in Newry in October 1924 after de Valera's arrest for violating an order banning him from entering Northern Ireland. He served one month in Belfast Jail for the offence.

19. A statue of a United Irishman in Wexford Town commemorating the Rebellion of 1798.

18. Mailing labels issued in 1972 to commemorate the 50th anniversary of the deaths of Michael Collins and Arthur Griffith, and an actual postage stamp for Collins, which was not issued until 1990.

be viewed as one of the most constructive interventions by a monarch into a crisis in modern British history, a conflict which the King himself described as 'a conflict which for generations embarrassed our forefathers'.[24]

However, an analysis of the events leading up to the King's speech suggests that a considerable impetus for scheduling the address came from within the Cabinet. Of equal importance is the fact that the Cabinet's secretarial staff were directly involved in drafting the speech. The record also raises the question of whether the speech by George V prompted the Coalition's decision to turn away from its policy of coercion or was instead part of the 'packaging' for a decision that had already been made by the Government. By reviewing the play of events leading up to the King's 22 June address, together with the circumstances that gradually led Lloyd George and his Cabinet to pursue a negotiated policy in Ireland, we might gain a better grasp of the motivations of the British Government in Ireland in mid-1921.

The consensus among historians concerning the significance of George V's speech is itself noteworthy, largely because of the perceived impact the address had in encouraging the Government to pursue a different course. Charles Mowat has noted that 'the Cabinet, urged on by the King, decided that the universally warm reception to the King's speech gave them the opportunity they needed, and on 24 June, Lloyd George wrote to de Valera and Sir James Craig inviting them to a conference in London'. But Mowat also points out that the 'sudden reversal of policy was more apparent than actual', indicating that the Lloyd George Government was attempting a change in approach to Ireland prior to the 22 June speech.[25]

A. J. P. Taylor gives credit to the role played by South African Prime Minister Jan Smuts in encouraging George V to deliver a conciliatory speech and in persuading Lloyd George to push for a negotiated settlement within the Coalition. Taylor writes: 'Smuts drafted a warm plea for civil peace and pressed it on Lloyd George ... Lloyd George therefore accepted Smuts' proposal and soon made it his own. George V deserves some of the credit. His initiative was perhaps the greatest service performed by a British monarch in modern times'.[26] It is not without irony that Dorothy Macardle, in her totally sympathetic work on the Irish Republican cause, also found praise for George V's speech. Macardle noted:

> King George happily had other views and had the humanity and courage to seize the opportunity to express them. The speech prepared for him to deliver on the occasion of the opening of the Northern Ireland Parliament did not satisfy him. He discussed its tenor with General Smuts, and in consultation with him revised the speech. The alteration was agreed to by members of the Cabinet, not without reluctance: its tone made it impossible for them to proceed with the full rigour of their plans.[27]

In his actions with respect to Irish policy, George V was guided by his Private Secretary, Lord Stamfordham. The King's intervention in the conduct of the British policy in Ireland began with the controversy following the Government's attempt to implement the Second Home Rule Act. From the outset, it served to underscore the fact that George V's involvement amounted to more than a passing interest in Anglo-Irish affairs. Indeed, it must be emphasised that George V's speech, its implicit call for a political solution to the Anglo-Irish conflict notwithstanding, was made at the date and place in which Britain's political division of Ireland into two units took effect. In essence, the British monarch served as the vehicle for the implementation of that division by presiding over the creation of a state specially created by British officialdom along religious lines. As Nicholas Mansergh has noted, with the active assistance of the British Government, 'at a favourable moment politically the minority [i.e. the Protestant minority of Ireland] were in consequence enabled to obtain not only a separate state but also the area for which they asked on the grounds that it was the largest in which a stable unionist government could be maintained'.[28]

The extent to which the King's appearance in Belfast can be viewed as the means by which Lloyd George and the Coalition Cabinet could embark on a different approach to Ireland must be evaluated largely on the basis of the Cabinet's involvement in the preparation of the King's speech, and in a review of the historical evidence indicating the development of a prevailing view within it that a political solution was necessary.

The record also indicates that Lloyd George was at this time aware, from reports he received directly from Hamar Greenwood in Ireland, that Eamon de Valera was also endeavouring to pursue a path to peace. 'Things are moving in the right direction here', Greenwood wrote on 5 June. 'De Valera wants to see [Sir James] Craig [the Ulster Unionist leader] and the latter will tonight decide as to place if agreeable.' Greenwood also informed the Prime Minister that their effort to put a different face on the Irish Administration by naming the Catholic Lord Fitzalan to replace Lord French was proceeding. 'The new Viceroy was duly sworn in, and is busy meeting heads of departments and others. He's doing well. I had him cinemeaographed [sic] today for the "Movies of the World" as the First R. C. [Roman Catholic] Lord Lieutenant.' At the same time, while Lloyd George may have been seeking a way out of the dead-end which the Government's policy had led to, Greenwood persisted, forever the diehard. 'The military and police are hitting hard and sure', he wrote in the same letter. Attacks on forces [sic] are rarely successful now, and the enemy finds it safer to attack civilians . . . Please leave me here as long as possible. I can keep my hand on things so much better'.[29] Indeed, as events would demonstrate, Greenwood, unlike his predecessors, was not to be replaced. Instead he was about to become Britain's last Chief Secretary for Ireland.

In the case of George V, it can be said to his credit that he made a con-scious effort not to endorse the excesses of the Government's coercion policy in Ireland during the Anglo-Irish War, inquiring of Greenwood at one stage, 'if this policy of reprisals is to be continued and, if so, where will it lead ... ?'[30] He also expressed his view that the Black and Tans should be disbanded. It is also significant that the discussions which the Coalition Cabinet held over the King's visit to Belfast, along with the considerable time devoted to preparing an acceptable draft of the King's remarks, represented one of the only instances for which there is any record of a monarch's views being mentioned at the Cabinet level during the first half of the twentieth century.[31]

The precedent for George V's initiation of the first session of the Northern Ireland Parliament was the opening of the Parliament of the Commonwealth of Australia by the Duke of York in 1902. Significantly, the royal opening marked the first instance where a British monarch opened a parliament other than Britain's.[32]

While the first draft of a speech for George V originated with Sir James Craig, Northern Ireland's first Prime Minister, it was rejected by the King and the Cabinet on 17 June on the grounds that it was tied too closely to local government issues in the new Northern state. It was agreed by Lord Stam-fordham (acting for the King) and Lloyd George that a speech was needed which would capture the moment and point the way for a new policy initia-tive by the Government. Three other versions of a speech for the King exist: firstly, a draft by South Africa's Prime Minister General Jan Smuts, who was in London for the Imperial Conference; secondly, a draft by Lord Balfour, serving as Lord President of the Council for the Cabinet; and thirdly, a final version written by Sir Edward Grigg, Lloyd George's Private Secretary, with the active assistance of Lord Stamfordham. That all three drafts were written between 16 and 17 June underscores the urgency with which the King and the Cabinet viewed the royal address in Belfast. The special Cabinet session called to order on the evening of 17 June for the preparation of a final draft of the King's address also included the active participation of the Prime Minis-ter himself, along with the visiting General Smuts.[33]

The actual text delivered by the King in Belfast on 22 June represented the exchange of views between the King, General Smuts and the Cabinet. The language in the text provided by Grigg attempted to have the monarch describe in heartfelt terms his sentiments for all of Ireland, and make a plea for peace with an allusion to a type of domestic autonomy for the rest of Ire-land. That this speech was largely the work of the same British Cabinet responsible for the Government's coercion policy in Ireland was nonetheless against a backdrop of euphoria that greeted the King's address seven decades ago.

At the outset of the Imperial Conference in London, General Smuts decided to initiate contact with Eamon de Valera directly. But Smuts' decision was not taken entirely on his own. He consulted with Lloyd George, who was 'delighted'. Nonetheless, the South African was not reluctant to let the British leader know how much he felt that the Government's handling of the Irish situation was damaging the Empire. In a 14 June letter to Lloyd George, to which he attached his draft of a speech for delivery by King George in Belfast, Smuts stated: 'I need not enlarge to you on the importance of the Irish question for the Empire as a whole. The present situation is an unmeasured calamity; it is in negation of all the principles of government which we have professed as the basis of Empire, and it must more and more tend to poison both our Empire [*sic*] relations and our foreign relations.'

Smuts also took the opportunity to lecture Lloyd George that 'the present methods are frightfully expensive in a financial, no less than a moral sense; and what is worse, they have failed. What is to be the next move, for the present situation may not last?' He then made two suggestions to the Prime Minister, which were important in light of developments during the next six months. First, he indicated that the establishment of the Northern Parliament 'definitely eliminates the coercion of Ulster, and the road is clear now to deal on the most statesmanlike lines with the rest of Ireland'. In addition, as he intimated to George V, Smuts suggested to Lloyd George that the King's visit to Belfast 'would be fully justified if the occasion were made use of by him to make a really important declaration on the whole question. I believe that in the present universal mistrust and estrangement the King could be made use of to give a most important lead, which would help you out of a situation which is nigh desperate.'[34]

The suggested context for the King's speech offered by Smuts rested on granting Dominion status to the whole of Ireland with a separate Ulster Parliament. 'I would suggest', Smuts wrote, 'that in his speech to the Ulster Parliament, the King should foreshadow the grant of Dominion status to Ireland, and point out that the removal of all possibility of coercing Ulster now renders such a solution possible ... Informal negotiations could then be set going with responsible Irish leaders.'[35] It should be noted here that despite essential differences in tone from the draft written by Balfour two days later, Smuts' effort was also supportive of maintaining the separate Ulster Parliament, with dominion status for Southern Ireland. On that essential point, the key drafters of George V's address were all in agreement. While the final text did not include the five sentence declaration by Smuts in favour of outright dominion status for Southern Ireland, it did of course support partition, consistent with the Government of Ireland Act (1920), and a key part of the rationale behind the King's visit to Northern Ireland itself.

At 6.30 p.m. on 17 June, the Cabinet held its final meeting to discuss 'a draft of the King's speech for the state opening of the Parliament for Northern Ireland, prepared by Mr Balfour'. Balfour, Greenwood, and Shortt attended an earlier meeting that day to discuss with Sir Nevil Macready, the British

Commander-in-Chief in Ireland, the extension of martial law throughout all of the counties of southern Ireland.[36] According to Tom Jones, in a presentation to the Irish Situation Committee on 16 June, Macready said that 'if coercion is to succeed at all it can only succeed by being applied with the utmost thoroughness', and that 'only by so doing can the spirit of the soldiers and police be sustained'. Macready stressed that while 'quiet members of the Dáil Éireann would not be arrested … the government must begin at the beginning, and de Valera when caught must be tried for his life'. Macready noted that he was 'losing his self respect'. For instance, it put him in an absurd position to be unable to buy English goods due to the boycott enforced by local merchants in Dublin, although he was Commander-in-Chief of the British forces.[37] Ostensibly, with the Cabinet's approval, martial law throughout the twenty-six counties was to be activated by 14 July if the Sinn Féin members elected in the general election of May 1921 refused to take the oath of allegiance to the King and join the Southern Parliament set up under the Government of Ireland Act.

It appeared politically impossible, however, given the objections both at home and abroad to Britain's policy of coercion in Ireland, that the 14 July date recommended by the Irish Situation Committee for implementing martial law would be met. But that such a discussion continued to take place among key members of the British Cabinet while the same ministers were also discussing the King's opening of the Northern Ireland Parliament must not be ignored. The question must be raised as to whether, in the view of some members of the British Cabinet, the move towards a truce was aimed more at slowing the pace of rebel activity and in turn placing Britain in a better position to regain control of Ireland by superior force, should a negotiated settlement in Britain's interest not be realised. It is with this question in mind that these comments, offered by Winston Churchill to the Cabinet one month earlier, take on particular relevance. Perhaps most significant, in light of the shift in focus that British policy would undergo within a matter of weeks, was Churchill's assessment of how a truce would help Britain militarily:

> An offer by the government to take the pressure off is an act of good faith. It would have considerable effect on British public opinion and on British Liberal opinion. Where is the disadvantage? There is no military disadvantage. Supposing you appeal to Irish honour. If you do attempt to appease, either the truce will be kept or it will be broken. If kept, you'll have tremendous advantage; they'll have great difficulty in getting men to go back; if they break, you are in a far stronger position with our public opinion; your troops are all in position; they can begin at any moment and in the interval you'll have got information. It is a matter of psychology when you should time it, but it should be very early and allow a gentler mood to prevail.[38]

Churchill's prescription for the use of 'psychology' in dealing with the Irish situation appears to have been a compelling one, especially to Lloyd George.

Perhaps Churchill's rationale for a change in policy was heightened by a greater awareness on the Cabinet's part of the actual military situation in Ireland. Sir Laming Worthington-Evans' 24 May warning as Secretary of State for War that there was a 'risk that a position of virtual stalemate may continue throughout the summer and that winter will be a time of decisive advantage to the rebels', struck a particular note of pessimism. The Cabinet meeting on the evening of 17 June, held to discuss the King's speech, saw Lloyd George in the chair. Prime Minister Smuts was also present. According to Sir Maurice Hankey, Lloyd George 'found himself in full agreement with the view of the Irish Situation Committee'. He stated that it was unlikely that 'the Sinn Féiners, who had perpetrated the act of vandalism of burning down the Custom House would listen to any appeal'. Against this backdrop the Prime Minister saw the King's Belfast visit 'as an occasion for a big gesture'. The Cabinet stated that 'general agreement was expressed that earlier passages in Sir Edward Grigg's draft introduced a personal element, calculated to appeal to Irish sentiment, and that they might usefully precede Mr Balfour's draft'.[39] This awareness shows an understanding within the Cabinet that a personal appeal was needed to break the logjam of British policy in Ireland, and should come directly from the King himself. The recent efforts by the Prime Minister, such as the call to the Irish to support a Southern Parliament under the Government of Ireland Act, received little support from the majority of Irish Nationalists – a situation not unlike the failure of the earlier Irish Convention.

The tone of the speech was clearly directed towards the prospect of a negotiated resolution of the conflict and away from the policy of coercion. It articulated a call for peace, yet a peace clearly on British terms. In calling for a solution for which 'the Parliament of the United Kingdom has in the fullest measure provided the powers', we see the Cabinet's intent. The King's speech emphasised the British intention to see a Southern Irish Parliament created under the terms of the Government of Ireland Act, attached as a dominion to Britain, while maintaining a separate Northern Ireland entity under British jurisdiction.

George V's comment that 'few things are more earnestly desired throughout the English-speaking world than a satisfactory solution of the age-long Irish problems which for generations embarrassed our forefathers' was a tacit admission of how much the Irish conflict had grown as a cause of concern for Britain in its relations with the Commonwealth nations and the United States.* But the monarch's hope that the Northern Ireland state's affairs 'will be managed with wisdom and with moderation, with fairness and due respect

---

* Jan Smuts, Lionel Curtis and Edward Grigg, because of their interest in a harmonious Imperial federation, communicated this message internally throughout the first six months of 1921.

to every faith and interest', were not to be echoed by Northern Ireland's first Premier, Sir James Craig. Craig later declared: 'All I boast is that we have a Protestant Parliament and a Protestant state.'[40] It was a hope which for Craig was to be essentially realised, as we shall see.*

While George V's speech was conciliatory, it sought to lay the blame for the conflict on the Irish themselves. In his 'appeal to all Irishmen to pause, to stretch out the hand of forebearance and conciliation, to forgive and forget, and to join in making for the land which they love a new era of peace, contentment and good will',[41] the monarch was in essence stating that the problem was not a conflict over the belief of a substantial majority in Ireland that Britain could no longer claim to govern Ireland, but was instead one of competing religious identities within Ireland itself. Following this logic, the conflict was a matter that could be resolved by internal goodwill among Irishmen of different faiths while they continued to live under British rule in some form.

The reaction to the King's speech was immediate and achieved the opening the Government sought: a grand gesture, achieving widespread attention, had opened the door for a change in British policy in Ireland. As Lionel Curtis had suggested for the benefit of Lloyd George and the Cabinet in the June 1921 edition of *The Round Table*, regarding the failure of British military policy in Ireland: 'It sometimes happens that a people intent on practical business and little accustomed to talk of ideas surprises the world and itself by responding to the call of great opportunity.'[42]

An editorial in *The Times* of London on 23 June 1921 hailed the royal visit to Belfast as a 'supreme and unqualified success'. 'His speech', the paper stated, 'was a triumph of tact and statesmanship – the statesmanship that is great enough to be human and obviously sincere.' *The Times*, however, was less complimentary towards Britain's political leadership, stating that 'on the day of the King's departure on June 21st, the Government by the mouth of the Lord Chancellor, ruthlessly dashed all hopes that their hearts might have changed and decreed intensified warfare in Ireland to the bitter end'. Troops, *The Times'* editorial also noted, 'are being poured into Ireland at all possible speed, and as plainly indicated, martial law will be applied to the whole country outside Ulster unless the Southern Parliament consents, as it is not likely to consent, to be established'. While *The Times* admitted that such action by the Government might yet be needed 'to the continuance of the

---

* Ironically, General Sir Henry Wilson declined Craig's invitation to attend the Northern Parliament's opening on the grounds that it might prove a conflict since he might soon be 'ordering thousands of troops to crush the rebellion in the South and West'. Instead, Wilson would soon be working directly for the Craig regime as its security advisor, a role which would see him intricately involved in the creation of the sectarian part-time Protestant militia known as the B-Specials. (See Dorothy Macardle, *Irish Republic*, p 460.)

Government's present policy ... it is astounding that it should be resolved upon and announced on the very eve of the King's appeal for peace in Ireland'.[43] Clearly *The Times* was unaware of the extent to which Lloyd George and a majority in the Coalition were working behind the scenes to shift British policy towards a different approach.

The Prime Minister's own comments gave him the appearance of a man who had anxiously awaited the outcome of the King's speech. In a letter to the King on the day following the address, Lloyd George let it be known how successful he thought the event was: 'None but the King could have made that personal appeal, none but the King could have evoked so instantaneous a response.'[44] Indeed, the King's appeal to 'all Irishmen to pause, to stretch out the hand of forbearance and conciliation, to forgive, and forget', stood in marked contrast to the British policy of coercion. It provided a striking contrast to Birkenhead's speech in the House of Lords the day before the King's visit to Belfast calling for increased repressive measures. But Birkenhead at the same time indicated why the Government wanted a resolution of the conflict. 'The history of the last three months is the history of the failure of our military methods to keep pace with, and to overcome, the military methods which have been taken by our opponents.'[45]

Following the monarch's address, Churchill wrote: 'No one responsible for the King's speech had contemplated immediate results in action, but in such declarations everything depends upon a sounding board.' The Government had now cast itself as a peacemaker. Churchill's earlier arguments now appeared more plausible. Were Sinn Féin to accept the open invitation to confer with the British Government, and the conference breakdown due to Sinn Féin demands for one independent Ireland, the Government could well win back public sympathy and pursue an even more aggressive policy of coercion in Ireland. It is perhaps for this reason that a dichotomy can be discerned between the positive reaction of the British press and public to the King's address and the interpretation of that reaction by some in the Cabinet. In Churchill's own note of praise to George V for the success of his address, he stated that he was sure that 'the results of the visit of Your Majesty accompanied by the Queen will help materially to facilitate the reunion of the two islands'.[46] On 24 June Lloyd George summoned a meeting of a select group of ministers, including Greenwood, Churchill, Shortt, Balfour, Anderson and Andy Cope of the Irish office. The session focused on the advantage provided to the Government by the King's speech. Lloyd George noted to his colleagues that 'the appeal [by the King] had received a favourable reception by the Irish Nationalist press'.[47] He also stated that 'in the course of the last three days, we have received indications that de Valera is in a frame of mind to discuss a settlement on a basis other than that of independence'.[48] Soon after the session, those present roundly approved of Lloyd George's suggestion that he prepare invitations to both Eamon de Valera and Sir James Craig to meet him in London.

In reviewing the sequence of these events it is important to note that Lloyd George, with or without the Cabinet's knowledge, had already been laying the groundwork for negotiations. On the afternoon of 22 June British troops on foot patrol searching a house in the Blackrock section of Dublin took into custody a man of uncertain identity. The man turned out to be President de Valera. But to General Macready's regret and de Valera's surprise the British Government ordered him released the following day. On 25 June, however, the reasoning behind the British decision became clear when de Valera received a letter from Lloyd George proposing a conference between them to explore the prospect for a settlement.[49] He accepted Lloyd George's offer for discussion, and as we will see, a truce was called by the British forces and the IRA, which took effect on 11 July. But it must be emphasised that the favourable publicity surrounding George V's speech and the truce itself did not lead at that point to an end to the support within the British Cabinet for a policy of coercion in Ireland. In a 13 August Cabinet meeting on the course of the discussions with Sinn Féin, Winston Churchill, speaking of Sinn Féin, said:

> They have a great fear in their hearts. I believe you will help them to reason if your reply brings them right up against it. I propose a direct question to them – 'If you wish to come to a conference on the basis of the integrity of the Empire, come, if not, not.' The Cabinet should not assume it is going to be a terrible war and I am fortified in my view by the language used by General Macready. It will not be much worse than what has gone on before. We have taken the ground which the world approves. My view was that coercion should be on fundamentals, not on finance.[50]

Churchill was true to the views he had expressed to the Cabinet the previous May. A truce that forced Sinn Féin to a debate on British terms, after a period in which public opinion could be swayed into believing that the British Government was the reasonable side, could provide the best climate for renewed warfare in Ireland. At the same time, if there was to be a negotiated approach to the conflict, the exclusion of northeast Ulster from the aegis of an Irish government in Dublin meant that the question of Irish territorial integrity would be effectively removed from the outset.

In short, the opportunity that George V's speech provided at the opening of the Northern Ireland Parliament led undeniably to a change in British policy. But it was a change that was not unanticipated by the Government. Lloyd George and all but the most optimistic members of his Cabinet were well aware by this point that they had reached a stalemate in Ireland. Against this backdrop, the British Cabinet, aided by the favourable publicity generated by King George V's speech and the more positive environment it helped create, could now more freely pursue other options.

8

The Anglo-Irish Truce

> Our respective positions have been stated and are understood, and we agree
> that conference, not correspondence, is the most practical ... way to under-
> standing. We accept the invitation, and our delegates will meet you in
> London ... to explore every possibility of settlement.
>
> Eamon de Valera to Lloyd George, 30 September 1921.

On 23 June 1921, one day after King George V's speech opening the Northern Ireland Parliament, there were no less than twenty-nine attacks on British
patrols, including assaults made upon troop trains, RIC Barracks, and various British patrols. Eight IRA men were killed in these encounters, while the
British suffered ten killed and thirty wounded.

Nonetheless, cooler heads on both sides had started to prevail, and the
momentum for a truce was sustained. While the initial offer for a cessation of
hostilities emanated from the British side, it was something that both sides
wanted. Indeed, so far as Collins and Mulcahy were concerned, without a
truce another 'Bloody Sunday' type effort aimed at eliminating a new wave of
British intelligence agents would be needed. Collins' intelligence network had,
by June 1921, undergone serious losses due to British pressure in the field,
particularly in Dublin and Britain. A key Republican agent inside Dublin
Castle was found out and jailed.

One benefit that would rebound to the interest of the British Government,
and one that was probably not unanticipated, was that of the truce itself. As
we have seen, the Irish independence movement was made up of a fragile
coalition containing various strands of Irish Nationalism. Ironically, its
binding agent, more often than not, was the pressure exerted on it by the
British Government. When those pressures were minimised the cohesion of
the Irish independence effort was affected. Likewise, the British benefitted
when large sections of the IRA, especially leaders like Michael Collins, came
out over time in the open.[1]

According to one estimate, by mid-July 1921 the IRA's manpower stood at
approximately 3,000 men, with 4,500 interned and 1,000 under prison sentence.[2] Given such realities, along with increasing difficulties in obtaining

arms and ammunition, there can be little doubt that General Headquarters was in the best position for assessing the IRA's overall military situation. It is in their exercising of such judgments that the differences in information and outlook between de Valera and the General Headquarters staff might be considered. An episode dating back to the earlier debate between de Valera and the IRA as to the timing for a truce is useful.

Following the death of Dick McKee, Commanding Officer of the Dublin Brigade, in November 1920, Ernie O'Malley found that J. J. 'Ginger' O'Connell, the IRA's Director of Training, 'was the only man on the H.Q. Staff whom one could discuss military problems with'. Ordered by O'Connell in January 1921 to a meeting with Michael Collins, Richard Mulcahy and President de Valera, recently returned from the United States, to discuss the military situation as well as IRA training needs in various parts of Ireland, O'Malley had to literally shoot his way to the rendezvous. His account is useful in shedding light on the differences in personality between Collins and de Valera, as well as the latter's lack of familiarity with many facets of the Republican guerrilla campaign. At the same time, O'Malley was sympathetic to de Valera.

> He [de Valera] had lost personal contact during the year and a half he had been away. We sat around a table ... The C. S. (Mulcahy) laid out a large map on the table ... He (de Valera) pointed to Tipperary. 'Tell us about the country. What are the military and police strengths? Our strengths?' I pointed out posts and barracks, outlined our battalion areas, gave, as far as I could remember, our armament and told him the support the people gave us. He had not the human qualities of Collins, the Big Fellow. Dev [*sic*] was more reserved, a scholarly type. He was cold and controlled. Collins might solve a problem boisterously, by improvisation, solve it by its own development. De Valera would find the solution mathematically, clearly, with logic. He questioned me about Clare, Limerick, Cork, Kilkenny. He did not know the names of our senior officers. His questions showed that he did not understand the situation in the South. The main strengths of the enemy he knew, but things had changed since he had been in Ireland.[3]

Following negotiations between the sides at the Mansion House a truce was at long last announced on 9 July. It took effect two days later, and was welcomed by a weary Irish population.* Likewise, for the British Cabinet it provided the opportunity for the saving of face. They knew, as the IRA knew, that the system of dual command which came to characterise the police and military effort to pacify Ireland had not succeeded, notwithstanding the

---

* Yet to some IRA men, there should have been little concern for public morale. Ernie O'Malley stated that 'we had never consulted the feelings of the people. If so, we would never have fired a shot. If we gave them a good strong lead, they would follow'. See Ernie O'Malley, *The Singing Flame* (Dublin, 1979), p. 25.

pressure which curfews imposed in urban districts and roving patrols had placed on the IRA's limited human and material resources. 'Why had the truce been ordered?', a 21-year-old Ernie O'Malley pondered. From his vantage point as a key IRA officer at the time in Tipperary: 'We were gaining ground, each day strengthened us and weakened our enemy; then why was it necessary to put a stop to hostilities?'[4] Yet Liam Lynch, ironically one who would play a key role in the armed opposition mounted by diehard Republicans to the Irish Free State, made it clear that the Republican effort at civilian government had all but collapsed before the truce.

> We must admit that all civil organisations, county councils, Sinn Féin clubs and all other organised bodies were an absolute failure during the last phase of hostilities. If anything, they were a burden on the army.[5]

To the annoyance of Sir James Craig and his Unionist regime the truce was also extended to Northern Ireland by the British Government. This was done without consultation with him. Thus the IRA came out in the open, drilled and re-organised within the six-county state as they had in the rest of Ireland. But the truce vexed the Unionists further because it slowed the transfer of power from the Crown to the Belfast departments. In addition, it served to stoke their ever-present fears that Britain would sell them out to Nationalist Ireland.[6]

Overall, the terms of the Anglo-Irish truce provided that attacks on Crown forces and civilians alike would cease, while there would be no more provocative displays of force on either side, curfew restrictions were removed and the sending of reinforcements from Britain to Ireland suspended. In Dublin City the Dublin Metropolitan Police were allowed to resume their normal police functions unimpeded, and British military activity was restricted to the support of the police in their normal civic duties. Aside from the civic lifting of curfews, perhaps the greatest breathing space obtained by the Irish civilian population and the IRA alike was the end to raids and searches by either the military or the RIC.[7]

Not surprisingly, disputes involving compliance with the terms of the truce often proved vexing to both sides. Throughout its duration, IRA General Headquarters continued to forward directives to all Brigade Commanders on a regular basis. Such actions, along with the drilling and acceptance of new recruits into the ranks that continued throughout the truce were consistent with the attitude on the part of Collins and Mulcahy, among others in the IRA's command sector, who saw the need for the maximum amount of preparedness possible should hostilities be renewed. While for the most part operating within the terms of the truce itself, General Headquarters was also well aware that with over 40,000 troops in Ireland and a virtually unlimited supply of resources to call upon, the British side would also make use of the truce in the event of a return to armed conflict. On 12 July 1921 a memorandum sent by Eamon Duggan, Chief Liaison Officer for the IRA during the truce, informed the local units that 'motor cars, bicycles and other articles commandeered prior to the truce period may not be returned at present except by special permission of the Divisional Commander'. The directive also contained these requirements:

> 1) Instances may come to notice where serious hardship is caused by the withholding of property so commandeered ... The O'C responsible should bear in mind that a state of war still exists and that the general return of commandeered property cannot at present be considered.
> 2) In all cases in which books, account books, etc., belonging to local authorities have been taken possession of by the army in order to prevent auditing by the enemy, they should now be returned at once to the proper local authorities.[8]

During the eighteen weeks that elapsed between the commencement of the Truce on 11 July 1921 and the signing of the Anglo-Irish Treaty, the ranks of the IRA increased dramatically. These truce-time enlistees into the ranks of the IRA would later become known as the 'Truceleers'.[9]

Monthly reports from IRA officers throughout the country forwarded to General Headquarters during the truce underscore the extent to which the lull in fighting made better training possible in some sections of the country. On 11 August 1921 the Brigade Adjutant for the Kilkenny Brigade observed that the 'day to day dispatch service through the Atts. [sic] is working splendid'. The IRA officer went on to note that 'all CC's are working well in the matters of training and recruiting. The civil duties of our police force are functioned [sic] in a satisfactory manner. Our courts are also functioning'.[10] One month later, the Brigade Adjutant noted some additional improvements:

> Most of the officers have been in training camp during the month and have now commenced a Training Camp in Battalion. Engineers have received instructions on munitions work in some of the company S. [sic] The Batt. [sic] has received about 50 rifles and bayonets (Italian pattern) and are engaged in cleaning and polishing same. Let me know if stuff can be procured for them.[11]

In East Clare, efforts at enhancing the military skills of the local volunteers also proceeded. The journal of one IRA scout in Kilfenora, Co. Clare, indicates that on 28 August he and his comrades found themselves taking instructions on how to implement 'a system of blockade for areas and other steps to be taken should hostilities be resumed'. The young IRA man was also learning at this time of the differences between standing, routine, and operating orders.[12]

IRA intelligence at the grass-roots level also continued regularly to apprise General Headquarters of the movements of the British forces. 'I have to report', the Brigade Adjutant for Kilkenny stated on 26 October 1921, while the Anglo-Irish negotiations became bogged down in London, 'that the Auxiliary Division, RIC received standing instructions to secure ample provisions as hostilities are likely to be resumed.' 'A barrack defence', he noted, 'was formed yesterday and detailed as to their duties, no more details available at present.' But there were also drawbacks for the IRA from the standpoint of discipline. It was the estimate of West Cork IRA Commander Tom Barry that there was 'at least a 30 per cent deterioration in our effectiveness and our structure, and morale'.[13] In short, despite Barry's own complaint, many IRA men as well as the great mass of the Irish public were happy that peace had broken out.

The observance of the truce by the IRA was a subject for concern within the Cabinet's Irish Situation Committee. Hamar Greenwood informed the Committee on 20 August that, while every breach of the truce had been made the immediate subject of protest, nonetheless, breaches were still occurring. The fact that IRA drilling continued to take place proved a source of consternation to the Committee. It was agreed that 'when it was felt that the situation had become grave and that the breaches were occurring in such numbers as to constitute a real challenge to the British Government, a stern protest should be made by the head of the Irish Government to de Valera'. Nonetheless, the group concluded that the 'gravity' of any acts committed by the Republicans would have to be 'fully shown before the British Government could break the truce'. In effect, the Government had little desire to force a break in negotiations. The Cabinet's Irish Situation Committee, for example, showed a clear ambivalence about the operation of the Republican Courts.

> It was not considered, for instance, that the establishment of Sinn Féin Courts in itself constituted a sufficiently grave reason for breaking the Truce if those Courts were confined to dealing with civil questions. If, however, the Courts usurped any criminal jurisdiction, the matter became a grave one and should be taken up at once.[14]

Sinn Féin came to know the British official attitude towards the Republican Courts by the start of the Anglo-Irish negotiations in October. Erskine Childers, the Irish delegation's Secretary, informed de Valera from London at the outset of the Anglo-Irish negotiations that the existence of the Republican Courts was, in the eyes of the British Government, less at issue than Sinn Féin's efforts to dramatise their existence. The Courts could continue to function in relation to the truce insofar 'as it is not done in such a way as to make it impossible to pretend not to know'.[15] Indeed, it was by this stage not so much the Courts, but their use as a propaganda exercise that most irked the Crown.

From Lord Fitzalan, Lord French's successor as Lord Lieutenant for Ireland now in place at Dublin Castle, Lloyd George was given a word of

caution on 23 August against any urging of a stiffer British reaction to violation of the Truce. Fitzalan was particularly concerned about instructions
given to General Macready. 'I cannot so far appreciate what you are at in the
proposals made to him. Insofar as I do understand them I hope they will not
be carried out.' Fitzalan added that while he was 'most anxious for every
arrangement being made for the possibility of a break, there won't be one
unless we or DeV. [*sic*] are more foolish than we need be'.[16]

If a break were to occur, the Irish Situation Committee was determined
that it would come 'only if rebel leaders were seen to be engaged in a deliberate attempt to usurp the function of Government under cover of the Truce'.
Tom Jones noted that 'the Committee fully realised the importance of, if
possible, delaying a rupture until the reply of Sinn Féin was received, and
then, if that should be necessary, joining the issue on a definite challenge of
the authority of the British Empire'. The British Government's intent to
implement partition in Ireland, however, was illustrated by the Committee's
decision that 'in the event of a rupture of negotiations with Sinn Féin, control
of the police in the Six Counties should be transferred to the Northern Government immediately'.[17]

Throughout this period Mark Sturgis revealed himself as critical of British
protestations concerning alleged truce violations by the Irish side. '[General]
Brind has, for the second time,' he wrote, 'rung up Duggan today and told
him of a breach of the Truce by an ambush and then found out that it is
stupid and worse to give away to them how stupid we are.' He noted further
in a diary entry of 22 July 1921:

> Macready, in his latest to the Army Council, deplores the fact that Sinn
> Féin is in a day of believing itself recognised as "an army at war," etc. But if
> this is so nobody is more answerable than Macready himself who stepped
> down to the Mansion House on the Friday unasked, fixed up a 'cessation of
> hostilities' [his words] and appointed his Brigadier Brind [*sic*] Chief Liaison
> Officer, making of what might have been a civilian unofficial truce a military
> armistice.

Sturgis went on to state that 'the whole question is much more bitter than
that, and we must be ready to swallow a lot if a real settlement can result'.[18]

During August, Andy Cope stated to Tom Jones that among his greatest
concerns was the possibility of an upsurge of public support for the more
extreme elements of Irish Republicanism, spurred on, ironically, by over-
reaction on the part of the British military to drilling by the IRA. 'The
fanatics who now stand in the way of a settlement are looking to Martial law
as their strongest ally', he wrote. 'They knew', he contended, 'that they have
not the country behind them at present, but they know that if the Government makes war on the whole Irish people the Irish people will again be
with them to a man'. In the view of the man who had worked as tirelessly as

anyone in Dublin Castle to extricate his country from its difficulties in Ireland, it was Cope's assessment that, 'the military mind as I have met with it over here is incurably stupid and crude when dealing with anything outside the ordinary routine of military administration'.[19]

In a secret correspondence with Lloyd George on 20 August, he argued that such activities amounted to more of a 'method of keeping control over the younger and wilder spirits than an intention to continue the fight'. 'The drilling', he added, 'is no preparation for such fighting as the IRA would have to go against our forces and their drilling in compact bodies if continued for fighting only means a better target'.[20] One week later, Fitzalan apprised Lloyd George of developments within the Dáil and Sinn Féin Cabinet.

Indeed, the IRA were preparing for the possibility of a break in the Truce. It is clear that, as late as October 1921, Óglaigh na h-Éireann (IRA Headquarters) emphasised the need for greater cooperation on the part of local IRA units with the local Sinn Féin organisation, and with the administrative apparatus which the civilian side of the separatist effort continued to attempt to give positive effect to throughout the Truce. General Headquarters' Directive No. 17 noted 'complaints received that volunteers are standing aloof from the work of the Sinn Féin clubs and have in some cases been given instructions by their officers not to assist in the work of the clubs'. 'This is not right', the document stated. 'Volunteers', it emphasised, 'are expected to take a very sympathetic interest in the work of the clubs and to help them in every possible way so that they function effectively and be imbued with a vigorous Republican spirit.' The apparent lack of cohesion between the military and civilian sectors of the Irish independence movement at the local level, in the eyes of General Headquarters, made for a dangerously weakened national effort: a result that was undesirable whether or not the Truce held up. 'It must be clearly understood', Circular No. 17 also stated, that 'our civil administration must function and that interference on the part of the enemy with this administration – whether it be with the work of courts etc. or with the work of the police is a distinct breach of the truce and all cases of such interference must be reported at once'.[21]

The development of an ability to assess a situation continued to form the basis for other IRA training memoranda. Training Directive No. 9 held that developing the ability to appreciate a situation fully was central for 'improving military knowledge – it further produces reasoning'. It laid special emphasis on the need for an officer to develop a 'clear and concise statement of the objective in view'. In addition, the following topics were covered in this order: 'A. Situation and Strengths of hostile and friendly forces; B. Distribution and topography; C. Armaments; D. Morale and influence on politics; E. Points which can be reached by yourself and the enemy in a given time; F. Lines of communication.'[22]

The maintenance of exemplary conduct in the course of the IRA's dealings with the citizenry during the Truce, specifically in the matter of unauthorised levies, was at the heart of another directive issued by Óglaigh na h-Éireann on 25 October 1921. Signed personally by Cathal Brugha as Republican Minister for Defence, it stated, 'Our national reputation for honor and discipline is involved in this matter ... We have received complaints that levies and forced collections for local Army funds are still being made in certain districts ... all such levies are unauthorised and are to be stopped.'[23]

The truce also provided a period of cooperation between the sides on such matters as the status of missing personnel. Mark Sturgis, writing from Dublin Castle to the IRA liaison on 1 November 1921, stated that 'The father of First Lieutenant Leonard French of the RAF ... has been of the opinion that it is possible that his son was killed since the Truce.' Sturgis was aware that the young officer had been tried by the IRA in County Kerry for 'espionage'.[24]

Operating under the assumption that hostilities could recur at any time, some IRA Brigade Headquarters proceeded to develop intelligence profiles of local individuals who could prove helpful in such an eventuality. Using a form provided by General Headquarters, the Kilkenny Brigade, in October, identified men by skill and by their disposition to the Republican movement.[25] At the end of that month, however, following an admonition from Lloyd George, the Irish delegation communicated their view to Dublin that in order to 'give evidence of our bonafides' the continued importation of arms should be stopped, since it placed both the truce and their own negotiating position, as they saw it, in jeopardy. As a result, shortly thereafter Cathal Brugha instructed Richard Mulcahy to halt the further importation of arms.[26]

On the subject of truce violations, one writer has characterised the attitude of many of the Volunteer units throughout the country as being 'indifferent to the high political preoccupations of the politicians in Dublin or London'. They were likewise 'oblivious to the prospect of peace by negotiation and insensitive to its delicate balance'. The inexperience of the Irish side at negotiating was shown from the outset of the truce, according to Sheila Lawlor, who has argued that 'by submitting on the issue of regularising the truce, the Irish enabled Lloyd George to transform the hitherto indefinite arrangement between Macready and themselves, into a formal agreement by which they were now bound, and which was drawn up and published as a Command Paper on 26 October'.[27] But such an argument underestimates the political reality of overseas opinion, which Lloyd George was very much aware of: while the British Government certainly had the firepower to unleash in Ireland, it was restrained from using it out of international concerns, particularly its relations with the United States. And while the Coalition might seek to expand the policy of coercion and martial law, using still more lethal force, there was no guarantee that such a policy would produce a result in the

Government's interest, hence the decision to enter into negotiations with the same party representing the Irish side that it had characterised as a 'murder gang' for much of the conflict.

A report on the status of the importance of munitions issued by Cathal Brugha as Republican Minister for Defence, and dated 19 December 1921 – compiled at his request in the midst of the Dáil's debates on the Anglo-Irish Treaty – is instructive in comparing the IRA's strength before and during the truce from a munitions standpoint. But given Brugha's personal dislike of Michael Collins and Arthur Griffith, along with his outright opposition to the Anglo-Irish Treaty from the outset, the report should at the same time be cautiously considered. Brugha stated: 'It is hoped that this hurried report will suffice to refute any allegations that have been made.' The following statement will show the quantity of arms and munitions imported and distributed since August 1920, and compares the eleven-month period ending with the truce period. It will be seen that the amount for the five-month period of the truce exceeds the previous eleven months.[28] The report stated:

Arms and Munitions Imported and Distributed 16 August, 1920–July 11, 1921; July 11, 1921–December 17, 1921

	August, 1920–July, 1921	July 1921–December, 1921
Machine Guns	6	51
Rifles	96	313
Revolvers and Automatics	522	637
Rifle Ammunition	21,672	18,232
Shotgun Ammunition	24,629	16,574

The Quartermaster General informed Brugha that 'The purchase of material is a simple matter compared with out transport difficulties. The difficulty in landing, storing and distributing materials in the country cannot be grasped by the average man, even in the army, but can only be realised by those who have overcome the difficulties.' The official's comments on the difficulties involved in the importation of arms and the problems inherent in the manufacture of hand grenades on a large-scale basis are also useful:

Take, for example, the purchase of one hundred weapons and see what it means to have them delivered here in Ireland with safety. First the clearance from a foreign port where you have enemy agents always on the alert, then on arrival at an Irish port you have even a looser net to get through, where every boat is carefully searched immediately on arrival. When you have them landed and distributed, what does it amount to? Merely two weapons per brigade. It is a tough job to get 100 weapons but it looks nothing when the Brigade gets its share, and the Brigade officers will always look at it from the two weapons point of view ... Grenades: This branch was developed when the Truce started. The only place working on the manufacture of grenades was the General Headquarters factory. During the five month period of the Truce, munitions plants have been set up all over the country under the supervision of the quartermasters, and most divisions are turning out their own grenades . . . [29]

He noted that some grenades, were cast without the benefit of a furnace, and provided the following information:

Grenade Manufacture
August 16, 1920–July 11, 1921/July 11, 1921–December 17, 1921
2,209 Complete (approximate)   15,000 complete
12,000 partially completed grenades (approximate)

For the manufacture of explosives, the Quartermaster General informed Brugha that 'The same remarks apply to explosives as to grenades and the following figures will show the progress that has been made.' He then noted these statistics: For the period 16 August 1920 through 11 July 1921, a total of 19,000 pounds of explosives had been produced, while during the period from 11 July 1921 to 17 December 1921, the figure more than doubled to 40,000 pounds. But 'the full weight of the Department in general', he informed the Minister for Defence, 'can be more fully realised when shown as follows: case value of materials purchased from August 16, 1920–July 11, 1921: 10,000 pounds or 1,000 per month; July 11, 1921–December 17, 1921: 30,000 pounds or 6,000 per month'.[30] The conclusion offered by the Quartermaster General also sought to underscore Brugha's work as Minister of Defence:

This statement would prove that there has been no slackness or neglect of duty in this Department. The Truce brought with it no facility for this Department which had to carry out the greater portion of its work under war conditions. The only advantage of the Truce was the freedom of movement and the advantage of being able to work at night as well as day.[31]

In effect, the document, while designed to bring no discredit to Brugha, then locked in disagreement with Collins and Griffith over their actions in London, conveys the reality that there would have been no easy road ahead for the IRA had hostilities resumed. Clearer still was Collins' comment uttered during the truce that 'If this fails, we're done.'[32] He was also aware that the very existence of the Truce had ended his ability, and that of those serving with him in the 'invisible army', to go undercover successfully again.

There were also contentious issues to be addressed, not just between Britain and Ireland, but within the ranks of Irish Nationalism. It was a discussion which the Anglo-Irish War had pushed off the agenda. As had other British accounts forwarded to the British Government, Andy Cope noted what he saw to be a view held by Republicans such as Cathal Brugha and Erskine

Childers, that the Government could force the Ulster Unionists into a settlement centred around a united Ireland.

> They seem unable to realise that whatever may be said as to the British Government's responsibility for creating the present Ulster problem, it is not within the power of the British Government to override Ulster's obstinacy without flagrant breach of faith, and even assuming that the Government were willing to repeal the Government of Ireland Act without Ulster's consent, the recessing Parliamentary support for such a course of action would certainly not be forthcoming.[33]

But Brugha and Childers were by no means alone in this view, as we shall see from the events of the following six months.

Soon after the truce took effect, Mark Sturgis opined in his diary that de Valera 'is having the role of liberator absolutely thrust on him from all sides, and it's hard to see how it can go wrong'.[34] But the time which the British Government had purchased with the truce allowed for philosophical differences, previously kept in check by Sinn Féin, to erupt and begin to split the national movement. So severe were the divisions that had developed within the Dáil Cabinet by July 1921 that separate alliances had taken shape in the small body, with Collins and Griffith on one side and Brugha and Stack on the other. De Valera sought to navigate between them, sometimes choosing sides. Increasingly he sided with Brugha and Stack. The merits of the issues that would come before the Cabinet aside, it is possible that de Valera may have needed Stack and Brugha more to secure his base among the nationalist hard core. Despite his credentials as the only surviving leader of the Easter Rising, the American-born leader of the Irish nation, and son of a Cuban father, carried with him a need to assert his Irishness. Given that Collins had also emerged to rival de Valera in the hearts and minds of Nationalist Ireland, particularly during the former's time spent in the United States, his tendency to agree with Brugha and Stack at Collins' expense may also have been personally motivated.

The extent to which the British Government was aware of these internal divisions within the Dáil Cabinet as the truce continued, is still uncertain. Writing in 1935, Frank Pakenham held that 'little in the way of useful information vis-a-vis what Sinn Féin's real position was appeared to have come from the secret negotiations conducted by Andy Cope and others. We incline to the view', he wrote, 'that two months of secret negotiations had probably brought Lloyd George some encouraging reports about probable attitudes, but no explicit assurances, and that he was nearly as far away as ever from realising the conditions under which he had calculated it would be safe to set on foot negotiations with a Dominion settlement as the goal'.[35] In general, Pakenham was right about the information the Prime Minister was receiving. Indeed, some of it, emanating from the highest level of British officialdom in

Ireland, proved simply wrong. On 28 August correspondence from Lord Fitzalan to Lloyd George, for example, was off the mark on a number of important points, as events would show. He told the Prime Minister of the likelihood that an Irish delegation headed by de Valera, and including Griffith and Barton, was being organised 'to come over and see you at your convenience'. 'They have left Childers out of the Government [sic] altogether', he went on to further misinform Lloyd George. 'This is good as he was dangerous, and I believe they make no secret that this is the reason, though they excuse it by saying that he is overwrought.' He was also wrong in his assessment of the position of Craig and the Ulster Unionists. Stating that while 'Ulster is going to be the difficulty when it comes to meeting', he offered, 'I think they will in the end come sufficiently far to meet the South'. It was an expression of wishful thinking that Fitzalan was not alone in making.[36]

Indeed, the man with the most direct access of all British officials to Sinn Féin expressed his frustration: 'Things are very uncertain here and I have considerable doubt which way they will go', Andy Cope stated in a letter to Tom Jones on 15 August. But in that same correspondence, Cope was better able to help the Government in understanding what the heart of Sinn Féin's position was. 'As we have seen all along, the fly in the ointment is the Ulster question and not the Republic.' 'With Ireland out,' Cope continued, 'the Republic would be in the shade, and the whole thing a walk-over, but with the 6 Counties out, Southern Ireland ... is disappointed and hesitates to accept our scheme.' Cope also advised Jones that Sinn Féin, 'having pushed for national determination and failed ... seek local determination and they are inclined to re-open the question of county option'. He stated that Fermanagh and Tyrone, both with a majority Catholic population, were likely to join with a Southern Irish state rather than remain in Northern Ireland if given the option.[37]

Cope also drove home the value of a protracted truce. He argued that a protracted period of inactivity would sap the efficiency and fighting spirit of the IRA, 'whose members would gradually return to their ordinary habits of civilian life'. 'The advantages of this situation from the Government's point of view', he argued, 'are such that I think they should take no action themselves to terminate the truce, but in view of the unlikelihood of such a situation lasting, they would meanwhile have to make their preparations for adopting one of the other alternatives at a moment's notice.'[38]

Of the alternatives which Cope outlined that the Government could turn to in the event the truce collapsed, he was adamant that 'a settlement imposed by force would have no moral sanction in the eyes of the people'. If that happened, Cope argued, 'one of the earliest acts of the Dominion Government when constituted and in full possession of the country would be to repudiate it and declare for a republic [sic]. The trouble would then begin anew with Britain's moral position badly shaken.'

But it is Cope's final recommendation, from the 24 August memorandum to Tom Jones suggesting that the Government 'evacuate the interior of the country, and hold the ports and strategic coast positions', that requires particular attention, in light of the settlement which an Irish delegation eventually signed four months later. In the memorandum, Cope held that 'the relinquishment of the administration of 90% [sic] of the country would of necessity compel the Sinn Féin [sic] to assure their administration themselves and a responsible Sinn Féin government would be brought into existence with whom we could do business while not recognising their republican pretensions'. Therefore, Cope argued that rather than 'impeding the Sinn Féin government, I should endeavour to cultivate amicable relations with them'. The ex-British customs detective suggested that 'railway and postal services could go on as usual unless Sinn Féin itself put difficulties in the way'. Under Cope's plan, outside Ulster, the RIC would be concentrated within the Irish ports of Dublin, Cork, Wexford, Waterford, Drogheda, and Galway among other areas, while at the same time the Government would relinquish to Sinn Féin 'All civil and fiscal administration of the interior of the country'. Such operations, in Cope's view 'could be carried out without bloodshed and without incurring censure from public opinion, in England and abroad'. 'No British interests', he added, 'would be sacrificed or imperilled. The scandal of England reconquering Ireland in the 20th century would be avoided with all its evil consequences.'[39] In essence, we see that the Government ultimately gained from Dáil Éireann the acceptance of a settlement which it ironically had in its power to effect anyway, had either the truce or the negotiations broken down.

The existence of such a communication from one of Lloyd George's chief contacts in Ireland, based on Cope's assessment of Sinn Féin's position at that time, casts doubt on the seriousness of Lloyd George's later threat made to members of the Irish delegation in Downing Street during the Anglo-Irish Conference of 'immediate and terrible war' and 'war within three days' if the draft Treaty, as it stood on 6 December 1921, was not signed by the Irish side. The Prime Minister was aware that without those signatures, and even with the collapse of the truce, many of the same circumstances sought by the Treaty could be garnered by a less costly yet strategically defined British posture in Southern Ireland, while the emergence of a more moderate body of Sinn Féin opinion was awaited. With this in mind, we should now focus on the developments that led to formal negotiations between the British and Irish sides.

De Valera and Lloyd George

If by 1 July 1921 Eamon de Valera felt that he was caught in a hurly burly of events beyond his control – in which he was arrested one day only to be released the next without explanation, and then given an invitation directly from Lloyd George to commence discussions leading to a settlement of the conflict – he had good reason for this feeling. Nonetheless, by 22 July, albeit with a precarious Anglo-Irish truce in place, de Valera was en route to London carrying the hope of an Irish nation, matched on the other side by the anxiety of a British Prime Minister intent upon ridding himself of the age-old 'Irish Problem'.

De Valera's visit, however, did not evolve the way Lloyd George had envisioned. The Prime Minister's invitation of 24 June to de Valera asked that he 'attend a conference here in London, in company with Sir James Craig, to explore to the utmost the possibility of settlement'.[40] The Irish leader, however, had no desire to be part of discussions in London where he would appear to represent one part of Ireland and Craig another. In fact, two months earlier, through the efforts of Andy Cope, de Valera had met with Craig, who was then about to become Prime Minister of the Northern Ireland state as established by the Government of Ireland Act (1920). The encounter did little but establish how far apart the two men were in relation to the future governance of Ireland. At the same time, prior to departing for London, de Valera invited Irish loyalist leaders to a separate meeting with him in Dublin. Lord Midleton, the prominent Southern Irish Unionist, came, but Sir James Craig declined. The latter appeared content with what he had already achieved: his own Protestant Unionist state secured by British guarantee.

In all, four meetings were held between de Valera and Lloyd George between 14 and 24 July 1921. The Irish leader's meetings with the Prime Minister were preceded by talks in Dublin on 5 July with South African Prime Minister Jan Smuts, the former Boer independence leader who had come to openly embrace his country's membership in the British Commonwealth. In Dublin, he sought to impress upon de Valera the need to accept that the British Government would never concede an Irish Republic, and that Dominion status similar to that enjoyed by South Africa was the most realistic option. As noted earlier, Smuts played a key role in encouraging George V, in the interest of greater harmony within that Commonwealth, to make a conciliatory speech in Belfast. In Britain for a meeting of the Commonwealth countries' prime ministers, he reported directly to Lloyd George about his meeting with de Valera. According to Smuts, de Valera stated on a conciliatory note that 'if the status of Dominion rule is offered, I will use all our machinery to get the people to accept it'.[41] If de Valera made such a remark, events were to show that it was more than a little disingenuous.

One week later, with the Anglo-Irish truce now in effect, de Valera was in London for his first meeting with Lloyd George. The two men met in the Cabinet Room at No. 10 Downing Street, and as in the case of their subsequent meetings, they met alone. The Cabinet Room was a site of Lloyd

George's choosing. His motive was a contrived one: to impress upon de Valera that the vacant chair at the long table would belong to an Irish Prime Minister who would lead Ireland formally into the Commonwealth of nations and take its place alongside Canada, South Africa, Australia, and the other Dominions. But de Valera, to Lloyd George's vexation, refused to take the bait. As Lloyd George gestured to the empty chair, the Irishman pretended to focus on his papers.*

In reality, more transpired between Lloyd George and de Valera in London than the former's attempts to cajole the latter. On 18 July, de Valera demanded that the British Government explain its attitude towards Sir James Craig's stated position that Northern Ireland was to remain separate and apart from the rest of Ireland's relationship with Britain. Lloyd George's answer was characteristically equivocal: it was a matter for the Irish, both the North and the South, to resolve.[43]

At their final meeting on 20 July, the Prime Minister presented de Valera with the British proposals. But de Valera refused to take them back with him to Dublin, arguing that they should be sent to Dublin separately.† The offer provided for limited Dominion status for a twenty-six county Southern Ireland. At the same time, the Government sought agreement from de Valera and his colleagues that Northern Ireland and its Parliament be accepted along with an agreement that a change in status could not occur without the approval of a majority in the six-county area. In addition to reiterating that Ireland's partition would continue, the British proposals of 20 July also provided for Dominion status, with safeguards built in for the Crown's defence. Provisions requiring that Ireland agree to free trade between the two countries and carry its share of 'the present debt of the United Kingdom' were also

---

* It was a ploy that Lloyd George would attempt again during the Anglo-Irish negotiations. Ironically, on that occasion the recipient of Lloyd George's attention was Michael Collins. In an interview in July 1985, the late Sean MacBride related to this writer the incongruous looking scene he witnessed in the Cabinet Room at the end of a meeting between the Prime Minister and Collins late in the negotiations. MacBride, in London as a member of Collins' personal security detail, stated that upon entering the room he found the two men looking up at a world map where the British Empire's holdings were colored in red. The much shorter Lloyd George stood with his arm around Collins' waist, speculating out loud as to what a great military leader Collins would make for the Empire. The younger man listened, and gave no reaction. Afterwards, alone with MacBride, Collins laughed off the Prime Minister's praise. But MacBride recalled wondering if the Welshman's compliments were actually going to Collins' head. MacBride himself later took up arms against Collins and the pro-Treaty side in the Irish Civil War. Indeed, as a member of the Anti-Treatyite party that kidnapped General 'Ginger' O'Connell off the streets of Dublin, while his colleagues occupied the Four Courts, he helped set the divisions in greater motion.
† In fact, they were delivered by Tom Jones in person to the rest of the Irish Delegation at their residence.

included.[44] In these proposals, the British Government was willing to grant a Southern Irish state a degree of autonomy not given the previous year in the Government of Ireland Act. Drafted largely by Lionel Curtis, the British proposals shown to de Valera on 20 July represented the essence of what was to become the Anglo-Irish Treaty. In the next chapter we will return to de Valera's meetings with Lloyd George, in attempting to assess how likely the Irish leader thought an actual settlement was.

Even before de Valera returned from London, the Dáil Cabinet rejected the British proposals out of hand, on the basis that it could not 'admit the right of the British Government to mutilate our country, either in its own interest or at the call of a section of our population'. Three weeks passed, however, before de Valera gave his official reply to the British Government. His answer of 10 August represented the first of a total of sixteen letters and telegrams exchanged by the two leaders, ending on 30 September. His considered response was also one of outright rejection, echoing the verbal rejection he gave Lloyd George on 20 July, when he first saw the proposals. His position was buoyed by unanimous resolutions from the Dáil and the Cabinet turning the British proposals down. 'The responsibility for initiating an honourable peace rests primarily not with our Government, but with yours', his letter of 10 August stated.[45] Nonetheless, the letter provided the basis for the long correspondence between de Valera and Lloyd George that in the end resulted in the substantive negotiations between the Irish and British representatives that began in London two months later.

Upon de Valera's return his actions on the question of attaining a settlement were governed by meetings with a divided Dáil Cabinet. It is apparent that by the time his exchange of correspondence with Lloyd George commenced, de Valera was well aware that hopes for the recognition of an Irish Republic by the British Government were in vain. Indeed, well before he had even met Lloyd George, de Valera cautioned Harry Boland, the Sinn Féin secretary, against excessive public demands for a Republic.

> In public statements, our policy should be not to make it easy for Lloyd George by proclaiming that nothing but so and so will satisfy us. Our position should be simply that we are insisting on only one right, and that is the right of the people of this country to determine for themselves how they should be governed. That sounds moderate, but includes everything.[46]

At a minimum, de Valera can be seen from that statement to have at least been preparing the groundwork for a shift from the demand of a Republic, if not an outright acknowledgement of its lack of viability at a conference.

De Valera sought to avoid the political mine-field he found in the Dáil Cabinet and elsewhere, in an effort to prevent a collapse of the truce. He used his correspondence with Lloyd George to propose his notion known as 'Free Association with the British Empire', a concept Erskine Childers devised and to which de Valera first made reference in a letter to Lloyd George on 10 August.

The letters continued between the two men. De Valera's correspondence of 12 September to Lloyd George, in response to Lloyd George's letter of 7 September, provided a hopeful sign for the British, stating:

> We have no hesitation in declaring our willingness to enter a conference to ascertain how the association of Ireland with the community of nations known as the British Empire can best be reconciled with Irish national aspirations ... We have summoned Dáil Éireann that we may submit to it for ratification the names of the representatives it is our intention to propose.[47]

However, the Irish leader's comment within that letter that 'our nation has formally declared its independence and recognises itself as a sovereign State' was clearly considered offensive by Lloyd George, to such an extent that he was hesitant to show it to his Cabinet during their meeting in Inverness.[48] It remained the major obstacle to a conference in the British view.

In fact, evidence that the Government sought to force a response on its own terms, through a threat of harsh action in the event Sinn Féin refused to compromise, is found in a secret communication sent by Tom Jones to Lloyd George in Inverness on 12 August 1921:

> I saw Mr Art O'Brien at noon to-day and told him you hoped to let Sinn Féin have the Government's reply on Sunday evening. We then discussed freely and quite informally Mr de Valera's reply for half an hour. I reiterated many times that no headway whatever could be made so long as Sinn Féin talked of 'amicable and absolute separation,' that Sinn Féin was asking for the shadow of nominal independence and throwing away the substance of real freedom offered them in the Government's proposals. I said that de Valera's document evicted the King and put Ulster outside the Empire and that this made the position much worse than it was a few weeks ago.[49]

We will also see how, during the subsequent Dáil debates on the Treaty, a central question revolved around whether the acceptance by the Irish delegates of the oath to the King repudiated the Republic. A possible return to armed conflict was averted by de Valera's correspondence to Lloyd George on 12 September. He accepted the Prime Minister's invitation to a conference to fulfil the Irish side's willingness to discuss how the association of Ireland with the British Empire could best be reconciled with 'Irish national aspirations'. Significantly, de Valera's letter included no prerequisite that the British Government should first recognise the existence of an Irish Republic.

It is clear that there existed a general agreement within the highest levels of the British Government as to the conditions for an Anglo-Irish conference. In reviewing the pertinent documents, Lord Stamfordham, King George V's

Private Secretary, writing on 20 September to Sir Edward Grigg, one of Lloyd George's principle secretaries, conveyed the monarch's approval of

> the reply sent to de Valera on the night of the 18th, which demonstrates that, not only were the previous conversations not unconditional, but that de Valera was invited as 'the chosen leader of the great majority in Southern Ireland,' and that at the very outset he was reminded that allegiance to the Throne and membership of the British Commonwealth were postulates to any conversations.

Stamfordham also noted that George V had also received de Valera's reply of 19 September, scouting out 'the idea of entrance into conference'. While Stamfordham noted de Valera's evasiveness on the requisite of allegiance to the Crown, the King believed that the reply offered 'further signs of conciliation'.[50]

On 20 September, Stamfordham received this response from Grigg on Lloyd George's behalf:

> The Prime Minister is in complete agreement with the King's view that de Valera's latest communication shows signs of a desire to conciliation. In fact, it is significant that the Prime Minister's most severely worded communications have produced a more conciliatory tone than has been heard on the Irish side in this correspondence before.[51]

Lloyd George's knowledge of de Valera's political situation at home was evident in Grigg's comment that 'the Prime Minister is most anxious to find some way of saving de Valera's face and helping him out of the impossible situation in which he has placed himself, provided the fundamental position of His Majesty's Government is not compromised'.[52] The letter, however, neglected to underscore the equally compelling need on the British Government's part to likewise pursue a negotiated settlement.

Lloyd George also received advice during this period from his Cabinet colleagues. Echoing the proposal outlined earlier by Andy Cope, H. A. L. Fisher urged the Prime Minister to allow de Valera the widest possible latitude in his communications since the 'whole sentiment of Ireland is passionately averse to a rupture of the truce'. For that reason he suggested that the Government not attach to de Valera's correspondence 'the sense which they appear to bear' but to accept his desire for an actual settlement.[53] In the event the truce was terminated, and Sinn Féin refused to give Britain the requisite outlets in Ireland for protecting its security, Fisher proposed that 'we leave Sinn Féin for the moment to their own devices'. In his estimate, such an approach could undermine the popularity of the Dáil Government by forcing Southern Ireland into a position of isolation.[54] But such a contingency did not prove necessary, given that de Valera appeared to show a greater willingness to bend in order that talks could begin.

Lloyd George's reply of 29 September to de Valera's letter of 19 September evidently had an impact on the Irish side and spurred on the commencement of the Anglo-Irish Conference. It was to be the last letter that Lloyd George sent to de Valera, and may well have been the one that induced the Irish leader to commence negotiations with the Government. The Prime Minister stated that, in spite of its 'sincere desire for peace, they [his government] cannot enter a conference on the basis of this correspondence'. De Valera's insistence on the sovereignty of Ireland was unacceptable to him. Lloyd George emphasised that

> notwithstanding your personal assurance to the contrary ... it might be argued in the future that the acceptance of a conference on this basis had involved them in a recognition which no British Government can accord. On this point they must guard themselves against any possible doubt. There is no purpose to be served by any further interchange of explanatory and argumentative communications upon this subject.[55]

The swiftness of de Valera's reply of 30 September to Lloyd George, and a full reading of it, suggests his earnest desire not to break with the Prime Minister. 'We accept the invitation, and our delegates will meet you in London on the date mentioned to explore every possibility of settlement by personal discussion.' Although de Valera's response includes his comment that 'their respective positions have been stated and are understood', he did not insist that Ireland be afforded the status of a sovereign nation in any discussions.[56]

At the same time, a significant milestone had been reached by de Valera and the Irish side. The same British Prime Minister who less than a year before had pledged at the London Guildhall not to compromise with the IRA, and who claimed that the Coalition's policies 'had murder by the throat', was now going to treat with the representatives of the Irish insurrectionists in formal conference. He would do so without preconditions. But what could not be achieved by the British Government through its failed dual policy, which combined a measure of Home Rule with counter-terror, would instead be switched to an attempt aimed at drawing the enemy into the British Dominions within the framework of a divided Ireland. British statecraft would now be the means used to attempt peace in Ireland. And if peace could not be achieved, then the Government would accept a result in which it could extricate itself from Ireland to the greatest extent possible, rendering the Irish problem a genuinely Irish one, and the casualties largely Irish.

9

The Anglo-Irish Treaty

I do solemnly swear true faith and allegiance to the Constitution of the Irish
Free State as by law established and that I will be faithful to H. M. King
George V, his heirs and successors by law, in virtue of the common citizenship
of Ireland with Great Britain and her adherence to and membership of the
group of nations forming the British Commonwealth of Nations.

Oath to the Crown as contained in Article IV of Anglo-Irish Treaty

The Anglo-Irish Conference itself, held at Downing Street between 11 October and 6 December 1921, produced the agreement which has in essence defined Anglo-Irish relations up to the present day, and therefore requires a careful analysis.

Frank Pakenham's distillation of the situation that confronted the Irish and British sides as the Conference opened remains most valuable.

At the time of the Treaty negotiations in 1921 two dominant problems confronted the negotiations on both sides. Both were severe; but one – the problem of reconciling Irish independence with Britain's ideas of her own security – was probably, in the circumstances of the time, insoluble without tragedy. The other – the problem of securing a United Ireland, accepted by all parts of Ireland – was admittedly very testing. The reason, however, why things did not take a different course has just been mentioned. It lay in the intractibility of the first issue.[1]

The Anglo-Irish Treaty validated what the Government of Ireland Act (1920) had already established: the division of Ireland into two separate states, each over time carrying its own institutionalised markings of sectarian religious sentiment. The new Northern Ireland state, owing to the manner in which its six-county area was carved out of the whole Province of Ulster, was attached directly to the Crown but, ironically enough, granted its own form of Home Rule. Indeed, the Northern Ireland governmental structure, with its own Prime Minister, two-house Parliament and civil service, was already in place several months before the Anglo-Irish Treaty was signed. At the same time, there would be much in the Anglo-Irish Treaty that went beyond the scope of the 1920 measure.

In discussing the Anglo-Irish negotiations of 1921, several issues need to be addressed. These include an examination of the composition of the two delegations to the Downing Street conference, with particular emphasis on the rationale behind de Valera's selection of the Irish side. This is necessary because of the friction that developed within the Dáil Cabinet well before the Irish Delegation departed for England, and indeed in light of the course of events in Ireland following the signing of the Treaty during the early hours of 6 December 1921. A discussion of the instructions given to the Irish side and the manner in which they followed those instructions, along with an analysis of the negotiations themselves and the Dáil debate which followed, are also important to a fuller understanding of the Anglo-Irish Treaty and its consequences.

De Valera: To Go Or Not To Go

The apparent role reversal that took place between Eamon de Valera and Michael Collins as heads of the Irish delegations to London in July and October, respectively, also requires discussion. In both cases, of course, the question of who would and would not attend, and who would lead, was driven by de Valera himself.

Understanding what, in fact, de Valera's actual bargaining position was up to the onset of the Anglo-Irish Treaty negotiations continues to defy ready characterisation. Indeed, his time spent in America on the public platform, and in dealing with a steady diet of interviews on various topics, proved highly useful in allowing him to develop a nuanced approach to complex questions. Such questions as whether the objective of the Irish struggle was indeed an unfettered Irish Republic, or if Dominion status in some form might prove acceptable, were met by his own brand of doublespeak. De Valera's finely honed skills in answering questions with half-answers, combined with his mathematician's brain, equipped him with a capacity for obfuscation. But these skills, while perhaps too often evident, do not alter the fact that de Valera's role in the Dáil Cabinet also required considerable efforts on his part to keep the disparate factions – represented by Stack and Brugha on the one hand, and Collins and Griffith on the other – from fighting in the open. He would remain effective in this position as long as he remained a neutral broker.

De Valera's experience in America influenced his thinking beyond the fact that he was born there. He felt a special attraction to that country because the mother he never really knew in childhood resided there with his only sibling – a half-brother who was by this time a Catholic priest. His nineteen months in the US also gave him a perspective on events outside Ireland, which in turn influenced his subsequent dealings with the British Government, and indeed with his own countrymen. He equated the title of President of the Irish Republic with the American presidential model – the strong executive in whom the aspirations of the nation were invested. And with that came a belief on de Valera's part that when it came to negotiating a settlement with the British Government, he would not stake his credibility on one gambit. This outlook appears, to some extent, to have weighed on his decision not to head the Irish delegation sent to London to negotiate with an extremely able British side led by Lloyd George. De Valera was quite aware of the setback suffered by American President Woodrow Wilson in Paris in 1919.

But in the end, de Valera's decision not to go to London in the autumn of 1921 as leader of the Irish Delegation was probably shaped most of all by the outcome of his own direct talks with Lloyd George in July of that year. As we have seen, the Irish leader met the British Prime Minister a total of four times in London, on 14, 15, 18, and 21 July 1921.[2] The British proposals were put to him in writing on 20 July, and were centred upon an offer of Dominion Home Rule. Although they excluded the Six Counties of Ulster, they were a considerable improvement on the Government of Ireland Act (1920). The proposal was, however, unacceptable to de Valera, who conveyed his view to Lloyd George directly. He was opposed outright to a formal recognition of the Crown, along with the fact that the offer did not respect Ireland's right to sovereignty. The Dáil Cabinet backed his position.

On 10 August de Valera countered with his proposal of External Association, which was probably drafted by Erskine Childers.* The idea was aimed at closing the chasm between the idea of a totally independent Irish Republic and the British proposal of Dominion status, and came to be known as External Association. In essence the proposal offered a treaty providing 'free association' for Ireland with the British Commonwealth. And while it would not require an oath of allegiance to the Crown, but instead merely acceptance of the Crown's position as head of the proposed association, it was de Valera's hope that it could also serve as a sufficient inducement to the Ulster Unionists

---

* Erskine Childers, 1870–1922, a respected author and former British official turned Irish patriot. Of Anglo-Irish background, Childers helped lead the Howth gun running incident in 1914. In 1919, he was elected for Kildare-Wicklow to the Dáil Éireann and later served as Director of Publicity for the Dáil Government and editor of the Republican propaganda organ, the *Irish Bulletin*, where he made an extremely effective contribution to the Irish independence effort. Childers developed a close affinity with Eamon de Valera. The latter's confidence in him led to his being named to the Irish negotiating team's Secretariat for the October–December 1921 Anglo-Irish negotiations. A strong opponent of the Treaty, he sided openly with the Republicans. Childers was arrested by Free State troops in November 1922 for possession of a revolver and executed one month later. Ironically, the weapon had been given to him by Michael Collins.

to participate in a unitary Irish state. But in short order the British Government made it clear that it rejected the proposal, while the Craig regime never directly responded to it. Ironically, a future British Government would draw on de Valera's External Association idea in dealing with the relationship of India and other countries to the Commonwealth.

In all, fifteen letters and telegrams were exchanged between de Valera and Lloyd George after the former's return to Dublin on 22 July 1921. The last communication came on 30 September when de Valera announced that he had accepted Lloyd George's invitation to begin formal negotiations. But this time around the Irish delegation would, of course, be without de Valera himself. It was a development that was crucial to the outcome of the negotiations, as far as Nationalist Ireland was concerned, a source of division both during and after the negotiations.

It remains difficult, even with the passage of time, to fully ascertain precisely what de Valera believed could ultimately be extracted from Britain in the way of the greatest possible degree of Irish independence between 11 July 1921, when he arrived in London, and 10 October, when the Irish Delegation arrived in Downing Street without him. We do, however, know what he knew. It is clear that he possessed a direct knowledge of what the British Government was prepared to concede for a settlement, and how hard and fast that position was. It is a point we will return to in greater detail. Lloyd George's offer of Dominion status in July, combined with the fact that the British Government did not move from this position during the succeeding weeks of communication with de Valera, appears to have shaped his decision not to involve himself directly in further negotiations. Whether this was out of a concern for Ireland's interest, his own, or indeed perhaps both, remains a matter for conjecture.

We know that on the one hand he spoke of avoiding 'the strait-jacket of a Republic' while, on the other, opposing the British offer of limited Dominion status. We also know that he was aware that his plan for External Association showed little hope of British acceptance at any stage. De Valera's views, at least up until the time of the Anglo-Irish Treaty, cannot be neatly packaged and contrasted with those of Michael Collins or anyone else. While Collins was no paragon of openness, his thoughts and actions are much easier to discern than de Valera's. It should be emphasised that the two men were separated by almost a decade in age – de Valera being the elder, as well as by characteristics of individual style and temperament.

On 9 September 1921 de Valera told the Dáil Cabinet what his reasons were for not going to London when the negotiations commenced. By remaining in Ireland, he argued, he could act as an important reserve to be called upon should the talks collapse. Furthermore, still hopeful that External Association might be accepted by the British, he argued that his presence in Ireland was important in persuading militant Republicans to accept such a provision. It should be noted that de Valera never put the idea of 'External Association' before the Dáil in open discussion, whether before or after the Treaty was referred back. By remaining in Dublin, de Valera contended he could give free expression to national feeling as the embodiment of an independent Irish nation. His additional argument for sending the more moderate Arthur Griffith as head of the delegation, given that his own views on the key issues were already well-known to the British, remains as incredible as it is ironic in light of the outcome.

Whether plausible or not, these reasons given by de Valera for not going to London as head of the Irish delegation – a decision that was in the end backed by a majority in the Dáil – remain useful in underscoring the extent to which he may have dwelt in the world of the theoretical. But arguments suggesting that this penchant for the theoretical formed the overriding basis for the hesitation he revealed during the period following his return from London, and before he finally accepted the British offer to negotiate terms, amount to an oversimplication; and to an extent they also diminish his responsibility for the course of action he pursued both during this period and after the Treaty was signed and ratified by Dáil Éireann. In the end, de Valera may well have misjudged the military and political dynamics of this crucial period. His actions were nonetheless informed by his own careful reading of the situation. His experience in the United States, as well as his own dealings with Lloyd George, and his discussions with the South African leader Jan Smuts and Northern Ireland Premier Sir James Craig, formed key parts of the equation for him. They were also experiences that were certainly unique for any Irish revolutionary leader. And while de Valera was in the United States for much of the War of Independence, and may not have been fully conversant with the IRA's guerilla campaign and the British counter-terrorist effort to suppress it, he was nonetheless back in the country a full six months before the Anglo-Irish truce commenced.

De Valera and Collins, on the surface at least, did indeed undergo something of a role reversal between July and October 1921, trading places as to which wore the mantles of dove and hawk. But the extent to which this might have been the British perception of the two men should not be exaggerated, given the fact that Collins, as we have seen, had been conducting discussions with British agents, such as Andy Cope, sent to Ireland by Lloyd George, to determine who it was he could strike a bargain with – even before the truce. That Collins' private view in favour of finding a way out of the conflict was at odds with his public image as the hardest of IRA hard men must have been apparent to many in the British Cabinet well before he entered No. 10 Downing Street in October. The British difficulty in attempting to read the far more enigmatic de Valera is best characterised by Lloyd George's still unparalleled description of dealing with the Irish leader as akin to 'Trying to pick up mercury with a fork.'[3]

In their July meetings in London, de Valera met on all four occasions with Lloyd George alone. As we have seen, de Valera proved frustratingly aloof to Lloyd George, while also coming away with the clearest of understandings of what the British position was. Some form of Dominion status was on offer as part of terms that could supersede the Government of Ireland Act (1920), but there could be no acceptance of an independent Irish Republic. This de Valera knew in July, even if the rest of his colleagues in the Dáil Cabinet and Dáil Éireann as a whole did not. And this knowledge de Valera would continue to possess during the eleven weeks that would pass between his return and the Irish delegation's mission, which he refused to lead, went to London as 'Plenipotentiaries'. No matter what terms were brought back, a compromise on the issue of an independent Irish Republic would clearly be necessary.[4]

The time that elapsed between de Valera's return from London and the arrival at Downing Street on 7 October of the Irish delegation for the Anglo-Irish negotiations was indeed crucial to the future of Ireland. As de Valera procrastinated, Lloyd George became more focused then ever on forcing an end to the conflict. He used the ensuing weeks to his advantage, while endeavouring to keep his rivals, both inside and outside the coalition, off balance.

In short, de Valera learned first hand from Lloyd George on the subject of an Irish Republic what he had gathered face-to-face from Sir James Craig, one month earlier, regarding the likelihood of a united Ireland: these two canons of the Irish struggle were irreconcilable with the prospects for a peaceful settlement at this time. But rather than accept these realities and work as the leader of Nationalist Ireland for a solution that would realise the greatest amount of freedom possible, he reacted to Lloyd George as he had to Craig. De Valera sought to remove himself from further direct negotiation with the Prime Minister. It was clear to him that the Republic was, as he termed it, 'a strait-jacket' from which he must escape. By his manoeuvring during the period following his return from London, de Valera was able to ease himself out of that strait-jacket, but the nation he claimed to lead – not just the delegation he sent to negotiate terms in London – was left struggling within it. The exchange of letters with Lloyd George became, in effect, a substitute for action. He could posture as the head of the Irish Government by trading weighty correspondence for public consumption with his British counterpart; but he did not have to confront Lloyd George again and undertake the risks inherent in ironing out a settlement. In a letter of 31 July 1921 to Jan Smuts, de Valera offered a stark look at his thinking on the importance attached to preserving the Republic which he himself would not again defend in England: 'The questions of procedure and form as distinguished from substance are very important.'[5] It was against such an obtuse standard that the performance of those who were sent to London would to a great extent be judged, and in its defence that Ireland would be plunged into still bloodier conflict.

The first intimation that de Valera had decided against going to London for the formal negotiations on a settlement came at a meeting of the Dáil Cabinet on 20 August. Instead, this time around, it was his decision that Michael Collins should go. Voting with de Valera were Cathal Brugha, Austin Stack and Robert Barton. Collins, objecting strenuously to the plan, was supported by Arthur Griffith and William T. Cosgrave. Also electing not to journey to London again as part of the Irish delegation was Austin Stack, along with Brugha, who would serve as one of the lightning rods in opposition to the terms which Collins, Griffith and their colleagues brought back.

With Collins and Griffith, the Dáil Cabinet voted to send an Irish delegation that included Robert Barton, Charles Gavan Duffey and Eamon Duggan. Named as Secretaries to the Delegation were Erskine Childers and John Chartres, the latter a little-known British patent lawyer, but nonetheless someone who had proved an invaluable intelligence source to Collins in Britain. Childers was a former high-ranking British civil servant who had defected to the Irish cause, and a cousin of Robert Barton; he also steadily earned the distrust of Collins and Griffith.

De Valera sought later to explain to Joe McGarrity, the leader of Clan na Gael in America, why he decided against going to London:

> Lest I might in any way compromise the position of the Republic and in order that I might be in a position to meet any tricks of Lloyd George, I remained home myself, but the plenipotentiaries had agreed with my view, had their instructions and even a preliminary draft treaty to guide them. So I thought everything quite safe.[6]*

De Valera's statement that the plenipotentiaries had all agreed that he should not join them in London is inaccurate. Collins was at the time just as clear that de Valera should go to London as that he himself should not. At the continued urging of de Valera, Collins nevertheless agreed to serve on the delegation. He had strenuously objected to the Cabinet's effort to press him into service as a negotiator on the grounds that his best contribution lay not in the political realm but by remaining in the background as a military figure and as an enigma to the British. In a private session of the Dáil on 14 September, during which his appointment was officially approved by the full body, Collins stated: 'To me, the task is a loathsome one. If I go, I go in the

---

* De Valera's letter to Joseph McGarrity of 27 December 1921, along with the private and public sessions of the Dáil Debates on the treaty, are an important primary account of this period. The letter represents de Valera's most open account in his own words of how and why the Irish delegates were chosen, why he decided not to participate in the Anglo-Irish Conference, and what the delegates' instructions were in his view.

spirit of a soldier who acts against his best judgment at the order of his superior.'[7] Few comments uttered by anyone in the months to come were to prove as poignant. But Collins might have known as early as August 1921 what was in store for him. At a meeting of the IRA Executive early in 1921, Harry Boland emphasised why Collins should be included in any delegation sent to London.

> At the present time, from what I have learned since I came back from America, you will not succeed in overthrowing the British militarily. If it is a question between peace and war, I'm for peace. If there are negotiations, I think Mick should go and I'll tell you why – in my opinion, a 'gunman' will screw better terms out of them than an ordinary politician.[8]

Boland's remarks are particularly significant in that some months prior to offering them he had returned from accompanying de Valera on his mission in the United States. By this point, Boland, who had prior to the United States tour been a close friend of Collins, was in de Valera's camp, although retained great admiration for Collins.*

Collins reserved critical comments about his selection until he had himself met with his associates on the IRA's Supreme Council. Within the counsels of this secret society his real views may be found, removed from the world of politicians and would-be diplomats. According to Sean O'Muirthile, Collins' friend as well as the Secretary of the Supreme Council, in November, during the negotiations, Collins told the organisation's hierarchy:

> I have been sent to London to do a thing which those who sent me know had to be done but had not the courage to do it themselves. We had not when these terms were offered, an average of one round of ammunition for each weapon we had. The fighting area in Cork ... was becoming daily more circumscribed, and they could not have carried on much longer.[9]

Collins rejected outright the warnings of some of his loyal followers within the IRB against his going to London, lest he be made a scapegoat later on. 'Let them make a scapegoat or anything they will of me', he said, adding: 'We have accepted the situation as it is and someone must go.'[10]

While, by the late summer of 1921, Collins may not have wished to go to London, an August 1921 memorandum to Arthur Griffith, outlining the damage he felt the partition of Ireland would cause, is useful in underscoring Collins' political astuteness. Indeed, it could be argued that Collins' analysis of the partition issue qualified him automatically for inclusion on the Irish team sent to London. Most importantly, perhaps, his arguments also showed

---

* Earlier the two men had vied for the affections of the same woman, Kitty Kiernan, with Collins emerging the winner.

him to be keenly aware of the possibility of using the Ulster issue as the basis for a 'break' with Britain, should such a need arise.

It was Collins' contention that, under the Government of Ireland Act (1920), the British Government had set up a 'parliament' in Northern Ireland, which 'nobody wanted'. Noting that the six-county state, comprising the Northeastern Irish counties of Fermanagh, Tyrone, Derry, Antrim, Armagh and Down, were carved out of Ulster's entire Province of nine counties to get 'a certain expression of opinion', he argued that partition was not even sought by the 'artificial' Unionist majority now created in the six counties. 'They accepted it [the result of the May 1921 election providing for separate parliaments for the North and the South], not as any expression of self-determination, but in order to prevent the wishes of the vast majority of their countrymen from being carried out: to use it as a means of preventing the real self determination of Ireland.'

Collins held that 'if the British Government says that such a Parliament must remain, it would indicate that it wishes to divide Ireland'. In his estimate, such a Northern Parliament, subservient to Westminster, 'would be a permanent danger to the future of the Nation'. At the same time, consistent with the views that he would attempt to convey two months later as leader of the Irish negotiating panel in London, he held that the creation of a Northern Ireland Parliament under an overall Irish Government was indeed possible: 'There would be no such danger in Ireland herself granting local autonomy to a section of the population that expressed a clear and genuine wish for such autonomy', he stated. But in relation to the action which the British Government had already taken, Collins argued further:

> The Irish Government cannot recognise conditions illegitimately set up by the British Government, a Government which has been repudiated by the Irish people and set up while the war was still in progress, and before terms of peace were discussed. When I read the Lloyd George offer, it seemed to me that it was not capable as it stood of being translated into a Treaty of Peace. That having made an offer to Ireland he could not make it a condition that it should not apply to one fifth of Ireland. His offer could be made to the 26 Counties and he could say that the status quo he had created in the Six Counties should remain intact.[11]

What Collins sought to accomplish, conscious of the delicate balance that kept the Anglo-Irish Truce alive while also not letting the pendulum of public opinion move away from himself and his colleagues, was 'a means of criticising his [the British Prime Minister's] proposals'. In the wider context, the Ulster Question offered the means for a 'break' – if necessary, a break that would keep public opinion on the Irish side. Collins held that Lloyd George 'cannot say that he is willing to withdraw his forces only on the condition that we abandon the object for which we have so far successfully engaged in war with him. That is asking for complete surrender on our part'. In his view, Lloyd George presented an offer wrapped in the trappings of peace while at the same time he insisted 'on the inviolability of his "Northern Parliament"'. 'A damaging exposure', Collins told Griffith, 'can be made which should make it impossible for the support of public opinion to be withdrawn from us on the plea that we are refusing "generous terms"'.[12]

Over the course of the negotiations, we will see that Collins' position on partition was to evolve, partially under the influence of Arthur Griffith. But it may have been due as much to his own pragmatic nature. 'Collins', Frank Pakenham wrote, 'more than any man in the Irish delegation was to come to the negotiations with the ordinary Irish outlook and the open mind. No man was to be so much influenced by the actual course that the negotiations ran.'[13]

One way or the other, the Ulster question would continue at the forefront of Collins' mind. In addition to representing a constituency from his native Cork in the Dáil, like de Valera, he was also elected for a Northern constituency. In visiting that constituency in County Armagh during the Truce, it is noteworthy that, also like de Valera, Collins stated that Sinn Féin did not seek to coerce the Ulster Unionists into a United Ireland.[14] At the same time he was concerned with the plight of Northern Ireland Nationalists, particularly those who were subject to pogroms by loyalist mobs. But whether or not Collins planned, as he and the delegation were later instructed by the Dáil Cabinet, to stage a 'break' over Ulster, it is clear that the British were well aware from the outset that Ulster was their Achilles heel in negotiations, and that keeping the agenda away from any focus on partition for as long as possible was key to the Government's negotiating strategy.

In contrast to the friction which existed within the Irish side, of which the British Government was not unaware, the British side possessed a greater degree of unity. They also held the strategic advantage of hosting the conference and setting many of its rules of engagement. At the same time, however, Lloyd George also had his own political demons to contend with. His desire for peace in Ireland was motivated by the need to consolidate his own political position. Hints of a break-up in the Coalition received increasing currency from mid-1921 onwards. In June, the *Manchester Guardian*, headed by the Prime Minister's recently reconciled ally, C. P. Scott, reported on a plot by Lloyd George's Tory partners to replace him with one of their own. The attempt was led by Lord Birkenhead and Winston Churchill, the latter of whom, one writer stated, being 'angry at not being given the Exchequer in [Austen] Chamberlain's place, held the mistaken belief that he could lead any government that succeeded Lloyd George's'.[15] By this point Bonar Law had already left the Coalition due to illness, with Chamberlain acceding to the Conservative's Party's leadership in his place.

In October 1921, the Prime Minister purchased some time by naming Birkenhead, Churchill and Chamberlain as members of the Government's negotiating panel for the Anglo-Irish Conference. In this fashion he kept them more than occupied in pursuits other than plotting his political demise. They were joined on the panel by Lloyd George himself, along with Sir Laming Worthington-Evans, Sir Hamar Greenwood, and Sir Gordon Stewart, with Tom Jones serving as the Prime Minister's Secretary.

Overall, the British side was a formidable one and would still have been so even if de Valera had joined the Irish delegation. The experience they combined no doubt also played a significant part on the outcome of the Conference, notwithstanding the best efforts of Collins, Griffith, and the rest of the Irish delegation.* But more than anything, the Anglo-Irish Truce itself provided the Government with an important window from which to view Sinn Féin and the IRA. In essence, they were flushed out in the open, a fact that Collins conceded in private conversation.

De Valera's letter to Joe McGarrity, written some three weeks after the Anglo-Irish Treaty was signed, offers a look at how he claimed he felt Griffith and Collins would perform in London at the time he appointed them to the Irish Delegation.

> That Griffith would accept the Crown under pressure I had no doubt. From the preliminary work which M. C. (Michael Collins) was doing with the I.R.B. I felt certain that he too was contemplating accepting the Crown, but I hoped that all this would simply make them both a better bait for Lloyd George – leading him further in our direction. I felt convinced on the other hand that as matters came to a close, we would be able to hold them from this side from crossing the line.[16]

But these remarks beg the question of why de Valera not only appointed Griffith and Collins as members of the delegation, but to lead it. If indeed he felt they would both waver on the vital issue of allegiance to the Crown, then on what did he base his view that the two could be held 'from this side from crossing the line' on that or any other issue? His letter to McGarrity sheds no light on this, nor is it explained by de Valera in any other account. By his own admission, Eamon Duggan and George Gavan Duffy were 'mere legal padding' amongst the panel.[17] At best, he felt, Gavan Duffy would lean more towards the fifth delegate, Robert Barton – a close friend and the cousin of Erskine Childers, the delegation's Secretary. Such a situation would surely be

---

* Indeed, Michael Collins appears to have impressed his opposite numbers at both the plenary and sub-conference level of the negotiations by his grasp of details, particularly as they related to financial issues. It should be remembered that he faced Lloyd George, Winston Churchill and company, albeit unwillingly, as a young man of thirty-one, with a limited formal education.

all the more reason why de Valera would want to appoint individuals to the panel who in his view would be more likely to fight to the end on the issues he had identified as vital to the Irish agenda. But such was not the case, given the fact that he made no effort to send Brugha or Stack to London.

The Irish delegation and its instructions

There can be little doubt that de Valera's decision to remain in Dublin was a source of confusion, especially in light of the fact that, as we shall see, the delegations were given two varying sets of instructions. Were they indeed plenipotentiaries with the authority to reach an agreement in London? Or were they simply delegates obliged to refer back to the Dáil Cabinet? The instructions given to the five-member Irish delegation to the Anglo-Irish Conference, and their interpretation of those instructions, are central to any focused discussion of Collins' and Griffith's performance during and after the negotiation of the Treaty.

In his work on the Treaty, Frank Pakenham has cautioned against any attempt 'to lay down binding conclusions about a whole situation which is generally held to have been sui generis', from the standpoint of how far the Irish delegates were actually accepted as 'Envoys Plenipotentiary' by the British Government.[18] From the British perspective the Irish delegates were not on an equal footing with those of a recognised government, but rather the spokesmen of an insurgency effort. But the question of whether the Irish signatories to the Anglo-Irish agreement exceeded their authority needs to be reviewed with regard to the instructions given to them by de Valera and the Dáil, and to the way in which they followed those instructions.[19]

Although remaining in Dublin, de Valera continued to play an important role in the course of events as they unfolded. The instructions he signed for the delegation, and which were approved by Dáil Éireann on 14 September, were as follows:

> In virtue of the authority, vested in me by Dáil Éireann, I hereby appoint Arthur Griffith T.D., Minister for Foreign Affairs, Michael Collins T.D., Minister for Finance, Robert Barton T.D., Minister for Economic Affairs, Edmund Duggan T.D., and George Gavan Duffy as Envoys Plenipotentiary from the elected government of the Republic of Ireland to negotiate and conclude on behalf of Ireland, with the representatives of His Majesty George V a treaty or treaties of settlement, association and accommodation between Ireland and the community of nations known as the British Empire.[20]

Further confusion would be sown by a unilateral action de Valera took on 7 October. His letter of credentials for the Irish delegation was approved by

Dáil Éireann on 14 September. During that session of the Dáil, a motion supported by Cathal Brugha and Austin Stack seeking to restrict the scope of the authority of the delegates was withdrawn under pressure from de Valera himself as President, who went so far to threaten to resign if the restrictions were added. In defence of that broad authority for the plenipotentiaries, de Valera's comments to the Dáil are significant in light of subsequent events. He stated in private session: 'Remember what you are asking them to do ... You are asking them to secure by negotiations what we were totally unable to secure by force of arms.'[21] Clearly, de Valera grasped the military realities and the severe limitations inherent in a return to armed conflict, at least to an extent that he apparently became unable to do after the signing of the Anglo-Irish Treaty. But for another reason his disagreement with them may have been unclear to Brugha and Stack: the less the delegation's accountability was to Dublin, the greater became his ability to reject any agreement they might sign afterwards.

In the end the Dáil approved the delegates' credentials, while Liam Cosgrave made one more attempt to get de Valera to go to London, on the basis that they could not afford to hold their ablest player 'in reserve'. In the end, de Valera won out.

In addition to the credentials which were approved by the Dáil, the Cabinet and de Valera, a further set of instructions was given to the delegates by de Valera himself. In the opening session of the Dáil Debates on the Treaty on 14 December 1921, he referred to 'instructions which I wrote with my own hand at the Cabinet meeting on the 7th of October'.[22] There remains no evidence that this latter set of instructions ever met with Dáil Éireann's approval on or before that date. Neither did any approval by the Cabinet occur. These final instructions, which encompassed five points in all, gave certain additional instructions to the delegates, but were, partially, inconsistent with the earlier letter of credentials giving the Irish representatives broad authority to act as Ireland's 'Envoys Plenipotentiary'. The instructions drafted by de Valera included the following provisions:

1. The Plenipotentiaries have full powers as defined in their credentials.
2. It is understood before decisions are finally reached on the main question, that a dispatch notifying the intention to make these decisions will be sent to members of the Cabinet in Dublin, and that a reply will be awaited by the Plenipotentiaries before final decision is made.
3. It is also understood that the complete text of the draft treaty about to be signed will be similarly submitted to Dublin and reply awaited.
4. In case of a break, the text of the final proposals from our side will be similarly submitted.
5. It is understood the Cabinet in Dublin will be kept regularly informed of the progress of the negotiations.[23]

The negotiations

The Irish delegation brought with it to London a set of proposals to counter the terms which Lloyd George offered de Valera on 20 July. The sum and substance of the Irish counter-proposal came under five headings: Trade, Finance, Defence, the Future of Ulster, and Ireland's Relationship with the Crown and Empire. While each of these issues would in their own right prove contentious, it was the latter two which evoked the widest disagreement – in the end, perhaps, more so within the Dáil Government than between the Irish and British sides.

For the Irish side, the negotiations centred on whether Ireland was to be a British Dominion or an externally associated Republic. But a necessary corollary to any association with the Crown would be an oath of allegiance to the Crown, the elements of which would be determined by the extent to which Ireland was affiliated with the Empire. Thus, de Valera's plan for external association became the optimum Irish objective in London, largely because it would involve the loosest possible form of allegiance to the Crown.

The Irish proposals were not designed to be straightforward. The document, however, had passages of bluntness: 'The claim of Ireland is not Dominion status, but if it were your proposals would not confer that status'. Similarly, the Irish document stated: 'You desire to safeguard the security of your Empire. Ireland is resolved to achieve her freedom. We offer you proposals for a treaty which will ensure the realisation of these ends'.[24] Significantly, the Irish document did not make an outright claim to the status of a Republic. At the same time, Britain was called upon 'to renounce all claim to authority over Ireland and Irish Affairs'. In essence, the issue for the Irish side centered on sovereignty, and for the first time the term Free State was used: 'We propose that Ireland shall be recognised as a Free State, that the British Government shall recognise Ireland's freedom and integrity, and that the League of Nations and the United States of America shall be invited to join in that guarantee'.[25]

The language in the Irish document on the Ulster question was perhaps the plainest of all: 'Freedom of choice must be given to the electorates within this area.' Partition through the instrument of the Government of Ireland Act (1920) 'has rendered an obstacle to peace and amity between the two nations'. In essence, Britain was asked outright to deny its grant of a loyalist veto to the Ulster Unionists and to instead allow the two parts of Ireland the opportunity to resolve their differences.

The British position remained unchanged throughout this first phase of the talks. Any Irish proposal aimed at receiving favourable consideration by the Government would need to include provisions for these three essentials: allegiance to the King, an expression of Irish willingness to enter the Empire freely of her own accord, and guaranteed British access to Irish ports for defensive reasons. Aside from having the entire negotiations conducted in their own venue, unimpeded by time spent on travel or communication constraints, Britain also held the advantage of an experienced negotiating team and also unity, both in the objectives sought and the strategy for achieving them. Lloyd George oversaw the strategy and the tactics employed.[26] He also had the benefit of Tom Jones as his Private Secretary, and Lionel Curtis, who served as Secretary to the British panel at the Conference and who had also been Colonial Affairs advisor, in addition to his work with the Liberal Round Table group. Jones' value has already been discussed. From Curtis, Lloyd George received an analysis offering the most advantageous strategy the British could pursue.

For Curtis, the status of Ireland in relation to Britain was the most important issue for the Government. It was, in fact, the approach Lloyd George followed. Curtis, in a memorandum of 21 September, cautioned the Prime Minister that from the outset the Government should avoid any appearance of equivocation by stating that 'while offering Dominion status it refuses to recognise the independence of Ireland'. Likewise, he stated, the Government should impress upon the Irish side the need to recognise the role of the King as sovereign for both Britain and Ireland. 'Nothing is to be gained', he wrote, 'by arguing this position with the Irish leaders. They are fanatics and their logical minds will cheerfully accept the embarrassment their claim would impose on Irishmen throughout the British dominions.'[27]

The British strategy wrongfooted the Irish delegation from the outset of the conference. It was in the Irish delegation's interest to raise the question of Irish unity first, and to have the issue of the Crown dealt with early on. Indeed, the British side sought to delay raising the question of partition until the issue of Ireland's status and the role of the Crown in Irish affairs was resolved at the conference. But Curtis' memorandum to Lloyd George indicates the decision may have been made more out of a practical grasp of the inherent divisiveness to an Irish settlement which the Ulster question posed than out of some deep-rooted desire to ensure a divided Ireland. He believed that recent experience, including the failure of Craig and de Valera to come to any understanding, had demonstrated how intractable the situation was.

> Some months ago the idea was advanced that Ulster might appear in the role of peacemaker and negotiate with Sinn Féin a settlement of the whole question acceptable to Great Britain ... on various occasions Ulster and Nationalist leaders have been brought face to face, but they have never succeeded in reaching the Ulster question. The negotiating always broke down on the relations of Ireland to Great Britain ... This being so, it may be wise to exclude all question of Ulster, so far as possible, until all the points previously raised have been provisionally settled. The present writer firmly believes that the whole of Ireland can and will be brought under one autonomous system. He sees, however, but little prospect that this can be done at the present

juncture. Southern Ireland must change its leaders or those leaders must greatly change their present outlook before it is conceivable that the men who now sit in office at Belfast and their constituents will place those in power at Dublin in control of their destinies. If ever both sets of men are brought into the same conference room, this fact will become apparent.[28]

Thus, through a combination of the British side's desire to defer the Ulster issue, and the Irish delegation being tactically prevented from doing so until late in the Conference, issues relating to partition and Irish unity became subordinated to the question of an oath to the King and Ireland's role within the Empire.

After the opening session on 11 October, subcommittees were set up covering financial relations and naval and air defence issues, as well as a subcommittee for observance of the truce. Collins was a member of each of these subcommittees. On the financial and naval subcommittees he was in fact Ireland's only representative. But while the issues covered in these subcommittees were often contentious, they were not the irreconcilable ones. Instead, it was the questions of sovereignty and partition which remained the most contentious, and indeed insoluble. The reality of a new Northern Ireland state, protected by the British Parliament, made it more than unlikely that any British Government would compel it into a united Ireland by force.[29] But as important as Ulster was to Sinn Féin, and indeed to every member of the Irish delegation, it was not the main concern raised by the Irish side during the negotiations, nor would it be in the later Dáil debates, both public and private, on the Anglo-Irish Treaty. The relationship of Ireland to the Crown was the overriding issue in Downing Street; and so it would be later in Dáil Éireann.

The negotiations revolved around several phases. From 11 to 24 October, seven plenary sessions were held, with no conclusive result. Between 24 October and 3 November, concessions were made by the Irish side to induce British pressure on the Ulster Unionists. This was followed by British attempts from 5 to 17 November to pressure Sir James Craig.* From 18 November to 30 December, the focus shifted to British pressure against Sinn Féin. The conference culminated in the events of 1 to 6 December as the Irish side underwent internal debate over the British final draft and received an ultimatum from Lloyd George threatening war.[30]

The format for engagement changed dramatically after the seventh and final plenary session, when the negotiations shifted to a sub-conference format. The change was due ostensibly to Lloyd George's desire for increased manoeuvrability within his own side, leaving him free of Worthington-Evans and Hamar Greenwood. But in reality the change was as likely due to the

---

* Throughout the Anglo-Irish Conference Craig held court at private offices in London, accompanied by senior officials of the Northern Ireland regime.

British intention to exclude Erskine Childers, who had shown himself to be more than a thorn in the British side at the Conference thus far, especially with his knowledge of the Dominions and their precise relationship to the Crown.[31] As a result of the sub-conference arrangement, the British met regularly with Collins and Griffith without encountering the rest of the delegation.

The tide changes

The early stages of the Conference might be described as the source of a false sense of optimism for the Irish side, at least as far as Griffith was concerned. The plenary session, held at 6.00 p.m. on 24 October – the eighth in all, but the first conducted throughout the British-instituted sub-conference – offers a valuable glimpse of how the British official tone had started to change. It was here that Lloyd George and his colleagues queried the Irish delegation in detail on the meaning of their proposals vis-à-vis the Crown and Ireland's relationship with or within the Empire, and on Sinn Féin's effort to develop for Ireland a position of neutrality in international conflicts involving Britain. Consider this exchange between Arthur Griffith and Lloyd George:

> Prime Minister: 'Consent to adhere.' Does that mean all other conditions being satisfactory, you are prepared to come within the British Empire as Canada?
>
> Arthur Griffith: We are prepared to be associated with the British Empire.
>
> Prime Minister: How do you differentiate?
>
> Arthur Griffith: We shall be associated with you and Dominions, but outside that we shall be a free people. Dominions are bound to you by luck of Crown, to be plain.
>
> Prime Minister: You adhere as allies?
>
> Arthur Griffith: More than that, as permanent allies.
>
> Prime Minister: But not as members of the same Empire?
>
> Arthur Griffith: Not as members, but we assume we should be represented at your Imperial Conference and take a decision on all these matters.
>
> Prime Minister: Take words 'agreed common concern'. What do you mean?
>
> Arthur Griffith: War and peace and large issues.
>
> Prime Minister: Do you mean the same as those we have with the Dominion?
>
> Arthur Griffith: I would not like to say. A Treaty would have to define.
>
> Prime Minister: French are here, we discuss Silesia etc., but with the Dominions, we discuss general defence of Empire.[32]

On 25 October, Arthur Griffith provided de Valera with a detailed account of a meeting that Collins and he had had with Lloyd George and Austen Chamberlain, separate from the rest of the delegation. Griffith's communication proved such a cause for concern to the President that he suggested immedi-ately joining the delegation in London himself. De Valera's reaction was motivated largely by Griffith's statement that no Irishmen could offer any recognition of the British Crown 'unless the essential unity of Ireland was agreed to by the dissidents. This should put them up against the Ulster die-hards.'[33] While the strategy of 'putting the British up against the Ulster diehards' was one Griffith could agree to, it was not de Valera's strategy. Griffith's suggestion of tacit recognition of the Crown was not acceptable to de Valera. In the Irish leader's view, the situation was compounded by the fact that the questions of Ulster and the Crown had come up so early. De Valera's alarm was possibly exacerbated by what he saw as Griffith's and Collins' willingness to recognise the Crown and not to push wholeheartedly for 'external association'. At the heart of his suggestion that he go to London himself was the expressed willingness of Griffith and Collins to admit even to him their possible recognition of the Crown.

The tone of the letter sent on 26 October by the entire delegation in response to de Valera made it clear that they saw his suggestion as an infrin-gement on the instructions given to each delegate by the Cabinet three weeks earlier. It also indicates that the delegates shared a clear view as to the meaning of the instructions written in de Valera's own hand and given to them on 7 October.

> The delegates regard the first paragraph of your letter No. 7 [*sic*] as tying their hands ... and as inconsistent with the powers given them on their appointment and numbers 1 and 2 of 'instructions to the Plenipotentiaries from the Cabinet' dated 7th of October ... Obviously any form of association necessitates discussion of recognition in some form or other of the head of the Association. Instruction 2 conferred this power of discussion but required before a decision was made reference to the members of the Cabinet in Dublin. The powers were given by the Cabinet as a whole. Having regard to the stage discussions have reached now, it is obvious that we could not con-tinue any longer in conference and should return to Dublin immediately if this, however, is withdrawn.[34]

Instruction No. 2 given by de Valera to each delegate stated: 'It is understood before decisions are finally reached on the main question, that a dispatch notifying the intention to make these decisions will be sent to members of the Cabinet in Dublin, and that a reply will be awaited by the Plenipotentiaries before final decision is made.' The response from the delegation to de Valera clearly implied a commitment to follow that instruction, assuaging de Valera's concern at the time regarding recognition of the Crown. This com-mitment, combined with the implied threat of resignation by the entire delegation, may well have dissuaded him from going to London. Indeed, the delegates voiced an expression of their frustration at the situation they found themselves in, as well as its extreme gravity. 'We strongly resent, in the position we are placed, the interference with our powers. The responsibility, if this interference breaks the very slight possibility there is of settlement, will not and must not rest on the plenipotentiaries.'[35]

Since the letter was apparently written by Griffith with Collins' cooperation, it may have reflected an outward manifestation by both men of a belief they had held from the outset of the negotiations: they had been deliberately ordered into an impossible situation. Accordingly, if the conference was to breakdown and if their authority as plenipotentiaries, as they understood, it was not to be adhered to by de Valera, then they were determined to let the blame fall on de Valera and their opponents in Dublin. In the end the delegates warned de Valera to come immediately if he were to come at all, and to do so only privately unless requested otherwise.[36] De Valera, taken aback by the delegation's response, replied that 'There is obviously a misunderstanding. There can be no question', he wrote, 'of tying the hands of the plenipotentiaries beyond the extent to which they are tied by their original instructions.'[37] He was unclear, however, as to whether he was referring to the Dáil's instructions or those he had issued himself.

De Valera, in fact, had first come to know about the determination of the British to press the matter of the Crown not through Griffith but from Childers. Much to the annoyance of Griffith and Collins, Childers regularly reported to him on the progress of the conference. In addition to including detailed accounts about the various Committee meetings, he also kept the Irish leader apprised, to the extent he could, of the separate meetings Griffith and Collins participated in with British officials. Childers, as early as 21 October, informed de Valera that the British had begun to raise the question of the Crown. Childers actually sought instructions from de Valera on the delegation's behalf 'as to which course to adopt'.[38] He made it clear that the action requested of the Irish delegation by the British in regard to the Crown was considered by the plenipotentiaries to be of vital import at 'the highly critical stage of the negotiations we have now reached ... The question of the Crown has now been directly raised by the British representatives and will come up at the Conference on Monday'. Childers also characterised the 'two courses' that were open to the delegation: 'A. To refuse to accept the Crown, B. Neither refuse it or accept it at the preliminary state but to say that if they are satisfied on the other points – Ulster, Defence, Trade, etc. – they will be predisposed to consider the question of the Crown'. Childers concluded by stating that the delegation 'requests instructions as to which course to accept. It must be added that the British representatives showed a strong disposition to press matters'. Despite the urgency underscored in that communication, the record shows that the Monday meeting of the Irish delegation with their British counterparts came and went without the requested instructions from Dublin. Childers' own copy of the memorandum to the President was initialed with the remark: 'No answer received.'[39]

By this point, Collins' sense of helplessness was worsening. 'What have we come for? I ask myself that question a dozen times a day'. These words were revealingly written by Collins in a letter to a friend in early November. They echoed a similar question posed by Arthur Griffith: 'What do we accept?' Indeed, Collins' frustrations with what had been achieved or not achieved thus far in the negotiations with the British were tempered by an awareness that Lloyd George knew of the difficulties which he and Griffith faced both in Dublin and amongst a divided Irish delegation in London. 'Not much achieved', Collins later observed, 'principally because P.M. recognises our overriding difficulty – Dublin.' In his estimation, Lloyd George did his utmost to exploit the situation to his own advantage.[40]

That Collins resented the unrealistic expectations which those who remained behind in Dublin still held while he and Griffith toiled in London is clear. At the same time he continued to harbour respect for Cathal Brugha, whom he characterised as 'a fighter – only he is misguided'.[41]

Collins' difficulties with Brugha and Stack had been evident long before the commencement of the Anglo-Irish Conference. Their differences were a source of considerable hostility. In regard to Stack, Collins' depiction of his administration of the Department of Home Affairs as a 'bloody joke' became too much for Stack to take. 'He's no "Big Fellow" to me', Stack was heard to say of Collins following the incident.[42]

Brugha apparently resented the legendary status Collins had engendered as the shadowy figure who directed the IRA's successful intelligence network while eluding arrest. He described Collins as 'a subordinate in a subordinate department of my office'. Although Brugha was Minister for Defence, Collins' role had grown to such an extent that he, rather then Brugha, was the person sought out by visiting IRA leaders to Dublin.[43] Brugha, in turn, infuriated Collins. He rejected Brugha's plan to take a team of IRA guerilla leaders to London for the purpose of assassinating the British Cabinet in the House of Commons. Collins' reaction was blunt: 'This is madness. Do you think that England has the makings of only one Cabinet.'[44]

At Winston Churchill's home on the evening of Sunday 30 October, Lloyd George held his first private meeting with Arthur Griffith. From Griffith the Prime Minister sought personal assurances that he would not stage a 'break' on the issues of the Crown and British access to Irish ports. In return Lloyd George would endeavor to secure Ireland's 'essential unity' and would press the Ulster Unionists to the utmost on the matter. Lloyd George's suggestion that a Boundary Commission would be devised to reduce the territory of the Northern Ireland State if Craig did not accept participation in an all-Ireland Parliament was yet to be raised.

But what Griffith did himself agree to in writing, combined with his later signed acceptance of proposals on Ulster outlined to him by Lloyd George, served to undermine the Irish delegation's negotiating strategy, as far as the essential unity of Ireland and achievement of the closest degree of external association with the Empire were concerned. In his 2 November letter to Lloyd George, Griffith personally stated his acceptance of a 'Free Partnership with the other states associated within the British Commonwealth'. In essence, he had agreed to support Ireland's inclusion within the British Empire as a Dominion. Nonetheless, in a later communication to de Valera, Griffith contended that he 'accepted this as it did not alter the essence of the formula'. It should be noted there was no immediate reply from de Valera indicating a position one way or the other.[45]

At the end of October Griffith described to de Valera a meeting with Lloyd George at which the Prime Minister suggested his Government might avoid censure in the House of Lords if, according to Griffith, he were given written assurances 'on the Crown, free partnership with the British Empire and facilities for the British navy on the Irish coast'.[46] The course of Griffith's actions in relation to the requests made by Lloyd George over the next forty-eight hours indicates that he had by this time already made certain promises to the British leader concerning the Crown. On 1 and 2 November, Griffith submitted two letters for Lloyd George's consideration. Oddly, the second letter had been prepared on House of Lords stationery. The two letters were fundamentally different in meaning, evidence apparently of another meeting which Griffith had had either with Lloyd George or a subordinate between the drafting of each. In the draft letter of 1 November, Griffith stated:

> In reply I assured you ... I was prepared to recognise a requirement of the Crown, the formula ... to be arrived at a later stage. I since agreed to recognise free participation with the British Commonwealth. I stated this action of mine was conditional on the recognition of the essential unity of Ireland ... but on no account would I recognise free association with the Crown or Empire, if the unity of Ireland were denied in word or fact.[47]

On the following day, Griffith embraced partition for the first time when he wrote: 'As for the Northeast of Ireland, while reserving for further discussion the question of area, I would agree to any safeguards.'[48] Griffith attempted to minimise his action by saying that it was 'intended to be personal', and not officially as Chairman of the Irish delegation. However, as Gavan Duffy noted afterwards to Griffith, 'The letter will necessarily be read by Mr George as indicating a weakening from the last memo of the Delegation, if not as superseding it as far as you, the head of our delegation is concerned.'[49] On 3 November Griffith attempted to explain to de Valera the reasons for the difference between the letters prepared for Lloyd George on 1 and 2 November.

> Following my conversation with Lloyd George on Sunday night he asked me to write him a letter embodying the personal assurances I gave him in order that he might take his stand against Craig and the 'Ulsterites' if they proved

> obdurate. Yesterday, I dispatched a letter and at Lord Birkenhead's request, I with Michael Collins, met him. He suggested some alterations, and we agreed to meet him and Lloyd George later.

Significantly, Griffith believed that on the basis of his second letter, the British were 'satisfied to face the Ulster question on it, and assure me that if Ulster proves unreasonable they are prepared to resign rather than use force against us. In any such event, no English Government is capable of formulating a war policy against Ireland.' He then attempted to provide a rationale for his actions on the basis that he had succeeded tactically in tying the question of Ulster to the question of the Crown. 'The British Government is now up against it,' he claimed to de Valera, 'and we for the moment are standing aside', 'If they secure Ulster', he argued, 'we shall have gained essential unity and the difference we shall be up against will be the formal language of association and recognition.'[50]

Whether Griffith actually believed this himself, or felt he could induce de Valera to accept this interpretation, remains unclear. His correspondence with de Valera a week later was less optimistic on the Ulster question, however. In it he cited Lloyd George's belief that the 'Ulsterites' were being encouraged to resist any form of Irish unity, 'possibly by Bonar Law'.[51] On the following day, Griffith first apprised Dublin of what would effectively become Britain's last offer.

> Lloyd George and his colleagues are sending further reply to the Ulstermen refusing their dominion proposal, but offering to create an All Ireland Parliament. Ulster to have a right to vote itself out within twelve months, but if it does, a Boundary Commission to be set up to delimit the area, and the part that remains after the Commission has acted to be subject to equal financial burdens with England. Lloyd George intimated this would be the last word on Ulster.[52]

Griffith's strategy had failed. On 13 November, he provided Lloyd George with a personal memorandum stating that he would sign and recommend an agreement that included formal recognition of the Crown along with provision for a Boundary Commission for Northeast Ulster to the Dáil. The statement would later be used by Lloyd George, with telling effect, against Griffith during the early hours of 6 December.

In the meantime, the British Government was proceeding with its own agenda, now with Griffith in tow. On 8 November, a day in which Griffith and Collins held an informal meeting with Tom Jones at the Grosvenor Hotel, Lloyd George and the British negotiating panel met specifically to discuss the position of Sir James Craig and the Ulster Unionists in relation to the British proposals. Craig's attitude had changed, a British Cabinet member wrote, 'from willingness to discuss All-Ireland Parliament to absolute non possumus'. Worthington-Evans suggested that in the event Ulster 'counter-offered to remain within the powers of the 1920 Act under U.K. and left the South free to take Dominion status "Shinners" [Sinn Féin] would probably withdraw their offer of allegiance and issue would be should we coerce Ulster to go in or coerce South who repudiated sovereignty'. At one point in the meeting Lloyd George suggested that while the Unionists could not be coerced, the Government might say to the King, 'We are pledged not to coerce Ulster but we cannot advise coercion of South – dominions – unions would be against you – U.S. would break up Washington Conference, go on building ships ...'

On 10 November, Lloyd George received a revised draft from Lionel Curtis of a submission the Prime Minister was to make to the Ulster Unionists outlining the Government's progress in the Anglo-Irish negotiations to date, with proposals relevant to the Northern Ireland state. In the end, Lloyd George asked Craig to support the Government's proposals out of an appeal to patriotism. Threats were not hinted at with the exception of official reference for the first time to a Boundary Commission in the event 'Ulster did not see her way to accept immediately the principle of a Parliament of All-Ireland'. In that event, Northern Ireland would continue to send representatives to the Westminster Parliament and to be subject to British taxation within the terms of the Government of Ireland Act (1920). 'In this case, however,' Lloyd George stated, 'it would be necessary to revise the boundary of Northern Ireland. This might be done by a Boundary Commission which would be directed to adjust the line both by inclusion and exclusion so as to make the Boundary conform as closely as possible to the wishes of the population.'[53]

But this reference to a Boundary Commission was the extent of the pressure on Craig to the Northern Unionists. Perhaps more important, a copy of this document was given to Arthur Griffith by Tom Jones in a private meeting two days after the former had met with Lloyd George and given a verbal commitment not to break with the Government on the Ulster question if the Prime Minister showed his willingness to use the Boundary Commission concept as leverage on the Ulster Unionists. We will return to Griffith's performance in this instance.

Craig's response to Lloyd George's offer was predictably negative, given that Northern Unionists had already gained under the Government of Ireland Act (1920) the best possible arrangement: their own specially manufactured state courtesy of the British Parliament, designed to ensure a Protestant majority. Craig stated his objection to the All-Ireland Parliament proposed by Lloyd George in his letter of 10 and 11 November by disingenuously stressing that the 1920 Act which established the Northern Ireland jurisdiction provided for the establishment of a Council of Ireland. That body, in fact, would never come into existence. Indeed, Craig's position would remain largely unchanged, despite seeking more concessions for

Northern Ireland from the Government on taxation and customs matters under the Treaty.[54]

In effect, the British exerted little pressure on Craig. Instead, with Griffith's promise in hand, rather than attempt to force Craig and the Ulster Unionists, it was the Nationalists who were the recipients of British coercive efforts from mid-November onwards, as the question of Southern Ireland's relationship to the Crown reached a boiling point. The threats from Lloyd George of a return to warfare now represented a stark reversal in the British approach to the Irish delegation. Only three days earlier, at a meeting with the Government and the Southern Unionists, Lord Midleton inquired of Lloyd George whether any time limit had been given to Sinn Féin. The Prime Minister answered 'No'.[55]

On Monday 28 November, the Irish delegation submitted another memorandum to the British advocating external association, consistent with earlier proposals for a limited connection with the British Empire:

> The proposal is that Ireland shall be associated with the British Commonwealth for purposes of common concern such as defence, peace, and war; and she shall recognise the British Crown as head of the association; and that, as a token of that recognition, she shall vote an annual sum to the King's Civic List. Her legislative and executive authority shall be derived exclusively from her elected representatives.[56]

By means of this article, de Valera was prepared, at worst, to accept 'recognition of the British King as head of the whole association, that is, we could swear to recognise him as a sort of President of the whole league'.[57] To whatever degree Collins or Griffith believed in the external association plan they had the responsibility of selling, the British Government still clearly refused to accept it. Lloyd George insisted that the Crown could not be excluded from domestic Irish affairs and, above all, that an oath of allegiance to the Crown was an immovable requirement.

The course of events between 28 November and 3 December proved fateful both for the Irish delegation and for the course of Anglo-Irish relations, as it was also for the course of relations between the Irish themselves. The British strategy during this period combined conciliation and force in a compact form. On the evening of 28 November they threw the Irish delegation off balance by offering them 'any phrase they liked which would ensure that the position of the Crown in Ireland should be no more than it was in Canada or in any other Dominion'.[58] By the end of the week the Irish delegation was compelled to go back to Dublin for consultation with the Cabinet after the British had given what was to prove their final terms, packaged by the threat of 'immediate and terrible war' if acceptance was not forthcoming upon their return to London.

By any reckoning, the day-long meeting between the Dáil Cabinet and the Irish delegation in Dublin on 3 December can be characterised as having been of crucial importance in light of the events that would unfold during the subsequent seventy-two hours. It was to be the last meeting in Dublin, and in effect the final contact between the delegation and the Dáil Cabinet, prior to the signing of the Articles of Agreement in London.[59] It was at this meeting that the British final offer was discussed in great detail for a period of several hours, and where the delegates agreed to act in accordance with the Cabinet's instructions tendered at that meeting.

From the outset of the meeting the split within the Irish delegation itself was plain to all in attendance. Griffith made it clear what his position was: he was determined to sign the Treaty in order to avoid committing Ireland to further warfare, and in light of his view that the Irish had wrung the maximum in the way of concessions from the British side. Robert Barton disputed Griffith on this point, arguing that 'England's last word had not been reached and she could not declare war on questions of allegiance'.[60] Gavan Duffy agreed with Barton's reading of the situation, stating that the British Government was 'bluffing' and that the Irish side could still make further advances. Collins, however, weighed in in favour of Griffith, contending that their refusal to accept the Treaty would be a gamble since Britain 'could arrange a war in Ireland within a week'. In an apparent contradiction of his earlier views against partition, Collins also agreed, according to the minutes of the meeting, that the 'sacrifice to North East Ulster made for the sake of essential unity was justified'. He held that further concessions could be gained on issues related to trade and defence. But on the question of the oath, Collins was somewhat equivocal. Since the oath would not come into effect for one year from the signing of the Treaty, Collins questioned whether it would be worthwhile 'taking that twelve months' and seeing how the Treaty would work. At the same time he suggested that the Dáil go to the country on the treaty, but recommending 'non-acceptance' of the oath.[61]

Soon after, and before the meeting adjourned temporarily, Cathal Brugha added heat to the already highly charged session by remarking, upon being told that it was the British Government's decision to hold meetings with Collins and Griffith separate from the rest of the delegation, 'Yes, the British Government selected their men'. An outraged Arthur Griffith walked over to Brugha and demanded that he withdraw the remark. It was withdrawn. But the incident was only a taste of the vituperation that was to follow.

After an internal discussion by the Dáil Cabinet, the meeting was resumed. It was then that de Valera made himself heard. He would deal with that 'present document exactly as with that of 20 July – say it cannot be accepted and put up counter-proposals'. De Valera stated that he could not accept the Oath of Allegiance nor could he 'sign any document which would give Northeast Ulster power to vote itself out of the Irish State'. He suggested, however, that with 'modifications' the Treaty might be accepted 'honorably'. Stating that the delegates had in his estimate done their 'utmost' it was now their responsibility 'to show that if document [was] not amended that they were prepared to face the consequences – war or no war'.[62] In effect, he would leave the delegates hanging.

Griffith countered that while he did not 'like' the document, he did not find it 'dishonourable'. Implying that there was no real alternative contained within their original external association proposal to justify the Treaty's rejection over the issue of Allegiance, like Collins, he offered the Machiavellian recommendation that the 'Delegation sign the Treaty and leave it to the President and Dáil to reject'. Thus, if a return to arms could not be avoided, Ireland would at least be responding on her own terms and in her own time. Griffith also stated that he would not take 'the responsibility of breaking on the Crown'.

It was then that an exchange took place between Griffith and Brugha that led to a pledge by the former to the Cabinet which contradicted his personal promise to Lloyd George in London on 12 November. According to Austin Stack, Brugha asked Griffith: 'Don't you realise that if you sign this thing, you will split Ireland from top to bottom?' The delegation Chairman answered: 'I suppose that's so. I'll tell you what I'll do. I'll go back to London. I'll not sign that document but I'll bring it back and submit it to the Dáil and, if necessary, to the people.' Griffith's statement served as a source of reassurance to the Cabinet and to de Valera that he would not sign any document that required allegiance to the Crown or Ireland's inclusion within the British Empire.[63] Griffith's pledge also gave de Valera the basis to decline Robert Barton's final appeal that he join the delegation in London. Instead, that evening the Dáil Cabinet rushed forward with a set of final instructions for the Plenipotentiaries. They were to 'carry out their final instructions with the same powers', and to inform the British that the Dáil Cabinet could not accept the Oath of Allegiance without amendment, the threat of renewed warfare notwithstanding.* Griffith was also instructed to inform Lloyd George that the document 'could not be signed and to state that it is now a matter for the Dáil, and to try and put the blame in Ulster'.[64] By different boats the Irish delegation headed back to London.

At 10 Downing Street, on the evening of 4 December, the Irish found an anxious Lloyd George and his colleagues waiting for them. Griffith attempted early on in the discussion to force a break over Ulster as he had promised in Dublin. But no sooner had he done so than his commitment of 12 November to Lloyd George not to force such a break was raised. Griffith backed away from the argument, and instead offered the Irish Amendments to the British proposal. In short order the proposed changes were rejected by the British side. To Lloyd George the Irish had merely re-packaged the proposals which had been rejected

---

* It bears noting that in the persons of Collins, Griffith and Barton, the Irish delegation contained three members of the Dáil Cabinet.

earlier. In essence, the Irish, he believed, were refusing to enter the Empire and to recognise the Crown. The meeting adjourned amid some acrimony.

The British gave the Irish counter-proposals short shrift. External association was again rejected outright. The British reply stated that it could not 'consider a change which would vitally affect the interests of all the self-governing countries of which the Empire is made up'. The Irish attempt to 'repudiate the Crown' was a source of particular consternation. The Government argued that the rejection of the oath would only further alienate the Ulster Unionists. 'It is difficult to conceive any measure more certainly fatal to the ultimate unity of Northern and Southern Ireland from the claim which the representatives of Southern Ireland now advance. So far from advancing Irish unity, which we had hoped to achieve as the early result of their negotiations,' the British response stated, 'this repudiation of the Crown will now make unity impossible.'[65]

But while the Government took a hard line, Lloyd George endeavoured to meet Collins privately. Collins' meeting with Lloyd George proved pivotal in assuring that Collins would vote in favour of the Treaty. Collins agreed to support the Treaty based on a British commitment to delimit Nationalist majority counties of Tyrone and Fermanagh from Northern Ireland under the Boundary Commission, if Craig refused to consent to Ireland's 'essential unity'. His agreeing to do so made the difference in the Irish delegation's decision to sign the Articles, and the Dáil later ratifying them. For so great a force was Collins to the Irish Revolution, the differences between the myth and the reality notwithstanding, that he had the ability at this moment to decide whether it should end or continue.

Given Collins' support for the British proposals, Ireland was poised to enter the Empire. In addition to the commitment Collins thought he had been given on the Boundary Commission, he was in fact given concessions by Lloyd George on trade and defence matters, though in the scheme of things these were not major breakthroughs towards a settlement. Significantly, in returning to his colleagues in the delegation later on that morning of 5 December, Collins did not raise his conversation with the Prime Minister vis-à-vis possible Boundary Commission changes as a selling point.

A detailed memorandum that Collins prepared immediately after his meeting with Lloyd George makes plain that the discussion, particularly as it related to North-East Ireland, had persuaded him to support the Treaty and, more importantly, to lobby actively for it in Ireland. But it remains unclear what new pledge, if any, the Prime Minister made to Collins on Ulster. Indeed, it is possible at this stage that Collins heard what he wanted to hear. His notes offer the following as the sum and substance of their exchange on Irish unity.

> Mr Lloyd George remarked that I myself pointed out on a previous occasion that the north would be forced economically to come in. I said that the posi-

tion was so serious, owing to certain recent happenings, that for my part I was anxious to secure a definite reply from Craig and his colleagues, and that I was agreeable to a reply, rejecting or accepting. In view of the former we should save Tyrone and Fermanagh, parts of Derry, Armagh and Down by the Boundary Commission and thus avoid such things as the raid on the Tyrone County Council and the ejection of the staff. Mr Lloyd George expressed the view that this might be put to Craig.[66]

From this account we see that it was Collins who placed the greatest emphasis on the proposed Boundary Commission as the vehicle for acquiring the Nationalist majority counties from the Northern states, along with parts of others. Nothing at all was given to him in writing by Lloyd George on this point – only a possible verbal commitment.

Later, Collins would lead his colleagues in the IRB Executive to believe, however, that Lloyd George had himself given him such a commitment. The IRB's support was of course crucial to the Dáil's acceptance of the Treaty. Collins would also claim publicly that the Boundary Commission would transfer that territory to Southern Ireland. But Lord Birkenhead later rejected Collins' claim in a letter to Balfour. Arguing that Collins was likely to have made the claim to garner support for his position on the Treaty, in reality the claim had 'no foundation whatsoever except in his overheated imagination'.[67] The final word, however, on what Lloyd George may or may not have promised Collins at that important meeting on that morning in December goes to Lloyd George himself. As the Irish Provisional Government set up its transitional government after the Treaty, when asked by Kevin O'Higgins what scale of territory Northern Ireland was likely to lose, he answered: 'Who am I to say what a judicial commission will decide?'[68]

It was at this juncture in the Conference that Collins had irrevocably moved from the company of the self-sacrifice school of Irish separatism. Instead, he came to subscribe to Griffith's doctrine of self-reliance. He had broken with Republican orthodoxy. Collins now stood for the new Ireland, the Ireland which aimed to succeed, not by eliciting sympathy, but by compelling respect.[69] To a great extent he had succeeded. He now sought to consolidate the gains the Irish Revolution had achieved to date, by securing a settlement that could be built upon incrementally. By the time he left his meeting with Lloyd George, his idea of using the Treaty as a 'stepping stone' to fuller freedom had probably already begun to take shape. He had opted for peace with Britain at this time.

The final act

At five o'clock on the afternoon of 5 December, Collins, Griffith and Barton met with Lloyd George, Chamberlain, Birkenhead and Churchill. The Irish delegation actually returned to the conference table for what would be the last meeting between the parties to treat with a Prime Minister who, since his meeting with Collins, had visited the King, held a Cabinet meeting, met the editor of the *Manchester Guardian,* and found the time to take a nap. Confident now of both Griffith's and Collins' support for the agreement, he sought to raise the stakes, by requiring acceptance by the rest of the Irish delegation. After a discussion of the Ulster issue in which Lloyd George reiterated the need to give to Sir James Craig the outcome of the Anglo-Irish Conference prior to the impending session of the Northern Ireland Parliament, he demanded an answer from the Irish side. Would they accept the Ulster proposals? Griffith endeavoured to hold out for a commitment by Craig to Ireland's 'essential unity' before a formal answer was given. But his pledge to Lloyd George not to 'break' on Ulster was thrown at him by Churchill and Birkenhead. The Prime Minister himself heated up the atmosphere of the Cabinet Room, feigning outrage over Griffith's broken promise. He and his colleagues had put their careers on the line by risking reproach by the Tory backbenches for the concessions they had already rendered to the Irish. He was now met not with compromise but, instead, the resurrection of the Irish threat to end the Conference over the Ulster Question.

After a discussion and general agreement on trade and defence issues, the British side left the room. Soon after they reappeared, Lloyd George at this time produced the assurance Griffith had given him three weeks earlier. A dumbfounded Robert Barton turned to Collins and asked him what the letter amounted to. 'I don't know what the hell it is', he gruffly responded.[70] The Irish were now wrong-footed. In the end Griffith acquiesced to an appeal from Lloyd George not to break on Ulster.

The discussion now moved to other issues, with the British conceding full fiscal autonomy to the Irish side. This provision represented a significant change in the document which the Dáil Cabinet had rejected two days earlier. But the points of agreement had reached an end. Lloyd George now produced for the Irish side the irreducible minimum: agree to come within the Empire or face war in three days. Craig must be given the result, the Prime Minister restated. 'We must know your answer by ten tonight. You can have until then, but no longer to decide whether you will give peace or war to your country', he declared.[71]

The conference adjourned until 10.00 p.m. that night and the Irish delegates headed back to their quarters for a final and painful meeting. The discussion centred around whether they would sign or not, accept Dominion status or run the risk of a return to conflict. Consideration of contacting Dublin by telephone was not given, nor to any suggestion that they must have the Cabinet's approval before signing any agreement. In this curious lapse, the seeds were sown for future bloodshed in Ireland.

It would be near midnight before the last of the Irish delegates, Robert Barton and Gavan Duffy, consented to sign the Treaty. At 2.30 a.m. on the morning of 6 December, what would become known as the Anglo-Irish Treaty was signed by both sides in a moment of high tension at No. 10 Downing Street. But this expression of unity on the part of the Irish was not to last.

Even greater tension would await the Irish plenipotentiaries in Ireland, where they would have to run a gauntlet organised for them within the Dáil Cabinet by Eamon de Valera and his allies, Cathal Brugha and Austin Stack.* In his heart of hearts, Michael Collins knew before he left London on 6 December that de Valera would not accept the agreement he had signed. At 8.00 p.m. the Articles of Agreement for a Treaty between Britain and Ireland were to be simultaneously published in the two countries. When urged to read a copy of the treaty handed to him by Eamon Duggan, with the explanation of its publication, de Valera, certainly within his rights as head of the Irish nation, complained, 'What, to be published whether I have seen it or not – whether I approve or not?'[72]

At noon on Thursday 8 December, the meeting of the Dáil Cabinet called by de Valera commenced. By a margin of four votes to three, the Dáil Cabinet voted in favour of the Treaty. Robert Barton, who would later repudiate his signature before the full Dáil, sided with Collins and Griffith, as did William Cosgrave. De Valera was supported by Brugha and Stack. Apparently, unshackled by any commitment to majority rule, whether in the Cabinet or in the Dáil, de Valera almost immediately issued a public statement repudiating the document. For his part, Arthur Griffith followed with a statement of his own and defended his action on the basis that 'What I have signed I will stand by in the belief that the end of the conflict is at hand.'

The debate on the Treaty

From 14 December 1921 until 6 January 1922, Dáil Éireann debated the Treaty in both public and private sessions. What precisely were the issues that Dáil Éireann was asked to decide on during the Treaty Debates? This question is crucial. A review of the Dáil Debates belies the myth that the choice was between a Republic or the Irish Free State, established by the terms of the Treaty. In reality, the issue facing the Dáil came down to a choice between Document No. 1 – that is, the Articles of Agreement signed by the plenipotentiaries in London – and Document No. 2 – the alternative proposal submitted to the Chamber by de Valera with its central focus on 'external association' with the British Empire. During the course of the Dáil Debates,

---

* Years later, de Valera would express his regret that he had not ordered the delegation's arrest immediately after they docked in Dublin.

one anti-Treatyite Dáil member said: 'People outside think that this is a question of the Republic against the treaty. It is not. It is a question of the treaty against Document No. 2, and there isn't a particle of difference between the two.'[73] But according to de Valera and the principal author of Document No. 2, Erskine Childers, 'external association' represented a profound difference from Dominion status. As Frank Pakenham has noted: 'The Irish contended that while in theory the Crown in Ireland would be identical with the Crown in the Dominions, yet in fact it would retain powers in Ireland that in the Dominions had long been obsolete.'[74]

In the private session of the Dáil on 14 December, Collins argued that he and his colleagues had fought fully for de Valera's proposal for 'external association'. 'We fought this with energy in London', he said, adding, 'no further delegation could have got better. Let the treaty be reported and put up this.'[75] For Collins, de Valera's persistence in raising Document No. 2 – the name by which 'external association' was now known – as an alternative to the Treaty as signed was evidently a matter of splitting hairs.

Document No. 2 differed from the Anglo-Irish Treaty in that it did not contain an oath to the Crown. The King was mentioned solely for the purposes of the association of Ireland with the British Commonwealth and the Commonwealth nations. The monarch was recognised by Ireland as head of the association. The fact that de Valera was able to win over such diehard Republicans in the Cabinet as Cathal Brugha and Austin Stack to 'external association' was no small accomplishment. But crucially, it did not win the British Government's backing.

Indeed, such a fine job of salesmanship had de Valera done in persuading Brugha to accept 'external association' that he actually spoke during the Treaty debates in favour of it. 'We are prepared to enter into an agreement', Brugha stated, 'with the British Commonwealth of Nations ... on the same or similar lines as that on which one business firm enters into association with another, or several others.' By entering such an arrangement, Brugha argued, 'we are not going into the British Empire; neither do we take any oath whatsoever; and there will be no representative of the British Crown in the shape of a Governor-General in Ireland'.[76] In short, what was for Arthur Griffith a 'quibble' with words – namely, as the differences between the Treaty's language and 'external association' – Brugha saw as the basis for justifying a major schism, not only within the ranks of Sinn Féin, but within Ireland itself.

The extent to which Eamon de Valera can be adjudged to have been disingenuous by arguments he advanced during the course of the Dáil Debates that the Treaty represented a betrayal of the 'Republic' is usefully chronicled by P. S. O'Hegarty, a Collins loyalist, IRB man, and Sinn Féin propagandist. Noting that de Valera expressed the desire long before the Anglo-Irish Conference began to get himself out of the 'strait-jacket of the Republic',

O'Hegarty took the Irish leader and his supporters to task for raising the issue of the Republic vis-à-vis the Treaty so divisively during the Dáil Debates.

> The opposition to the treaty in the Dáil was wholly dishonest. It had been made plain to the Deputies by Mr de Valera, in public and in private session, that they were negotiating for terms, and that he himself would not be bound rigidly by the oath to the republic. They had before them, when they finally agreed to terms, Mr de Valera's own letters to Lloyd George, in which he was obviously bluffing in order to save his face, in which every time he went a bit too far he immediately wriggled, and in which he mentions the word Republic only to assure Lloyd George that he was not asking England to recognise it ... The time to overthrow the treaty was before it had been signed, when it was merely threatened. The time to vote against it was at the meeting of the Dáil after the Lloyd George letter. Those who heard there Mr de Valera's explanations, his threats to resign if he were bound to his oath knew perfectly well they were abandoning the Republic.[77]

Collins and Griffith raised these arguments during the course of the Dáil Debate on the Treaty. To them the question of discussing the recognition of the Irish Republic at the London conference had never been an issue. It had been set aside before the first meeting between the parties ever took place. And it was clear from de Valera's correspondence with Lloyd George, they argued, that the British Government would not participate in a conference in which a Republic was sought.

During the first Dáil Debate on the Treaty, de Valera stated the view that the delegates had followed their instructions 'with the exception of paragraph three'. The delegates, he argued, did not in fact submit the complete text of the draft Treaty to Dublin and await a reply before they took further action. It is this particular instruction which flew in the face of the original credentials in which he stated that as 'envoys Plenipotentiary' they had the authority to 'negotiate and conclude on behalf of Ireland ... a treaty or treaties' with Britain. In his argument in support of the need to carry out paragraph three of their instructions, de Valera stated in the Dáil what he was to reiterate in his 27 December letter to Joe McGarrity:

> My idea was when the plenipotentiaries had arrived at an agreement, and had a rough draft which they were prepared to sign, that document in its full text, would be submitted [to the Dáil] because in the case of a treaty, even verbal, the exact form of words is of tremendous importance. I have only to say with respect to paragraph Three that the final text was not submitted.[78]

The letter of credentials which the Dáil had approved, and which had preceded de Valera's handwritten instructions of 7 October, was not mentioned in the Dáil's opening session until Michael Collins raised it. De Valera had taken the floor first, as President, and had read aloud the five handwritten instructions he had given the delegates in addition to their individual credentials letter of 7 October. Collins countered that 'the original terms that were served on each member of the delegation have not been read out. This thing has already taken on an unfair aspect and I am against a private session'. Collins was directing the latter comment at de Valera's earlier recommendation that the Dáil go into private session to discuss, among other things, the President said, 'the circumstances under which the plenipotentiaries were appointed, and to explain the terms of reference ... or directions given to them and to explain them insofar as I can do so, consistent with public interest'. When he raised the matter of the approved credentials letters in the Dáil, Collins was asked by de Valera whether the credentials were ever actually presented to Lloyd George, and whether the letters were given 'in order to get the British Government to recognise the Irish Republic'. 'Was that document giving the credentials of the accredited representatives from the Irish government to the British government presented to and accepted by the British delegates?' de Valera asked. Collins responded that 'the original credentials were presented'.[79] He then read them aloud.

On a strict interpretation of paragraph three of the handwritten instructions given by de Valera, which called for the 'complete text' of any draft treaty to be submitted to the Dáil before being signed by the delegation – along with Griffith's promise not to sign an agreement including Dominion status without Dáil approval – it can be argued that the delegation acted outside the scope of their instructions. However, in the context of the original credentials given to the delegation as plenipotentiaries, with the broad authority granted to them to 'negotiate and conclude on behalf of Ireland ... a treaty, or treaties, of settlement, association and accommodation between Ireland and the community of nations known as the British Empire', the Irish representatives acted in consonance with the only officially approved instructions they were given, Griffith's 3 December pledge to the Cabinet notwithstanding.

The Articles of Agreement concluded by the Irish and British parties on 6 December 1921 were clearly within the authority outlined in the letter of credentials as approved by Dáil Éireann. The inherent confusion that the two varying sets of instructions to the delegates provoked was one of the most tragic consequences of the October–December Anglo-Irish Conference, especially so far as Ireland and its future were concerned.

De Valera's own views on many of the issues facing the delegation were less than definitive, particularly on the Ulster question, even after the signing of the Treaty. In answer to a hypothetical question posed by one of the signatories at the 8 December meeting of the Dáil Cabinet as to whether he would 'opt' for the Treaty if Ulster came in on it, he replied, according to Childers, that 'this was one consideration that might affect his judgment. He said that he did not despair of winning better terms yet. Threat of war he regarded as natural and inevitable. Lloyd George threatened him. He presumed all who signed did so under the threat of force.'[80] Evidently, de Valera wished the 'signing under duress' argument to become one that could be used by the delegation while the Dáil repudiated the treaty and could provide the chance to seek 'better terms'. It is here that de Valera's letter to McGarrity on 27 December takes on special significance, since it also indicates that de Valera was himself willing to accept an agreement that might not have been totally consistent with the requirement of the submission of any draft, as set forth in paragraph three of his handwritten instructions to the delegates:

> On Monday night in Limerick, I heard over the telephone that some agreement had been reached, and I felt like throwing my hat in the air. I felt certain, on account of Griffith's understanding [that he would not accept the oath to the Crown] that our proposals had been accepted. I was in the same high spirits on Tuesday, until about 7.30 p.m. when the text of the treaty as signed was put in my hands at the Mansion House by one of the plenipotentiaries who had just brought it over ... Comment is unnecessary.[81]

Despite the obvious note of dejection, de Valera implies that if he could have found acceptable the terms which the delegates had agreed to, he would have supported the result, even though the Irish representatives would still not have followed the requisites of paragraph three: submission to Dublin for a reply before final action was taken. The document that was signed, de Valera argued, meant that

> A chance greater than I had dared to hope for was lost – a chance which England's imperial needs and her consequent desire to peace, Lloyd George's political needs and his political imagination, the British Coalition which precluded the usual Tory opposition – all these made a combination of factors that occurs but once in history. It was lost because Lloyd George wanted not merely all the best trumps but the joker as well for his political hand and our plenipotentiaries were not bold enough to dare 'to make a heap of all their winnings' and stake it.[82]

Given that de Valera clearly knew by this time about British opposition to his proposal for 'external association', his raising of the issue must be seen as misleading at first.

De Valera's criticism to McGarrity written during a break in the Dáil Debates on the treaty that 'our plenipotentiaries were not bold enough to dare to make a heap of all their winnings and stake it', begs the question as to what were 'the winnings' which they were to make 'a heap of'? As the reports the delegates brought back to Dublin indicated to de Valera and the Cabinet, the negotiations had not produced any acceptance by the British of the Irish side's proposal for external association. Assuming that de Valera knew the mindset of Griffith and Collins as far as their desire to compromise was concerned, why did he expect them to attempt an all-or-nothing strategy? And what would the consequences be for Ireland if Lloyd George was not bluffing about this threat of 'war in three days'? De Valera's comments to McGarrity concerning Lloyd George's political situation also reflected an extremely limited understanding of the realities the Prime Minister faced as the head of a Coalition which included a significant amount of pro-Unionist sentiment within both the Cabinet and Parliament.

Collins told the Dáil in the 14 December Debate that he and the other plenipotentiaries 'did not sign it [the document] as a treaty, but did sign on the understanding that such signatory would recommend it to the Dáil for acceptance'. Later in that session, he added that 'if the Dáil does not accept it, I as one of the signatories will be relieved of all responsibility for myself, but I am bound to recommend it over my signature and of course we are bound to take action, whatever action was implied by our signatures'.[83] But Collins' account before Dáil Éireann was somewhat different from his remark made to a friend from London on the day he signed the Treaty: 'I will tell you this – early this morning, I signed my death warrant. I thought at the time how odd, how ridiculous – a bullet may just have done the job five years ago.'[84]

The performance and motives of Michael Collins throughout the Anglo-Irish Conference continue to raise questions for the analysts of the period. Given his unique background as a leader of the physical force movement loyal to the Irish Republican Brotherhood, in addition to his role as Finance Minister of the Dáil Government, it is evident that Collins was not averse to acting outside of instructions which originated in the civil sector. One of the inherent difficulties of the internal functioning of the revolutionary movement – namely, the effort to subjugate its military component to civilian control – was personified by Michael Collins. He remained, first and foremost, a leading member of the Irish Republican Brotherhood's Executive. Unlike his opponents in the Cabinet and consistent with the doctrine of the IRB, he was prepared to consolidate the gains which the Irish struggle had already made and to take advantage of any practical opportunity that would lead to the attainment of full Irish freedom. Collins' pragmatism was no doubt inspired by what he saw as the military realities confronting the IRA. He made no secret of this in the Cabinet meeting held on 8 December. According to Childers, Collins said 'his position was that in a contest between a great Empire and a small nation, this was as far as the small nation could get until the British Empire was destroyed. Ireland could get no more.'[85]

Collins' conduct, together with that of the IRB. Executive, was the basis for severe criticism afterwards by Ernie O'Malley, the young guerrilla fighter whom the IRA General Headquarters had come to rely on before the truce as an organiser in many sections of the country. Collins and Mulcahy, among others supporting the treaty within the General Headquarters staff, he wrote, 'did not compare with the Easter Week men, with Pearse, Connolly,

MacDonagh, Sean MacDermott and Plunkett'. To O'Malley, they lacked an element of "intellect and spirituality". 'What made the Irish Republican Brotherhood accept the treaty and force it through?' he asked. 'Why break the back of the sacrifice? What did Collins mean to himself?'[86]

The IRB's Supreme Council's action in support of the Treaty was also condemned by de Valera. In his letter to Joe McGarrity, he referred to the organisation's directive to its Dáil members: 'The members of the IRB were told that acceptance of the Treaty would be the quickest way to the Republic, and a lot of this stuff which time only will explode ... Curse secret societies!'[87]

De Valera's suspicions concerning Michael Collins' activities within the IRB during the Anglo-Irish negotiations were well-founded. The influence of Michael Collins on the IRB, as a member of its Executive, manifested itself to the detriment of the anti-Treatyites. This is clear in an action taken by the IRB Supreme Council on 12 December, which proved significant to the Treaty's ratification in the Dáil. After a vote of eleven in favour, with four against, the Supreme Council issued the following instructions to those members of Dáil Éireann who were also members of the IRB: 'The Supreme Council, having due regard to the Constitution of the Organisation has decided that the present peace treaty between Ireland and Great Britain should be ratified. Members of the Organisation, however, who are to take public action as representatives, are given freedom of action in the matter.'[88] Given that the Treaty passed the Dáil by a majority of only seven votes, the endorsement by the IRB's Supreme Council was significant indeed. It is also noteworthy that throughout the course of the Anglo-Irish negotiations, Collins kept the Supreme Council aware of developments on a regular basis.[89]

This is not surprising, considering Collins' belief that the IRB was the body to which he owed his first loyalty. According to one source, 'shortly after the treaty agreement, Collins told a meeting ... of the IRB circle, of which he was the centre, how his position had arisen. He thought it necessary to do this because, as he said, his first obligation was to the IRB and he cared nothing for any other opinion.'[90] Overall, his efforts to apprise the IRB of developments of the London conference, and also to seek out their views, provided him with an important standard of measurement for the action he would ultimately take. It might also be inferred from this that no matter what set of instructions Collins was given by Dáil Éireann, the IRB would have been the controlling factor in his conduct.

It should be emphasised that the IRB never deviated from its stated belief that the real head of the Irish Republic was not the President of Dáil Éireann but the president of the Irish Republican Brotherhood. This difference was minimised during the course of the Anglo-Irish War out of the Irish independence movement's interest in presenting as unified a front as possible, both militarily and politically. But the IRB continued, as Collins apparently did, to owe its primary loyalty to the Constitution of its own organisation rather than to that enacted by Dáil Éireann.[91] During November 1920, while de Valera was in America, Collins became acting President of the Dáil. At this time, he was also President of the Supreme Council of the IRB. As Dorothy MacArdle and León Ó Broin have both noted, in accordance with IRB tradition, when he assumed the leadership of the civilian sector, Collins was merely acceding officially to the role which was reserved for the head of the physical force movement. For all intents and purposes, he was clearly the head of that movement by this time.[92]

To the vast majority of the IRB's Supreme Council, support for the Treaty was justified because the organisation's Constitution allowed for the support of any advance designed to achieve the cause of Irish freedom. In essence, Collins' incrementalist argument that the Treaty 'gives us freedom, not the ultimate freedom that all nations desire and develop to, but the freedom to achieve it', proved in the end consistent with the objectives of the Irish Republican Brotherhood.[93] In effect, the Treaty was to be approved by the Supreme Council for the same reason that it had approved the truce. In the gross terms of military reality, the IRA's guerrilla campaign had achieved as much as it could. Michael Collins, as Director of Intelligence for the IRA, and Richard Mulcahy, IRA Chief of Staff, were acutely aware of this. On the acceptance of the truce in July, and with the hope for a negotiated settlement, O'Muirthile said that 'the Truce was agreed to because it was felt that the military campaign against the British could have no further success, and that perhaps terms could be obtained that would put Ireland in a position from which she could develop on lines that would enable her to achieve complete independence'.[94]

Collins was also less than sanguine about the reliability and scale of American support needed if hostilities were to resume. He reminded the Dáil during the Treaty debates that 'America did not recognise the Irish Republic'. Part of his thinking in signing the Treaty was shaped by whether they were 'going to go on with this fight without referring it to the Irish people, for the sake of propaganda in America'. Collins also sought to meet pledges of American support if he voted to scuttle the Treaty head on:

> I understand that my name is pretty well known in America, and what I am going to say will make me unpopular there for the rest of my life ... I received a telegram from San Francisco saying 'Stand fast, we will send you a million dollars a month.' Well, my reply to that is, 'Send us half a million and send us a thousand men fully equipped.'[95]

What of the argument advanced by de Valera in the course of the Dáil Debates that the plenipotentiaries had signed the treaty under 'duress'? The argument was given credence by Robert Barton, who repudiated his signature before the Dáil due to 'duress' inflicted in the form of British threats. Based on a reading of Childers' own diary during the final meeting of the delegation on the evening of 6 December, and immediately prior to the signing of the Treaty document, he did not try to dissuade his cousin from signing the document. Instead, Childers suggested that if Barton signed, he should later claim it was done under duress.[96] This reference in Childers' diary provides the first instance where the 'signing under duress' argument appears; and it actually occurred before the Treaty was signed. The claim of duress was clearly rejected by Collins several times later during the course of the Dáil Debates on the Treaty. At one point Collins stated: 'It has also been suggested that the Delegation broke down before the first bit of English bluff ... England put up quite a good bluff for the last five years and I did not break down before that bluff.'[97]

A review of both the private and public sessions of the Dáil Debates in the Treaty underscores how little the issue of partition was raised. Ironically, this was particularly the case with Eamon de Valera. One who did rise to make partition a major focus was Sean MacEntee, a native of Belfast. In light of the conflict that was to afflict Northern Ireland from 1969 onward, his comments take on something of a prophetic nature. MacEntee argued that since the Treaty 'perpetuates partition it must fail utterly to do what it is ostensibly intended to do – reconcile the ... Irish people to association with the British Empire'. 'When did the achievement of our nation's unification cease to be one of our national aspirations', he asked. In MacEntee's view, partition, with its provision for two separate states on the island of Ireland, was key to British attempts to keep the Irish people permanently divided along religious lines:

> the provisions of this treaty mean this: that in the North of Ireland certain people differing from us somewhat in tradition, and differing in religion, which are very vital elements in nationality, are going to be driven, in order to maintain their separate identity, to demarcate themselves from us, while we, in order to preserve ourselves against the encroachment of English culture, are going to be driven to demarcate ourselves so far as ever from them ... The Minister for Finance [Michael Collins] referring again to the problem of secessionist Ulster, more or less washed his hands of the whole matter when he said, 'Well, after all, what are we to do with these people? ... of all the things I may have done this one thing I would not do: I would not let them go. I would not traffic in my nation's independence without at least securing my nation's unity.'[98]

Ironically, MacEntee, who also criticised the Irish supporters of the Treaty for sanctioning the partition of Ireland and the partition of Ulster as well, had echoed Collins' own stated criticism of Britain's partition plan in his memorandum to Arthur Griffith the previous August. At that time, Collins saw the measure as aimed at dividing Ireland into separate interests. But the Michael Collins who rose in the Dáil in defence of the articles he had signed in London now offered the practical realities which he saw on the Ulster question.

We have stated we would not coerce the northeast, we have stated it officially in our correspondence. I have stated it in Armagh. What did we mean? ... What was the use of talking big phrases about not agreeing to the partition of our country? Surely we recognise that the northeast corner does exist and surely our intention was that we should take such steps as would sooner or later lead to mutual understanding. The treaty has made an effort to deal with it, and has made an effort, in my opinion, to deal with it on lines that will lead rapidly to good will and the entry of the northeast under the Irish Parliament [applause]. I don't say it is an ideal arrangement, but if our policy is, as has been stated, a policy of non-coercion, then let somebody else get a better way out of it.[99]

But the unlikelihood of the Boundary Commission providing Southern Ireland with the two majority Nationalist counties within Northern Ireland, if the Ulster Unionists proved obstinate on the question of Ireland's unity, was underscored with what must be described as remarkable prescience by MacEntee. Arguing against the implied promises of Lloyd George and his Government as to the extent the Boundary Commission could work in the interests of Nationalist Ireland, in the Dáil Debate of 22 December he quoted Lloyd George's own words in the House of Commons on the Coalition's determination to ensure a Unionist majority within the six-county state:

We were of the opinion, and we were not alone in that opinion, because there are friends of Ulster who take the same view, that it is desirable of Ulster to remain a separate unit, that there should be an adjustment of boundaries ... we propose that Ulster should have a readjustment of boundaries which would take into account the existence of a homogeneous population, and considering all these circumstances we think it is in the interest of Ulster that she should have people within her who should work with her and help her.[100]

In Westminster, the debate on the Treaty was less contentious as the House of Commons approved it on 16 December by a four-to-one margin. The result also served to underscore that Lloyd George's earlier intimations of widespread Tory opposition to his efforts were somewhat exaggerated.

In the days leading up to the Dáil's vote on the Treaty, Lord Fitzalan's analysis from the Viceroy's office seemed as misleading as that offered to Lloyd George before the Anglo-Irish Conference got underway. On 27 December he told the Prime Minister that there seemed 'little doubt the Dáil will approve [the Treaty], and by a larger majority than was anticipated last week'. At the same time he apprised Lloyd George correctly of Griffith's and Collins' desire to avoid 'visiting Dublin Castle: for the present and not have it said they have been in touch with me till the decision is taken by the Dáil'.[101]

By a margin of seven votes, Dáil Éireann ratified the Anglo-Irish Treaty on 7 January, electing Arthur Griffith as its President after Eamon de Valera had resigned that post in opposition to the Dáil's action.* Soon after this, Michael Collins became Chairman of the Provisional Government that took over the seat of British power in Ireland from the Lord Lieutenant. He was also effectively still the head of the IRB. For Collins and for Ireland, it was an undeniable accomplishment. On behalf of an Irish Government he presided over the transfer to it of the central symbol of British authority in Ireland: Dublin Castle. Ironically, his young life was to end tragically in the months following the creation of the Irish Free State and the resulting conflict between Irishmen. Many of the principal actors on both sides of the Dáil debate on the Treaty would be dead before 1922 was out.

In sum, what Ireland received under the terms of the Anglo-Irish Treaty was limited Dominion status. The Irish Free State thus created was granted fiscal autonomy and its own army, while Britain was granted naval facilities at strategic locations. Article XII of the Treaty essentially validated the partition of Northeast Ulster that had commenced under the Government of Ireland Act (1920). Almost immediately after the Treaty's ratification by the Dáil Éireann and the British House of Commons, Northern Ireland exercised its option to stay out of a unitary state. But, as we have seen, it was the Treaty's Article IV, requiring an oath to the monarch, that became the foremost cause of division within the ranks of Sinn Féin.

Lloyd George stated that the Treaty represented 'the greatest day in the history of the British Empire'.[102] But while the Anglo-Irish Treaty can be termed a success, at least within the short run, for Britain, for Ireland itself the agony of violence would continue.

Lloyd George and the Treaty

That political realities tempered Lloyd George's attitude towards Ireland became clear once again during the Anglo-Irish negotiations. By this time, his dependence on the Conservatives for support of an Irish settlement for the Coalition overall was particularly acute. He began his discussions in October 1921 with the Irish delegates by offering an All-Ireland Parliament in exchange for an oath to the King and membership within the Empire. This proposition clearly caught the interest of Sinn Féin's representatives. However, when the Conservative Party Conference in mid-November made it clear that any effort to place Northern Ireland under Dublin control was unacceptable, he withdrew this proposal from the British agenda. In the end, as we have seen, Lloyd George resorted instead to a threat of 'immediate and terrible war' and 'war within three days' in his dealings with Irish

---

* It was an ironic reversal, given that de Valera had defeated Griffith for the Presidency of Sinn Féin in 1917.

representatives, if the British draft proposal was not accepted. Lloyd George thus demonstrated that he was more willing to confront the Nationalist majority in Ireland than the Unionist minority, with their conservative allies in Britain.

It is significant that, in the Anglo-Irish negotiations of 1921, Lloyd George reverted to secret diplomacy similar to that which he had used during his negotiations with Carson and Redmond some three years earlier. Late in 1921, he sought to avoid openly addressing the issue of whether Ireland would be partitioned. The means by which he achieved that result in the case of the October–December 1921 Conference between the Irish and British representatives provides a classic example of his considerable political skills and his ability to follow through on a hidden agenda. The device of a 'Boundary Commission', as suggested by Tom Jones for the British side on 8 and 9 November, induced Arthur Griffith, and later Michael Collins, to accept the British argument that in the event of a reduction of the area of Northern Ireland, the Unionists would be forced to come within the rubric of a united Ireland. Having secured Arthur Griffith's agreement in writing to support such a 'Boundary Commission' provision, Lloyd George then assured Ulster Unionists and British Conservatives that he would not allow the coercion of Ulster into a United Ireland.

In the eight decades since the end of the Coalition Government and the signing of the Anglo-Irish Treaty, which established in essence two separate political jurisdictions for a partitioned Ireland, Lloyd George's attitude towards Ireland remains ambiguous. Perhaps the ultimate authority that can be cited as to the shortcomings of the approach followed by Britain in Ireland during much of 1919–21 is David Lloyd George himself. The explanation he offered shortly after the collapse of the Coalition of why he had decided to truck with the same men the Government had previously labelled murderers and subversives stands as stark testimony to his own sense of realpolitik, as well as tacit admission that the path pursued by Britain had not succeeded. His comments form the most explicit statement by the British statesman most responsible for the Government's reversal in Ireland:

> The British Government was prepared to meet in discussion any representatives of the Irish people who could 'deliver the goods,' and sustain a bargain when it was made ... We were warned not to confer with men who were engaged in repudiating the authority of the Crown and were associated with deeds which we abhorred. But with whom would our critics have conferred? We did confer with the Southern unionists, very well known and very distinguished men ... but they could not put through an arrangement for Ireland ... But if you object to men because of the methods of their election then there is an end to the British Constitution.[103]

Perhaps Lloyd George made his most revealing remark of all when he stated that 'we all knew that the sympathies of Ireland were behind Sinn Féin, and all we could do was regard them as the duly elected representatives of the people'. 'Clearly,' he argued, 'there was no one else in Ireland with whom we could deal'.[104]

In closing this chapter on the Treaty, we are summoned back to the Dáil Debates to hear again the divergent visions of two young men, united in the Irish War of Independence, but rendered enemies by the Treaty. The first, Michael Collins, would die within less than a year as head of the Irish Free State. The second, Sean MacEntee, would survive to become a Cabinet minister in successive Irish governments later in the century. Collins' words are particularly poignant in light of both the short, but no doubt torturous, road that lay ahead for him, and the further bloodshed that would envelop Ireland.

> Deputies have spoken about whether dead men would approve of it [the Treaty], and they have spoken of whether children yet unborn will approve of it, but few of them have spoken of whether the living approve of it. In my own small way I tried to have before my mind what the whole lot of them would think of it ... There is no one here who has more regard for the dead men that I have ... I think the decision ought to be a clear decision on the documents as they are before us – on the treaty as it is before us ... Don't let us put the responsibility, the individual responsibility, upon anybody else. Let us take that responsibility ourselves and let us in God's name abide by the decision.[105]

Sean MacEntee was no less eloquent:

> All men of principle, they are asking you to vote for this measure upon grounds of expediency. It was upon grounds of expediency that the Catholic Bishops supported the Act of Union. It was upon grounds of expediency – and I ask the Irish people to remember this – it was upon grounds of expediency that Parnell was overthrown. It was on grounds of expediency that Redmond and the Irish people through him supported England in the late war. It is upon grounds of expediency that we are asked to approve of this treaty and recommend it to the Irish people for acceptance. Ah! I tell you that history is full of notable cases and great careers that were wrecked upon the shifting sands of expediency. There are many men in this Dáil who, by their valour and devotions, have won an honoured and glorious place in their country's history. Some of them have declared that upon the grounds of expediency they are going to vote for this treaty.[106]

Thus the terms for division among Irishmen and women over the Treaty had been set. It was to be a split that would wound Ireland deeply, as the pendulum swung away from the floor of Dáil Éireann to more lethal venues.

The Bitter Harvest

The Cabinet instructed me to send you a formal communication expressing their growing anxiety at the spread of disorder in the 26 counties. Instead of this, I write to you as man to man ... It is difficult for us over here to measure it truly [the erosion of support for de Valera] but it is obvious that in the long run, Government ... must assert itself or perish and be replaced by some other [form] of control.

Winston Churchill to Michael Collins, 12 April 1922 [SPO Dublin]

We have seen how the myriad of events which formed the years 1919–21 in Anglo-Irish relations, and which gave rise to the creation of an independent Irish state within the context of a divided Ireland, were the product of many different dynamics. There was indeed the protracted violent conflict that pitted the IRA against the superior forces of the British Empire. The violence which typified the War of Independence was often sporadic. In the end it resulted in stalemate, with the British Government agreeing to a negotiated settlement after having sought one through various channels. But, significantly, we have also seen that there were other aspects of the Irish struggle that were not tied to physical force. The active support by important elements in the Irish labour movement for the cause of an independent Ireland, the founding of Dáil Éireann – after Sinn Féin secured a significant electoral mandate in the 1918 general election – along with the rudiments of a system of native-controlled local government were also key factors in undermining British rule in Ireland. The development of the Republican Courts and their acceptance by a great number of Irish citizens at the expense of the King's writ was another manifestation of what were, in fact, the non-violent aspects of the Irish independence effort.

In effect, the Anglo-Irish conflict during these years was about more than a violent revolt and the British response to it. In the aggregate, the Irish War of Independence and its outcome continues, not so surprisingly, as the object of differing interpretations. Roy Foster has written that 'whether the bloody catalogue of assassination and war from 1919–21 was necessary in order to negotiate [the 1921 Anglo-Irish Treaty] may be fairly questioned'.[1] The matter is indeed one for conjecture. Ronan Fanning has argued, conversely, that 'history cannot prove that the British would have conceded the substance of the Treaty if there had been no War of Independence'.[2] In arguing against Roy Foster's interpretation of the Irish Revolution, Fanning contends that 'there is no shred of evidence to suggest that the British would have moved beyond the niggardliness of the Home Rule proposals finally enacted in the Government of Ireland Act of 1920, to the larger, if still imperfect generosity of the Treaty if they had not wished to bring an end to the Anglo-Irish War'.[3] Fanning lays particular emphasis on the fact that, despite widespread evidence that the majority of the Irish people wanted Home Rule, as validated by successive general elections between 1900 and 1918, the British Government showed itself unwilling to meet this constitutionally expressed desire until Irish Nationalism resorted to more drastic methods.

> Those whose historical perspective is essentially conditioned by a determination to uphold the democratic process would do well to recall ... that the British Government finally enacted Home Rule (in the 1920 Act) only two years after the 1918 election when the Irish voters withdrew the democratic mandate held for so long by the Home Rule Party and instead conferred it upon Sinn Féin. They might further recall that the Volunteers of the IRA in 1919–1921 conceived of their campaign as being designed to defend that new Irish democracy which found expression in the inauguration of the First Dáil on 21st January, 1919 – the same day as the Soloheadbeg Ambush, afterwards regarded as the beginning of the War of Independence.[4]

For this writer, the weight of historical evidence leads to the conclusion that the War of Independence indeed led to a greater degree of Irish freedom than that offered by the Government of Ireland Act (1920), and certainly beyond that offered by the false promise of Home Rule. An examination of the assessments used by the British Government to determine whether to pursue its violent campaign in Ireland and to seek a negotiated settlement bears this out.

A paper prepared by Lionel Curtis on 8 November 1921 for Lloyd George to Sir James Craig, outlining proposals relative to Ulster and the rest of Ireland, offered what may have been one of the most candid verdicts rendered by a British official on the conflict: 'The poison thus accumulated in the veins of the body politic [in Ireland] has been brought to a dangerous head by the cataclysm of the Great War. The results have been seen in a struggle conducted on lines to which future generations of both races will look back with remorse.'

Curtis' language was amended, however, after a reading by the Prime Minister. Instead, the second sentence, which acknowledged that the name of Britain had also been sullied in the conflict was changed* to read: 'The results

---

* If not by Lloyd George himself, then by a Cabinet member with Lloyd George's approval, the document having already been discussed by Curtis with Tom Jones and Sir Edward Grigg.

have been seen in the internecine conflict which has raged in Ireland for the last few years.' As in the case of the text of George V's address opening the Northern Ireland Parliament, the Irish conflict was again to be characterised as an 'internecine' one in which Irishmen were fighting Irishmen.[5]

If for nothing else, the episode is useful in illustrating the British Government's desire not only to deny its own culpability in the violence and destruction during the years 1919–21, but also to confine the conflict and whatever 'troubles' Ireland North or South presented as solely a problem of Irish manufacture.

While power changed hands by the attainment of independence for most of Ireland in 1922 under the terms of the Anglo-Irish Treaty, it did not result in a radical transformation of Irish society. This was due to the fact that Sinn Féin did not itself advocate a program of fundamental change. In essence, the Democratic Programme, with its promises of social reform, remained a policy statement, not a blueprint for action. Indeed, the relatively conservative policies embraced by Sinn Féin on such issues have in the end proved to be a key reason for its success in gaining the support of significant sections of the Irish mercantile and middle classes, and also that of the Catholic clergy and hierarchy. That a major transition did occur in Ireland during the years 1919–21 is a matter of fact. The reins of power passed from the British Government to a native administration in most of Ireland, led by individuals who in many cases had taken up arms against the Crown. But their pedigree was not that of constitutional Nationalism. It lay instead in the physical force tradition, rooted in the doctrine of the Irish Republican Brotherhood and in the loosely defined objectives of Sinn Féin. At the same time, the kind of revolution that actually was waged was aimed at achieving radical social and economic change. Brian Farrell's analysis is useful in grasping this point:

> Many modern historians ... have attempted to place the events of the formative years into a more coherent and continuous course of Irish history. But in the main, the underlying assumption that there was a break and a new beginning in the creation of the new state has remained unchanged. Desmond Williams, for example, says that the Civil War 'was preceded by a political revolution extending from the 1916 rising to the treaty' and F. S. L. Lyons writes of 'the Road to Revolution.' 'Revolution' is acknowledged as an ambiguous term ... But however defined, there seems a valid distinction between revolutions that involve some large cataclysmic social changes and other forms of 'internal war' that simply change the structure and personnel of government.[6]

The lack of social and structural change generated by the Irish Revolution continues to serve as a subject for our attention.

In essence, the immediate outcome of the Irish Revolution itself remains the stuff of ongoing debate. Several years after the signing of the Anglo-Irish

Treaty, and with many of the principals on both sides of the Anglo-Irish War either dead or out of office, Winston Churchill wrote that, 'No act of British State policy in which I have been concerned aroused more violently conflicting emotions than the Irish settlement.'[7] What followed in his remarks merits quotation, since they represent the views of a man who was involved in matters related to Ireland longer than any senior British elected official during the years 1910–25.

> For a system of human government so vast and so variously composed as the British Empire to compact with open rebellion in the peculiar form in which it was developed in Ireland, was an event which might well have shaken to its foundations that authority upon which the peace and order of hundreds of millions of people of many races and communities were erected. Servants of the Crown in the faithful performance of their duty had been and were cruelly murdered as a feature in a deliberately adopted method of warfare. It was only possible to say of those responsible for these acts that they were not actuated by selfish or sordid motives; they were ready to lay down their own lives; and that in the main they were supported by the sentiment of their fellow countrymen. To receive the leaders of such men at Council Board, and to attempt to form through their agency the government of a civilised state, must be regarded as one of the most questionable and hazardous experiments upon which a great Empire in the plentitude of its power had ever embarked.[8]

Yet treat with the very men whom they had previously labelled 'murderers' is precisely what the British Government did. We have seen from Lloyd George's own comments that this decision was motivated by the reality that Sinn Féin was the only viable party in Nationalist Ireland with whom they could make peace. He was matched in pragmatism by Ulster Unionism's acceptance under Craig's leadership of a six-county Northern Ireland entity as the most realistic option for safeguarding the greatest degree of Protestant hegemony. In essence, to guarantee their politics of 'No Surrender!' the Unionists of Northeast Ulster surrendered their brethren in the South and in three other Ulster counties to the control of a Catholic Ireland. Nonetheless, Sir Edward Carson's public remarks, uttered during the debate in the House of Lords on the Anglo-Irish Treaty on 14 December 1921, at least on the surface, expressed both bitterness and fear at what the Treaty represented for the Empire:

> we are told that the reason why they had to pass the terms of the Treaty and the reason why they could not put down crime in Ireland was because they had neither the men, nor the money, nor the backing. Let me say that this is an awful confession to make to the British Empire. If you tell your Empire in India, in Egypt, and all over the world that you have not got the men, the money, the pluck, the inclination, and the backing to restore order in a country within 20 miles of your shore, you may as well abandon the attempt to prevail throughout the Empire at all.[9]

The view that the degree of independence granted the twenty-six counties that formed the Irish Free State marked the beginning of the end of the British Empire is a view that has been given currency elsewhere.[10] It was indeed the irony of ironies that the same Empire that had been one of the principle victors in the 'Great War' found itself in short order as having to seek terms with the rebel forces of a substantially smaller nation it had previously held in check for over seven centuries. But what was not achieved at the barrel of a gun was negotiated in the end by superior statecraft and the threat of superior force by Britain, against a far less experienced adversary in the realm of diplomacy.

Following de Valera's remarkable return to power in 1932, Frank Pakenham observed that 'it has become impossible to argue that the treaty satisfied Ireland as a permanent settlement'.[11] With the passage of time, Pakenham's argument has increased in currency. At the same time, accounts critical of Collins and Griffith for succumbing to Lloyd George's threat of 'immediate and terrible war' ignore not only their inability at the time to ascertain the veracity of his threat, but also the weakened position of the Irish independence movement, especially the IRA, a position that Collins appears to have understood far better than de Valera.

Taking a wider view of Ireland's position vis-à-vis Britain, in Collins' estimate the dismemberment of the British Empire had already commenced. The exploitation of that process by the Irish side did not necessarily require further revolt in Ireland.[12] Indeed, Collins' desire to consolidate the gains that had been made in the revolution he had helped lead also placed him in a position, perhaps better than anybody else on the Irish side, to understand the limits of further armed resistance. But his assessment of such realities, and his view that the Treaty afforded the best means available to further Irish freedom, was not shared by an increasingly militant minority.

The Dáil's ratification of the Treaty by a margin of seven votes left no impression on de Valera. Furthermore, the narrowness of the majority in favour of the Treaty did not reflect the vast majority in the nation as a whole who favoured it. Indeed, he had so acquiesced to the almost theological incantations of the most militant Republicans inside and outside the Dáil that it is unlikely that de Valera would have accepted the wishes of a majority in Dáil Éireann even if they had been expressed by a greater margin. His own choice of words was hardly less mystical or more accepting of reality than the most uncompromising utterances of Mary MacSwiney. 'Whenever I wanted to know what the Irish people wanted,' de Valera proclaimed, 'I had only to examine my own heart and it told me what the Irish wanted.' He was holding unswervingly to the Republican orthodoxy he claimed 'because if I was the only man left of those of 1916 – as I was the senior officer left – I will go down in that creed to my grave'.[13]

The matter is of course not so simple as assuming that if the Treaty had not been signed in London, the state of affairs would have resorted to that which it had been before the Irish delegation left for London. In the persons of Collins and de Valera, two ruthless men were now locked in what was fundamentally a mortal struggle for the soul and future of the nation. Similarly, in the case of de Valera and Arthur Griffith, it can be said that two autocratic personalities, both older than Collins, had helped shape the dynamic Ireland was now in.

And what if Lloyd George had made good on his threat of 'war in three days', had the Irish delegation not signed the Treaty? The concern of Collins, Mulcahy and others that the IRA would have then had to face a much stronger British army was lost on the Treaty's opponents, as anti-Treaty speaker after speaker made evident during the Dáil Debates. De Valera's actions before even the Dáil Debates on the Treaty had commenced demonstrate his unwillingness to even contemplate making work the agreement which he would end up accepting a decade later after a horrific cost in Irish lives and resources resulting from internecine conflict.

He was to utter words that were more harsh and divisive in nature than his comments in Dáil Éireann. By any standard, de Valera's speech in Thurles, Co. Tipperary, on St Patrick's Day 1922, must be viewed as incendiary.

> If they accept the Treaty, and if the Volunteers of the future tried to complete the work the Volunteers of the last four years had been attempting, they would have to complete it, not over the bodies of foreign soldiers, but over the dead bodies of their own countrymen. They would have to wade through Irish blood, through the blood of the soldiers of the Irish Government, and through perhaps, the blood of some members of the Government, in order to get Irish freedom.[14]

That de Valera acknowledged that the soldiers of the Provisional Government were in fact soldiers of 'the Irish Government' is in itself significant to the extent that he would still, at least tacitly, condone an attack on those forces by a minority claiming it was acting to uphold a concept of a Republic which only months before he had termed a 'strait-jacket'. In Killarney, soon after, although tempering his remarks, de Valera still granted an important cover to those who would seek to do violence to the fledgling Irish state. 'Acts had been performed in the name of the Republic', he stated, 'which would be immoral if the Republic did not exist. Men and women had been shot for helping the enemy [the Free State] and there would be no justification for the shooting of these if the Republic did not exist.'[15] Elsewhere, in defence of what was de Valera's apparent repudiation of the right of the majority of the Irish people to see the Treaty enforced, he argued that 'there are rights which a minority may justly uphold, even by arms against a majority'. In a comment laying bare a most atavistic sense of paternalism, he argued that 'the people have never a right to do wrong'.[16]

Militant Irish Republicans held a longstanding contempt for parliamentary politics. It was therefore perhaps not surprising that, in the case of the Anglo-Irish Treaty settlement, its willingness to accept even the outcome of an intense and open deliberation by Dáil Éireann was no less hostile. If there was one individual who could have risen to the occasion when finding himself on the losing side of the democratic ledger it was Eamon de Valera, the most senior surviving leader of the 'Easter Rising' and the leader of Sinn Féin, as well as President of the Republic. But it was an occasion he would not rise to. Instead, he would oppose the Treaty at every interval, while helping in no small part to unleash a bloody course of events where Irishmen and women did more damage to each other, along with thwarting the prospect of Ireland's peaceful advancement, than did the Black and Tans. At the same time, while de Valera helped fuel the opposition to the Treaty by infusing it with credibility, in the end he was reduced to the role of a foot-soldier in the Civil War that would come.

Dublin Castle was handed over to Collins and the fledgling Provisional Government on 16 January 1922. From the outset the clouds of Civil War weighed down over Ireland as the more militant opponents of the Treaty refused to concede the democratic right of the majority within or without the Dáil to accept it. In the early hours of the morning on 1 February, the armed forces supporting the Treaty took possession of Dublin's Beggars Bush Barracks as the British evacuated it. Their objective was to prevent the anti-Treaty forces from taking it first. The pattern was repeated throughout Ireland in the coming weeks.*

The effort to find a reason for de Valera's conduct following the Treaty's approval by the Dáil, and his subsequent defeat by Arthur Griffith for the presidency, is a subject that must be defined by more than a reading of his statements in the Dáil during the Treaty debates and after. By any estimation, Eamon de Valera was a complex individual. His actions, as we have seen, were often governed by a certain obtuseness in problem solving. As one writer has observed, the 'truth may be that de Valera, disappointed and suddenly taken down from his eminence, gave way to the less noble side of his complex nature'.[17]

The years 1916–22 marked a period of almost total metamorphosis for de Valera, aged forty-two at the end of this period. Reared in rural poverty, he spent years as a mathematics teacher at secondary school level, and had been rejected for university lecturing. He began his duty as a leader of the Easter Rising with every expectation that his own death was a certain outcome, while leaving behind a young widow and several small children. During the

---

* Ironically, of the forty-six men who walked past Michael Collins on that day to take possession of the barracks, seven were later to fight for the anti-Treaty side.

'Rising', de Valera showed undeniable courage and leadership acumen, with the men under his command inflicting the worst casualties of the revolt on the British forces at Mount Street Bridge. As the most senior leader to survive he became an instant hero of the Rising. Then it would be on to British jails where he would be elected Commandant by the prisoners. Upon his release, de Valera was elected President of both Sinn Féin and the Irish Volunteers. He was arrested in 1918 during the 'German Plot' and sent to Lincoln Prison, from which he escaped. He returned to Dublin and was elected President of the First Dáil. Soon after, he journeyed to America for the next eighteen months, where he lived in an almost unreal atmosphere, being treated there as a head of state and appearing before millions. And then it came to an end with the Anglo-Irish Treaty. Added to this there appears to have been some jealousy of the position Michael Collins had come to occupy in the hearts and minds of the Irish people.

The Provisional Government, as provided for in the Treaty, was established with the objective of effecting a transition of power from the British Government to a native Irish one in the twenty-six county State. But the means by which the Provisional Government was formed was more galling to some defenders of the Republic then the Treaty itself, its oath to the King included. The formation of the Provisional regime meant the liquidation of the Irish Republic. Whether the Republic was a reality or not was not for them the issue – it was the ideal for which they had strived. Now it was not a British Government but their former colleagues who were pledged to that Republic who were presiding over its destruction. Since the Treaty did not recognise the Republic, it likewise did not recognise the Second Dáil. Instead it was the Southern Parliament provided for under the Government of Ireland Act (1920) which was to serve as the legislature for Southern Ireland. Hence, the constitutional situation was shifting into murky waters.

The first meeting of the Provisional Government was held at the Mansion House on 14 January 1922, with the sixty-four Dáil Deputies in attendance who had voted in favor of the Treaty joined by two Unionist members elected for Dublin University. Given that the Second Dáil still existed and was now headed by a Dáil Cabinet of which Arthur Griffith was now President, Southern Ireland in effect had a dual government. But real power moved swiftly to the Provisional Government, with Collins as its Chairman and Minister of Finance. Griffith's role in replacing de Valera as President of the Republic, while Collins at virtually the same time assumed the Chairmanship of the Provisional Government of the Irish Free State, arguably created the impression as one writer has acerbically commented that the independent republic 'had gone into liquidation'.[18]

Among those selected to serve with Collins in various ministries were: W. T. Cosgrave (Local Government), Kevin O'Higgins (Economic Affairs), Eamon Duggan (Home Affairs), Patrick Hogan (Agriculture), Fionan Lynch

(Education), Joseph McGrath (Labour). Given that Collins moved quickly to assume power in the name of the Provisional Government under the Treaty, combined with the fact that the British Government had already turned over its military barracks to an Irish Army, it became clear that the new regime had the authority and sufficient gravitas to make decisions for the country. With Griffith's obvious acquiescence, the Dáil Cabinet was co-opted by the Provisional Government's decision to allow Ministers of the Dáil Cabinet to attend its sessions. The Dáil Cabinet met only nine more times between 27 February and 28 April 1922.[19] But, at the same time, the Provisional Government existed independent of accountability to any Parliamentary body, since the Provisional Parliament was not yet operative. In effect, the Third Dáil did not meet until September 1922. Circumstances had conspired, including a decision made by Collins and Griffith with the support of the British Government, so that the Provisional Government could consolidate its position beyond what was called for by the Treaty, and by the reality of the Civil War.

The Provisional Government, as set up by the Anglo-Irish Treaty, operated as described elsewhere in 'obscure constitutional and administrative circumstances'.[20] But the ability to make those circumstances any less obscure was not aided by the reality of obstructionism at the outset, leading to armed revolt on the part of the Treaty's opponents. Joe Lee has surmised that 'If the Civil War illustrated with a vengeance the potential for autocracy lurking in Irish political culture, it illustrated even more emphatically the potential for democracy.'[21] While the roots of the Provisional Government may not have been pristinely rooted in democracy itself, as its advocates have claimed, the judgment of history should rest on their side, given the fact that the majority of a war-weary Irish nation, and not merely the merchant class and the Catholic hierarchy, favoured the Treaty.

There was confusion over what body governed Ireland, and there was also the even more dangerous situation that there were now two armies claiming to defend it – for distinctly different reasons. Each force challenged the legitimacy of the other.* The first to move in, laying claim to the South as the British withdrew, was the Provisional Government, when on 31 January 1922 it established an army headquartered at Dublin's Beggars Bush Barracks. At the outset, it was an army virtually in name and uniform only, since despite having a command structure headed by Richard Mulcahy, it was outmanned in sheer numbers by those IRA members opposed to the Treaty.

---

* For a more detailed discussion of the division within the IRA at this time and of the Irish Civil War in general, consult Michael Hopkinson, *Green Against Green* (Dublin, 1988); Eoin Neeson, *The Civil War in Ireland* (Cork, 1966); and Carlton Younger, *The Irish Civil War* (London, 1969); and Tom Garvin's *The Birth of Irish Democracy*, (Dublin, 1996).

Indeed, it was the reality that two armies existed which drove the political divisions further apart, and which in the end made a political resolution of the differences between the proponents and opponents of the Treaty untenable. One of the first major threats to the Provisional Government and its forces occurred in Limerick City on 23 February 1922, when that City's IRA units, joined by reinforcements from County Tipperary, took control of the barracks there from the departing British garrison. A majority in Limerick apparently opposed the Treaty. Nonetheless, the Provisional Government could not allow a major city on the mouth of the River Shannon to remain out of its control, and so it dispatched the IRA's pro-Treaty Mid-Clare Brigade. Within hours, 700 armed Irishmen on each side of the Treaty divide confronted each other. Bloodshed was averted with Mulcahy's personal intervention, and the city turned over to the Pro-Treaty garrison. But the Anti-Treaty IRA units withdrew with both their numbers and weapons intact. The stage for what would tragically become the Irish Civil War or Cogadh na gCairde, the Irish for 'War of the Friends', was rapidly being set.

On 26 March an IRA Army Convention featuring both sides was ordered to be cancelled by Mulcahy, largely out of a concern that the Pro-Treaty supporters would be outvoted. But at the urging of Rory O'Connor a separate Convention went forward, attended by some 200 IRA officers opposing the Treaty. It openly repudiated the authority of the majority in Dáil Éireann. Soon after, O'Connor claimed to have the support of some eighty per cent of the IRA's rank and file, including that of 200 Brigades. On 9 April a separate constitution for the Anti-Treaty IRA members was drafted and an Executive of its own announced. Liam Lynch was named Chief of Staff, with O'Connor, joined by Liam Mellowes, and such famed guerrilla leaders from the War of Independence as Sean Moylan and Liam Deasy, also signing on.

Collins offered his own assessment of the uncertain situation to Joe McGarrity in Philadelphia, who had also kept the lines of communication open with de Valera.

> Politically, there is scarcely any clearing on the horizon. Both sides are holding meetings. The others held two before we started, and now there is a veritable campaign facing us. There have not really been any serious incidences [sic], but a few situations have arisen which might have had very unpleasant endings only we managed to keep things easy.[22]

A measure of how matters had deteriorated in the space of only two weeks is provided in a letter of Collins to McGarrity on 4 April. 'The Opposition policy is making it almost impossible for us to hold useful meetings', he stated. 'The crowds assemble all right, but twenty, or thirty, or forty, interrupters succeeded in most places in preventing the speakers from being heard.' 'That apparently is the official policy,' he added, 'accompanied by blocked roads and torn up railways.' In a remark filled as much with frustration as anger,

Collins stated, 'Some of our Volunteer cars were fired on in Dublin yesterday. I greatly fear that the civil war which they have been threatening is now close at hand. So far as we can see the result of that will really mean the destruction of all our hopes, and the return of the English.'[23]

The return of the British in fact, as events will show, was the result that Rory O'Connor and other opponents of the Treaty actually wanted. At one stage Michael Collins found himself almost reduced to pleading with his opposition for the right to be heard at public events. In Castlebar on 16 April he asked: 'If Mr de Valera and his friends will not join us, if they will not cooperate in the work to be done, can they not accept the policy of live and let live?'[24] Collins also expressed outrage that shots were fired by opponents of the Treaty while he addressed a rally in Cork in April. Later he disarmed a man who attempted to shoot him in a bid to steal his vehicle. In Cork City, Collins' opponents also succeeded in blocking his entry to Terence MacSwiney's grave.

On the economic front, Collins singled out the need for increased capital formation to help fuel Ireland's economic expansion. Here he brought his knowledge of finance to the fore. Conversely, his ideas also underscored how destructive a civil war would be from the standpoint of the country's development.

> Millions of Irish money are lying idle in banks. The deposits in Irish joint stock banks increased in the aggregate by £7,318,999 during the half year ended December 31, 1921. At that date, the total of deposits and cash balances in Irish banks was £194,391,000 to which in addition there was a sum of almost £14,000 in the post office Savings Bank. If Irish money were invested in Irish industries, to assist existing ones, there would be an enormous development of Irish commerce ... the Irish people have a large amount of capital invested abroad. With scope for our energies, with restoration of confidence, the inevitable tendency will be toward return of this capital to Ireland.[25]

Collins also advanced a vision of Ireland that transcended a mere focus on balance sheets. It was a picture that also gave a glimpse of how well he could have served his country and its people had he been given the benefit of a full life. In an extensive memorandum sent to Desmond Fitzgerald five weeks before his death, Collins outlined a vision of what he termed 'practical nationalism' tied to Ireland's economic development. At the core of his ideas lay the use of the cinema as a tool for educating the mass of the people, he wrote, through 'educational films ... with the object of focusing the people's minds on the great problems of construction and retrenchment'.

Collins proposed the development of native Irish industries 'which it could be economic for us to create [including] soap works, great tanneries, beet root sugar factories, great frozen meat factories including potted meats'. He also suggested the use of 'picturesque photos showing the broad seas, calm, wild, etc. with such captions as the 'Atlantic Goldmine,' full of wealth for the taking'. They were to be contrasted with other film segments 'showing the poor, ill equipped little fleets of the poor people ... show the reason they are so poor or go as harvesters to England and Scotland'. 'Show them', he noted, 'the well equipped, up-to-date trawlers of Great Britain which poach on them.' But Collins also showed in his memo to Fitzgerald, then the government's Director of Publicity, an understanding of the poor living conditions afflicting many Irish rural and urban dwellers. He wanted the Irish public to see photos 'showing the appalling distress in Connemara [sic], Donegal and other maritime counties ... the awful little huts of the people ... their poor dress, food, their barren fields, showing corn growing among great boulders as I have seen in Donegal'. Of the hard life lived by many in Dublin City he wanted images 'showing the terrible slums, the long ranks of unemployed with counter-pictures of the little garden suburbs they will have to be turned into'. Of all the Irish leaders to emerge during the Irish Revolution, this glimpse at Collins' thinking indicates that he may have been the one most willing to have tried to make the promises outlined in the First Dáil's Democratic Programme a reality. But in tackling the ambitious economic and social agenda he sketched, Collins also emphasised, 'we must have peace and stable conditions in the country'.[26]

Regrettably for Ireland, Collins' arguments in support of a practical nationalism that would use the Treaty as a 'stepping stone to freedom' by making economic advances which would encourage the North to join with the rest of Ireland were lost on Liam Mellowes and other opponents of the Treaty. 'We do not seek to make this country a materially great country at the expense of its honour', Mellowes stated. 'We would rather have this country poor and indigent, we would rather have the people of Ireland eking out a poor existence on the soil, as long as they possessed their souls, their minds, and their honour ...'. Whatever the Irish people may have wanted, Mellowes evidently believed he knew better.[27] He drew an analogy between the biblical account in which the Devil tempted Christ with the world's earthly possessions if he would worship him. Mellowes wrote that 'we are told that we will get these things in return for ... selling the honour of Ireland for this mess of pottage contained in the Treaty'.[28] To Mellowes and his cohorts, politics then was something to be feared and not supported by their own active involvement.

It would not be until six months after the Anglo-Irish Treaty was signed that the issue was put before the Irish people for a vote. It was a situation in which Michael Collins, and to a lesser extent Arthur Griffith, shared responsibility. It was against a backdrop of increasing anarchy that Collins, Griffith and their colleagues attempted to accomplish a transition from British rule and establish the Provisional Government that would exist on an interim basis, as provided by the Treaty, before a Free State with its own constitution was established. While the leaders forming the new government would have welcomed the necessary referendum on the Treaty in February, Griffith supported Collins' efforts to defer a vote in the hope that common ground might be achieved with de Valera and the disaster of a split averted. Instead, the election was scheduled for 16 June that year. Collins at the same time showed little tolerance for de Valera's incitement of violence, terming it 'the language of a madness'. He was no less harsh on Cathal Brugha and Austin Stack for fomenting a split in the IRA's leadership and encouraging systematic disruption in Southern Ireland. In his view, these were the tactics of a 'discredited and defeated faction'.[29]

Nonetheless, Collins sought to do everything possible to avoid the outbreak of a Civil War. But while Collins, the soldier, sought to heal the rift with the men he had to a great extent led, Griffith, a democrat to the core, sought to deal with the opponents of the people's will at the earliest possible opportunity, so that the task of nation-building could eventually begin. But if in the end a Civil War could not be avoided, then Collins wanted to confront his former comrades on the strongest possible military terms. Many of what had been the most active IRA units were still opposed to the Treaty.

In late April, at the invitation of the Archbishop of Dublin, Collins and Griffith met with de Valera and Brugha with the objective of setting a date for an election, unencumbered by disruption. But no agreement was forthcoming, given the anti-Treatyites' continued unwillingness to face an election which they believed they would lose. Hence the objective of derailing the Treaty by any means, including the denial of the Irish people's right to express themselves, continued. In light of the independence campaign in which de Valera and Brugha had both risked their lives for the Irish peoples' right to self-determination, their unwillingness to now consult those same people is ironic. The cause itself had come to outweigh its objective.

The Free State's inability early on to check the anti-Treatyites' local outbreaks in the country was explained in graphic terms by one of the men most closely associated with its foundation. Kevin O'Higgins, at first the Provisional Government's Minister for Economic Affairs, and later its Attorney General and Vice Chairman, remarked that at this point

> there was no State and no organised forces. The Provisional Government was simply eight young men in the City Hall standing amidst the ruins of one administration, with the foundations of another not yet laid, and with wild men screaming through the keyhole. No police force was functioning through the country, no system of justice operating, the wheels of administration hung idle, battered out of recognition by the clash of rival jurisdictions.[30]

Against these developments there was also the reality of British pressure being exerted on the Provisional Government to act aggressively against the

Republicans. As the situation remained uncertain into the spring, the British Government became more anxious about the Provisional regime's performance. On 12 April Winston Churchill – by then charged with the task of implementing the Treaty from the British side – cloaked that concern with an optimistic outlook. He told Collins, 'on the whole, my impression is that public opinion is increasingly mobilising and asserting itself in Ireland and that you will get very strong national support in defending your just and lawful position'. But clearly he also felt it was time for Collins and his colleagues to move more swiftly against their opponents. In his approach to the Irish leader, we see again what Churchill had earlier referred to as the 'use of psychology' in dealing with Irish Nationalist leaders, and with Collins in particular. 'The Cabinet instructed me', he wrote, 'to send you a formal communication expressing their growing anxiety at the spread of disorder in the 26 Counties. Instead of this, however, I write to you as man to man.' Churchill proceeded to outline a list of developments in the South which he viewed as counterproductive to the Provisional Government's ability to impose a stable order. His analysis also came with a warning, and it was one of several, pressuring Collins, that Churchill and Lloyd George would forward to the Provisional Government during the next several weeks.

> There is no doubt that capital is taking flight. Credits are shutting up, railways are slowing down, business and enterprise are baffled. The wealth of Ireland is undergoing woeful shrinkage. Up to a certain point no doubt these facts may have the beneficial effect of rousing all classes to defend their own material interests, and Mr de Valera may gradually become to personify not a cause but a catastrophe. It is difficult for us over here to measure it truly, but it is obvious that in the long run, Government [sic], however patient, must assert itself or perish and be replaced by some other form of control.[31]

Churchill, by now the British Colonial Secretary, also offered Collins some direct advice on what might be done. 'Ought you not rally round the Free State', he asked, 'all the elements in Ireland which will whole-heartedly adhere to the Treaty and therein sign the declaration attaching to it irrespective of what their former attitudes have been?' Churchill went so far as to suggest how the Irish abroad might be motivated to support the Free State: 'Ought you not summon your "far flung people" to your aid? In America, Australia, Canada, New Zealand, there must be hundreds of Irishmen intensely devoted to the welfare of their native land who would come to see fair play over the elections and make sure that the people had a free vote.' Against the recognition of the role that Irish exiles abroad had played in both morally and financially supporting the Irish independence effort in the Anglo-Irish War, Churchill's latter comments might be viewed as somewhat gratuitous.[32]

Still, Collins adhered to his own course in the increasingly unlikely hope that the Treaty could be implemented and civil war averted. He may also have sought the chance to bide his time until the Free State Army was sufficiently armed and equipped to defend the fledgling state against attack.

The extent to which the methods developed successfully by the IRA during the War of Independence could now be turned with equally lethal effect on the institutions of the new Irish state was described by Kevin O'Higgins. 'In our struggle with the British,' he pointed out, 'we developed a type of war by which a comparatively small number of men can harass and hamper a government and finally reduce it to impotence and futility.' O'Higgins was clearly concerned that if the anti-Treatyite forces were successful in provoking 'increased stagnation and consequent unemployment ... the situation would be ripe for British intervention and the world's applause'.[33] A crucial difference of course between the IRA of the War of Independence and those who would wage war against their fellow Irishmen lay in the fact that in the case of the former the support of the people at large was much more forthcoming at a grass-roots level than it was for the latter.

Nonetheless, forcing a situation in which the Provisional Government would collapse and the British forces re-enter Ireland on a large scale was indeed the scenario sought by the anti-Treaty officers Volunteer Executive, dating from their formation at a convention in Dublin's Mansion House on 18 March 1922. The disruption of commerce, the destruction of railway lines and printing presses, bank robberies, and the general promotion of a state of anarchy formed a central part of the agenda sanctioned by Cathal Brugha as the anti-Treatyite's senior officer, and was a complete reversal of a pledge he had made before the Dáil in a private session on 14 December, when he stated that while he opposed the Treaty, 'The army must abide by the decision of the Dáil.'[34]

The justification for taking up arms against those with whom they had served in the war against the British, and who now wore the uniform of an Irish State, was reduced to this simple formula by Ernie O'Malley: 'We gave the men who had fought and worked credit for the past, but when their present action negatived [sic] the past, they were only a danger to the cause they had once served.'[35] But any belief that affairs could have reverted to the situation that existed before the Treaty was signed remains the height of fantasy. The likelihood of Lloyd George carrying out his threat of immediate and terrible war notwithstanding, circumstances had changed dramatically. As we have seen, a substantial portion of the British garrison had already left Ireland as early as the end of 1922, including the hated Auxiliaries and Black and Tans. Both developments were provided for under the Treaty. Rudiments of a native Irish Government had begun to take root. Most important, that fledgling native government – election or no election by this point – enjoyed significant popular support. Most of all, just as they had during the truce, following the announcement that the Treaty was signed, the majority of the Irish people still wanted peace.

Confrontations between pro-Treaty and anti-Treaty forces occurred during April in Counties Galway and Offaly, but the most daring and provocative action was to occur on the evening of 13 April, when the Four Courts were seized by anti-Treaty members of the Dublin No. 1 Brigade. They acted under orders of the Army's Executive Council. It was the situation that the Provisional Government feared most, given that the great majority of the Dublin No. 1 Brigade opposed the Treaty, and the Provisional Government forces in Dublin were powerless to stop their takeover of the Four Courts.

The Four Courts were home to the courts of Chancery, King's Bench, Common Pleas and Exchequer. Twenty-four columns helped support the dome of the classic Georgian structure. Its appearance would soon face a serious alteration, however, while serving as a terrible metaphor for the next several months of life in Ireland. The takeover of the Four Courts marked the first large-scale attack on the authority of the Provisional Government. It also made clear that the IRA had physically split over the Treaty, as the members of the Second Dáil had earlier.

Once inside the Four Courts the rebels, under Rory O'Connor's direction, fortified their position and made their removal particularly difficult. Ernie O'Malley's recollection of himself entering the building with his colleagues describes the outlook of the young diehards who acted with him. Likening his late-night entry to the Four Courts with Liam Mellowes and men from the Dublin and Tipperary brigades to a 'Hans Anderson' [*sic*] fairy tale, Ernie O'Malley wrote: 'I entered room after room on the second story. "This will do", I thought. A nice little suite of rooms. I pinned a sheet of paper on the door: "Officer of the D/O." I opened other doors. I found more suitable quarters. I pinned another sheet on the door. I went further; a yet better office.' He noted that 'We all had offices now, roll-topped desks, typewriters, bookcases, comfortable upholstered and leather chairs, good lighting.'[36] The apparent spaciousness of the Four Courts was an improvement over the quarters they had occupied previously at the Orange Hall on the other side of the city. But the relative quality of their surroundings appeared less to occupy the minds of the other young men within the upper echelons of the Provisional Government, charged with the task of completing a transition of power with the British, while on the other hand fighting off the threat posed by O'Malley and his colleagues to their authority.

The seizure of the Four Courts was also of great symbolic importance because the occupation of this major public building underscored the impotence of the Provisional Government to act. And if the supporters of the Treaty were unable or unwilling to act, O'Connor hoped that the action of his men would force a British attack, leading to a return to a full-scale resumption of the British military role in Ireland. To expedite such a development snipers from the Four Courts regularly shot at British military personnel as they proceeded along the River Liffey, killing some and wounding others.

From their position at the Four Courts, the anti-Treatyite Executive led by Rory O'Connor, Liam Mellowes and Ernie O'Malley issued demands to the Provisional Government including a commitment not to hold elections 'while the threat of war with England exists'. They ominously characterised their demands as the last for 'saving the country from Civil War, now threatened by those who have abandoned the Republic'.[37]

And where was Eamon de Valera during these developments? Not wishing to join the anti-Treatyite fray directly as a combatant, he found himself trying to regain the prestige he had lost overall. To such extremists as Rory O'Connor he was only marginally better than Collins and Griffith, with Document No. 2 being viewed as only a demonstration of weakness. In fact, the Four Courts were seized without any consultation between the Anti-Treatyite Army Executive and de Valera. Politicians were no longer necessary, and certainly not to be trusted. De Valera admitted he had no control over the actions of the IRA.

Nonetheless, the occurrences in Dublin were the logical consequence of his earlier actions in the Dáil. In essence he had provided the Treaty's most militant opponents with a powerful example that the will of the majority could be discounted and that those who supported the Treaty and were now intent upon setting up a Provisional Government consistent with its terms were usurpers who had betrayed the Republic.

Nonetheless, Collins still hoped to make a deal with de Valera. But Churchill made it clear to Collins that any effort to supplicate de Valera by resurrecting the hopes of an Irish Republic would be met by his Government's resistance.

> I am glad to see you have arranged a meeting with de Valera; but I hope you will understand that we cannot go any further in any respect. We have run every risk and made every effort and fulfilled every stipulation according to the agreement we signed with you. But that is the absolute end so far as we are concerned, and everyone of us will swing round with every scrap of influence we can command against a Republic or any inroad upon the Treaty structure.[38]

In this expression of vehemence against Collins' efforts to come to terms with de Valera, the British Government conveyed quite candidly how low the goal of reconciliation amongst the Irish Nationalists factions was on its agenda.

Nonetheless, the seven-month delay between the ratification of the Treaty by the Dáil and the holding of a national election served to obfuscate what the electorate was asked to decide. The fundamental choice between adhering to majority rule as represented by Dáil Éireann, and the right of the Provisional Government to build a native administration in the name of the Irish people, or to repudiate the Treaty and resume the struggle for full National independence, was well obscured by June 1922. One writer has commented that it is 'doubtful if the majority were aware of what they voted for'.[39] By then the choice was simply between war and peace, with the mood of the country clearly in favour of maintaining the peace with each passing month.

Despite his incendiary comments, de Valera still sought a way in which political channels could be kept open, and he politically alive with them. Such a vehicle was provided by the Collins–de Valera Pact. It was also designed to take the initiative away from the activities of the Four Courts. Under its terms, a national panel of Sinn Féin candidates was selected. There were reasons why Collins, Griffith (perhaps unwillingly) and de Valera were involved in a long period of procrastination between February and June 1922. The pact was perhaps the best chance for de Valera and Collins to restore some semblance of unity to what had been the Irish independence effort. Under its terms both sides of Sinn Féin would be represented on a single Sinn Féin slate, in proportion to their respective strength in the Dáil as of May 1922. Following the June 1922 election they would form a Coalition Cabinet. The body would consist of a total of ten ministers, five from the majority, four from the minority, with a Minister of Defence specifically representing the IRA, and a President elected by a majority in the Dáil. The untenability of this arrangement has been a subject for discussion elsewhere. One writer has described it as part of a 'fantasy world' which, by doing little more than restoring the situation as it had existed in the previous January, 'would seem bound to result in recriminatory deadlock'.[40]

The pact was useful to de Valera in that it kept the political process open as a vehicle for resolution. As Joe Lee has aptly noted, de Valera 'could hope to retrieve something of his former authority only if politics remained the medium of exchange'.[41] Civil war meant marginalisation for him. And with the collapse of the pact, marginalised is what he increasingly became. In fact, Collins, like Kevin O'Higgins, had an interest in keeping de Valera within the realm of democratic politics, since it would serve to split the anti-Treatyites.

For Collins there were other reasons in addition to the avoidance of civil strife. Overall, as the actual leader of the Provisional Government, he risked a break with Britain, and with Churchill in particular. Collins' manoeuvres during this period, as we have seen, were kept under close watch by Churchill as the guardian of British interests in Ireland. He was not swayed by the Irishman's explanation that the new Dáil, which the Pact would return, would amount to little more than a constituent assembly to be charged with drafting a constitution under the terms of the Anglo-Irish Treaty. Churchill termed the pact 'an outrage of democratic principles'. The criticism offered by the British Government added a note rich in hypocrisy given that the wishes of a majority in Ireland had not mattered to it before. Likewise, the prospects of Irishmen wading through each other's blood did not exactly excite a negative reaction in the British Government's private counsels.

Despite the gravity of the situation, there were still glimpses of humour peeping through the fabric of Irish life. Perhaps surprising in itself, the 24 June edition of the Provisional Government-owned organ, *The Free State*, carried an advertisement placed by 'The People's Own Tailors', which proclaimed that 'Treaty or No Treaty' all were agreed that the shop 'is the best House in Dublin for Ladies and Gentlemen's Tailoring'. The advertisement also offered 'Specialties to members of IRA' [*sic*] whether 'in uniform or mufti', which implied that the apparel needs of either side could be suitably met.[42]

In the end the Collins–de Valera Pact was upset by the will of the people to the extent the gains made by Labour and the Farmer's Party worked against the anti-Treatyites electorally. The pro-Treaty party won fifty-eight seats outright in the 'Pact' election. But the election of thirty-four other pro-Treaty representatives to the Irish Parliament from the ranks of Irish Labour – which had now re-entered Irish politics – and the Farmer's Party, undermined the position of de Valera and his total of thirty-six seats. Collins and Griffith were now determined to turn this clear popular mandate for the Treaty towards developing the machinery of a democratic government. The results of the Pact Election played an important role, as has been noted elsewhere, in legitimising the Treaty and the status of the Provisional Government. Once it became apparent that the will of the people, by a margin of 486,469 to 133,864,* approved of the agreement, the new regime was able to take on the mantle of a democratically elected government in its own right. Rather than seek to compromise with its opponents it could now characterise the opposition as deliberately seeking to thwart the will of the people.

The new assembly created effectively became the Third Dáil. But to irredentists refusing to accept the verdict in favour of the Anglo-Irish Treaty, the Second Dáil had never legally been disestablished. As a practical matter, the Pact was probably the only way that an election on the Treaty could be held. A majority of the anti-Treaty forces clearly sought to overthrow the result.[43]

In the end Collins failed in his goal of achieving a constitution based on conciliation. He did not publish the document, owing no doubt to its most controversial provisions – including the oath to the Crown and the acceptance of a British Governor General until the morning of the election. In fact, he had conceded the British objections. Again his actions were tempered by British pressure, with a threat to consider the Free State a dead letter combined with military re-intervention in Ireland. And so vanished Collins' slim hope of formulating an essentially Republican constitution that both the British and the anti-Treatyites could accept. Indeed, the divisions within the ranks of the former partners in the Irish independence movement encouraged

---

* These figures were based on the proportional representation system, its first application in Ireland coming in the Pact Election.

the more atavistic impulses of the British Government, with Churchill leading the chorus. The prospect of Irish Nationalists killing each other was still by no means unpalatable at Downing Street.

The British rejection of Collins' Constitution guaranteed that Civil War would be the inevitable result for Ireland. At the same time, the overall results of the Pact Election left de Valera in a greatly deteriorated position from a democratic standpoint. His anti-Treaty group lost a total of twenty-two seats, including those of Constance Markievicz and Erskine Childers, while the Collins–Griffith pro-Treaty faction won fifty-eight seats, gaining an overall majority of eight. They were joined, however, by other combinations also in favour of the Treaty. Labour had seventeen seats, and an assortment of seventeen more representing farmers, independents and unionists. It is clear that much of the action taken by the anti-Treatyite Executive was predicated on a leap in the dark.

The results of the election were predictable enough, and did little to dissuade those within the Four Courts from continuing their challenge under arms against the authority of the new Irish State. If anything, the Four Courts Executive became more anxious to take widespread action, with the objective of forcing Britain back into the conflict. Ernie O'Malley offers the best first-hand account of the mindset within that Republican fortress at this time.

> At the meeting of the Executive the situation was discussed endlessly. Some favoured an attack on the British in the north, giving them two days notice first. Others thought we should attack them in Dublin. A fight would probably unite the Staters and Republicans; some of the Staters would probably want to fight with us. The only solution appeared to be the British. They would, we expected, attack us before the two days had elapsed.[44]

In one face-to-face exchange with a member of the Civic Guards – the police force set in motion by the Provisional Government – O'Malley argued, 'If we don't fight [the British] before the British leave the country, we will be left to face each other.' His comment led a lorry load of the new Irish police to turn over their weapons to him.[45] What is perhaps most remarkable about this incident is the fact that, as late as 24 June, the leadership of the Four Courts garrison and their men continued to travel freely to and from the structure in pursuit of their activities, particularly the collection of arms. The Four Courts, aside from serving as the centre of the armed Republican resistance to the authority of the Provisional Government, also acted as a clearing house from which weapons were routed around the country, Northern Ireland included.

A split within a split occurred at a convention of IRA officers opposing the Treaty called by Liam Lynch on 18 June. A narrow majority voted to reject a resolution that proposed a declaration of war on Britain, while giving both the British and Provisional governments a seventy-two hour notice prior to hostilities. Rory O'Connor showed himself no more ready to follow the dictates of a Republican majority than he did a large mandate from the Irish people. Joined by a group of the most militant IRA officers he returned to the Four Courts and prepared to take violent action. To underscore that only those who adhered totally to their point of view would be tolerated, O'Connor and his colleagues ordered that no members of the anti-Treaty IRA Executive who had voted against their resolution would be admitted to the structure. In all, the Four Courts garrison contained no more than 190 men.[46]

Richard Mulcahy proposed what was to prove a last-ditch effort to keep the IRA together. A plan he sent to the Four Courts Executive would have kept a unified IRA structure within a chain of command in which the Minister of Defence and Chief of Staff positions were kept within the ranks of the pro-Treaty side. The offer was rejected within the Four Courts by a vote of four to three. O'Connor and his followers stated instead that talks with the Provisional Government would end at noon on 12 June. Mulcahy was stung by the rejection and implied in a note sent to Ernie O'Malley that the effort had eroded his own position within the Provisional Government, which was probably the case.[47]

Ensconced in the Four Courts, the anti-Treaty Executive sought to open a second front, partly as a diversionary tactic, but also out of a continuing desire to both unify the pre-Treaty IRA membership and to draw Britain back into the fray. In June they launched a concerted attack in the territory of the Northern Ireland Government by holding a forty-mile section of County Fermanagh, including the towns of Beleek and Pettigo. The area – a Nationalist stronghold – was held for a period of a week before the IRA were repelled across the border by a British counter-attack. Their objective appears to have been one which Michael Collins, at least for a while, shared, consistent with his predilection for furtive activities. The basis for claiming that Collins had prior knowledge of the attack, if not outright connivance, lies largely in the fact that many of the weapons used by the IRA units in Fermanagh were routed to them by the Free State Army, which had previously acquired them from the British Government for the purpose of defeating the anti-Treatyites.

But in the end Collins did not openly side with the IRA. Buoyed by the electoral success enjoyed by the Provisional Government in the June elections, he would instead accept British military assistance, which he would in the end use to drive the IRA out of the Four Courts.

The IRA attack on Fermanagh represented the first and last major IRA attack upon Northern Ireland territory during the Irish Civil War. Indeed, other than actions aimed at protecting Catholics in Belfast from pogroms launched by the Unionists, often with the help of the British-sanctioned B-Specials under ex-British General Solly Flood, at the urging of General Sir Henry Wilson, IRA activity in Northern Ireland came to a virtual standstill.

Instead, the preponderance of the action shifted to the south-western counties of Kerry, Cork, Limerick and Tipperary, with a lesser degree of activity in the West.

Some of Collins' requests to the British Government on the subject of munitions proved a cause of concern to Churchill. They also raised broader questions about Collins' own agenda at this time: was he actively and quite boldly seeking British weapons that could in turn be used later by a unified Republican effort against the six-county regime? Or was he in fact so ruthless in his desire to eradicate the opposition to the Free State by his former comrades in arms that he would use any resources made available by Britain? The record shows that by mid-April 1922 the still evolving Free State Army was also the beneficiary of a substantial amount of weaponry at Collins' apparent request through General Emmet Dalton. Churchill told Collins that he had been informed by Andy Cope, who was still attached to the Chief Secretary for Ireland's staff, that he issued 4,500 rifles. 'He has authority to issue up to 6,000', Churchill stated, 'and as soon as they have been placed in trustworthy hands, I shall be quite ready to issue two or three thousand more with proportionate ammunition.' But Churchill rejected a request from Collins via Dalton for 25,000 Mills bombs and 5,000 rifle grenades. The rejection also came with an admonishment, as if directed at a subordinate: 'These are the weapons far more of a revolution than of Government [sic]. If they fall into bad hands they become a most terrible means of aggression on the civil population. I am quite ready to issue a small number for the defence of particular posts. Perhaps you will talk it over with Cope tomorrow. You never know whom a bomb will kill; very likely a woman, probably a widow.'

A further note of displeasure was sounded by Churchill when he reminded Collins that 'We have already issued you one armoured car, which has unhappily fallen into bad hands. Cope tells me a second car has been placed at your disposal.' But it is Churchill's next comment on the subject of armoured cars that is particularly useful in revealing the uneasiness with which Collins and his approach to his former comrades was viewed by the British Government: 'We have only got four left; but if the need is serious you can arrange with Cope to take two of these on the basis of your personal guarantee that they will be kept in Treaty hands at all costs. I am enquiring about two tanks. We will issue the ten lorries.'[48] The tanks and lorries were also apparently requested of the British by Collins.

In his correspondence with Collins of 12 April, Churchill emphasised that he was 'counting' on him 'to let me know if you think a crisis is imminent. My feeling is ... that we shall get through Easter without an explosion.' The prediction, however, proved wishful thinking on the Englishman's part.

Collins also had good reason to feel that the British Government was retreating from its commitment under the Treaty to grant the Northern Ireland Parliament no more authority than was contained in the Government of Ireland Act (1920). The onset of the Civil War and the energies it required on the part of the Free State Government gave Britain wider latitude to assist the Northern Ireland Government in ways that appeared to contravene the commitments made under the Anglo-Irish Treaty. Despite his own efforts to avert a civil war, Michael Collins also monitored developments on a number of fronts. The British Government's activities in allowing the Northern Ireland Government to set up its own agency for the monitoring of animal diseases, in effect undermining the jurisdiction of the Council of Ireland promised under the Treaty, drew Collins' ire.[49] But of far greater concern was the treatment of Northern Ireland Nationalists and the attacks on their lives by loyalist mobs.

In May 1922 with British Government sanction, the Craig regime embarked on a policy directed overwhelmingly at Catholics of nationalist hues. 500 arrests were made with internment without trial put into operation. The internees first were held in Belfast Gaol and later on the prison ship *Argenta*. The group included doctors, lawyers, and teachers, as well as suspected IRA members. That Craig's draconian measures were directed solely against Catholics only exacerbated the horror that Collins felt on 31 May of that year when Craig's Special Police Constables, following an IRA attack on two of their number, opened fire on the predominantly Catholic population of Belfast's Millfield district. By the end of the day ten were killed, including two Protestants. The action was accompanied by a police riot that saw the looting of Catholic-owned businesses and Church property.

Collins was not alone in these sentiments. Indeed, within Lloyd George's own inner sanctum, Tom Jones and Lionel Curtis made the Prime Minister aware of their misgivings over the latitude Sir James Craig had been given to establish his own special Constabulary – the B-Specials – and to recruit them as a totally sectarian force. In the Spring of 1922 Jones informed Lloyd George that 'Curtis and I are very disquieted at the position we are moving into in relation to Ulster'. Jones reminded him of Austen Chamberlain's explicit statement to Craig in December that 'If Northern Ireland remains part of Great Britain the British Government will be responsible for the maintenance and control of all military forces which may be needed to support the civil authority in Northern Ireland ... The British Government will not permit the organisation of military forces by any other authority.' Jones warned that the Government was 'departing from the spirit of the bargain with the South and will be changed by the world with one more breach of faith if we continue the present policy ...'. That policy in fact consisted of the Crown's Exchequer paying for the Special Constables, making related grants to the Northern Ireland Government, allowing the B-Specials to operate under the cover of a police force, and as Jones stated, 'allowing Henry Wilson to proceed unchallenged to prepare his "scheme" for which the Northern Parliament is voting £2,000,000 ... and bringing us back to the position of

1914 with the advantage that the Field Marshall is making his preparations legally with the money of the British Government and without protest'. The Prime Minister's Private Secretary asked whether it was not the day 'of the British Government to undertake the control of the border and to remove all justification from the Northern Ireland Government for these swollen police forces?'[50]

From Sir James Craig, however, there was much reason for gratitude. He not only had a Protestant Parliament for a Protestant people, but he also had a Protestant police force to go with it, accompanied by the British Government's blessing. In a letter to Winston Churchill on 28 May, Craig stated 'You have been splendid about meeting our requirements and I write to tender grateful thanks.' 'Solly Flood', he wrote, 'is gradually but surely obtaining the upper hand, and the other side is feeling the strain. With the provision you and the British Government have now approved we will be able to go ahead with the utmost confidence.'[51]

Nothing in the historical record indicates that Lloyd George offered anything but acquiescence to Craig and Wilson's activities, while allowing the British Exchequer to underwrite them. In short order Tom Jones' worst fears were confirmed as the B-Specials undertook, with General Wilson's training, a campaign of random violence against the Northern Nationalists. But Michael Collins would show himself willing to take more aggressive action against Wilson than would the General's British critics. It appears that the Field Marshal's assassination in June by two members of a London IRA unit was done with Collins' full knowledge.

If Lloyd George had any sense, at the time he sent a communication to Collins shortly after General Wilson's death, that the Irishman had any involvement in the killing, he was careful to hide it. The Prime Minister viewed Wilson's assassination as part of a larger effort by the IRA 'irregulars' to widen a campaign of attack upon British lives and property in Britain and Northern Ireland. 'I am desired by His Majesty's Government to inform you that documents have been found upon the murderers of Field Marshal Sir Henry Wilson which clearly connect the assassins with the Irish Republican Army and which further reveal the existence of a definite conspiracy against the peace and order of this country.' What the situation called for, in Lloyd George's estimate, was a full-scale assault by the Provisional Government on anti-Treatyite positions in the Four Courts. 'The ambiguous position', he said, 'of the Irish Republican Army can no longer be ignored by the British Government. Still less can Mr Rory O'Connor be permitted to remain with his followers and his arsenal in open rebellion in the heart of Dublin in possession of the Courts of Justice organising and sending out from this centre enterprises of murder not only in the area of your Government but also in the six northern counties and in Great Britain.'[52]

Lloyd George's letter bordered on an ultimatum to the Provisional Government. Ironically, the man to whom he was delivering the message may have had more to do with General Wilson's death than did Rory O'Connor and his companions in the Four Courts.* The Prime Minister stated:

> His Majesty cannot consent to a continuance of this state of things and they feel entitled to ask you formally to bring it to an end forthwith ... His Majesty's Government are prepared to place at your disposal the necessary pieces of artillery which may be required, or otherwise to assist you as may be arranged. But I am to inform you that they regard the continued toleration of this rebellious defiance of the principles of the treaty as incompatible with its faithful execution.[53]

Risking a total loss of control of the situation, Collins in the end accepted the British Government's offer of artillery. But his decision to attack his former colleagues was also driven by the kidnapping of J. J. 'Ginger' O'Connell, an Adjutant General of the Free State Army and close friend of Collins, by members of the Dublin No. 1 Brigade.†

When Lloyd George's letter reached Dublin, Collins was in Cork dealing with an attempt by anti-Treatyite sympathisers to tamper with his constituency's ballot papers. The task fell to a subordinate to offer a response. The rationale given for not launching an attack on the anti-Treatyites in the Four Courts is of interest to the extent that it indicates that as late as 2 June the Provisional Government, at Collins' direction, continued to adopt a policy of inaction. In response to Lloyd George, the Provisional Government believed that the forces lodged inside the courts 'contained within themselves elements of disruption which given time would accomplish their complete disintegration and relieve the [Free State] Government of the necessity of employing methods of suppression which would have perhaps evoked a certain amount of misplaced sympathy for them'. Moreover, the response proposed that the Provisional Government hold out until after the elections for a result that would strengthen its hand in taking the necessary steps to restore order in the country.[54]

At 4.29 a.m. on the morning of 28 June 1922, the bombardment of the Four Courts began with shells fired from two British field guns. Shortly after, guns firing eighteen-pound shells were brought into action. At first they were

---

* Rex Taylor's in-depth analysis of the Wilson assassination demonstrates that at a minimum Collins had ordered the Field Marshal's death prior to the Truce and forgot to call it off. In Britain, Dunne and Joseph O'Sullivan carried out their assignment on the basis that the order remained current. But given Collins' notorious reputation for detail, it is implausible that he would have overlooked an assassination order upon such a prominent figure. See Rex Taylor, *Assassination*, (London, 1961).
† The kidnappers included Sean MacBride, later to become a prominent jurist and Foreign Minister of the 1948–51 Coalition Government.

fired at five-minute intervals in an effort on the part of the Provisional Army to conserve their ammunition. In what added a level of black comedy to the appalling vista of Irishmen bombarding Irishmen on the streets of Dublin, many of the shells missed the structure of the Four Courts altogether, while others barely scratched its surface due to the inexperienced aim of the Free State officers. A review of photographs and newsreel footage from the bombardment also shows how some of the men were literally knocked back and deafened by the recoil from the artillery pieces, something for which they were apparently unprepared.

It is significant that the first time that Michael Collins actually demanded that the Republicans leave the Four Courts was in a message delivered to Rory O'Connor at 3.40 a.m. on the morning of 28 June. Minutes later the government opened fire on their opponents when the order was refused.

But that effort was not enough to bring about a surrender by the Republicans inside. Collins was forced to seek further munitions assistance from the British. Macready refused to provide that support without further approval by the War Office, leading Collins to telephone Churchill, then the Colonial Secretary, directly.* Churchill in turn set in motion the transfer of 300 more shells from the British Barracks in Dublin while Macready hoarded a supply of 5,000 such shells with which to defend his own garrison, should the Republicans in the end triumph. On 29 June, Churchill, acting under the Cabinets' instructions, urged Collins to make maximum use of the 300 additional shells and warned that 'they will be little use without heavier guns and good runners ... Do not fail to take both. Both are available.' Churchill also noted that airplanes would also be available from the next day.[55]

On 30 June, aided by the additional British support, the Free State Government recaptured the Four Courts. But it was not without considerable destruction to this building, which housed much of the legal records of Ireland. Aside from the exterior damage caused by the Free States forces' steady bombardment for almost two days, the Republicans, cognizant of the tenuousness of their position, set the historic structure afire from within, prior to their surrender.

Asked to provide details on the destruction that had ensued in the Four Courts, Churchill told the House of Commons on 30 June: 'When men are fighting about matters so important as the foundations of their country, buildings and records will often suffer ... I have no further information at present. I will only say this – that a State without archives is better than archives without a State.'[56]

---

* Macready was probably holding on to the shells in the event he needed them himself. On 24 June he had gone so far as to draft a proclamation laying the basis for the British Army clearing the Four Courts itself.

Despite assurances from Churchill to the effect that the Free State's attack on the Republicans in the Four Courts held 'the possibilities of very great hope for the peace and ultimate unity of Ireland, objects which are very dear to your British cosignatories', the consolidation of Northern Ireland by James Craig into a sectarian regime proceeded unimpeded by the British Government.[57]

Indeed, the course of events in northeast Ulster suggested that, rather than seeking Irish unity, British policy was instead in favour of consolidating partition. On 9 August, in a communication with Churchill, Collins returned to the development he had warned against in June: the Northern Ireland Local Government Bill and Craig's effort at gerrymandering within the six-county area. Collins emphasised that the net effect of allowing Craig to divide the area into several Protestant constituencies, and Catholic areas into one single constituency, would be 'to prejudice the Catholic and Nationalist position in the whole of the North Eastern Counties'.[58] That Collins fully understood the implications of what was happening in the setting up of the North's local government constituencies could not have been made more apparent, perhaps to his own detriment in the eyes of the British Government.

> Do you not see, or have His Majesty's advisors not disclosed the true meaning of all this? Not merely is it intended to oust the Catholic and Nationalist people of the Six Counties from their rightful share in local administration, but it is, beyond all question, intended to paint the Counties of Tyrone and Fermanagh with a deep Orange tint in anticipation of the operation of the 'Ulster Month' and the Boundary Commission, and so, to try to defraud these people of the benefits of the Treaty.

Collins then asked Churchill to use his voice against the legislature's Northern Ireland Bill. 'This was especially necessary', he wrote, 'when we are seeking any gleam of hope that we can meet the Irishmen of the North East upon some working basis of union.'[59] The British Cabinet, however, did not feel able to put pressure on Craig to change the Local Government franchise. Collins' appeal thus fell on deaf ears. That the Coalition was at this time in no better position to persuade the Ulster Unionists, and most importantly their Conservative allies in Parliament, into entering into a form of all-Ireland arrangement is fairly certain. However, the fact that the Government took no step to prevent the development of the Northern state along sectarian lines must have made it bitterly clear to Collins that the inclusion of the Boundary Commission as part of the Anglo-Irish Treaty amounted to little more than a device to entice Michael Collins and Arthur Griffith into signing the agreement. In that context, the Government's willingness to allow James Craig a free hand in ensuring an absolute Protestant majority at Stormont, with a bare minimum of Nationalist representation, leads to the inescapable conclusion that, aside from the threat posed by Bonar Law and his Unionist colleagues to survival of the Coalition, the division of Ireland into two states, with different religious majorities, had in fact become a policy objective of the British Government.

The form in which the Northern Ireland Government was allowed to emerge was now evident to Collins. The beast which he received as his part of the bargain in the Anglo-Irish Treaty amounted to something less than 'a stepping-stone' to full Irish freedom. Walled in on the one side by Republican extremists oblivious to the unfavourable position the effort at armed struggle had reached by mid-1921, and on the other by a British Government that apparently distrusted his motives as much as he distrusted theirs, Collins found little room for manoeuvre. His situation was further compounded, as we have seen, by the fact that there appeared to be elements within the Free State Government who were less than comfortable with his actions.

From the British standpoint, there was undoubtedly much in Collins' conduct, as the dominant personality of the Free State Government, that left them uneasy. Much has been written about instances in which weapons issued to the Free State Army by the British Government found their way across the border into the hands of the IRA's Northern Command. While the ease with which IRA units crossed the border from the South without resistance by the Free State Army during April–August 1922 may have been due as much to natural sympathy among some in the Free State ranks, Collins's at least tacit support of IRA activity in Northeast Ulster cannot be overlooked. Up to the end of his life, he was undoubtedly considered a serious threat by the Northern Ireland Government. If the British Government was not going to take steps to thwart Craig's effort at gerrymandering, or end the pogroms by Unionist mobs against Northern Catholics, then he was going to continue supporting efforts aimed at disrupting the Northern State. In effect, the presence of Collins as head of the Free State Government served as a source of countervailing pressure against the worst excesses of the Craig regime, excesses the British Government was unwilling to confront.

Few areas serve to underscore Collins' capacity for duplicity, as well as revealing the almost surreal cooperation between the two Irish armies, more than the actions taken to undermine the Craig regime. In the spring of 1922, the IRA's two divisions in Northern Ireland contained some 8,000 men. Three other divisions had operated near the border. Since the signing of the Treaty it had certainly been the objective of Collins to keep the Northern Ireland divisions as loyal to him as possible – an objective he largely succeeded in. Indeed, Collins had shown that he was intent upon protecting the rights and safety of Northern Ireland nationalists – which more than the debate in the South over the oath, was the overriding concern of many Catholics in the six counties. He sought to do this, firstly, by lobbying the British Government and the Craig regime for protection against discrimination and attacks by loyalist mobs, and secondly by covert support of the IRA in Northern Ireland. It was through the latter approach that he was able to keep the lines of communication, and indeed cooperation, open with the irregular forces in the South. Whether Collins actually believed that under-mining the Craig regime, at a maximum, or the need to protect Northern Nationalists, at a minimum, would serve as a catalyst for averting a full-scale rift between the two IRA factions in the South is a matter for conjecture. But the fact remains that he did take steps to keep the IRA in the North armed – in direct contravention of the Treaty – and that he did so without his collea-gues in the Provisional Government knowing, while colluding with the same forces who were challenging it's authority.

Collins had his reasons for seeking to make life uncomfortable for Craig. While he had facilitated an end to the Belfast boycott by Southern merchants under a pact with Craig, the latter had not honoured a commitment to ensure that the 9,000 Catholic Belfast shipyard workers driven from their jobs be allowed to return safely. Indeed he was outraged that not even a single worker had been allowed to return. Collins' efforts included official protests, as we shall see, both to Craig and the British Government over what he saw as a litany of wrongs perpetrated against Northern Nationalists. At the same time, within the Provisional Government he sought to ensure a policy of non-cooperation with the Northern Government at virtually every level. Collins went so far as to fund nationalist teachers within the six-county jurisdiction from the Provisional Government Exchequer

But it was Collins' collusion with anti-Treatyite elements in providing weapons to the IRA's Northern Divisions that represents the most serious action. While waging an effort, on the one hand, to institutionalise a Free State Government he worked, on the other, to route arms to the IRA in the North through the IRA in the South. While most of the arms and equipment for the Northern IRA divisions came through Liam Lynch's anti-Treatyite forces, Collins also actually provided rifles issued by the British to the Provi-sional Government, as one writer has noted, in return for weapons obtained earlier from other outlets by anti-Treatyite IRA brigades in Cork.[60] The actions of some elements within the Free State Army, particularly along the border areas, were not surprising given that many members of the IRB, now associated with the Provisional Government, backed the Treaty solely out of loyalty to Collins.* In all, Collins' actions vis-à-vis Northern Ireland had the effect of co-opting the IRA's Northern Divisions and confusing his Southern opponents.[61]

Overall Collins' Northern policy can be seen to have been shaped by the view that for the foreseeable future the Northern Ireland state would remain

* When Collins died they were left leaderless. The split between those elements of the Army still loyal to Collins, and his view that the Treaty was a stepping stone toward a Republic, were significant factors in the mutiny within the Free State Army in 1924.

a reality and had become so before the Ango-Irish Treaty itself. But to the end of his life Collins was also committed to a policy of making Northern Ireland unworkable while paying official obeisance to the terms of the Treaty. His attempt to include a provision that would have allowed Northern nationalist MPs to sit in the Free State Parliament under the constitution he crafted with Eamon de Valera during the 1922 pact raises a question as to his real motives in this instance. It may have been an attempt to compensate for his neglect at not having insisted on a requirement for a county by county plebiscite for the six Northeast Ulster counties under the Anglo-Irish Treaty. Nonetheless, more than any other Sinn Féin leader during the years 1917–22 Collins still showed himself to be the most consistently and practically concerned with the rights of Northern nationalists.[62]

The clock runs out for Collins

On 12 July 1922 Collins took the extraordinary step of resigning from the Cabinet, effectively removing himself from his ministerial capacity. He announced that he would assume responsibility as Commander-in-Chief of the Army in prosecuting the Civil War to its conclusion. By his own design, he took up authority immediately as head of a 'War Council' of three that also included Richard Mulcahy as Chief of Staff and Minister of Defence, and Eoin O'Duffy as Commander of the Southwest Division. O'Duffy, an Ulsterman who had won Collins' confidence during the Anglo-Irish War, was sent to the Southwest because it was the latter's view that it was there that the crux of the Republican threat to peace remained. Eliminate the problem there, he argued, and Dáil Éireann could assert its authority, with the National Army falling back to a subordinate position.[63]

Yet Collins' decision to leave the Cabinet at this stage may have been motivated as much by his frustrations within that body as by a desire to bring the Civil War to a conclusion. One month previously, he argued openly with Ernest Blythe, with the latter taking the lead in an attack claiming that the constitution Collins had initially drafted was that of an independent Republic rather than that of a state such as that provided for by the Treaty. It was argued, with Collins present, that the Collins–de Valera Pact, combined with the shooting of British soldiers and ex-servicemen in Ireland, produced an attitude on the part of the British Government that was 'one of suspicion and the Constitution was interpreted by them from this point of view'. Significantly, with Collins' earlier activities in working behind the scenes with his former colleagues to attack British positions in Northern Ireland in mind, the Cabinet 'decided that no troops from the 26 Counties, either those under official Cabinet control or attached to the Executive, should be permitted to invade the six county area.'[64]

Although removed from the day-to-day workings of the Provisional Government, Collins clearly continued to intervene when the situation demanded. He likewise proved himself to be just as hard on the Ministry of the Free State as he had been on his colleagues in the Dáil Cabinet during the Anglo-Irish War. The need for the swift and effective establishment of the Civic Guards as the police force of the new state drew his attention from the Civil War theatre. 'I am afraid the matter is being dealt with rather casually', he wrote to Liam Cosgrave as Acting Chairman of the Provisional Government on 3 August. He added, 'I would like to see something a little more definite.'[65]

Recognising how little room he now had for manoeuvring within the Provisional and British Governments alike, and with his pact with de Valera long since collapsed, the ever-enigmatic Collins decided to strike out on his own. That he sought to make contact with his old comrades in arms, either directly or through intermediaries, is fairly clear. That such an enterprise may have contributed to the loss of his own life also remains possible.

The period from 12 to 22 August was a definitive one for the future of the Irish Free State. On the first date, Arthur Griffith died of a cerebral haemorrhage at a Dublin nursing home. Collins replaced him as head of the Government, but did not return to the Cabinet, instead electing to remain in the field as Commander-in-Chief. But he returned to Dublin for Griffith's funeral. As Collins walked behind Griffith's funeral cortege as the new leader of an independent Ireland, the two men he had in all probability directed to assassinate General Sir Henry Wilson were readied for the gallows in London.[66] It was an irony that transcended Collins' earlier works of intrigue, and which also belied a certain hubris on his part.

Collins' assumption of power in the Free State could not be seen as a reassuring development for the British Government, especially to Churchill, who as we have seen had become locked in a running feud with the phlegmatic leader over the treatment of Nationalists in Northern Ireland. But his new position was important to the new state, given his close association with the War of Independence. At the end of June 1922, while making use of Churchill's assistance to bombard his former colleagues out of the Four Courts, Collins still found himself contending with the same man over British policy in Northern Ireland. It was a debate that would go on between the two for the next several weeks. But on the evening of 22 August 1922 the Irish landscape shifted dramatically again as Collins was assassinated in an ambush hastily set by anti-Treaty Republican forces in his native West Cork. The forces of violence in Ireland which he had helped unleash and later sought to tame had now taken him. But even in death, Collins helped solidify the identity and legitimacy of the Free State.

The news of Collins' death provoked public expressions of regret from Churchill, among others in the British Government. But the private comments uttered about Collins' demise were probably closer to British official sentiments. In a note to Andy Cope, Lionel Curtis wrote how Collins 'once said that the best service he could render the RIC would be to get murdered, which was fine of him'.[67] A comment offered by Curtis two years later to Churchill is even more revealing of his attitude to Collins. He wrote:

> I have never thought that Collins tried to meet you squarely on the Treaty. I am not sure he was responsible for those atrocities [the shooting of British soldiers in Dublin during the Four Courts occupation, April–June 1922] but his own hands were so red with blood he could not bring himself to the murder of British soldiers very sincerely except when it threatened his own political power.[68]

Perhaps a more genuine reaction to the news of the 'Big Fellow's' demise came, ironically, from some of his former comrades, who were seen to kneel in prayer in various prisons where IRA men were incarcerated that August.

Still, the death of Collins, while not openly welcomed by the leaders of the anti-Treatyite forces in the field, met with an at best clinical reaction. Liam Lynch's response to Liam Deasy's report on the events at Béal na Bláth is a case in point.

> Considering the very small number of men engaged this was a most successful operation, and they are to be complimented on the fight made under such heavy fire, and against such odds. Considering you were aware of the fact that the convoy contained an armoured car, it is surprising you had not mines laid to get this. Nothing could bring home more forcibly the awful unfortunate national situation at present than the fact that it has become necessary for Irishmen and former comrades to shoot such men as M. Collins who rendered such splendid service to the Republic in the late war against England. It is to be hoped our present enemies will realise the folly in trying to crush the Republic before it is too late.[69]

But Lynch's allowance for the necessity of shooting Collins to save his vision of the Republic was altered quite drastically the following spring. After receiving a mortal wound himself, in that instance from Free State Forces, Lynch uttered: 'All this is a pity. It should never have happened.'[70]

On the surface, at least, Collins' death threatened to undermine the Provisional Government. While Cosgrave succeeded Collins as its Chair, a position he had already nominally held since Collins had resigned from the Cabinet in July, Kevin O'Higgins emerged as the driving force in the Government. O'Higgins' reserve was needed since there were times after Collins' death when Cosgrave appeared to weaken. Early in September, for example, Cosgrave joined Mulcahy in communicating a message to the Republicans which implied that if they disbanded the Provisional Government would allow them to keep their arms.[71]* On 5 September, Mulcahy engaged de Valera in private talks, apparently unsanctioned by either side, with both men vouching for the safe conduct of the other. The meeting bore little fruit, especially since de Valera still showed little desire to recognise the legitimacy of the Free State or the Third Dáil.

After Collins' assassination, those who remained behind him in the Government's civil sector resorted to living their lives in a virtual state of siege. Ironically, not unlike the heads of Britain's last Irish Administration at Dublin Castle, the leaders of the soon-to-be-formed Irish Free State were forced both to live and work in Government buildings. At night, while attempting to smoke a cigarette on a rooftop, they were subject to attack by snipers.[72]

Executions

Those Republicans imprisoned in various Irish prisons who mourned the death of Collins would soon be bemoaning the faith of others who had fought with them against their former leader. For after Collins' death there was unleashed by the Free State a degree of ferocity against the 'irregular' forces not previously seen in the Civil War.

A Public Safety Bill was enacted by the Dáil in October 1922. It represented the Free State's harshest attempt to protect itself, and offered a bloody response to the Republicans. The measure provided for a system of military courts with the power to order executions for crimes including illegal arms possession. There is little reason to believe that Collins would have countenanced what would become the large-scale execution of his former comrades. An October amnesty offered by the Government to those wishing to accept its authority and lay down their arms was largely ignored. While Ernest Blythe and Kevin O'Higgins have generally been cited as the Free State leaders most responsible for the 'Executions' policy, Richard Mulcahy also embraced the enterprise. 'There can be no question', he said, 'but that I personally was the ultimate and supreme authority for these and at all times accepted the supreme responsibility.'[73] The Catholic hierarchy also weighed in in support of the Government's policy.

In all, seventy-seven Republican prisoners would be executed by the Free State, many of them summarily. Among the most prominent were the leaders of the Four Courts Executive: Rory O'Connor, Liam Mellowes, Joseph McKelvey and Joseph Barrett, who had been in prison since June. That they had taken part in no actions since the Civil War began was an argument Kevin O'Higgins found unconvincing.† Instead, he forced a broadening of the

---

* In the end the arms would be dumped, not surrendered.
† Rory O'Connor was the best man at O'Higgins' wedding.

executions to the local level on the basis that there should be 'executions in every county', since local executions, he held, would have an even more dramatic impact on the Republican grass roots.[74] O'Higgins also succeeded with his argument that even the youngest and most lowly in rank should face the firing squad. But despite the harsh language issued by O'Higgins and others in the Free State Government, the executions of these leaders in Mountjoy prison were extra-legal. They also showed that the Government was gripped as much by fear as a desire for revenge. The Treaty was still in jeopardy, as was their own position. In short, the effort can be viewed as a desperate act, in part brought about by Collins' death.

There is little doubt that the executions had a lingering impact. Some months later, with an order for his own execution the following day hanging over him, Liam Deasy, the IRA's Deputy Chief of Staff and one of its principal leaders in Southwest Munster, agreed to sign a statement drafted by Free State authorities calling on the IRA to surrender its arms. In the document Deasy stated: 'I will accept and I will aid immediate and unconditional surrender of guns and men as required by General Mulcahy.' He then called on the Republican leadership by name to join him. To O'Malley, inside the walls of a prison hospital, Deasy's action represented a 'stunning blow'. Yet he urged Liam Lynch and others not to accept Deasy's capitulation, and to write him and all other Republican prisoners off as 'casualties'. But while Deasy's statement no doubt served to weaken the Republican effort, the statement had little impact on the IRA's leadership, in or out of prison. Lynch continued to act as Chief of Staff, with little hesitation. In the spring of 1922 he was himself shot dead by Free State forces on a hillside on the Limerick–Tipperary border.[75] At first, the Free State party that came upon the mortally wounded Lynch mistook him for Eamon de Valera.

The feeling of being hunted down by one's former comrades is graphically described by Ernie O'Malley, who on the day of his capture by Free State forces was hidden in a secret room, its passage concealed behind a coat closet in a suburban Dublin house.

> My hand was shaking but my mind was clear as I moved the .45 cartridges in a row of six on the table beside the bed. Then I put a cardboard file of my most important papers on a chair. I would bring them with me if I broke through or burn them in a bucket ... I knelt on one knee to pray for courage; then I sat on the end of the bed, the revolver in my hand, listening in the darkness.[76]

But an attempt by the rebel leader to shoot his way out of the house ended in the death of at least two Free State soldiers, and with O'Malley riddled with bullets, looking up at his captors in a semi-conscious state. 'I could see green uniforms around me', he recalled later. 'One soldier', O'Malley remarked, 'took up the rifle which lay beside me. He ejected an empty cartridge case and pointed the muzzle at my body, and then very slowly I saw the bolt move forward and heard the snap as he turned down the bolt.' But another soldier, recognising the wounded man, pushed the soldier away and said, 'That's O'Malley and you'd better leave him alone while I'm here.'[77] O'Malley would spend the next eighteen months between the walls of various prison hospitals and jails. A death sentence delivered against him by a military tribunal was rescinded.

By the spring of 1923, the anti-Treatyites found themselves not only out-gunned and outmanned but lacking in support from the people in most rural areas which a unified IRA was able to count on during the War of Independence. A campaign of guerrilla war without indigenous support could continue to inflict physical and economic damage against the Free State. But the victims of such tactics more often than not were Irish men, women and children.

The death of Liam Lynch in April 1923 paved the way for Eamon de Valera to seize the initiative by calling on his comrades to cease hostilities. While their arms would not be surrendered, it marked the unofficial end of the Irish Civil War. But de Valera's statement marked a tacit admission of defeat, at least on the battlefield.

> Soldiers of the Republic, Legion of the Rearguard ... The Republic can no longer be defended successfully by your arms ... victory must be allowed to rest for the moment with those who have destroyed the Republic ... Much that you have set out to accomplish has been achieved. You have saved the nation's honour and kept open the road to independence ... Seven years of intense effort have exhausted our people ... If they have turned aside and have not given you their active support which alone could bring victory in the last year, it is because they saw overwhelming forces against them ...[78]

The havoc which the Civil War had wreaked on Ireland was enormous in terms of death and injuries, destruction of railroads, and the losses it inflicted on Irish trade and agriculture. In the eleven-month period that spanned the Irish Civil War, more Irishmen were killed at the hands of their fellow countrymen than there were Volunteers lost to the British forces during the entire two and a half years of the Anglo-Irish War. In comparison to a total of seventy-seven executions that were carried out by the Free State against their former comrades, only twenty-four executions had been carried out by the British authorities during the entire Anglo-Irish War. From the ranks of the Irish Free State army there were 800 killed alone, with the number of IRA dead unknown, but probably higher. It is also likely that the total number of casualties, both military and civilian, during the Civil War vastly exceeded those of the War of Independence period.[79]

But Republicanism in Ireland did not die with the April 1923 arms dump, nor was it to be simply co-opted by future manifestations of the IRA. The ideal of an independent Irish Republic, despite the hardships which the Treaty's more militant opponents were in large measure responsible for inflicting on the country during the Civil War, was an objective that a significant number of Irish people expressed support for at the ballot box. And despite the fact that de Valera was well established by the conflict's end as a polarising figure, his stock was still high with those Irish men and women who felt on purely democratic terms that the Treaty settlement was not enough. To the deep surprise of Cosgrave's Cumann na nGaedheal Party, as the pro-Treaty Party was by now called, the appeal of Republicanism was made clear by the results of a snap election which Cosgrave had ironically called in August 1923. The electorate contained four hundred thousand more voters over the registrar of the 1918 Election, Cumann na nGaedheal won sixty-three seats against a surprisingly strong forty-four seats for Sinn Féin. The fact that Cosgrave's governing party added only five seats in a contest that included twenty-five new constituencies, represented a disappointing showing, especially given the fact that Eamon de Valera and some 10,000 Republican activists were in jail and Sinn Féin was without an effective political organisation. Fortunately for Cumann na nGaedheal, Sinn Féin continued its abstentionist policy. But it was an approach which de Valera would depart from over time.

The results of the 1923 election indicated to de Valera that he still had a political future. It also led to his breaking with the rump that remained of Sinn Féin and the formation of the Fianna Fáil Party in 1926. That year de Valera entered the Dáil with forty-three other Fianna Fáil TD's, taking the same oath to the King over which he had helped provoke the Anglo-Irish Treaty split less than six years earlier. But de Valera's decision to enter the Dáil was driven by more than election returns alone. Ironically, they were pushed into doing so by the actions of the Cosgrave Government. The passage of the Public Safety and Electoral Act by the Dáil in August 1927, in the aftermath of the assassination of Kevin O'Higgins by an IRA faction, along with a Declaration of Emergency, severely shortened what slack remained on de Valera's political rope. Faced with the prospect of Fianna Fáil's election results being invalidated because of its policy of abstention, within a day of the Declaration of Emergency's passage de Valera announced that he and his colleagues would take the oath. Hence on 12 August, Fianna Fáil entered the Dáil as what Sean Lemass termed a 'slightly constitutional party'. Nonetheless it was the effective commencement of a parliamentary democracy reflecting all segments of opinion in the South, and the beginning of a decades-long rivalry in Dáil Éireann between Cosgrave's pro-Treaty party – later to become Fine Gael – and Fianna Fáil, with Labour continuing on as a weaker third force and sometimes Coalition partner.

During the Dáil Debate on the Emergency legislation, Ernest Blythe remarked that 'the object of the Government is to put a cold shiver of fear down the backs of the terrorists'. Cosgrave himself made clear his determination to suspend the Constitution in order to ensure in the long run that 'liberty would be retained'.[80] And so extremism in defence of freedom was now as stretched in Ireland, as an excuse by the party in power, as it would be elsewhere at other times in the twentieth century. Under the Public Safety Act (1927) the Free State Government was given the power to restrict freedom of the press, including proscription of the Republican organ *An Phoblacht*, which in its 25 August issue lashed out at the dead O'Higgins as 'a traitor who took Liam Mellowes and his comrades who were helpless in his power and murdered them on the Feast of the Immaculate Conception'.[81] Quite astutely, in a report sent to his superiors in the State Department, the then US Consul General in Dublin commented that, while the measure might give the Government the authority 'to prevent the publication of such statements ... it will not give them power to prevent men's [*sic*] cherishing such beliefs'.[82]

11

Epilogue

> We do not pretend to be able to do it [end partition] ... All we can do is try
> our best to bring about union but no one can say how it inevitably can be
> done. The question for us is how far we [the South] should deny ourselves in
> order to bring it about ...
>
> Remarks of Eamon de Valera before Dáil Éireann, 29 May 1935. *Dáil Debates*
> Vol. 56, pp. 2,112–2,116.

The role played by William T. Cosgrave in making it possible for Eamon de
Valera and his colleagues actually to enter the Dáil should not be eclipsed by
a fast-forwarding to the latter's decision to embark on a course driven by
political expediency. While it is not the intention of this chapter to chronicle
the history of the Irish Free State, certain events during the years 1923–27
require a wider discussion of its achievements.

The persona of Michael Collins continued to be felt in Ireland in the years
following his death. This was particularly the case within the ranks of the
Free State Government, and perhaps even more predictably in its army. As in
the Government's execution of its harsh Civil War policy in the aftermath of
Collins' death, Kevin O'Higgins continued as the Free State's dynamo, the
polar opposite to the retiring Cosgrave, who admitted himself to be 'no leader
of men'.[1] While the Government worked at home to rebuild the railways and
other elements of the country's infrastructure left in tatters by the Civil War,
O'Higgins proceeded to carve out an active role for the Free State within the
British Commonwealth.

Whether or not Cosgrave and his colleagues viewed Fianna Fáil's entry as a
source of long-term stability for the State, the fact was they did not move to
thwart their erstwhile opponents from entering the Dáil. The formation of
Fianna Fáil and its participation in the autumn 1927 election had a stabilising effect. It meant that neither the IRA nor the rump of the old Sinn Féin
organisation, who then rejected de Valera as leader, could claim to be the sole
heirs of the Republican orthodoxy. There was now a constitutional alternative, and – if only half-heartedly – de Valera and Fianna Fáil were part of
it. Ironically, this was perhaps the result that Collins had hoped to achieve by

engaging de Valera seven years earlier, in an electoral pact, prior to the out-break of the Civil War.

In the Dáil, as what Sean Lemass termed a 'slightly constitutional party', Fianna Fáil, under de Valera's stewardship, played at being both constitutional and Republican. They accepted the Free State Dáil as a necessary evil, holding on to a belief that the Second Dáil had been illegally disestablished. But within Leinster House the party developed a program in opposition that was not merely confined to the oath. It emphasised economic self-sufficiency both in agriculture and industry, and opposed the Cosgrave Government on issues involving tariff policy and old-age pensions.

Fundamentally, Cosgrave's Cumann na nGaedheal regime was a conservative one. Aside from its emphasis on maintaining law and order, the government adhered largely to a programme favouring free trade, and showed little willingness to embrace an activist role in social policy. With the exception of the Ard na Crusha Power scheme, designed to harness the River Shannon, there was little to be found in the actual record of the Cosgrave Government that was based on a reading of Collins' earlier broad plans for the country's economic and social development. But to the ever-lasting credit of the unassuming Cosgrave, there was a fundamental commitment to following the democratic process, even when it worked to his disadvantage.

In February 1932, with the country beset by high unemployment and relative economic stagnation, he was forced to fight another general election against de Valera. Taking seventy-two seats, Fianna Fáil became the largest party in the new Dáil. And through a coalition with Labor and other smaller parties, de Valera came to replace Cosgrave as the head of the Free State. A swift and peaceful transition ensued, with Cosgrave and his colleagues stepping aside without obstruction.[2]

There were also tests to the Cosgrave Government from within. Once again, the shadow of Collins could be felt. The time was the spring of 1924, when disgruntled officers in the Free State Army, who had served previously as members of Collins' elite assassination squad, set the stage for a mutiny. Ostensibly the officers, including Liam Tobin and Tom Cullen, held that the Government had betrayed Collins' commitment to lead the state towards an all-Ireland Republic. But below the surface, the core issues appear to have had more to do with preferment and the fact that these Collins loyalists believed that they had been shunted aside in favour of those who had entered the Army with no prior service in the independence struggle. The Government moved quickly to remove the malcontents. But Richard Mulcahy also fared badly in the events. Criticised on the one hand by O'Higgins for allowing the situation to develop in which the pro-Collins element felt free to manoeuvre, he was reviled on the other by the mutineers for having himself betrayed Collins' legacy. In the end Mulcahy resigned his post and, showing considerable restraint, began a period in political oblivion.* Britain itself was by this time ruled by a Tory administration, Lloyd George's Coalition having collapsed within a year of the signing of the Anglo-Irish Treaty. Indeed, the treaty was the overriding factor in the Coalition's demise, owing to back-bench Tory revulsion at the agreement. Now the British parties of all stripes had a new context in which to handle Ireland. As Deirdre MacMahon has astutely noted, the British

> tactic of getting Irish moderates to deal with Irish extremists was a hallowed one, certainly as old as O'Connell as in the case of the new Irish Free State the tactic had been a success. It resulted in ten years of comparatively har-monious relations with the Cosgrave government and only a minority of die-hard Tories were now heard to lament the Treaty and all it stood for. In 1932, Cosgrave and Cuman na nGaedheal symbolised stability and security to the British Government, and no British Minister of whatever party was inclined to tolerate a disturbance of the status quo. British officials felt a real gratitude and loyalty to Cosgrave and from the day that de Valera took office scanned the political horizon anxiously for signs of his return.[3]

The Boundary Commission

The pressures that weighed on Michael Collins at the end of his life were in no way eased by his awareness of the Boundary Commission's limitations. According to Kevin O'Shiel, the law advisor to the Free State Government, 'The late General never made any secret of his distrust in the Boundary Commission as a means of settlement per se.' O'Shiel quoted Collins as say-ing, 'The Boundary Commission will settle nothing.'[4] Those comments, of course, were totally at variance with Collins' public statements in support of the Boundary Commission as a basis for achieving Irish unity, uttered during the Dáil Debates on the Treaty, and afterwards with the establishment of the Provisional Government.[†] But perhaps even more compelling in relation to his attitude toward the Boundary Commission is O'Shiel's estimate that Collins knew that the problems of Northeast Ulster transcended whatever actions the Commission might take in the end.

> He realised that even after the Boundary Commission had sat and made its decisions, and even if those decisions conceded to us our ultimate claim there

---

* For a fuller account of the Army 'mutiny' consult Mary Valivuilius, *Richard Mulcahy*, (Dublin, 1992).
† According to an article published in An Phoblacht on December 4, 1925 in defence of the Treaty on February 4th, 1922, Collins made this claim: 'Under the Treaty, Ireland is about to become a fully constituted nation. The whole of Ireland as one nation is to com-pose the Irish Free State ... That is the whole basis of the Treaty.'

would still be an 'Hibernia Irredenta' [*sic*] to disturb the peace of future generations. Not only that, but there would be an increased feeling of intense hatred amongst the Northern Ireland secessionist populations [the Unionists] against the rest of Ireland. Though the territory of the Saorstat [state] might be broadened, the gulf between Saorstat and those populations would also be broadened. So fully aware of all this was the late General that on a number of occasions he went out of his way to establish contact with the Belfast Authorities in the hope that such contact would lead to a better and more enduring settlement between Irishmen.[5]

However, true to his penchant for duplicity in dealing with many of the problems he confronted at this time, in his role as leader of the Provisional Government Collins acted to persuade Catholic teachers in Northern Ireland to ignore the authority of the Department of Education in the Six Counties, offering the assurance that the Southern Government would fully compensate them whether they were *fired* or not. Likewise, in a further attempt to make Northern Ireland unworkable, he urged all County and Urban District Councils with a Nationalist majority to ignore the jurisdiction of the Northern Ireland Local Government Authority.[6]

Indeed, Collins' low expectations for the Boundary Commission may have driven him to conclude in his first pact with Sir James Craig to abandon the Boundary Commission, replacing it with representatives from the Southern and Northern Governments, who would then seek to conclude a private resolution of boundary disputes.[7]

Oddly enough, the death of Collins helped force the Boundary Commission into existence. Repression against Catholics in Northern Ireland intensified after he died, virtually without criticism by the British Government. But the Free State Government, now firmly in the hands of more moderate leaders, offered the Northern Nationalists little assistance, even after the end of the Civil War. Driven more by frustration than anything else, by mid-1923 Nationalist leaders in the North exhorted the Free State Government to call the Boundary Commission to order. Despite the advice of Kevin O'Shiel, the Cabinet's law advisor and the awareness that it was highly unlikely that the Commission would cede any significant new territory to the Free State, the Government moved forward nonetheless in favour of activating the body. The Irish Government, through its Boundary Commissioner Eoin MacNeill, in fact, lodged a maximum claim that would have reduced the Northern State to a land area containing only Eastern Tyrone, North Antrim, North Down and North Armagh. The Unionists for their part offered to exchange heavily Catholic and staunchly Republican South Armagh for the predominantly Protestant enclave of North Monaghan.

The three member Boundary Commission, chaired by the English-born South African jurist Richard Feetham, did not actually commence its investigations until November 1924. In effect, the pro-British Imperialist Feetham, a close friend of Lionel Curtis, a key adviser to the British cabinet, acted as tie-breaker between the Northern and Southern representatives. He opted for an interpretation of the intent behind Article XII of the Anglo-Irish Treaty which provided for the Boundary Commission. His interpretation heavily favoured the Unionist viewpoint and that of the by now Tory government. Feetham's finding left Northern Ireland essentially as it had been defined by the Government of Ireland Act (1920). By October 1925 by which time, the Commission had concluded its efforts, Bonar Law was succeeded by another Tory Prime Minister, Stanley Baldwin. Thus the combination of political circumstances in Britain, coupled with the fact that the longer the Northern Ireland State operated under the boundaries defined by the 1920 Act the less likely were those boundaries to be tampered with, militated against any concession to the Free State Government. Furthermore, as Michael Laffan has noted, the Free State government 'seemed less anxious to acquire the Catholic areas of the north than the unionists were to retain them, and it brought no comparable pressure to bear on the Commission'.[8] In effect, in Collin's absence, the Ulster Unionists felt no challenge from the South.

Although the official report of the Boundary Commission would not be published for decades, at the Free State Government's request, a leak of the agreement found its way into the pages of the pro-Tory organ, *The Morning Post* on 7 November 1925. That added to the embarrassment of the poor result the Free State had received. A last-ditch effort by Cosgrave to achieve a negotiated settlement with Craig and the British Government outside of the parameters of the Commission changed little from the situation as it had existed in 1921. In what was essentially a face-saving measure granted by the British to allow Cosgrave to ward off a domestic upheaval, the Free State was allowed a substantial reduction in the annual payments towards the Empire's public debt, as provided for under Article V of the Anglo-Irish Treaty. To Republicans in the South, the concession amounted to a 'Selling of the Six Counties for cash'. A lead article in *An Phoblacht*, the journalistic voice of Irish Republicanism, concluded:

> Every sign points to the fact that the F.S. [Free State] Ministers have lost the battle. Rather than take the nation into their confidence and organise against this British treachery as they organised in 1918 against Conscription, they have surrendered every road of the Six Counties to Sir James Craig ... thus themselves dishonouring the whole spirit of the 'Treaty' in whose name they executed seventy-seven Republican soldiers.[9]

As pointed as this statement was, it bears emphasis again that partition did not feature as a major point in the Republicans' early opposition to the Treaty. In fact, de Valera and Childers in 'Document 2' tacitly accepted a six-county state. But on the question of surrendering their claim for more territory in exchange for a reduction in their share of Britain's debt, the Free

State Government was nonetheless vulnerable. Kevin O'Higgins went so far as to concede that the allegation was probably more than half true.[10]

The final settlement of the border, as agreed between the Free State and the British Government, in conjunction with the Northern Ireland Government, was the same as that agreed to in 1921. It meant that 500,000 Nationalists, or more than one-third of the Six Counties' population, would remain within the confines of a jurisdiction they never wanted, and which for the most part they would refuse to accept as legitimate.* The Free State was freed from its obligations towards meeting the Imperial debt, but the Council of Ireland, the vaguely defined body that was the sole all-Ireland institution provided for under the Anglo-Irish Treaty, was abolished before it got off the ground. The latter action was a further concession by the British Government to the Craig regime. What powers the Council was to have had in agriculture, fisheries and other sectors were delegated to the separate departments in both the South and the North.

Whatever measure of short-term comfort the agreement may have afforded to its signatories, the record shows that it yielded a bitter harvest, not least within Northern Ireland itself. It did however, for the better part of five decades, alter the calculus of the Anglo-Irish conflict to the extent that the respective and successive governments in Ireland and Britain were able to 'confine' the problem to within the six-county entity itself. This would remain so until the combination of internal upheaval and external pressures would force the British Government to revisit the offspring it had midwifed called Northern Ireland, forcing it to impose direct rule in 1972.

Questions of identity

The outcome of the statutory partition of Ireland by Act of the British Parliament, which divided Ireland into two separate states, renders the warning given to the British Government in May 1916 by James Campbell, the Crown's Attorney General for Ireland and a southern Irish Protestant, eerily prescient against the backdrop of the conflict that raged in Northern Ireland for the last three decades of the twentieth century.

> Englishmen may well think that the experiment is worth the risk, but no Irishman who is conscious of the dreadful results that must inevitably follow from its failure can regard it as anything short of a desperate and dangerous gamble, while its success must permanently divide the Irish nation into two

---

* Fionnula O'Connor's study of the attitudes of a diverse slice of Northern Nationalists in *In Search of a State* (Blackstaff Press, 1994) provides a significant look at the question of nationalist identity in the context prior to the 1998 Good Friday Agreement.

hostile sections, each bearing the statutory brand of a distinctive religious sentiment. One side or the other is going to be deceived in this matter, with the inevitable consequences of bitter recrimination and renewed agitation.[11]

Indeed, rather than facilitate Ireland's 'essential unity', as some within the ranks of the British Government argued in advocating the creation of two separate states under the Government of Ireland Act (1920), the prospect of developing a sense of Irishness among Catholics and Protestants throughout Ireland was seriously weakened. Other factors had, of course, conspired before the imposition of partition by the British Government to make the fostering of a common sense of Irish identity in the twentieth century difficult. Whether intended or not, Daniel O'Connell's campaign in the previous century for Catholic emancipation resulted in a definition of what and who constituted the 'Irish people' as synonymous with Catholic Ireland. By the mid-nineteenth century, the United Irishman's vision of an Ireland that would see the end of 'all past dissensions and ... substitute the common name of Irishman in place of the denominations of Protestant, Catholic and Dissenter', was without any serious prospect of attainment. Conversely, the more the Catholic hierarchy came to be identified as leading on issues of concern to Irish Nationalism, as became particularly the case after the fall of Parnell, the less likely were Irish Protestants to consider themselves truly Irish. Cardinal Cullen's pronouncement that Irish Protestants were in his view foreigners and not part of Ireland, irrespective of the duration of their family's residence in the country, can only be viewed as counter-productive to the fostering of any sense of a common Irish identity. Eamon de Valera's choice of words was no more inclusive when he described Ulster Unionists during the War of Independence as 'not Irish people'.[12]

At the same time, a progression of events saw a more confident and inspired Irish Catholic community by the end of the nineteenth century embrace Irish cultural and social movements, including the Irish language and especially Gaelic games. These provided a sense of Irishness that held a wider appeal for Catholics. Nonetheless, it was partition as an active policy of the British Government that ensured a divided Ireland socially, culturally, and politically. Partition was not devised by Britain to keep two warring tribes apart. As we have seen from the earlier analysis of the drafting of the Government of Ireland Act (1920) the six-county state and its border were drawn in order to ensure Unionist hegemony. Such hegemony would not have been possible for long in a nine county Ulster where Catholics would be in the clear majority. From the initial drawing of the border, there evolved the long-standing practice of the gerrymandering of electoral boundaries to ensure Protestant control over communities that were predominately Catholic. Ironically, the fact that Northern Nationalists of a more Republican bent adhered to a long-standing policy of abstention from the

Northern Ireland Parliament at Stormont and the regime's government departments probably guaranteed even greater overall discrimination against Nationalists.[13]

Consequently, accepting the reality of a Southern State that effectively cut itself off from the Nationalist population of Northern Ireland, just as Northern Unionists had already embarked upon developing their own political model without their Unionist brethren in the historic Province of Ulster's other three counties, the leaders of the Irish Free State went in their own direction after the Irish Civil War. Successive Irish governments, regardless of their Civil War politics, made use of the independence the South had gained to develop an official Irish identity modelled after some of the original 'Irish Ireland', ideas of the late nineteenth-century Dungannon clubs and the original Sinn Féin movement. The Irish language was given a special place in the new State and the Nationalist and Republican aspects of Irish history and culture were emphasised not only in the rhetoric and symbols of the new state but also in the school curriculum. Hence, while still influenced greatly by many British institutions, an independent Irish identity had the chance to take root in the Free State.[14]

While partition in the short run led to acclaim for the British Government at home and beyond, it purchased conflict and outright embarrassment for Britain in the future. Churchill's contention that an essentially benign British Government had been forced to devise the partition plan that emerged out of what he characterised as Irish recalcitrance, best epitomised by his description of 'the dreary steeples of Fermanagh and Tyrone' is disengenuous at best. While the British statesman spoke of the 'integrity of the quarrel' within the population of Northern Ireland, that quarrel was exacerbated all too often by British policy, rather than ameliorated to any genuine extent.[15]

The recent conflict which has raged in Northern Ireland for more than three decades has its origins to a great extent in the events that occurred and the decisions made during the years 1919–21. At the same time the legacy of the Irish Civil War itself must be seen as conflict between ideological commitment to the ideal of an Irish Republic and political pragmatism. In essence, military leaders like Michael Collins and Richard Mulcahy gained a place for those advocating Irish independence at the conference table not out of an unquenchable resolve that there should be an independent Irish Republic, but because they developed tactics that were based on a realistic understanding of the limits of their resources. In gross terms it can be stated that Michael Collins shot his way to the Conference table at No. 10 Downing Street, even though he would rather not have gone himself. Perhaps more graphically, much to the chagrin of Eamon de Valera and Cathal Brugha, who thought the Irish cause should be served by a more ennobling type of warfare, Collins and his adherents seized and held Britain's attention by a steady diet of assassinations and ambushes. The point was not lost on the later incarnation of the IRA in its campaign in Northern Ireland and Britain itself. But by the early 1990s, political violence in the context of Northern Ireland came to be seen as counterproductive by the Republican leadership. That it took so long for this realisation to occur, resulting in the needless deaths of so many, has compounded the tragedy of 'the Troubles'.

Writing more than a decade after the signing of the Anglo-Irish Treaty, Frank Pakenham speculated on how the future historian might assess its effect on Ireland.

> The universal historian will be moved to few congratulations. For he will feel certain that the Treaty, signed as it was, must always have divided Ireland with bitter discord, torn her with conflict between cruel exacting loyalties, and so preserved her for a space for the British Commonwealth with an economy of lives.[16]

As this writer pens the conclusion to this volume some eight decades after that Treaty was signed, another British Government, with the involvement of the Government of an independent Twenty-Six-County Irish Republic, grapples with history and the future in the search for peace by creating new instrumentalities that include provision for cross-border institutions between the two parts of Ireland and participation in a Council for Ireland, Northern Ireland, England, Scotland and Wales. The 1998 Anglo-Irish Agreement demonstrated an understanding on the part of all British political parties that another Agreement seeking to contain the Anglo-Irish problem exclusively within the boundaries of a six-county Northern Ireland state is no longer acceptable. For its part the Irish Government, supported by the vast majority of the electorate in the Irish Republic, removed the Constitutional claim to the territory of Northern Ireland, replacing it in 1998 with aspirational language.

Yet more needs to be said in a historical context about the evolution of a culture of partition on both sides of the Irish border. While the Northern Ireland government embarked with a free hand to fashion a Protestant state for a Protestant people, to the virtual exclusion of Catholics within the six counties from positions of power within the regime, and aided unwittingly by the decision of many Nationalist leaders to abstain as far as possible from participating in the life of Northern Ireland, successive Governments in Southern Ireland – albeit with far less sectarian intent – proceeded to build institutions driven by a strongly Catholic ethos.

In a provocative analysis of this period and the years that followed, Ronan Fanning has written that for the South 'the achievement of sovereignty took precedence over the aspiration to unity in the minds of those who controlled the destiny of independent Ireland. And the exclusivist values of that independent Ireland – exclusive at least of Protestant opinion north and south of the border in that they were professedly Catholic.'[17] No substantial differences were to be found between Cosgrave's Cumann na nGaedheal Party [later Fine Gael] and de Valera's Fianna Fáil on the relationship between the Irish State and the Catholic Church. But while the Constitution that governed the Irish Free State was a direct product of the 1921 Anglo-Irish Treaty, the Constitution which Eamon de Valera was able to enact when in power in 1937 was able to reflect Catholic teachings within the letter of the law on matters ranging from divorce to education. The document defining an independent Ireland thereby equated Irishness with Catholicism.

Conversely, in Northern Ireland partition provided for the development of a governmental and cultural view that saw this section of Ulster as almost exclusively 'British', and which denied a sense of Irish identity: British symbols were held up while Irish culture was ignored; in state schools Irish history was at best glossed over. But Northern Catholics by and large continued to cling to their identity. In essence, as a substantial minority within the six-county regime, Northern Catholics were able to maintain a separate existence within Northern Ireland, even though their status was characterised by glaring inequalities, particularly in relation to access to private and public sector employment opportunities, and voting rights.

Within fifty years of Northern Ireland's formation, another British Government found it necessary to abolish the Stormont Government and impose direct rule from Westminster, after internecine violence and some of the worst excesses of the Unionist regime rendered local autonomy for Northern Ireland untenable. Direct rule from Westminster would last twenty-eight years. Since the 1921 Anglo-Irish Treaty, there have been several other measures affecting the balance of Anglo-Irish relations. In 1948 the Republic of Ireland Act, enacted by Dáil Éireann, effectively removed the Twenty-Six-County Southern State from the British Commonwealth. Britain countered in the following year with the Ireland Act, in which Northern Ireland's constitutional position as part of the United Kingdom was formally guaranteed. The measure also shut the door on any prospect of those counties with a Nationalist majority being able to opt out of a Northern Ireland state in favour of the Republic by its affirmation that 'in no event will Northern Ireland or any part thereof cease to be part of His Majesty's Dominions and of the United Kingdom without the consent of the Parliament of Northern Ireland'.** The language was no doubt offensive to all political parties in Dublin. But in reality the Republic of Ireland Act, while providing the South with greater sovereignty, produced an outcome in which Irish unity was even less likely. Although the Republic of Ireland Act was enacted not under a Fianna Fáil Government, but under the leadership of John A. Costello's Fine Gael-led

---

* Provision for the re-implementation of direct rule and the suspension of the institutions of the 1998 agreement by the British Government continues.
** See appendices for this and other relevant Anglo-Irish documents since 1920.

Inter-Party Government, its philosophy was consistent with de Valera's. The main parties in the Irish Republic, while opposing partition as a matter of record, were determined at the same time by their actions to take no steps that would show even the most moderate elements of Northern Ireland's Unionists, or the Northern Nationalists whose interests they claimed to espouse, that they would seek to end partition by accommodation. In fact, fourteen years earlier, de Valera rejected outright arguments that Fianna Fáil's policies in the South should reflect a desire not to render Northern Unionists more hostile:

> We do not pretend to be able to do it [end partition] ... All we can do is try our best to bring about union but no one can say how it can inevitably be done. The question for us is how far we should deny ourselves in order to bring it about ...[18]

And yet, in his last visit to London as Prime Minister of Ireland in 1958, de Valera implied to the British Government that in exchange for an end to partition he would support Ireland's re-entry into the British Commonwealth. There were no British takers, however, perhaps because de Valera's suggestion was proferred not as a direct proposal from him, but more by an inference that the British Government should initiate it.[19] Such a suggestion by de Valera indeed appears supremely incongruous, given the fact that he more than anyone else helped perpetuate the division within the ranks of Irish Nationalism that resulted in the brutal and draining Civil War that followed his rejection of the Anglo-Irish Treaty thirty-eight years earlier. Nonetheless, it was de Valera who during the 1921 Anglo-Irish negotiations sought to advance the notion of 'external association' with the British Empire as an alternative to Dominion status. Given the path which India, Zimbabwe and more recently South Africa have travelled within the British Commonwealth, while emerging to the status of a Republic, de Valera's external association concept was indeed ahead of its time from the standpoint of the Commonwealth's evolution. While the issue of the Irish Republic's re-entry into the British Commonwealth has been revisited as a topic in recent years, receiving the tacit support of Irish ex-President Mary Robinson, such an occurrence is highly unlikely given the Republic's position within the European Union, and the hope that new cross border institutions within the island of Ireland itself will lead to a deeper sense of cooperation and understanding. In short, there is no impetus within the Irish Republic for British Commonwealth re-entry.

In the 'Downing Street Declaration', announced by the Irish and British Governments on 17 December 1993, another Conservative Government stated that it held 'no selfish strategic or economic interest in Northern Ireland'.[20] This marked a significant departure for a party that had whole-heartedly supported the partition of Ireland for three quarters of a century.

To some Unionist leaders the Downing Street Declaration left their position within the Union not unlike that of the devoted spouse who is assured of their partner's affection but is then told 'But of course darling, if you want to go I won't stop you.'

By the mid-1990s events in Northern Ireland saw such unprecedented developments as an American official intervention, a Presidential visit, and the willingness of the British Tory and Labour governments for the first time to accept outside intervention in Northern Ireland, first via the international panel on the decommissioning of paramilitary weapons headed by former US Senator George Mitchell, following ceasefires by the Provisional IRA and their loyalist counterparts; Mitchell later as chairman of the all-party talks that produced the 1998 'Good Friday' Agreement. The heightened focus which Northern Ireland has occupied in Anglo-Irish relations, particularly since 1992, gives fresh meaning to Lord Rosebery's contention that the Irish question 'never passes into history because it never leaves politics'. But for British Prime Minister Tony Blair, elected in 1997, it has meant a lion-hearted effort to alter that dictum.

The complexity of the matters to be dealt with, not the least of which continues to include the accommodation of the identities of both Catholics and Protestants in Northern Ireland, and the relationship of Northern Ireland Protestants to the island itself, makes a clear-cut solution still quite difficult. Such considerations of identity require an attempt at analysis here. Despite having a separate state with a guaranteed Protestant majority since its inception, under-written by successive British Governments, Northern Ireland Unionists have projected the image of a threatened minority on the island. As Garret FitzGerald has aptly noted, theirs has not been the image of 'a secure majority within Northern Ireland'.[21] That insecurity, in addition to outright bigotry, was often at the bottom of the effort to keep Northern Ireland Catholics in the position of second-class citizenship throughout the fifty-two-year existence of the Stormont regime. Conversely, for FitzGerald, a former Taoiseach and Irish Foreign Minister, intimately involved in the shaping of both the Sunningdale Agreement (1974) and the Anglo-Irish Agreement (1985), those Unionist insecurities have been 'contrasted vividly with the manner in which at an equally fundamental level ... Southern nationalists after the establishment of their state, quickly lost any real sense of living within an all-Ireland context'.[22]

The ready conversion to the Twenty-Six-County state has ironically served to create a dynamic in which Southern Nationalism has in its own way helped consolidate the island's partition. FitzGerald provides a useful and personal illustration of this development. 'From the time the state was founded', he writes, 'its laws and practices were moulded along partitionist, but not ... sectarian lines, that made no allowance for and were found to alienate Northern unionists.' While the state's founders (in Cumann na nGaelheal) saw Irish as an essential subject in national schools, FitzGerald asks 'was any thought given by my father [Desmond FitzGerald] or any of his colleagues in that administration to the effect this [compulsory Irish] would have in reinforcing the newly created border?' 'The further reinforcement', he adds, 'of these measures by that first government's decision to make Irish an essential subject for entry and promotion within the public sector served brutal notice on Northern Unionists – and indeed in practice on most Northern Nationalists also – that so far as the administration of a united Ireland might be concerned, they would be likely to be second class citizens, effectively excluded from public office.'[23]

Given the high level of expenditure annually by Britain in administering Northern Ireland, and the lingering sense of dependency those expenditures have fostered the Irish Republic's overall insulation from the 'Troubles' may have aided its economic rebirth as well as political stability. The disintegration of the former nations of Czechoslovakia and Yugoslavia due to ethnic hatred in recent times is offered an example of the kind of calamity the Irish Republic has thus far been able to avoid. It begs the question of whether, in the eyes of the Republic's main political parties, de Valera's Fianna Fáil included, re-unification is a goal to be prayed for but never actively pursued.

From an economic standpoint, the Irish Republic overtook Northern Ireland long ago in the industrial sector. Its membership in the European Union since 1972 has been a contributing factor to a new-found confidence that has marked an end to its economic dependence on Britain. By 1998 the Irish Republic had for several years been the fastest-growing economy in Europe. Ironically, by the mid 1990s, more British firms were located in the Irish Republic than in Northern Ireland. Indeed in 1997 the Republic's manufacturing output was about twice that of Northern Ireland, a complete reversal of how things had stood in 1960. In the area of computer software 'localisation' the Republic is now second only to the United States, globally.

In effect, the island of Ireland's economic needs and realities helped to drive forward a political solution to the Northern Ireland conflict and free both parts of the island from decades of political baggage. One writer has commented with particular astuteness on the economic realities encompassing both parts of Ireland.

> Economic logic is beginning to offer an all-island future in a way very different from that imagined by Irish nationalists. Growth corridors, firm networks, industrial clusters and state-led initiatives must come if the North is to turn itself round. It is not because the Republic needs the six counties that there will be new political structures in Ireland; but because the six counties need the South to break out of decline. The challenge is to manage this process politically; but it has rarely looked more obvious.[24]

But again, such a discussion unavoidably raises the question of how much the Irish Republic, and its political establishment in particular, desires the creation of a united Ireland? From 1922 Anglo-Irish relations, and the relationships between the greater number of Irish Catholics and Irish Protestants, was largely defined by the Anglo-Irish Treaty (1921) and the Government of Ireland Act (1920). At the same time, the evolution of an independent Ireland within a twenty-six-county state, together with the role the Republic of Ireland plays within the European Community and the international community at large including the UN Security Council, is testimony to the state's resilience as a democratic entity. In April 1994 an international trade and tariff agreement was hammered out under the leadership of a former Irish Attorney General and European Commission member, Peter Sutherland. Significantly, the British Government joined the rest of the European Community in supporting an agreement that was the fruit of the Irishman's labours. Overall, the economic achievements of the Irish Republic in the last decade of the twentieth century may finally be bearing witness to Michael Collins' prediction that an independent South would with time overtake the British-dependent North. It remains to be seen whether such a development may offer a further stimulant to some form of pan-Irish federation motivated by practical considerations.

In 1996 an electrical transformer that helps generate electricity on a cross-border basis was reconnected, following the first ceasefire declared by the Provisional IRA on 29 August 1994. The transformer had been blown up by the IRA on several prior occasions during the conflict. Other, more substantive North–South ties involving the island's tourism, agriculture, and economic development agencies under new cross-border bodies appear likely. Indeed, there was evidence of this before the 1998 Anglo-Irish accord. In February 1996, the scientific agencies of the Republic and Northern Ireland established a formal cooperative focus for technology development under the RADIAN program (Research and Development in Ireland America North), funded by the International Fund for Ireland and driven by Irish – American software entrepreneur John Cullinane, a supporter of then US President Bill Clinton. Soon after a formal working partnership in the two health departments on the island came into effect.

The 1993 Downing Street Declaration issued by the Irish and British Governments clearly established a parameter according to which the Constitutional status of Northern Ireland will not change unless a majority there desire it to. This position was solidified by the 1998 Good Friday Agreement between the two Governments, which was ratified in a June referendum that year by vast majorities on both sides of the border. Of great significance was the overwhelming approval by a majority in the Irish Republic of the removal of the territorial claim to Northern Ireland, inherent since 1937 in the Irish Constitution and its replacement with aspirational language.

The 1998 Agreement expresses a commitment to 'partnership, equality and mutual respect on the basis of relationships within Northern Ireland, between

North and South, and between these islands' (From 'Declaration of Support'; contained in the 1998 Anglo-Irish Agreement). It provides for the replacement of British direct rule, in force since the abolition of the Stormont Parliament in 1972, with a 108-seat assembly and Cabinet-style government led by a First Minister. While the amendments of Articles 2 and 3 of the Irish Constitution were aimed at assuaging longstanding Unionist fears about the intentions of the Irish government, the creation of a North–South ministerial council under the Agreement, with specified executive responsibilities, was received by most Nationalists in Northern Ireland as proof that the 1998 agreement at long last had recognised their Irish identity.

Against this backdrop a Northern Ireland state may yet emerge that will be antithetical to the sectarian society designed by James Craig and his fellow Unionists, with British acquiescence, eight decades earlier.

Recognising the great distances yet to cover, virtually all the signatories to the 1998 Accord characterised the document as 'an agreement', but not a settlement. For most Unionists there is security to be derived from the formal acceptance of the Irish government, and the Nationalist signatories to the document from within Northern Ireland, that the constitutional status of Northern Ireland will not change without the consent of a majority within it. For Nationalists there is the willingness to hope, based on the creation of new institutions, that Northern Ireland can be reformed into a society where equality at all levels will become a reality.

Are those sentiments incompatible with the aspirations of the Unionist tradition in Northern Ireland? In the words of Seamus Heaney, will 'hope and history rhyme' within a space where hope will indeed be able to grow? As a new order is being set in motion often against severe stumbling blocks and the persistence of sectarian hatred, the author asks the reader to hear the words of Edward Carson, arch-defender of the union, directed to Winston Churchill in the House of Commons on 24 April 1914. As uncharacteristic as they may appear in relation to the Carson we have seen earlier, his words have relevance to the possibilities for the Ireland that may yet come to pass.

> If Home Rule is to pass, much as I detest it, and little as I will take the responsibility for the passing of it, my earnest hope, and indeed I could say, my earnest prayer would be that the Government of Ireland for the South and West [sic] would prove and might prove such a success in the future, notwithstanding all our anticipations, that it might even be for the interests of Ulster itself to move forward that Government, and come in under it and form one unit in relation to Ireland. May I say something more than that? I would be glad to see such a state of things arising in Ireland in which you would find mutual confidence and good will between all classes in Ireland as would lead to a stronger Ireland in a federal scheme.

The attainment of steady progress will require more from all the parties involved. With it must come an acceptance of the need for developing strong cross-border links throughout Ireland in such areas as economic development.

In the end, the ongoing need for economic growth throughout the island of Ireland is more likely to spur cooperation than the bromides and violence that have helped to poison relations among people on both sides of the border. Such an evolution must be encouraged further by the British and Irish Governments.

The full development of the island of Ireland's economic potential has been deeply affected by the Northern Ireland conflict. The 'Troubles' that raged in both communities brought forth various forms of strife and malevolence for much of the period from 1969 to 1996. That conflict indeed found its roots in the events chronicled in this discussion of the Irish Revolution, and in the British attempts to deal with that conflict in a way that proved ineffective. The decline in sectarian violence since 1997, combined with the creation of new bodies for governance within Northern Ireland, offers a harbinger that lasting peace may be on a shore that is not too distant. From the pain endured by all sections of the communities in Northern Ireland may thus come wisdom as well as a realisation by those that have killed and maimed that they must cease forever.

As US President Bill Clinton shared a platform with British Prime Minister Tony Blair during his second visit to Northern Ireland in September 1998, an inkling that these sentiments could find new meaning came from Northern Ireland's First Minister David Trimble, the leader of the Ulster Unionist Party. In words doubtless constructed to ameliorate Sir James Craig's stark declaration that the parliament he headed in Northern Ireland would rule solely for a 'Protestant people', the Northern Ireland Assembly would represent instead a 'pluralist Assembly for a pluralist people'.

Many instances during the years 1969 to 1996 in particular fed a cycle of violence and despair fuelled by paramilitary and official acts of violence. Some official acts of violence continue a legacy of pain among nationalists especially given that some actions were accompanied by a persistent pattern of official denial and cover-ups. Most notable was the killing of fourteen unarmed civilians shot dead in cold blood on the streets of Derry in January 1972 by British paratroopers. At the time of writing a new inquiry is underway. The horror of the episode was encapsulated by SDLP Party leader John Hume who has stood out as a voice of non-violence and common sense throughout the conflict: 'This was the only atrocity justified and ratified by the state. Its victims were vilified. These were all innocent people. It traumatised the whole island.'

As Ireland moves further into a new century it does so less quietly than it entered the last one. On much of the island we have seen how an independent Ireland fuelled in its early days by a spirit driving towards an 'Irish Ireland', has taken root economically and is now part of a greater European community. Ireland, through its citizens, whether as part of independent Irish humanitarian aid organisations or through the work of Irish religious orders, is also making a significant contribution to the world community. Its army has long been regarded as an effective peace-keeping force; indeed, no single day in the past four decades has passed without an Irish peace-keeping presence in some corner of the globe. Britain itself is now a partner with the Irish Republic in a new Europe.

On 26 November 1998 Tony Blair became the first Prime Minister to address both houses of the Irish Parliament. 'After keeping us apart for so long,' Blair stated, 'Northern Ireland is now helping to bring us closer together.' At the same time he noted that Northern Ireland should not be allowed to 'define the relationship between us'.[25] But while Irish and British interest transcend Northern Ireland on many fronts, the fact remains that for some time Northern Ireland will continue to define relations between the Irish and British peoples.

On 13 December 1999 Armagh City was the host of the Inauguaral Meeting of the North South Ministerial Council. The occasion marked the first time in Irish History that a body with a North–South political mandate met. The Council for Ireland provided for in the Government of Ireland Act(1920) was never implemented owing to unionist political manoeuvring, while a similar body called for in the 1973 Sunningdale Agreement died with the collapse of that agreement itself. Indeed many of the features of Sunningdale, including the requirement for power sharing within a Northern Ireland Executive were resurrected with the Good Friday Agreement. It is indeed a matter of great sadness that, between the collapse of the Sunningdale Agreement and the signing of the 1998 Good Friday Agreement, more than 2,500 men, women and children died on all sides in Northern Ireland, most of them killed by loyalist and Republican paramilitaries.

As tenuous as it is, the new dispensation now under way in Northern Ireland has been driven by the slow building of trust between unionism and nationalism. This building process must take place within Northern Ireland itself first and then in the island as a whole.

Only time and the behaviour of the residents of Northern Ireland towards each other will tell if they are ready and willing to give positive effect to the intent of the Good Friday Agreement as a vehicle for enabling them to share the same space. Or will they pull each other back to the abyss? Not unlike other conflicts where divided peoples inhabit the same piece of earth the essence of what has been conveniently called the 'constitutional question' in Northern Ireland remains territory. A clear need remains for more enlightened leadership from the grass roots up who will help in large part to determine whether Northern Ireland in the early part of the twenty-first century will actually undergo conflict resolution for the good of all or conflict transformation in which one population replaces the other with a crude majority.

Such leadership, more so than the promising prose of any agreement struck between political parties and governments, will also help end the culture in which gains made by one community are viewed as proof of the downfall of the other. And in that vein, for Ulster unionism in particular, the question remains as to whether its own leadership will reach a sufficient level of generosity to accept that what was a 'cold house' for nationalists does indeed require more than cosmetic alteration in the interest of all and that shared institutions point to the best way for stability. The slow but steady introduction of normal politics to Northern Ireland has allowed it to belatedly join the rest of the island in entering global society.

In the early days of the twenty-first century, the island that for most of the previous one had been one of the most conservative societies has become one of the most outward looking. The pace and scope of international investment cited earlier have helped serve as a mid-wife to this development perhaps more so than any other factor. The sheer volume of that investment has spawned an Ireland that would be unrecognisable to the founders of the Irish independence movement and perhaps quite at variance with Arthur Griffith and the original Sinn Féin movement's adherence to its doctrine of 'Ourselves Alone'. At the same time the widespread evidence of political and corporate corruption that has accompanied the pace of change and modernisation in the Republic would likewise be a source of dismay to many of the original shapers of the Irish independence struggle.

This volume has focused on the circumstances that produced the 1921 Anglo-Irish Treaty, which in essence has defined the political identity of Ireland until the last days of the twentieth century. The new institutions for governance set up under the 1998 agreement are the product in large measure of an independent Irish Government negotiating on an equal footing with its British counterpart. Indeed the international context in which this agreement was arrived at, driven by the need for an inclusive settlement in the interest of all communities on the island of Ireland, stood in stark contrast to the circumstances which pertained to the Anglo-Irish negotiations of eight decades ago. This author believes that evolution of the relationship between Ireland and Britain is made evident by the documents found at the end of this book which outline the efforts made at finding a lasting settlement over the course of the twentieth century. In the meantime the obligation to hope does indeed continue.

Notes

Preface

1. *Winston Churchill, Vol. IV, 1916–1922*, ed. Martin Gilbert (Boston, 1969), pp. 190–201 *passim*.

Chapter 1

1. James Fintan Lalor, letter in *The Irish Felon*, 24 June 1848, reprinted in *James Fintan Lalor* (Dublin, 1918), pp. 59–65.
2. Rudyard Kipling 'Ulster 1912' as published in the *Morning Post*, 9 April 1912, cited in A. Mitchell and P. O'Snodaigh (eds), *Irish Political Documents 1869–1916* (Dublin, 1989), pp. 134–5.
3. A. T. Q. Stewart, *The Ulster Crisis* (London, 1966), p. 141.
4. James Carty (ed.), *Ireland: From Famine to Treaty*, Vol. 3 (Dublin, 1958), p. 95.
5. Oliver MacDonagh, *Ireland: The Union and its Aftermath* (London, 1979), pp. 78–9.
6. F. S. L. Lyons, *Ireland Since the Famine* (London, 1971), pp. 102–3.
7. Brian Murphy, 'Pearse and 1916', *Irish Times*, 18 October 1990.
8. Ibid.
9. Erhard Rumpf with A. C. Hepburn, *Nationalism and Sovereignty in Ireland* (Liverpool, 1977), p. 165.
10. Ibid.
11. J. J. Lee, *Ireland 1912–1985: Politics and Society* (New York, 1989), p. 19.
12. Donal McCartney, 'The Sinn Féin Movement', in Kevin B. Nowlan (ed.), *The Making of 1916: Studies in the History of the Rising*, p. 311.
13. 'Gaelic Athletic Association Convention at Thurles', Report by Inspector A. W. Waters, cited in W. F. Mandle, *The Gaelic Athletic Association and Irish Nationalist Politics 1884–1924* (London, 1987), p. 10.
14. Thomas Markham, cited in the *Irish Press*, 14 April 1934, p. 56.
15. Richard Davis, *Arthur Griffith and Non-Violent Sinn Féin* (Dublin, 1974), p. 9.
16. F. X. Martin, 'The Origins of the Irish Rising of 1916', in Desmond Williams (ed.), *The Irish Struggle, 1916–1926* (Toronto, 1966), p. 4.
17. Roy Foster, *Modern Ireland, 1600–1972* (London, 1988).
18. Ibid., p. 57.
19. *An Claidheamh Soluis*, 8 November 1913.

20. Ibid.
21. Davis, *Arthur Griffith*, p. 33.
22. McCartney, 'The Sinn Féin Movement', p. 33.
23. Arthur Griffith, *The Resurrection of Hungary: A Parallel for Ireland* (Dublin, 1918), p. 116–19.
24. Ernie O'Malley, *The Singing Flame* (Dublin, 1978) p. 278.
25. Ibid.
26. Cited in Patrick O'Farrell, *Ireland's English Question: Anglo-Irish Relations, 1534–1970* (New York, 1971), p. 231.
27. Ibid., p. 231–2.
28. Sean Cronin, *Irish Nationalism: A History of its Roots and Ideology* (Dublin, 1980), p. 109.
29. James Carty (ed.), *Ireland from the Great Famine to the Treaty, 1851–1921*, Vol. III (Dublin, 1958), p. 111.
30. Ibid.
31. Joseph McGarrity Papers, National Library of Ireland, letter of Tom Clarke to McGarrity, November 1914.
32. MacDonagh, *Ireland*, p. 49.
33. Ibid.
34. Ibid., p. 55.
35. Collins to Barret, 9 Aug. 1919, Military History Bureau A/6362.
36. Pearse to Devoy, *loc. cit.* (Eire/Ireland), p. 54.
37. Ibid, p. 54.
38. Bulmer Hobson, *Ireland Yesterday and Tomorrow* (Tralee, 1968), p. 70.
39. Ibid.
40. Ibid.
41. Ibid., p. 74.
42. It is unclear, however, if all seven actually assented to the Easter Proclamation, since a signed copy has not been found to date.
43. Sean Cronin, 'Connolly's Great Leap in the Dark', *The Capuchin Annual*, 1977, p. 309.
44. Tom Garvin, *Nationalist Revolutionaries in Ireland 1858–1928* (Dublin, 1986), p. 55.
45. Memorandum from Walter Long to Cabinet, 19 May 1916, CAB 37/150.
46. Thomas Coffey, *Agony At Easter: The 1916 Uprising* (New York, 1969), pp. 254–5.
47. Sean O'Mahoney, *Frongoch: University of Revolution* (Dublin, 1987), p. 62.
48. T. Ryle Dwyer, *Michael Collins: The Man who Won the War* (Cork, 1990), p. 24.
49. Walter Long to British Cabinet, 19 May 1916.
50. Memorandum of James Campbell to Cabinet, 24 June 1916, CAB 37/150.
51. *Irish Worker*, 14 March 1914.
52. Records of the Irish Convention, The Horace Plunkett Papers, National Library of Ireland.
53. George Dangerfield, *The Damnable Question: A Study in Anglo-Irish Relations* (Boston, 1976), p. 249.
54. Liam de Paor, *On the Easter Proclamation and Other Dedications* (Dublin, 1997), p. 28.
55. 'To My Daughter Betty, The Gift of God', by Thomas Kettle, as published in *The Easter Rising* (London, 1968), p. 100.
56. O'Farrell, *Ireland's English Question*, pp. 282–3.
57. Garvin, *Nationalist Revolutionaries*, p. 278.
58. Ibid., p. 277.
59. Joost Augusteijn, 'The Importance of Being Irish: Ideas and the Volunteers', in David Fitzpatrick (ed.), *Revolution? Ireland 1917–1923* (Dublin, 1990), p. 31.

60. Ibid., p. 7.
61. De Valera Papers, Franciscan Institute for Celtic Studies and Historical Research, Killiney, County Dublin.
62. Dwyer, *Michael Collins*, p. 32.
63. See Tim Pat Coogan's *De Valera: Long Fellow, Long Shadow* (London, 1993), pp. 95–6.
64. Ibid.
65. Diarmuid Lynch, *The I.R.B. and the 1916 Insurrection* (Cork, 1957), p. 33.
66. P. S. O'Hegarty, *The History of Ireland Under the Union* (New York, 1951), p. 719.
67. Ibid.
68. Ibid., pp. 488–91.
69. Max Beloff, *Imperial Sunset*, Vol. I, *Britain's Liberal Empire, 1897–1921* (New York, 1970), p. 317.
70. John McColgan, *British Policy and the Irish Administration, 1920–1922* (London, 1983), p. 1.

Chapter 2

1. Keith Middlemas, *Politics in Industrial Society: The Experience of the British System Since 1911* (London, 1979), p. 108.
2. Henry Duke to Lloyd George, 22 March 1918, HCRO, Lloyd George Collection F/37/4/10, cited in Sheila Lawlor, *Britain and Ireland 1914–23* (Totowa, NJ, 1983) p. 16.
3. Henry Duke to Lloyd George, 16 April 1918, HLRO, Lloyd George Collection F/37/4/51.
4. From Report of Ulster Unionist delegates to Irish Convention, 5 April 1918.
5. Horace Plunkett to Lloyd George, 8 April 1918, Irish Convention Report Cd. 9019.
6. Dangerfield, *The Damnable Question*, p. 281.
7. Minutes of Sinn Féin Standing Committee, 6 May 1918, cited in Lawlor, *Britain and Ireland*, p 21.
8. Lionel Curtis, 'Ireland', *The Round Table*, Vol. 20 (June 1921), p. 485.
9. Christopher M. Andrew, *Her Majesty's Secret Service: The Making of the British Intelligence Community* (New York, 1987), p. 249.
10. Ibid., p. 50.
11. See Command Paper No. 1108, 'Documents Relative to the Sinn Féin Movement', and No. 1326, 'Bolshevism and Sinn Féin' (His Majesty's Stationery Office).
12. US Consul Charles Hathaway to US Secretary of State, 12 September 1918, US Legation, Files 841.00/94.
13. Ibid.
14. Patrick Kavanagh, *The Green Fool* (London, 1938 [1971]), p. 104.
15. Sinn Féin 1918 general election Manifesto.
16. See Statement of John Dillon as reported in the *Irish Independent*, 26 November 1918.
17. *Irish Times*, 30 November 1918.
18. Kavanagh, *Green Fool*, pp. 107–8.
19. John A. Murphy, *Ireland in the Twentieth Century* (Dublin, 1975), pp. 4–5.
20. P. S. O'Hegarty, *The Victory of Sinn Féin: How it Won it and How it Used it* (Dublin, 1924).
21. Dan Breen, *My Fight for Irish Freedom* (Dublin, 1981), p. 27.
22. Ibid.
23. Davis, *Arthur Griffith*, p. 168.

24. Breen, *My Fight*, pp. 27–9.
25. Ibid.
26. Ibid.
27. Piaras Béaslaí, *Michael Collins and the Making of a New Ireland* (New York, 1926), Vol. I, p. 270.
28. Ulick O'Connor, *Oliver St. John Gogarty* (London, 1964), p. 185.
29. Curtis, 'Ireland', p. 480.
30. Frank Pakenham, *Peace By Ordeal* (London, 1972), p. 39.
31. Curtis, 'Ireland', *The Round Table* (June 1921).
32. Ibid.
33. *An t-Oglach*, 31 January 1919.
34. Frank Barrett to Michael Collins, 1 August 1919; Military History Bureau; A/6362, Dublin.
35. Michael Collins to Frank Barrett.
36. Augusteijn, 'The Importance of Being Irish', p. 41.
37. See Peter Hart, 'Youth, Culture and the Cork IRA' in Fitzpatrick (ed.), *Revolution?*, p. 13.
38. Breen, *My Fight*, p. 21.
39. Thomas McGrath, *Pictures from Ireland* (1889), pp. 170–4 cited in *Garvin, Nationalist Revolutionairies*, p. 102.
40. George A. Birmingham, *An Irishman* (London, 1926), pp. 135–6.
41. See Coogan, *De Valera*, p. 137.
42. Ibid.
43. Conor Cruise O'Brien, *The Atlantic Monthly*, July 1994.
44. Mr Lindsay to Earl Curzon, 28 June 1919; Records of the British Legation in the United States, F.O. 414/243.
45. Mr Lindsay to Earl Curzon, 5 March 1920, F.O. 417/246.
46. Sir Auckland Geddes to British Foreign Office, 23 November 1920, F.O. 371/4559.
47. Cited in Coogan, *De Valera*, p. 195, F.O. 371/424, p. 195.
48. See J. M. MacCarthy (ed.), *Limerick's Fighting Story* (Tralee, 1966), p. 60.
49. Charles Townshend, *The British Military Campaign in Ireland 1919–1929* (London, 1975), p. 65.
50. Ibid.
51. *Parliamentary Debates* (Lords), Vol. 58 (1921), Col. 2038.
52. Ibid.
53. P. S. O'Hegarty to Óglaigh na h-Éireann, 18 March 1921, Mulcahy Collection, UCD, P7A/5.
54. Ibid.
55. Ibid.
56. *Parliamentary Debates* (Hansard), Vol. 134 (18 November 1920), col. 2115.
57. Ibid., 22 July 1920.
58. D. G. Boyce, *Englishmen and Irish Troubles British Public Opinion and the Making of Irish Policy* (Cambridge, 1972), p. 58.
59. British Cabinet Minutes, 21 April 1921.
60. Notes of Walter Hume-Long from Meeting of Irish Situation Committee, April 1920, CAB 23/22.
61. British Cabinet Minutes, 15 August 1919, CAB 23/15.
62. Ibid.

63. Dáil Éireann Minutes, 29 January 1920.
64. See McCartan, *With De Valera in America*, pp. 216–250.
65. *Documents Relative to the Sinn Fein Movement*, Cmd. 1108 (1921), and I.B.C. p. 361.
66. C. J. C. Street ('I. O.' pseud.) *Ireland in 1921* (London, 1922), p. 361.
67. Ibid.
68. Ibid.
69. Michael Laffan, '*Labor Must Wait: Ireland's Conservative Revolution*', in Patrick Cornish, (ed.), *Radicals, Rebels and Establishments* (Belfast, 1985).

Chapter 3

1. Anthony Clayton, *The British Empire as a Superpower 1919–1929* (Athens, GA, 1984), p. 88.
2. Arthur Mitchell, *Revolutionary Government in Ireland: Dáil Éireann 1919–1922* (Dublin, 1995), p. 154.
3. Report of Sir Warren Fisher to the British Government, 3 May 1920, HLRO Lloyd George Papers F/33/1.
4. Charles Townshend, *The British Campaign in Ireland, 1919–1921: The Development of Political and Military Policies* (London, 1975), p. 25.
5. Long to A. F. Blood, 16 June 1920, cited in Richard Murphy, 'Walter Hume Long and the Making of the Government of Ireland Act', *Irish Historical Studies*, Vol. XXV, No. 97, May 1986, p. 95.
6. Long to Cardinal Bourne, 11 May 1918 (Long Papers, WRO 947/161), cited in ibid.
7. Long to Lloyd George, 18 June 1920, Long Papers, WRO 947/240 cited in ibid.
8. Report of the Committee on the Government of Ireland Act Amendment Bill, 4 November 1919, C.P. 56, CAB 27/68.
9. 'Ulster and Home Rule: No Partition of Ulster', Statement by Delegates for Cavan, Donegal and Monaghan. PRONI, Montgomery Papers D 627/435 cited in A. C. Hepburn, *The Conflict of Nationality in Modern Ireland* (New York, 1980), p. 118.
10. Joseph Lee, *Ireland 1912–1985: Politics and Society* (Cambridge, 1989), p. 44.
11. Nicholas Mansergh, *The Irish Question, 1840–1921* (London, 1965), p. 330.
12. Ibid.
13. Ibid.
14. *The Times*, 18 May 1920.
15. Charles Mowat, *Britain Between the Wars, 1918–1940* (Chicago, 1955).
16. Lloyd George in the House of Commons, 11 November 1920: Hansard 5 CXXXIV pp. 1430–1, 1433–4.
17. John W. Wheeler-Bennett, *John Anderson, Viscount Waverley* (New York, 1962), p. 60.
18. Joseph Curran, *The Birth of the Irish Free State 1921–1923* (Alabama, 1980), pp. 371–424.
19. Wheeler-Bennett, *John Anderson*, p. 62.
20. Ibid., p. 62–3.
21. Clayton, *The British Empire as Super Power*, p. 90.
22. Richard Bennett, *The Black and Tans* (London, 1959), p. 31–8, and pp. 92–131.
23. Street, *Ireland in 1921*, pp. 214–15.
24. Tom Barry, *Guerilla Days in Ireland* (Dublin, 1949), p. 23.

25. Ibid.
26. Hayden Talbot, *Michael Collins' Own Story* (London, 1923), pp. 124–5.
27. Frank Crozier, *Ireland for Ever* (London, 1932), p. 218.
28. Irish Situation Committee, Minutes, 20 July 1920, with notes by W. H. Long, CP 1672, CAB 27, Vol. 107.
29. Ibid.
30. From Report of British General Staff in Ireland to Irish Situation Committee, 15 June 1920, CP 1467, CAB 24, Vol. 107.
31. Tom Jones, *Whitehall Diary*, K. Middelmas (ed.) (London, 1969) Vol. III, p. 18.
32. Ibid., p. 19.
33. Ibid., pp. 19–20.
34. Ibid., p. 17.
35. Sinn Fein Bulletin, 13 July 1920, cited in Dorothy MacArdle, *The Irish Republic: A Documented Cronicle of the Anglo-Irish Conflict and the Partitioning of Ireland* (New York, 1965), pp. 359–61.
36. Ibid.
37. Ibid., p. 359.
38. Bennett, *The Black and Tans*.
39. Telegram of Chief Secretary for Ireland to Lord Privy Seal, 22 June 1920, CAB 27/107.
40. Dáil Loan prospectus issued by Dáil Éireann, 1919, and Dáil Éireann Files, SPO.
41. Jones, *Whitehall Diary*, Vol. III, p. 33.
42. Bennett, *The Black and Tans*, p. 68.
43. See letter of Terence MacSwiney to Michael Collins, Dáil Éireann Files, SPO.
44. Jones, *Whitehall Diary*, Vol. III, p. 33.
45. Ibid.
46. Dáil Loan Prospectus issued by Dáil Éireann in 1919, Dáil Éireann Files, SPO.
47. *Irish Times*, 1 May 1920.
48. Records of Conversation by Walter Long, Irish Situation Committee, 30 June 1920, S.I.C. 3, CAB 27, Vol. 108.
49. General Sir Neville Macready to Sir Hamar Greenwood, 17 July 1920; Lloyd George Collection, HLRO File 19/2/2.
50. Ibid.
51. Sir John Anderson to Sir Hamar Greenwood, 20 July 1920; Lloyd George Collection, HLRO 19/2/14.
52. Ibid.
53. Sir John Anderson to the Cabinet, 25 July 1920; CO 904/188.
54. Ibid.
55. Memorandum of General Neville Macready to Irish Situation Committee, 26 July 1920, and 6 August 1920, C.O. 904/188.
56. 'Extracts from the Conclusions of a meeting of the Cabinet', 13 August 1920; CAB 23/22.
57. Letter of Complaint Submitted by RIC Rank-and-File at Athlone Station Depot to Police Executive under General Tudor, August 1920, C.O. 904.
58. Ibid.
59. Michael Farrell, *Northern Ireland, The Orange State* (London, 1976) p. 91.
60. W. E. Wylie, Law Advisor to the Irish Administration, Memorandum to Hamar Greenwood, September 1920.
61. 'Survey of Conditions in Ireland', for week ending 30 August 1920, C.O. 904/168.

62. *Cork Examiner*, 28 September 1920.
63. Ibid.; Mowat, *Britain Between the Wars*, p. 73.
64. Meda Ryan, *The Real Chief: The Story of Liam Lynch* (Cork, 1986), p. 49.
65. Diary of Sir Henry Wilson, 29 September 1920.
66. *The Times*, 28 September 1920.
67. *Cork Examiner*, 30 October 1920.
68. Statement of C. A. Walsh, Deputy Inspector General RIC undated, from fall 1920, C.O. 904/168.
69. Remarks of Sir Hamar Greenwood to Dublin Agents of RIC, fall, 1920, undated; C.O. 904/168.
70. Notes of a Conference held at 10 Downing Street, 1 October 1920; C. A. B. 23/22.
71. Sir John Anderson's Files, Irish Executive, C. O. 904/168.
72. Ibid.
73. Crozier, *Ireland for Ever*, pp. 220–1.
74. Letter of J. S. Callister to Arthur Griffith, October 1920, (undated) Sir John Anderson's Files, C. O. 904/168.
75. Adjutant General Oglaigh na h-Éireann General Headquarters, November 9, 1920/ Captured document in files of Sir John Anderson, C. O. 904/168.
76. Florence O'Donoghue, *No Other Law* (Dublin, 1986), pp. 154–5.
77. See David Nelligan, *Spy in the Castle* (Dublin, 1979) and also account of Sean Kavanagh in Kenneth Griffith and Timothy O'Grady (eds), *Curious Journey: An Oral History of Ireland's Unfinished Revolution* (London, 1982), pp. 135–7.
78. Breen, *My Fight*, pp. 165–6.
79. Letter of Kevin Barry, undated, while awaiting execution at Mountjoy Jail, National Museum of Ireland.
80. Piaras Béaslaí, *Michael Collins and the Making of a New Ireland* (New York, 1926), Vol. II, p. 67.
81. Report of Dublin Metropolitan Police, 21 November 1920; C. O. 904/168.
82. 'Bloody Sunday', Account of Mrs. B. C. P. Keenlyside, 21 November 1921, C. O. 904/168.
83. Ibid.
84. C. S. Andrews, *Dublin Made Me: An Autobiography* (Dublin, 1979), p. 151.
85. Ibid.
86. Talbot, *Michael Collins' Own Story*, p. 93.
87. Ibid.
88. From 'Report on the General Situation in Ireland by the General Officer Commanding-In-Chief for week ending 27 November 1920' (CAB 27/107).
89. Wheeler-Bennett, *John Anderson*, p. 73.
90. Irish Situation Committee Report, 27 November 1920, CAB 27/107.
91. *Freemans Journal*, 22 November 1920.
92. W. F. Mandle, *The Gaelic Athletic Association and Irish Nationalist Politics, 1884–1984* (London, 1987), p. 193.
93. Ibid.
94. Crozier, *Ireland for Ever*, p. 148.
95. CAS 27/107, Report of General Macready to the Irish Situation Committee, 27/11/ 1920.
96. Ibid.
97. Ibid.

98. Report of Sir Hamar Greenwood to the Irish Situation Committee, 22 November 1920 (CAB 27/107).
99. Michael Collins to Richard Mulcahy, 7 April 1922; Military History Bureau, Irish Department of Defence.
100. Sir Auckland Geddes to Foreign Office, 24 November 1920; Public Record Office, London, A8224.
101. Foreign Office 'Minutes' for 29 November 1920; Public Record Office, London A8313.
102. Ibid.
103. Macready, Report to Irish Situation Committee, 27 November 1920 (CAB 27/107).
104. Files of Sir John Anderson, C. O. 904/168.
105. Tom Barry, *Guerilla Days in Ireland*.
106. Ibid., p. 44.
107. British Cabinet Minutes, 5 December 1920.
108. Michael Hopkinson, *Green Against Green: The Irish Civil War* (Dublin, 1988), pp. 10–11.
109. Crozier, *Ireland for Ever*, p. 179.
110. Ibid., p. 177. See also Piaras Béaslaí, *Michael Collins and the Making of a New Ireland*, Vol. I (Dublin, 1926), pp. 103–6.
111. Irish Situation Committee Weekly Survey, 20 December 1920, CAB 27/107.
112. Mark Sturgis' Diary, 14 December 1920, PRO, London.
113. Ernie O'Malley, *Raids and Rallies* (Dublin, 1982), p. 91.
114. General Macready to Irish Situation Committee, 25 December 1920, CAB 27/107.

Chapter 4

1. Mowat, *Britain Between the Wars*, p. 81.
2. *The Times*, 20 November 1920.
3. *Irish Independent*, 20 October 1920.
4. See Alan J. Ward, *Ireland and Anglo-American Relations, 1899–1921* (London, 1969), pp. 238–9. Also, F. M. Carroll, 'All Standards of Human Conduct: The American Commission on Conditions in Ireland 1920–1921', *Eire/Ireland*, Vol. 16 (Fall 1981), p. 59.
5. See William Maloney's Memorandum on Washington Commission on British Atrocities cited in McCartan, *With De Valera in America*, pp. 259–62.
6. See Carroll, 'All Standards of Human Conduct', p. 65.
7. Geddes to Foreign Office, 16 September 1920, FO 371/4552. Sir Auckland Geddes, British Ambassador to the US, 1920–24, served prior to that as Minister of National Service in Lloyd George's Coalition Government, 1917–18, and as President of the Board of Trade, 1919. His brother, Sir Eric Geddes, was appointed on 16 August 1921, to head a committee of leading British business leaders to make recommendations on the economic recovery policies the Coalition Government should pursue.
8. Mary MacSwiney travelled for the Commission on a multi-city US tour articulating the cause of Irish Nationalism. Her travels in the US spanned both coasts, including visits as far south as New Orleans.
9. See *Interim Report, American Commission on Conditions in Ireland, 1921*, pp. 99–101.
10. F. M. Carroll, 'All Standards of Human Conduct'.
11. See *Report of the Labor Commission to Ireland*, Jan. 1921, p. 1.

12. Ibid., p. 65.
13. Ibid., p. 56.
14. Ibid.
15. See Middlemas, *Politics and Industrial Society* (London, 1959), pp. 166–7.
16. See Report on the Situation in Ireland, by the General Officer Commander-in-Chief for the week ending 1 January 1921, CAB 27/107, p. 27, declassified secret document S.I.C. 68.
17. See *Report of the Labour Commission to Ireland* (London, 1921), pp. 6–7.
18. MacCarthy, *Limerick's Fighting Story*, p. 203.
19. Ibid., pp. 199–218; see also Crozier, *Ireland for Ever*, p. 290.
20. See Crozier, *Ireland for Ever*, Appendix to letter of Michael Fogarty, Bishop of Killahoe to General Crozier, 24 October 1930.
21. Wheeler-Bennett, *John Anderson*, p. 72.
22. Sir John Anderson to Bonar Law, Lord Privy Seal, 5 November 1920, CO 904/188.
23. Ibid.
24. Bonar Law to Sir John Anderson, 9 November 1920, CO 904/188; 'Conclusions of a Meeting of the Cabinet held in Bonar Law's Office', 6 December 1920, CAB 23/22.
25. Memorandum of C. J. Phillips, British Foreign Office Intelligence Department, 19 November 1920, Lloyd George Collection, HLRO, 102/7/6.
26. Henry Wickham Steed, *Through Thirty Years, 1982–1922* (London, 1924), p. 353.
27. Ibid., pp. 353–8.
28. *The Times*, 10 November 1920.
29. 'Conclusions of a Meeting of the Cabinet held at Bonar Law's Room', 6 December 1920, CAB 23/22.
30. Memorandum of Fr Michael O'Flanagan to British Government, 26 January 1921, Lloyd George Collection, HLRO, F/19/3/2.
31. Lloyd George Collection, HLRO, F/19/3–F/102/6.
32. Ibid.
33. Ibid.
34. Lloyd George to Hamar Greenwood, 2 December 1920, HLRO, F/102/6/2.
35. Talbot, *Michael Collins' Own Story*, p. 123.
36. Ibid.
37. Telegram of Basil Clarke to C. J. C. Street, 16 December 1920; Lloyd George Collection, HLRO, 102/6/16.
38. Memorandum of Michael Collins as Minister of Finance to Dáil Éireann, 31 December 1920, Mulcahy Collection, UCD Archives.
39. Dáil Éireann Report, released 15 February 1921, State Papers Office (hereinafter referred to as SPO), Dáil Éireann Files.
40. Superintendent of London Police, Intelligence Department to Home Secretary, 5 January 1921, Lloyd George Collection, HLRO, F/46/9/19.
41. H. Greenwood to Lloyd George, 26 January 1921, Lloyd George Collection, HLRO, F/19/3/2.
42. Memorandum of Fr Michael O'Flanagan to British Government, 26 January 1921, Lloyd George Collection, HLRO, F/19/3/2.
43. H. Greenwood to Lloyd George.
44. Ibid.
45. J. T. Davies to Irish Situation Committee, 12 February 1921, Lloyd George Collection, HLRO, F/181/1/1.
46. Michael Collins to P. O'Keefe, 21 January 1921, SPO/Dáil Éireann Files.

47. Dáil Éireann Files, private sessions, January 1921.
48. Ibid.; See also Jones, *Whitehall Diary*, Vol. III, pp. 45–8 for a wider focus on the British version of these events.
49. Jones, *Whitehall Diary*, Vol. III, p. 47.
50. See letter to Sir John Anderson, 2 November 1920, CO 904/188.
51. Jones, *Whitehall Diary*, Vol. III, p. 48.
52. Ibid., pp. 49–50.
53. Ibid.
54. David Lloyd George to Sir Hamar Greenwood, 25 February 1921, Lloyd George Collection, HLRO F/19/13/4.
55. Talbot, *Michael Collins' Own Story*, p. 135.
56. Ibid., p. 135.
57. León Ó Broin, *W. E. Wylie and the Irish Revolution* (Dublin, 1989), pp. 77–81.
58. Ibid.
59. O'Malley Collection UCD Archives, 17A/132.
60. Ibid.
61. Ibid.
62. O'Malley Collection, UCD Archives, 17a/107. Óglaigh Na h-Éireann January 1921, Instructions on Training of Active Service Units from IRA General Headquarters.
63. Ibid.
64. 'Short Digest of Mr. Charles Dumont's [American Consul, Dublin] Report No. 195 of March 24, 1921', Records of US Legation, State Department Files, 841.00/340.
65. Ibid.
66. Report of US Consul, 23 April 1921, Records of US Legation, State Department Files, 841.00/351.
67. Ibid.
68. Ibid.
69. Ibid.
70. Todd Andrews, *Dublin Made Me* (Dublin, 1979), p. 144.
71. Wheeler-Bennett, *John Anderson*, p. 73.
72. See Christopher Andrew, *Her Majesty's Secret Service* (London, 1987), p. 255.
73. Sturgis' Diary, 5 March 1921, PRO, 39/50–60.
74. Ernie O'Malley, *On Another Man's Wound* (Dublin, 1978), p. 294.
75. Irish Situation Committee, CAB 27/108 and CAB 24.
76. Wheeler-Bennett, *John Anderson*, p. 75.
77. Sturgis' Diary, 16 February 1921, PRO, 35/50–60.
78. Ibid.; See also Michael Hopkinson (ed.), *The Last Days of Dublin Castle: The Diaries of Mark Sturgis* (Dublin 1999), p. 39.
79. Ibid.
80. Uinseann MacEoin, *Survivors: The Story of Ireland's Struggle as Told Through some of Her Outstanding People* (Dublin, 1987), p. 502.
81. Sturgis' Diary, 5 March 1921.
82. Michael Collins's Interview with Carl Ackerman, *Philadelphia Bulletin*, 21 April 1921.
83. Sturgis' Diary, 6 March 1921.
84. Ibid.
85. See Ryan, *The Real Chief*, p. 60.
86. Bennett, *The Black and Tans*, p. 178.
87. Memorandum of Richard Mulcahy, IRA Chief of Staff, 7 March 1921; Mulcahy Collection, UCD Archives, P7/A/32.

88. Ibid.
89. Richard Mulcahy to Michael Collins, 16/3/21; Mulcahy Collection, UCD, P/A/13, Nos. 43–8.
90. Michael Collins to Richard Mulcahy, 21 March 1921; Mulcahy Collection, UCD P/A/13, Nos. 43–8.
91. Tom Barry to Adjutant General, IRA General Headquarters, 21 March 1921, Mulcahy Collection, UCD, P7/A/13, Nos. 43–50.
92. General Headquarters Staff, 'The War as a Whole', 24 March 1921, Mulcahy Collection, UCD P7/A/32.
93. Ibid.
94. Ibid.
95. Ibid.
96. IRA General Headquarters Analysis of British Civil Service Expenditures in Ireland through period ending 31 March 1921. Military History Bureau, Irish Department of Defence.
97. Ibid.
98. Sturgis' Diary, April 1921, PRO 39/50–60.
99. Ibid.
100. Ibid.
101. Ibid. See p. 55 of Sturgis' Diary for 1921, PRO 39/50–60.
102. Rory O'Connor to Richard Mulcahy, 4 April 1921, Mulcahy Collection, UCD, P7/A/B.
103. Ibid.
104. O'Malley Collection, UCD, 132/17A.
105. Sturgis' Diary, undated for April 1921, PRO 39/50–60.
106. Sturgis' Diary, 17 May 1921, PRO 39/50–60.
107. Sturgis' Diary, 26 May 1921.
108. Ibid.
109. Military History Bureau, Irish Department of Defence.
110. Account of Vincent Byrne, in An t-Óglach, Custom House Memorial Issue, Vol. I, No. 5, 1962.
111. Ibid.
112. From a letter given to the author by a relative.
113. O'Broin, W. E. Wylie, p. 47–53.
114. See Neville Macready, Annals of an Active Life (London, 1925), Vol. II, p. 53.
115. 'Ireland and the General Military Situation', Memorandum by Worthington-Evans, 24 May 1921, C. P. 2964, CAB 23, Vol. 108.
116. Report of No. 1 Brigade, 1st Northern Division, to IRA General Headquarters, 5/22/2/, Military History Bureau.
117. Richard Mulcahy to Brigade Commander, East Connemara, 1 June 1921. Mulcahy Collection, UCD Archives.
118. M. Collins to R. Mulcahy, 15 April 1921, Mulcahy Collection, UCD Archives.
119. Richard Mulcahy to Brigade Commander, East Connemara, 1 June 1921, Mulcahy Collection, UCD Archives.
120. IRA General Headquarters memorandum 30/6/21, Military History Bureau Files, Irish Department of Defence.
121. Mid-Clare Brigade Commander to Mulcahy, Military History Bureau Files, 30/6.
122. General Order issued by Richard Mulcahy, June 1921, Mulcahy Collection, UCD Archives.

123. IRA 3rd Battalion, Galway Brigade C.O. to General Headquarters, 29 May 1921, Mulcahy Collection, UCD, P7/A/18–31.
124. Communication from West Connemara Brigade IRA to General Headquarters, 14 February 1921, Mulcahy Collection, UCD, 7/A16–20.
125. Richard Mulcahy to Commandant, Kilkenny Brigade, 1 June 1921, Mulcahy Collection, UCD Archives.
126. Reports of Dublin Brigade IRA to General Headquarters, 15–18 June 1921, Military History Bureau, Irish Department of Defence.
127. Richard Mulcahy Memorandum from General Headquarters, Mulcahy Collection, UCD Archives.
128. Report of Cork No. 3 Brigade, 7 June 1921, to General Headquarters, Military History Bureau, Irish Department of Defence.
129. Report of Dublin Brigade IRA, June 1921, to General Headquarters Military History Bureau, Irish Department of Defence.
130. Mulcahy Collection, UCD Archives, 7/A13–14.
131. Sturgis' Diary, June 1921, PRO 39/50–60.
132. Ibid.
133. Curtis, 'Ireland'.
134. See Jones, *Whitehall Diary*, Vol. III, p. 227.
135. Lionel Curtis, 'Ireland'.
136. Ibid.
137. Ibid., p. 507.
138. Macready to Cabinet, May 1921, CAB 27/108.
139. Winston Churchill, *The World Crisis, 1919–1928: The Aftermath* (London, 1929), p. 294.
140. Mulcahy papers, UCD P7/A.
141. Report of O/C Dublin Brigade to IRA General Headquarters, 30 May 1921, Mulcahy Collection, UCD, P7/A/19–32.
142. Mulcahy Collection, P7/A/49, UCD Archives.
143. Collins to Mulcahy, 21 June 1921, Mulcahy Collection, UCD Archives.
144. Rory O'Connor to General Headquarters, 3 June 1921, Mulcahy Collection, P7/A/13–19.
145. Ibid.
146. Ibid.
147. Mulcahy to Collins, 10 June 1921, May 1921, P7/A19–32, Mulcahy Collection, UCD.
148. Mulcahy to Collins, 10 June 1921.
149. Ibid.
150. Richard Mulcahy to Sligo Brigade Commander, May 1921, Military History Bureau, P7/A/28–32.
151. Mulcahy Collection, UCD, P7A/19.
152. Manuscript of Sean O'Muirithile, p. 141, Mulcahy Collection UCD.
153. Memorandum of Dublin Castle Executive to British Cabinet, 23 September 1920, CO 904/168.
154. Manuscript of Sean O'Muirithile, pp. 141–2; Mulcahy Collection, UCD.
155. Irish Intelligence Summary, Report No. 259, 1 July 1921, Lloyd George Collection, HLRO, F/46/9/25.
156. Ibid.
157. Ibid.

158. Sturgis' Diary, July 1921, PRO 39/51–60.
159. Ibid.
160. Ernie O'Malley, *The Singing Flame* (Dublin, 1978), p. 16.

Chapter 5

1. From an account in The *Freeman's Journal* of an address by Thomas Johnson, 17 October 1919.
2. Adrian Pimley, 'Working Class and Revolution, 1896–1923', in D. G. Boyce (ed.), *The Revolution in Ireland, 1879–1923* (London, 1988), p. 205.
3. Ibid., p. 210.
4. Austen Morgan, *James Connolly: A Political Biography* (Manchester, 1988), p. 173.
5. Ibid., p. 98.
6. Charles Desmond Greaves, *The Life and Times of James Connolly* (New York, 1976), p. 420.
7. MacDonagh, *Ireland: The Union and Its Aftermath*, p. 76.
8. Ibid.
9. Morgan, *James Connolly*, p. 196.
10. Ibid.
11. MacDonagh, *Ireland*, pp. 80–1.
12. Ibid., p. 81.
13. Sean Cronin, *Irish Nationalism* (Dublin, 1980), p. 110.
14. Sean Cronin, *Young Connolly* (Dublin, 1978), pp. 35–6, 110.
15. D. G. Boyce, *Englishmen and Irish Troubles: British Public Opinion and the Making of Irish Policy* (Cambridge, 1972), pp. 30–59.
16. See James Connolly, *Labour in Ireland* (Dublin, 1917).
17. Patrick Lynch, 'The Social Revolution That Never Was', in Williams, *The Irish Struggle*, p. 45.
18. Cronin, *Irish Nationalism*, p. 110.
19. J. J. Lee, *The Modernization of Irish Society 1848–1914* (Dublin, 1973), p. 151.
20. Michael Laffan, 'Labour Must Wait: Ireland's Conservative Revolution', in Patrick Corish (ed.), *Radicals, Rebels and Establishments* (Belfast, 1985), p. 212.
21. Paul Bew, 'Sinn Fein, Agrarian Radicalism and the War of Independence, 1919–1921', in D. G. Boyce (ed), *The Revolution in Ireland* (London, 1988), p. 220.
22. David Fitzpatrick, *Politics and Irish Life, 1913–1921: The Provincial Experience of War and Revolution* (Dublin, 1977) p. 207.
23. Ibid., pp. 207–8.
24. From Statement of Irish Labour Party National Executive, *Voice of Labour*, 9/11/1918.
25. Ibid.
26. See Brian Farrell, 'Labour and the Irish Political Party System: A Suggested Approach to Analysis', in *The Economic and Social Review* (Fall 1970), pp. 477–502.
27. From Statement of Irish Labour Party National Executive, Vol. 1, *Voice of Labour* 9/11/1918.
28. Report of the Irish Labour Party and Trades Union Congress, 1918, p. 168.
29. Farrell, 'Labour and the Irish Political Party System'.
30. Report of Irish Trades Union Congress 6–8 August 1917, as cited by Brian Farrell, 'Labour and the Irish Political Party System'.
31. See Emmet O'Connor, *Syndicalism in Ireland: 1917–1923* (Cork, 1989).

32. Ibid.
33. Ibid.
34. Ibid.
35. Pimley, 'Working Class and Revolution', p. 208.
36. Laffan, 'Labour Must Wait', p. 217.
37. Pimley, 'Working Class and Revolution', p. 211.
38. D. R. O'Connor Lysaght, *The Republic of Ireland: An Hypothesis in Eight Chapters and Two Intermissions* (Cork, 1970), p. 63.
39. Ibid.
40. Farrell, 'Labour and the Irish Political Party System', pp. 487–9.
41. Ibid.
42. Presidential Address of Fr Michael O'Flanagan to Sinn Féin Convention, 14 October 1938, cited in 'Labour and the Irish Political Party System', p. 487.
43. Lysaght, *Republic of Ireland*, p. 62.
44. Ibid.
45. Ibid., p. 64.
46. Greaves, *James Connolly*, p. 167.
47. John A. Murphy, *Ireland in the Twentieth Century* (Dublin, 1975), p. 9.
48. Ibid.
49. Boyce, *Nationalism in Ireland*, p. 327.
50. Ibid.
51. Lysaght, *Republic of Ireland*, p. 63.
52. Laffan, 'Labour Must Wait', p. 204.
53. J. C. McCracken, *Representative Government in Ireland* (Oxford, 1948), pp. 33–4.
54. Laffan, 'Labour Must Wait'.
55. Lysaght, *Republic of Ireland*, p. 64.
56. Murphy, *Ireland in the Twentieth Century*, p. 9.
57. Pearse, Patrick, *The Sovereign People* (Dublin, 1916).
58. Proceedings of Dáil Éireann 1919–1921, pp. 22–3 cited in A. Mitchell and P. O'Snodaigh, *Irish Political Documents 1916–1949* (Dublin, 1985), pp. 59–60.
59. Murphy, *Ireland in the Twentieth Century*, p. 10.
60. Lynch, 'The Social Revolution that Never Was', p. 46.
61. Greaves, *James Connolly*, p. 167.
62. Dáil Debates, January 1919.
63. Murphy, *Ireland in the Twentieth Century*, p. 10.
64. Rumpf and Hepburn, *Nationalism and Socialism in Twentieth Century Ireland* (Liverpool, 1977), p. 24.
65. Boyce, *Nationalism in Ireland*, p. 173.
66. Lynch, 'Social Revolution', p. 41.
67. Henry Patterson, *The Politics of Illusion: Republicanism and Socialism in Modern Ireland* (London, 1989), p. 10, 18.
68. Pimley, 'The Working Class Movement and The Irish Revolution, 1896–1923', p. 212.
69. Henry Patterson, *Politics of Illusion*, p. 11.
70. Michael Brennan, *The War in Clare 1911–1921: Personal Memoirs of the Irish War of Independence* (Dublin, 1980), cited in Hopkinson, *Green Against Green*, p. 45.
71. Patterson, *Politics of Illusion*, p. 15.
72. Laffan, 'Labour Must Wait', p. 205.
73. *Dáil Decree*, 29 June 1920.

74. Peadar O'Donnell, in *An Phoblacht*, 15 November 1930.
75. Patterson, *Politics of Illusion*, p. 15.
76. Rumpf and Hepburn, *Nationalism and Socialism*, p. 55.
77. Patterson, *Politics of Illusion*, p. 15.
78. David Fitzpatrick, 'The Geography of Irish Nationalism,' *Past & Present*, No. 78 (February 1978), p. 119.
79. Pearse, *The Sovereign People*.
80. Darrel Figgis, *Recollections of the Irish War* (New York, 1925), p. 293.
81. David Fitzpatrick, 'Strikes in Ireland, 1914–1921' in *Saothar: The Journal of the Irish Labour History Society* No. 6 (1980), pp. 87–101.
82. See Emmet O'Connor 'Agrarian Unrest and the Labour Movement in County Waterford 1917–1923 in *Saothar Journal of Irish Labour History Society*, No. 6 (1980).
83. Fitzpatrick, 'Geography of Irish Nationalism', p. 32.
84. Laffan, 'Labour Must Wait', p. 214.
85. James McDonagh, Acting Minister for Labour to the Cabinet, S.P.O. Dáil Éireann Files DE/2/5.
86. Emmet O'Connor, *Syndicalism in Ireland 1917–1923* (Cork, 1989), p. 148.
87. Jacqueline Van Voris, *Constance Markievicz: Cork. In the Cause of Ireland* (Amherst, 1967), p. 297.
88. O'Connor, *Syndicalism in Ireland*, p. 92. See also SPO Dublin, Dáil Éireann MSS, Department of Labour report, 19 May 1921, DE/2/5.
89. Proceedings of Dáil Éireann, 23 August 1921. Also see O'Connor, *Syndicalism in Ireland*, p. 92.
90. *Irish Bulletin*, 29 November 1921.
91. Van Voris, *Constance Markievicz*, p. 298.
92. Constance Markievicz Memorandum to Cabinet, 1921, State Papers Office DE2/483.
93. See Pimley, 'Working Class and Revolution', p. 209.
94. Arthur Mitchell, *Labour in Irish Politics* (New York, 1974), p. 212.
95. *Freeman's Journal*, 19 June 1920.
96. *ITUC Report*, 1921.
97. *Irish Times*, 27 May 1920.
98. *Freeman's Journal*, 6 June 1920.
99. *Irish Times*, 7 June 1920.
100. *Freeman's Journal*, 12 June 1920.
101. British Cabinet Papers, CAB 23/22; CAB 24/109; C.P. 1891.
102. Ibid.
103. Ibid.
104. Jones, *Whitehall Diary*, Vol. III, p. 32.
105. CAB 24/109 cited in Charles Townshend 'The Irish Railway Strike of 1920', *Irish Historical Studies* (March, 1979) p. 276.
106. CAB 27/108 and C.O. 904/157 cited in Townshend 'The Irish Railway Strike of 1920', p. 277.
107. *Freeman's Journal*, 17 November 1920.
108. *Irish Times*, 17 November, 1920.
109. *Freeman's Journal*, 3 December 1920.
110. 'Report of the Irish Trade Union Congress' (Dublin, 1921), pp. 7–70 passim.
111. Ibid.
112. Ibid.

113. Ibid.
114. Ibid.
115. Ibid.
116. Ibid.
117. Ibid.
118. Ibid.
119. Townshend, 'Irish Railway Strike', p. 281.
120. Béaslaí, *Michael Collins*, Vol. II, p. 38.
121. O'Donoghue, *No Other Law*, p. 79.
122. Michael Collins to William O'Brien, 6 July 1921, National Library of Ireland.
123. Michael Collins to Art O'Brien, 6 July 1921, National Library of Ireland.
124. Jones, *Whitehall Diary*, Vol. III, pp. 58–9.
125. Captured letter of James Fitzgerald to Terence MacSwiney, 25 May 1920 C.O. 904/168.
126. Ibid.
127. Article by Dr Patrick McCartan, *Kerryman*, 25 December 1938.
128. O'Connor, *Syndicalism in Ireland*, pp. 16–17.
129. Pimley, 'Working Class and Revolution'', p. 206, 207. See Donal Nevin 'Labour and the Political Revolution' in *The Years of the Great Test 1926–39*, Francis McManus (ed.) (Cork, 1978), p. 61.
130. Ibid.
131. O'Malley, *The Singing Flame*, p. 286.

Chapter 6

1. Griffith, *Resurrection of Hungary*, p. 156.
2. Ibid., pp. 156–7.
3. MacArdle, *The Irish Republic*, p. 303.
4. Conor Maguire, 'The Republican Courts', *Capuchin Annual*, 1969, p. 378.
5. Mary Kotsonouris, *Retreat from Revolution: The Dáil Courts, 1920–1924* (Dublin, 1994), cited in the *Irish Times*, 21 January 1994, p. 16.
6. James Casey, 'The Republican Courts in Ireland 1919–1922, *Irish Jurist*, Vol. 19 (1972), pp. 321–4.
7. Dermott O'Hegarty to Austin Stack, 17 June 1920, Dáil Éireann Files, S.P.O. Dublin.
8. Austin Stack to Dáil Secretariat, August 1919, Dáil Éireann Files, S.P.O. Dublin.
9. Figgis, *Recollections of the Irish War*, p. 294.
10. See Leo Kohn, *The Constitution of the Irish Free State* (London, 1932), pp. 38–9.
11. Charles Desmond Greaves, *Liam Mellowes and the Irish Revolution* (London, 1971), pp. 115–17.
12. Department of Home Affairs, Emigration Statement, MS. 15374A, National Library of Ireland, August 1920.
13. Stack to Maguire, 7 September 1920, MS 15374B, National Library of Ireland.
14. Greaves, *Liam Mellowes*, p. 142.
15. *Irish Times*, 24 May 1920.
16. MacCarthy, *Limerick's Fighting Story*, p. 253.
17. Greaves, *Liam Mellowes*, p. 172.
18. Michael Collins, *The Path to Freedom* (Dublin, 1922), p. 133.
19. Béaslaí, *Michael Collins*, Vol. II, p. 340.

20. MacCarthy, *Limerick's Fighting Story*, p. 253.
21. From correspondence of Austin Stack, 9 March 1920, on the matter of Laoghaire v. Madame Markievicz and others. Dáil Éireann Files, S.P.O. Dublin.
22. Padraig Colum, *Arthur Griffith* (Dublin, 1959), p. 216.
23. Saorstat na hÉireann, 'Judiciary: Rules and Forms, Parish and District Court'. Published by the Department of Home Affairs, 1921.
24. Ó Broin, *W. E. Wylie*, p. 47.
25. Letter of P. S. O'Hegarty, 17 February 1920, as cited by Casey, 'Republican Courts', p. 332.
26. MacArdle, *Irish Republic*, p. 303.
27. Figgis, *Recollections of the Irish War*, p. 293.
28. *Irish Times*, 20 May 1921.
29. Cahir Davitt, 'The Civil Jurisdiction of the Courts of Justice of the Irish Republic, 1920–1922', *Irish Jurist*, (1968), pp. 121–2.
30. CAB 27/108, S.I.C. 24, 7 June 1920.
31. Ibid.
32. CAB 27/108, S.I.C. 1693, Reports, June–July 1920.
33. Ibid.
34. Ibid.
35. Ibid.
36. *Irish Times*, 24 May 1920.
37. *Irish Times*, 20 April 1920.
38. Remarks of W. E. Wylie, S.I.C. 1693, 23 July 1920, letter to Walter Long, 30 June 1920, CAB 23/22.
39. Ibid.
40. *Irish Times*, 7 April 1920.
41. *Irish Times*, 31 May 1920.
42. *Parliamentary Debates* (Hansard) Vol. 130 (1920), cols. 1419–80.
43. Ibid.
44. *Parliamentary Debates* (Hansard), Vol. 131 (1920), cols. 619–23.
45. Irish Situation Committee Minutes, June–July, 1920, CAB 22/23.
46. Irish Situation Committee Minutes, June–July 1920, S.I.C. 1693. CAB 22/23.
47. Ibid.
48. Ibid.
49. Colum, *Arthur Griffith*, p. 216.
50. MacCarthy, *Limerick's Fighting Story*, p. 253.
51. Statement from Dublin Castle, 8 October 1920, CO 904/168.
52. *The Times*, cited in Béaslaí, *Michael Collins*, Vol. II, pp. 445–6.
53. Ibid., Vol. II, p. 39.
54. Maguire, 'Republican Courts', pp. 380–1.
55. Stack to Maguire, 18 September 1920, National Library of Ireland, MS. 115374.
56. Maguire, 'Republican Courts', p. 385.
57. Ibid., p. 385.
58. Cahir Davitt, 'The Civil Jurisdiction of the Courts of Justice of the Irish Republic, 1920–22', p. 123. *Irish Jurist*, Vol. 17 (April 1968).
59. Hopkinson, *Green Against Green*, p. 7.
60. Colum, *Arthur Griffith*, p. 252.
61. Ó Broin, *W. E. Wylie*, p. 47.
62. Lyons, *Ireland Since the Famine*, p. 408.

63. MacArdle, *The Irish Republic*, pp. 768–70.
64. Dáil Debates, April–July 1922.
65. MacArdle, *Irish Republic*, pp. 768–71.
66. Extract from Conclusions of a meeting held at 10 Downing Street, 13 August 1920, CAB 23/22.

Chapter 7

1. Kenneth Morgan, *Consensus and Disunity* (Oxford, 1979), p. 124.
2. CAB 232/23, 13 October 1920.
3. *The Times*, 31 July 1920.
4. Lionel Curtis, 'Ireland', p. 482.
5. D. G. Boyce, 'How to Settle the Irish Question', in A. J. P. Taylor (ed.), *Lloyd George, Twelve Essays* (London, 1971) pp. 140–2.
6. A. J. P. Taylor, *English History 1919–1945* (London, 1965) p. 145.
7. Ibid., p. 131.
8. See Martin Gilbert, *The Stricken World, 1916–1922* (Boston, 1975), p. 450 and further discussion on pp. 709–710, 738; Lawlor, *Britain and Ireland*, pp. 123–38, and also CAB 43, the official records of the British Cabinet on the Anglo-Irish Conference of 1921.
9. Kenneth Morgan, *Consensus and Disunity*, p. 132.
10. Trevor Wilson, *The Political Diaries of C. P. Scott* (Ithaca, NY, 1970), pp. 385–6.
11. Lawlor, *Britain and Ireland*, p. 78. See also Townshend, *The British Campaign in Ireland*, p. 82, also pp. 97–100.
12. C. S. I. Weekly Survey Irish Situation Com., Greenwood to Com., 6 June 1921.
13. *Diary of Sir Maurice Hankey*, Vol. II, p. 120.
14. C. E. Callwell, *Field-Marshal Sir Henry Wilson* (New York, 1927), Vol. II, p. 251.
15. See Townshend, *The British Campaign in Ireland*, p. 100.
16. Ibid., pp. 100–1.
17. Jones, *Whitehall Diary*, Vol. III, p. 73.
18. See Neville Macready, *Annals of an Active Life* (London, 1924), Vol. III, p. 490.
19. See Jones, *Whitehall Diary*, Vol. III. p. 99; for fuller discussion, see pp. 89–103.
20. Boyce, 'The Irish Question', p. 150.
21. Jones, *Whitehall Diary*, Vol. III, pp. 67–8.
22. Ibid., pp. 67–9.
23. See Martin Gilbert, (ed.), *Winston Churchill, The Stricken World 1916–1922* (Boston, 1975) pp. 666–7.
24. Text of King George V's speech at Stormont, 22 June 1921, in Jones, *Whitehall Diary*, Vol. III p. 74; See Frank Hardie, *The Political Influence of the British Monarchy* (London, 1972), pp. 161–2.
25. Mowat, *Britain Between the Wars*, p. 85.
26. Taylor, *English History*. pp. 156–7.
27. MacArdle, *The Irish Republic*, p. 466.
28. Mansergh, *The Irish Question*, p. 328.
29. Ibid.
30. Harold Nicolson, *King George the Fifth: His Life and Reign* (London, 1952), p. 348.
31. Hardie, *Political Influence*, pp. 160–3.
32. Jones, *Whitehall Diary*, Vol. III, p. 74.

33. Conclusions of a meeting at 10 Downing Street, 17 June 1921, CAB 27/107.
34. F. S. Crafford, *Jan Smuts: A Biography* (London, 1943), p. 188; W. K. Hancock, *Smuts, Vol. II The Fields of Force, 1919–1950* (Cambridge, 1968), pp. 50–3.
35. Jones, *Whitehall Diary*, p. 75.
36. Ibid., pp. 69–70.
37. 'Record of the Irish Situation Committee', 16 June 1921. CAB 27/107.
38. Jones, *Whitehall Diary*, pp. 69–70.
39. 'Ireland and the General Military Situation', Memorandum of Worthington-Evans, 24 May 1921, C. P. 2964 CAB 24/123. Minutes of Irish Situation Committee, 16 June 1921, CAB 27/107. "Conclusions of a meeting at 10 Downing Street, 17 June 1921, 6:45 P.M., CAB 27/107'.
40. Text of King George V's Opening Session Speech, Northern Ireland Parliament at Stormont, 22 June 1921, cited in Michael Farrell, *Northern Ireland: The Orange State,* (London, 1983), p. 92.
41. Text of King George V at Stormont.
42. Curtis, 'Ireland'.
43. *The Times*, 23 June 1921.
44. Ibid.
45. *Parlimentary Debates* (Lords), 21 June 1921.
46. Martin Gilbert (ed.), *Winston Churchill* (Boston, 1971), Vol. III, p. 665.
47. Cabinet Minutes, 24 June 1921, CAB 27/107.
48. Gilbert, *Churchill*, Vol. III., p. 665.
49. Macready, *Annals of An Active Life*, p. 589; and Béaslaí, *Michael Collins*, p. 242. According to Macready in his memoir of the period, when de Valera, whom he described as 'the Spanish-Hibernian President of the Irish Republic', was arrested, 'he told the officer that if he had known how small the party was he would have made a bolt for it. It is to be regretted that he did not, as in all probability he would have been shot and much trouble and bloodshed been thereby averted in the future. Piaras Beaslai in his biography of Michael Collins cites a letter from the officer arresting de Valera which states that de Valera was intercepted by one of Collins' men on the mail boat. He stated that 'the orders to release de Valera came from Lloyd George. It seems there was an understanding he was not to be arrested'. The letter from the arresting officer concluded 'this is sure to reach you safely, as I am sending it in an armoured car to the boat'. According to Beaslai, the letter was obtained on the boat.
50. Churchill, *The Stricken World*, pp. 666–7.

Chapter 8

1. See Tom Garvin, *Nationalist Revolutionaries in Ireland 1858–1928* (Oxford, 1987).
2. Hopkinson, *Green Against Green*, p. 8.
3. Ernie O'Malley, *On Another Man's Wound* (Dublin, 1979), p. 293.
4. O'Malley, *The Singing Flame*, p. 13.
5. Hopkinson, *Green Against Green*.
6. See Michael Farrell, *Arming the Protestants: The Formation of the Ulster Special Constabulary and the Royal Ulster Constabulary* (London, 1983) p. 61.
7. Texts of Anglo-Irish truce, 11 July 1921, published in *Irish Political Documents*, Arthur Mitchell and Patraig O'Snodaigh (eds) (Dublin, 1984), pp. 113–14.

8. Memorandum of Eamon Duggan, Óglaigh na h-Éireann, 12 July 1921, Mulcahy Collection, UCD PA7/47.
9. Michael Hopkinson notes that by 21 November 1921, there were 72,363 IRA members, but at the declaration of the Anglo-Irish Truce, 11 July 1921, there were probably 30,000 in all.
10. Brigade Adjutant, Kilkenny Brigade to Second Southern Division, 8 August 1921, Ernie O'Malley Papers, UCD, p. 9/147.
11. Kilkenny Brigade Adjutant to IRA General Headquarters, 11 August 1921, O'Malley Papers, UCD, p. 9/124.
12. Notebook of Frank Brewe, Mid-Clare Brigade, in author's possession.
13. Kilkenny Brigade Adjutant to IRA General Headquarters, 26 October 1921, O'Malley Papers, UCD, P9/136.
14. Notes of Tom Jones from Irish Situation Committee Meeting, 20 August 1921, Tom Jones Collection, National University of Wales. Class GG/Vol. I, Nos. 1–2.
15. Mulcahy Collection, UCD Archives, 7a/12.
16. Lord Fitzalan to Lloyd George, 23 August 1921, Lloyd George Collection HLRO P/17/2/10.
17. Jones, *Whitehall Diary*, Vol. III, pp. 98–103.
18. Sturgis' Diary, 22 June 1921, PRO 29/50–60.
19. Andy Cope to Tom Jones, 24 August 1921, Tom Jones Collection, National University of Wales, Class GG/Vol. II.
20. Viscount Fitzalan to Lloyd George, 2 August 1921, HLRO, F/17/2/9.
21. Circular No. 17 issued by Óglaigh na h-Éireann, October 1921, Mulcahy Collection, UCD Archives.
22. IRA Training Memorandum No. 9, November 1921, issued by Óglaigh na h-Éireann, Mulcahy Collection, UCD.
23. Order of Cathal Brugha, issued October 25, 1921, Mulcahy Collection, UCD.
24. Letter of Mark Sturgis, 1 November 1921, Mulcahy Collection, P9/101.
25. Records of Kilkenny Brigade, IRA Headquarters, 30 October 1921, O'Malley Papers, UCD, p. 9/139.
26. See Sheila Lawlor, 'Ireland From Truce to Treaty: War or Peace?' *Irish Historical Studies*, Vol. 35 (Fall, 1980), pp. 56–65.
27. Ibid., p. 65.
28. Report to Minister of Defence from Quartermaster General, 19 December 1921, O'Malley Collection, UCD Archives.
29. Ibid.
30. Ibid.
31. Ibid.
32. Rex Taylor, *Michael Collins* (London, 1958), p. 113.
33. Sturgis' Diary, undated, PRO, 39/50–60.
34. Ibid.
35. Frank Pakenham, *Peace by Ordeal: An Account from First-hand Sources of the Negotiation and Signature of the Anglo-Irish Treaty* (Dublin, 1972), p 68.
36. Lord FitzAlan to Lloyd George, 28 August 1921; Lloyd George Collection HLRO F/17/2/11.
37. Andy Cope to Tom Jones, 15 August 1921, Tom Jones Papers, National University of Wales.
38. Andy Cope to Tom Jones, 24 August 1921; Tom Jones Papers, National University of Wales.

39. Ibid.
40. Lloyd George to Eamon De Valera, 24 June 1921.
41. See W. K. Hancock, *Smuts, Vol. II, The Fields of Force 1919–1950* (Cambridge, 1968).
42. Pakenham, *Peace by Ordeal*, p. 74.
43. Michael Farrell, *Northern Ireland.*
44. Command Document 14760, 'Proposals of His Majesty's Government for an Irish Settlement'. British Stationery Office.
45. Command 1470, ibid.
46. Letter from De Valera to Harry Boland quoted in correspondence with James O'Mara on 3/29/31, 'The O'Mara Papers', MS 21 (549), National Library of Ireland, cited in T. R. Dwyer, *Michael Collins and the Treaty: His Differences with De Valera* (Dublin, 1981), p. 30.
47. Ibid.
48. Letter from De Valera to Harry Boland quoted in correspondence with James O'Mara on 29/3/31, 'The O'Mara Papers', MS 21 (549), National Library of Ireland, cited in Dwyer, *Michael Collins and the Treaty*, p. 30.
49. Letter of Tom Jones to Lloyd George, 12 August 1921. Lloyd George Collections HLRO, C/25/2/3.
50. Letter of Lord Stamfordham to Edward Grigg, 9/20/21, Edward Grigg Collection, Widener Library, Harvard University.
51. Letter of Edward Grigg to Lord Stamfordham, 9/20/21.
52. Ibid.
53. H. A. L. Fisher to Lloyd George, 4 September 1921. Lloyd George Collection HLRO F/25/2).
54. Ibid.
55. U. K. 1921, Proposals for an Irish Settlement CMD 1470, p. 194.
56. Letter of Eamon De Valera to Lloyd George, 30 September 1921, *Proposals for An Irish Settlement*, Cmd. 1470 (1921), p. 11.

Chapter 9

1. From an address by Lord Pakenham at University College, Cork, 22 December 1967, U.C.C. Press.
2. Pakenham, *Peace by Ordeal*, p 71.
3. Ibid., p. 74.
4. For a wider understanding of these developments of De Valera's performance at this time, a reading of Chapters eleven and twelve of Coogan, *De Valera*, is recommended.
5. Eamon De Valera to Jan Smuts, 31 July 1921, cited in Coogan, *De Valera*, p. 241.
6. De Valera to McGarrity, 27 December 1921, cited in Sean Cronin, *The McGarrity Papers*, p. 106.
7. See Béaslaí, *Michael Collins*, Vol. II, p. 293.
8. From Manuscript of Sean O'Muirthile, p. 160, Mulcahy Collection, U.C.D. p. 7/013.
9. Sean O'Muirthile, *Memoir*, Mulcahy Collection, UCD P7/52.
10. Ibid., p. 161.
11. Memorandum of Michael Collins to Arthur Griffith, August 1921, SPO, Dáil Éireann Files.
12. Ibid.
13. Pakenham, *Peace by Ordeal*, p. 101.

14. Dáil Debates, 14–24 December 1921.
15. George Dangerfield, *The Damnable Question*, p. 328.
16. Cronin, *McGarrity Papers*, p. 110.
17. Ibid.
18. Pakenham, *Peace by Ordeal*, p. 88.
19. According to Béaslaí, *Michael Collins*, Vol. II, p. 295, some members of the Irish delegation noted how, at the opening of the conference, Lloyd George referred to Dáil Éireann as 'your Parliament' and the Cabinet as 'your Ministry'.
20. From letter of Credentials for Irish delegation members to the Anglo-Irish Conference, 1921, *Dáil Debates*, 14 December 1921 to 10 January 1922.
21. Béaslaí, *Michael Collins*, Vol. II, p. 281.
22. *Dáil Debates*, Dáil Éireann Session, 14 December 1921–7 January 1922, p. 8. The Dáil Debates on the Treaty began on 14 December and resulted in the approval of the 'articles of Agreement' brought back by the plenipotentiaries on 7 January 1922. The Dáil that ratified the document continued to meet up to 10 January, during which time Arthur Griffith was selected as President over De Valera, who had resigned in protest at the imminent demise of the Irish Republic in favour of the new Free States.
23. *Dáil Debates*, December 1921–January 1922, p. 8.
24. Pakenham, *Peace by Ordeal*, pp. 143–4.
25. Ibid.
26. Pakenham, *Peace by Ordeal*, p. 119.
27. Tom Jones Collection, National Library of Wales.
28. Ibid.
29. Pakenham, *Peace by Ordeal*, p. 91.
30. Ibid., p. 306.
31. Ibid., p. 146.
32. Lloyd George Collection, HLRO PO154–5.
33. Letter of Arthur Griffith to President De Valera, 25 October 1921, Childers collection, TCD, 7790.
34. Irish Delegation to President De Valera, 27 October 1921, Childers Collection TCD, 7790.
35. Ibid.
36. Ibid.
37. De Valera to Irish Delegation, 26 October 1921; Childers Collection, UCD, and Minutes of Private Session of Dáil Éireann, 14 December 1921, *Dáil Debates*, p. 103.
38. Childers to De Valera, 'Memo No. 5', 21 October 1921, TCD.
39. Ibid.
40. Tim Pat Coogan, *Michael Collins: A Biography* (London, 1990) p. 242.
41. Ibid.
42. Pakenham, *Peace By Ordeal*, p. 74.
43. In addition, British officials had their own way of demonstrating which of the two men was the most dangerous to their efforts. From the middle of 1920, a prize of £10,000 was offered for the capture of Michael Collins, dead or alive, while there is no record of any bounty having been offered for Cathal Brugha's life, although his arrest was often sought. See Ó Broin, *Revolutionary Underground*, p. 201.
44. Dwyer, *Michael Collins and the Treaty*, p. 32.
45. Pakenham, *Peace by Ordeal*, p. 157.

46. Letter of Arthur Griffith to Eamon De Valera, Childers Collection, TCD, 31 October 1921.
47. Griffith to DeValera, 1 and 2 November 1921, Childers Collection, TCD.
48. Ibid.
49. Gavan Duffy, letter to Griffith, 11/6/21, Childers Collection, TCD.
50. Griffith to De Valera, 3 November 1921, Childers Collection, TCD.
51. Griffith to De Valera, 11 November 1921, Childers' Collection, TCD.
52. Ibid.
53. Lloyd George to Sir James Craig, 10 November 1921; Lloyd George Collection, HLRO, F/181/4/1.
54. Worthington-Evans to Lloyd George, 12 November 1921. Worthington-Evans Papers, Bodleian Library.
55. Notes from a meeting with Southern Unionists, 15 November 1921; Worthington-Evans Papers, Bodleian Library.
56. Pakenham, *Peace by Ordeal*, p. 246.
57. Cronin, *McGarrity Papers*, pp. 106–8.
58. Pakenham, *Peace by Ordeal*, p. 201.
59. Ibid., p. 242.
60. Minutes of meeting of Cabinet and Delegation, 3 December 1921, compiled by Colum O'Murchada, Assistant Secretary of the Dáil Cabinet, SPO P4/492.
61. Ibid.
62. Ibid.
63. See account of Austin Stack as cited by Pakenham, *Peace by Ordeal*, p. 210.
64. Minutes of 3 December meeting of the Cabinet and Delegation; SPO/P4/492.
65. British Government response to irish Amendments in Anglo-Irish Treaty proposal, 4 December 1921, CAB p. 209; see also Pakenham, *Peace by Ordeal*, pp. 215–16.
66. Pakenham, *Peace by Ordeal*, p. 221.
67. Birkenhead to Balfour, 3 May 1922, as cited by Dwyer, *Michael Collins and the Treaty*, p. 156.
68. Dwyer, *Michael Collins and the Treaty*, p. 157.
69. Pakenham, *Peace by Ordeal*, p. 224.
70. Ibid., p. 236.
71. Ibid., pp. 239–40.
72. Coogan, *The Man Who Made Ireland* (Dublin, 1990), p. 295.
73. O'Hegarty, *The Victory of Sinn Fein*, p. 85.
74. Pakenham, *Peace By Ordeal*, p. 246.
75. See Erskine Childers, TCD Collection, Dáil Minutes and Private Sessions, 14 December 1921, 7.00 p.m.
76. Dáil Debates, 7 January 1922, p. 7.
77. Ibid., pp. 8–14.
78. *Dáil Debates*, p. 8.
79. *Dáil Debates*, Public Session, 14 December, 1921, p. 8.
80. Childers Collection, TCD, Notes on Special Cabinet Meeting, 8 December 1921.
81. Letter to Joe McGarrity, 27 December 1921, cited in Cronin, *The McGarrity Papers*, p. 108.
82. Ibid.
83. Childer's Collection, TCD, Notes on Special Cabinet Meeting, 8 December 1921.
84. Rex Taylor, *Michael Collins*, p. 189.
85. Childers Collection, TCD, Notes on Special Cabinet Meeting, 8 December 1921.

86. O'Malley, *The Singing Flame*, pp. 286–7.
87. De Valera to Joe McGarrity, 27 December 1921, cited in Cronin, *The McGarrity Papers*, p. 108.
88. Instructions of IRB Supreme Council as cited in Ó Broin, *Revolutionary Underground*, pp. 199–200.
89. Ó Broin, *Revolutionary Underground*, pp. 196–9.
90. O'Hegarty, *A History of Ireland Under the Union 1801–1922* (Dublin, 1952), pp. 758–9.
91. McArdle, *Irish Republic*, p. 406.
92. Ibid.
93. *Dáil Debates*, 19 December 1921, p. 32.
94. Sean O'Muirthile Memoir, The Mulcahy Papers, P7/C13.
95. *Dáil Debates*, 22 December 1921, p. 35.
96. From the personal diary of Erskine Childers, 6 December 1921, Trinity College, Dublin 7814.
97. See *Dáil Debates*, 19 December 1921, p. 31.
98. *Dáil Debates*, 22 December 1921, pp. 152–8.
99. *Dáil Debates*, 19 December 1921, p. 35.
100. *Dáil Debates*, December 1921, p. 155.
101. Fitzalan to Lloyd George, 27 December 1921, Lloyd George Collection, HLRO P/17/2/27.
102. William G. Fitzgerald (ed.), *The Voice of Ireland: A Survey of the Race and Nation from all Angles by the Foremost Leaders of Home and Abroad* (Dublin, 1923) pp. 3–4. This volume was published to commemorate the Anglo-Irish Treaty.
103. Ibid.
104. Ibid.
105. *Dáil Debates*, 19 December 1921, p. 36.
106. *Dáil Debates*, 22 December 1921, p. 153.

Chapter 10

1. Roy F. Foster, *Modern Ireland 1600–1972* (London, 1988), p. 506.
2. Ronan Fanning 'Michael Collins, Revolutionary Democrat', *Sunday Independent*, 14 October 1990.
3. Ibid.
4. Ibid.
5. Draft of Lionel Curtis prepared for Lloyd George, 8 November 1921, Lloyd George Collection HLRO.
6. Brian Farrell, *The Founding of Dáil Éireann: Parliament and National Building* (Dublin, 1971).
7. Churchill, *The Aftermath*, p. 295.
8. Parliamentary Debates (Lords), 14 December 1921.
9. Ibid.
10. See Edward Grierson, The Death of the Imperial Dream (New York, 1972).
11. Pakenham, *Peace by Ordeal*, p. 15.
12. See 'Interview with Michael Collins and U. S. Senator James Phelan of California, July 31, 1922'. Phelan Papers, University of California at Berkeley.
13. Ronan Fanning, *Independent Ireland* (Dublin, 1983), p. 7.

14. David Hogan (pseudonym for Frank Gallagher), *The Four Glorious Years* (Dublin, 1953), p. 169.
15. Ibid.
16. Terence de Vere White, *Kevin O'Higgins* (Dublin, 1966), p. 87.
17. White, *Kevin O'Higgins*, pp. 87–8.
18. Hepburn, *The Conflict of Nationality*, p. 127.
19. See Fanning, *Independent Ireland*, pp. 8–9.
20. See McColgan, *British Policy*.
21. Lee, *Ireland 1912–1985*, p. 68.
22. Michael Collins to Joe McGarrity, 25 March 1922, NLI, MS 17436.
23. Michael Collins to Joe McGarrity, 4 April 1922, NLI, MS 17436.
24. *Freeman's Journal*, 17 April 1922.
25. Michael Collins, *The Path to Freedom*, pp. 116–17.
26. Michael Collins to Desmond Fitzgerald, 12 July 1922, SPO Dublin.
27. Fanning, *Independent Ireland*, p. 5.
28. Ibid.
29. White, *Kevin O'Higgins*, p. 89.
30. Kevin O'Higgins, Address to the Irish Society at Oxford University, 1924, cited in White, *Kevin O'Higgins*, p. 84.
31. Churchill to Collins, 12 April 1922, SPO Dublin S1322.
32. Ibid.
33. White, *Kevin O'Higgins*, pp. 91–2.
34. Dáil Debates, Private Session, 14 December 1921.
35. O'Malley, *The Singing Flame*, p. 86.
36. Ibid., pp. 70–1.
37. Hopkinson, *Green Against Green*, p. 72.
38. Churchill to Collins, 12 April 1922. SPO Dublin S1322.
39. Foin Neeson, *The Civil War in Ireland* (Cork, 1966), p. 43.
40. Lee, *Ireland 1912–1985*, p. 58.
41. Ibid.
42. *The Free State*, June, 1924 p. 8.
43. For a wider discussion see Sean Cronin, *Irish Nationalism: A History of its Roots and Ideology* (Dublin, 1980).
44. Ernie O'Malley, *The Singing Flame*, p. 80.
45. Ibid., p. 81.
46. Ibid., p. 98.
47. Maryann Gialanella Valiulis, *Portrait of a Revolutionary: General Richard Mulcahy and the Founding of the Irish Free State* (Dublin, 1992), p. 151.
48. Churchill to Collins, 12 April 1911. SPO Dublin. Sec. 1322.
49. Collins to Churchill, 27 July 1922. SPO Dublin, P24/65.
50. Tom Jones to Lloyd George, 17 March 1922. Lloyd George Papers HLRO F/26/1.
51. James Craig to Winston Churchill, 28 May 1922; Lloyd George Collection, HLRO F/10/2/80.
52. Lloyd George to Michael Collins undated from June 1922, but following Field Marshal Henry Wilson's death that month. SPO Dublin, P24/66.
53. Ibid.
54. Provisional Government to Lloyd George, 23 June 1922. SPO Dublin, P24/66.
55. See Churchill, *The Stricken World*, 1916–22, p. 741.
56. See Churchill Speeches, Vol. IV, p. 3342.

57. Churchill to Collins, 7 July 1922, p. 742.
58. Collins to Churchill, 9 August 1922, in *The Stricken World*, p. 744.
59. Ibid.
60. See Calton Younger, *Ireland's Civil War* (Glasgow, 1979), p. 261.
61. See Peter Young 'Michael Collins – A Military Leader' *An Cosantoir Review*, 1997, p. 136.
62. See Eamon Phoenix, 'Michael Collins: The Northern Question 1916–1922', in Gabriel Doherty and Dermot Keogh, *Michael Collins and the Making of the Irish State* (Cork, 1998).
63. Hopkinson, *Green Against Green*, p. 172.
64. Minutes of the Cabinet, 2 June 1922, SPO Dáil Éireann Files.
65. Collins to Cosgrave, 3 August 1922. SPO Dublin, P24/67.
66. See Rex Taylor, *Assassination: The Death of Sir Henry Wilson and the Tragedy of Ireland* (London, 1961).
67. Lionel Curtis to Alfred Cope, 23 August 1922, Tom Jones Collection, National Library of Wales.
68. Lionel Curtis to Winston Churchill, 19 August 1924, Lionel Curtis Collection, Bodleian Library, Oxford University.
69. Liam Lynch to Liam Deasy, 28 August 1922, Military History Bureau, Irish Department of Defense 'Lot 4, no. 160'.
70. Ryan, *The Real Chief*, p. 165.
71. Hopkinson, *Green against Green*, p. 183.
72. White, *Kevin O'Higgins*, p. 109.
73. Hopkinson, *Green against Green*, p. 181.
74. Memorandum of Kevin O'Higgins, 11 January 1925, Mulcahy Collection P7/C/21.
75. p. 298.
76. O'Malley, *The Singing Flame*, p. 181.
77. Ibid. p. 187.
78. Neeson, *The Irish Civil War*, p. 75.
79. See Hopkinson, *Green Against Green*, p. 22.
80. *Irish Times*, 11 August 1922.
81. *An Phoblacht*, 25 August 1922.
82. Report of US Consul Charles Hathaway, Dublin to the State Department, 11 August 1927; 841 d. 00/923, State Dept. Files.

Chapter 11

1. Lee, *Modern Ireland*, pp. 96–105.
2. See Kevin Nowlan, 'President Cosgrave's Last Administration', in Francis MacManus (ed.), *The Years of the Great Test* (Cork, 1967), pp. 7–18.
3. Ibid., p. 20.
4. See Memorandum of Kevin O'Shiel, 10 February 1923 at McGuire Papers P/35/B/132 17 May 1923, Mulcahy Collection P7/B/288; and June 5, 1923, SPO G 2/2.
5. Ibid.
6. See Frank Aiken to Richard Mulcahy, August 1922, Frank Aiken Papers, NLI.
7. See Michael Laffan, *The Partition of Ireland 1911–1925* (Dublin, 1983), p. 92.
8. Michael Laffan, *Partition of Ireland*, p. 102.
9. *An Phoblacht*, 4 December 1925.
10. Laffan, *Partition of Ireland*, p. 104.

11. James Campbell to the British Cabinet, British Cabinet Records, May 1916.
12. See Brian Walker, 'How Irishness Came to be Equated with Catholicism', *Irish Times*, 4 January 1994.
13. See also Lee, *Ireland 1912–1985*, pp. 45–6.
14. *Irish Times*, 4 January 1994.
15. Lee, *Ireland 1912–1985*, p. 46.
16. Pakenham, *Peace by Ordeal*, p. 267.
17. Fanning, *Independent Ireland*, p. 180.
18. Remarks of Eamon de Valera as Prime Minister in Dáil Éireann, 29 May 1935, Dáil Debates, Vol. 56, pp. 2112–6 cited in John Bowman, *De Valera and the Ulster Question, 1917–1973* (Oxford, 1982), p. 129.
19. Coogan, *DeValera*, p. 646.
20. From Article IV Anglo-Irish Joint Declaration, 17 December 1993 as released by the Office of the Taoiseach, Dublin.
21. Garret FitzGerald, 'The Double Paradox of Irish Divisions', *Irish Times*, 17 September 1994.
22. Ibid.
23. Ibid.
24. Will Hutton, reprinted from the *Manchester Guardian* in the *Irish Times*, 14 February 1994.
25. *Irish Times*, 27 November 1998.

Bibliography

Books

Andrew, Christopher M., *Her Majesty's Secret Service: The Making of the British Intelligence Community* (New York, 1987).

Andrews, C. S., *Dublin Made Me: An Autobiography* (Dublin, 1979).

Augusteijn, Joost, *From Public Defiance to Guerilla Warfare: The Radicalisation of the Irish Republican Army, A Comparative Analysis, 1916–1921* (Amsterdam, 1994).

Barry, Tom, *Guerilla Days in Ireland* (Dublin, 1949).

Béaslaí, Piaras, *Michael Collins and the Making of a New Ireland*, 2 Vols. (New York, 1926).

Beaverbrook, Lord, *The Decline and Fall of Lloyd George* (New York, 1963).

Beckett, J. C. *The Making of Modern Ireland, 1603–1923* (London, 1966).

Beloff, Max, *Imperial Sunset*, 2 Vols. (New York, 1970).

Bennett, Richard, *The Black and Tans* (London, 1959).

Blake, Robert, *The Forgotten Prime Minister. The Life and Times of Andrew Bonar Law* (London, 1955).

Bowman, John, *De Valera and the Ulster Question 1917–1923* (Oxford, 1982).

Boyce, D. G., *Englishmen and Irish Troubles: British Public Opinion and the Making of Irish Policy* (Cambridge, 1972).

— *Nationalism in Ireland* (Baltimore, 1982).

Boyce, D. G. (ed.), *The Revolution in Ireland, 1879–1923* (London, 1988).

Breen, Dan, *My Fight for Irish Freedom* (Dublin, 1981).

Brennan, Michael, *The War in Clare 1911–1921: Personal Memoirs of the Irish War of Independence* (Dublin, 1980).

Bromage, Mary Cogan, *DeValera and the March of a Nation* (New York, 1957).

Callanan, Frank, *T. M. Healy* (Cork, 1996).

Callwell, C. E., *Field-Marshal Sir Henry Wilson* (New York, 1927).

Campbell, John, *F. E. Smith: First Earl of Birkenhead* (London, 1983).

Canning, Paul, *British Policy Towards Ireland 1921–1941* (Oxford, 1985).

Carroll, F. M., *American Opinion and the Irish Question, 1910–23: A Study in Opinion and Policy* (Dublin, 1978).

Carty, James (ed.), *Ireland from the Great Famine to the Treaty 1851–1921*, Vol. III (Dublin, 1958).

Churchill, Winston, *The World Crisis, 1918–1928: The Aftermath* (London, 1929).

Clayton, Anthony, *The British Empire as Superpower, 1919–1939* (Athens, GA, 1984).

Coffey, Thomas, *Agony at Easter: The 1916 Uprising* (New York, 1969).

Coldrey, Barry, *Faith and Fatherland: The Christian Brothers and Irish Nationalism, 1838–1921* (Dublin, 1977).

Collins, Michael, *The Path to Freedom* (Dublin, 1922).

Colum, Padraig, *Arthur Griffith* (Dublin, 1959).

Connolly, James, *Labour in Ireland* (Dublin, 1917).

Coogan, Tim Pat, *Michael Collins: A Biography* (London, 1990).

— *De Valera: Long Fellow, Long Shadow* (London, 1993).

Corish, Patrick (ed.), *Radicals, Rebels and Establishments* (Belfast, 1985).

Costello, Francis, *Enduring the Most: The Life and Death of Terence MacSwiney* (Dublin, 1995).

Costello, Francis (ed.), *Michael Collins, In His Own Words* (Dublin, 1997).

Costello, Peter, *The Heart Grown Brutal: The Irish Revolution in Literature from Parnell to the Death of Yeats* (Dublin, 1977).

Crafford, F. S., *Jan Smuts: A Biography* (London, 1943).

Cronin, Sean, *The McGarrity Papers* (Tralee, 1972).

— *Young Connolly* (Dublin, 1978).

— *Irish Nationalism: A History of its Roots and Ideology* (Dublin, 1980).

Crozier, Joseph, *Ireland for Ever* (London, 1932).

Curran, Joseph, *The Birth of the Irish Free State, 1921–1923* (Alabama, 1980).

Dangerfield, George, *The Damnable Question: A Study in Anglo-Irish Relations* (Boston, 1976).

Davis, Richard, *Arthur Griffith and Non-Violent Sinn Féin* (Dublin, 1974).

Deacy, Liam, *Toward Ireland Free* (Dublin, 1965).

De Paor, Liam, *On the Easter Proclamation and Other Declarations* (Dublin, 1997).

Dwyer, T. R., *Michael Collins: The Man who Won the War* (Cork, 1990).

— *DeValera: The Man and the Myths* (Dublin, 1992).

— *Michael Collins and the Treaty: His Differences with De Valera* (Dublin, 1981).

Edwards, Owen Dudley, *Eamon De Valera* (Cardiff, 1987).

English, Richard, *Ernie O'Malley: IRA Intellectual* (Oxford, 1998).

Fanning, Ronan, *Independent Ireland* (Dublin, 1983).

— *The Irish Department of Finance 1922–58* (Dublin, 1978).

Farrell, Brian, *The Founding of Dail Eireann; Parliament and Nation Building* (Dublin, 1971).

Farrell, Michael, *Northern Ireland, The Orange State* (London, 1976).

— *Arming the Protestants: The Formation of the Ulster Special Constabulary and the Royal Ulster Constabulary* (London, 1983).

Figgis, Darrell, *Recollections of the Irish War* (New York, 1925).

— *The Economic Case for Irish Independence* (Dublin, 1920).

Fitz-Gerald, William G. (ed.), *The Voice of Ireland: A Survey of the Race and Nation from all Angles by the Foremost Leaders at Home and Abroad* (Dublin, 1923).

Fitzpatrick, David, *Politics and Irish Life, 1913–1921: The Provincial Experience of War and Revolution* (Dublin, 1977).

Fitzpatrick, David (ed.), *Revolution? Ireland 1917–1923* (Dublin, 1990).

Foster, Roy F., *Modern Ireland, 1600–1972* (London, 1988).

Garvin, Tom, *Nationalist Revolutionaries in Ireland 1858–1928* (Dublin, 1986).

— *The Birth of Irish Democracy* (Dublin, 1996).

Gilbert, Martin (ed.), *Winston S. Churchill: The Stricken World* (Boston, 1969).

Greaves, Charles Desmond, *The Life and Times of James Connolly* (New York, 1976).

— *Liam Mellowes and the Irish Revolution* (London, 1971).

Grierson, Edward, *The Imperial Dream: The British Commonwealth and Empire 1775–1969* (New York, 1972).

Griffith, Arthur, *The Resurrection of Hungary: A Parallel for Ireland* (Dublin, 1918).
Griffith, Kenneth and Timothy E. O'Grady, *Curious Journey: An Oral History of Ireland's Unfinished Revolution* (London, 1982).
Hancock, W. K., *Smuts, Vol. II, The Fields of Force 1919–1950* (Cambridge, 1968).
Hardie, Frank, *The Political Influence of the British Monarchy, 1868–1952* (London, 1972).
Harkness, D. W., *The Restless Dominion: The Irish Free State and the British Commonwealth of Nations 1921–31* (London, 1969).
Hart, Peter, *The I.R.A. and its Enemies: Violence and Community in Cork, 1916–1923* (Oxford, 1998).
Hepburn, A. C., *The Conflict of Nationality in Modern Ireland* (New York, 1980).
Hobson, Bulmer, *Ireland Yesterday and Tomorrow* (Tralee, 1968).
Hogan, David (pseudonym for Frank Gallagher), *The Four Glorious Years* (Dublin, 1953).
Hopkinson, Michael, *Green Against Green: The Irish Civil War* (Dublin, 1988).
Hopkinson, Michael (ed.), *The Last Days of Dublin Castle: The Diaries of Mark Sturgis* (Dublin, 1999).
Humphries, Tom, *Green Fields: Gaelic Sport in Ireland* (London, 1996).
Jones, Thomas, *Whitehall Diary*, K. Middlemas (ed.) (London, 1969).
Kavanagh, Patrick, *The Green Fool* (London, 1938 [1971]).
Kee, Robert, *The Green Flag* (New York, 1972).
— *The Jewel and The Ivy* (London, 1993).
Keogh, Dermot, *Twentieth Century Ireland: Nation and State* (Dublin, 1994).
Kohn, Leo, *The Constitution of the Irish Free State* (London, 1932).
Kotsonouris, Mary, *Retreat From Revolution: The Dail Courts 1920–1924* (Dublin, 1994).
Laffan, Michael, *The Resurrection of Ireland: The Sinn Féin Party 1916–1923* (Cambridge, 1999).
— *The Partition of Ireland 1911–25* (Dublin, 1983).
Lawlor, Sheila, *Britain and Ireland 1914–23* (Princeton, 1983).
Lee, J. J., *Ireland 1912–1985: Politics and Society* (Cambridge, 1989).
— *The Modernisation of Irish Society, 1848–1914* (Dublin, 1973).
Lynch, Diarmuid, *The I.R.B. and the 1916 Insurrection* (Cork, 1957).
Lysaght, D. R. O'Connor, *The Republic of Ireland* (Cork, 1970).
Lyons, F. S. L, *Ireland Since the Famine* (London, 1971).
MacArdle, Dorothy, *The Irish Republic: a Documented Cronicle of the Anglo-Irish Conflict and the Partitioning of Ireland* (New York, 1965).
McCaffrey, Lawrence, *The Irish Question, 1800–1922* (Washington, DC, 1984).
MacCartan, Patrick, *With De Valera in America* (New York, 1932).
MacCarthy, J. M. (ed.), *Limerick's Fighting Story* (Tralee, 1966).
McColgan, John, *British Policy and the Irish Administration, 1920–1922* (London, 1983).
McCracken, J. C., *Representative Government in Ireland* (Oxford, 1948).
MacDonagh, Oliver, *Ireland: The Union and Its Aftermath* (London, 1979).
McDowell, R. B., *The Irish Connection* (London, 1970).
MacEoin, Uinseann, *Survivors: The Story of Ireland's Struggle as Told Through Some of Her Outstanding People* (Dublin, 1987)
McMahon, Deirdre, *Republicans and Imperialists: Anglo-Irish Relations in the 1930s* (Dublin, 1987).
MacManus, Francis (ed.), *The Years of the Great Test* (Cork, 1978).
Macready, Neville, *Annals of an Active Life*, 2 Vols. (London, 1924).
Mandle, W. F., *The Gaelic Athletic Association and Irish Nationalist Politics, 1884–1984* (London, 1987).

Mansergh, Nicholas, *The Irish Question, 1840–1921* (London, 1965).
— *The Commonwealth Experience* (Toronto, 1982).
— *The Anglo-Irish Question and its Undoing, 1912–19* (New Haven, 1991).
Martin, F. X. (ed.), *Eoin MacNeill: The Scholar Revolutionary* (Shannon, 1973).
Maye, Brian, *Arthur Griffith* (Dublin, 1998).
Middlemas, Keith, *Politics in Industrial Society: The Experience of the British System Since 1911* (London, 1979).
Mitchell, Arthur, *Labor in Irish Politics* (New York, 1974).
— *Revolutionary Government in Ireland: Dail Eireann 1919–1922* (Dublin, 1995).
Mitchell, Arthur and Pádraig Ó Snodaigh (eds.), *Irish Political Documents 1916–1949* (Blackrock, 1985).
Mowat, Charles, *Britain Between the Wars, 1918–1940* (Chicago, 1955).
Morgan, Austen, *James Connolly: A Political Biography* (Manchester, 1988).
Morgan, Kenneth, *Consensus and Disunity* (Oxford, 1979).
Murphy, John A., *Ireland in the Twentieth Century* (Dublin, 1975).
Neeson, Eoin, *The Civil War in Ireland* (Cork, 1966).
Neligan, David, *Spy in the Castle* (London, 1968).
Nicolson, Harold, *King George the Fifth: His Life and Reign* (London, 1971).
Nowlan, Kevin, B. (ed.), *The Making of 1916: Studies in the History of the Rising* (Dublin, 1969).
O'Brien, Conor Cruise (ed.), *The Shaping of Modern Ireland* (London, 1961).
Ó Broin, León, *Revolutionary Underground: The Story of the Irish Republican Brotherhood, 1858–1924* (Dublin, 1976).
— *W. E. Wylie and the Irish Revolution, 1916–1921* (Dublin, 1989).
O'Carroll, J. P. and John A. Murphy (ed.), *DeValera and His Times* (Cork, 1983).
O'Connor, Emmet, *Syndicalism in Ireland: 1917–1923* (Cork, 1989).
O'Connor, Frank, *The Big Fellow: Michael Collins and the Irish Revolution* (Dublin, 1968).
O'Connor, Ulick, *Oliver St. John Gogarty* (London, 1964).
O'Donoghue, Florence, *No Other Law* (Dublin, 1986).
O'Farrell, Patrick, *Ireland's English Question: Anglo-Irish Relations, 1534–1970* (New York, 1971).
O'Halpin, E. *The Decline of the Union: British Government in Ireland 1892–1920* (Dublin, 1987).
O'Hegarty, P. S., *The Victory of Sinn Fein: How it Won and How it Used it* (Dublin, 1925).
— *The History of Ireland Under the Union, 1801–1922* (London, 1952).
O'Mahoney, Sean, *Frongoch: University of Revolution* (Dublin, 1987).
O'Malley, Ernie, *The Singing Flame* (Dublin, 1978).
— *On Another Man's Wound* (Dublin, 1979).
— *Raids and Rallies* (Dublin, 1982).
O'Neill, T. P. and Frank Pakenham, *DeValera* (London, 1972).
Pakenham, Frank, *Peace By Ordeal: An Account, From First-hand Sources of the Negotiation and Signature of the Anglo-Irish Treaty* (Dublin, 1972).
Patterson, Henry, *The Politics of Illusion: Republicanism and Socialism in Modern Ireland* (London, 1989).
Pearse, Patrick, *The Sovereign People* (Dublin, 1916).
Phoenix, Eamon, *Northern Nationalism* (Belfast, 1994).
Rowland, Peter, *Lloyd George* (London, 1975).
Rumpf, Erhard and A. C. Hepburn, *Nationalism and Socialism in Twentieth Century Ireland* (Liverpool, 1977).
Ryan, Meda, *The Real Chief: The Story of Liam Lynch* (Cork, 1986).

Steed, Henry Wickham, *Through Thirty Years, 1982–1922* Vol. II (New York, 1924).
Street, C. J. C. ('I.O.' pseud.), *Ireland in 1921* (London, 1922).
Stevenson, Frances, *Lloyd George: A Diary*, A. J. P. Taylor (ed.) (London, 1971).
Stewart, A. T. Q. *The Ulster Crisis* (London, 1966).
Talbot, Hayden, *Michael Collins' Own Story* (London, 1923).
Taylor, A. J. P. (ed.), *Lloyd George: Twelve Essays* (London, 1971).
— *English History 1914–1945* (London, 1965).
Taylor, Rex, *Michael Collins* (London, 1958).
— *Association: the Death of Sir Henry Wilson and the Tragedy of Ireland* (London, 1961).
Townshend, Charles, *The British Campaign in Ireland 1919–1921: The Development of Political and Military Policies* (London, 1975).
Townshend, Charles, *Political Violence in Ireland* (Oxford, 1988).
Valiulis, Maryann Gialanella, *Portrait of a Revolutionary: General Richard Mulcahy and the Founding of the Irish Free State* (Dublin, 1992).
Van Voris, Jacqueline, *Constance Markievicz: In the Cause of Ireland* (Amherst, 1967).
Ward, Alan J., *Ireland and Anglo-American Relations, 1899–1921* (London, 1969).
West, Trevor and Horace Plunkett, *Cooperation and Politics* (Washington, 1986).
Wheeler-Bennett, John W., *John Anderson, Viscount Waverley* (New York, 1970).
White, Terence de Vere, *Kevin O'Higgins* (Dublin, 1966).
Williams, Desmond (ed.), *The Irish Struggle, 1916–1926* (Toronto, 1966).
Wilson, Trevor (ed.), *The Political Diaries of C. P. Scott* (Ithaca, NY, 1970).
Winter, Sir Ormonde, *Winter's Tale: An Autobiography* (London, 1955).
Younger, Calton, *Ireland's Civil War* (Glasgow, 1979).

Articles

Augusteijn, Joost, 'The Importance of Being Irish: Ideas and the Volunteers', in David Fitzpatrick (ed.), *Revolution? Ireland 1917–1923* (Dublin, 1990), pp. 31–7.
Bew, Paul, 'Moderate Nationalism and the Irish Revolution 1916–1923', *The Historical Journal*, Vol. 42 (1999), pp. 729–49.
— 'Sinn Fein and Agrarian Radicalism', in D. G. Boyce (ed.), *The Making of Modern Ireland* (London, 1988), pp. 311–22.
Boyce, D. G., 'How to Settle the Irish Question', in A. J. P. Taylor (ed.), *Lloyd George: Twelve Essays* (London, 1971), pp. 140–2.
Carroll, F. M., 'All Standards of Human Conduct: The American Commission on Conditions in Ireland, 1920–21', *Eire/Ireland*, Vol. 16 (Fall 1981), pp. 65–78.
Casey, James, 'The Republican Courts in Ireland, 1919–1922', *Irish Jurist*, Vol. 19 (October 1970), pp. 321–41.
Casey, J. P., 'The Genesis of the Dail Courts', *Irish Jurist*, Vol. 218 (April 1979), pp. 326–8.
Costello, Francis, 'Nurturing Irish Unity', *Boston Globe*, 1 October 1994.
— 'Ireland as a Commonwealth Nation?' *Chicago Tribune*, 5 August 1994.
— 'King George V's Speech at Belfast, 1921: Prelude to the Anglo-Irish Truce', *Eire/Ireland*, Vol. 22 (Fall 1987), pp. 43–57.
— 'The Role of Propaganda in the Anglo-Irish War, 1919–1921', *The Canadian Journal of Irish Studies*, Vol. 14 (January 1909), pp. 5–24.
— 'The Irish Representatives to the London Anglo-Irish Conference 1921: Violators of their Authority of Victims or Contradictory Instructions?', *Eire/Ireland*, Vol. 24 (Summer 1989).

Cronin, Sean, 'Connolly's Great Leap in the Dark', *The Capuchin Annual* (1977), p. 309.

Curtis, Lionel, 'Ireland', *The Round Table*, Vol. 20 (June 1921).

Davis, Eoghan, 'The Guerrilla Mind', in D. Fitzpatrick (ed.), *Revolution? Ireland 1917–1923* (Dublin, 1990), pp. 43–9.

Davitt, Cahir, 'The Civil Jurisdiction of the Courts of Justice of the Irish Republic, 1929–1922', *Irish Jurist*, Vol. 17 (April 1968), pp. 121–31.

Dillon, Myles, Douglas Hyde, in Conor Cruise O'Brien (ed.), *The Shaping of Modern Ireland* (London, 1950), pp. 57–1.

Fanning, Ronan, 'Michael Collins, Revolutionary Democrat', *Sunday Independent*, 14 October 1990.

Farrell, Brian, 'Labour and the Irish Political Party System', *Economic and Social Review*, Vol. 1 (Fall, 1970), pp. 477–502.

FitzGerald, Garret, 'Weak Northern Ireland Economy Needs South Link', *Irish Times*, 28 November 1998.

Fitzpatrick, David, 'The Geography of Irish Nationalism', *Past and Present*, No. 78 (February 1978), pp. 114–37.

— 'Strikes in Ireland, 1914–1921', *Saothar, The Journal of the Irish Labour History Society*, Vol. 6 (1980), pp. 87–101.

Laffan, Michael, 'The Unification of Sinn Fein in 1917', *Irish Historical Studies*, Vol. 26 (Summer 1971), pp. 353–79.

— 'Labour Must Wait: Ireland's Conservative Revolution', in Patrick Cornish (ed.), *Radicals, Rebels, and Establishments* (Belfast, 1985), pp. 217–29.

Lalor, James Fintan, Letter in *The Irish Felon*, 24 June 1848.

Lawlor, Sheila, 'Ireland from Truce to Treaty: War or Peace', *Irish Historical Studies*, Vol. 35 (Fall 1980), pp. 49–64.

Lyons, F. S. L., 'The Two Faces of Home Rule', in Kevin B. Nowlan (ed.), *The Making of 1916: Studies in the History of the Rising* (Dublin, 1969), pp. 110–23.

Lynch, Patrick, 'The Social Revolution that Never Was', in Desmond Williams (ed.), *The Irish Struggle 1916–1926* (Toronto, 1966), pp. 45–53.

McCarthy, John P., 'The Friends of Irish Freedom' and 'The Founding of the Irish Free State', *The Recorder*, Vol. 6, No. 2 (Fall 1993), p. 117.

McCartney, Donal, 'The Sinn Fein Movement', in Kevin B. Nowlan (ed.), *The Making of 1916: Studies in the History of the Rising* (Dublin, 1969), pp. 311–22.

Maguire, Conor, 'The Republican Courts', *Capuchin Annual* (1969), pp. 380–1.

Martin, F. X., 'The Origins of the Irish Rising of 1916', in Desmond Williams (ed.), *The Irish Struggle, 1916–1926* (Toronto, 1966).

Murphy, Brian, 'Pearse and 1916', Letter in *The Irish Times*, 18 October 1990.

Murphy, Richard, 'Walter Hume Long and the Making of the Government of Ireland Act, 1919–1920', *Irish Historical Studies*, Vol. 40 (Spring 1986), pp. 82–96.

Nevin, Donal, 'Labour and the Political Revolution', in Francis MacManus (ed.), *The Years of the Great Test* (Cork, 1978), pp. 86–93.

Nowlan, Kevin B., 'President Cosgrave's Last Administration', in F. McManus (ed.), *The Years of the Great Test 1926–1939* (Cork, 1978), pp. 7–18.

Phoenix, Eamon, 'Michael Collins: The Northern Question 1916–1922', in Gabriel Doherty and Dermot Keogh (eds), *Michael Collins and the Making of the Irish State* (Cork, 1998).

Pimley, Adrian, 'Working Class and Revolution, 1896–1923', in D. G. Boyce (ed.), *The Revolution in Ireland, 1879–1923* (London, 1988), p. 205.

Townshend, Charles, 'The Irish Railway Strike of 1920', *Irish Historical Studies* (March, 1979).

Young, Peter, 'Michael Collins – A Military Leader?', *An Cosantoir Review*, 1997, pp. 130–43.

Official records

British Cabinet Office Records 1916–1922, Public Record Office, London, CAB 11–24; CAB 217 CAB 42–3.

British Colonial Office Records, CO 904 Series.

British Foreign Office Files, Records of the British Legation to the US 1916–1921, Public Record Office, London.

Dail Eireann Files, State Papers Office, Irish Government Archives, Dublin.

Records of the Military History Bureau, Irish Department of Defence, Dublin.

US State Department, US Legation Files, Northern European Affairs, 841.00 Series.

Newspapers and periodicals

Irish:

> *An Phoblact*
> *An tÓglach*
> *Cork Examiner*, 1919–98
> *Freeman's Journal*, 1916–22
> *Irish Independent*, 1916–22 and *The Sunday Independent*, 1990–7
> *Irish News*, Belfast, 1920–98, *The Belfast Telegraph*, 1920–98
> *Irish Press*
> *Irish Times*, 1916–98
> *Sinn Fein Bulletin*, 1920–21

British:

> *Daily News*, London, 1919–21
> *Manchester Guardian*, 1916–22
> *The Times*, London, 1916–22

American:

> *Boston Globe*, 1916–22.
> *Nation*, New York, 1920–21.
> *New York Times*, 1916–22.

Official reports and publications

'The Sinn Féin Movement', His Majesty's Stationery Office, 1918 (Comd. 1108).

'Proposals for an Irish Settlement', His Majesty's Stationery Office, 1921 (Comd. 1470).

'Articles of Agreement for a Treaty Between Great Britain and Ireland, 1921', His Majesty's Stationery Office (Comd. 1560).

Parliamentary Debates Fifth Series, Vols. 144–9 (House of Commons) and Vols. 43–52 (House of Lords) 1916–22.

'Proceedings of Dail Eireann, Private and Public Sessions, 1919–22' (The Stationery Office, Dublin).

'Report of the Proceedings of the Irish Convention', His Majesty's Stationery Office, 1918 (Comd. 9019).

'Report of the Labour Commission to Ireland' (London: Labour Party, 1921).

'Report of the US Commission on Conditions in Ireland' (Washington, 1922).

'Report of the Irish Trade Union Congress' (Dublin, 1921).

Chronological Record of Irish Political Events 1914–1923

5 March Home Rule Bill introduced a third time in the House of Commons.

March The Curragh Mutiny. General Gough and other cavalry officers at the Curragh Camp refuse to obey orders which would entail their proceeding to Ulster to enforce the law. British Government accepts their terms.

8 September Home Rule Act becomes law under the Parliament Act without the consent of the House of Lords, but a Suspensory Act is passed at the same time suspending its operation till after the war.

1916
20 April Attempt to land arms in Ireland from German steamer the *Aud*. Landing of Sir Roger Casement from a German submarine and his subsequent arrest.

24 April Easter 'Rising' in Dublin. General Post Office and other points seized by Irish volunteers and the Citizen Army under command of Pearse and Connolly. Proclamation of an Irish Republic. Professor John MacNeill, the commander of the Irish Volunteers, attempts to stop the rebellion and succeeds in confining it to Dublin.

1917
7 March Major William Redmond makes his last speech in House of Commons appealing on behalf of the Irish soldiers for peace and liberty in Ireland. Mr Lloyd George, Prime Minister, replying for the Government states that the Government would not take any action to enforce Home Rule on that part of Ireland to which it was repugnant. The Nationalist Party, led by Mr Redmond, left the House of Commons as a protest against the Government's attitude.

17 May	Government proposals submitted by Mr Lloyd George to both Irish parties who agree to take part in an Irish Convention for the purpose of producing a scheme of Irish self-government within the Empire. Mr Bonar Law explains in the House of Commons that the Government's pledge not to coerce Ulster still holds good and that they will not act on the Convention's report unless it is practically unanimous.
17 June	Irish prisoners in England released under an act of amnesty.
10 July	Eamon de Valera elected in by-election for East Clare, Major Redmond's constituency.

1918

5 April	Report of Irish Convention submitted to Prime Minister embodying a scheme of Irish self-government agreed to by Nationalists and Southern Unionists. Mr Lloyd George announces Government's intention to apply conscription to Ireland.
16 April	Irish Conscription Act passed. Irish Party withdraw from the House of Commons as a protest.
18 April	Mansion House Conference of all Nationalist leaders agrees to resist conscription by the most effective means.
17 May	Lord French announces discovery of 'German plot' and suspension of conscription. Sinn Féin leaders arrested and interned without trial.
15 December	General election. Sinn Féin captures seventy-four seats, including every seat in Southern Ireland except one.

1919

January	Irish Republic established.
January–December	Development of Dáil Government.
	Anglo-Irish War begins.

1920

March	British Government introduces Black and Tans to Ireland, increasing nationalist alienation.
	Lord Mayor Tomas MacCurtain assassinated, apparently by British undercover agents. British House of Commons passes Government of Ireland Act establishing a Southern Irish Parliament while also allowing for the creation of a six-county Northeast Ulster state, effectively providing basis for Ireland's partition. House of Lords approve (Bill at end of the year)
May	Sir John Anderson named Under Secretary for British administration in Dublin along with appointment of subordinates Andy Cope and Mark Sturgis to begin process of informally exploring avenues for reaching a settlement with Sinn Féin.

June	British Cabinet forms Irish Situation Committee to monitor developments in Ireland.
July	'Restoration of Order' Act in Ireland implemented by British Government in Ireland, abolishing coroner's juries and providing for wider application of martial law in southern Ireland. Measure is a further manifestation of policy combining coercion with search for political settlement.
August	Terence MacSwiney, MacCurtain's successor as Lord Mayor begins what would be a seventy-four-day hunger strike to the death.
October	Sean Treacy, Third Tipperary Brigade leader killed in Dublin ambush by British Auxiliaries.
November	Kevin Barry hanged in Mountoy Jail. Large squads of British forces ambushed in Longford and Cork.
21 November	Marked Bloody Sunday in Dublin as IRA's Dublin Brigade combined with Michael Collins' assassination squad to assassinate fourteen alleged British intelligence officers. British respond with attack later in day at Croke Park Gaelic football match, killing thirteen people and wounding sixty others.
December	Cork City is burned and looted by a combined force of British regulars, auxiliaries and Black and Tans in apparent reprisal for IRA ambushed.

1921

7 June	Northern Ireland Government comes into existence under Government of Ireland Act (1920).
24 June	Lloyd George invites de Valera into Conference.
11 July	Anglo-Irish Truce.
14–21 July	Lloyd George–de Valera meetings in London.
20 July	British present Dominion terms.
10 August	Dáil Government refuses Dominion terms.
10 August–30 September	Lloyd George–de Valera correspondence.
11 October–6 December	Anglo-Irish negotiations in London.
5 December	Lloyd George ultimatum: Dominion Status or immediate war.
6 December	Treaty signed.
8 December	Dublin Cabinet meeting. De Valera publishes repudiation of Treaty.

1922

7 January	Dáil agrees to Treaty, sixty-four votes to fifty-seven.
28 June	Civil War begins in Ireland.
6 December	Irish Free State established.
7 December	Northern Ireland opts out under Treaty.

The Government of Ireland Act, 1920

An Act to provide for the better Government of Ireland. 23rd December 1920.

Be it enacted by the King's most Excellent Majesty, by and with the advice and consent of the Lords Spiritual and Temporal, and Commons, in this present Parliament assembled, and by the authority of the same, as follows:

ESTABLISHMENT OF PARLIAMENTS FOR SOUTHERN IRELAND AND NORTHERN IRELAND AND A COUNCIL OF IRELAND.

1. – (1) On and after the appointed day there shall be established for Southern Ireland a Parliament to be called the Parliament of Southern Ireland consisting of His Majesty, the Senate of Southern Ireland, and the House of Commons of Southern Ireland, and there shall be established for Northern Ireland a Parliament to be called the Parliament of Northern Ireland consisting of His Majesty, the Senate of Northern Ireland, and the House of Commons of Northern Ireland.

(2) For the purpose of this Act, Northern Ireland shall consist of the parliamentary counties of Antrim, Armagh, Down, Fermanagh, Londonderry and Tyrone, and the parliamentary boroughs of Belfast and Londonderry, and Southern Ireland shall consist of so much of Ireland as is not comprised within the said parliamentary counties and boroughs.

2. – (1) With a view to the eventual establishment of a Parliament for the whole of Ireland, and to bringing about harmonious action between the parliaments and governments of Southern Ireland and Northern Ireland, and to the promotion of mutual intercourse and uniformity in relation to matters affecting the whole of Ireland, and to providing for the administration of services which the two parliaments mutually agree should be administered uniformly throughout the whole of Ireland, or which by virtue of this Act are to be so administered, there shall be constituted, as soon as may be after the appointed day, a Council to be called the Council of Ireland.

(2) Subject as hereinafter provided, the Council of Ireland shall consist of a person nominated by the Lord Lieutenant acting in accordance with instructions from His Majesty who shall be President and forty other persons,

of whom seven shall be members of the Senate of Southern Ireland, thirteen shall be members of the House of Commons of Southern Ireland, seven shall be members of the Senate of Northern Ireland, and thirteen shall be members of the House of Commons of Northern Ireland.

The members of the Council of Ireland shall be elected in each case by the members of that House of the Parliament of Southern Ireland or Northern Ireland of which they are members. The election of members of the Council of Ireland shall be the first business of the Senates and Houses of Commons of Southern Ireland and Northern Ireland.

A member of the Council shall, on ceasing to be a member of that House of Parliament of Southern Ireland or Northern Ireland by which he was elected a member of the Council, cease to be a member of the Council: Provided that, on the dissolution of the Parliament of Southern Ireland or Northern Ireland, the persons who are members of the Council elected by either House of that Parliament shall continue to hold office as members of the Council until the date of the first meeting of the new Parliament and shall then retire unless re-elected.

The President of the Council shall preside at each meeting of the Council at which he is present and shall be entitled to vote in case of an equality of votes, but not otherwise.

The first meeting of the Council shall be held at such time and place as may be appointed by the Lord Lieutenant.

The Council may act notwithstanding a vacancy in their number, and the quorum of the Council shall be fifteen, subject as aforesaid, the Council may regulate their own procedure, including the delegation of powers to committees.

(3) The constitution of the Council of Ireland may from time to time be varied by identical Acts passed by the Parliament of Southern Ireland and the Parliament of Northern Ireland, and the Acts may provide for all or any of the members of the Council of Ireland being elected by parliamentary electors, and determine the constituencies by which the several elective members are to be returned and the number of the members are to be returned by the several constituencies and the method of election.

Power to Establish a Parliament for the Whole of Ireland

3. – (1) The Parliaments of Southern Ireland and Northern Ireland may, by identical Acts agreed to by an absolute majority of members of the House of Commons of each Parliament at the third reading (hereinafter referred to as constituent Acts), establish, in lieu of the Council of Ireland, a Parliament for the whole of Ireland consisting of His Majesty and two Houses (which shall be called and known as the Parliament of Ireland), and may determine

the number of members thereof and the manner in which the members are to be appointed or elected, and the constituencies for which the several elective members are to be returned, and the number of members to be returned by the several constituencies, and the method of appointment or election, and the relations of the two Houses to one another; and the date at which the Parliament of Ireland is established is hereinafter referred to as the date of Irish union:

Provided that the Bill for a constituent Act shall not be introduced except upon a resolution passed at a previous meeting of the House in which the Bill is to be introduced.

(2) On the date of Irish union the Council of Ireland shall cease to exist and there shall be transferred to the Parliament and Government of Ireland all powers then exercisable by the Council of Ireland, and (except so far as the constituent Acts otherwise provide) the matters which under this Act cease to be reserved matters at the date of Irish union, and any other powers for the joint exercise of which by the Parliaments or Governments of Southern and Northern Ireland provision has been made under this Act.

(3) There shall also be transferred to the Parliament and Government of Ireland, except so far as the constituent Acts otherwise provide, all the powers and duties of the Parliaments and Governments of Southern Ireland and Northern Ireland, including all powers as to taxation, and, unless any powers and duties are retained by the Parliaments and Governments of Southern Ireland and Northern Ireland under the constituent Acts, those Parliaments and Governments shall cease to exist:

Provided that, if any powers and duties are so retained, the constituent Acts shall make provision with respect to the financial relations between the Exchequers of Southern and Northern Ireland on the one hand and the Irish Exchequer on the other.

(4) If by the constituent Acts any powers and duties are so retained as aforesaid, the Parliaments of Southern Ireland and Northern Ireland may subsequently by identical Acts transfer any of those powers and duties to the Government and Parliament of Ireland, and, in the event of all such powers and duties being so transferred, the Parliaments and Governments of Southern Ireland and Northern Ireland shall cease to exist.

Legislative Powers

4. – (1) Subject to the provisions of this Act, the Parliament of Southern Ireland and the Parliament of Northern Ireland shall respectively have power to make laws for the peace, order, and good government of Southern Ireland and Northern Ireland with the following limitations, namely, that they shall not have power to make laws except in respect of matters exclusively relating

to the portion of Ireland within their jurisdiction, or some part thereof, and (without prejudice to that general limitation) that they shall not have power to make laws in respect of the following matters in particular, namely:

(1) The Crown or the succession to the Crown, or a regency, or the property of the Crown (including foreshore vested in the Crown), or the Lord Lieutenant, except as respects the exercise of his executive power in relation to Irish services as defined for the purposes of this Act; or

(2) The making of peace or war, or matters arising from a state of war; or the regulation of the conduct of any portion of His Majesty's subjects during the existence of hostilities between foreign states with which His Majesty is at peace, in relation to those hostilities; or

(3) The navy, the army, the air force, the territorial force, or any other naval, military, or air force, or the defence of the realm, or any other naval, military, or air force matter (including any pensions and allowances payable to persons who have been members of or in respect of service in any such force or their widows or dependents, and provision for the training, education, employment and assistance for the reinstatement in civil life of persons who have ceased to be members of any such force); or

(4) Treaties, or any relations with foreign states, or relations with other parts of His Majesty's dominions, or matters involving the contravention of treaties or agreements with foreign states or any part of His Majesty's dominions, or offences connected with any such treaties or relations, or procedure connected with the extradition of criminals under any treaty, or the return of fugitive offenders from or to any part of His Majesty's dominions; or

(5) Dignities or titles of honour; or

(6) Treason, treason felony, alienage, naturalisation, or aliens as such, or domicile; or

(7) Trade with any place out of the part of Ireland within their jurisdiction, except so far as trade may be affected by the exercise of the powers of taxation given to the said parliaments, or by regulations made for the sole purpose or preventing contagious disease, or by steps taken by means of inquiries or agencies out of the part of Ireland within their jurisdiction for the improvement of the trade of that part or for the protection of traders of that part from fraud; the granting of bounties on the export of goods; quarantine, navigation, including merchant shipping (except as respect inland waters, the regulation of harbours, and local health regulations); or

(8) Submarine cables; or

(9) Wireless telegraphy; or

(10) Aerial navigation; or

(11) Lighthouses, buoys, or beacons (except so far as they can consistently with any general Act of the parliament of the United Kingdom be constructed or maintained by a local harbour authority); or

(12) Coinage; legal tender; negotiable instruments (including bank notes) except so far as negotiable instruments may be affected by the exercise of the powers of taxation given to the said Parliaments; or any change in the standard of weights and measures; or

(13) Trade marks, designs, merchandise marks, copyright, or patent rights; or

(14) Any matter which by this Act is declared to be a reserved matter, so long as it remains reserved. Any law made in contravention of the limitations imposed by this section shall, so far as it contravenes those limitations, be void.

(2) The limitation on the powers of the said Parliaments to the making of laws with respect to matters exclusively relating to the portion of Ireland within their respective jurisdiction shall not be construed so as to prevent the said Parliaments by identical legislation making laws respecting matters affecting both Southern and Northern Ireland.

5. – (1) In the exercise of their power to make laws under this Act neither the Parliament of Southern Ireland nor the Parliament of Northern Ireland shall make a law so as either directly or indirectly to establish or endow any religion, or prohibit or restrict the free exercise thereof or give a preference, privilege, or advantage, or impose any disability or disadvantage, on account of religious belief or religious or ecclesiastical status, or make any religious belief or religious ceremony a condition of the validity of any marriage, or affect prejudicially the right of any child to attend a school receiving public money without attending the religious instruction at the schools, or alter the constitution of any religious body except where the alteration is approved on behalf of the religious body by the governing body thereof, or divert from any religious denomination the fabric of cathedral churches, or, except for the purpose of roads, railways, lighting, water, or drainage works, or other works of public utility upon payment of compensation, any other property, or take any property without compensation. Any law made in contravention of the restrictions imposed by this subsection shall, so far as it contravenes those restrictions, be void.

(2) Any existing enactment by which any penalty, disadvantage, or disability is imposed on account of religious belief or on a member of any religious order as such shall, as from the appointed day, cease to have effect in Ireland.

6. – (1) Neither the Parliament of Southern Ireland nor the Parliament of Northern Ireland shall have power to repeal or alter any provision of this Act (except as is specially provided by this Act), or of any Act passed by the

Parliament of the United Kingdom after the appointed day and extending to the part of Ireland within their jurisdiction, although that provision deals with a matter with respect to which the parliament have power to make laws.

(2) Where any Act of the Parliament of Southern Ireland or the Parliament of Northern Ireland deals with any matter with respect to which that Parliament has power to make laws which is dealt with by any Act of the Parliament of the United Kingdom passed after the appointed day and extending to the part of Ireland within its jurisdiction, the Act of the Parliament of Southern Ireland or the Parliament of Northern Ireland shall be read subject to the Act of the Parliament of the United Kingdom, and so far as it is repugnant to that Act, but no further, shall be void.

(3) Any order, rule or regulation made in pursuance of, or having the force of, an Act of Parliament of the United Kingdom shall be deemed to be a provision of an Act within the meaning of this section.

7. – (1) The Council of Ireland shall have power to make orders with respect to matters affecting interests both in Southern Ireland and Northern Ireland, in any case where the matter –

(a) is of such a nature that if it had affected interests in one of those areas only it would have been within the powers of the Parliament for that area; and

(b) is a matter to affect which, it would, apart from this provision, have been necessary to apply to the Parliament of the United Kingdom by petition for leave to bring in a private Bill.

(2) The provisions contained in the first Schedule to this Act shall have effect with respect to the procedure for making such orders.

(3) Any order so made by the Council of Ireland under this section shall be presented to the Lord Lieutenant for His Majesty's assent, in like manner as a Bill passed by the Senate and House of Commons of Southern Ireland or Northern Ireland, and, on such assent being given, the order shall have effect in Southern and Northern Ireland respectively, as if enacted by the Parliament of Southern Ireland or Northern Ireland, as the case may be.

Executive Authority

8. – (1) The executive power in Southern Ireland and in Northern Ireland shall continue vested in His Majesty the King, and nothing in this Act shall affect the exercise of that power.

ARTICLES OF AGREEMENT
For a
TREATY BETWEEN GREAT BRITAIN AND IRELAND
Signed in London
on the 6th December 1921

ARTICLES OF AGREEMENT.

1. Ireland shall have the same constitutional status in the Community of Nations known as the British Empire, as the Dominion of New Zealand, and the Union of South Africa, with a Parliament having powers to make laws for the peace order and good government of Ireland and an Executive responsible to that Parliament, and shall be styled and known as the Irish Free State.
2. Subject to the provisions hereinafter set out the position of the Irish Free State in relation to the Imperial Parliament and Government and otherwise shall be that of the Dominion of Canada, and the law, practice and constitutional usage governing the relationship of the Crown or the representative of the Crown and of the Imperial Parliament to the Dominion of Canada shall govern their relationship to the Irish Free State.
3. The representative of the Crown in Ireland shall be appointed in like manner as the Governor-General of Canada and in accordance with the practice observed in the making of such appointments.
4. The oath to be taken by Members of the Parliament of the Irish Free State shall be in the following form:

> I .... do solemnly swear true faith and allegiance to the Constitution of the Irish Free State as by law established and that I will be faithful to H.M. King George V., his heirs and successors by law, in virtue of the common citizenship of Ireland with Great Britain and her adherence to and membership of the group of nations forming the British Commonwealth of Nations.

5. The Irish Free State shall assume liability for the service of the Public Debt of the United Kingdom as existing at the date hereof and towards the payment of war pensions as existing at that date in such proportion as may be fair and equitable, having regard to any just claims on the part of Ireland by way of set off or counter-claim, the amount of such sums being determined in default of agreement by the arbitration of one or more independent persons being citizens of the British Empire.

6. Until an arrangement has been made between the British and Irish Governments whereby the Irish Free State undertakes her own coastal defence, the defence by sea of Great Britain and Ireland shall be undertaken by His Majesty's Imperial Forces. But this shall not prevent the construction or maintenance by the Government of the Irish Free State of such vessels as are necessary for the protection of the Revenue or the Fisheries.

The foregoing provisions of this Article shall be reviewed at a Conference of Representatives of the British and Irish Governments to be held at the expiration of five years from the date hereof with a view to the undertaking by Ireland of a share in her own coastal defence.

7. The Government of the Irish Free State shall afford to His Majesty's Imperial Forces:

(a) In time of peace such harbour and other facilities as are indicated in the Annex hereto, or such other facilities as may from time to time be agreed between the British Government and the Government of the Irish Free State; and

(b) In time of war or of strained relations with a Foreign Power such harbour and other facilities as the British Government may require for the purposes of such defence as aforesaid.

8. With a view to securing the observance of the principle of international limitation of armaments, if the Government of the Irish Free State establishes and maintains a military defence force, the establishments thereof shall not exceed in size such proportion of the population of Ireland bears to the population of Great Britain.

9. The ports of Great Britain and the Irish Free State shall be freely open to the ships of the other country on payment of the customary port and other dues.

10. The Government of the Irish Free State agrees to pay fair compensation on terms not less favourable than those accorded by the Act of 1920 to judges, officials, members of Police Forces and other Public Servants who are discharged by it or who retire in consequence of the change of government effected in pursuance hereof.

Provided that this agreement shall not apply to members of the Auxiliary Police Force or to persons recruited in Great Britain for the Royal Irish Constabulary during the two years next preceding the date hereof. The British Government will assume responsibility for such compensation or pensions as may be payable to any of these excepted persons.

11. Until the expiration of one month from the passing of the Act of Parliament for the ratification of this instrument, the powers of the Parliament and the government of the Irish Free State shall not be exercisable as respects Northern Ireland and the provisions of the Government of Ireland Act, 1920, shall, so far as they relate to Northern Ireland, remain of full force and effect, and no election shall be held for the return of members to serve in the Parliament of the Irish Free State constituencies in Northern Ireland, unless a resolution is passed by both Houses of the Parliament of Northern Ireland in favour of the holding of such election before the end of the said month.

12. If before the expiration of the said month, an address is presented to His Majesty by both Houses of the Parliament of Northern Ireland to that effect, the powers of the Parliament and Government of the Irish Free State shall no longer extend to Northern Ireland, and the provisions of the Government of Ireland Act, 1920, (including those relating to the Council of Ireland) shall so far as they relate to Northern Ireland, continue to be of full force and effect, and this instrument shall have effect subject to the necessary modifications.

Provided that if such an address is so presented a Commission consisting of three persons, one to be appointed by the Government of the Irish Free State, one to be appointed by the Government of Northern Ireland and one who shall be Chairman to be appointed by the British Government shall determine in accordance with the wishes of the inhabitants, so far as may be compatible with economic and geographic conditions, the boundaries between Northern Ireland the rest of Ireland, and for the purposes of the Government of Ireland Act, 1920, and of this instrument, the boundary of Northern Ireland shall be such as may be determined by such Commission.

13. For the purpose of the last foregoing article, the powers of the Parliament of Southern Ireland under the Government of Ireland Act, 1920, to elect members of the Council of Ireland shall after the Parliament of the Irish Free State is constituted be exercised by that Parliament.

14. After the expiration of the said month, if no such address as is mentioned in Article 12 hereof is presented, the Parliament and Government of Northern Ireland shall continue to exercise as respects Northern Ireland the powers conferred on them by the Government of Ireland Act, 1920 but the Parliament and Government of the Irish Free State shall in Northern Ireland have in relation to matters in respect of which the Parliament of Northern Ireland has not power to make laws under that Act (including matters which under the said Act are within the jurisdiction of the Council of Ireland) the same powers as in the rest of Ireland, subject to such other provisions as may be agreed in manner hereinafter appearing.

15. At any time after the date hereof the Government of Northern Ireland and the provisional Government of Southern Ireland hereinafter constituted

may meet for the purpose of discussing the provisions subject to which the last foregoing article is to operate in the event of no such address as is therein mentioned being presented and those provisions may include:

(a) Safeguards with regard to patronage in Northern Ireland;

(b) Safeguards with regard to the collection of revenue in Northern Ireland;

(c) Safeguards with regard to import and export duties affecting the trade or industry of Northern Ireland;

(d) Safeguards for minorities in Northern Ireland;

(e) The settlement of the financial relations between Northern Ireland the Irish Free State;

(f) The establishment and powers of a local militia in Northern Ireland and the relation of the Defence Forces of the Irish Free State and of Northern Ireland respectively;

and if at any such meeting provisions are agreed to, the same shall have effects as if they were included amongst the provisions subject to which the Powers of the Parliament and Government of the Irish Free State are to be exercisable in Northern Ireland under Article 14 hereof.

16. Neither the Parliament of the Irish Free State nor the Parliament of Northern Ireland shall make any law so as either directly or indirectly to endow any religion or prohibit or restrict the free exercise thereof or given any preference or impose any disability on account of religious belief or religious status or affect prejudicially the right of any child to attend a school receiving public money without attending the religious instruction at the school or make any discrimination as respects state aid between schools under the management of different religious denominations or divert from any religious denomination or any educational institution any of its property except for public utility purposes and on payment of compensation.

17. By way of provisional arrangement for the administration of Southern Ireland during the interval which must elapse between the date hereof and the constitution of a Parliament and Government of the Irish Free State in accordance therewith, steps shall be taken forthwith for summoning a meeting of members of Parliament elected for constituencies in Southern Ireland since the passing of the Government of Ireland Act, 1920, and for constituting a provisional Government, and the British Government shall take steps necessary to transfer to such provisional Government the powers and machinery requisite for the discharge of its duties, provided that every member of such provisional Government shall have signified in writing his or her acceptance of this instrument. But this arrangement shall not continue in force beyond the expiration of twelve months from the date hereof.

18. This instrument shall be submitted forthwith by his Majesty's Government for the approval of Parliament and by the Irish signatories to a meeting summoned for the purpose of the members elected to sit in the House of

Commons of Southern Ireland, and if approved shall be ratified by the necessary legislation.

On behalf of the Irish Delegation	On behalf of the British Delegation
ART O GRIOBHTHA	D. LLOYD GEORGE
(ARTHUR GRIFFITH)	AUSTEN CHAMBERLAIN
MICHEAL O COILEAIN	BIRKENHEAD
RIOBARD BARTUN	WINSTON S. CHURCHILL
EUDHMONN S. O DUGAIN	
SEORSA GHABHAIN UI DHUBHTHAIGH	

December 6, 1921.

ANNEX

1. The following are the specific facilities required.

Dockyard port at Berehaven.

(a) Admiralty property and rights to be retained as at the date hereof. Harbour defences to remain in charge of British care and maintenance parties.

Queenstown

(b) Harbour defences to remain in charge of British care and maintenance parties. Certain mooring buoys to be retained for use of His Majesty's ships.

Belfast Lough

(c) Harbour defences to remain in charge of British care and maintenance parties.

Lough Swilly

(d) Harbour defences to remain in charge of British care and maintenance parties.

Aviation

(e) Facilities in the neighbourhood of the above Ports for coastal defence by air.

Oil Fuel Storage

(f) Haulbowline	To be offered for sale to commercial companies under guarantee that
Rathmullen	purchasers shall maintain a certain minimum stock for Admiralty purposes.

2. A Convention shall be made between the British Government and the Government of the Irish Free State to give effect to the following conditions:-

(a) That submarine cables shall not be landed or wireless stations for communication with places outside Ireland be established except by agreement with the British Government; that the existing cable landing rights and wireless concessions shall not be withdrawn except by agreement with the British Government, and that the British Government shall be entitled to land additional submarine cables or establish additional wireless stations for communication with places outside Ireland.

(b) That lighthouses, buoys, beacons, and any navigational marks or navigational aids shall be maintained by the Government of the Irish Free State as at the date hereof and shall not be removed or added to except by agreement with the British Government.

(c) That war signal stations shall be closed down and left in charge of care and maintenance parties, the Government of the Irish Free State being offered the option of taking them over and working them for commercial purposes subject to Admiralty inspection, and guaranteeing the upkeep of existing telegraphic communication therewith.

3. A Convention shall be made between the same Governments for the regulation of Civil Communication by Air.

D.Ll.G   B   W.S.C.   A.G.
                                                                M.O.C.
A.C.   R.B.

Ireland Withdraws from the Commonwealth – The Republic of Ireland Bill (1948)

Dáil Éireann debates, vol 113, cols 394–398. 24 November 1948

...The Bill is a simple Bill but it has tremendous and, I believe and hope, very beneficial results. The first section repeal the External Relations Act. I have dealt fully with that. Section Two provides: 'It is hereby declared that the description of the State shall be the Republic of Ireland.' That section is so obviously necessary that it requires no advocacy on my part to commend it to the Dáil. Deputies will recall that under the Constitution the name of the State is Eire or, according to Article Four, the name of the State is Eire or, in the English language, Ireland. Now, this section does not purport, as it could not, to repeal the Constitution. There is the name of the State and there is the description of the State. The name of the State is Ireland and the description of the State is the Republic of Ireland. That is the description of its constitutional and international status. Deputies are probably aware of the fact that tremendous confusion has been caused by the use of the work 'Eire' in Article 4. By a misuse by malicious people of that word, 'Eire', they have identified it with the Twenty-Six Counties and not with the State that was set up under this Constitution of 1937.

In documents of a legal character, such as, for instance, policies of insurance, there is always difficulty in putting in what word one wants to describe the State referred to. Section 2 provides a solution for these difficulties, and those malicious newspapers who want to refer in derogatory tones to this country as 'Eire' and who have coined these contemptuous adjectives about it, such as 'Éireannish' and 'Eirish', and all the rest of it, will have to conform to the legal direction here in this Bill.

Section 2 does these subsidiary things but it does more than that. It does something fundamental. It declares to the world that when this Bill is passed this State is unequivocally a republic. It states that as something that cannot be controverted or argued about and we can rely, I think and I hope, on international courtesy to prevent in future this contemptuous reference to us and the name of our State being used for contemptuous purposes, as it has been, by some people and by some organs in the last few years.

Section 3 merely provides that the President, on the authority and on the advice of the Government, may exercise the executive power or any executive function of the State in or in connection with its external relations. We now, and we will under this clause and under this Bill, have clarified our international position. No longer will there by letters of credence sent furtively across to Buckingham Palace. Diplomatic representatives will be received by the President of Ireland, the head of the State. We now have the unambiguous position that the President is head of the State and, if there are heads of State treaties to be entered into, if he goes abroad, he will go abroad as the head of this State, the head of the Republic of Ireland.

Section 4 says: 'This Act shall come into operation on such day as the Government may by Order appoint.'

When this Bill is enacted there will be no reason for those fears, those apprehensions which have been so assiduously set abroad by the poisonous sections of the Press, but there will be certain difficulties though not of a major character. I can hardly call them difficulties because they are not difficulties but merely legal matters that have to be cleared up and which may necessitate legislation here perhaps or perhaps in Canada, Australia, or Great Britain and we must provide a time limit, a breathing space within which these matters of detail can be carried out in concord and agreement. There are no very important matters; they are matters of detail, legal technicalities, not matters of difficulty or controversy. They will take some little time. I cannot say how long it will take to have these details brought into operation and accordingly, however much we would like to see this Bill come into immediate operation, we will have to have a breathing space for the various Parliaments to settle up the details which require to be settled up. They are not matters of difficulty.

As I said before and now repeat, I recommend this Bill to the Dáil and ask for its unanimous acceptance by the Dáil. It will, I believe, if it is passed in a spirit of goodwill, if it is passed unanimously, do and achieve what its primary purpose hopes for: to bring peace here in this part of our country and by bringing this country well on to the international stage, by lifting this problem of Partition from the domestic arena and putting it on the international scene, give us not a faint hope but a clear prospect of bringing about the unity of Ireland.

I should like to say one more thing in conclusion. There have been sometimes smug, sometimes fearsome declarations by British Ministers or British Governments that the problem of Partition is an Irish problem, that must be settled between Irishmen. That Pilate-like attitude can no longer be held by statesmen with the courage and decency to look facts in the face. This problem was created by an Act of the British Parliament, the Government of Ireland Act, 1920. It may be insisting on the obvious, but I have had occasion to insist very strongly on the obvious in recent months. That Act of 1920 was passed before the Treaty of 1921 and it is surprising how many people think that the Partition of our country was effected by the Treaty of 1921. The problem was created by the British Government and the British Parliament and it is for them to solve the problem. They cannot wash their hands of it and clear themselves of responsibility for it. The Act of 1920 is a very poor title for a claim which is not based upon morality and justice. The Government of the six northeastern counties claim that and assert it by virtue of a majority, a statutorily created majority, a majority created deliberately under the Act of 1920 to coerce and keep within the bounds of their so-called State masses of our Catholic people and fellow Irishmen who do not want to be there. That Act of 1920 was put on the Statute Book and brought into operation without a single vote cast in its favour by any Irish representative in the British Parliament or without anybody North or South wanting it. Therefore the problem of undoing that wrong devolves upon the British Government. We are doing our part down here. We are doing our part by this Bill.

The whole basis of the case I make for this Bill is founded, on goodwill, is founded on the end of bitterness. It is founded on a sincere desire to have greater goodwill with Great Britain. We hope through the creation of that goodwill, through fostering further goodwill, that that will help materially to induce the British Government and Great Britain to take a hand in the undoing of the wrong for which their predecessors were responsible in 1920. We believe that this Bill, by creating conditions on which that goodwill can increase, will help towards the solution of the problem of Partition. We hold out, as I said here earlier today, the hand of friendship to the decent people of Northern Ireland and they can be assured if they come in here, end this great wrong and come into a unified Ireland, they will be doing good work for themselves, for the whole of Ireland and for that country to which they proclaim their intense loyalty, Great Britain, and the Commonwealth of Nations and be giving a lasting contribution to the peace of the world.

IRELAND ACT, 1949 [enacted by the British Parliament]

An Act to recognise and declare the constitutional position as to the part of Ireland heretofore known as Eire, and to make provisions as to the name by which it may be known and the manner in which the law is to apply in relation to it; to declare and affirm the constitutional position and the territorial integrity of Northern Ireland and to amend, as respects the Parliament of the United Kingdom, the law relating to the qualifications of electors in constituencies in Northern Ireland; and for purposes connected with the matters aforesaid. (2nd June 1949)

Be in enacted by the King's most Excellent Majesty, by and with the advice and consent of the Lords Spiritual and Temporal, and Commons, in this present Parliament assembled, and by the authority of the same, as follows:-

1. – (1) It is hereby recognised and declared that the part of Ireland heretofore known as Eire ceased, as from the eighteenth day of April, nineteen hundred and forty-nine, to be part of His Majesty's dominions.

(2) It is hereby declared that Northern Ireland remains part of His Majesty's dominions and of the United Kingdom and it is hereby affirmed that in no event will Northern Ireland or any part thereof cease to be part of His Majesty's dominions and of the United Kingdom without the consent of the Parliament of Northern Ireland.

(3) The part of Ireland referred to in subsection (1) of this section is hereafter in this Act referred to, and may in any Act, enactment or instrument passed or made after the passing of this Act be referred to, by the name attributed thereto by the law thereof, that is to say, as the Republic of Ireland.

2. – (1) It is hereby declared that, notwithstanding that the Republic of Ireland is not part of His Majesty's dominions, the Republic of Ireland is not a foreign country for the purposes of any law in force in any part of the United Kingdom or in any colony, protectorate or United Kingdom trust territory, whether by virtue of a rule of law in force in any part of the United Kingdom or in any colony, protectorate or United Kingdom trust territory, whether by virtue of a rule of law or of an Act of Parliament or any other enactment or instrument whatsoever, whether passed or made before or after the passing of this Act, and references in any Act of Parliament, other enactment or instrument whatsoever, whether passed or made before or after the passing of this Act, to foreigners, aliens, foreign countries, and foreign or foreign-built ships or aircraft shall be construed accordingly.

(2) The person who, in the United Kingdom, is the chief representative of the Republic of Ireland or of the Government thereof shall, whatever the style of his office, have the same privileges and exemptions as to taxation and otherwise as fall to be accorded under the law for the time being in force to High Commissions and Agents General within the meaning of section nine-

teen of the Finance Act, 1923, and his staff shall have the same privileges and exemptions as to taxation and otherwise as fall to be accorded under the laws for the time being in force to their staffs.

3. – (1) It is hereby declared that

(a) the operation of the following statutory provisions, that is to say:

(i) The British Nationality Act, 1948 (and in particular, and without prejudice to the generality of the preceding words, sections two, three and six thereof);

(ii) so much of any Act, or of any Act of the Parliament of Northern Ireland, as gives effect, or enables effect to be given, to agreements or arrangements made at any time after the coming into operation of the original constitution of the Irish Free State, being agreements or arrangements made with the Government of, or otherwise affecting, the part of Ireland which now forms the Republic of Ireland, including agreements or arrangements made after the commencement of this Act; and

(iii) the Orders in Council made under sections five and six of the Irish Free State (Consequential Provisions Act, 1922 (Session 2), is not affected by the fact that the Republic of Ireland is not part of His Majesty's dominions; and

(b) that, in the said provisions and in any Act of parliament or other enactment or instrument whatsoever, so far as it operates as part of the law of, or of any part of, the United Kingdom or any colony, protectorate or United Kingdom trust territory, references to citizens of Eire include, on their true construction, references to citizens of the Republic of Ireland.

(2) Until provision to the contrary is made by Parliament or by some other authority having power in that behalf, the following provisions shall have as respects any Act of Parliament or other enactment or instrument whatsoever passed or made before the passing of this Act, so far as it operates as part of the law of, or any part of, the United Kingdom or any colony, protectorate or United Kingdom trust territory that is to say –

(a) if it contains a reference to His Majesty's dominions, or to any parts thereof, which would have extended so as in any way to include the Republic of Ireland had that part of Ireland remained part of His Majesty's dominions, it shall have effect, with any necessary adaptations, as if that reference did extend so as in that way to include the Republic of Ireland, notwithstanding that that part of Ireland is no longer part of His Majesty's dominions; and

(b) in particular and without prejudice to the generality of the preceding paragraph, if it contains a reference to all, or to any class or descriptions of, British or British-built ships or aircraft which would have extended so as in any way to include all, or any classes or descriptions of, the ships or aircraft of or built in the Republic of Ireland had that part of Ireland remained part of His Majesty's dominions, it shall have effect, with any necessary adaptations, as if that reference did extend so as in that way to include all, or that class or description of, the ships or aircraft of or built in the Republic of Ireland, as the case may be, notwithstanding that that part of Ireland is no longer part of His Majesty's dominions.

(3) The last preceding subsection shall not apply to so much of section two of the Regency Act, 1937, as requires that a declaration under that section of the incapacity or unavailability of the Sovereign should be communicated to the Governments of His Majesty's dominions, and nothing in this section shall be construed as implying that any alteration in the law touching the Succession to the Throne or the Royal Style and Titles requires the assent of the Parliament of the Republic of Ireland.

4. – (1) Subject to the provisions of subsection (4) of this section, subsection (2) of section three of the British Nationality Act, 1948 (which relates to the effect of existing Acts of Parliament and other enactments and instruments) shall have effect in relation to Acts, enactments or instruments passed or made before the end of the year nineteen hundred and forty-nine as it has effect in relation to Acts, enactments or instruments in force at the date of the commencement of that Act.

(2) Subject to the provisions of subsection (4) of this section, subsection (2) of the last preceding section shall have effect in relation to Acts, enactments or instruments passed or made before the end of the year nineteen hundred and forty-nine as it has effect in relation to Acts, enactments or instruments passed or made before the passing of this Act.

(3) Where, whether by virtue of the preceding provisions of this section or otherwise, subsection (2) of section three of the British Nationality Act, 1948, or subsection (2) of the last preceding section has effect in relation to any Act, enactment or instrument, it shall, subject to the provisions of subsection (4) of this section, have effect also in relation to any other Act, enactment or instrument which, whether expressly or by implications, is required to be construed in the same way as that Act, enactment or instrument.

(4) The preceding provision of this section have effect in relation to any Act, enactment or instrument only in so far as a contrary intention does not appear in that Act, enactment or instrument:

Provided that the fact that an Act, enactment or instrument refers to a British subject, or to, or to any part of, His Majesty's dominions, or to a British or British-built ship or aircraft, without referring to a citizen of the Republic of Ireland, to the Republic of Ireland or to a ship or aircraft of or built in the Republic of Ireland shall not of itself be taken as indicating a contrary intention for the purposes of this subsection, and the same principle of construction shall be applied to other similar expressions.

APPENDICES

5. – (1) A person who (a) was born before the sixth day of December, nineteen hundred and twenty-two, in the part of Ireland which now forms the Republic of Ireland; and (b) was a British subject immediately before the date of the commencement of the British Nationality Act, 1948, shall not be deemed to have ceased to be a British subject on the coming into force of that Act unless either –

> (i) he was, on the said sixth day of December, domiciled in the part of Ireland which now forms the Republic of Ireland; or (ii) he was, on or after the tenth day of April nineteen hundred and thirty-five and before the date of the commencement of that Act, permanently resident in that part of Ireland; or (iii) he had, before the date of commencement of that Act, been registered as a citizen of Eire under the laws of that part of Ireland relating to citizenship.

(2) In relation to persons born before the sixth day of December in the part of Ireland which now forms the Republic of Ireland, being persons who do not satisfy any of the conditions specified in paragraphs (i), (ii) and (iii) of subsection (1) of this sections twelve and thirteen of the said Act (which relate to citizenship of the United Kingdom and Colonies and to British subjects without citizenship) shall have effect and be deemed always to have effect as if, in paragraph (a) of subsection (4) of the said section twelve, the words 'or a citizen of Eire' and in subsection (1) of the said section thirteen, the words 'or of Eire' were omitted.

(3) So much of the said Act as has the effect of providing that a person is, in specified circumstances, to be treated for the purposes of that Act as having been a British subject immediately before the commencement thereof shall apply also for the purposes of this section.

(4) Nothing in this section affects the position of any person who, on the coming into force of the British Nationality Act, 1948, became a citizen of the United Kingdom and Colonies or a British subject without citizenship apart from the provisions of this section.

6. – (1) Notwithstanding anything in the Representation of the People Act, 1948, a person shall not be entitled to vote as an elector of an election of a person to serve as a Member of the Parliament of the United Kingdom for a constituency in Northern Ireland unless he was resident in Northern Ireland during the whole of the period of three months ending on the qualifying date for that election.

(2) Subsection (2) of section two of the Representation of the People Act, 1948 (which specifies the cases where a person's residence is not be deemed to be interrupted) and subsection (3) of that section (which provides that a person detained in a mental hospital or prison is not to be treated as resident there) shall apply for the purposes of the preceding subsection as they apply for the purposes of section one of that Act.

(3) The preceding provisions of this section shall not affect the right to vote of any service voter, and a person ceasing to have a service qualification shall

393

be treated for the purposes of subsection (1) of this section as if he were resident in Northern Ireland during the period during which he had a service qualification.

(4) The register of parliamentary electors shall, for the purposes of Part 1 of the Representation of the People Act, 1948, be conclusive on the question whether or not a person registered as an elector in a constituency in Northern Ireland was resident in Northern Ireland during the whole of the period of three months ending on the qualifying date.

(5) This section shall be construed as if enacted in Part 1 of the Representation of the People Act, 1948:

Provided that this section shall not have effect with respect to the first register to be prepared under that Act or the elections, if any, for which that register is used.

7. – (1) This Act may be cited as the Ireland Act, 1949.

(2) References in this Act to colonies, protectorates and United Kingdom trust territories hail be construed as if they were references contained in the British Nationalist Act, 1948.

(3) Save as otherwise expressly provided, this Act shall be deemed to have had effect as from the eighteenth day of April, nineteen hundred and forty-nine.

ANGLO-IRISH AGREEMENT
15 November 1985

The Government of the United Kingdom of Great Britain and Northern Ireland and the Government of the Republic of Ireland;

Wishing further to develop the unique relationship between their peoples and the close cooperation between their countries as friendly neighbours and as partners in the European Community;

Recognising the major interest of both their countries and, above all, of the people of Northern Ireland in diminishing the divisions there and achieving lasting peace and stability;

Recognising the need for continuing efforts to reconcile and to acknowledge the rights of the two major traditions that exist in Ireland, represented on the one hand by those who wish for no change in the present status of Northern Ireland and on the other hand by those who aspire to a sovereign united Ireland achieved by peaceful means and through agreement;

Reaffirming their total rejection of any attempt to promote political objectives by violence or the threat of violence and their determination to work together to ensure that those who adopt or support such methods do not succeed;

Recognising that a condition of genuine reconciliation and dialogue between unionists and nationalists is mutual recognition and acceptance of each other's rights;

Recognising and respecting the identities of the two communities in Northern Ireland, and the right of each to pursue its aspirations by peaceful and constitutional means;

Reaffirming their commitment to a society in Northern Ireland of which all may live in peace, free from discrimination and intolerance, and with the opportunity for both communities to participate fully in the structures and processes of government;

Have accordingly agreed as follows:

A STATUS OF NORTHERN IRELAND

Article 1

The two Governments

(a) affirm that any change in the status of Northern Ireland would only come about with the consent of a majority of the people of Northern Ireland;

(b) recognise that the present wish of a majority of the people of Northern Ireland is for no change in the status of Northern Ireland;

(c) declare that, if in the future a majority of the people of Northern Ireland clearly wish for and formally consent to the establishment of a united Ireland, they will introduce and support in the respective Parliaments legislation to give effect to that wish.

B THE INTERGOVERNMENTAL CONFERENCE

Article 2

(a) There is hereby established, within the framework of the Anglo-Irish Intergovernmental Council set up after the meeting between the two heads of Government on 6 November 1981, an Intergovernmental Conference (hereinafter referred to as 'the Conference'), concerned with Northern Ireland and with relations between the two parts of the island of Ireland, to deal, as set out in this Agreement, on a regular basis with: (i) political matters; (ii) security and related matters; (iii) legal matters, including the administration of justice; (iv) the promotion of cross-border cooperation.

(b) The United Kingdom Government accept that the Irish Government will put forward views and proposals on matters relating to Northern Ireland within the field of activity of the Conference in so far as those matters are not the responsibility of a devolved administration in Northern Ireland. In the interest of promoting peace and stability, determined effort shall be made through the Conference to resolve any differences. The Conference will be mainly concerned with Northern Ireland; but some of the matters under consideration will involve cooperative action in both parts of the island of Ireland, and possibly also in Great Britain. Some of the proposals considered in respect of Northern Ireland may also be found to have application by the Irish Government. There is no derogation from the sovereignty of either the United Kingdom Government or the Irish Government, and each retains responsibility for the decisions and administration of government within its own jurisdiction.

Article 3

The Conference shall meet at ministerial or official level, as required. The business of the Conference will thus receive attention at the highest level. Regular and frequent ministerial meetings shall be held, and in particular special meetings shall be convened at the request of either side. Officials may meet in subordinate groups. Membership of the Conference and of sub-groups shall be small and flexible. When the Conference meets at ministerial level the Secretary of State for Northern Ireland and an Irish minister designated as the Permanent Irish Ministerial Representative shall be joint chairmen. Within the framework of the Conference other British and Irish ministers may hold or attend meetings as appropriate; when legal matters are under consideration the Attorneys General may attend. Ministers may be accompanied by their officials and their professional advisers; for example, when questions of security policy or security cooperation are being discussed, they may be accompanied by the Chief Constable of the Royal Ulster Constabulary and the Commissioner of the Garda Siochána or when questions of economic or social policy or cooperation are being discussed, they may be accompanied by officials of the relevant departments. A Secretariat shall be established by the two Governments to service the Conference on a continuing basis in the discharge of its functions as set out in this Agreement.

Article 4

(a) In relation to matters coming within its field of activity, the Conference shall be a framework within which the United Kingdom Government and the Irish Government work together

(i) for the accommodations of the rights and identities of the two traditions which exist in Northern Ireland; and

(ii) for peace, stability and prosperity throughout the island of Ireland by promoting reconciliation, respect for human rights, cooperation against terrorism and the development of economic, social and cultural cooperation.

(b) It is the declared policy of the United Kingdom Government that responsibility in respect of certain matters within the powers of the Secretary of State for Northern Ireland should be devolved within Northern Ireland on a basis which would secure widespread acceptance throughout the community. The Irish Government support that policy.

(c) Both Governments recognise that devolution can be achieved only with the cooperation of constitutional representatives within Northern Ireland of both traditions there. The Conference shall be a framework within which the Irish Government may put forward views and proposals on the modalities of bringing about devolution in Northern Ireland, in so far as they relate to the interests of the minority community.

C POLITICAL MATTERS

Article 5

(a) The Conference shall concern itself with measures to recognise and accommodate the rights and identities of the two traditions in Northern Ireland, to protect human rights and to prevent discrimination. Matters to be considered in this area include measures to foster the cultural heritage of both traditions, changes in electoral arrangements, the use of flags and emblems, the avoidance of economic and social discrimination and the advantages and disadvantages of a Bill of Rights in some form in Northern Ireland.

(b) The discussion of these matters shall be mainly concerned with Northern Ireland, but the possible application of any measures pursuant to this Article by the Irish Government in their jurisdiction shall not be excluded.

(c) If it should prove impossible to achieve and sustain devolution on a basis which secures widespread acceptance in Northern Ireland, the Conference shall be a framework within which the Irish Government may, where the interests of the minority community are significantly or especially affected, put forward views on proposals for major legislation and on major policy issues, which are within the purview of the Northern Ireland departments and which remain the responsibility of the Secretary of State for Northern Ireland.

Article 6

The conference shall be a framework within which the Irish Government may put forward views and proposals on the role and composition of bodies appointed by the Secretary of State for Northern Ireland or by departments subject to his direction and control, including: the Standing Advisory Commission on Human Rights; the Fair Employment Agency; the Equal Opportunities Commission; the Police Authority for Northern Ireland; the Police Complaints Board.

D SECURITY AND RELATED MATTERS

Article 7

(a) The Conference shall consider: (i) security policy; (ii) relations between the security forces and the community; (iii) prisons policy.

(b) The Conference shall consider the security situation at its regular meetings and thus provide an opportunity to address policy issues, serious incidents and forthcoming events.

(c) The two Governments agree that there is a need for a programme of special measures in Northern Ireland to improve relations between the security forces and the community, with the object in particular of making the security forces more readily accepted by the nationalist community. Such a programme shall be developed, for the Conference's consideration, and may include the establishment of local consultative machinery, training in community relations, crime prevention schemes involving the community, improvements in arrangements for handling complaints, and action to increase the proportion of members of the minority in the Royal Ulster Constabulary. Elements of the programme may be considered by the Irish Government suitable for application within their jurisdiction.

(d) The Conference may consider policy issues relating to prisons. Individual cases may be raised as appropriate, so that information can be provided or enquiries instituted.

E LEGAL MATTERS, INCLUDING THE ADMINISTRATION OF JUSTICE

Article 8

The Conference shall deal with issues of concern to both countries relating to the enforcement of the criminal law. In particular, it shall consider whether there are areas of the criminal law applying in the North and in the South respectively which might with benefit be harmonised. The two Governments agree on the importance of public confidence in the administration of justice. The Conference shall seek, with the help of advice from experts as appropriate, measures which would give substantial expression to this aim, considering inter alia the possibility of mixed courts in both jurisdictions for the trial of certain offences. The Conference shall also be concerned with policy aspects of extradition and extra-territorial jurisdiction as between North and South.

F CROSS-BORDER COOPERATION ON SECURITY, ECONOMIC, SOCIAL AND CULTURAL MATTERS

Article 9

(a) With a view to enhancing cross-border co-operation on security matters, the Conference shall set in hand a programme of work to be undertaken by the Chief Constable of the Royal Ulster Constabulary and the Commissioner of the Garda Siochána and, where appropriate, groups of officials in such areas as threat assessments, exchange of information, liaison structures, technical cooperation, training of personnel, and operational resources.

(b) The Conference shall have no operational responsibilities; responsibility for police operations shall remain with the heads of the respective police forces, the Chief Constable of the Royal Ulster Constabulary maintaining his links with the Secretary of State for Northern Ireland and the Commissioner of the Garda Siochána his links with the Minister for Justice.

Article 10

(a) The two Governments shall cooperate to promote the economic and social development of those areas of both parts of Ireland which have suffered most severely from the consequences of the instability of recent years, and shall consider the possibility of securing international support for this work.

(b) If it should prove impossible to achieve and sustain devolution on a basis which secures widespread acceptance in Northern Ireland, the Conference shall be a framework for the promotion of cooperation between the two parts of Ireland concerning cross-border aspects of economic, social and cultural matters in relation to which the Secretary of State for Northern Ireland continues to exercise authority.

(c) If responsibility is devolved in respect of certain matters in the economic, social or cultural areas currently within the responsibility of the Secretary of

State for Northern Ireland, machinery will need to be established by the responsible authorities in the North and South for practical cooperation in respect of cross-border aspects of these issues.

G ARRANGEMENTS FOR REVIEW

Article 11

At the end of three years from signature of this Agreement, or earlier if requested by either Government, the working of the Conference shall be reviewed by the two Governments to see whether any changes in the scope and nature of its activities are desirable.

H INTERPARLIAMENTARY RELATIONS

Article 12

It will be for parliamentary decisions in Westminster and in Dublin whether to establish an Anglo-Irish parliamentary body of the kind adumbrated in the Anglo-Irish Studies Report of November 1981. The two Governments agree that they would give support as appropriate to such a body, if it were to be established.

J FINAL CLAUSES

Article 13

This Agreement shall enter into force on the date on which the two Governments exchange notifications of their acceptance of this Agreement.

ANGLO-IRISH JOINT DECLARATION
15 December 1993

1. The Taoiseach, Mr. Albert Reynolds, TD, and the Prime Minister, the Rt. Hon. John Major MP, acknowledge that the most urgent and important issue facing the people of Ireland, North and South, and the British and Irish Governments together, is to remove the causes of conflict, to overcome the legacy of history and to heal the divisions which have resulted, recognising that the absence of a lasting and satisfactory settlement of relationships between the peoples of both islands has contributed to continuing tragedy and suffering. They believe that the development of an agreed framework for peace, which has been discussed between them since early last year, and which is based on a number of key principles articulated by the two Governments over the past 20 years, together with the adaptation of other widely accepted principles, provides the starting point of a peace process designed to culminate in a political settlement.

2. The Taoiseach and the Prime Minister are convinced of the inestimable value to both their peoples, and particularly for the next generation, of healing divisions in Ireland and of ending a conflict which has been so manifestly to the detriment of all. Both recognise that the ending of divisions can come about only through the agreement and cooperation of the people, North and South, representing both traditions in Ireland. They therefore make a solemn commitment to promote cooperation at all levels on the basis of the fundamental principles, undertakings, obligations under international agreements, to which they have jointly committed themselves, and the guarantees which each Government has given and now reaffirms, including Northern Ireland's statutory constitutional guarantee. It is their aim to foster agreement and reconciliation, leading to a new political framework founded on consent and encompassing arrangements within Northern Ireland, for the whole island and between these islands.

3. They also consider that the development of Europe will, of itself, require new approaches to serve interests common to both parts of the island of Ireland, and to Ireland and the United Kingdom as partners in the European Union.

4. The Prime Minister, on behalf of the British Government, reaffirms that they will uphold the democratic wish of a greater number of the people of Northern Ireland on the issue of whether they prefer to support the Union or a sovereign united Ireland. On this basis, he reiterates, on behalf of the British Government, that they have no selfish strategic or economic interest in Northern Ireland. Their primary interest is to see peace, stability and reconciliation established by agreement among all the people who inhabit the island, and they will work together with the Irish Government to achieve such an agreement, which will embrace the totality of relationships. The role of the British Government will be to encourage, facilitate and enable the achievement of such agreement over a period through a process of dialogue and cooperation based on full respect for the rights and identities of both traditions in Ireland. They accept that such agreement may, as of right, take the form of agreed structures for the island as a whole, including a united Ireland achieved by peaceful means on the following basis. The British Government agree that it is for the people of the island of Ireland alone, by agreement between the two parts respectively, to exercise their right of self-determination on the basis of consent, freely and concurrently given, North and South, to bring about a united Ireland, if that is their wish. They reaffirm as a binding obligation that they will, for their part, introduce the necessary legislation to give effect to this, or equality to any measure of agreement on future relationships in Ireland which the people living in Ireland may themselves freely so determine without external impediment. They believe that the people of Britain would wish, in friendship to all sides, to enable the people of Ireland to reach agreement on how they may live together in harmony and in partnership, with respect for their diverse traditions, and will full recognition of the special links and the unique relationship which exist between the peoples of Britain and Ireland.

5. The Taoiseach, on behalf of the Irish Government, considers that the lessons of Irish history, and especially of Northern Ireland, show that stability and well-being will not be found under any political system which is refused allegiance or rejected on grounds of identity by a significant minority of those governed by it. For this reason, it would be wrong to attempt to impose a united Ireland, in the absence of the freely given consent of a majority of the people of Northern Ireland. He accepts, on behalf of the Irish Government, that the democratic right of self-determination by the people of Ireland as a whole must be achieved and exercised with and subject to the agreement and consent of a majority of the people of Northern Ireland and must, consistent with justice and equity, respect the democratic dignity and the civil rights and religious liberties of both communities, including:
  - the right of free political thought;
  - the right of freedom and expression of religion;
  - the right to pursue democratically national and political aspirations;

- the right to seek constitutional change by peaceful and legitimate means;
- the right to live wherever one chooses without hindrance;
- the right to equal opportunity in all social and economic activity, regardless of class, creed, sex or colour.

These would be reflected in any future political and constitutional arrangements emerging from a new and more broadly based agreement.

6. The Taoiseach however recognises the genuine difficulties and barriers to building relationships of trust either within or beyond Northern Ireland, from which both traditions suffer. He will work to create a new era of trust, in which suspicion of the motives or actions of others is removed on the part of either community. He considers that the future of the island depends on the nature of the relationship between the two main traditions that inhabit it. Every effort must be made to build a new sense of trust between those communities. In recognition of the fears of the Unionist community and as a token of his willingness to make a personal contribution to the building up of that necessary trust, the Taoiseach will examine with his colleagues any elements in the democratic life and organisation of the Irish State that can be represented to the Irish Government in the course of political dialogue as a real and substantial threat to their way of life and ethos, or that can be represented as not being fully consistent with a modern democratic and pluralist society, and undertakes to examine any possible ways of removing such obstacles. Such an examination would of course have due regard to the desire to preserve those inherited values that are largely shared throughout the island or that belong to the cultural and historical roots of the people of this island in all their diversity. The Taoiseach hopes that over time a meeting of hearts and minds will develop, which will bring all the people of Ireland together, and will work towards that objective, but he pledges in the meantime that as a result of the efforts that will be made to build mutual confidence no Northern Unionist should ever have to fear in future that this ideal will be pursued either by threat or coercion.

7. Both Governments accept that Irish unity would be achieved only by those who favour this outcome persuading those who do not, peacefully and without coercion or violence, and that, if it in the future a majority of the people of Northern Ireland are so persuaded, both Governments will support and give legislative effect to their wish. But, notwithstanding the solemn affirmation by both Governments in the Anglo-Irish Agreement that any change in the status of Northern Ireland would only come about with the consent of a majority of the people of Northern Ireland, the Taoiseach also recognises the continuing uncertainties and misgivings which dominate so much of Northern Unionist attitudes towards the rest of Ireland. He believes that we stand at a stage of our history when the genuine feelings of all traditions in the North must be recognised and acknowledged. He appeals to both traditions at this

time to grasp the opportunity for a fresh start and a new beginning, which could hold such promise for all our lives and the generations to come. He asks the people of Northern Ireland to look on the people of the Republic as friends, who share their grief and shame over all the suffering of the last quarter of a century, and who want to develop the best possible relationship with them, a relationship in which trust and new understanding can flourish and grow. The Taoiseach also acknowledges the presence in the Constitution of the Republic of elements which are deeply resented by Northern Unionists, but which at the same time reflect the hopes and ideals which lie deep in the heart of many Irish men and women North and South. But as we move towards a new era of understanding in which new relationships of trust may grow and bring peace to the island of Ireland, the Taoiseach believes that the time has come to consider together how best the hopes and identities of all can be expressed in more balanced ways, which no longer engender division and the lack of trust to which he has referred. He confirms that, in the event of an overall settlement, the Irish Government will, as part of a balanced constitutional accommodation, put forward and support proposals for change in the Irish Constitution which would fully reflect the principle of consent in Northern Ireland.

8. The Taoiseach recognises the need to engage in dialogue which would address with honesty and integrity the fears of all traditions. But that dialogue, both within the North and between the people and their representatives of both parts of Ireland, must be entered into with an acknowledgement that the future security and welfare of the people of the island will depend on an open, frank and balanced approach to all the problems which for too long have caused division.

9. The British and Irish Governments will seek, along with the Northern Ireland constitutional parties through a process of political dialogue, to create institutions and structures which, while respecting the diversity of the people of Ireland, would enable them to work together in all areas of common interest. This will help over a period to build the trust necessary to end past divisions, leading to an agreed and peaceful future. Such structures would, of course, include institutional recognition of the special links that exist between the peoples of Britain and Ireland as part of the totality of relationships, while taking account of newly forged links with the rest of Europe.

10. The British and Irish Governments reiterate that the achievements of peace must involve a permanent end to the use of, or support for, paramilitary violence. They confirm that, in these circumstances, democratically mandated parties which establish a commitment to exclusively peaceful methods and which have shown that they abide by the democratic process, are free to participate fully in democratic politics and to join in dialogue in due course between the Governments and the political parties on the way ahead.

11. The Irish Government would make their own arrangements within their jurisdiction to enable democratic parties to consult together and share in dialogue about the political future. The Taoiseach's intention is that these arrangements could include the establishment, in consultation with other parties, of a Forum for Peace and Reconciliation to make recommendations on ways in which agreement and trust between both traditions in Ireland can be promoted and established.

12. The Taoiseach and the Prime Minister are determined to build on the fervent wish of both their peoples to see old fears and animosities replaced by a climate of peace. They believe the framework they have set out offers the people of Ireland, North and South, whatever their tradition, the basis to agree that from now on their differences can be negotiated and resolved exclusively by peaceful political means. They appeal to all concerned to grasp the opportunity for a new departure. That step would compromise no position or principle, nor prejudice the future for either community. On the contrary, it would be an incomparable gain for all. It would break decisively the cycle of violence and the intolerable suffering it entails for the people of these islands, particularly for both communities in Northern Ireland. It would allow the process of economic and social cooperation on the island to realise its full potential for prosperity and mutual understanding. It would transform the prospects for building on the progress already made in the Talks process, involving the two Governments and the constitutional parties in Northern Ireland. The Taoiseach and the Prime Minister believe that these arrangements offer an opportunity to lay the foundations for a more peaceful and harmonious future, devoid of the violence and bitter divisions which have scarred the past generation. They commit themselves and their Governments to continue to work together, unremittingly, towards that objective.

THE ANGLO-IRISH AGREEMENT 1998

AGREEMENT REACHED IN THE MULTI-PARTY NEGOTIATIONS

ANNEX A
DRAFT CLAUSES/SCHEDULES FOR INCORPORATION IN BRITISH LEGISLATION

1. (1) It is hereby declared that Northern Ireland in its entirety remains part of the United Kingdom and shall not cease to be so without the consent of a majority of the people of Northern Ireland voting in a poll held for the purposes of this section in accordance with Schedule 1.

    (2) But if the wish expressed by a majority in such a poll is that Northern Ireland should cease to be part of the United Kingdom and form part of a united Ireland, the Secretary of State shall lay before Parliament such proposals to give effect to that wish as may be agreed between Her Majesty's Government in the United Kingdom and the Government of Ireland.

2. The Government of Ireland Act 1920 is repealed; and this Act shall have effect notwithstanding any other previous enactment.

SCHEDULE 1
POLLS FOR THE PURPOSE OF SECTION 1

1. The Secretary of State may by order direct the holding of a poll for the purposes of section 1 on a date specified in the order.

2. Subject to paragraph 3, the Secretary of State shall exercise the power under paragraph 1 if at any time it appears likely to him that a majority of those voting would express a wish that Northern Ireland should cease to be part of the United Kingdom and form part of a united Ireland.

3. The Secretary of State shall not make an order under paragraph 1 earlier than seven years after the holding of a previous poll under this Schedule.

4. (Remaining paragraphs along the lines of paragraph 2 and 3 of existing Schedule I to 1973 Act.)

ANNEX B
IRISH GOVERNMENT DRAFT LEGISLATION TO AMEND THE CONSTITUTION

Add to Article 29 the following sections:

1. The State may consent to be bound by the British-Irish Agreement done at Belfast on the day of 1998, hereinafter called the Agreement.

2. Any institution established by or under the Agreement may exercise the powers and functions thereby conferred on it in respect of all or any part of the island of Ireland notwithstanding any other provision of this Constitution conferring a like power or function on any person or any organ of State appointed under or created or established by or under this Constitution. Any power or function conferred on such an institution in relation to the settlement or resolution of disputes or controversies may be in addition to or in substitution for any like power or function conferred by this Constitution on any such person or organ of State as aforesaid.

3. If the Government declare that the State has become obliged, pursuant to the Agreement, to give effect to the amendment of this Constitution referred to therein, then, notwithstanding Article 46 hereof, this Constitution shall be amended as follows:

    i.   the following Articles shall be substituted for Articles 2 and 3 of the Irish text:
    "2. [Irish text to be inserted here]
    3. [Irish text to be inserted here]"

    ii. The following Articles shall be substituted for Articles 2 and 3 of the English text:

    Article 2
    It is the entitlement and birthright of every person born in the island of Ireland, which includes its islands and seas, to be part of the Irish nation. That is also the entitlement of all persons otherwise qualified in accordance with law to be citizens of Ireland. Furthermore, the Irish national cherishes its special affinity with people of Irish ancestry living abroad who share its cultural identity and heritage.

    Article 3
    1. It is the firm will of the Irish nation, in harmony and friendship, to unite all the people who share the territory of the island of Ireland, in all the diversity of their identities and traditions, recognizing that a united Ireland shall be brought about only by peaceful means with the consent of a majority of the people, democratically expressed, in both jurisdictions in the island. Until then, the laws enacted by the Parliament established by this Constitution shall have the like area and extent of application as

the laws enacted by the Parliament that existed immediately before the coming into operation of this Constitution.

2. Institutions with executive powers and functions that are shared between those jurisdictions may be established by their respective responsible authorities for stated purposes and may exercise powers and functions in respect of all or any part of the island.

iii. the following section shall be added to the Irish text of this Article:

"8. [Irish text to be inserted here]"

and

iv. The following section shall be added to the English test of this Article:

"8. The State may exercise extra-territorial jurisdiction in accordance with the generally recognised principles of international law."

4. If a declaration under this section is made, this subsection and subsection 3, other than the amendment of this Constitution effected thereby, and subsection 5 of this section shall be omitted from every official text of this Constitution published thereafter, but notwithstanding such omission this section shall continue to have the force of law.

5. If such a declaration is not made within twelve months of this section being added to this Constitution or such longer period as may be provided for by law, this section shall cease to have effect and shall be omitted from every official text of this Constitution published thereafter.

STRAND ONE

DEMOCRATIC INSTITUTIONS IN NORTHERN IRELAND

1. This agreement provides for a democratically elected Assembly in Northern Ireland which is inclusive in its membership, capable of exercising executive and legislative authority, and subject to safeguards to protect the rights and interests of all sides of the community.

The Assembly

2. A 108-member Assembly will be elected by PR(STV) from existing Westminster constituencies.
3. The Assembly will exercise full legislative and executive authority in respect of those matters currently within the responsibility of the six Northern Ireland Government Departments, with the possibility of taking on responsibility for other matters as detailed elsewhere in this agreement.
4. The Assembly – operating where appropriate on a cross-community basis – will be the prime source of authority in respect of all devolved responsibilities.

Safeguards

5. There will be safeguards to ensure that all sections of the community can participate and work together successfully in the operating of these institutions and that all sections of the community are protected, including:
   (a) allocations of Committee Chairs, Ministers and Committee membership in proportion to party strengths;
   (b) the European Convention on Human Rights (ECHR) and any Bill of Rights for Northern Ireland supplementing it, which neither the

Assembly nor public bodies can infringe, together with a Human Rights Commission;

(c) arrangements to provide that key decisions and legislation are proofed to ensure that they do not infringe the ECHR and any Bill of Rights for Northern Ireland;

(d) arrangements to ensure key decisions are taken on a cross-community basis;

    (i) **either** parallel consent, i.e. a majority of those members present and voting, including a majority of the unionist and nationalist designations present and voting;

    (ii) **or** a weighted majority (60%) of members present and voting, including at least 40% of each of the nationalist and unionist designations present and voting.

    Key decisions requiring cross-community support will be designated in advance, including election of the Chair of the Assembly, the First Minister and Deputy First Ministers, standing orders and budget allocations. In other cases such decisions could be triggered by a petition of concern brought by a significant minority of Assembly members (30/108).

(e) an Equality commission to monitor a statutory obligation to promote equality of opportunity in specified areas and parity of esteem between the two main communities and to investigate

Operation of the Assembly

6. At their first meeting, members of the Assembly will register a designation of identity – nationalist, unionist or other – for the purposes of measuring cross-community support in Assembly votes under the relevant provisions above.

7. The Chair and Deputy Chair of the Assembly will be elected on a cross-community basis, as set out in paragraph 5(d) above.

8. There will be a Committee for each of the main executive functions of the Northern Ireland Administration. The Chairs and Deputy Chairs of the Assembly Committees will be allocated proportionally, using the d'Hondt System. Membership of the Committees will be in broad proportion to party strengths in the Assembly to ensure that the opportunity of Committee places is available to all members.

9. The Committees will have a scrutiny, policy development and consultation role with respect to the Department with which each is associated, and will have a role in initiation of legislation. They will have the power to:

    • consider and advise on Departmental budgets and Annual Plans in the context of the overall budget allocation;

- approve relevant secondary legislation and take the Committee stage of relevant primary legislation;
- call for persons and papers;
- initiate enquiries and make reports;
- consider and advise on matters brought to the Committee by its Minister.

10. Standing Committees other than Department Committees may be established as may be required from time to time.

11. The Assembly may appoint a special Committee to examine and report on whether a measure or proposal for legislation is in conformity with equality requirements, including the ECHR/Bill of Rights. The Committee shall have the power to call people and papers to assist in its consideration of the matter. The Assembly shall then consider the report of the Committee and can determine the matter in accordance with the cross-community consent procedure.

12. The above special procedure shall be followed when required by the Executive Committee, or by the relevant Departmental Committee, voting on a cross-community basis.

13. When there is a petition of concern as in 5(d) above, the Assembly shall vote to determine whether the measure may proceed without reference to this special procedure. If this fails to achieve support on a cross-community basis, as in 5(d)(i) above, the special procedure shall be followed.

Executive Authority

14. Executive authority to be discharged on behalf of the Assembly by a First Minister and Deputy First Minister and up to ten Ministers with Departmental responsibilities.

15. The First Minister and Deputy First Minister shall be jointly elected into office by the Assembly voting on a cross-community basis, according to 5(d)(i) above.

16. Following the election of the First Minister and Deputy First Minister, the posts of Ministers will be allocated to parties on the basis of the d'Hondt system by reference to the number of seats each party has in the Assembly.

17. The Ministers will constitute an Executive Committee, which will be convened, and presided over, by the First Minister and Deputy First Minister.

18. The duties of the First Minister and Deputy First Minister will include, inter alia, dealing with and coordinating the work of the Executive Committee and the response of the Northern Ireland administration to external relationships.

19. The Executive Committee will provide a forum for the discussion of, and agreement on, issues which cut across the responsibilities of two or more Ministers, for prioritising executive and legislative proposals and for

recommending a common position where necessary (e.g. in dealing with external relationships).

20. The Executive Committee will seek to agree each year, and review as necessary, a programme incorporating an agreed budget linked to policies and programmes, subject to approval by the Assembly, after scrutiny in Assembly Committees, on a cross-community basis.

21. A party may decline the opportunity to nominate a person to serve as a Minister or may subsequently change its nominee.

22. All of the Northern Ireland Departments will be headed by a Minister. All Ministers will liaise regularly with their respective Committee.

23. As a condition of appointment, Ministers, including the First Minister and Deputy First Minister, will affirm the terms of a Pledge of Office (Annex A) undertaking to discharge effectively and in good faith all the responsibilities attaching to their office.

24. Ministers will have full executive authority in their respective areas of responsibility, within any broad programme agreed by the Executive Committee and endorsed by the Assembly as a whole.

25. An individual may be removed from office following a decision of the Assembly taken on a cross-community basis, if (s)he loses the confidence of the Assembly, voting on a cross-community basis, for failure to meet his or her responsibilities including, inter alia, those set out in the Pledge of Office. Those who hold office should use only democratic, non-violent means, and those who do not should be excluded or removed from office under these provisions.

Legislation

26. The Assembly will have authority to pass primary legislation for Northern Ireland in devolved areas, subject to:
    (a) the ECHR and any Bill of Rights for Northern Ireland supplementing it which, if the courts found to be breached, would render the relevant legislation null and void;
    (b) decisions by simple majority of members voting, except when decision on a cross-community basis is required;
    (c) detailed scrutiny and approval in the relevant Departmental Committee;
    (d) mechanisms, based on arrangements proposed for the Scottish Parliament, to ensure suitable co-ordination, and avoid disputes, between the Assembly and the Westminster Parliament;
    (e) option of the Assembly seeking to include Northern Ireland provisions in United Kingdom-wide legislation in the Westminster Parliament, especially on devolved issues where parity is normally maintained (e.g. social security, company law).

27. The Assembly will have authority to legislate in reserved areas with the approval of the Secretary of State and subject to Parliamentary control.
28. Disputes over legislative competence will be decided by the Courts.
29. Legislation could be initiated by an individual, a Committee or a Minister.

Relations with other institutions

30. Arrangements to represent the Assembly as a whole, at Summit level and in dealings with other institutions, will be in accordance with paragraph 18, and will be such as to ensure cross-community involvement.
31. Terms will be agreed between appropriate Assembly representatives and the Government of the United Kingdom to ensure effective co-ordination and input by Ministers to national policy making, including on EU issues.
32. Role of Secretary of State:
    (a) to remain responsible for NIO matters not devolved to the Assembly, subject to regular consultation with the Assembly and Ministers;
    (b) to approve and lay before the Westminister Parliament any Assembly legislation on reserved matters;
    (c) to represent Northern Ireland interest in the United Kingdom Cabinet;
    (d) to have the right to attend the Assembly at their invitation.
33. The Westminister Parliament (whose power to make legislation for Northern Ireland would remain unaffected) will:
    (a) legislate for non-devolved issues, other than where the Assembly legislates with the approval of the Secretary of State and subject to the control of Parliament;
    (b) to legislate as necessary to ensure the United Kingdom's international obligations are met in respect of Northern Ireland;
    (c) scrutinise, including through the Northern Ireland Grand and Select Committees, the responsibilities of the Secretary of State.
34. A consultative Civic Forum will be established. It will comprise representatives of the business, trade union and voluntary sectors, and such other sectors as agreed by the First Minister and the Deputy First Minister. It will act as a consultative mechanism on social, economic and cultural issues. The First Minister and the Deputy First Minster will by agreement provide administrative support for the Civic Forum and establish guidelines for the selection of representatives to the Civic Forum

Transitional Arrangements

35. The Assembly will meet first for the purpose of organisation, without legislative or executive powers, to resolve its standing orders and working

practices and make preparations for the effective functioning of the Assembly, the British–Irish Council and the North/South Ministerial Council and associated implementation bodies. In this transitional period, those members of the Assembly serving as shadow Ministers shall affirm their commitment to non-violence and exclusively peaceful and democratic means and their opposition to any use or threat of force by others for any political purpose; to work in good faith to bring the new arrangements into being, and to observe the spirit of the Pledge of Office applying to appointed Ministers.

Review

36. After a specified period there will be a review of these arrangements, including the details of electoral arrangements and of the Assembly's procedures, with a view to agreeing any adjustments necessary in the interests of efficiency and fairness.

ANNEX A
PLEDGE OF OFFICE

To pledge:
(a) to discharge in good faith all the duties of office;
(b) commitment to non-violence and exclusively peaceful and democratic means;
(c) to serve all the people of Northern Ireland equally, and to act in accordance with the general obligations on government to promote equality and prevent discrimination;
(d) to participate with colleagues in the preparation of a programme for government;
(e) to operate within the framework of that programme when agreed within the Executive Committee and endorsed by the Assembly;
(f) to support, and to act in accordance with, all decisions of the Executive Committee and Assembly;
(g) to comply with the Ministerial Code of Conduct.

CODE OF CONDUCT

Ministers must at all times:
• observe the highest standards of propriety and regularity involving impartiality, integrity and objectivity in relationship to the stewardship of public funds;

- be accountable to users of services, the community and, through the Assembly, for the activities within their responsibilities, their stewardship of public funds and the extent to which key performance targets and objectives have been met;
- ensure all reasonable requests for information from the Assembly, users of services and individual citizens are complied with; and that Departments and their staff conduct their dealings with the public in an open and responsible way;
- follow the seven principles of public life set out by the Committee on Standards in Public Life;
- comply with this code and with rules relating to the use of public funds;
- operate in a way conducive to promoting good community relations and equality of treatment;
- not use information gained in the course of their service for personal gain; not seek to use the opportunity of public service to promote their private interests;
- ensure they comply with any rules on the acceptance of gifts and hospitality that might be offered;
- declare any personal or business interests which may conflict with their responsibilities. The Assembly will retain a Register of Interests. Individuals must ensure that any direct or indirect pecuniary interests which members of the public might reasonably think could influence their judgement are listed in the Register of Interests.

STRAND TWO

NORTH/SOUTH MINISTERIAL COUNCIL

1. Under a new British/Irish Agreement dealing with the totality of relationships, and related legislation at Westminster and in the Oireachtas, a North/South Ministerial Council to be established to bring together those with executive responsibilities in Northern Ireland and the Irish Government, to develop consultation, cooperation and action within the island of Ireland – including through implementation on an all-island and cross-border basis – on matters of mutual interest within the competence of the Administrations, North and South.

2. All Council decisions to be by agreement between the two sides. Northern Ireland to be represented by the First Minister, Deputy First Minister and any relevant Ministers, the Irish Government by the Taoiseach and relevant Ministers, all operating in accordance with the rules for democratic authority and accountability in force in the Northern Ireland Assembly and the Oireachtas respectively. Participation in the Council to be one of the essential responsibilities attaching to relevant posts in the two Administrations. If a holder of a relevant post will not participate normally in the Council, the Taoiseach in the case of the Irish Government and the First and Deputy First Minister in the case of Northern Ireland Administration to be able to make alternative arrangements.

3. The Council to meet in different formats:
   (i)   in plenary format twice a year, with Northern Ireland representation led by the First Minister and deputy First Minister and the Irish Government led by the Taoiseach;
   (ii) in specific sectoral formats on a regular and frequent basis with each side represented by the appropriate Minister;
   (iii) in an appropriate format to consider institutional or cross-sectoral matters (including in relation to the EU) and to resolve disagreement.

4. Agendas for all meetings to be settled by prior agreement between the two sides, but it will be open to either to propose any matter for consideration or action.

5. The Council:
   (i)   to exchange information, discuss and consult with a view to coop-erating on matters of mutual interest within the competence of both Administrations, North and South;
   (ii) to use best endeavours to reach agreement on the adoption of com-mon policies, in areas where there is a mutual cross-border and all-island benefit, and which are within the competence of both Administrations, North and South, making determined efforts to overcome any disagreements;
   (iii) to take decisions by agreement on policies for implementation sepa-rately in each jurisdiction, in relevant meaningful areas within the competence of both Administrations, North and South;
   (iv) to take decisions by agreement on policies and action at an all-island and cross-border level to be implemented by the bodies to be estab-lished as set out in paragraphs 8 and 9 below.

6. Each side to be in a position to take decisions in the Council within the defined authority of those attending, through the arrangements in place for coordination of executive functions within each jurisdiction. Each side to remain accountable to the Assembly and Oireachtas respectively, whose approval, through the arrangements in place on either side, would be required for decisions beyond the defined authority of those attending.

7. As soon as practically possible after elections to the Northern Ireland Assembly, inaugural meeting will take place of the Assembly, the British/ Irish Council and the North/South Ministerial Council in their transi-tional forms. All three institutions will meet regularly and frequently on this basis during the period between the elections to the Assembly, and the transfer of powers to the Assembly, in order to establish their modus operandi.

8. During the transitional period between the elections to the Northern Ireland Assembly and the transfer of power to it, representatives of the Northern Ireland transitional Administration and the Irish Government operating in the North/South Ministerial Council will undertake a work programme, in consultation with the British Government, covering at least 12 subject areas, with a view to identifying and agreeing by 31 October 1998 areas where co-operation and implementations for mutual benefit will take place. Such areas may include matters in the list set out in the Annex.

9. As part of the work programme, the Council will identify and agree at least 6 matters for cooperation and implementation in each of the following categories:

(i) Matters where existing bodies will be the appropriate mechanisms for cooperation in each separate jurisdiction;

(ii) Matters where the cooperation will take place through agreed implementation bodies on a cross-border or all-island level.

10. The two Governments will make necessary legislative and other enabling preparations to ensure, as an absolute commitment, that these bodies, which have been agreed as a result of the work programme, function at the time of the inception of the British/Irish Agreement and the transfer of powers, with legislative authority for these bodies transferred to the Assembly as soon as possible thereafter. Other arrangements for the agreed cooperation will also commence contemporaneously with the transfer of powers to the Assembly.

11. The implementation bodies will have a clear operational remit. They will implement on an all-island and cross-border basis policies agreed in the Council.

12. Any further development of these arrangements to be by agreement in the Council and with the specific endorsement of the Northern Ireland Assembly and Oireachtas, subject to the extent of the competences and responsibility of the two Administrations.

13. It is understood that the North/South Ministerial Council and the Northern Ireland Assembly are mutually inter-dependent, and that one cannot successfully function without the other.

14. Disagreements within the Counsel to be addressed in the format described as paragraph 3(iii) above or in the plenary format. By agreement between the two sides, experts could be appointed to consider a particular matter and report.

15. Funding to be provided by the two Administrations on the basis that the Council and the implementation bodies constitute a necessary public function.

16. The Council to be supported by a standing joint Secretariat, staffed by members of the Northern Ireland Civil Service and the Irish Civil Service.

17. The Council to consider the European Union dimension of relevant matters, including the implementation of EU policies and programmes and proposals under consideration in the EU framework. Arrangements to be made to ensure that the views of the Council are taken into account and represented appropriately at relevant EU meetings.

18. The Northern Ireland Assembly and the Oireachtas to consider developing a joint parliamentary forum, bringing together equal numbers from both institutions for discussion of matters of mutual interest and concern.

19. Consideration to be given to the establishment of an independent consultative forum appointed by the two Administrations, representative of

civil society, comprising the social partners and other members with expertise in social, cultural, economic and other issues.

ANNEX

Areas for North/South cooperation and implementation may include the following:
1. Agriculture – animal and plant health.
2. Education – teacher qualifications and exchange.
3. Transport – strategic transport planning.
4. Environment – environmental protection, pollution, water quality, and waste management.
5. Waterways – inland waterways.
6. Social Security/Social Welfare – entitlements of cross-border workers and fraud control.
7. Tourism – promotion, marketing, research and product development.
8. Relevant EU Programmes such as SPPR, INTERREG, Leader II and their successors.
9. Inland Fisheries.
10. Aquaculture and marine matters.
11. Health: accident and emergency services and other related cross-border issues.
12. Urban and rural development.
Others to be considered by the shadow North/South Council.

STRAND THREE

BRITISH-IRISH COUNCIL

1. A British–Irish Council (BIC) will be established under a new British-Irish Agreement to promote the harmonious and mutually beneficial development of the totality of relationships among the peoples of these islands.
2. Membership of the BIC will comprise representatives of the British and Irish Governments, devolved institutions in Northern Ireland, Scotland and Wales, when established, and, if appropriate, elsewhere in the United Kingdom, together with representatives of the Isle of Man and the Channel islands.
3. The BIC will meet in different formats: at summit level, twice per year, in specific sectoral formats on a regular basis, with each side represented by the appropriate Minister; in an appropriate format to consider cross-sectoral matters.
4. Representatives of members will operate in accordance with whatever procedures for democratic authority and accountability are in force in their respective elected institutions.
5. The BIC will exchange information, discuss, consult and use best endeavours to reach agreement on cooperation on matters of mutual interest within the competence of the relevant Administrations. Suitable issues for early discussion in the BIC could include transport links, agricultural issues, environmental issues, cultural issues, health issues, education issues and approaches to EU issues. Suitable arrangements to be made for practical cooperation on agreed policies.
6. It will be open to the BIC to agree common policies or common actions. Individual members may opt not to participate in such common policies and common action.
7. The BIC normally will operate by consensus. In relation to decisions on common policies or common actions, including their means of implementation, it will operate by agreement of all members participating in such policies or actions.

8. The members of the BIC, on a basis to be agreed between them, will provide such financial support as it may require.
9. A secretariat for the BIC will be provided by the British and Irish Governments in coordination with officials of each of the other members.
10. In addition to the structures provided for under this agreement, it will be open to two or more members to develop bilateral or multilateral arrangements between them. Such arrangements could include, subject to the agreement of the members concerned, mechanisms to enable consultation, cooperation and joint decision-making on matters of mutual interest; and mechanisms to implement any joint decisions they may reach. These arrangements will not require the prior approval of the BIC as a whole and will operate independently of it.
11. The elected institutions of the members will be encouraged to develop interparliamentary links, perhaps building on the British-Irish Interparliamentary Body.
12. The full membership of the BIC will keep under review the workings of the Council, including a formal published review at an appropriate time after the Agreement comes into effect, and will contribute as appropriate to any review of the overall political agreement arising from the multiparty negotiations.

BRITISH–IRISH INTERGOVERNMENTAL CONFERENCE

1. There will be a new British–Irish Agreement dealing with the totality of relationships. It will establish a standing British–Irish Intergovernmental Conference, which will subsume both the Anglo–Irish Intergovernmental Council and the Intergovernmental Conference established under the 1985 Agreement.
2. The Conference will bring together the British and Irish Governments to promote bilateral cooperation at all levels on all matters of mutual interest within the competence of both Governments.
3. The Conference will meet as required at Summit level (Prime Minister and Taoiseach). Otherwise, Governments will be represented by appropriate Ministers, Advisers, including police and security advisers will attend as appropriate.
4. All decisions will be by agreement between both Governments. The Governments will make determined efforts to resolve disagreements between them. There will be no derogation from the sovereignty of either Government.
5. In recognition of the Irish Government's special interest in Northern Ireland and of the extent to which issues of mutual concern arise in relation to Northern Ireland, there will be regular and frequent meetings of

the Conference concerned with non-devolved Northern Ireland matters, on which the Irish Government may put forward views and proposals. These meetings, to be co-chaired by the Minister for Foreign Affairs and the Secretary of State for Northern Ireland, would also deal with all-island and cross-border cooperation on non-devolved issues.

6. Cooperation within the framework of the Conference will include facilitation of cooperation in security matters. The Conference also will address, in particular, the areas of rights, justice, prisons and policing in Northern Ireland (unless and until responsibility is devolved to a Northern Ireland administration) and will intensify cooperation between the two Governments on the all-island or cross-border aspects of these matters.

7. Relevant executive members of the Northern Ireland Administration will be involved in meetings of the Conference, and in the reviews referred to in paragraph 9 below to discuss non-devolved Northern Ireland matters.

8. The Conference will be supported by officials of the British and Irish Governments, including by a standing joint Secretariat of officials dealing with non-devolved Northern Ireland matters.

9. The Conference will keep under review the workings of the new British-Irish Agreement and the machinery and institutions established under it, including a formal published review three years after the Agreement comes into effect. Representatives of the Northern Ireland Administration will be invited to express views to the Conference in this context. The Conference will contribute as appropriate to any review of the overall political agreement arising from the multi-party negotiations but will have no power to override the democratic arrangements set up by this Agreement.

RIGHTS, SAFEGUARDS AND EQUALITY OF OPPORTUNITY

Human Rights

1. The parties affirm their commitment to the mutual respect, the civil rights and the religious liberties of everyone in the community. Against the background of the recent history of communal conflict, the parties affirm in particular:
   - the right of free political thought;
   - the right to freedom and expression of religion;
   - the right to pursue democratically national and political aspirations;
   - the right to seek constitutional change by peaceful and legitimate means;
   - the right to freely choose one's place of residence;
   - the right to equal opportunity in all social and economic activity, regardless of class, creed, disability, gender or ethnicity;

- the right to freedom from sectarian harassment; and
- the right of women to full and equal political participation.

United Kingdom Legislation

2. The British Government will complete incorporation into Northern Ireland law of the European Convention on Human Rights (ECHR), with direct access to the courts, and remedies for breach of the Convention, including power for the courts to overrule Assembly legislation on grounds of inconsistency.

3. Subject to the outcome of public consultation underway, the British Government intends, as a particular priority, to create a statutory obligation on public authorities in Northern Ireland to carry out all their functions with due regard to the need to promote equality of opportunity in relation to religion and political opinion; gender; race; disability; age; marital status; dependents; and sexual orientation. Public bodies would be required to draw up statutory schemes showing how they would implement this obligation. Such schemes would cover arrangements for policy appraisal, including an assessment of impact on relevant categories, public consultation, public access to information and services, monitoring and timetables.

4. The new Northern Ireland Human Rights Commission (see paragraph 5 below) will be invited to consult and to advise on the scope for defining, in Westminster legislation, rights supplementary to those in the European Convention on Human Rights, to reflect the particular circumstances of Northern Ireland, drawing as appropriate on international instruments and experience. These additional rights to reflect the principles of mutual respect for the identity and ethos of both communities and parity of esteem, and – taken together with the ECHR – to constitute a Bill of Rights for Northern Ireland. Among the issues for consideration by the Commission will be:

   - The formulation of a general obligation on government and public bodies fully to respect, on the basis of equality of treatment, the identity and ethos of both communities in Norther Ireland; and
   - a clear formulation of the rights not to be discriminated against and to equality of opportunity in both the public and private sectors.

New Institutions in Northern Ireland

5. A new Northern Ireland Human Rights Commission, with membership from Northern Ireland reflecting the community balance, will be established by Westminster legislation, independent of Government, with an extended and enhanced role beyond that currently exercised by the

Standing Advisory commission on Human Rights, to include keeping under review the adequacy and effectiveness of laws and practices, making recommendations to Government as necessary; providing information and promoting awareness of human rights; considering draft legislation referred to them by the new Assembly; and, in appropriate cases, bringing court proceedings or providing assistance to individuals doing so.

6. Subject to the outcome of public consultation currently underway, the British Government intends a new statutory Equality Commission to replace the Fair Employment Commission, the Equal Opportunities Commission (NI), the Commission of Racial Equality (NI) and the Disability Council. Such a unified Commission will advise on, validate and monitor the statutory obligation and will Investigate complaints of default.

7. It would be open to a new Northern Ireland Assembly to consider bringing together its responsibilities for these matters into a dedicated Department of Equality.

8. These improvements will build on existing protections in Westminister legislation in respect of the judiciary, the system of justice and policing.

Comparable Steps by the Irish Government

9. The Irish Government will also take steps to further strengthen the protection of human rights in its jurisdiction. The Government will, taking account of the work of the All-Party Oireachtas Committee on the Constitution and the Report of the Constitution Review Group, bring forward measures to strengthen and underpin the constitutional protection of human rights. These proposals will draw on the European Convention of Human Rights and other international legal instruments in the field of human rights and the question of the incorporation of the ECHR will be further examined in this context. The measures brought forward would ensure at least an equivalent level of protection of human rights as will pertain in Northern Ireland. In addition, the Irish Government will:

- establish a Human Rights Commission with a mandate and remit equivalent to that within Northern Ireland;
- proceed with arrangements as quickly as possible to ratify the Council of Europe Framework Convention on National Minorities (already ratified by the UK);
- implement enhanced employment equality legislation;
- introduce enhanced employment equality legislation;
- introduce equal status legislation; and
- continue to take further active steps to demonstrate its respect for the different traditions in the island of Ireland.

A Joint Committee

10. It is envisaged that there would be a joint committee of representatives of the two Human Rights Commissions, North and South,
as a forum for consideration of human rights issues in the island of
Ireland. The joint committee will consider, among other matters, the
possibility of establishing a charter, open to signature by all democratic political parties, reflecting and endorsing agreed measure for the
protection of the fundamental rights of everyone living in the island of
Ireland.

Reconciliation and Victims of Violence

11. The participants believe that it is essential to acknowledge and address
the suffering of the victims of violence as a necessary element of reconciliation. They look forward to the results of the work of the Northern Ireland Victim's Commission.

12 It is recognised that victims have a right to remember as well as to contribute to a changed society. The achievement of a peaceful and just
society would be the true memorial to the victims of violence. The participants particularly recognise that young people from areas affected by
the troubles face particular difficulties and will support the development
of special community-based initiatives based on international best practice. The provision of services that are supportive and sensitive to the
needs of victims will also be a critical element and that support will need
to be channeled through both statutory and community-based voluntary
organisations facilitating locally-based self-help and support networks.
This will require the allocation of sufficient resources, including statutory
funding as necessary, to meet the needs of victims and to provide for
community-based support programmes.

13. The participants recognise and value the work being done by many
organisations to develop reconciliation and mutual understanding and
respect between and within communities and traditions, in Northern
Ireland and between North and South, and they see such work as having
a vital role in consolidating peace and political agreement. Accordingly,
they pledge their continuing support to such organisations and will posi-
tively examine the case for enhanced financial assistance for the work of
reconciliation process is the promotion of a culture of tolerance at every
level of society, including initiatives to facilitate and encourage integrated
education and mixed housing.

RIGHTS, SAFEGUARDS AND EQUALITY OF OPPORTUNITY

Economic, Social and Cultural Issues

1. Pending the devolution of powers to a new Northern Ireland Assembly, the British Government will pursue board policies for sustained economic growth and stability in Northern Ireland and for promoting social inclusion, including in particular community development and the advancement of women in public life.

2. Subject to the public consultation currently under way, the British Government will make rapid progress with:
   (i) A new regional development strategy for Northern Ireland, for consideration in due course by the Assembly, tackling the problems of a divided society and social cohesion in urban, rural and border areas, protecting and enhancing the environment, producing new approaches to transport issues, strengthening the physical infrastructure of the region, developing the advantages and resources of rural areas and rejuvenating major urban centres;
   (ii) a new economic development strategy for Northern Ireland, for consideration in due course by the Assembly, which would provide for short and medium term economic planning linked as appropriate to the regional development strategy; and
   (iii) measures on employment equality included in the recent White paper ('Partnership for Equality') and covering the extension and strengthening of anti-discrimination legislation, a review of the national security aspects of the present fair employment legislation at the earliest possible time, a new more focused Targeting Social Need initiative and a range of measures aimed at combating unemployment and progressively eliminating the differential in unemployment rates between the two communities by targeting objective need.

3. All participants recognise the importance of respect, understanding and tolerance in relation to linguistic diversity, including in Northern Ireland, the Irish language, Ulster-Scots and the languages of the various ethnic communities, all of which are part of the cultural wealth of the island of Ireland.

4. In the context of active consideration currently being given to the UK signing the Council of Europe Charter for Regional or Minority Languages, the British Government will in particular in relation to the Irish language, where appropriate and where people so desire it:
   • take resolute action to promote the language;
   • facilitate and encourage the use of the language in speech and writing in public and private life where there is appropriate demand;

- seek to remove, where possible, restrictions which would discourage or work against the maintenance or development of the language;
- make provision for liaising with the Irish language community, representing their views to public authorities and investigating complaints;
- place a statutory duty on the Department of Education to encourage and facilitate Irish medium education in line with current provision for integrated education;
- explore urgently with the relevant British authorities, and in co-operation with the Irish broadcasting authorities, the scope for achieving more widespread availability of Teilifís na Gaeilge in Northern Ireland;
- seek more effective ways to encourage and provide financial support for Irish language film and television production in Northern Ireland; and
- encourage the parties to secure agreement that this commitment will be sustained by a new Assembly in a way which takes account of the desires and sensitivities of the community.

5. All participants acknowledge the sensitivity of the use of symbols and emblems for public purposes, and the need in particular in creating the new institutions to ensure that such symbols and emblems are used in a manner which promotes mutual respect rather than division. Arrangements will be made to monitor this issue and consider what action might be required.

DECOMMISSIONING

1. Participants recall their agreement in the Procedural Motion adopted on 24 September 1997 'that the resolution of the decommissioning issue is an indispensable part of the process of negotiation', and also recall the provisions of paragraph 25 of Strand One above.

2. They note the progress made by the Independent International Commission on Decommissioning and the Governments in developing schemes which can represent a workable basis for achieving the decommissioning of illegally held arms in the possession of paramilitary groups.

3. All participants accordingly reaffirm their commitment to the total disarmament of all paramilitary organisations. They also confirm their intention to continue to work constructively and in good faith with the Independent Commission, and to use any influence they may have, to achieve the decommissioning of all paramilitary arms within two years following endorsement in referendums North and South of the agreement and in the context of the implementation of the overall settlement.

4. The Independent Commission will monitor, review and verify progress on decommissioning of illegal arms, and will report to both Governments at regular intervals.

5. Both Governments will take all necessary steps to facilitate the decommissioning process to include bringing the relevant schemes into force by the end of June.

SECURITY

1. The participants note that the development of a peaceful environment on the basis of this agreement can and should mean a normalisation of security arrangements and practices.

2. The British Government will make progress towards the objective of as early a return as possible to normal security arrangements in Northern Ireland, consistent with the level of threat and with a published overall strategy, dealing with:
    (i)   the reduction of the numbers and role of the Armed Forces deployed in Northern Ireland to levels compatible with a normal peaceful society;
    (ii) the removal of security installations;
    (iii) the removal of emergency powers in Norther Ireland; and
    (iv) other measures appropriate to and compatible with a normal peaceful society.

3. The Secretary of State will consult regularly on progress, and the response to any continuing paramilitary activity, with the Irish Government and the political parties, as appropriate.

4. The British Government will continue its consultation on firearms regulations and control on the basis of the document published on 2 April 1998.

5. The Irish Government will initiate a wide-ranging review of the Offences Against the State Acts 1939–85 with a view to both reform and dispensing with those elements no longer required as circumstances permit.

POLICING AND JUSTICE

1. The participants recognise that policing is a central issue in any society. They equally recognise that Northern Ireland's history of deep divisions has made it highly emotive, with great hurt suffered and sacrifices made by many individuals and their families, including those in the RUC and other public servants. They believe that the agreement provides the opportunity for a new beginning to policing in Northern Ireland with a police service capable of attracting and sustaining support from the community as a whole. They also believe that this agreement offers a

unique opportunity to bring about a new political dispensation which will recognise the full and equal legitimacy and worth of the identities, senses of allegiance and ethos of all sections of the community in Northern Ireland. They consider that this opportunity should inform and underpin the development of a police service representative in terms of the make-up of the community as a whole and which, in a peaceful environment, should be routinely unarmed.

2. The participants believe it essential that policing structures and arrangements are such that the police service is professional, effective and efficient, fair and impartial, free from partisan political control; accountable, both under the law for its actions and to the community it serves; representative of the society it polices, and operates with a coherent and cooperative criminal justice system, which conforms with human rights norms. The participants also believe that those structures and arrangements must be capable of maintaining law and order including responding effectively to crime and to any terrorist threat and to public order problems. A police service which cannot do so will fail to win public confidence and acceptance. They believe that any such structures and arrangements should be capable of delivering a policing service, in constructive and inclusive partnerships with the community at all levels, and with the maximum delegation of authority and responsibility, consistent with the foregoing principles. These arrangements should be based on principles of protection of human rights and professional integrity and should be unambiguously accepted and actively supported by the entire community.

3. An independent Commission will be established to make recommendations for future policing arrangements in Northern Ireland including means of encouraging widespread community support for these arrangements within the agreed framework of principles reflected in the paragraphs above and in accordance with the terms of reference at Annex A. The Commission will be broadly representative with expert and international representation among its membership and will be asked to consult widely and to report no later than Summer 1999.

4. The participants believe that the aims of the criminal justice system are to:
   - deliver a fair and impartial system of justice to the community;
   - be responsible to the community's concerns, and encouraging community involvement where appropriate;
   - have the confidence of all parts of the community; and
   - deliver justice efficiently and effectively.

5. There will be a parallel wide-ranging review of criminal justice (other than policing and those aspects of the system relating to the emergency legislation) to be carried out by the British Government through a mechanism with an independent element, in consultation with the political parties and others. The review will commence as soon as possible, will include

wide consultation, and a report will be made to the Secretary of State no later than Autumn 1999. Terms of Reference are attached at Annex B.

6. Implementation of the recommendations arising from both reviews will be discussed with the political parties and with the Irish Government.

7. The participants also note that the British Government remains ready in principle, with the broad support of the political parties, and after consultation, as appropriate, with the Irish Government, in the context of ongoing implementation of the relevant recommendations, to devolve responsibility for policing and justice issues.

ANNEX A

COMMISSION ON POLICING FOR NORTHERN IRELAND

Terms of Reference

Taking account of the principles on policing as set out in the Agreement, the Commission will inquire into policing in Northern Ireland and, on the basis of its findings, bring forward proposals for future policing structures and arrangements, including means of encouraging widespread community support for those arrangements.

Its proposals on policing should be designed to ensure that policing arrangements, including composition, recruitment, training, culture, ethos and symbols, are such that in a new approach Northern Ireland has a police service that can enjoy widespread support from, and is seen as an integral part of, the community as a whole.

Its proposals should include recommendations covering any issues such as re-training, job placement and educational and professional development required in the transition to policing in a peaceful society.

Its proposals should also be designed to ensure that:
- the police service is structured, managed and resourced so that it can be effective in discharging its full range of functions (including proposals on any necessary arrangements for the transition to policing in a normal peaceful society);
- the police service is delivered in constructive and inclusive partnerships with the community at all levels with the maximum delegation of authority and responsibility;

- the legislative and constitutional framework requires the impartial discharge of policing functions and conforms with internationally accepted norms in relation to policing standards;
- the police operate within a clear framework of accountability to the law and the community they serve, so:
- they are constrained by, accountable to and act only within the law;
- their powers and procedures, like the law they enforce, are clearly established and publicly available;
- there are open, accessible and independent means of investigating and adjudicating upon complaints against the police;
- there are clearly established arrangements enabling local people, and their political representatives, to articulate their views and concerns about policing and to establish publicly policing priorities and influence policing policies, subject to safeguards to ensure police impartiality and freedom from partisan political control;
- there are arrangements for accountability and for the effective, efficient and economic use of resource in achieving policing objectives;
- there are means to ensure independent professional scrutiny and inspection of the police service to ensure that proper professional standards are maintained
- the scope for structured cooperation with the Garda Siochána and other police forces is addressed; and
- the management of public order events which can impose exceptional demands on policing resources is also addressed.

The Commission should focus on policing issues, but if it identifies other aspects of the criminal justice system relevant to its work on policing, including the role of the police in prosecution, then it should draw the attention of the Government to those matters.

The Commission should consult widely, including with non-governmental expert organisations, and through such focus groups as they consider it appropriate to establish.

The Government proposes to establish the Commission as soon as possible, with the aim of it starting work as soon as possible and publishing its final report by Summer 1999.

ANNEX B

REVIEW OF THE CRIMINAL JUSTICE SYSTEM

Terms of Reference

Taking account of the aims of the criminal justice system as set out in the Agreement, the review will address the structure, management and resourcing of publicly funded elements of the criminal justice system and will bring forward proposals for future criminal justice arrangements (other than policing and those aspects of the system relating to emergency legislation, which the Government is considering separately) covering such issues as:

- the arrangement for making appointments to the judiciary and magistracy, and safeguards for protecting their independence;
- the arrangements for the organisation and supervision of the prosecution process, and for safeguarding its independence:
- measures to improve the responsiveness and accountability of, and any lay participation in the criminal justice system.
- mechanisms for addressing law reform;
- the scope for structured cooperation between the criminal justice agencies on both parts of the island; and
- the structure and organisation of criminal justice functions that might be devolved to an Assembly, including the possibility of establishing a Department of Justice, while safeguarding the essential independence of many of the key functions in this area.

The Government proposes to commence the review as soon as possible, consulting with the political parties and others, including non-governmental expert organisations. The review will be completed by August 1999.

PRISONERS

1. Both Governments will put in place mechanisms to provide for an accelerated programme for the release of prisoners, including transferred prisoners, convicted of scheduled offences in Northern Ireland or, in the case of those sentenced outside Northern Ireland, similar offences (referred to hereafter as qualifying prisoners). Any such arrangements will protect the rights of individual prisoners under national and international law.

2. Prisoners affiliated to organisations which have not established or are not maintaining a complete and unequivocal ceasefire will not benefit from the arrangements. The situation in this regard will be kept under review.

3. Both Governments will complete a review process within a fixed time frame and set prospective release dates for all qualifying prisoners. The review

process would provide for the advance of the release dates of qualifying prisoners while allowing account to be taken of the seriousness of the offences for which the person was convicted and the need to protect the community. In addition, the intention would be that should the circumstances allow it, any qualifying prisoners who remained in custody two years after the commencement of the scheme would be released at that point.

4. The Governments will seek to enact the appropriate legislation to give effect to these arrangements by the end of June 1998.

5. The Governments continue to recognise the importance of measures to facilitate the reintegration of prisoners into the community by providing support both prior to and after release, including assistance directed towards availing of employment opportunities, retraining and/or re-skilling, and further education.

VALIDATION, IMPLEMENTATION AND REVIEW

VALIDATION AND IMPLEMENTATION

1. The two Governments will as soon as possible sign a new British–Irish Agreement replacing the 1985 Anglo-Irish Agreement, embodying understandings on constitutional issues and affirming their solemn commitment to support and, where appropriate, implement the agreement reached by the participants in the negotiations which shall be annexed to the British-Irish Agreement.

2. Each Government will organise a referendum on 22 May 1998. Subject to Parliamentary approval, a consultative referendum in Northern Ireland, organised under the terms of the Northern Ireland (Entry to Negotiations, etc.) Act 1996, will address the question: 'Do you support the agreement reached in the multi-party talks on Northern Ireland and set out in Command Page 3883?' The Irish Government will introduce and support in the Oireachtas a Bill to amend the Constitution as described in paragraph 2 of the section "Constitutional Issues" and in Annex B, as follows: (a) to amend Articles 2 and 3 as described in paragraph 8.1 in Annex B above and (b) to amend Article 29 to permit the Government to ratify the new British-Irish Agreement. On passage by the Oireachtas, the Bill will be put to referendum.

3. If majorities of those voting in each of the referendums support this agreement, the Governments will then introduce and support, in their respective parliaments, such legislation as may be necessary to give effect to all aspects of this agreement, and will take whatever ancillary steps as may be required including the holding of elections on 25 June, subject to parliamentary approval, to the Assembly, which would meet initially in a

'shadow' mode. The establishment of the North-South Ministerial Council, implementation bodies, the British-Irish council and the British-Irish Intergovernmental Conference and the assumption by the Assembly of its legislative and executive powers will take place at the same time on the entry into force of the British-Irish Agreement.

4. In the interim, aspects of the implementation of the multi-party agreement will be reviewed at meetings of those parties relevant in the particular case (taking into account, once Assembly elections have been held, the results of those elections), under the chairmanship of the British Government or the two Governments, as may be appropriate; and representatives of the two Governments and all relevant parties may meet under independent chairmanship to review implementation of the agreement as a whole.

Review procedures following implementation

5. Each institution may, at any time, review any problems that may arise in its operation and, where no other institution is affected, take remedial action in consultation as necessary with the relevant Government or Governments. It will be for each institution to determine its procedures for review.

6. If there are difficulties in the operation of a particular institution, which may have implications for another institution, they may review their operations separately and jointly and agree on remedial action to be taken under their respective authorities.

7. If difficulties arise which require remedial action across the range of institutions, or otherwise require amendment of the British–Irish Agreement or relevant legislation, the process of review will fall to the two Governments in consultation with the parties in the Assembly. Each Government will be responsible for action in its own jurisdiction.

8. Notwithstanding the above, each institution will publish an annual report on its operations. In addition, the two Governments and the parties in the Assembly will convene a conference 4 years after the Agreement comes into effect, to review and report on its operation.

AGREEMENT BETWEEN THE GOVERNMENT OF THE UNITED KINGDOM OF GREAT BRITAIN AND NORTHERN IRELAND AND THE GOVERNMENT OF IRELAND

The British and Irish Governments:

Welcoming the strong commitment to the Agreement reached on 10th April 1998 by themselves and other participants in the multi-party talks and set out in Annex 1 to this Agreement (hereinafter the Multi-Party Agreement);

Considering that the Multi-Party Agreement offers an opportunity for a new beginning in relationships within Northern Ireland, within the island of Ireland and between the peoples of these islands;

Wishing to develop still further the unique relationship between their peoples and the close cooperation between their countries as friendly neighbours and as partners in the European Union;

Reaffirming their total commitment to the principles of democracy and non-violence which have been fundamental to the multi-party talks;

Reaffirming their commitment to the principles of partnership, equality and mutual respect and to the protection of civil, political, social, economic and cultural rights in their respective jurisdictions;

Have agreed as follows:

Article 1

The two Governments

(i) recognize the legitimacy of whatever choice is freely exercised by a majority of the people of Northern Ireland with regard to its status, whether they prefer to continue to support the Union with Great Britain or a sovereign united Ireland;

(ii) recognise that it is for the people of the island of Ireland alone, by agreement between the two parts respectively and without external impediment, to exercise their right of self-determination on the basis of consent, freely and concurrently given, North and South, to bring about a united Ireland, if that is their wish, accepting that this right must be achieved and exercised with and subject to the agreement and consent of a majority of the people of Northern Ireland;

(iii) acknowledge that while a substantial section of the people in Northern Ireland share the legitimate wish of a majority of the people of the island of Ireland for a united Ireland, the present wish of a majority of the people of Northern Ireland, freely exercised and legitimate, is to maintain the Union and accordingly, that Northern Ireland's status as part of the United Kingdom reflects and relies upon that wish; and that it would be wrong to make any change in the status of Northern Ireland save with the consent of a majority of its people;

(iv) affirm that, if in the future, the people of Ireland exercise their right of self-determination on the basis set out in sections (I) and (ii) above to bring about a united Ireland, it will be a binding obligation on both Governments to introduce and support in their respective Parliaments legislation to give effect to that wish;

(v) affirm that whatever choice is freely exercised by a majority of the people of Northern Ireland, the power of the sovereign government with jurisdiction there shall be exercised with rigorous impartiality on behalf of the people in the diversity of their identities and traditions and shall be founded on the principles of full respect for, and equality of, civil, political, social and cultural rights, of freedom from discrimination for all citizens, and of parity of esteem and of just and equal treatment for the identity, ethos and aspirations of both communities.

(vi) recognise the birthright of all the people of Northern Ireland to identify themselves and be accepted as Irish or British, or both, as they may so choose, and accordingly confirm that their right to hold both British and Irish citizenship is accepted by both Governments and would not be affected by any further change in the status of Northern Ireland.

Article 2

The two Governments affirm their solemn commitment to support, and where appropriate implement, the provisions of the Multi-Party Agreement. In particular there shall be established in accordance with the provisions of the Multi-Party Agreement immediately on the entry into force of this Agreement, the following institutions:
  (i) a North/South Ministerial Council;
 (ii) the implementation bodies referred to in paragraph 9 (ii) of the section entitled Strand Two of the Multi-Party Agreement;
(iii) a British–Irish Council;
(iv) a British–Irish Intergovernmental Conference.

Article 3

(1) This Agreement shall replace the Agreement between the British and Irish Governments done at Hillsborough on 15 November 1985 which shall cease to have effect on entry into force of this Agreement.
(2) The Intergovernmental Conference established by Article 2 of the aforementioned Agreement done on 15 November 1985 shall cease to exist on entry into force of this Agreement.

Article 4

(1) It shall be a requirement for entry into force of this Agreement that:
  (a) British legislation shall have been enacted for the purpose of implementing the provisions of Annex A to the section entitled 'Constitutional Issues' of the Multi-Party Agreement;
  (b) the amendments to the Constitution of Ireland set out in Annex B to the section entitled 'Constitutional Issues' of the Multi-Party Agreement shall have been approved by Referendum;
  (c) such legislation shall have been enacted as may be required to establish the institutions referred to in Article 2 of this Agreement.
(2) Each Government shall notify the other in writing of the completion, so far as it is concerned, of the requirements for entry into force of this Agreement. This Agreement shall enter into force on the date of the receipt of the later of the two notifications.
(3) Immediately on entry into force of this Agreement, the Irish Government shall ensure that the amendments to the Constitution of Ireland set out in Annex B to the section entitled 'Constitutional Issues' of the Multi-Party Agreement take effect.

In witness thereof the undersigned, being duty authorised thereto by the respective Governments, have signed this Agreement.

Done in two originals at Belfast on the 10th day of April 1998.

For the Government of the United Kingdom of Great Britain and Northern Ireland	For the Government of Ireland

INDEX